Strategic Survey

2006

published by

Routledge
Taylor & Francis Group

for

The International Institute for Strategic Studies
Arundel House | 13–15 Arundel Street | Temple Place | London | WC2R 3DX | UK

The International Institute for Strategic Studies
Arundel House | 13–15 Arundel Street | Temple Place | London | WC2R 3DX | UK

Strategic Survey 2006

First published August 2006 by **Routledge**
4 Park Square, Milton Park, Abingdon, Oxon, OX14 4RN

for **The International Institute for Strategic Studies**
Arundel House, 13–15 Arundel Street, Temple Place, London, WC2R 3DX, UK

Simultaneously published in the USA and Canada by **Routledge**
270 Madison Ave., New York, NY 10016

Routledge is an imprint of Taylor & Francis, an Informa business

© 2006 The International Institute for Strategic Studies

DIRECTOR-GENERAL AND CHIEF EXECUTIVE Dr John Chipman
EDITOR Alexander Nicoll

ASSISTANT EDITOR Dr Jeffrey Mazo
MAP EDITOR James Hackett
CONTRIBUTING EDITOR Jonathan Stevenson
MANAGER FOR EDITORIAL SERVICES Dr Ayse Abdullah
DESIGNER Jesse Simon
MAP RESEARCH Jessica Delaney, Catherine Micklethwaite, James Howarth
CARTOGRAPHY Steven Bernard

COVER IMAGES AP/Wide World Photos/Empics
PRINTED AND BOUND IN GREAT BRITAIN BY Bell & Bain Ltd, Thornliebank, Glasgow

This publication has been prepared by the Director-General of the Institute and his Staff, who accept full responsibility for its contents, which describe and analyse events up to 30 June 2006. These do not, and indeed cannot, represent a consensus of views among the worldwide membership of the Institute as a whole.

British Library Cataloguing in Publication Data
A catalogue record for this book is available from the British Library

Library of Congress Cataloguing in Publication Data

ISBN 1-85743-400-5
ISSN 0459-7230

Contents

Index of Regional Maps

Index of Maps

Index of Tables

Strategic Geography

Events at a Glance
May 2005–May 2006

May 2005

5   **UK:** Labour party re-elected with reduced majority.

13   **Uzbekistan:** Troops open fire on demonstrators in eastern city of Andijan, killing hundreds.

27   **US:** Five-yearly review conference of Nuclear Non-Proliferation Treaty ends without substantive agreement.

29   **France:** French voters reject EU constitution in referendum, prompting resignation of Prime Minister Jean-Pierre Raffarin, replaced by Dominique de Villepin.

June 2005

1   **Netherlands:** Dutch voters reject EU constitutional treaty in referendum.

15   **Iran:** International Atomic Energy Agency (IΛEA) says Iran admitted experimenting with reprocessing plutonium as recently as 1998, five years more recently than previously admitted.

23   **UK:** Prime Minister Tony Blair tells European Parliament of his commitment to a 'political' Europe but says EU must respond to peoples' aspirations. Calls for reforms to economies, subsidies, labour and EU budget.

24   **Iran:** Mahmoud Ahmadinejad, conservative Mayor of Tehran, easily wins presidential election in a run-off against Akbar Hashemi Rafsanjani.

28   **France:** After 20 years of wrangling, France is chosen by a 30-nation consortium to host the world's first nuclear fusion reactor using deuterium extracted from seawater as main fuel.

July 2005

5   **China:** Shanghai Cooperation Organisation, which includes China, Russia, Kazakhstan, Kyrgyzstan, Tajikistan and Uzbekistan, calls at a summit for US and coalition members to set a date for withdrawal from bases in Uzbekistan and Kyrgyzstan.

7   **UK:** Four bombs explode in London, three on Underground trains and one on a bus, killing 52 people and injuring 700. Killers are identified as three-British-born Muslims of Pakistani origin and a Jamaica-born Muslim convert brought up in England.

8   **UK:** Leaders of the G8, meeting at Gleneagles, Scotland, agree to double development aid to $50 billion a year by 2010 and to hold talks, including India and China, on global warming.

21   **China:** China says yuan will no longer be pegged to dollar, revalues it 2.1%.

21   **UK:** Four men try and fail to explode bombs in London, three on Underground trains and one on a bus. Suspects are later arrested.

22   **UK:** British police shoot dead Brazilian man on Underground train, mistaking him for a suicide bomber.

22   **Egypt:** Multiple bombings kill 89 in Egyptian resort of Sharm-al-Sheikh.

28   **UK:** Irish Republican Army formally declares end to armed struggle.

31   **Iran:** Government says it will resume uranium enrichment.

August 2005

1   **UK:** Government announces reduction of troop levels in Northern Ireland from 10,500 to 5,000 over two years.

1   **Sudan:** Vice President John Garang killed in helicopter crash.

1   **Saudi Arabia:** King Fahd dies, succeeded by King Abdullah.

6   **UK:** Britain announces plans to deport clerics fostering hatred and violence, and to ban two Muslim extremist organisations.

7   **India/Pakistan:** Governments agree to set up telephone hotline to notify each other of ballistic missile tests.

14   **Indonesia:** Government and rebels of the Free Aceh Movement sign peace agreement mediated by former Finnish president Martti Ahtisaari.

14   **Sri Lanka:** Foreign Minister Lakshman Kudirgamar assassinated.

17   **Bangladesh:** More than 100 small bomb attacks in Bangladesh kill two.

22   **Israel:** Withdrawal of settlers from Gaza completed.

28   **Iraq:** Parliament approves draft constitution.

29   **US:** Hurricane Katrina bursts levees in New Orleans, flooding city and killing more than 1,600 people in Louisiana and Mississippi.

31   **Iraq:** Nearly 1,000 Shi'ite pilgrims killed in stampede on bridge in Baghdad.

September 2005

4 **US:** Chief Justice William Rehnquist dies. John Roberts later succeeds him.

7 **United Nations:** Final report by independent inquiry committee on UN oil-for-food programme in Iraq calls for large-scale reforms to improve management and oversight of UN organisation.

11 **Japan:** Liberal Democratic Party, led by Junichiro Koizumi, retains power in general election.

18 **Afghanistan:** Parliamentary elections held.

18 **Germany:** General elections produce no clear result, setting negotiations in motion on forming a coalition government.

19 **North Korea:** Government agrees to give up nuclear weapons and return to Non-proliferation Treaty in return for security guarantees and energy aid. Says later it will not give up nuclear weapons until it gets light water reactor.

28 **Iran:** UK Foreign Secretary Jack Straw says military action against Iran 'inconceivable'.

30 **Uzbekistan:** EU imposes sanctions on Uzbekistan five months after Andijan killings.

October 2005

1 **Indonesia:** Three suicide bomb blasts at two resorts in Bali kill 32.

3 **Turkey:** EU membership talks formally begin.

8 **Pakistan:** Earthquake kills at least 75,000 people.

10 **Germany:** Angela Merkel announces agreement on grand coalition headed by herself.

12 **Syria:** Interior Minister Ghazi Kanaan dead in apparent suicide.

17 **Japan:** Japanese Prime Minister Junichiro Koizumi again visits Yasukuni Shrine war memorial, prompting protests from China and others.

19 **Iraq:** Trial of Saddam Hussein begins.

20 **India:** Bomb attacks in Delhi kill more than 60.

23 **Poland:** Lech Kaczyinski elected president.

25 **Lebanon:** UN investigator Detlev Mehlis releases report on assassination of former Lebanese prime minister Rafik Hariri, strongly implicating Syria.

25 **Iraq:** Constitution approved in referendum.

26 **Iran:** President Mahmoud Ahmadinejad says Israel should be 'wiped off the map'.

28 **US:** I. Lewis 'Scooter' Libby, Jr, chief of staff to Vice President Dick Cheney, resigns after special prosecutor says he will bring criminal charges over leak case.

November 2005

4   **Argentina:** Anti-Bush protests greet Summit of the Americas, which fails to reach trade deal.

6   **Azerbaijan:** Ruling party claims victory in elections denounced by opposition and international observers.

7   **India:** Foreign Minister Natwar Singh resigns over UN oil-for-food programme.

7   **Palestine:** EU agrees to monitor Rafah border crossing between Gaza and Egypt.

8   **France:** Government declares state of emergency, declares curfews after 12 days of rioting and car-burning in suburbs of cities.

10 **Liberia:** Ellen Johnson-Sirleaf elected president.

10 **Jordan:** Suicide bombs in Amman, claimed by al-Qaeda in Mesopotamia, kill 59, sparking protests in Jordan.

15 **Iraq:** US troops find secret jail with 200 prisoners in Iraqi Interior Ministry.

15 **Israel:** US Secretary of State Condoleezza Rice secures Israel–Palestine agreement on border controls for Gaza strip.

16 **Iraq:** US acknowledges it may have killed Iraqis in Falluja with white phosphorus.

17 **Iran:** Uranium processing resumed at Isfahan.

18 **Iraq:** South Korea says it will cut Iraq troops from 3,200 to 2,000.

18 **Iran:** IAEA chief Mohamed ElBaradei says document in Iran showed it possessed plans to build a nuclear weapon, acquired from A.Q. Khan network.

18 **Sri Lanka:** Mahinda Rajapakse elected president.

21 **Israel:** Prime Minister Ariel Sharon quits Likud party to set up Kadima party.

22 **Germany:** Angela Merkel takes office as chancellor.

22 **US:** José Padilla charged with conspiring to murder people overseas, three years after being held without charge supposedly in connection with radiological bomb plan.

23 **Kenya:** President Mwai Kibaki dismisses cabinet after defeat in referendum on constitution.

23 **Uzbekistan:** Government tells NATO members they can no longer use Uzbek airspace to support Afghanistan operations.

23 **Indonesia:** US lifts arms embargo.

25 **Russia:** Duma passes law requiring all foreign non-governmental organisations to register with a state body with authority to investigate and close them down.

28 **Spain:** Spain agrees to sell military aircraft and ships to Venezuela.

30 **Belgium:** Police arrest 11 people on suspicion of planning terrorist attacks in Iraq after disclosure that a Belgian woman carried out suicide bombing in Baghdad.

December 2005

5   **US:** Final report of 9/11 Commission details shortcomings of US government response to 2001 attacks and says progress is disappointing.

5   **US:** Secretary of State Condoleezza Rice issues statement on renditions and treatment of detainees. Says US does not authorise or condone torture.

7   **Eritrea:** Government orders US, Canadian, European and Russian members of UN peacekeeping force to leave the country.

8   **Saudi Arabia:** King Abdullah convenes leaders of 50 Muslim nations to address 'malaise' in Muslim world.

8   **Iran:** President Mahmoud Ahmadinejad says Israel should be relocated in Germany and Austria, and that the holocaust did not take place.

8   **Afghanistan:** NATO ministers agree to deploy extra 6,000 troops.

15   **Iraq:** Iraqis vote in parliamentary elections.

17   **US:** *New York Times* reveals George W. Bush administration conducted extensive secret wire-tapping programme after 11 September 2001 attacks.

17   **Hong Kong:** World Trade Organisation negotiators agree limited deal.

18   **Bolivia:** Presidential election results in win for Evo Morales.

January 2006

1   **Ukraine:** Russia reduces gas supplies to Ukraine over price dispute, affecting supplies to several European countries. Dispute resolved on January 4.

4   **United Arab Emirates:** Emir of Dubai, Sheikh Maktoum bin Rashid al-Maktoum, dies in Australia. Succeeded by Sheikh Mohammed Bin Rashid al-Maktoum.

4   **Israel:** Prime Minister Ariel Sharon incapacitated by stroke, Ehud Olmert takes over as acting prime minister.

7   **US:** Tom DeLay, US Republican Congressman, steps down as House majority leader after being indicted for violation of election laws. In April, after aides plead guilty to corruption charges, he says he will resign his seat.

10   **Iran:** After giving notification on 3 January, Iran removes IAEA seals from three nuclear facilities and resumes enrichment activity at Natanz.

11   **China:** China and India agree to cooperate to secure crude oil reserves overseas.

12   **Saudi Arabia:** Stampede kills 345 in Mecca during Haj.

15   **Chile:** Michelle Bachelet wins presidential election.

15   **Pakistan:** US bombs Pakistani village in failed attempt to kill senior al-Qaeda figure Ayman al-Zawahiri.

16   **Kuwait:** Emir, Sheikh Jaber al-Ahmad al-Sabah, dies. On 24 January, parliament votes his heir out of office and replaces him as emir with Prime Minister Sheikh Sabah al-Ahmad al-Jaber al-Sabah.

19   **Iraq:** Italy says it will withdraw its 3,000 troops from Iraq by year end.

19   **France:** President Jacques Chirac says France would consider a nuclear response against any state-backed terrorist strike against its interests.

23   **Canada:** Conservative Party wins 40% of seats in parliamentary elections, and forms minority government led by Stephen Harper.

25   **Palestine:** Hamas wins majority of seats in parliamentary election.

26   **UK:** Government announces plans to deploy 4,000 extra soldiers to Afghanistan, with peak number at 5,700.

31   **US:** President Bush, in State of the Union Address, says US must end 'addiction to oil'.

February 2006

5   **Yemen:** 13 al-Qaeda members, convicted of USS *Cole* attack, escape from jail.

5   **Iran:** Government announces it will resume some suspended nuclear activities and will not accept snap IAEA inspections.

5   **Denmark:** Nordic embassies in Middle East attacked in reaction to publication in 2005 of cartoons in a Danish newspaper depicting Prophet Mohammad. Cartoons also provoke protests in Europe.

6   **US:** Ben Bernanke replaces Alan Greenspan as Federal Reserve Board chairman.

21   **Russia:** Aircraft manufacturers merged into single state-run holding company.

22   **Iraq:** Attack on Shia Golden Mosque in Samarra sparks widespread violence.

24   **Philippines:** President Gloria Macapagal-Arroyo declares state of emergency after coup attempt.

24   **Saudi Arabia:** Suicide bomb attack on Abqaiq oil processing facilities foiled.

March 2006

2   **India:** President Bush, in New Delhi, agrees deal allowing India to import US nuclear technology in exchange for opening civilian nuclear facilities to international inspections. Requires approves by Indian parliament and US Congress.

8   **Austria:** International Atomic Energy Agency board sends Iran issue to UN Security Council.

9   **US:** Dubai Ports says it will transfer six US ports, acquired in takeover of British company P&O, to US ownership, after heated US political opposition to deal Bush supported.

9   **Iraq:** US announces plans to close Abu Ghraib prison.

11   **Serbia:** Former president Slobodan Milosevic dies in cell in The Hague, Netherlands.

12   **Sudan:** African foreign ministers agree to extend African Union troops' mandate in Darfur for six months, fending off deployment of UN peacekeepers.

13   **UK:** Government announces plans to cut forces in Iraq by 10% to about 7,000.

16   **Iraq:** Parliament holds first session after election, in spite of failure to form government. US, Iraqi forces mount offensive near Samarra, as US and Iran agree to hold direct talks on Iraq. However, these talks are indefinitely postponed.

19   **Belarus:** Election win for President Alexander Lukashenko provokes protests followed by crackdown.

21   **Russia:** President Vladimir Putin says Russia will build two gas pipelines to China.

22   **Spain:** Basque separatist group ETA announces 'permanent' cease-fire after 38-year violent campaign.

23   **Eritrea:** Government expels three foreign NGOs.

26   **Ukraine:** President Viktor Yushchenko suffers setback in parliamentary elections.

28   **US:** Bush administration personnel shakeup begins as White House Chief of Staff Andrew Card resigns and is replaced by Joshua Bolten.

28   **Israel:** Kadima party wins 29 out of 120 seats in Israeli elections, forms coalition headed by Ehud Olmert. Likud party wins 12 seats.

29   **Nigeria:** Former Liberian leader Charles Taylor attempts to flee from exile in Nigeria, is captured on border with Cameroon and flown to Sierra Leone for trial by special court on war-crimes charges.

29   **Iran:** UN Security Council issues Presidential Statement urging Iran to suspend nuclear activity.

April 2006

2   **Thailand:** Prime Minister Thaksin Shinawatra suffers setback in surprise elections he called, announces he will not continue as PM. However, he remains PM and elections are annulled.

10   **France:** Weeks of demonstrations force government to withdraw First Job Contract legislation that would have made it easier to fire employees under 26.

11   **Spain:** Spanish judge indicts 29 people over Madrid train bombings on 11 March 2004.

19   **Italy:** Court upholds narrow victory of Romano Prodi in 10 April general election, defeating Silvio Berlusconi. In May, Prodi forms government.

23   **US:** Finance ministers agree to reform International Monetary Fund, giving developing countries a bigger role in decision-making and reforming economic surveillance.

24   **Egypt:** Three suicide bombers kill 20 in Sinai resort of Dahab.

24   **Nepal:** King Gyanendra, following days of street protests, agrees to reinstate parliament after removing it in 2005.

25   **Sri Lanka:** Suicide bomber kills 11 and seriously wounds Army chief Lt-Gen. Sarath Fonseka.

28   **Iran:** IAEA says Iran has failed to comply with UN demand to halt uranium enrichment.

May 2006

1   **Bolivia:** President Evo Morales nationalises energy industry and orders troops into gas and oil fields.

3   **US:** Zacarias Moussaoui, only person indicted for 11 September attacks, given life sentence.

5   **US:** Porter Goss, head of Central Intelligence Agency, resigns. General Michael Hayden, deputy director of national intelligence, nominated to succeed him.

8   **Iran:** President Mahmoud Ahmadinejad writes letter to US President Bush.

15   **Libya:** US restores full diplomatic relations.

15   **Sudan:** Following 5 May partial peace deal, African Union agrees to transfer peacekeeping force to UN control.

20   **Iraq:** Government headed by Prime Minister Nouri al-Maliki sworn in. He promises 'maximum force' to deal with insurgency.

21   **Serbia:** Voters in Montenegro approve secession from Serbia.

1 | **Perspectives**

The Persian Gulf dominated international affairs in the year to mid-2006. The obstinate conflict in Iraq worsened as internecine attacks and insurgency exacted a heavy toll that foreign and Iraqi forces seemed powerless to stem. Across the border in Iran, the government defied international pressure by lifting its voluntary suspension of uranium conversion and enrichment activities, arousing renewed concern that the country could have a nuclear weapon by the turn of the decade, or even earlier. Five years after the 11 September 2001 attacks by al-Qaeda against the United States, Islamic extremism remained a potent threat to many countries: the degree of success of the US 'global war on terrorism' in countering violent radicalism was unclear, underlining the difficulties inherent in declaring a 'war' in which no definitive final victory could ever be determined.

During the year, the perception grew in the United States – it was already prevalent in much of the rest of the world – that the Iraq War had been a costly mistake, had been undertaken on false pretences and had damaged rather than advanced US strategic interests. American officials could not help but be acutely aware of the loss of prestige that their country had suffered and of the outright enmity aroused not only by the war, but by the abuse of prisoners at Abu Ghraib prison in Iraq and the detention without charge of hundreds of suspects at Guantanamo Bay in Cuba. The United States, in pursuing what it saw as a war against terrorism primarily by military means, had succeeded in fanning the flames of radicalism. Its abuses appeared to most people irreconcilable with America's exhortation to other countries to embrace democracy and human rights. Therefore, it was not surprising that, as the first year of President George W. Bush's second term unfolded, changes in Washington's approach began to be seen. Steadily, Condoleezza Rice, as secretary of state, grasped control of US foreign policy and steered Bush along a line that saw him owning up to some of the administration's past mistakes and adopting a more consultative and multilateral tone on key issues such as Iran's nuclear programme. In truth, he had little option but to shift away from the unilateralist, neo-conservative doctrine of his first term as he came under heavy fire from mainstream Republican Senators.

The United States remained, as it will for many years, the world's only superpower, with a very large, resilient economy as well as military power unassailable by that of any other country or, probably, any grouping of countries. But its ability to use that position benignly to exert change in the world has been badly damaged by failures and abuses: its casting of the world's essential challenge as a 'war on terror' – re-branded by the Pentagon in 2006 as 'the long war' – struck few chords outside the United States. Terrorism, in the view of others, is simply a tactic, and its uses should almost always be treated as a series of crimes that are symptomatic of more or less local political tensions rather than as a global challenge to be addressed militarily. To the rest of the world, the really dangerous issues seemed much more chronic and familiar: nuclear proliferation, regional and national struggles, climate change, poverty and disease. In addition, a world in which the United States had steadily lost credibility was also one in which the established order was undergoing change, with emergent powers expanding their international relations and pressing their interests. The problem for the international system was that the United States could not lead on the basis of the strategy of the first Bush administration, yet the rest of the world was unable to construct any other order that did not involve a central role for the United States. The unavoidable conclusion was that the United States would need to understand, and build into its global strategy, the very different concerns that preoccupied much of the rest of the world. Conversely, those of America's critics who wanted Washington to continue to play a pivotal role would have to better appreciate and address its concerns.

Iraq: politics and insecurity

Three years after the US-led invasion of Iraq, large parts of the country remained in the grip of violence, with government institutions yet to resume effective management after disintegrating at the fall of Saddam Hussein's regime. The lack of security meant that, to the extent that central Iraqi control was exerted, it continued to be from the heavily fortified Green Zone, a ten square kilometre area of central Baghdad. This picture of disorder was not uniform: the northern Kurdish areas of Iraq, as was the case under Saddam, enjoyed considerable autonomy and mostly peaceful order.

The elections of December 2005, followed eventually by the formation of a government in May 2006, represented important steps forward. The United States, mainly through its Ambassador Zalmay Khalilzad, played a key role in harrying and supporting the long bargaining that led to Nouri al-Maliki's emergence as prime minister and his appointment of a cabinet. This culminated in Bush's lightning excursion to Baghdad on 13 June 2006 to express support for al-Maliki. The visit enabled the Bush administration to cast progress in Iraq in a far more favourable light than had been possible through the darker days of the preceding year. But it also highlighted both the lack of security in Iraq and the client status of the country's supposedly sovereign government: until it became public knowledge, the trip was a tight secret among a very few people, and was disguised by a misleading account of Bush's plans for the day; al-Maliki as prime minister had no knowledge of the arrival of a foreign head of state until moments before he met him.

The establishment in three years of a new democracy in a nation torn by sectarian strife and without a democratic tradition may justly be regarded as an achievement both for Iraqi politicians, many of them previously long-term exiles, and for their foreign abettors. Turnout in the 15 December 2005 elections reached 76%, indicating that voters included significant numbers of the Sunni minority that had governed the country under Saddam and had most to fear from Shia domination. Al-Maliki's cabinet represented a cross-section of the nation, with representatives from all the main ethnic and religious groups. It included members of the different factions of the Shia majority, as well as a Sunni defence minister, a Kurdish foreign minister, and an oil minister who, though Shia, was not allied to any political party. The government included representatives of militia forces that had been heavily involved in fighting against American forces or violence against fellow Iraqis. From out of the chaos of the US-led occupation, a political process had thus developed and had produced a representative government, albeit one operating from behind heavily defended barricades.

However, the government's writ did not yet extend far beyond the Green Zone. Much of the country was afflicted by a profound absence of security. Acts of sectarian violence and murder were commonplace, leading many to believe that the country was either on the point of descending into civil war, or had in fact already done so. Several distinct strands were interwoven. Organised crime was rampant on the streets. Militias continued to operate, ranging from self-defence groups formed by residents to patrol their neighbourhoods to substantial, well-established organisations like the Mahdi Army and the Badr Brigade. The militias had infiltrated Iraqi security forces, leading for example to the imprisonment and torture of large numbers of Sunni Arabs in Shia-controlled Interior Ministry cells. Layered into the criminal gangs and militias was an insurgency that sought to fuel sectarian strife, to disrupt the advance of democracy and to target the 150,000 foreign troops in Iraq. The insurgency had formed around several groups that fused nationalism with Salafist Islamic views. Amid daily suicide bombings and other attacks, its most effective strike during the past year was the February 2006 bombing of the al-Askariyya Mosque in Samarra, one of Shia Islam's holiest shrines, an act that set off a wave of sectarian killing and destruction in which hundreds died. Non-Iraqi Arab fighters, and in particular the Jordanian Abu Musab al-Zarqawi, played a key role in marshalling the insurgency. But US and Iraqi forces made a breakthrough on 8 June 2006 when an American air strike killed Zarqawi in a village near Baquba, 65km north of Baghdad. Although a new leader of al-Qaeda in Mesopotamia – almost certainly another foreigner – was immediately announced, there were signs that the movement was finding itself under increasing pressure from US and Iraqi forces.

The Iraq conflict remained disturbing and disruptive for the rest of the Arab world, which simultaneously was nervously observing Iran's role in Iraq and Tehran's accelerated pursuit of nuclear capabilities. The United States repeatedly charged Iran with meddling in Iraq. Indeed, Iranian influence could hardly be avoided: one of Iraq's main Shia political parties, the Supreme Council for the Islamic Revolution in Iraq, had been based in Iran before the fall of Saddam. The United States and the United Kingdom alleged that technology originating in Iran had been found in bomb devices in southern Iraq. The Arab world, however, seemed to have few levers to influence either events in Iraq or tensions with Iran.

Iran: looming conflict or long-term negotiation?

Since the 1979–81 hostage crisis, few relationships have been as fraught with confrontation and a lack of mutual understanding as that between the United States and Iran. Over the past year, their stand-off has escalated because of Tehran's more determined pursuit of nuclear capabilities, as well as its alleged interference in Iraqi affairs, its continued sponsoring of terrorist groups, and the provocative rhetoric of President Mahmoud Ahmadinejad. The irony of this situation is that the United States and Iran – as well as many other countries – in fact have regional security interests in common. Both would benefit from a more stable Iraq, a Shia-dominated democracy from which foreign troops could withdraw; both require a quiet Gulf in which oil can flow uninterrupted; both want an orderly Afghanistan in which terrorism, drugs and foreign troops are not prevalent. Yet as this chapter of *Strategic Survey* was being written, the confrontation between Iran and the United States over Tehran's nuclear programme seemed to pose a serious risk of eventual conflict. Tehran was considering a package of incentives devised by France, Germany and the United Kingdom and agreed by the United States, China and Russia.

That permanent agreement on the nuclear issue is almost impossible under current circumstances is evident from Tehran's absolute belief – on which the government has strong popular support – in its right and need to be self-sufficient in uranium enrichment. While it denies that its purpose is to build nuclear weapons, its past concealment, its missile programmes, evidence of military linkages and the illogic of its uranium activities lead experts to believe that it has this end in view.

On the other side, the Western world, Russia and China are united in the view that Iran must not have nuclear weapons; among them, the only issue is about how this should be prevented. France, Germany and the United Kingdom, taking the lead in negotiations with Iran, have in essence held the view that the best option was to delay Iranian activities for as long as possible in the hope of changes in political circumstances that could permit a permanent cessation. This led to the Paris agreement of November 2004, under which Iran agreed to a voluntary suspension of all uranium enrichment-related and reprocessing activities.

In 2005 and 2006, Tehran took a series of steps that had the effect of ending the Paris agreement. In August 2005, the newly elected Ahmadinejad derisively rejected a European package of incentives including political and security cooperation, support for a civil nuclear programme, and economic and technical cooperation, but also proposed a binding commitment by Iran not to pursue fuel-cycle activities other than the construction and operation of light-water power and research reactors. In the same month, Iran resumed conversion of uranium yellow-cake into compounds for enrichment. In January 2006, Iran resumed enrichment R&D, and in April it announced that it had enriched uranium in a 164-machine cascade, that it planned a 3,000-machine cascade and that its conversion activities had produced 110 tonnes of uranium hexafluoride to feed into the cascades. These and other announcements and actions indicated Iran was heading towards a feared 'break-out' capacity for nuclear weapons, and that it was seeking decisively to alter the 'facts on the ground' upon which international talks would be based.

The Iranian moves led inevitably to a decision by the board of the International Atomic Energy Agency (IAEA) to refer the matter to the United Nations Security Council, which in March 2006 called for an IAEA-verified suspension of uranium enrichment and related activities. This was followed by the offer of the new package of incentives agreed by the five permanent members of the Security Council plus Germany, under consideration by Iran in mid-June. Russia and China prevented any language that could allow the Council statement to be interpreted as providing a trigger for eventual military action.

Iran's progress on enrichment, made by omitting lengthy testing processes that would be customary, brought forward in most experts' minds the earliest possible time by which – assuming similar continued progress on enrichment and other fronts – Iran might possess a nuclear weapon. The US assessment was that this could be about the turn of the decade, though some assessments in Europe estimated an earlier timeframe. The implication of these estimates is that time remains for diplomacy – but not much. This explains, perhaps, the striking consensus of the international community, including Russia and China. Bush made a remarkable concession to the desire for unity and diplomacy when he agreed to associate Washington with the package of incentives and to join negotiations if Iran first suspended all enrichment activity – the first such direct contact between the two countries since the 1970s. The fact of US involvement clearly must give Tehran pause for thought. Although Ahmadinejad's fiery statements – such as that Israel must be 'wiped off the map' – have attracted the most attention, the nuclear issue falls under the control of the Supreme Leader, Ayatollah Sayyid Ali Khamenei. Nevertheless, it is hard to identify the potential points of a lasting compromise, and the most likely path seems a reversion to the Security Council and attempts at a Chapter VII resolution that would make suspension mandatory, followed by sanctions provisions if Iran still refused – always with the possibility that Bush could opt for pre-emptive bombing of nuclear facilities.

International terrorism: difficult policy issues

While almost no government would follow the example of the United States in making a 'war on terror' the central tenet of its foreign and security policy, many would agree that the potential for terrorist acts committed by Islamic extremists remains a serious threat. The premise of the American response to the 11 September 2001 attacks on New York City and Washington was that the threat was external, and could be eliminated mostly by military action abroad, as well as isolating terrorists by, for example, preventing their movements and cutting off sources of funds. Since the initial focus of the response was on military action in Afghanistan because it had provided safe haven to al-Qaeda, it was an easy decision for other countries to express solidarity with the United States and to take part in that action. In the nearly five years that have since passed, however, the situation has become far more complex.

For many countries, the terrorist threat simply forms part of domestic and regional affairs – and would not necessarily be seen as the most serious danger to national security. In Muslim countries, and those that have significant Muslim minorities, the risk is that small numbers of people may become radicalised, espousing an al-Qaeda-inspired 'universalist' view of Islam that paints the religion as being under attack everywhere from a Western conspiracy, and demands a global and violent response. But while the appeal to extremists may lie in a view that seeks to transcend localities and nations, the effects and responses are national and local. Arab governments, often managing delicate political, factional or sectarian balances, fear that people returning from Iraq may adversely affect these balances – but cannot afford to alienate, through excessive responses, large elements of their populations. European governments also do not wish their responses to provide fodder for extremist arguments. For all countries threatened, appropriate responses include vigilance and action by intelligence agencies and security forces, and sharing of information with other relevant countries. But they also see the need to embrace social and economic policies, as well as religious teachings, that seek to counter alienation or, if it occurs, to prevent it from leading to violence. The most effective response to the terrorist threat is for governments to have policies that are widely seen to be just.

The difficulties and dilemmas posed by Islamic extremism have been in sharp focus in European countries, many of which have large Muslim minorities. The 7 July 2005 bombings in London, which killed 52 people and injured 700, shocked Britons because all four attackers had been brought up entirely in England: three were born there to Pakistani immigrants, and the fourth had moved from Jamaica as a baby. They appeared to have become radicalised in the course of their daily life around the northern city of Leeds: no evidence had yet been found to connect their adoption of extremist views directly with al-Qaeda or other foreigners, although two of them had visited Pakistan. The leader, Mohammad Sidique Khan, made a suicide video in which he said: 'Your democratically elected governments continuously perpetuate atrocities against my people all over the world.' His reference to 'my people' – identifying himself with Muslims worldwide, rather than with his nationality or family – gave pause for thought about the success or otherwise of the government's 'multicultural' approach to integrating immigrant communities into British society. This approach respects and even encourages different cultures, customs and languages of ethnic groups, which together make up a diverse entity that forms a nation. Critics argue, however, that it does not adequately create a sense of national identity and citizenship – Khan seemed to provide evidence for this argument. Equally, the opposite method of integration, known as 'assimilation', seemed to be having, at best, mixed success. France's emphasis on French customs and language seeks to discourage differences between cultures and customs and to foster a single nationhood. But over the past year it has suffered serious violence among disadvantaged immigrant communities. While a serious act of Islamic extremist terrorism had not occurred in France, many suspects have been arrested and deported by the country's tough judicial authorities. Governments across Europe were in mid-2006 striving to understand the motivations behind tendencies towards extremist violence within their countries, and to adjust social and judicial policies to address the threats. However, in doing so they ran up against civil-liberty concerns – that in, for example, increasing surveillance activities and extending periods of detention without charge, they could be dismantling the open societies that were, in themselves, the best advertisement against illiberal extremist beliefs.

The London bombings, as well as other acts and plots around Europe, underlined what had already been the clear trend since al-Qaeda's leadership was scattered or killed by the 2001 invasion of Afghanistan. It has increasingly become a 'virtual', atomised organisation, inspiring rather than initiating or carrying out terrorist acts. The Internet plays a very important role in facilitating the communication of ideology, information, encouragement, fellow-feeling and technical know-how. Such a network may be penetrable by intelligence and law-enforcement agencies, but is not obviously vulnerable to military action. However, the approach of the United States, elaborated in the 2006 Quadrennial Defense Review, continues to emphasise military capabilities, such as those of US Special Operations Forces, which are to receive additional resources.

The international order in question

Fundamental differences between nations about how to view and tackle terrorism are indicative of deeper fissures. World leaders seem scarcely able to make an international speech without referring to globalisation, to the increasing interdependence of nations, to the need for common approaches to shared problems. The implication is that this need is not being met by the intersecting network of organisations, treaties and structures through which, since the Second World War, the world has sought to address international issues: the United Nations (UN) and its specialist agencies, the North Atlantic Treaty Organisation (NATO), the Nuclear Non-proliferation Treaty (NPT), the International Monetary Fund (IMF), the World Bank, and more recently the World Trade Organisation (WTO). This architecture has been put increasingly in question since Bush took office in 2001 – though his aggressive unilateralism perhaps accelerated and exposed institutional inadequacies as much as it created them. The composition of the UN Security Council no longer reflects global power balances; the UN itself has been weakened by corruption and the perceived ineffectiveness of some of its agencies; NATO leaders have not settled on a post-Cold War role for the Alliance even though it is an active deployer of troops; the IMF and World Bank are being reformed after providing solutions to developing countries' problems that were not popularly acceptable; the current round of WTO negotiations has been stuttering.

The structures have not seemed adequate to manage current trends. These include globalisation, with its potential for disruption in one part of the world to damage another; the growing role of an undemocratic but wealthy China in a globalised world; the proliferation of nuclear weapons; Islamic extremism; climate change; and chronic problems of poverty and disease. Instead of the shared approach for which leaders call, globalisation has over the past year provoked alarming instances of economic nationalism, such as the successful Congressional opposition to an Arab purchase of American ports. While the West has sought to tie increased aid for Africa to improved governance in African nations, China is ploughing in large investments to expand its trade and energy supplies without regard to politics or governance. The rise of China has produced an exceptional degree of economic interdependence with the United States, but this is of questionable durability given that the two nations continue to spar with each other cagily on security issues, and that the future of Taiwan remains unresolved. Nuclear proliferation has not been contained: though there was progress with Libya's renunciation of a nuclear programme, India and Pakistan have built weapons, North Korea claims to have done so, and Iran has recently accelerated efforts to develop the technologies that would allow it to build them. Finally, the growth of Islamic extremism has evoked the contrasting responses mentioned above: the US 'global war on terrorism' is more alienating than inspiring to the rest of the world.

Though the United States did not by itself create these divisions and inadequacies, the Bush administration's policies appear at least to have created diversions that have hampered effective common action to address them. The world since the Cold War has been anchored on American power. But the Iraqi adventure has revealed limits to American military clout and strategic leverage. The Bush doctrine of pre-emption, the invasion of Iraq on what appeared later to be false pretences, as well as abuses at Abu Ghraib prison in Iraq and Guantanamo Bay in Cuba, have combined to accentuate in the minds of many people the overweening aspects of US power and its perceived disregard for international law and global norms. Notwithstanding the large loss of American life on 11 September and the risk of terrorists acquiring nuclear, biological, chemical or radiological weapons, the threat of terrorism is overshadowed for much of humanity by more immediate threats. For example, on one issue of global concern, climate change, the Bush administration has adopted an attitude of ostentatious indifference.

Washington, meanwhile, pressed a theme of its own: democratisation as a central means of eradicating terrorism. The neo-conservative belief was that the creation of democracy in Iraq would be swiftly followed by similar moves throughout the region, which in turn would remove the ground from beneath Islamic radicalism. But Iraq has shown the difficulties of this project, and governments in the Arab world, many of which have defence agreements with the United States, have not surprisingly been unenthusiastic. That terrorism has developed anew in Europe's open, democratic societies is awkward and discomfiting for the Bush thesis. The Bush administration's continued support – for traditional reasons of realpolitik – of authoritarian leaders in Central Asia also sits poorly with its democracy project. While the United States is correct to argue that nuclear weapons in the hands of Iran would be far more dangerous than their current possession by Israel, it is curiously indifferent to how this double standard is perceived throughout the world.

The effect was to create a sense of the world's most powerful country, rather than leading ways to address the shared problems of a globalised world in a cooperative manner, pursuing instead an isolated track that appeared, by turns, ineffective, irrelevant and objectionable. Its unilateralism had put in question the legitimacy of its actions. It was seen to have over-reached itself. It was losing friends even among its natural allies, for example in Latin America. While this posed profound questions about the future of America's hegemonic role, it also raised the prospect of a world in which fundamental structures and systems had been undermined, with no indication of what was to replace them. This sense of a world operating without a system is one that leaders need urgently to counter, almost certainly by reasserting the primacy of the world's institutions, while ensuring that these are, and are seen to be, relevant to the world's most pressing issues. But such leadership seems beyond the ambitions, mindset or political capacities of current leaders.

America's changing tune

America's lost prestige and damaged credibility have been disconcerting for those who want to see it as a benign guarantor of security in many parts of the world. It has been depressing for American officials who see honest efforts to preserve security amidst many specific disputes and tensions discredited and undermined. However, a change of tack in Washington under the second Bush administration is already showing signs of bringing about rehabilitation.

Part of Washington's problem during its period of 11-September-induced dislocation was that its closest allies failed to be sufficiently frank with it, partly because they risked a humiliating public rebuke like Defense Secretary Donald Rumsfeld's description of France and Germany as 'old Europe'. This contributed to the muddled rationale for the Iraq invasion, the diplomatic train-wreck that preceded it, and the incompetent execution of the occupation – all of which have since haunted the United States and its coalition partners. Over the past year, the administration – admittedly, mainly because of domestic pressures – has shown willingness to admit errors, and allies have been more open in their criticism of Washington. The somewhat paradoxical effect has been to forge greater unity, as has been seen, for example, with regard to Iran.

This change has come about as Rice, who replaced Colin Powell as secretary of state in the second Bush administration, has steadily taken control of foreign policy, using access unrivalled among her Cabinet colleagues to the president's attention and trust. Her deputy as national security adviser in the first administration, Stephen Hadley, succeeded her in the White House post, ensuring a strong White House–State Department axis that has appeared to reduce the importance of Vice President Dick Cheney and of Rumsfeld, who between them had secured the Pentagon's control of the Iraq occupation. Cheney was weakened by the resignation and indictment over a leak inquiry of his chief of staff, Lewis 'Scooter' Libby, Jr, in October 2005. During a March 2006 visit to the United Kingdom, Rice said of Iraq: 'I know we've made tactical errors – thousands of them, I'm sure.' Rumsfeld gave public vent to his irritation. He then endured criticism of his performance from a string of retired generals. When the two secretaries visited Baghdad together the following month, Rice energetically took the clear lead, and the *Washington Post* reported that they 'often seemed in separate orbits'.

Meanwhile, America's allies became bolder. In May 2006, Peter Goldsmith, who holds the UK Cabinet position of attorney general, attacked the detention facility at Guantanamo Bay, where several British detainees have been held. He said it was 'unacceptable' and should close: 'The historic tradition of the United States as a beacon of freedom, liberty and justice deserves the removal of this symbol.' German Chancellor Angela Merkel made a similar call, to which Bush responded: 'I would very much like to end Guantanamo. I would very much like to get people to a court.'

The National Security Strategy published in March 2006 revealed evidence of a shift back to more normal American priorities and international relations. While referring to a 'long struggle' against Islamic extremism, the Strategy did not cast the 'war on terror' – and certainly not its military pursuit – as the dominant guiding factor. Instead, it presented a far more traditional mix of promotion of human rights, democracy, economic growth and counter-proliferation, and stressed the need for international cooperation. Rice had signalled a more pragmatic approach in January with her announcement of a new mission for the State Department that she called 'transformational diplomacy'. This, she said, was 'rooted in partnership, not in paternalism'. The new policy involved shifting more diplomatic posts to fast-growing developing countries and into cities without American representation, as well as rebuilding the role and morale of her department.

There can be no doubt that if these signs of a more cooperative approach are borne out in practice – Bush's approach to Iran at mid-2006 suggested that this may be happening – it is likely to be embraced. Because of the size of America's markets and its importance in dealing with any global crisis, it remains a priority for almost all governments to have a comfortable relationship with the United States.

Persistent security issues

The continuing need for international cooperation is evident from the significant number of persistent conflicts and disputes that threaten international security. In addition to Iraq, Iran and Islamic extremism, these include Afghanistan, North Korea's nuclear programme, conflicts in Sudan, the Democratic Republic of the Congo and other African nations, and the Israel–Palestine stand-off.

- Construction of a new state in Afghanistan remained at serious risk from Taliban violence – spurred, according to Kabul, by Pakistan – and economic dependence on opium. In 2006, NATO expanded its presence into southern Afghanistan and re-styled the mission of the American troops it replaced to focus more on providing a secure environment for ordinary Afghans. But the Taliban's domination of some rural areas made the NATO mission fraught with risk.

- Little progress was made over the past year in resolving the stand-off over North Korea's nuclear-weapons programme. In mid-2006 Pyongyang carried out a missile test that increased tensions. Although the Six-Party Talks framework produced agreement in September 2005 on a Joint Statement of Principles, it later emerged that this had not really resolved differences, and the stalemate continued.

- Though Africa as a whole benefited from renewed investment and aid from industrialised countries and China, several African conflicts continued to defy resolution, with a heavy presence of peacekeeping troops across the continent. The conflict in the Darfur area of Sudan claimed many lives and spilled into neighbouring Chad. There were difficulties in implementing Sudan's 2005 Comprehensive Peace Agreement and unrest in several parts of the country.

- Elections in Israel, following Ariel Sharon's incapacitation by illness, and in Palestine, where Hamas won control of parliament, left an uncertain outlook as Ehud Olmert, the new Israeli prime minister, planned to press ahead with unilateral withdrawals of settlers from parts of the West Bank.

Questions about rising powers

'The rise of China' has been the most over-used phrase in international relations over the past year – but nevertheless demands attention, particularly in light of the concomitant decline in American prestige. Chinese economic growth has continued apace, and so too has the expansion of its international relationships, driven partly by the growth of its trade and a desire to guarantee long-term access to sources of oil. In April 2006 President Hu Jintao called for a strategic partnership with Africa: China's investments in energy exploration and infrastructure have enabled it to deepen relations with Angola, Kenya, Morocco, Sudan and Nigeria. Its economic power has also won new regional influence: for example, in 2005 Indonesia entered into a wide-ranging bilateral partnership with both security and economic aspects. Beijing's adherence to the non-interference principle and its skilful blending of economic and politico-security elements have distinguished its foreign policy from that of the United States in the developing world. For example, it has been unwilling to exert political influence over Sudan's regime, which exports 60% of its oil to China, even as the West sought to stop genocide in Darfur.

Many countries, unsure whether China's international aspirations are disruptive or not, have responded to its push for heightened engagement with a cautious approach termed 'hedged integration' – engaging Beijing for economic reasons and in the hope of its eventual embrace of international norms, but remaining alert to the possibility of less welcome outcomes and recognising that China's ultimate designs are unknown. While the Chinese leadership may be looking increasingly outwards, it is also concerned with its own survival and with domestic matters such as the growing strains between a still-impoverished interior and thriving coastal provinces and cities, as well as tensions with ethnic minorities.

In February 2006, the Pentagon's Quadrennial Defense Review identified China as the country with 'the greatest potential to compete militarily with the United States and field disruptive military technologies that could over time offset traditional US military advantages'. It noted that Beijing's military modernisation programme was putting 'regional military balances at risk' and called for greater transparency in defence spending. However, American–Chinese commercial and financial engagement is already extremely deep, and the consequences of any confrontation would be very costly for both China and the United States. American companies have invested heavily in China, which, with a very large trade surplus deriving principally from American imports of low-cost Chinese goods, has invested heavily in US government securities. Washington says it wants China to be a responsible 'stakeholder' in the international system, but Beijing has not made a clear response to this request. A policy of hedged integration will probably remain a prudent way to approach China for some time to come.

China's rise is twinned in common parlance with that of India, which has remained a power in waiting for so long mainly because of its own diffidence about playing a distinctive role on the world stage. India has begun to fulfil some of its economic potential, though it remains well behind China in this respect. It has also moved beyond an obsessional preoccupation with Pakistan to expand its international presence in a number of ways, not least by declaring itself a nuclear-weapons state following test explosions in 1998. This produced first an intense, mostly private dialogue between officials representing then Prime Minister Atal Behari Vajpayee and US President Bill Clinton, followed by the development a full-fledged strategic relationship under President Bush, which continued after Manmohan Singh's Congress Party-led government was elected in 2004. From Washington's viewpoint, India – a democracy that now has a more open economy as well as large diaspora and student community in the United States – seems a natural ally and perhaps a counter-balance to China's growing power. US–Indian military cooperation is growing, particularly in the maritime sphere as the Indian Navy has acquired more power projection capability.

However, the central element of the relationship – and thus the greatest risk to it – has become the proposed nuclear agreement agreed between Singh and Bush in Washington in July 2005 and again in New Delhi in February 2006. The agreement is intended to end India's nuclear isolation by giving it access to nuclear fuel and technology in return for placing most of its nuclear reactors under international supervision while separating civilian and military nuclear programmes.

This accommodation of the nuclear status of India, which is not a member of the NPT, has been criticised as fatally undermining the non-proliferation regime of which the NPT is the core, and as increasing incentives for proliferation. However American supporters argued it would strengthen non-proliferation by agreeing curbs with and monitoring of a country that would not join the NPT and would not abandon nuclear weapons. The deal required approval from the US Congress and the 45-nation Nuclear Suppliers' Group.

While moving closer to Washington, New Delhi has also been building ties with Beijing and Moscow. Economic and political accords were signed when Chinese Premier Wen Jiabao visited India in April 2005. However, India is acutely conscious that China has intensified commercial and security relations with the states surrounding India – Bangladesh, the Maldives, Myanmar, Nepal, Pakistan and Sri Lanka – and has been securing access to Central Asian oil.

Russia, too, has been flexing newfound muscles that result in its case from oil and gas wealth. As its foreign-exchange reserves and its economy have rapidly grown, dependence on foreign finance and advice during the 1990s has been replaced by assertiveness and a deterioration of relations with the United States and Europe. A temporary cut-off of gas supplies to Ukraine in January 2006 over a price dispute was seen in the West as an alarming sign of Russian willingness to use energy resources as a political tool. US Vice President Dick Cheney accused Moscow of 'intimidation and blackmail'. Russia has been rebuilding relationships in Central Asia and with China, to which President Vladimir Putin agreed in 2006 to build two natural gas pipelines. The two countries jointly called for the withdrawal of US forces from Central Asia through the medium of the Shanghai Cooperation Organisation, a regional body that is likely to attract increasing attention. However, there are important question marks over Russia's ability to sustain its clout: oil and gas output is likely to decline in the absence of large investment to develop unexploited reserves, and the country's progress is held back by corruption and other domestic challenges. Much will hang on the outcome of presidential elections in 2008, in which Putin is constitutionally barred from seeking a third term.

Though the past year has been characterised by lost American prestige and a spreading of wings by resurgent China, Russia and India, it is probably premature to discern a fundamental revision of the established world order. The signs are that the United States' post-Cold War dominance of the international system may not be unshakeable in the long term. But Washington – particularly with a revitalised and more traditional foreign policy – is certainly not accepting a drift into decline as a fait accompli. In particular, US diplomatic efforts across Asia indicate that it is attempting to recoup its strategic position by bolstering relations with states of all sizes that it sees as key allies and associates in its hedging strategy vis-à-vis China. Whatever some in Washington might fear, there is no risk of a Cold-War-like strategic convergence among the rising powers of China, Russia and India that would directly challenge American dominance: tensions, suspicions and disputes among them persist.

Nagging questions remain, however, about long-standing American common interests with Europe and Latin America. At a time of so much jostling for power and influence among old and new powers, Europe is in a poor position. Its much-vaunted potential to act as a concerted actor on the world stage – which Washington has long claimed to want to see – has been set back by the halt to European Union integration brought about by French and Dutch voters' rejection of a proposed constitutional treaty. Simultaneously, the main European countries have been going through periods of introspection and domestic political transition. Willingness of European governments to play the role in international security that Washington seeks has been seen in expanded deployments of troops to Afghanistan and other European defence initiatives, as well as the strong and united stance taken by Europe on Iran's nuclear programme. However, Washington's desire to turn NATO into a more global security body, perhaps with special status for Australia and New Zealand and possibly Japan and South Korea, has not been greeted with enthusiasm. Meanwhile, Washington's influence in South America has been undermined by the populism of Venezuelan President Hugo Chávez, who has embarked on an international anti-American crusade buoyed by oil wealth. Other regional leaders mostly do not like his intervention in their affairs but cannot ignore his populist appeal.

These trends leave Washington with an opportunity to rebuild its international standing on the basis of more familiar foreign-policy positions that leave behind the unilateralism, neo-conservatism and international dislocation of Bush's first term. Improvements in security in Iraq and signs of the containment of Iran would help in a return to normality, and would provide a breathing space in which to arrest the current sense of deleterious global drift, which can only give encouragement to those who are inclined to cause disruption. The United States may not for some time – perhaps not ever – be able to reassume the same unquestioned dominance that it enjoyed in the years after the Cold War. But it will be a vital part of any new dispensation of power.

2 | Strategic Policy Issues

The Campaign against Terrorism: Five Years after 11 September

Nearly 3,000 people died in the terrorist attacks on the United States on 11 September 2001. In the five years that have elapsed since, the priority for the United States, Russia, Europe and other key targets has understandably been self-protection and, therefore, 'hard' security and counter-terrorism. The United States prosecuted what it called the 'Global War on Terrorism' with some vigour and tactical coordination (for example, through counter-terrorism intelligence centres established between the United States and other governments), but with a deficit of strategic direction. Hard power – military counter-insurgency in Iraq, Afghanistan and elsewhere; law enforcement and intelligence cooperation; homeland security – still constituted the bulk of the overall effort. Yet, since the US-led takedown of al-Qaeda and the Taliban in Afghanistan in late 2001 and early 2002, the indisputable overall tendency of the global Islamist terrorist network has been to disperse and atomise. This means that groups in Europe and potentially the United States, inspired by 11 September and other spectacular jihadist operations, will spring up more or less autonomously and spontaneously in largely urban areas, manned more by 'local talent' than by imports. The attacks in Madrid in 2004 and London in 2005 were consistent with this pattern. The current overall approach to counter-terrorism appears inadequate to address this development.

US counter-terrorism strategy

As of early 2006, the United States still seemed intent on militarising counter-terrorism. While acknowledging that defeating terrorism required winning the war of ideas in the long run, the new National Security Strategy, released on 16 March 2006, tended to stress military means for preventing attacks; denying terrorists support, sanctuary and access to weapons of mass destruction; and denying them control of any nation or territory that they might use as a base and a platform. The Department of Defense (DoD)'s 2006 Quadrennial Defense Review (QDR), though acknowledging that transnational terrorists 'cannot be defeated solely through military force', broadly embodied the view that the so-called 'Global War on Terrorism', now re-branded 'the Long War', integrally involved the military in that aggressive intervention abroad was necessary to forestall terrorist operations in US territory. The QDR envisaged a long war not against nation-states but rather against non-state networks, which called for a US capability to engage enemies in countries with which it was not at war 'in many operations characterised by irregular warfare' and an ability 'to operate clandestinely and to sustain a persistent but low-visibility presence'. Accordingly, 'long-duration, complex operations involving the U.S. military, other government agencies and international partners will be waged simultaneously in multiple countries around the world, relying on a combination of direct (visible) and indirect (clandestine) approaches'. The QDR further asserted that 'maintaining a long-term, low-visibility presence in many areas of the world where US forces do not traditionally operate will be required'. Corresponding premiums are placed on, for example, accurate real-time intelligence, proactive military train-and-equip programmes with key countries, quick global response capabilities, and riverine warfare capacities to help foreign security forces deny terrorists territorial access. Maritime-domain awareness and interdiction are also priorities, embodied in the US-led and now strongly multilateral Proliferation Security Initiative.

The QDR's principal prescribed counter-terrorist instruments are special-operations forces (SOF), which 'will possess an expanded organic ability to locate, tag and track dangerous individuals and other high-value targets globally'. This mission was reinforced by organisation changes: US Special Operations Command (SOCOM) became a 'supported' as well as a 'supporting' combatant command, with substantial budgetary and operational independence from the regional combatant commands, and was assigned the lead military counter-terrorist role under the 2004 Unified Command Plan. In addition, the 9/11 Commission recommended that the military should take over the Central Intelligence Agency (CIA)'s paramilitary division, and Congress decided in 2005 to provide SOCOM with $25 million annually in discretionary money that can be used to buy foreign allegiances – a function previously the CIA's alone. In turn, the National Military Strategic Plan for the War on Terrorism, promulgated in early 2006, tasks SOCOM with preparing a 'Global Strategic Plan' for the 'war on terror' that will become the centrepiece of the American counter-terrorist enterprise. Consistent with this plan, SOCOM is now the only supported command with a geographically unlimited remit.

By the end of the 2006 fiscal year, US SOF are expected to number 52,846 – the troop strength of three or four infantry divisions. SOCOM's baseline budget has increased 81% since 2001, and for fiscal-year 2006 will come to $6.6 billion. Over the next five years, the DoD plans to increase its personnel by more than 13,000 (15%), and to add $9bn to SOCOM's budget. The DoD will also increase the number of active-duty US Army Special Forces battalions by a third; expand psychological operations and civil-affairs units by 3,700 personnel, or 33%; establish a 2,600-strong Marine Corps Special Operations Command; establish an SOF unmanned aerial vehicle squadron; and enhance SOF capabilities for insertion into and extraction from denied areas from strategic distances. Underlining SOCOM's institutional significance is Secretary of Defense Donald Rumsfeld's inclusion of the SOCOM deputy commander on the 12-person Deputies Advisory Working Group, which was made a permanent part of the DoD's senior management structure in March 2006. No other combatant commander was so privileged.

The Pentagon now allows SOF to operate as 'military liaison elements', with considerable independence, in countries with which the United States has a full diplomatic and civilian intelligence presence. Advocates of SOCOM's growing role in the campaign against terrorism believe that SOF should be engaged in all of the 60-odd countries in which jihadist cells are believed to operate. In the counter-terrorism arena, then, the Pentagon has continued to win the bureaucratic contest with the State Department and the CIA. While the Bush administration paid lip-service to the importance of public diplomacy in the campaign against terrorism, it has not expedited its pursuit. Karen Hughes, the undersecretary of state for public diplomacy and public affairs, did not assume her post for six months following her nomination. Her disastrous 'listening tour' in September–October 2005 merely confirmed to Muslim populations American naiveté and ignorance about Islam and the impact of US policies.

Counter-arguments

Some governments have acknowledged the need for more focused and inventive applications of soft power, particularly in the form of public diplomacy in the Muslim world and more integrative state outreach to Muslim communities in Europe. But the intensifying jihadist-assisted insurgency in Iraq and the July 2005 London bombings (and attempted bombings) indicated that actual efforts in those areas were proving insufficient to stem jihadist recruitment and activity. The global jihad has continued its post-Afghanistan evolution as a horizontal, atomised network in which the core al-Qaeda leadership, headed by Osama bin Laden and Ayman al-Zawahiri, had diminished command and control but could inspire and influence regional insurgencies (e.g., al-Qaeda in Mesopotamia, Kashmiri separatists, and several Southeast Asian groups) and local upstart groups (like those that staged the Madrid and London bombings). This pattern, driven by Internet-spread propaganda and further accelerated by the ongoing US-led military occupation of Iraq, is likely to continue. While a flat structure makes the network less capable than it was with its base in Afghanistan of pulling off a large-scale coordinated attack on the order of 11 September, it also makes the network less vulnerable to military power and harder to neutralise decisively. After settling for targets of opportunity immediately after the Afghanistan intervention, an ever more dispersed jihadist network now appears capable of striking a wider range of targets in addition to Iraq (e.g., Jeddah, Saudi Arabia, December 2004; London, UK, July

Table 2.1 **International terrorism: significant attacks associated with al-Qaeda, 1993–2006**

Date	Location	Summary
26 Feb 1993	USA (New York)	First World Trade Center bombing planned by Ramzi Youssef. Six killed, over 1,000 injured.
11 Dec 1994	Philippines	Small bomb on Philippines Airlines flight; one Japanese businessman killed, 10 people injured.
29 Jul 1995	France (Paris and Lyon)	Four-month bombing campaign. Attacks on the Paris metro, the Arc de Triomphe and outside a Jewish school in Lyon.
13 Nov 1995	Saudi Arabia (Riyadh)	Car bombs at military compound.
18 Sep 1997	Egypt (Cairo)	Gunmen attack a tourist bus. Nine Germans and one Egyptian killed.
17 Nov 1997	Egypt (Luxor)	Gunmen attack tourists. c. 70 killed.
7 Aug 1998	Kenya (Nairobi) and Tanzania (Dar-es-Salaam)	Truck bomb attack against US embassies. Over 200 people killed, thousands injured.
12 Oct 2000	Yemen	Boat bomb attack on the USS *Cole* in the port of Aden. 17 US soldiers killed, 39 wounded.
11 Sep 2001	USA (New York and Washington)	Hijacked planes crashed into the two World Trade Center towers and the Pentagon. A fourth plane crashes into a field in Pennsylvania. c. 3,000 killed.
11 Apr 2002	Tunisia	Vehicle bomb attack against a synagogue on the resort island of Djerba. c. 21 killed.
8 May 2002	Pakistan (Karachi)	Bomb attack against bus carrying French engineers near Sheraton Hotel.
14 Jun 2002	Pakistan (Karachi)	Truck bomb attack against US Consulate. 12 killed, 51 injured.
6 Oct 2002	Yemen	Boat bomb attack against French oil tanker MV *Limburg* off Ash Shahir port. One killed.
12 Oct 2002	Indonesia (Bali)	Attacks against US Consulate, Sari Club and Paddy's Bar. 202 killed.
28 Nov 2002	Kenya (Mombasa)	Attack on an Israeli-owned hotel. 12 killed. Surface-to-air missile launched at Israeli airliner the same day.
12 May 2003	Saudi Arabia (Riyadh)	Attacks at three compounds housing expatriates. Over 30 killed.
16 May 2003	Morocco (Casablanca)	Multiple suicide bombings against Spanish club, hotel and sites. 45 dead, c. 100 injured.
5 Aug 2003	Indonesia (Jakarta)	Vehicle bomb attack against Marriott Hotel. c. 12 killed, 100 injured.
8 Nov 2003	Saudi Arabia (Riyadh)	Vehicle bomb attack against residential compound housing mainly expatriate workers from other Arab countries. 17 killed, over 80 injured.

2005; Sharm al-Sheikh, Egypt, July 2005; Bali, Indonesia, October 2005; Amman, Jordan, November 2005) over the course of a year.

While terrorist operations continue and protective measures remain important, it is equally central to countering terrorism to determine what applications of softer forms of power will lead to the diminution of transnational political violence. And although Americans and others tend to view counter-terrorism as an endeavour closely akin to a war, Europeans and others still are inclined to see it as a law-enforcement and public-policy challenge. However, most parties agree that each approach has its merits, and neither should be discarded. Both

Table 2.1 **International terrorism: significant attacks associated with al-Qaeda, 1993–2006**

Date	Location	Summary
15 Nov 2003	Turkey (Istanbul)	Two vehicle bomb attacks at Jewish synagogues.
20 Nov 2003	Turkey (Istanbul)	Two vehicle bombs at HSBC Bank and British Consulate. Together with 15 November attack, over 60 people killed.
11 Mar 2004	Spain (Madrid)	Bomb attacks against four trains kill 199.
1 May 2004	Saudi Arabia (Yanbu)	Attack on expatriate oil workers. Six foreign nationals and 1 Saudi killed.
30 May 2004	Saudi Arabia (Al Khobar)	Four attacks target oil companies and compound.
9 Sep 2004	Indonesia (Jakarta)	Vehicle bomb outside Australian Embassy. Nine killed, over 100 injured.
8 Oct 2004	Egypt	Explosions at Hilton Hotel in Taba and at two campsites in the Sinai area. Over 30 killed.
28 Oct 2004	Pakistan (Islamabad)	Explosion at Marriott Hotel. 7 injured.
6 Dec 2004	Saudi Arabia (Jeddah)	Up to 13 armed men attack the US Consulate with guns and hand grenades; four of the attackers and five consulate employees (none American) killed.
19 Mar 2005	Qatar (Doha)	Vehicle bomb attack outside the Doha Players' Theatre. One (British national) killed, 12 injured.
07 Apr 2005	Egypt (Cairo)	Attack near tourist bazaar in Cairo. Two French nationals and one American killed, c.18 injured.
30 Apr 2005	Egypt (Cairo)	Tourist bus fired on in Cairo. Eight injured.
07 Jul 2005	UK (London)	Four explosions – three in Underground trains, kill 52, injure 700.
23 Jul 2005	Egypt (Sharm al-Sheikh)	Suicide-bomb attacks on two hotels and a market. 67 dead, over 200 injured
1 Oct 2005	Indonesia	Suicide-bomb attacks on three outdoor restaurants. Up to 27 dead, over 100 injured.
9 Nov 2005	Jordan (Amman)	Suicide-bomb attacks on three hotels. At least 59 dead, over 200 injured.
24 Apr 2006	Egypt (Dahab)	Three explosions in a resort area. 18 dead, 85 injured.

Source: Prime Minister's Office, UK, 13 July 2005, http://www.pm.gov.uk/output/page7930.asp. The December 2004 Jeddah attack and all attacks subsequent to the original publication have been added. Some of those listed were directly linked to bin Laden or other al-Qaeda leaders, but many were conducted by terrorists inspired by al-Qaeda. Attacks in Afghanistan and Iraq have been excluded.

foreign policy and domestic policy are therefore critical. Arguably the greatest impediment to prospective gains in the 'war on terror' is the Bush administration's reluctance to recognise the galvanising effect the Iraq occupation has had on terrorist recruitment, morale and capability. The most salient impact of the Iraq intervention, as perceived by some European governments, is that it has reinforced bin Laden's narrative depicting the United States and its allies as seeking to establish Western hegemony in the Arab and wider Muslim world, to loot Islam's oil, and to support Israel against its largely Muslim neighbours. Furthermore, the US, Canadian and European intelligence communities broadly agree that Iraq has replaced Afghanistan as a training ground for jihadist terrorists. The Iraq engagement allowed a charismatic jihadist leader, Abu Musab al-Zarqawi, to emerge, until he was killed by an American airstrike in June 2006. And it has arguably led the United States to neglect other areas, such as sub-Saharan Africa, ripe for growth in terrorism recruitment or activity.

Perhaps the most salient and sobering development in 2005–06 has been Islamist terrorists' consolidation of Europe as a 'field of jihad'. The social, economic and political marginalisation of Muslims in a number of European countries has made Muslim communities susceptible to radicalisation. These countries have tried various mixtures of integration and tolerance, none to adequate effect. There are distinctly different views of the breadth and depth of the Muslim radicalisation problem in Europe, with the French considering the problem less dire than the British and the Spanish. What is undisputed is the fact that some young Muslim men placed in limbo between home country and European host country were following radical leaders' exhortations to seek an authentic and more satisfying identity in the Islamic *umma*.

Europe's crisis

The population of the European Union includes roughly 15m Muslims (about 4%), and the Muslim share is set to double by 2025 – a consequence of both immigration and high fertility rates. It has become less and less likely that the perpetrator of a terrorist attack in Europe will be a member of, or affiliated with, a pre-existing terrorist organisation; that is to say, European Muslim terrorists are increasingly home grown. The overriding factors that lie behind Muslim radicalisation in Europe are probably structural. Colonial legacies help determine the geographical distribution of Muslims in Europe, and some of the violently inclined take their cue from various home conflicts (e.g., British Muslims from Pakistan's political and religious strife, French Muslims from Algeria's, Spanish Muslims from Morocco's, and perhaps Dutch Muslims from Indonesia's). But by perpetuating social, economic and political marginalisation, most major European nations have also fuelled Muslim grievances. Muslims in Europe tend to be segregated in Muslim 'ghettos', and disproportionately unemployed, imprisoned and under-educated.

Furthermore, while first-generation refugees tend to stay connected to their home countries, Muslim citizens or permanent residents who have been in Europe for longer generally do not maintain close links. Thus, second- and third-generation Muslims find themselves in an unsettling limbo, whereby they are not fully integrated into their European home countries but have no affinity for the language, culture or politics of the countries of their forebears. It is harder for Muslims to assimilate in Europe than in the United States, a nation founded on immigration. Older European Muslims simply become insular, but younger ones undertake a more aggressive search for alternative identities that feel more authentic. When they encounter the tendency of non-Muslim society not to integrate Muslims, they can find radical Islam an attractive option.

European intelligence agencies generally agree that most European jihadists (roughly two-thirds) are not under-achievers who may have resorted to criminality, but are upwardly mobile in society – for example, university undergraduates with technical qualifications. Historically, university students have typically been the first to be radicalised – even in groups like the Baader–Meinhof Gang or the Red Brigades that styled themselves proletarian. In the context of social marginalisation, Muslims moving up the social ladder are more likely to run into significant discrimination or racism as they venture outside their own religious and ethnic circles. This means that government programmes maintaining a high level of education, while important, will not by themselves diminish terrorism. Finding neither their home countries nor their host countries especially hospitable, some European Muslims seek a home in the *umma* (that is, the notional single nation comprising Muslim believers worldwide), where bin Laden's worldview now flourishes independently of his personal fate or actions. While the al-Qaeda leadership may have given the Madrid and London bombings its blessing because of Spain's and the UK's participation in the Iraq War, more significant is the likelihood that the bombings would have occurred regardless of that leadership's specific sanction.

On top of adding fuel to the jihadist argument that Western bellicosity warrants the mobilisation of Muslims, the Iraq issue has led many Middle Eastern governments, worried about their respective 'streets', to distance themselves publicly from the United States and its allies. It has also stoked *secular* European anti-American anger and rejection of war. Iraq, then, is a triply potent motivational factor for European Muslims, among whom the war has been broadly and deeply unpopular. The irony is that the European political bond against the war has now crossed ethnic lines. It is true, as French scholar Olivier Roy has noted, that other conflicts (e.g., Israel–Palestine, Kashmir, Chechnya) and more general circumstances (structural marginalisation) gave rise to European Muslims' radicalisation and violent activity before the Iraq War. Non-Muslim European anti-Americanism also predated Iraq. But Iraq confirmed and intensified the jihadist narrative of Muslim humiliation and subjugation by presenting the acute antagonism of Americans killing Arabs, and offering the possibility of a triumphant moment during which a Muslim can kill an American in battle. So far, at most only 200–300 European Muslims are believed to have joined the jihad in Iraq, and few returnees have surfaced in Europe. Those who do return, however, are likely to have a unique cachet and the ability to increase terrorist recruitment, capability and activity. And they will find at least passive political sympathy in Europe's non-Muslim population. Overall, Europe appears to be approaching a tipping point at which localised Muslim insurgencies – potentially coordinated by knowledgeable veterans of the Iraq jihad – could become a fact of life.

Whether this happens depends on the directions of Muslim communities and security apparatuses in three key countries: France, the UK and the Netherlands. These countries cover the spectrum of domestic national counter-terrorism approaches in Europe, from, respectively, enforced assimilation, to a balance of encouraged assimilation and hard enforcement, to liberal integration. The rise of Islamic radicalism in Europe, however, has challenged the status quo in each country. The Netherlands seems to have responded the most dramatically, with far stricter enforcement and more aggressively assimilative requirements than elsewhere. France, by contrast, has resisted – though not entirely discounted – empirical indications that its Muslim population is becoming more vulnerable to radicalisation, and has defaulted to rigorous intelligence collection and law enforcement as the principal instruments of counter-terrorism. The UK has recognised that even its ramped-up programme combining community outreach, infiltration and prevention was insufficient to stop the July 2005 terrorist bombings, but appears to have concluded essentially that the central problem is one of execution rather than design. On balance, then, the Netherlands is moving expeditiously to the UK's middle position while France is moving towards that position more slowly. Given the nature of Europe's current Muslim crisis, this trend is a positive one. Security would likely be improved, however, if France adopted a mixed approach on a more accelerated basis.

There are more than 4m Muslims in France, constituting about 6% of the population. About three-quarters originate from the Maghreb, over 1.5m from Algeria. Over half of France's Muslims are French citizens. But Muslim immigrants are twice as likely as non-Muslim immigrants to be unemployed. France's domestic state policy of resolute secularism – *laïcité* – dictates an immigration policy of strict assimilation: Muslims, like others, are required to pass a French language and culture test in order to be naturalised, and are pushed to embrace French civil ideals and to keep their religion private. In response to the looming problem of radicalisation and potential Islamist terrorism, however, the French Council for the Muslim Religion was established in May 2003 as an integrative moderating mechanism for the nation's Muslims and as Muslims' official interlocutor with the government. The council is increasingly pressing the government to respond to Muslims' religious grievances. But its effectiveness is unclear, as many Muslims – radical and moderate alike – view it as potentially reinforcing marginalisation. France has not otherwise compromised its official secularity. For example, it has not moved to allow a greater degree of religious expression in schools, and has thus far given little energy to initiatives for improving public religious education or the training of France's broadly unassimilated imams (though this may be changing). The problem is that the policy of assimilation has not been coupled to an effective 'affirmative action' type policy to assist it.

The French government's muscular, centrally controlled and integrated counter-terrorism apparatus has undoubtedly produced positive security results. French authorities have arrested over 230 terrorist suspects since 2002. They have prevented numerous major terrorist operations, including the bombing of the Eiffel Tower and that of the US embassy in Paris, and dealt highly disruptive blows to Europe-wide al-Qaeda facilitation and recruitment networks. Unlike Spain and the UK, France has not suffered a major attack since 11 September. By the same token, however, France's aggressive approach to hard counter-terrorism, combined with an institutionalised intolerance of overt piety that is at odds with the sensibilities of many Muslims and certainly those attracted to Salafism, appears to have rendered significant portions of its Muslim population hostile to the state – or at least reinforced their hostility. Evidence includes the autumn 2005 urban riots – which the government tends to think were about religious and racial discrimination, rather than bin Ladenism per se – and the Muslim community's anger over France's ban on headscarves in public schools. More pronounced government outreach to the Muslim community to assist rather than merely proclaim assimilation is desirable.

In the Netherlands there are approximately 700,000 Muslims, making up almost 5% of the population. Dutch Muslims come primarily from Turkey and Morocco and are concentrated in particular in the four largest cities: Amsterdam, Rotterdam, The Hague and Utrecht. Dutch Muslims' unemployment levels are high and their educational achievement low. The Netherlands, however, has adopted a broadly liberal policy towards religion. Church and state are separate, freedom of religion legally enshrined, and religiously based discrimination illegal. At the same time, the state does provide certain religious groups – including Muslims – with funding and resources for schools (which must still fulfil a secular national curriculum) and other activities. Dutch liberalism and multiculturalism, however, are under siege. The murder of filmmaker Theo Van Gogh in November 2004 by a Moroccan Muslim, in reaction to what much of the Muslim community considered a blasphemous portrayal of Muslim women, precipitated a steep and reactionary increase in anti-Muslim hostility and violence, and rendered inter-communal relations in the Netherlands far more tense than they had been. Furthermore, the General Intelligence and Security Service (AIVD), which has primary operational responsibility for domestic counter-terrorism, has established that radical Islam has taken root in Dutch society and that extirpating it will be a long and arduous task.

The authorities responded to these realisations in a measured rather than a reactionary way, bolstering security without appearing to become tools of right-wing extremists who had been gaining favour even before 11 September. The government's working hypothesis is that such groups are generally not directly operationally linked to any global network, but will often develop transnational relationships with similar groups – or with individual members of al-Qaeda – and thus form new, flatter networks. One such local entity in the Netherlands was the so-called 'Hofstad group', with which Van Gogh's assassin was associated. The Dutch threat perception is also marked by an assessment that the Hofstad group is interested not only in mass Western casualties but also in targeting key individuals (politicians or pundits) – a departure for jihadis. In addition, the AIVD became worried about sectarian backlash, noting that arson attacks on churches, mosques and schools had been virtually unheard of in the Netherlands until the Van Gogh murder. These realisations – along with the discovery of plans for attacking several targets, among them an AIVD office, during the arrest on suspicion of robbery of a key Hofstad group member – led to expanded and tightened security in public buildings and sites and to a tougher preventive enforcement policy. The AIVD has also become directly involved in monitoring immigrants, in cooperation with four other government organisations.

The AIVD has been proactive in addressing deeper social problems contributing to radicalisation and terrorism. The agency initiated and spearheaded an investigative study, conducted under the auspices of the EU Counter Terrorism Group, of jihadist recruitment in Europe, focusing on methods of recruitment, characteristics of recruits, and recruiting locales. A 2004 AIVD study entitled 'From Dawa to Jihad' further chronicled modes (Saudi Wahhabi missionary organisations, itinerant Salafist preachers, the Internet, etc.) of radical indoctrination and recruitment in the Netherlands. This path appears to have had qualified positive effects. Both anti-Muslim sentiment and Islamist radicalisation may have levelled off, and there have been no major terrorist attacks in the Netherlands. To counter the inter-communal divisions and mistrust that have emerged, however, the government will probably have to intensify affirmative steps to bring Muslims into mainstream social, economic and political life.

The UK has long experience in combating the Provisional Irish Republican Army (IRA), and has tough counter-terrorism legislation in place – amplified after 11 September – that has facilitated its counter-terrorism effort. The vexing operational challenge has been to strike a balance between tough enforcement, which is necessary for the immediate protection of the public, and tolerance for the free expression of often inflammatory ideology or religious beliefs, which is viewed as conducive to longer-term conciliation between Muslim and non-Muslim Britons. The developing jihadist threat to the British homeland has rendered the optimal balance even harder to achieve. Thus, although December 2001 legislation substantially increased UK authorities' latitude for detaining terrorist suspects, they have not used their detention power too liberally. France, in particular, criticised the UK for being too lax, and the UK authorities began to undertake more preventive arrests and detentions starting in late 2002. Shortly after the Madrid bombings in March 2004, British security services seized a 1,600kg cache of ammonium nitrate fertiliser, an ingredient of home-made explosives, in a raid on a self-storage facility in West London. This discovery prompted the United Kingdom's Foreign and Commonwealth Office (FCO) and Home Office jointly to undertake a detailed examination – entitled 'Young Muslims and Extremism' and leaked to the *Times* of London after the London Underground bombings of 7 July 2005 – of the security risks posed by the UK's Muslim population.

In addition to setting out the social marginalisation of British Muslims, the presence of radical Islamist groups and their recruitment activity, the FCO–Home Office paper cited two primary policy goals: 'to isolate extremists within the Muslim community, and to provide support to moderates' and 'to help prevent young Muslims from becoming ensnared or bullied into participation in terrorist or extremist activity'. A programme, codenamed *Operation Contest*, emerged. The Security Service, MI5, would lead an all-out inter-agency effort to win Muslim hearts and minds while also more directly preventing imminent radicalisation. The FCO and the Home Office continued to conduct very public community-relations and anti-discrimination efforts, and added focus groups to their repertoire. In addition, however, MI5 and other law-enforcement and intelligence agencies dispatched hundreds of undercover officers in regional 'intelligence cells' or 'Muslim Contact Units' to monitor suspected terrorists and mapped the 'terrorist career path' with an eye towards developing a comprehensive 'interventions strategy' whereby government agencies would confront Muslims at 'key trigger points' before they were drawn into the radical fold.

The bombings in London on 7 July appeared to skew the balance even more decisively towards enforcement. Nevertheless, the UK's mixture of rigorous intelligence and law enforcement and forward-looking social policies worked well in taming the IRA's insurgency, and British officials tend to perceive Northern Ireland as highly relevant to, even if very different from, the global jihadist challenge. The UK is likely to stick to its mixed approach, resolving simply to apply it more efficiently and comprehensively. (For a discussion of Britain's 'multicultural' approach to integration of ethnic minorities, see pages 143–7). This mixed approach, under which soft and hard policies complement each other, makes the most sense in a dynamic security environment in which both short- and long-term risks must be managed and cannot be completely eliminated. It could be observed that because Britain has suffered a major jihadist terrorist attack while the other two countries mentioned have not, its counter-terrorism strategy might be questionable. But the UK's singularly close strategic alignment – especially as to Iraq – with the United States also made it a higher-value target. In that light, its strategy may appear more efficacious. While the EU provides some coordinative security mechanisms and baseline standards for social policy, its supranational power – diminished by the recent constitutional crisis – realistically cannot supplant national authority over counter-terrorism matters.

America's dilemma

US counter-terrorism strategy continues to pivot on the application of military force to engage terrorists outside US borders and thereby deny them access to US territory. Analytically, this makes a certain kind of sense: the US, unlike Europe, has not been infiltrated. As a group, Muslims in the United States have shown no sign of violent protest, let alone terrorism. The US Muslim population, though multi-ethnic and variable in terms of income, is generally prosperous and assimilated. Whereas European Muslims' average income is generally below the poverty line, that of American Muslims is slightly above the national average. Their reaction to 11 September was, on balance, constructive and patriotic. In short, Muslim violence within the United States is indeed more likely to come from foreigners, so the military denial strategy is logical. In practice, however, the strategy is failing. Its first expression occurred against a country – Iraq – that turned out not to pose a serious security threat to the United States. This single fact allowed radically inclined Muslims to think the worst about America's true intentions, which won al-Qaeda recruits and followers. America cannot rewind the tape, and now faces a dilemma. It can either withdraw expeditiously from Iraq or stay there indefinitely to complete the task of state building. Either way, the jihadists are handed a propaganda victory: withdrawal would be interpreted as a superpower's humiliation, ongoing occupation as imperialism. The only hope seems to be for the United States to stay long enough to prove itself a benevolent midwife rather than a malign hegemon.

While Iraq presents a more difficult and lethal operating environment for jihadists than did pre-11 September Afghanistan, the fear is that some jihadists will survive US-led counter-insurgency efforts and relocate in Saudi Arabia, Jordan, Europe and possibly the United States, better trained and motivated to perpetrate and direct terrorist operations. Although few, if any, have surfaced in Europe and none have turned up in the United States, a number have returned to Saudi Arabia and Jordan and staged attacks – notably the suicide bombings in Amman in November 2005 carried out by Iraqi terrorists under the aegis of al-Qaeda in Mesopotamia. More generally, events in Iraq also prompted jihadists to refine and propagate urban-warfare techniques, and they may choose to apply them robustly to cities elsewhere.

The received view is that the insurgency in Iraq opposing American, other coalition and new Iraqi government forces is primarily and in substantial majority an indigenous movement composed of Sunni Arab Iraqis associated with Saddam Hussein's Ba'athist regime. This group fears domination and reprisals from a reconstituted Iraqi government controlled mainly by Shi'ite Arab Iraqis, who make up about 65% of Iraq's population, and to a lesser degree by Iraqi Kurds, who account for roughly 23% of the population, both of which Saddam's regime brutally oppressed. It is also generally accepted that the jihadists led by Zarqawi – a Jordanian, and al-Qaeda's anointed representative in Iraq – infiltrated the network of Ba'athist holdouts driving the insurgency and incrementally gained influence within the movement. This latter view is fairly well substantiated, but largely inferential. It is drawn from the increasing incidence of suicide attacks, which are consistent with jihadist tactics and psychology, and from the rising proportion of attacks on Shi'ite religious and political figures and sites, which squares with a memorandum, apparently written by Zarqawi, intercepted and leaked by US intelligence in February 2004, indicating that a Sunni–Shi'ite civil war is necessary if the US effort to create a US-friendly state in Iraq is to be thwarted.

An important aspect of the insurgency on which there is less reliable intelligence, and no real consensus, is the mindset of Zarqawi's former followers. A large number of the jihadist fighters are native Iraqis. In addition to al-Qaeda in Mesopotamia – led until his death by Zarqawi – two of the best known and most active insurgent groups are Ansar al-Sunna and the Islamic Army of Iraq, both of which are homegrown. This probably reflects a broader reality: that, like the rest of the Arab world, a substantial portion of the Sunni population of Iraq had been pressured to Islamise since the Gulf War. Recordings of the sermons of radical preachers widely circulated in the Arab world have been available in Iraq. Just as other Arab leaders used Islam to enhance their claim to authority or outflank political competitors, Saddam and his Ba'ath party began a 'Faith Campaign' in 1993 in the realisation that the Ba'ath Party's secular ideology (which turned on pan-Arab nationalism, Iraqi patriotism and Sunni tribal patronage) was losing steam, and political Islam was on the rise in the Arab world. A minority of those who turned to religion espoused radical views. Despite its secularist roots, the regime tolerated these groups because they were anti-Saudi and thus were politically useful to Saddam. Thus, it is likely that Zarqawi and a small network of foreign jihadists gained some influence over Iraqi Sunnis *before* the United States and its coalition partners invaded and occupied Iraq. While there is no evidence of a substantial, planning-level connection between Saddam and bin Laden, Zarqawi was present in Iraq before 2003. US officials considered Iraqi Sunnis essentially secular, and therefore did not entertain the possibility of serious jihadist penetration.

In the run-up to the invasion of Iraq, the Bush administration described Zarqawi as being closely tied to both al-Qaeda and Saddam Hussein, though the Saddam connection was denied by the CIA. In fact, it transpired that Zarqawi was more of a rival to bin Laden than anything else: Trotsky to bin Laden's Lenin. Although both men stressed jihad, Zarqawi concentrated on the Middle East while bin Laden thought in global terms. Reports that bin Laden wanted someone else to run jihadist operations in Iraq and even sent someone to replace Zarqawi should be given some weight. Ultimately, the two men found common cause. For Zarqawi, bin Laden's imprimatur elevated his stature; for bin Laden, whose command and control of dispersed assets was constrained, a link to activity in Iraq ensured that he would remain a major player in the most active jihadist campaign. Bin Laden may also have been financially motivated. Wealthy donors – especially Saudis – could have been reluctant to give to an entity that appeared operationally crippled after the Afghanistan intervention in late 2001. Thus, in 2004, Zarqawi's Tawhid w'al Jihad (Monotheism and Jihad) became al-Qaeda in Mesopotamia.

A March 2005 analysis based on data from jihadist websites by Reuven Paz, an Israeli, suggested that most of the suicide attackers were not Iraqis but Saudis, who constituted 61% of the 154 Arab jihadists killed in Iraq during the previous six months, with Syrians, Iraqis and Kuwaitis making up another 25%. A *Washington Post* Internet survey produced broadly comparable numbers, with Saudis constituting a strong 44% plurality. This indicates that Zarqawi was able to attract literate young people from the entire Arab world, including Iraq. Most Iraqi insurgents as well as foreign jihadists appear to derive much of their energy and commitment from radical Islam. They are not easily distinguishable from foreign jihadists. Indeed, given the substantial and early infiltration of Iraqi society by the foreigners and the pre-existing trend of Islamisation, the distinction seems less germane, from a counter-terrorism point of view, than coalition forces and the Iraqi government have thought. Iraq has become a melting pot for terrorists and terrorist know-how and materiel, and the insurgency's talent pool has thus become homogenised.

Several other motivations drive the insurgents' participation in anti-coalition and anti-government violence in Iraq. Some Sunnis are acting principally out of revenge for having been toppled from positions of political and social supremacy. Others are disenchanted by their economic situation, and still others are simply common criminals motivated by greed. Neither revenge nor economic deprivation is inconsistent with jihadism or Sunni nationalism. Each may constitute an independent basis for involvement in the insurgency, but they are more likely to coalesce with religious and ideological influences and give them greater psychological traction. Economic hardship in particular, however, has been overrated as a motive for jihadism itself. Poverty is more likely simply to induce criminality. The US Army estimates that criminality is to blame for 80% of all violence in Iraq. The organised criminal groups predate regime change, having come to prominence in the mid-1990s at the peak of the social and economic suffering caused by sanctions, when Saddam Hussein's grip on society was at its weakest. These groups have been revitalised by the lawlessness of present-day Iraq, in which they can capitalise on readily available weapons, the absence of an efficient police force and the coalition's sketchy intelligence about Iraqi society. But criminals are at best ancillary support players in the insurgency, hired or paid bounty by higher-level planners with ideological convictions. Islamists appear to be the decisive players in the Iraqi insurgency.

On balance, most Iraqi insurgents are probably now focused on first things first: preserving Sunni Arab primacy within Iraq and wresting Iraq from perceived American control and undoubted US influence. Because many have been radicalised and indoctrinated with the jihadist point of view, though, a majority is likely to be amenable to eventually broadening the geographical scope of their activities. Such a shift would be a reasonable possibility if they achieved their primary Iraq-centric objectives. Yet it could well be even more likely if they see themselves as *failing* to achieve them: much as the defeat of political Islam in Egypt, Jordan and elsewhere prompted the transnationalisation of the movement, the defeat of both Sunni nationalism and political Islam in Iraq could transnationalise both Iraqi jihadists and their foreign abettors.

Saudi Arabia: continuing challenge

Saudi Arabia, owing to the complex and tenuous mutual dependency between the ruling family and the conservative Wahhabi clerical establishment, was extremely slow to acknowledge the gravity of the transnational Islamist militants' regional and local threat, and to deal with it. Attacks in May and November 2003 provided a reality check, and Riyadh has since taken counter-terrorism seriously. Al-Qaeda militants in the Arabian Peninsula killed other Saudi Muslims – reducing local sympathy for their cause – and have been labelled 'deviants' by the Saudi government. A soft, muted information-warfare approach has accounted for the lion's share of the effective counter-terrorism effort, and hard counter-terrorism only a small portion. But, while there have been successes in rolling up cells, up to a thousand Saudis have gone to Iraq to join the jihad there. The fear is that when the Iraq conflict dies down, experienced Saudi jihadis will return and start an insurgency that could dislodge the House of Saud.

From a regional geopolitical perspective, Saudi Arabia is subject to frustrating crosscurrents. Iraq and the rising price of oil are matters of the most immediate worry. There is a battle for influence in the Gulf between the Saudis and the Iranians. This competition emerged from the Cold War, when the Saudis fought the 'godless communists' alongside the United States, and in the 1980s and 1990s it primarily took the form of financial support for terrorist groups.

Now, for Riyadh, US state-building in Iraq raises concerns about a rising Shia crescent, as Iraq could become a Shia power backed by Iran. One logical counter to this development would be to fund anti-Shia terrorism within Saudi Arabia and perhaps beyond its borders. In turn, while high oil prices provide Saudi Arabia with more resources to invest in security, they also provide supporters of radical Islam with more funds for financing terrorism. Now, having experienced 'blowback', the Saudi Arabian government has made real strides in controlling terrorist financing – e.g., taking collection boxes out of mosques and tightening government control over large Saudi charities. These restrictions appear, however, to have marginally increased support for domestic terrorism.

Perhaps the most important counter-terrorism development overall has been the elevation, with the death of King Fahd bin Abdulaziz Al Saud, of Crown Prince Abdullah bin Abdul Aziz Al Saud to king, as he appreciates the need for both political reform and the eradication of terrorist cells. This factor may have helped stabilise US–Saudi relations, which remain grounded in reciprocal oil interests. However, ongoing and mainly American military activity in Iraq and the Israeli–Palestinian conflict were major sources of antagonism for Muslims and spurs to jihadist recruitment. While some reports say that 3,000 Saudis are fighting in Iraq, the real number is probably hundreds or perhaps 1,000 – but that is still considerable. Saudi jihadists – having drawn back after the al-Qaeda Organisation in the Arabian Peninsula was compromised by effective Saudi counter-terrorism – have opted not to hit the Saudi regime hard. But fighters returning from Iraq would logically have less restraint, and might be keen on the prospect of US intervention in the event of the collapse of the House of Saud. Further, there remain individual Saudis who support terrorism abroad. To an extent, they are able to channel funds through multilateral bodies – e.g., the Islamic Relief Organisation – that fall between the cracks of government regulatory authority. According to Saudi legislators, such organisations are not charities as such, and cannot be regulated as strictly. As long as this interpretation governs Riyadh's oversight of terrorist financing, Saudi Arabia will remain, notwithstanding the strides it has made in effective counter-terrorism, a source of terrorist finance.

Finally, Saudi clerics – 'Islamic Awakening' sheikhs of Muslim Brotherhood origins – who resist the customary alliance of convenience with the House of Saud are gaining power. These clerics are more critical of the United States and the US–Saudi strategic relationship. Thus, the Saudi *ulema* – that is, its scholarly religious elite – is increasingly nationalistic. Coupled with rising Sunni–Shi'ite tensions (sectarianism spreading from Iraq), this development makes Saudi Arabia less stable. The 'Islamic Awakening' sheikhs spoke against the US presence and the House of Saud starting in the early 1990s, and they are now among the most influential voices in Saudi Arabia. The House of Saud chose to bring the Islamic Awakening sheikhs into government. While they embrace the principle of jihad for use in daily life, and reject the notion that politics has a place among humans, they are now diluting these views because they have been accorded political power. They see Saudi Arabia's experimentation with democratisation at the United States' behest as an opportunity – clerics composed the lists for the 2005 municipal council elections – and would like to shape a national policy framed by hostility to the United States. At the same time, voters in Riyadh and Jeddah chose not the most militant candidates but rather moderate Islamists. Saudi Shi'ites appear to be playing the national unity card, but probably would not object to foreign forces' intervening to liberate them. On balance, then, Saudi Arabia remains a counter-terrorism 'partner of concern', subject to a variety of crosscutting and complex influences.

Pakistan and Central Asia: delicate balance

Afghanistan, al-Qaeda's former headquarters, has become a focal point for US and European state-building efforts motivated by counter-terrorism. Terrorism-related problems within Afghanistan include neo-Taliban operations as well as opium production and heroin processing, which finance Islamist terrorism. Military operations to kill or capture bin Laden, al-Zawahiri and other jihadist leaders believed to be hiding in Pakistan's 'tribal areas' near the Afghan border are ongoing. But they are constrained by the need to keep domestic Islamist pressure off secular Pakistani President Pervez Musharraf, an important counter-terrorism partner of the West. The salience of the global jihad in Pakistan, however, has been exaggerated. Some Islamist terrorist outfits operate with some degree of support from the Inter-Services Intelligence directorate (ISI). Musharraf has gained little traction on the ISI, and has attempted to de-Islamise the army. Musharraf has to manage popular sensitivities deftly, and needs American help, in the form of forbearance, in doing so. The fact that this consideration has trumped the all-out pursuit of bin Laden reflects his dwindling operational and perhaps even inspirational importance.

While the al-Qaeda-linked Islamic Movement of Uzbekistan (IMU) was evis-cerated by US forces in Kunduz, Afghanistan, in 2001, Islamist terrorism in the wider Central Asian region is far from extinguished. A core of radicalised Uzbeks in the Fergana Valley want to overthrow authoritarian Uzbekistan President Islam Karimov and Islamise government and law. They do not appear to be working as a coordinated force, and probably have not been penetrated by the security services. While they have some popular regional support, they do not appear to have the capability to mount a sustained guerrilla insurrection. They have been able to undertake isolated operations in Tashkent and Andijan. These militants seem to have no substantial links to neo-Taliban forces in Afghanistan, although a hard core may have fought there in the past. They are primarily a product of frustration with elite corruption and political neglect in their home country, rather than part of a global terrorist movement. Still, the Uzbek radicals could inspire radicalism elsewhere.

Although Kyrgyzstan's 'Tulip Revolution' expunged the authoritarian regime, the state is now chronically weak and vulnerable to radicalising influences. Accordingly, a fluid nexus of organised crime, arms and drug trafficking, and radical Islam is coalescing in the south of the country. At the same time, former president Askar Akayev's erstwhile patrons in the north have recently turned to crime bosses to extract political concessions from the government by force.

Tajikistan is faring somewhat better. The security forces have been regularly cracking local cells of Hizb-ut Tahrir al Islami (Islamic Party of Liberation) – an internationally based militant fundamentalist movement that gained strength in Central Asia, particularly among ethnic Uzbeks, after the collapse of the Soviet Union, and seeks to dismantle secular governments and establish an Asian caliphate. But, in the absence of a robust civil society, Hizb-ut Tahrir offers otherwise aimless young men an alternative to criminality.

Geopolitically, the United States and its partners face growing sensitivity on Russia's part over the American military presence in Central Asia, an area still within Russia's sphere of influence. In effect, these developments increase the counter-terrorism burden on Russia. Russia's special challenge boils down to resisting an institutionalised inclination to rubber-stamp the policies of authoritarian regimes (like Karimov's) and a fundamentally secular (in fact, residually atheistic) impulse that crowds out moderate Islam. So far, it has not managed to do so, and radical Islam has found traction as a unifying force in multi-ethnic, multi-tribal locales. Many Central Asian Muslims see a regional Islamic caliphate (advocated by both the IMU and Hizb-ut Tahrir) as a noble alternative to corrupt secular autocracy and clan and tribe domination. Whether the United States or Russia is the region's overarching security manager, the goals are likely to be the same: stable political reform in regimes that are able to contribute to their own security and willing to cooperate.

The principal regional counter-terrorism vehicle is the Shanghai Cooperation Organisation (SCO), which includes Russia, China and four of the five Central Asian countries (excluding isolationist Turkmenistan). At a landmark summit in Astana on 5 July 2005, the SCO admitted India, Pakistan, Afghanistan and Mongolia to observer status, and refined its counter-terrorism concept. A key part of this programme is the establishment of a permanent anti-terrorist centre in Uzbekistan, a secretariat and the ramping up of joint exercises. Each country has its own perception of the terrorist threat, but the umbrella terms used by the SCO are separatism (alluding mainly to Chechnya and Xinjiang Autonomous Region), terrorism (principally referencing Islamist groups in Uzbekistan, but also organised-crime and drug-trafficking networks) and extremism (pro-democracy opposition parties in Uzbekistan and China, and radical Islamist sects such as Hizb ut-Tahrir and Akramiya, principally in the cross-border Fergana Valley region in eastern Uzbekistan, Kyrgyzstan and Tajikistan). The SCO is politically callow and bureaucratically awkward, and probably unable to deal effectively with most of these threats at this stage. Bilateral exercises of the sort recently undertaken between Russia and Tajikistan, however, could have a short-term effect.

Quieter Southeast Asia

On balance, while Islamist terrorists still pose a serious threat to regional security in Southeast Asia, the weight of their involvement in the global jihad has diminished due to both their attenuated connections to the Arab-dominated political centre of the global movement and effective counter-terrorism. The latter has occurred primarily at the national level but also through bilateral relationships with major powers (in particular, the United States and Australia) and, more erratically, through the Association of Southeast Asian Nations.

Between 11 September 2001 and the rise of the Iraq insurgency, the Indonesia-based group Jemaah Islamiah (JI) was probably the most dangerous and effective trans-national Islamist terrorist group, having committed the bombings in Bali that killed over 200 people in October 2002 and alarmed most Southeast Asian governments – especially Singapore's and Malaysia's. Due to counter-terrorism efforts stimulated by JI's high political ambitions (i.e., a regional caliphate), and its ideological and operational links to al-Qaeda's core leadership, however, the group has become factionalised and its command and control has been compromised. In particular, the 2003 arrest in Thailand of Riduan Isamuddin (known commonly as Hambali) – the liaison between al-Qaeda and JI and the only Southeast Asian member of al-Qaeda's council (*shura*) – compromised JI's operations and frayed its connections with al-Qaeda. Bin Laden's loss of command and control over operational al-Qaeda assets and the consequent shift of the jihadist network's centre of gravity from Central Asia to Iraq appears to have had a similar effect. JI now gets less financial and operational support from the al-Qaeda nucleus. More broadly, Southeast Asia has always been considered the Islamic fringe, and there is an active debate as to how closely aligned JI is with al-Qaeda. The one aims for a regional caliphate, the other for a global one – which suggests that at some point their agenda will diverge. JI is, to be sure, still active. It is suspected of committing the September 2004 bombing of the Australian embassy in Jakarta, and the October 2005 bombings in Bali. In the Philippines, the Moro Islamic Liberation Front (MILF) is still operating terrorist training camps for JI, and Abu Sayyaf appears to be regaining some of its radical Islamist identity and re-forging links with JI. But the movement of the global jihad's focus away from Southeast Asia, Indonesia's domestic mobilisation against terrorism (over 200 arrests; the detention of spiritual leader Bashir), and an even more robust sub-regional effort (Singapore and Malaysia have adopted effective and professional approaches to counter-terrorism, and substantially rolled up JI affiliates) seem to have produced internal discord about ideology and the use of political violence. Indonesian analysts identify two broad groupings within JI: terrorists (bombers) and proselytisers. In Australia, some cells providing support to JI were discovered, but they were well short of being operational. Australia remains an attractive target, though, in light of its close strategic alignment with the United States.

Islamist terrorism in Thailand is a growing problem. While still primarily a local matter – the three southern Muslim-majority provinces have long wanted autonomy – the situation invites the global jihad, and some Thai Muslims have already been radicalised. Thus, the southern Thai groups have become a serious regional concern. There is considerable regional social connectivity between them and other players like JI and Abu Sayyaf, fugitives from which have taken refuge in Thailand. The insurgency is also taxing the counter-terrorism capacity of the Thai state. Bangkok declared victory in the early 1990s, when the Muslim groups were largely secular and leftist (some members having been trained in Syria). Subsequently, however, a steady infusion of Salafism changed their character. Whereas Indonesia has a robust and broadly moderate Islamic national system – a potential source of control – Thailand and the Philippines have none, which means young devout Muslims have to go to Pakistan or Saudi Arabia for training. The Thai groups' technical capabilities (e.g., bombs) have shown real momentum and progress. Politically, however, the groups behave oddly. They have stated no demands, and have not claimed public credit for attacks. Islamic piety (women wearing veils, gloves) is definitely on the rise, yet it does not appear popular, so compliance may be coerced.

While Iraq is among the most virulent sources of radical Muslim grievance in the Arab world and Europe, it appears to be less of a factor in Southeast Asia. Like the Israeli–Palestinian conflict, it surfaces more as a pretext (cited, for instance, as a reason for the Jakarta embassy attack) than a genuine motivator of terrorist activity. Some regional experts argue that Iraq is largely irrelevant to the terrorist challenge in Southeast Asia, which is instead a long-term one driven by an affirmative Islamist vision of Western exclusion. Indeed, most Southeast Asian government officials discount the connection between national Islamic resistance groups and bin Ladenism. Some MILF members do admire al-Qaeda and practice or impose Salafism in their areas. There have also been thin and rather obscure links established between European and Southeast Asian cells, as well as connections between JI and the Pakistani group Lashkar e-Toiba. Overall, however, Abu Sayyaf, the MILF and the Thai groups seem to have kept some distance from the global jihad. The prevailing rationale may be that a loose association can be useful for recruitment and political purposes and to give national authorities some pause, but a closer one unleashes too many counter-terrorism resources – e.g., US assistance – to be beneficial to the terrorist group in question.

For example, given Manila's historical failure to deliver on peace agreements and Mindanao's ungovernability, it has been a cost-effective purchase of leverage and options for the MILF to have ties to Ramzi Yousef's cell and Khalid Sheikh Mohammed, and to run camps for JI. But the MILF has also been careful not to draw too much attention. JI trainees now number only 10–20 per class, and the fact that the camps are mobile provides plausible deniability.

Political hazards and opportunities

Some people have been tempted to frame the counter-terrorism problem in exclusionary competitive terms, as a stand-off between 'Islam and the West'. But indulging this temptation is likely to lose Muslim 'hearts and minds' and should be resisted, insofar as it caters to the vision of a 'clash of civilisations' that bin Laden so fervently desires. Hard counter-terrorism enforcement, while indispensable, also imposes political costs. One of the most vexing quandaries facing counter-terrorism officials is that of gauging the trade-offs involved in curtailing civil liberties. Outright torture such as that perpetrated by US personnel at Abu Ghraib prison alienates Muslims to such a degree that it presents no perceptible net advantages. Less flagrant restrictions – such as indefinite detentions without full due process of law at Guantanamo Bay and elsewhere – are harder to assess. So are more selective if harsh measures, like American 'rendition' arrangements whereby suspects apprehended by the United States or an ally are sent to a country that employs brutal interrogation techniques. But publicity surrounding even these practices has damaged US credibility in the wider Muslim world. As a result, the US Congress in 2006 passed new legislation expressly barring US personnel outside as well as inside US borders from using 'cruel, inhuman and degrading' treatment on detainees.

Beyond the legal arena, serious American and European attention in the areas of diplomacy and domestic policy intimately related to the 'war on terror' in 2006 appears urgent. More promising diplomatic opportunities may be materialising with respect to the two conflicts that constitute the most antagonistic and radicalising influences in the Muslim world: the Israeli–Palestinian conflict and Iraq. Israel's withdrawal from Gaza has breathed new life into the Israeli–Palestinian peace process. The United States and its European partners, however, will have to immerse themselves to a greater extent in direct political brokering than they have since 11 September for Israel's initiative to fulfil its political potential. In November 2005, the US Congress passed legislation requiring that the government make 2006 'a period of significant transition to full Iraqi sovereignty'. While the Bush administration has been rhetorically resistant to deadlines – insisting that the United States must 'stay the course' – the president's historically low approval ratings (which plummeted to under 30%, according to some polls, in May 2006) and the growing disinclination of coalition partners to linger in Iraq limit the Bush team's freedom of action.

To salvage the Iraq enterprise, the United States will want to leave a stable unitary democratic state with a capable army and police service. Accordingly, it plans to accelerate its security training programmes in Iraq and ramp up its efforts to bridge differences on constitutional matters among Iraqi Shi'ites, Sunnis and Kurds. For their part, most European capitals appreciate the need to prevent Europe from becoming the platform for manning, planning and staging major attacks on the United States that it was before 11 September. Doing so requires the reversal of the radicalising trend in Europe through greater Muslim integration and assimilation, but there is no clear agreement on a coordinated course of action. At the same time, contrary to some assumptions, democratisation might not necessarily mean a decrease in terrorism. In fact, US democracy promotion may have perversely raised radical Islamist expectations that they could gain politically via an open political process. The political success of Hizbullah and more recently Hamas may have the same effect. Accordingly, the global jihad could conceivably evolve into a more subtle political instrument – a virtual caliphate, so to speak – that leverages terrorism selectively. Such an eventuality would make the strongly military approach to counter-terrorism that the US now favours even less plausible.

Outlook

In taking stock of counter-terrorism five years on from 11 September, a grim picture emerges, with three main features.

The first is the United States' persistent characterisation of the American-led campaign against transnational Islamist terrorism as a 'war'. Militarising counter-terrorism through military involvement in local security environments is liable to encourage the radical *umma* to graft those local confrontations onto the larger global one, such that those conflicts become part of a global war against Islam and serve to justify the 'defensive jihad' asserted by bin Laden and his adherents, as the Iraq War has so conveniently done.

Secondly, in conjunction with the Internet, the Iraq conflict has facilitated jihadis' propagation of urban-warfare techniques throughout the world. In the extreme case, more aggressive military activity would only accelerate this trend, which, if unchecked, would render cities all the more unruly, necessitate more provocative military action, and perpetuate a spiral of polarising confrontation between US-led and Islamist forces. The upshot is that while the United States and its counter-terrorism partners do have to ameliorate local conflicts (especially Israel–Palestine, Chechnya, Kashmir and of course Iraq itself), favouring diplomacy over force would help deny bin Laden traction in the *umma*. Hard counter-terrorist measures, some of them military, are undeniably indispensable, but they should be as inconspicuous and politically uninflammatory as possible.

Thirdly, the most alarming sub-trend of the transnational Islamist terrorist network's ongoing dispersal is the jihadist infiltration of Europe. Europe served very effectively as a recruitment, planning and staging area for al-Qaeda's attacks on US interests prior to 11 September 2001. If the jihadist infiltration of Europe continues, it could once again become a platform for striking the United States and its assets, as well as European and perhaps other countries.

Given the defensive advantages that have accrued to the global jihadist movement from its dispersal – undetectability, virtuality, operational flexibility – the most likely eventuality is for terrorists to remain distributed in cities and states in which sovereign authority in varying degrees still operates. In those places, military operations of any kind – including the irregular variety associated with SOF – will be exceedingly difficult to sustain. Most Western governments – including those hit hardest by Islamist terrorists – have an entrenched reluctance to allow the insinuation of state military power into homeland security. Even stronger reservations would logically extend to the armed forces of a foreign country. There are, of course, situations in which SOF could be counter-terrorist assets of early resort. For example, even if the jihadi network continues to favour dispersal rather than coalescence, it will need at least small training camps and will find countries with weak law enforcement, intelligence and military capabilities the easiest operating environments for establishing the necessary sites. This would call for discriminate, discreet, time-sensitive transnational applications of military force – for instance, the takedown of a training camp, or the 'snatch' of a terrorist suspect in open territory or in a country whose government is reluctant for political reasons to detain the suspect itself – which the US Special Operations Command is especially well suited to provide. Such situations, however, are likely to be comparatively few and far between. The *Predator* strike killing six al-Qaeda members in Yemen in November 2002, though actually executed by CIA officers, remains a stark example of the effective use of special operations to neutralise terrorists. Yet so far it has not been repeated.

Flaws in US counter-terrorism strategy mean that dangerous strategic incoherence afflicts counter-terrorism overall. But consensus is building among major Western powers that the acceptable period of reaction and adjustment to the 11 September attacks is coming to a close, that the counter-terrorism coalition assembled after 11 September has been weakened by Iraq, and that the coalition must now find a strategic direction that has thus far been elusive. The United States has understood the counter-terrorism enterprise essentially as a war-like campaign entailing the muscular promotion of democracy, while Europe has tended to view it as a public-policy and law-enforcement challenge. Iraq and, for example, the ascent of Islamists in Egypt's slowly liberalising political system have demonstrated that, contrary to what some US officials might wish, democratisation is at best an unreliable counter-terrorism instrument. At the same time, the rising terrorist threat in Europe and the jihadist network's adaptability and propagation have shown that the network demands both robust domestic integration and interdiction policies and a concerted international response. The coming year, therefore, may bring a degree of transatlantic strategic re-convergence on the counter-terrorism front. That, in turn, could unify the broader counter-terrorism coalition, which has found a consensus approach to the task of defeating transnational terrorism so difficult to forge.

An emerging consensus should recognise that US, European and Russian foreign and domestic policies have a profound effect on Muslim perceptions of the West and on the scope for stimulating greater political activism among moderate Muslims. Policies must take into account that promotion of democracy could lead to Islamists gaining sway through political participation. Given that globalised media and Internet connectivity propel Islamic radicalisation, diplomatic efforts that explain policy changes need to be carefully mounted. This would particularly apply to any moves to reduce the US and coalition presence in Iraq, which is currently the most important animator of Islamic radicalisation. The fact that this has led some to participate in the Iraqi insurgency and they are likely to return home from there must have an influence on domestic security polices in Europe, and in particular Saudi Arabia. Linked with this is the pressing need for European countries to make more intensive efforts to integrate immigrant communities into their societies so that domestic grievances are not translated into violent extremism.

The Oil Price Rise: Geopolitical and Structural Issues

Energy supply and pricing emerged as a key global challenge in 2006 as oil prices rose from $37 a barrel at the end of 2004 to over $70 by May 2006. While tensions in the Middle East and severe storms in the Gulf of Mexico triggered price volatility, there were also fundamental, long-term structural reasons for the steady rise in oil prices. Over the past few years, rising demand in the United States and Asia has met infrastructure constraints throughout the energy supply chain. The world is using almost all currently available oil production and refining capacity, and has underinvested in future new capacity to exploit still-substantial oil reserves. The oil-price rise, while acting as a constraint on consumption, also signals new global vulnerability.

Security of energy supply has thus risen rapidly up many governments' lists of concerns, and has become an increasingly important focus of foreign policy. While difficult relations between oil suppliers and oil consumers have been a feature of international strategic debate since the 1970s, recent strains in energy markets have prompted energy consumers to consider new steps to ensure supplies, including new arrangements with suppliers and new plans for pipelines, and energy suppliers to consider ways to maximise the benefits, both political and economic, of their new-found market power. A striking exercise of producer power came at the beginning of 2006, when Russia temporarily turned off gas supplies to Ukraine, causing knock-on effects across Europe and dramatically awakening governments in Europe and elsewhere to the strategic importance of energy. In April 2006, Bolivia nationalised its energy industry. Such acts prompted many consumer governments to pay increased attention to energy conservation and alternatives to existing energy sources.

Policy constraints and international tensions limit and delay much-needed investment in energy resources and implementation of consumer conservation measures. Energy markets functioned smoothly in the 1980s and 1990s, in contrast to earlier market failures when politics determined the ownership and flow of oil. The trend is again towards a politicisation of oil. The impetus to find alternatives, whether through nuclear or renewable energy, will therefore be even stronger.

Rising demand for oil

Global demand for oil has soared as a result of long and widespread economic growth. A decline in US domestic oil production has left the United States more dependent than ever on foreign oil, leading Bush to call in his 2006 State of the Union Address for a solution to America's 'addiction' to oil. The United States imported 12.9m barrels per day (b/d) in 2004, or about 63% of its total consumption of roughly 20.5m b/d, almost twice the level America faced during the oil crisis of 1973. The US Department of Energy (DoE) projects oil imports to grow to

Map 2.1 **Global energy consumption**

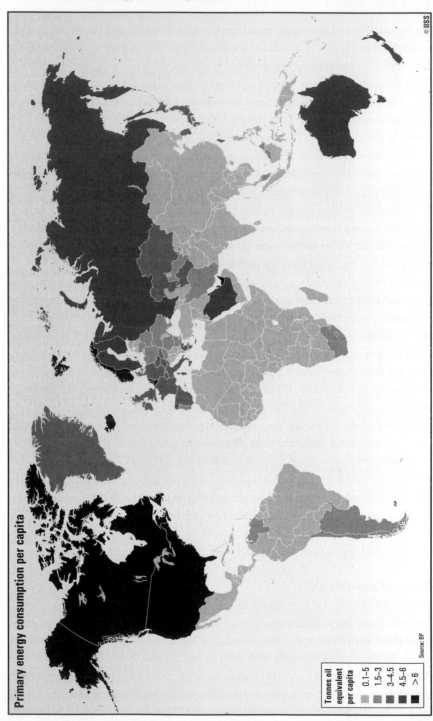

Primary energy consumption per capita

Tonnes oil equivalent per capita
- 0.1–5
- 1.5–3
- 3–4.5
- 4.5–6
- > 6

Source: BP

© IISS

close to 70% of consumption by 2020. Significantly, US imports from the Persian Gulf are expected to rise from 2.5m b/d (22% of total US imports) in 2003 to 4.2m b/d (62%) by 2020.

Much of this oil will be needed to fuel the US transport sector, which has been registering 2–3% annual growth in demand for many years. However, in response to rising prices US oil demand has actually been falling in 2006, by over 1% against the same date 12 months earlier. Any change in US policy that would curb growth in oil demand would have a significant impact on the global supply picture. But there has been no such policy change, either in the administration or Congress.

In Asia, China's oil demand has reached about 7m b/d, rising by about 4% a year, while India's oil demand is running at about 2.7m b/d, rising by about 2% a year. Despite high oil prices, the world economy continues to grow at about 4%, with energy efficiency and a shift to more service-oriented industries allowing this growth to take place against a lower increase in oil use than in the past. Still, by 2010, Asian oil demand is anticipated to increase by 50% to 29m b/d, representing roughly 35% of world oil demand, against 25% at present. Already, at over 21m b/d, Asia's oil consumption exceeds that of the United States. Per capita energy use in Asia remains markedly lower than in the industrialised West: India's total primary energy consumption per person, for example, averages roughly 13.3m British Thermal Units in comparison to the US average of 339.1m. More than half of future growth in Asian energy demand is expected to come from the transportation sector where, barring a technological breakthrough, increased reliance on oil-related products will be unavoidable.

Long-term oil supply remains abundant...
The dramatic rise in oil prices has rekindled the debate over whether the world might soon run dry. Several scientists, notably geologist Kenneth Deffeyes of Princeton and physicist David Goodstein of the California Institute of Technology, argue that the world's conventional oil resources are nearing the 'peak' – that a plateau level of maximum production will be followed by a gradual decline in output levels. However, oil company behaviour, oil reserve asset markets and scientific consensus suggest that the planet will not soon run out. The US Geological Survey, which conducts a comprehensive survey of global oil resources, has reported a long-term upward trend in reserve estimates. Its 2000 survey estimated total resources outside the United States at 2,659bn barrels (including those that have not yet been discovered, but are estimated by geologists). Proven world reserves are currently 42 times annual production levels, substantially higher than in 1972. In addition to conventional resources, an International Energy Agency (IEA) assessment published in 1998 noted an additional 1.7bn barrels of unconventional tar sands and oil shale remaining to be exploited. Canadian tar-sand production is averaging about 800,000 b/d,

expected to rise to 1.5m b/d by 2010, and exploitation of oil shale in the United States is also rising. Given technological advances, exploitation of these unconventional oil resources will remain commercially viable even if oil prices fall back to the $20–25 per barrel level.

While large oil resources remain available for exploitation, more than 75% of undiscovered resources outside the Organisation of Petroleum-Exporting Countries (OPEC) are located offshore, according to the US Geological Survey, lending credence to contentions that much of the 'easy' oil has already been found. Experts generally agree that world dependence on Middle East oil is likely to grow over time, since the natural peak has been reached for oil and gas production in the United States and the North Sea. North Sea production has declined from 6.39m b/d in 2000 to under 2.11m b/d at the end 2005. US domestic oil production averaged 5.12m b/d in 2005, down from 6.48m b/d ten years earlier. However, some recovery in US production is expected over the next few years, as new deep-water fields come on line in the Gulf of Mexico.

...but growth of oil supplies has been limited

The rise in prices clearly signals that more oil is badly needed. But the world's largest oil producers in the Persian Gulf and South America are not investing sufficiently to meet the expected rise in demand. The US DoE, the IEA and others predict that the international community will need a substantially higher supply from OPEC in coming years to balance rising demand, with OPEC needing to increase its actual output from 28–29m b/d currently to 40–50m b/d by 2025. However, OPEC has failed to increase its potential capacity substantially over the last 30 years: indeed it has fallen from 38.8m b/d in 1979 to roughly 31m b/d currently.

Table 2.2 **OPEC Supply Capacity, 1979–2005** (million b/d)

Member Country	1979	1983	1990	1997	1998	2000	2001	2003	2005
Saudi Arabia	10.84	11.30	8.00	9.65	9.80	9.50	9.90	10.15	10.30
Iran	7.00	3.00	3.10	3.70	3.70	3.75	3.80	3.80	4.00
Iraq	4.00	1.50	3.60	2.30	2.80	2.90	3.05	2.20	1.80
Kuwait	3.34	2.80	2.40	2.40	2.40	2.40	2.40	2.50	2.60
UAE	2.50	2.90	2.20	2.40	2.40	2.40	2.45	2.50	2.40
Qatar	0.65	0.65	0.40	0.71	0.72	0.73	0.75	0.75	0.82
Venezuela	2.40	2.50	2.60	3.45	3.30	2.98	3.10	2.50	2.50
Nigeria	2.50	2.40	1.80	2.00	2.05	2.10	2.30	2.30	2.30
Indonesia	1.80	1.60	1.25	1.40	1.35	1.35	1.30	1.15	0.90
Libya	2.50	2.00	1.50	1.45	1.45	1.45	1.45	1.45	1.60
Algeria	1.23	1.10	0.75	0.88	0.88	0.88	0.88	1.15	1.35
Total	38.76	31.75	27.60	30.34	30.85	30.44	31.38	30.45	30.57
Call on OPEC	34.01	16.65	22.20	27.59	25.85	30.04	28.23	29.20	29.87
Spare Capacity	4.75	15.10	5.40	2.75	5.00	0.40	3.15	1.25	0.70

Source: James A. Baker III Institute for Public Policy.

Table 2.3 **Non-OPEC Supply Growth, Recent and Projected** (in million b/d)					
Area	2002	2003	2004	2005	2006
Canada	2.89	2.99	3.06	3.06	3.21
Mexico	3.59	3.79	3.83	3.77	3.77
USA	7.63	7.45	7.65	7.31	7.53
South America	3.72	3.75	3.95	4.12	4.18
Europe	6.68	6.41	6.16	5.71	5.43
Middle East	1.98	1.96	1.77	1.72	1.67
Asia-Pacific	6.62	6.58	6.76	6.87	6.86
Africa	2.89	2.97	3.35	3.66	4.16
Former Soviet Union	9.38	10.37	11.16	11.53	11.61
(of which Russia)	7.69	8.54	9.19	9.38	9.35
Total	45.38	46.27	47.69	47.75	48.42
Increase		0.89	1.42	0.06	0.67
Increase without Russia		0.04	0.77	-0.13	0.70

Source: Hetco.

OPEC is currently operating at well over 90% of its crude-oil productive capacity, compared with 80% just before Iraq's invasion of Kuwait in 1990. This leaves markets with greater exposure to sudden disruptions in oil supply. With very little capacity to raise output, OPEC cannot make up for lost supplies, with the effect that loss of output anywhere in the world registers instantly in higher prices. The problem is more severe than past crises in 1973, 1979 and 1990, when ample spare production capacity and larger commercial oil inventories partially countered sudden supply disruptions.

Non-OPEC production has shown only a small increase in recent years, mainly as a result of production gains in Russia. US and North Sea production has declined, with the supply picture further clouded by two summers of hurricanes in the Gulf of Mexico. Over the past year, the market has seen several supply disruptions that could not be countered by increases in OPEC production and have therefore contributed to the rise in oil prices to historic highs. Prices were already rising when Hurricane Katrina hit the Louisiana coast on 29 August 2005. Growing worldwide demand, coupled with tight US and global refining capacity, had helped push New York Harbor gasoline futures prices up $0.43 per gallon between June and August while US retail prices had climbed to $2.59 a gallon. By 1 September, New York Harbor gasoline spot prices rose to just over $3.00 per gallon, up by $1.16 per gallon since the hurricane. US mean retail prices peaked at $3.12 per gallon. In the aftermath of Katrina, Gulf coast refinery production of finished gasoline (Padd 3) had fallen by 700,000 b/d against the same date the previous year. Hurricane Rita made landfall in Texas on 24 September and resulted in an additional, larger loss of refining capability. For the week ending 30 September, finished gasoline production was down by 1.4m b/d versus levels a year earlier. Some 75 days after the hurricanes, over 90m barrels of crude oil and 175m barrels of refined products had been lost from the market. In December, close to 750,000 b/d of US refining capacity was still affected by the aftermath of the hurricanes and did not come back on line until spring 2006.

These were not the only market disruptions. In early 2006, oil installations and personnel were attacked by rebels in Nigeria's Niger Delta region. The unrest led to the shutdown of exports from the Forcados field and a drop in Nigerian production from mid-February through March 2006 of 420,000 b/d of crude oil. In Iraq, sabotage and bad weather caused an additional 100,000 b/d drop in exports from already reduced levels: prospects for a recovery in output were clouded by insurgents' attacks that were preventing repairs and improvements to ailing infrastructure. A major pipeline spill at Alaska's Prudhoe Bay contributed to a temporary disruption of production, while technical problems at two installations in Canada temporarily slowed tar-sands oil output. Seasonal cyclones hit production in Australia, Malaysia and India, and output in Ecuador was also reduced.

Oil markets remain susceptible to temporary supply disruptions, small and large. They also react to perceived threats to supplies. Among the most serious is the potential for terrorist attacks on key Saudi oil infrastructure, as well as the stand-off between Iran and the West over Tehran's pursuit of a nuclear-weapons capability. Saudi Arabia is the world's largest oil exporter, and maintains between 500,000 and 1,000,000 b/d of idle capacity for emergencies. In February 2006, al-Qaeda staged a failed attack on the key crude-oil collection and processing area of Abqaiq – the world's largest central oil-gathering centre, heavily guarded by the Saudi military. Some 6–7m b/d of Saudi oil passes through the Abqaiq pipeline junction and central-processing facilities before heading to export from Saudi loading terminals at Ras Tanura and Ju'aymah. The size of the facility limits the damage that could be caused by a single missile, bomb or similar attack. However, markets were unnerved that al-Qaeda bombers were apparently able to penetrate the facility's outer perimeter before being stopped. A successful attack on Abqaiq would force industrialised nations to tap into strategic government stockpiles and implement emergency rationing plans.

With a diplomatic solution to the Iranian nuclear issue still elusive in mid-2006, market prices were inflated by worries that international sanctions could halt Iranian oil sales or disrupt the flow of oil via the Straits of Hormuz, through which about 17m b/d day pass. It is hardly surprising that policy makers in the US and Europe have shown renewed concern about dependence on Middle East oil.

Investment in future oil production is too low
In the past, sustained oil-supply shortages caused stepped-up exploration in the developing world by Western companies. This is not occurring to a sufficient degree. Nationalist or protectionist sentiment, is limiting foreign investors' access to oil resources. Moves to restrict foreign investment have been made by

populist leaders such as Hugo Chávez of Venezuela and Evo Morales of Bolivia. Open investment climates tend to promote greater and faster resource development than can be achieved by state monopolies. But according to PFC Energy Consultants of Washington DC, only 7% of global oil and gas reserves are open to full international oil company access and exploitation. Over 70% of oil and gas reserves are controlled by national oil monopolies, with outside investors not permitted to acquire equity in exploration activities. Another 17% of reserves are held by Russian companies, while the remaining 6% belong to state firms that allow some equity access to foreign investors, but with bureaucratic, legal and other investment barriers.

The inability of national oil companies to promote resource development represents an important barrier to efforts to meet rising demand. Pressure has been applied by big consuming nations on producing countries to open up to private participation, but with mixed results. Some international oil companies have tried to gain better access to closed or partially closed domains through strategic alliances or partnerships with national oil companies of producing nations. Royal Dutch Shell's efforts to partner with state-owned China National Petroleum Corporation on a gas pipeline across China ended with the company withdrawing with nothing to show for its investment. Several companies have registered losses from efforts to collaborate in Russia. Some companies have offered technical assistance but, as producers have many options for drilling technologies, the offers are only seen as having value in specialised situations such as deep-water exploration. A new approach is for international oil companies to consider stock or asset swaps with Russian and Chinese firms, following the lead of BP which forged a 50–50 partnership with Russian companies to form TNK-BP, Russia's second largest oil company. ConocoPhillips in the United States has struck a strategic partnership with Russia's Lukoil.

Foreign companies have invested in Africa and the Caspian Sea. If some of these moves are successful, they open the possibility for supply increases in future years. African oil production could rise by as much as 3m b/d by 2010 with the reopening of Libya to American investment and continued large investments in Angola and Nigeria's offshore areas. Nigeria is expecting to add 1.5m b/d of new capacity by 2010. Caspian production is also on the rise, with the opening of the Baku–Ceyhan pipeline expected later this year. Azerbaijan's production is expected to increase by 500,000 b/d to 1m b/d by 2010, up from 313,000 b/d in 2003. Kazakhstan's production could rise from 1.1m b/d in 2003 to over 3.5m b/d by 2015 if renegotiations of investment terms for key fields do not disrupt development schedules.

An additional constraint on investment in new capacity has been underinvestment in new exploration by the largest oil companies. Stock-market expectations can discourage investment by emphasising total returns – higher share prices and dividends. This can lead US companies to return cash to shareholders through share buy-backs rather than making capital investments in long-term capacity. Such approaches divert cash away from exploration and production activities. In the United States, stock buy-backs doubled in 2004, exceeding exploration spending. By the end of 2005, buy-backs had reached their highest levels ever, leading some critics to call on Congress to pass a windfall-profits tax on high industry earnings. ExxonMobil, for example, spent $5.5bn in the third quarter of 2005 on buying back its stock. The largest companies still spend a large amount on new exploration, but in inflation-adjusted terms their capital expenditure is less than half the level of 1981, according to John S. Herold, an energy research company. Their share of the worldwide investment in exploration has fallen from two-thirds to two-fifths over the last decade, according to Wood Mackenzie Consultants. This leaves the world's oil security more vulnerable to the invest-ment policies of OPEC members and other countries where national monopolies dominate, such as Mexico and Brazil.

Newly privatised Russian oil firms have been bucking this trend. Following privatisation, Russian production rose from a low of 6m b/d in the late 1990s to 9.19m b/d in 2004. But internal political changes in Russia are affecting growth rates. The Kremlin's attempts to rein in the private sector have slowed expan-sion of investment by companies, including Surgutneftegas, TNK and the now-dismantled Yukos. State-controlled firms have enjoyed a resurgence in the dispensation of major oil and gas projects. Proposed East Siberian projects are in limbo due to political interference and jockeying by state entities: even foreign investors in the distant Sakhalin Islands are finding new barriers in Moscow. Russian oil production was 9.38m b/d in 2005 and is not expected to expand significantly, if at all, in 2006.

The cloudy outlook for sustained large expansion in non-OPEC produc-tion, given limited access to prolific basins controlled by national oil companies coupled with a limited increase in exploration spending among the largest oil firms, means that the world is unlikely to see a repeat of the 1980s, when increased spending on non-OPEC resources created competition with OPEC for market share and brought down prices sharply. Instead, oil prices are likely to remain vulnerable to extreme volatility.

An additional problem is that infrastructure projects such as liquefied natural gas (LNG) terminals and investments to meet tightening refined product specifi-cations are competing for the available investment funds, leaving oil exploration with a shrinking percentage of capital spending. Nor is the capacity problem only in oil supplies. Oil refining worldwide is also close to full capacity, with key regions such as the United States, European Union and China currently oper-ating at above 90% capacity, compared to 75–85% in 1990. World demand for refined products averaged around 81m b/d in the fourth quarter of 2004, against world refining capacity of 84m b/d. The operation of the global refining industry at levels so close to capacity means that unexpected outages can quickly lead to price spikes and regional shortages.

Increasing demand for gas

The tightness and insecurity of oil markets is a further incentive to countries that were already looking to increase use of natural gas in key sectors like electricity generation and manufacturing. World gas demand is projected to grow by more than three-quarters over the next two decades, and the share of gas in world primary energy demand is expected to increase from one-fifth today to over one-quarter in 2020. Natural gas has become a larger part of Asia's overall energy mix, expanding from 5.5% to over 10% of annual energy consumption between 1980 and 2000, and is expected to continue to make significant gains. From 1990–2000, natural-gas consumption has grown at an average annual rate of 6.7% in Asia, with demand growing fastest in South Korea (20.1%), Thailand (11.9%) and Malaysia (8.8%).

Delivering more natural gas to major centres of demand will require massive investment in infrastructure. At present, the largest gas resources are generally far removed from where the need is greatest. Gas demand is projected to grow most rapidly in Western Europe, North America, South Asia and China but local resources in those areas are on the decline. Over two-thirds of proven gas reserves are located in Russia and the Middle East. Delivering this gas to end-use markets will require the construction of expensive pipelines and LNG facilities. The IEA's assessment of future investment in energy found that about $3 trillion in investment will be needed to meet the growing demand for natural gas between now and 2030.

Russia's role as a gas supplier

Russia's unequalled proven gas reserves give it the potential to increase its exports. The European Union buys about half of its gas imports from Russia. The degree of dependency has become a matter of discussion within the EU and in individual European countries, particularly after Russia heavy-handedly stopped supplies to Ukraine on 1 January 2006 over a price dispute. Russia had been supplying gas to Ukraine at heavily subsidised prices of $50 per 1,000 cubic metres compared to the market rate of about $230. The action by state-controlled Gazprom temporarily reduced supplies to western Europe. Austria, France, Germany, Hungary, Italy, Poland and Slovakia reported drops of up to 30% in gas supplies at the peak of winter demand. Moscow blamed Kiev for illegally diverting gas supplies meant for other countries, but Ukraine insisted that it was simply taking quantities it had previously contracted with Turkmenistan, as well as the percentage of gas due to it as transit fees for Russian gas exported to the West.

Gazprom worked out a settlement with Ukraine within days, but the affair prompted questions about the wisdom of relying too heavily on Russian gas, as well as discussions about alternatives. Gazprom's moves to invest in European gas distribution companies also attracted renewed attention – for example, in April 2006 it struck a deal with BASF giving it a share in German gas distribution in return for a stake in development of a Siberian gas field. Gazprom increasingly links future long-term gas supplies with its ability to acquire stakes and in some cases control over domestic gas distribution companies in Western Europe.

Gazprom's chief executive, Alexei Miller, underlined what was at stake when he held a meeting in April 2006 with 25 EU ambassadors in Moscow: 'Attempts to limit Gazprom's activities in the European market and politicise questions of gas supply, which in fact are of an entirely economic nature, will not lead to good results.' While it would honour its European supply contracts, he said, 'it should not be forgotten that we are actively familiarising ourselves with new markets, such as North America and China. Gas producers in Central Asia are also paying attention to the Chinese market. This is not by chance: competition for energy resources is growing.' Indeed, Russia signalled plans to expand oil and gas exports to China during President Vladimir Putin's visit to Beijing in March 2006 when he signed a deal on pipelines, which could begin supply within five years, and which would deliver up to 80bn cubic metres of gas annually to China from Russia's West and East Siberian fields. While East Siberian gas fields are yet to be developed for commercial production, West Siberian fields are the key source of gas exports to Europe. Therefore, any major increase of exports from those fields to China could put into doubt Moscow's ability to honour its obligation to European importers. Russia's policy, however, appeared to be to deliberately play the China card to soften European criticism of its energy policies and to remove obstacles to Gazprom's expansion in Europe.

The argument continued when Putin expressed displeasure with European moves to block Gazprom from acquiring stakes in distribution companies. This followed reports that Britain was considering special legislation to block Gazprom from acquiring a UK gas distributor – though the UK government made clear it had no such plans. Putin said: 'When [European] companies come to us it's called investment and globalisation, but when we go there it's called expansion by Russian companies.' US Vice-President Dick Cheney weighed in a week later in a speech in Lithuania, in which he attacked Russian progress on democracy and human rights and said: 'No legitimate interest is served when oil and gas become tools of intimidation or blackmail.' Putin's response was both angry and restrained.

European hopes that rising Russian gas output can fill the gaps in their energy needs may in any case be misplaced. Russian natural-gas production and consumption have been relatively flat since the early 1990s due to the slow pace of organisational reform and delays in new investments. Questions have emerged about Gazprom's ability to carry out gas-export projects like the $35–40bn development of the Bovanenskoye and Kharasaveiskoye fields of the Yamal Peninsula and the $20bn Stokman LNG project in the Barents Sea, especially since the Kremlin is pressing Gazprom to give priority to construction of pipelines to underdeveloped Russian domestic regions. The fate of other projects targeting Asian markets, such as the Talakanskoye field or the very large Kovykta field also remains cloudy. TNK-BP, through its major shareholding in Russia Petroleum, has been lobbying for an $18bn development plan for Kovykta, including plans for major exports to China and South Korea. While Gazprom – like other Russian energy companies – has plentiful access to financing from Western markets, its ability to increase production sharply also depends on acquiring additional industrial and management expertise.

Uncertain outlook for gas-pipeline schemes

Asian and American demand for natural gas will depend on the fate of pipeline projects to transport gas to major consumer areas. Unstable relations between major consuming governments and regimes in Bolivia, Venezuela and Iran call into question the viability of a widely expanding natural gas pipeline grid.

A number of gas-pipeline schemes have been held up by political factors. Domestic opposition scuttled plans for Bolivia to build a gas pipeline to a Chilean port for an LNG export programme. Continuing tense relations between Pakistan and India, and Iran's confrontation with the West over its nuclear development programme remain roadblocks to the development of pipelines to carry Iranian gas to the subcontinent. Similar proposals to bring Turkmen gas to Pakistan and India have the added barrier of continued instability in Afghanistan. It also remains unclear whether Turkmenistan will be able to export gas to China via Uzbekistan and Kazakhstan under an agreement signed by Chinese President Hu Jintao in April 2006.

Policy responses: sense and nonsense

The general issue of energy security has, over the past year, climbed steadily higher up the political agenda of the world's major importers of fossil fuels. But they have tended to react in different ways, none of them very successful.

The big Asian oil users – China and India – have embarked on a serious scramble for resources. Both are seeking out bilateral energy relationships with oil-exporting countries. China's three major national oil companies have invested over $40bn in oil-field and downstream refining ventures in Africa, Latin America, Central Asia and the Middle East since 1996. One of them, the China National Offshore Oil Corporation, went a step further and bid for the US company Unocal, arousing Congressional opposition until an American purchaser, Chevron, was eventually found. India has embarked on the same road. Its national oil company, Oil and Natural Gas Corporation, has invested as much as $3bn since 2000 in overseas exploration and energy projects. Such acquisitions of 'equity oil' – supplies in which the consumer has a financial investment – are understandable, but may give less security in terms of guaranteeing stable prices and quantities than Beijing and Delhi hope. These emerging big powers may, it is true, be able to bring political influence to bear on oil-exporting governments. But the latter will still want to get the maximum return on their oil, even if it means raising royalties or taxes on equity oil or breaking bilateral sales agreements in order to sell the oil to the highest bidder. In other words, owning or part-owning foreign oil does not always guarantee getting it, or getting it cheaply.

President George Bush made a big impact when he used his State of the Union speech to decry the oil 'addiction' of the United States, the world's biggest oil user and importer, though he made it clear that it was US dependence on specifically Arab oil that chiefly worried him. But he has since done no more to wean America off its drug. The United States still refuses to tax oil use in a way that could substantially reduce demand. Instead of using the market tool of price or tax, the United States continues to rely on an administrative system of car fuel efficiency standards that it has failed to tighten significantly for many years.

The European Union's chief new energy-security concern is its increasing reliance on Russian gas, an issue earlier highlighted by the Reagan administration. But instead of developing a collective response to this problem, many EU states have devoted most effort over the past year to strengthening their own gas and electricity companies, and in several cases encouraging them to merge into national energy champions. This in turn is frustrating EU energy-market liberalisation that would at least enable Europe to make the most efficient use of its available resources.

Several policy avenues suggest themselves to deal with the various energy supply challenges.

Oil

Even though countries that are net importers are home to major international companies, supply is really not in their hands but in those of the world's national oil companies, which sit on the bulk of reserves. It is therefore only the demand side of the equation that oil-importing countries can directly influence. Their main instrument is tax. Europe and Japan have long levied high taxes on oil products, to considerable effect in terms of fuel saving and efficiency. China broke new ground for an emerging economy when in April 2006 it imposed a progressive tax on car size, rising to 20% for the biggest. However, far from taxing oil products, there are still a number of developing countries that still *subsidise* them, an idea that was also attractive to some in the US Congress in spring 2006. There is no prospect of international agreement on oil taxation; such international agreement as there is is limited to the emergency oil stockpile system of mainly oil-importing countries, run by the International Energy Agency. But there have been calls in Europe to tax aviation fuel (chiefly to reduce atmospheric pollution), even though international conventions currently forbid taxing this product. More plausible, because more limited, was the UK suggestion in 2005 that the EU Emissions Trading System should be expanded to cover aviation emissions inside Europe.

Natural gas

In recent years gas has been the most popular fossil fuel for power generation, because it is the least polluting. The politics of the trade in gas have also been considered less naturally adversarial than for oil. Gas is mostly carried in fixed pipelines that require fixed long-term commercial relationships with close, direct contact between suppler and user: hence the fact that there is no OPEC equivalent for gas. However, these assumptions were somewhat shaken by Russia's abrupt behaviour towards Ukraine in early 2006 and worries by other European customers about over-reliance on Gazprom, and in the case of the UK about over-reliance on gas in general. Britain's concern is that it has rapidly become the biggest single national consumer in the EU of gas, which accounts for 40% of its power generation – and a much higher proportion in the future if it does not replace its ageing nuclear reactors. This matters all the more because the UK is now a net importer of gas, and has built far less gas storage than its continental European partners.

Nuclear/renewable energies

Supporters of these two forms of energy are usually at loggerheads. But they should be treated together, because they are each being driven by the same two worries: dependence on foreign fossil fuels (the United States is especially concerned about the Middle East, Europe about Russia); and high-carbon fuels contributing to climate change. Nuclear energy and renewable energy – such as wind or solar power – are both low carbon and essentially indigenous. Nuclear power depends on uranium fuel, which most countries need to import, but in very small quantities relative to either fossil fuels or relative to the overall cost of nuclear reactors.

As a result, the case for nuclear power is being favourably reconsidered, most immediately in the UK where the government in mid-2006 pronounced itself in favour of a new generation of reactors to replace those going out of commission in the next 15 years. It is also being re-examined in the United States, where no new reactor has been built for 30 years, and even in some continental European countries that had previously decided to phase out nuclear power. Renewables also attract interest: unlike nuclear energy, they cannot provide a strong, steady base-load of power, but they can provide extra power during peak demand.

There are other complementarities. Both nuclear and renewable energies have found it hard to survive in liberalised markets with volatile prices, and both probably need some kind of market support. The same instrument can be used for both – that is, a tax on carbon that benefits low-carbon alternatives. Such a tax exists in Europe's Emissions Trading System (ETS), the main mechanism with which the EU hopes to implement the Kyoto Treaty, because the price at which carbon pollution permits trade at on the ETS is effectively a tax on carbon. Unfortunately, the ETS hit serious teething problems in April–May 2006 when it became clear that most EU governments had been too generous to their national industries and had allowed their supply of pollution permits to outstrip demand. This led to a slump in the price of permits. EU governments will clearly have to be more self-disciplined when, at the start of 2008, the ETS becomes the centrepiece of Kyoto compliance.

For the duration of the Bush administration, the United States is certain to stay outside the Kyoto Treaty or any similar arrangement. However, it is just this sort of ETS trading system or quasi carbon tax that Bush needs to underpin the 'technological' solutions that he wants for climate change. If new technologies are to combat climate change, low-or-no-carbon technology will be required, and the United States is very well placed to provide it. Such technology will be expensive to develop and spread: companies will need an incentive to adopt it, and a carbon tax would be the best means to provide one.

Europe Interrupted

2007 marks the 50th anniversary of the Treaty of Rome, which created a six-member European Economic Community that evolved into today's 25-member European Union. Over the last half-century, member states proceeded towards closer integration through a series of additional treaties: the Single European Act of 1987 that completed the internal market; the Maastricht Treaty of 1992 that launched monetary union and created the three 'pillars' of competence to deal with social and economic issues, foreign policy and police and judicial cooperation; and the 2001 Treaty of Nice which modified the institutions so that the Union could function more efficiently after its 2004 enlargement to 25 members. But in 2005, the European project of steady integration ground suddenly and unexpectedly to a halt when the latest proposed treaty, in the form of a draft constitution, was decisively rejected by voters in France and the Netherlands. The outcome of those referendums halted plans for another in the United Kingdom, where voters would almost certainly have also rejected the treaty.

Europe has thus reached an important turning point where the European project needs to be redefined and new, probably more modest, goals set for the future. This requires strong political leadership from the European Union's largest members, but such leadership has unfortunately been in short supply and seems unlikely to emerge.

This is by no means the EU's first crisis; indeed, crises have been an essential part of the European integration process. Out of failures have come new ambitions, but this may prove the exception to the rule. The Treaty of Rome was partly a reaction to the collapse of the European Defence Community in 1954; after the Srebrenica massacre of 1995 came the launching of the European Security and Defence Policy (ESDP); after disagreements within Europe and across the Atlantic over the Iraq War in 2003, a European Security Strategy (ESS) was drafted and a new EU ambition in world affairs declared. The negotiation of treaties has been a powerful instrument of the integration process, which in turn set the terms for the expansion of the Union, and thus provided an extraordinarily potent means of generating social change and economic reform and growth in candidate and new member countries. The constitutional treaty that French and Dutch voters rejected in 2005 was supposed to bring the deepening and the widening of the Union together into one process. With its next steps unclear, the EU is now left without a sense of direction. The malaise created by the failure of the constitutional treaty seems more profound than in previous gridlocks.

The treaty would have simplified the organisational structure of the Union, putting an end to the rotating presidency; granted the Union a legal personality; and brought together the foreign-affairs functions of the Commission and the Council under a new EU foreign minister. The treaty had been drafted by a panel of senior politicians and officials in a convention headed by the former French president Valéry Giscard D'Estaing – ironically, because it was thought necessary 'to bring Europe closer to the people'. It is not clear that the treaty is completely dead. The European Council, which brings together member states' political leaders, called 'a pause for reflection', and no European leader has so far shown any desire that this pause should come to an end. There is a wide divergence of views on what should happen next. Some EU members want to drop the treaty entirely: Britain, Ireland, Sweden, Denmark, Poland and the Czech Republic have no intention to ratify the text. However, no serious alternative is under consideration. Others suggest saving what they perceived as the important measures in the draft, particularly in the area of foreign affairs. The 15 member states that have ratified the text are keen for the treaty to proceed. Some people, including Giscard d'Estaing, simply want the text put to new referendums in France and the Netherlands. However, Angela Merkel, the German chancellor who has been a strong supporter of the treaty, has recognised the lack of consensus and the need for more 'reflection'. She will take on the rotating presidency of the Union for the first half of 2007. The European Commission, the EU's appointed executive body, proposed that EU leaders should sign in 2007 a new formal declaration setting out the Union's core values and objectives on the occasion of the Treaty of Rome's 50th anniversary, and begin a new debate on institutional reforms: the Treaty of Nice now in force would in any case have to be amended if Croatia were admitted to membership.

Popular discontent

The rejection of the draft constitutional treaty by voters in important member countries indicated deep popular discontent with the European integration project that went well beyond disagreement with the precise terms of the treaty. The sources of such discontent appeared to vary greatly from country to country. The French 'non' and the Dutch 'nee' had few points in common. In France, the 'no' vote sprang primarily from domestic issues and was only secondly about Europe; in the Netherlands, it was the other way around. French people were expressing their dissatisfaction to a government that seemed incapable of improving economic conditions and of reducing the level of unemployment. The vote was also a condemnation of the main political parties, and sent a message of mistrust to President Jacques Chirac, whose popularity has waned as he approaches the end of his term in 2007. The French vote was also directed against what is seen in France as 'Anglo-Saxon' economic liberalisation threatening the more statist French social model. French voters also believed that France's influence was being diluted in a 25-member Union, and that Turkey's membership, on which formal negotiations have begun, would accelerate this. In addition, a controversial EU directive designed to create a free market in services triggered nationalist feelings, epitomised by the image of the 'Polish plumber' invading the French employment market.

In the Netherlands, which is the highest net contributor per capita to the EU budget, voters were unhappy that the stability and growth pact, under which countries that adopted the euro as a common currency were supposed to adhere to national budget deficit limits, had been ignored by France and Germany. This suggested that there was one rule for the big countries, and another for the rest. The Dutch were also upset that the euro, launched into circulation in 2002, had not brought the expected benefits. As in France, however, the vote was also influenced by domestic factors. The assassination of film director Theo Van Gogh in November 2004 by a Dutch Muslim radical of Moroccan descent prompted a debate about immigration and claims that liberal policies designed to enhance social integration had failed. This contributed to wariness about further enlargement of the Union. Whatever their differences, the votes did indicate that people in both France and the Netherlands wanted a more 'national flavour' to European policy, and a less 'directed' approach from Brussels. This is what the British had long called 'subsidiarity'.

There are signs that confidence among the European public in the Brussels institutions has reached an all-time low. Elections to the European Parliament in 2004 saw a record low turn out. According to a recent poll by the European Commission of nearly 30,000 Europeans, only 47% had a positive image of the Union. In a Eurobarometer poll published in May 2006, the Union was viewed as modern and democratic (67%), but almost half of the respondents thought it was technocratic (49%) and inefficient (43%). The EU is viewed by its critics as being too narrowly focused on small interest groups, like farmers; and as adding another layer of unnecessary, opaque, unaccountable bureaucracy. In short, Brussels is perceived by many people as not adding value. Austrian Chancellor Wolfgang Schüssel, holding the rotating EU presidency in the first half of 2006, admitted that 2005 had been 'catastrophic' for the EU in public opinion terms, saying: 'If we don't win over the public to [the] European project, then Europe has come to an end'. In the early 1990s, surveys showed that more than 70% of Europeans were in favour of the EU. Today, just over half considers that their country's membership in the EU is 'a good thing', with results varying considerably among countries, from Luxembourg (71%) and Ireland (68%) as the greatest EU enthusiasts to France (44%), Finland (36%), the UK (33%) and Austria (31%) as the leading sceptics.

There has been an institutional response: the European Commission launched a 'citizens agenda for Europe' in May 2006, aimed at rebuilding a climate of confidence and trust and to respond to citizens' expectations with 'concrete results'. The Commission wants, working within existing treaties, to strengthen its role in justice and home affairs to better protect citizens against terrorism; to boost competitiveness and remove remaining barriers to a single market; and to enhance the transparency of the EU decision-making process by transmitting legislation proposals directly to national parliaments.

However, increasing nationalism, fanned by politicians anxious to protect jobs, is also a factor in general disaffection with the European integration project. For example, France, Spain and Poland have each sought to prevent takeovers of companies by other European companies. In 2006 France announced plans to merge the private-sector utility company Suez with state-controlled Gaz de France after Italy's Enel expressed interest in buying Suez. Dominique de Villepin, the French prime minister, spoke unabashedly of the need for national champions. Spain made regulatory changes in an attempt to prevent a takeover of power company Endesa by Germany's E.ON. The Polish government sought to block plans by Italy's UniCredito for a transaction in Poland. Neelie Kroes, the EU's competition commissioner, said such developments 'risk taking Europe into a 1930s-style downward spiral of tit-for-tat protectionism'. However, European integration has come so far that the legality of all such moves is ultimately decided in Brussels. Thus protectionist moves within Europe can have, under present rules, only a limited effect: they represent, in effect, commercial and political jockeying for position in a heavily rule-bound environment.

A trend towards nationaism springs partly from poor implementation of the Lisbon Agenda, agreed by EU leaders in 2000. The Lisbon Agenda was a development plan intended to make Europe 'the most dynamic and competitive knowledge-based economy in the world' by 2010. The aim was to create faster economic growth and 20m jobs over ten years, with support for small businesses, reduced regulation and efforts to step up liberalisation of economies. Responsibility for action lay principally with national governments, and action has been limited at best. France and Germany in particular have found such moves politically sensitive.

It is obvious that a resurgence of populist nationalism casting fellow EU members as its targets would severely undermine the European project: hence the need for strong political leadership following the failure of the constitutional treaty in 2005. Calling the treaty a 'constitution' was not merely a factual but a political error, as it suggested that European integration was advancing definitively to a new stage – something that sceptics would reflexively reject. They did so just as governments in the main European countries were weak for different reasons. In Britain, the scrapping of referendum plans came as a relief to Prime Minister Tony Blair, as he faced persistent criticism over the Iraq War, suffered a drop in his party's parliamentary majority in the May 2005 general election, and would probably have suffered a damaging defeat if the EU referendum had been held. Germany in mid-2005 was in the run-up to elections that resulted in a swing to the right and a change of chancellor from Gerhard Schröder to Angela Merkel, though both were strong pro-Europeans. The disaffection of the French populace with Chirac's government was clearly seen in the 29 May 2005 referendum result, which in effect turned Chirac into a lame duck. Over the coming year, similar constraints will apply: Blair at mid-2006 faced a persistent if undeclared leadership challenge from Gordon Brown; France was increasingly occupied with pre-election jockeying that focused on domestic issues and scandal; Germany's Merkel, though forging a strong foreign policy, was keen to remake the country's relationship with the United States and thus to assert the importance of NATO; Italy at mid-2006 had a new government headed by Romano Prodi, elected by the narrowest of margins. None of these leaders were in a position to invest political capital in the future of the European Union, an issue so controversial that, in the judgement of each, it would be best left alone for the time being.

Limits to integration

That strong political leadership can drive the EU forward has been shown by the European Union's moves into the defence field over the past eight years. At St Malo in December 1998, an agreement between Chirac and Blair, the leaders of the two main European military powers, quickly resulted in the development of the ESDP, under which the EU is now involved in developing new European capabilities and deploying a wide range of crisis-management missions. Another productive initiative was Britain, France and Germany forging a common front on Iran's nuclear programme and negotiating jointly with Tehran.

However, the treaty fiasco, as well as the 2003 disagreements over Iraq, have demonstrated limits to European integration that other powers would do well to note. Harking back to Henry Kissinger's calls in the 1970s for Europe to have a telephone number, Washington has yearned for a more concerted European foreign policy with scope for united action to support its goals. US Secretary of Defense Donald Rumsfeld revealed similar frustrations in January 2003 when he characterised France and Germany as 'old Europe' because of their opposition to the Iraq War. For Washington in 2006, the current inward-looking tendency in European countries is irksome at a time when the Bush administration has demonstrated a renewed willingness to build bridges with traditional allies and a new emphasis on diplomacy rather than force. Significantly, in February 2005 Bush made the first visit by any American president to the European Commission. But European countries are distracted by domestic problems and constrained by limited resources, and each remains keen to forge its own relationship with Washington. Moreover, a significant portion of the European political elite and a large part of public opinion still considers the United States as part of the problem rather than the solution to global challenges. To be sure, this picture is not at all black and white: there has been considerable and improving transatlantic cooperation on Afghanistan, Iran, the Middle East and counter-terrorism. However, Washington remains sceptical that Europe can develop adequate capabilities and devote sufficient resources to play a full role in confronting security problems. It

is not clear to Americans why a European institution is able to impose a significant fine on Microsoft, but Europe is unable to send many troops abroad.

The treaty's failure set back efforts to create a more effective and coherent
EU foreign policy. The creation of a European foreign minister, the European
External Action Service and a new mechanism to allow closer integration in
defence have all had to be shelved. While these moves were not controversial in
most countries, resuscitating them at this stage would clearly make a mockery of
public opinion and would reinforce the image of a Brussels bureaucracy alienated from European citizens.

The post of European foreign minister was supposed to combine several key
roles. It would have taken on the functions of Javier Solana, high representative,
in leading the Common Foreign and Security Policy and ESDP; the chairmanship
of the Foreign Affairs Council now held by the rotating presidency; responsibility for tasks currently held by the commissioner for external relations; and
the running of the proposed European External Action Service, which would
combine some current functions of the Commission and the Council Secretariat
with the aim of providing unified policy briefing and analysis to the minister
and commissioners. The objective was to put external actions of the Council
and Commission under the same umbrella, so that the Union could speak with
one voice in the international arena. This cannot be done without a new treaty.
However, pragmatic solutions are available if backed by European leaders. For
example, the awkward institutional relationship between the high representative
and the commissioner for external relations, currently Benita Ferrero-Waldner of
Austria, could be improved. With a budget of €62m, Solana is not in a strong
position to initiate crisis-management operations, and has to rely on Commission
funding, which is conditional and spent according to a different logic. These
institutional issues are not well understood outside the Union and contribute
to an image of inefficiency and weakness. If the European Union is to be a more
important actor in world affairs in its own right, it will have to better integrate
diplomatic, defence, aid and trade policies and prevent the discontinuities that
come, for example, with a presidency rotating every six months. Kissinger
wanted one telephone line, not a call centre.

Limits to enlargement

A further casualty of an inward-looking Europe could be the enlargement process,
probably the EU's biggest success of recent years, but also its biggest political lia-
bility among the population of some member states. Olli Rehn, the commissioner
in charge of enlargement, has said: 'It would be utterly irresponsible to wobble
in our commitments and disrupt a valuable process which is helping to build
stable and effective partners in the most unstable parts of Europe.' There can be
no doubt that the appeal of EU membership has been a catalyst for large-scale

democratic and free-market reforms and economic growth in many countries of eastern Europe, and continues to be so for possible future member states in the Balkans. The enlargement process has been Europe's most efficient tool to transform its neighbourhood and to unite the continent. But according to one recent poll, 53% of Europeans viewed the enlargement process with 'indifference, fear, annoyance or frustration'. Among candidate countries are Romania and Bulgaria, which are far advanced in the process and seem likely to be admitted, although with more debate than would have taken place in earlier years. Croatia and other Balkan nations are early in the accession process, and Turkey began formal accession talks in June 2006.

France, citing what it calls the 'absorption capacity' of the EU, has passed a law that will oblige it to hold a referendum on further enlargement. The Dutch, Germans, Austrians and others at present overwhelmingly oppose the accession of Turkey and western Balkans countries. Overall, only 35% of Europeans support Turkey's membership while 52% oppose it. German Chancellor Merkel has argued for a 'privileged partnership' for Turkey instead of full membership, a position echoed by Nicolas Sarkozy, French interior minister and presidential candidate. There appear to be several reasons behind this new apprehension about the admission of new EU members. These include socio-economic factors such as the fear of job losses; a sense of lost national identity in the wake of increased immigration; and new insecurities linked to terrorism and organised crime.

Turkey will clearly be the most sensitive case for some years to come. The prospect of joining the EU has played a crucial role in modernising the country's institutions in recent years. If it were to shut the door to a secular, Muslim country, Europe would force a NATO member with a 70m population to rethink its entire strategic approach, with considerable implications for Turkish domestic politics. In the Balkans, enlargement is a strong instrument to encourage reforms and state-building; political instability and organised crime, which have demonstrable capacity to threaten European security, will be more difficult to tackle without the prospect of EU membership.

Alternatives to enlargement, such as the EU's 'stabilisation policy' promoting general regional cooperation and partnerships, provide limited tools to promote good democratic governance and political reforms. For example, in 1995 the Euro-Mediterranean Partnership was launched between EU members and a dozen states: Algeria, Cyprus, Egypt, Israel, Jordan, Lebanon, Malta, Morocco, Syria, Tunisia, Turkey and the Palestinian Authority. (Malta and Cyprus have since joined the EU.) The aim of the so-called 'Barcelona Process' was to prevent instability in the region and to mitigate its consequences in terms of immigration, trafficking and, since 2001, terrorism. Fundamentally a dialogue between governments, the process depended very much on the goodwill of leaders. In December 2005, with terrorism high on the agenda, eight of the ten Mediterranean leaders invited to a Euro-Mediterranean Summit stayed away. Separately, in March 2003 the European Commission adopted a new framework for relations with Russia, the newly independent states (Ukraine, Moldova and Belarus, and later including Armenia, Azerbaijan and Georgia), and the southern Mediterranean countries. This framework aimed to develop a zone of prosperity and a friendly neighbourhood, a 'ring of friends'. In return for demonstrable progress on shared values and effective implementation of political, economic and institutional reforms, all non-member countries involved were to be offered 'the prospect of a stake' in the Union's internal market. Seven bilateral action plans, with Israel, Jordan, Moldova, Morocco, the Palestinian Authority, Tunisia and Ukraine, were agreed, setting out an agenda of political and economic reforms. But granting access to the EU market remains slow and difficult, especially for agricultural products. A third initiative launched by the Commission in May 2004 was a neighbourhood policy in which democracy and good governance were underlined as key objectives. Yet such reforms were supposed to be implemented by governments that are in some cases robustly authoritarian; there is no real incentive for them to comply with democratic and human-rights standards. When civil-rights issues arise in such countries, the EU's role tends to be marginal. For example, when the 'Orange Revolution' erupted in Ukraine in 2004, the EU played some part in resolving the political crisis, but the roles of Poland, Lithuania and the United States were more important. In Belarus, the EU invested €2m to set up a radio programme that started to broadcast just three weeks before the March 2006 presidential election. Overall, the emphasis of the stabilisation approach is on order rather than democratic reforms and transforming the 'neighbourhood'.

While these approaches have only limited effect on non-member European countries by comparison with the prospect of full membership, there are more flexible options that could be attempted. Indeed, these already occur within the European Union. Only 12 of the 25 members use the euro; the Schengen agreement on border controls covers 15 countries, two of which – Iceland and Norway – are not EU members. Forms of flexible membership could be an interim and pragmatic solution: instead of negotiating opt-outs from a huge and fixed package, candidates could be allowed to adopt parts of the *acquis communautaire* (the accumulated body of EU law). In particular, the ability to opt in could be useful in the defence area; numerous non-members already contribute to EU (as well as NATO) missions and co-opting them more fully could add to the strategic weight and defence culture of the Union. While endless enlargement may not be practical, neither is the closing of the EU's borders likely to solve its problems.

The effect on Europe's external relations

For the world outside the EU, the most important question surrounding these internal setbacks and uncertainties about further European integration will be the effect on Europe's capacity as an actor – whether as individual countries or together – in international affairs. In spite of the 2003 disagreements over Iraq, the EU's advances in the defence and security arena, beginning with the 1998 Chirac–Blair St Malo agreement, have shown how much progress can be made under existing treaties, even though much more still needs to be done.

In keeping with its tradition, the EU produced an institutional and bureaucratic response to the political failure of 2003 when its political leaders split over the Iraq War, resulting in a tremendous loss of credibility in Washington. Even though it came out of the EU bureaucracy, however, the European Security Strategy (ESS) developed by Solana was a step forward. Agreed by EU leaders in December 2003, it began with the premise that 'the European Union is, like it or not, a global actor; it should be ready to share in the responsibility for global security.'

Such an idea was taboo during the Cold War, when NATO solidarity was vital to defeat the Soviet threat. It still remains controversial. But the EU's emergence as a security actor is forcing a new, uneasy balance to be struck between the two Brussels-based institutions. While this process has already passed important milestones, such as the 'Berlin Plus' arrangements that allow the EU to draw upon NATO assets in operations, it remains fraught with tension and difficulties, with France in particular wishing to limit NATO's role to that of a military alliance and to expand ESDP functions as much as possible. Nevertheless, strategic imperatives and immediate practicalities suggest the process will continue. The first stage came with the Balkan conflicts of the 1990s, in which Europe showed itself to be manifestly incapable of dealing with regional strife on its own doorstep. European governments realised that new instruments and capabilities were required, and that the United States might not be willing to step in to help solve future European problems. The second stage came with the 11 September 2001 attacks on the United States, which caused US strategic priorities and foreign-policy goals to be changed and a 'war on terror' to be declared. Europe, while appreciating the terrorist threat, saw different means of dealing with it and different pressing issues. The third stage was the division within Europe over the Iraq War, which rendered the EU irrelevant and powerless just at the time when officials were discussing ways, through the eventual draft treaty, to bring more coherence to European foreign policy.

This was the background behind the drafting of the ESS, an attempt to look outwards and to assess for the first time threats to Europe as a whole, and to show that Europe understood threats to global security just as much as the United States. Restoration of credibility in Washington was an important part of the strategy's motivation. Achieving consensus among 25 member states with widely differing strategic postures and threat environments was no small challenge for EU officials. This explained the document's relatively narrow focus. It identified five major threats: international terrorism, proliferation of weapons of mass destruction, regional conflicts, failed states and organised crime, but had little to say, for example, about the Middle East. If the threats seemed similar to those identified by Washington, the EU approach to them was not. In the Union's view, the means of addressing them could not be limited to military force, though this was certainly not excluded. The ESS noted: 'In an era of globalisation, distant threats may be as much a concern as those that are near at hand … Terrorists and criminals are now able to operate world-wide: their activities in central or southeast Asia may be a threat to European countries or their citizens.' However, because European vulnerabilities were inside as well as outside the continent, the Union put a premium on a soft-power approach, in contrast to the US 'war on terror' which assumed threats were external and distant. A specially appointed Group of Personalities reported to the European Commission: 'These threats can evolve rapidly. They may or may not include a military dimension, are often asymmetric, and can threaten the security of member states both from outside and inside EU territory. The distinction between external and internal security becomes increasingly blurred … Military instruments can and do play a role, but in most cases intelligence, police, judicial, economic, financial, scientific and diplomatic means will be at least as important.' The EU's crisis-management approach to regional conflicts and failing states thus seeks to combine civil, military and economic instruments. On terrorism, the emphasis is on law enforcement. Regarding proliferation of weapons of mass destruction, the EU approach is that diplomacy and strengthening international regimes remain the best tools, even if there are elements of a pre-emptive strategy in the doctrine of some European countries.

The ESS was based on two essential concepts: 'preventive engagement' and 'effective multilateralism'. The first – the word 'preventive' was preferred to 'pre-emptive' – referred to the Union's approach to stabilisation and nation-building, including rapid deployment of troops, humanitarian assistance, policing operations, enhancement of the rule of law and economic aid. For example, the Union has a reserve of 5,000 police personnel available for deployment, as well as civil administrators and judicial officers, and five member states have agreed to set up a European gendarmerie that will be able to conduct peacekeeping operations not requiring soldiers. Here lies in principle the Union's added value and its specific know-how. The second concept, 'effective multilateralism', captures the essence of the Union's rule-based security culture. The ESS stresses that 'the fundamental framework for international relations is the United Nations Charter. Strengthening the United Nations, equipping it to fulfil its responsibilities and to act effectively, is a European priority.' The Union affirms that the UN Security

Council should be the forum for legitimising the use of force, but also recognises that rules require enforcement: 'We want international organisations, regimes and treaties to be effective in confronting threats to international peace and security, and must therefore be ready to act when their rules are broken.' This implies a recognition that in emergency situations immediate actions, such as the 1999 Kosovo campaign for which there was no UN mandate, are not always compatible with the formal application of international law.

The ESS was an important step forward in what might be termed the 'strategic awakening' of Europe. However, it was essentially a bureaucratic response and its actual impact has been limited. There are, however, signs of political lessons being learned: for example, the united diplomacy of France, Germany and the United Kingdom on Iran contrasts with the divisions over Iraq, with Solana conveying their position to other EU members and sometimes to Tehran. This united front has been as important in dealing with Washington as with Tehran, putting weight behind the continuation of dialogue.

If, following Basil H. Liddell Hart, grand strategy is defined as 'the art of distributing and applying military means to fulfil the ends of policy', it is clear that the ESS is not a grand strategy. By its very nature, the Union will remain for the foreseeable future an unusual strategic actor, composed as it is of 25 individual countries whose leaders decide collectively whether to deploy collective force, and individually whether to deploy troops or other resources as part of the common endeavour.

The EU's parallel steps to develop defence capabilities have been similarly significant but similarly limited. The ESDP process that sprang from the St Malo agreement set capability targets that would enable the EU to carry out with reasonable speed the so-called 'Petersberg tasks' – a range of humanitarian and peacekeeping missions. While these crisis-management tasks fell well short of warfighting, they still required considerable transformation of European armed forces to be more flexible, deployable and better equipped. Progress has been patchy and too slow, but the number of European troops available for deployment on such missions has steadily increased, as has the number of operations involving European troops, whether under the banner of NATO, the EU or the UN, or in coalitions. The EU's biggest task so far has been to take over from NATO the responsibility for peacekeeping in Bosnia.

The EU's progress in the defence field, while it could be faster and more substantial, represents nevertheless an example of what can be achieved within the Brussels structure, with or without the constitutional treaty. A European Defence Agency has been established as a catalyst to improvements in national capabilities, as well as industry rationalisation and research spending. EU member states have made commitments to provide troops for 18 'battlegroups' of 1,500 people each, available for rapid deployment as an early step to prevent conflict, especially in Africa, or for humanitarian missions. The EU has set new targets for defence capabilities to be achieved by 2010 and for civilian capabilities by 2008. These targets put pressure on governments. The EU has considerably expanded the geographical range of its missions (see list of missions on pages 168–9).

However, some of these missions have been more symbolic than substantial, and could have been carried out by individual countries. Each proposed mission that involves danger to military or other personnel requires lengthy discussion. In spite of the ESS, consensus on the use of force remains fragile, and nations put constraining caveats on how forces can be used, whether by NATO or the EU. There remain important gaps in the capabilities required to carry out missions. Moreover, the logic of the battlegroups initiative is questionable, particularly in regard to the African deployments for which they were mainly designed. For many European states, Africa is a theatre of secondary importance where troops should not be deployed. Battlegroups are intended for 'quick-in, quick-out' deployments – restoring order, then leaving the rest to African peacekeepers. This may not be realistic: rapid exits from such deployments have proved difficult, and would rely on the African Union providing replacement troops. African conflicts are complex, and the African Union may lack the authority and the capacity to restore order.

The EU operation in the Democratic Republic of the Congo (DRC) due to get under way in July 2006 was a case in point. It took six months to get the mission off the ground, following a UN request in December 2005 to enhance the security of elections. Agreement was reached in June to send 2,000 soldiers to reinforce a 17,000-strong UN mission already in place. Germany and France were providing more than two-thirds of the force, with the remaining third contributed by 16 other European states, including Turkey. However, the troops were not intended to be deployed to the east of the DRC, where troubles were most likely to occur. Rather than meeting urgent security needs, the mission perhaps had more to do with cementing Franco-German cohesion and with an attempt by Brussels to bolster ESDP after the treaty fiasco.

Countering terrorism
Similar questions can be raised about the efficacy of the European Union as an actor in countering terrorism. The 11 September 2001 attacks, planned and executed by a cell that became radicalised in Hamburg; the 11 March 2004 Madrid bombings carried out mainly by Moroccans living in Spain; and the 7 July 2005 London bombings, carried out by British citizens mostly of Pakistani extraction, showed that Europe could be both a platform and a target for terrorism originating in Europe. The integration of about 15m Muslims living in Europe has become a security issue. Threat perceptions differ widely across Europe, and responses are seen as being mainly a matter for national governments, particu-

larly as they involve policies in social, economic, judicial and local government arenas that are country specific and go well beyond pure counter-terrorism.

However, Europe is an open society where freedom of movement is guaranteed, and EU members have vulnerable points in common, from seaports to porous borders. The EU has set up a Joint Situation Centre in Brussels to produce intelligence analyses. Intelligence-sharing is vital but problematic among 25 EU members, with the result that much cooperation tends to be bilateral. Since May 2003, the interior ministers of Britain, France, Germany, Italy and Spain, with the recent addition of Poland, have met regularly in the so-called G6 group to discuss counter-terrorism.

Governments also agree that cooperation at the EU level is desirable: the Madrid bombings prompted the creation of a large Action Plan to counter terrorism. The EU can play several important roles: it can coordinate and harmonise national policies, laws and standards, providing for example a common legal definition of terrorism. The European Arrest Warrant introduced in 2004 simplified surrender procedures between judicial authorities of member states, based upon the principle of mutual recognition of judicial decisions. An arrest warrant issued in one country is now valid in other EU nations. The Action Plan contained a list of over 150 proposed EU-wide measures, including an information-exchange network, moves to obstruct terrorist financing, and measures to better control explosives and firearms, but it is a long way from being fully implemented. The EU can also help to provide common concepts: for example, in December 2005 it adopted an approach closely modelled on the UK's 'Four P' (prevention, pursuit, protection and preparation) counter-terrorism strategy, an approach that seeks to reduce both threats and vulnerabilities. If this were to have an effect on national policies of EU members, it would mean that the EU was becoming involved in strategic planning to counter the terrorist threat. The EU can also provide practical advice to countries that lack infrastructure and resources.

There have been additional counter-terrorism moves at the European level. Gijs de Vries, a Dutch former deputy interior minister, was appointed European counter-terrorism coordinator but was given a limited mandate and no meaningful budget: he cannot propose legislation, nor does he chair ministerial meetings to set the anti-terrorism agenda. Other institutions were created: Eurojust to coordinate the fight against organised crime; Frontex to coordinate border control; and an EU Police Chiefs Task Force.

While this may represent a long list of counter-terrorist action at the EU level, much more could be done, particularly in light of the potential for an incident in one European country to affect others. As in other areas, there is scope for the EU, working within existing treaties, to take important steps that would assist in both strategic and tactical responses, given political impetus. A high representative for internal security could be appointed. A Crisis Management Centre could be set up in Brussels to act as the central institution for the secure exchange and coordination of information. The EU should also work with important partner countries such as the United States to develop links between terrorism analysis centres and share analysis of risks and counter-measures.

Steps to the next phase of the European project

The rejection of the constitutional treaty suggested that, for many Europeans, the European integration project had become irrelevant, or even damaging to their interests. This was perhaps inevitable for a European Union whose membership had grown and so profoundly changed. The EU now faces a period in which any additional moves towards integration and enlargement will be more thoroughly examined and tested by its member governments and their electors. It may be that a European Union of 25 members or more will not for the foreseeable future be able to contemplate further great steps in which all members stride forward together. This suggests that it may be time for a period of more flexible integration. Indeed, such an era has already begun with the partial adoption of the single currency. In the past, the European project's architects strongly opposed ideas of a 'multi-speed' or 'multi-core' Europe, fearing that this could set back the whole concept. But the EU's institutions and treaties are strong and binding, its marketplace open and formidably large. Europe's political leaders may now find flexible integration to be a more practical and effective means for nations to get the best out of Europe in the eyes of taxpayers and voters.

3 | The Americas

The United States: Beyond the Bush Doctrine?

In the six decades since Franklin Roosevelt's four election victories inspired a constitutional amendment limiting presidents to two, only Dwight Eisenhower, Ronald Reagan and Bill Clinton have finished two full terms. George W. Bush is set to become the fourth in this line, yet his low public approval at a time of national gloom is more reminiscent of those who failed to win re-election or were driven from office: Truman, Johnson, Nixon, Carter and Bush's own father.

All of those former embattled presidents can lay some claim to a stronger place in history than in their contemporaries' esteem. Lyndon Johnson, through his passionate commitment to civil-rights legislation, shares credit for the substantial completion of the American Revolution. Richard Nixon, by his opening to China and détente with the Soviet Union, laid out an architecture of evolving world powers that well compensated, in strategic terms, for the loss of Vietnam. Jimmy Carter established the human-rights discourse and the military build-up under which his successor is said to have 'won' the Cold War. And George H.W. Bush skilfully managed the diplomatic end of the Cold War, the reunification of Germany and the assembly of a UN-blessed coalition to reverse Saddam Hussein's invasion of Kuwait.

It is the presidency of Harry Truman that Bush supporters most commonly evoke as historical context for the current president's unpopularity. Like Truman, they claim, Bush has both the moral vision and the common sense to grasp the threat from totalitarian enemies and the central American role in confronting them. Like Truman, they say, he will be remembered as a great leader despite the short-sighted griping of his contemporaries. Like Truman,

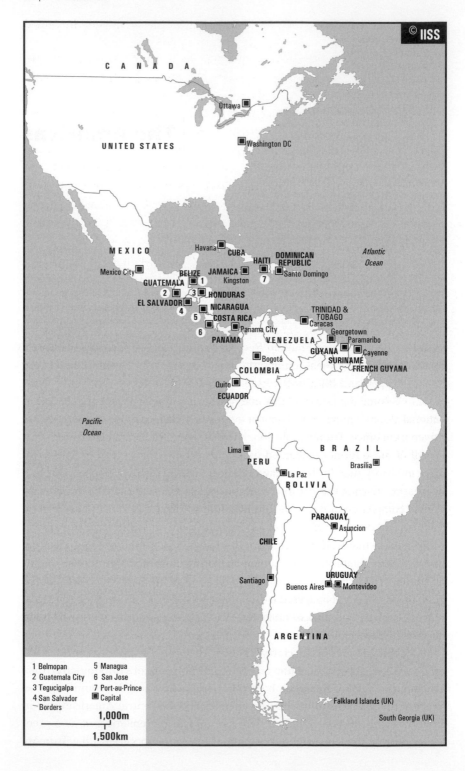

© IISS

CANADA

UNITED STATES

Ottawa

Washington DC

MEXICO

Havana

CUBA

HAITI

DOMINICAN REPUBLIC

Atlantic Ocean

Mexico City

BELIZE

JAMAICA

GUATEMALA 1

Kingston

2

3 HONDURAS

EL SALVADOR

4

5

NICARAGUA

COSTA RICA

6

Santo Domingo

7

TRINIDAD & TOBAGO

Caracas

PANAMA

Panama City

VENEZUELA

Georgetown

Paramaribo

GUYANA

Cayenne

SURINAME

FRENCH GUYANA

Bogotá

COLOMBIA

Quito

ECUADOR

Pacific Ocean

Lima

BRAZIL

PERU

Brasília

La Paz

BOLIVIA

PARAGUAY

Asuncion

CHILE

Santiago

URUGUAY

Buenos Aires

Montevideo

ARGENTINA

Falkland Islands (UK)

South Georgia (UK)

1 Belmopan   5 Managua
2 Guatemala City 6 San Jose
3 Tegucigalpa   7 Port-au-Prince
4 San Salvador   ■ Capital
— Borders

1,000m

1,500km

he was barely re-elected after a bitter campaign, and the voting public turned on him thereafter.

Bush was re-elected in the midst of a difficult war, and he might well have looked on his second term as a poisoned chalice. But the president is famously immune to second thoughts or self-doubt. 'We had an accountability moment, and that is called the 2004 elections', Bush said soon thereafter, brushing off criticisms of his conduct over Iraq. Re-election, he insisted, gave him 'political capital' that he intended to spend. On 20 January 2005, in his second inaugural address, the president proclaimed an American goal 'of ending tyranny in our world'.

The boldness of the Bush administration's governing philosophy has rested on three interlocking propositions. The first combines a theory about US global leadership with a distinct reading of what history teaches about the dangers of appeasement. Second is a conviction that 11 September 2001 ushered in an era of national emergency, requiring new ways of defending America, new approaches to the laws of war, a different reading of domestic civil liberties, and an expansive view of executive power in wartime. Finally, administration strategists have made the political judgement that the terrorist threat, along with the automatic advantage that voters tend to accord Republicans on national security issues, can be used to help consolidate an emerging conservative majority in the United States. This melding of domestic political and national security strategies rests also on the assumption, common among US conservatives, that American exceptionalism contains exceptional religious faith, often involving the kind of personal relationship with Jesus Christ that is professed by the current president of the United States.

The president looms large on the American scene, and great national dramas are usually mirrored as personal dramas for the president. The year 2005 was traumatic for the United States and demoralising for the Bush presidency. Alongside terrifying carnage in Iraq, the most damaging moment of the year was the administration's inadequate response and Bush's own rather feckless demeanour during the drowning of New Orleans, as waters stirred by Hurricane Katrina breached the levees in August. Whether Bush's image will recover in the remaining two years of his presidency depends in part on the direction of national morale, which will be determined by events that are impossible to predict. But it depends also on the administration's ability to move beyond the constraints and limits of the three propositions that have underpinned Bush's certainty. By mid-2006, there were some signs of a pragmatic adjustment and – particularly in the State Department under Secretary of State Condoleezza Rice – an understanding that there was little time, and much ground to be regained in both domestic and international credibility.

Leadership and appeasement

The bold claims of Bush's second inaugural address coincided with a modest increase of optimism about the consequences of his foreign policy. On 30 January

2005 millions of Iraqis braved the threat of terrorism to vote in their first free elections ever (or, depending on one's definition of free, for almost half a century). To be sure, the turnout was mainly Kurds and Shi'ites ready to inherit the state that had brutally repressed them under Saddam; embittered Sunnis did not, by and large, vote. Still, the courage and evident joy of Iraqis waving ink-stained fingers, their proud badge of political participation, was followed by what appeared to be portentous ripple effects: in Lebanon, where the assassination of former prime minister Rafik Hariri led to popular protests and Franco-American diplomacy to get Syrian troops out of the country; in Saudi Arabia, with some stirrings of political reform; in Egypt, where the regime conceded at least the principle of multi-party elections; and in Palestine, where the death of Yassir Arafat opened the way for the reformist and more moderate leadership of Mahmoud Abbas.

This moment was the closest that the administration has yet come to vindicating what might be called the neo-conservative theory of leadership: this is that with virtue – and overwhelming power – on America's side, it is not necessary, ante facto, to convince the rest of the world; unilateral success will generate multilateral support. In early 2005, in that faint breeze of an Arab Spring, even some of America's harsh critics among Arab intellectuals started to draw – or at least concede – a link between regime change in Iraq and democratic stirrings among its neighbours.

Though neither Bush nor any member of his cabinet can properly be labelled neo-conservative, the neo-conservative theory of American leadership fit the president's world view and religious convictions. Bush proclaimed often his faith in God, in America's innate goodness and in the universality of human yearnings for democracy. Immediately following his re-election, Bush invited the right-wing Israeli politician and former Soviet dissident, Natan Sharansky, for an Oval Office discussion of Sharansky's book, *The Case for Democracy*. 'If you want a glimpse of how I think about foreign policy read Natan Sharansky's book', Bush told a journalist. In her Senate confirmation hearings to become secretary of state, Condoleezza Rice focused on Sharansky's 'town square test'. '[If] a person cannot walk into the middle of the town square and express his or her views without fear of arrest, imprisonment, or physical harm, then that person is living in a fear society, not a free society', said Rice. 'We cannot rest until every person living in a "fear society" has finally won their freedom.' If dauntingly ambitious, the sentiment was nonetheless in line with an American rhetorical tradition extending through Ronald Reagan and John F. Kennedy back at least to Franklin Roosevelt. But Rice went on to attack the allegedly cynical realpolitik of all of those presidents, including – implicitly – the current President Bush's own father:

> In the Middle East, President Bush has broken with six decades of excusing and accommodating the lack of freedom in the hope of purchasing stability at the price of liberty. The stakes could not be higher. As long as the broader Middle

East remains a region of tyranny and despair and anger, it will produce extremists and movements that threaten the safety of Americans and our friends.

If Iraq had no weapons of mass destruction, the *casus belli* for the invasion, then an equally serious cause was needed to justify the ongoing expense of blood and treasure there. Rice and other administration officials invoked as precedent the American role in destroying fascist dictatorships and establishing stable democracies in Germany and Japan. But there was a historical sleight of hand here that masked the truly radical nature of a war for democracy in the Middle East. Leaving aside the Anglo-American alliance with Stalin's Russia, it was broadly true that the Second World War pitted democracies against dictatorships. But the United States joined that war for the proximate reason that it was attacked at Pearl Harbor, and for the broader purpose of countering Hitler's bid for mastery over Europe. The closest the United States had come to a war with the main purpose of defending human rights was the 1999 air war over Kosovo, but even in this case any effect on democratisation of Serbia was strictly indirect.

Americans had not signed on to a war for the democratisation of Iraq, and their support would be all the more difficult to sustain as the prospect unfolded there, not of stable democracy, but of sectarian civil war. By June 2005 a significant public opinion milestone was crossed, as for the first time a majority of surveyed Americans said the war in Iraq had not made America safer. In November, John Murtha, a hawkish Democratic Congressman from Pennsylvania, stood up in the House of Representatives to call for an early withdrawal of US troops. Murtha, who had been visiting wounded soldiers in Washington on a weekly basis, asserted that 'the reason for our going to war has been discredited', that the insurgency was being fuelled by the perception of occupation, and that the war was dangerously overstretching US forces. 'The future of our military is at risk', he concluded. Murtha's appeal caused a national stir not least because he was a Marine Corps Vietnam veteran with continuing close links to the US military. He was denounced by Republicans and praised, in personal terms, by Democrats, but the Democrat leadership in Congress did not back his proposal. The presumptive frontrunner for the 2008 Democratic presidential nomination, Senator Hillary Clinton, argued that a withdrawal would cause more problems than it would solve. 'It will matter to us if Iraq totally collapses into civil war, if it becomes a failed state the way Afghanistan was, where terrorists are free to basically set up camp and launch attacks against us', she said. Even former Vice President Al Gore, the highest-level Democrat to have opposed the war before it happened, was arguing in June 2006 that 'setting a deadline [for withdrawal] could set in motion forces that would make [the prospect of civil war] even worse … My guess is that a deadline is probably not the right approach.'

Until spring 2006, then, the consensus held among leaders of both parties that early withdrawal would make many things worse, not least the sagging prestige and position of the United States in the world. This judgement became increasingly plausible as the dominant character of violence in Iraq shifted from an anti-occupation insurgency to a conflict of ethnic cleansing and sectarian revenge. The watershed event in this incipient civil war was the terrorist destruction on 22 February 2006 of the Shi'ite al-Askariyya shrine in Samarra. The grisly aftermath included rival militias' culling of innocent civilians by sect, execution-style slayings and the most hideous forms of murder by torture, involving, inter alia, electric-drill holes in human faces and the conflict's trademark severing of human heads.

Watching this carnage, with no conscionable way to leave, Washington also had no obvious plan for what US troops could accomplish by staying. '[As] the Iraqi security forces stand up, coalition forces can stand down – and when our mission of defeating the terrorists in Iraq is complete, our troops will return home to a proud nation', Bush said in a 30 November 2005 speech to the US Naval Academy. But leaving aside questions of capability, the Iraqi forces standing up were overwhelmingly Shi'ite or Kurd, and included many of the sectarian militias implicated in the internecine horrors. The effect in America was a climate of helplessness, gloom and bitter recrimination. In April 2006 a succession of recently retired generals took very public aim at the civilian leadership of the war, venting their anger specifically on Defense Secretary Donald Rumsfeld. Retired Marine General Anthony Zinni, whose last command had been head of US Central Command, started the officers' revolt by calling on Rumsfeld to resign. Then Army Major-General Paul Eaton, who had been in charge of the programme to train Iraqi forces, published a *New York Times* editorial excoriating Rumsfeld as 'incompetent strategically, operationally and tactically', with a 'Cold Warrior's view of the world, and … unrealistic confidence in technology to replace manpower'. Several others joined the chorus. Most astonishing was the broadside from Lieutenant-General Greg Newbold, the former operations director for the Joint Chiefs of Staff, who in a *Time Magazine* essay criticised the decision to go to war as well as the administration's management of it, and even urged serving officers to join the rebellion.

> I now regret that I did not more openly challenge those who were determined to invade a country whose actions were peripheral to the real threat – al-Qaeda. … [T]he Pentagon's military leaders … with few exceptions, acted timidly when their voices urgently needed to be heard. When they knew the plan was flawed, saw intelligence distorted to justify a rationale for war, or witnessed arrogant micromanagement that at times crippled the military's effectiveness, many leaders who wore the uniform chose inaction. … It is time for senior military leaders to discard caution in expressing their views and ensure that the President hears them clearly. And that we won't be fooled again.

The most direct effect of this rebellion was probably to ensure that Rumsfeld would stay in office until the end of the Bush presidency. Civilian supremacy over war-making is a hallowed American principle, not least since President Truman had relieved General Douglas MacArthur of his Korean War command because MacArthur publicly, and insubordinately, advocated a drive across the 38th parallel and against China. Still, the criticisms were more evidence of the Iraq problem's growing political volatility.

Despite the fact that there were few truly competitive districts, Republicans started to fear that a sour public mood on Iraq – compounded by the president's unpopularity and their own low poll ratings – might after all cost them control of at least the House of Representatives in the November 2006 elections. But they also knew how to turn the Iraq quagmire into an uncomfortable issue for the Democrats, who were aware how easily they could be boxed into the image of the party of defeatism and appeasement. In June, as Democrats tried to cast a resolution calling for a drawdown, but not a firm 'deadline' for withdrawal, Republicans introduced their own resolution stating that America is 'engaged in a global war on terror, a long and demanding struggle against an adversary that is driven by hatred of American values and that is committed to imposing, by the use of terror, its repressive ideology throughout the world'. The resolution also stated that 'the terrorists have declared Iraq to be the central front in their war against all who oppose their ideology'. The partisan purpose of this language was made clear in the bitter floor debate. 'Many, but not all, on the other side of the aisle lack the will to win', Representative Charlie Norwood, Republican of Georgia, said of the Democrats. 'The American people need to know precisely who they are ... It is time to stand up and vote. Is it Al Qaeda, or is it America?' Bush made clear at about this time that he expected to hand the Iraq war to his successor. That statement prompted Richard Holbrooke, the former senior State Department official, to reflect on the Iraq War as a nightmare that could extend over several administrations, overshadowing and poisoning American politics until 2012 or beyond. In strategic terms, he said, it was 'worse than Vietnam'.

It was certainly the case that America was now caught in a credibility trap reminiscent of the war in Indochina. To leave behind a failed state would be to hand al-Qaeda and like-minded jihadists not just a training ground and base of operations, but a morale-boosting victory on a mythical par with their dispatching of the Soviets from Afghanistan. Yet, through 'staying the course' without visible success, America's image and credibility would suffer just as surely. Moreover, an endless war of counter-insurgency would demoralise and brutalise the US military. In a nightmarish echo of the Vietnam conflict, reports emerged that in Haditha in western Iraq, the heartland of the Sunni insurgency, a US marine was killed in November 2005 by a roadside bomb, and his comrades responded by shooting to death 24 civilians, including women and children.

The Churchillian posture posed other problems. Election gains by Hamas in Palestine, the Muslim Brotherhood in Egypt, and Shi'ite Islamists in Iraq were reminders that religious fundamentalism would, at the very least, compete with democratic enlightenment. One flaw with the Sharansky thesis as popularised by President Bush and Secretary Rice was the baleful truth that in much of the Islamic world, resentment and humiliation were more powerful factors than the yearning for democratic freedoms. Palestinians wanted to be free of Israeli occupation as much or more than they wanted to have working, democratic institutions. Sharansky's insistence that they could not have the former before developing the latter may not be a very astute reading of the psychology of democratic development.

Likewise, the ripple effect of Iraqi democracy depended on Iraqi democracy being established. Even in that best case, moreover, there remained the prospect of counter-waves of resentment and resistance to foreign occupation. These competing effects would be hard to quantify, but they could be glimpsed in reports such as one from The *Washington Post's* Anthony Shahid, who, in June 2006, reported that Tripoli, Lebanon was a 'city being transformed by growing radicalism and religious fervor'. From Tripoli Shahid assessed the Iraq war's 'profound legacy across the Arab world: fear and suspicion over Iraq's repercussions, a generation that casts the Bush administration's policy as an unquestioned war on Islam, and a subterranean reserve of men who … declare that the fight against the United States in Iraq is a model for the future'.

Simple propositions about standing firm and the dangers of appeasement were confounded by the situation that the United States now found itself in vis à vis Iran, featured in the administration's 2006 iteration of the US National Security Strategy as the 'single country' posing perhaps the greatest challenge to the United States. America's bargaining position had deteriorated dramatically over the course of three years. Just after US troops took Baghdad in April 2003, Iran had sent through the Swiss ambassador in Tehran a missive to the United States proposing 'comprehensive negotiations' to resolve disputes on nuclear safeguards, terrorism, the situation in Iraq, and 'material support' for Palestinian armed resistance along with the principle of a two-state solution to the Israeli–Palestinian dispute. It is impossible to say that such talks would have been successful. The Bush administration ignored the overture because many of its officials believed that Iran's clerical dictatorship was ripe for collapse, a result that American firmness on the back of its Iraq victory would hasten. But three years later, Iran was flush with oil revenues and defiant about its determination to pursue nuclear enrichment. America was flailing in Iraq, where Tehran had increasing influence. It was from this position of much greater weakness that the Bush administration decided it had no choice but to join the Europeans in direct talks with the Iranians about their nuclear programme.

Still, there was palpable relief among European allies that the United States finally seemed to take the negotiations route seriously, rather than counting on regime collapse or 'surgical strikes' for dealing with the problem. There were other signs of greater pragmatism. The movement of Rice from national security adviser to chief diplomat had a certain empowering effect on the State Department, due to Rice's close relationship with the president. Rice led a greater US engagement in the Israel–Palestine conflict, pressing Prime Minister Ariel Sharon and, after Sharon was stricken by a coma, his successor Ehud Olmert to negotiate with Palestinian President Mahmoud Abbas. On Olmert's first visit as prime minister to the White House, on 23 May 2006, the US side gave a distinctly reserved reaction to Olmert's vision for withdrawing without negotiations from parts of the West Bank and thereby unilaterally setting Israel's final borders.

The United States also softened, slightly, its dogmatic opposition to the International Criminal Court, insofar as it abstained from, rather than opposed, a UN Security Council resolution that called for the court to have a role in judging humanitarian crimes in the Darfur region of Sudan. It committed greater diplomatic resources, notably in the form of veteran diplomat Christopher Hill, to the Six-Party Talks on North Korea's nuclear programme – though, to be sure, those talks continued to go nowhere. In Latin America, having rather ineptly welcomed a short-lived coup against Venezuelan President Hugo Chávez in 2002, the administration more wisely refrained from being exercised by Chávez' demagogic anti-American exhortations in 2006, or his links to Cuba's regime and Nicaragua's Sandinista opposition. On China, which many neo-conservative strategists regard as the inevitable future challenger to America's global primacy, the administration also took a measured tone. Defense Secretary Rumsfeld, in a June 2006 speech to the IISS Shangri-La Dialogue in Singapore, expressed a more benign interpretation of the Chinese military posture than he had expressed from the same platform one year earlier. The signature statement of administration moderation on this score was perhaps a 21 September 2005 speech by then Deputy Secretary of State Robert Zoellick, inviting Beijing to exercise the responsibilities of a 'stake-holder' in international society.

State of emergency

The second proposition sustaining the Bush administration's approach to statecraft was summarised by journalist Ron Suskind as 'the one percent doctrine'. In a book with that title, Suskind paraphrased Vice President Dick Cheney as arguing after 11 September that 'if there was even a 1 percent chance of terrorists getting a weapon of mass destruction – and there has been a small probability of such an occurrence for some time – the United States must now act as if it were a certainty'. 'Response' was more important than 'analysis', and the old ways of laborious inter-agency deliberation to avoid policy mistakes had to give way to the new imperative of executive action to forestall and pre-empt the terrorist threat.

This doctrine famously led to stress in relations between the White House and Pentagon, on the one hand, and agencies such as the CIA, on the other. On 29 October 2005, this particular area of tension was exposed in the indictment of I. Lewis 'Scooter' Libby, Jr, an aide to Cheney, on perjury charges related to the outing of CIA operative Valerie Plame. Plame's husband, former American diplomat Joe Wilson, was a harsh critic of the Iraq War and, in particular, of some spurious claims the president had made regarding efforts by Saddam Hussein to acquire uranium in Niger. The motive for leaking information about his wife's covert status was murky, but it may have been meant either as retaliation for Wilson's public criticisms, or a warning shot to restive CIA analysts, or both. The poisoned relationship between the administration and the CIA continued to fester under the directorship of Porter Goss, who upon taking over in November 2004 sent a message to CIA employees warning, that '[we] support the administration and its policies in our work. As agency employees we do not identify with, support or champion opposition to the administration or its policies.' Under Goss there was a spate of high-level resignations. (Goss himself was eased out in May 2006, after less than two years in the job.)

But the proposition that the US executive had to act on the basis of a permanent state of national emergency went beyond questions of intelligence analysis or bureaucratic discipline to more fundamental questions of presidential power and the rule of law. In late 2001 and over the course of 2002 and 2003, administration lawyers including Alberto Gonzales (later attorney general) and John Yoo of the Justice Department drafted a series of legal memos arguing, first, that detainees in the 'war on terror' were neither prisoners of war subject to the Geneva Conventions nor criminal defendants subject to the usual protections under American law. Secondly, these lawyers argued that the president's inherent powers as commander-in-chief in wartime gave him the legal authority to override domestic and international laws against torture. These explosive arguments set off a furious campaign of opposition from Judge Advocate Generals, the US military lawyers, and from some high-level officials such as then Secretary of State Colin Powell. But the Gonzales and Yoo positions were backed crucially by Cheney and Rumsfeld, becoming, in effect, administration policy.

The notorious consequences constituted the largest blow to American moral prestige since the Second World War. They include hundreds of reported cases of prisoner abuse, most infamously at the Abu Ghraib prison in Iraq, and dozens of homicides. In 2005 and 2006 there was a struggle to undo some of this damage. The most important effort came in the form of an amendment to the FY 2006 Defense Appropriations Bill, sponsored by Republican Senator John McCain, himself a former prisoner of war who had been tortured by his Vietnamese captors. The McCain amendment prohibited 'cruel, inhuman, or degrading treatment or punishment' of any 'individual in the custody or under the physical control of United States Government, regardless of nationality or physical location'. It also barred any interrogation techniques 'not authorized by and listed in the United States Army Field Manual on Intelligence Interrogation'. The Bush administration, with Cheney's office in the lead, threatened to veto the amendment, and then worked behind the scenes to water it down. But it passed both Houses of Congress in October 2005 by overwhelming, veto-proof majorities – one of the very rare instances in which the Republican Congress had defied the president. Bush duly signed the bill containing the amendment, but he raised more questions about the administration's intentions when he attached a so-called 'signing statement', stipulating that '[the] executive branch shall construe [the law] in a manner consistent with the constitutional authority of the President ... as Commander in Chief' and 'the shared objective of the Congress and the President ... of protecting the American people from further terrorist attacks'. In June 2006, moreover, it was reported that the Pentagon was considering changing its Army Field Manual to delete the ban on 'humiliating and degrading treatment'.

The debate over torture, therefore, was not finished. It was clear that many in the administration, including Rice and much of the State Department, realised what huge damage had been done to America's reputation. Bush himself, on a June 2006 trip to Europe, said he wanted to close the prison at Guantanamo Bay, Cuba that housed detainees that the administration had put outside US territory and, purportedly, outside the reach of US law. But the administration as a whole, and Vice President Cheney's office in particular, was unwilling to give up on the expanded view of executive power, reasserted – in their view – in a national emergency to recover some of the ground lost to congressional overreaching after Vietnam. Thus, when the *New York Times* revealed in December 2005 that Bush had secretly authorised the National Security Agency to conduct a huge domestic surveillance programme in clear contravention of the Foreign Intelligence Surveillance Act passed in the 1970s, the administration claimed, again, that all was authorised under the president's inherent powers as commander-in-chief, and had been reconfirmed by Congress in its September 2001 resolution urging the president to fight terrorism.

On 29 June 2006 the US Supreme Court handed down a decision that appeared on first reading to refute such sweeping claims of executive authority. The narrow question addressed by *Hamdan vs Rumsfeld* was the constitutionality of military commissions set up to try detainees at Guantanamo, and the impact might be limited insofar as Congress could pass legislation to make the commissions pass Supreme Court muster. However, the reasoning of the five-judge majority appeared to suggest a broader rejection of claims from the president and his lawyers that his inherent powers as commander in chief authorised him, for example, to circumvent or reinterpret laws on torture – including even a refusal to comply with the

McCain Amendment. How this reasoning would play out, however, in the actual practices of the administration, and the precedents set for future administrations, was a matter of considerable debate among constitutional scholars.

The Bush administration often accused its critics of being mired in a 'pre-9/11' mindset. The extraordinary state of war, in its view, introduced new imperatives. Yet it was precisely the prospect of a wartime expansion of executive power that the founding drafters of the American constitution had in mind when they worried that a strong executive might lead to tyranny. The question some 217 years later came down to this: was the threat from al-Qaeda so far out of proportion to anything that America had previously faced, including the Cold War balance of nuclear terror, so as to outweigh this founding principle of the republic?

A conservative majority?

Bush entered his second term with strengthened Republican majorities in both Houses of Congress. The likelihood of at least two retirements from the Supreme Court offered him scope to cast the federal judiciary in a decisively more conservative direction. Conservatives were delighted with the prospect of implementing their agenda.

But the top item on that agenda quickly failed. The president's January 2005 State of the Union Address had been the beginning of his campaign to sell the idea of partially privatising Social Security, the state pensions scheme, by allowing younger workers to divert a portion of their payroll taxes into private pension accounts. Social Security, a linchpin of the New Deal welfare state, had long been a target of American conservatives, but was extremely popular among the public at large. Bush toured the country for several months to promote his plan. Democrats in Congress stood firm in opposing the idea, and key Republicans refused to back it. In his 2006 State of the Union speech, Bush acknowlegded this failure, to loud cheers from the Democratic side of the House.

Another contentious welfare-state controversy was impending. In 2003 the Republican-controlled Congress had passed, and Bush signed, a hugely expensive new benefit for the elderly – government-subsidised insurance to cover prescription drugs. As advanced pharmacology became an increasingly central part of medical care, it became correspondingly untenable that drugs were not paid for by Medicare, the free government health programme for people over 65. But in keeping with the Republicans' anti-government philosophy, and with their close links with business, the new benefit was devised in a Byzantine fashion as a system of subsidy to private insurance plans. Moreover, Medicare under the new law was expressly prohibited from using the federal government's vast purchasing power to bargain with drug companies for lower prices. In another twist, the benefit contained what came to be known as a 'donut hole': yearly drug expenses were covered up to $2,250, but then not covered until reaching $5,100, and beneficiaries were prohibited from buying supplemental insurance to cover the hole.

A bubbling up of anxiety was reported as the elderly in late 2005 tried to navigate an array of complex choices under the plan from private insurance companies. Anxiety turned to anger, and then panic, as the plan went into effect in January 2006: tens of thousands of the elderly poor found that their prescriptions, which Medicare had covered for low-income old people, either were no longer eligible, or their pharmacies would not take the chance because they did not know if they were eligible. Conservatives characterised this fiasco as another boondoggle of government spending. Moderates and liberals, remembering how the entire original Medicare programme was launched smoothly in 1966, said it was the result of having a big-government programme instituted by a party that was philosophically opposed to government welfare programmes.

The administration's philosophy of limited government had already taken a battering along the northern coast of the Gulf of Mexico. First, the flooding of New Orleans by Hurricane Katrina was a reminder that 40 years after the civil-rights movement and landmark legislation, there was still a large, poor, extremely vulnerable – and, in the case of New Orleans, overwhelmingly black – underclass. Evacuation plans relied on people escaping in their own cars, a commodity that the white population of the city by and large possessed. The carless were left to sink or swim, in some cases literally. Those who made it to the main designated refuge, the Superdome sports arena, soon found themselves in a foetid nightmare, with virtually no water, no food, no sanitation and no protection. It was, in moral terms, a national disgrace.

In strategic terms, it was a frightening revelation. FEMA, the Federal Emergency Management Agency, had performed well in the Clinton administration. Under Bush it was downgraded from a cabinet-level department and folded into the newly created Department of Homeland Security. As the agency proved unable to cope with Katrina, it emerged that the director was a political appointee with no disaster management experience, whose previous job was as legal counsel for the Arabian Horses Association. Bush did himself no favours the week of the disaster: he was filmed cutting a cake for Senator McCain, air-strumming a guitar with country music singer Mark Wills, returning to his vacation in Texas – and then, when he did turn his attention to the crisis, saying in an interview that 'I don't think anybody anticipated the breach of the levees'. In fact, that threat had been anticipated for decades, and there was film of him being briefed on it just hours before the storm's landfall. Beyond stumbling leadership was a stark reality: four years after 11 September, years during which the US executive branch had warned incessantly that terrorist enemies were planning a chemical, biological or nuclear attack in an urban area, the US government was unable to evacuate a middle-sized city following a disaster for which there was abundant and specific warning.

Restrained somewhat by both the social-justice and homeland-security implications of this fiasco, the Republican leadership in Congress temporarily shelved the next big item on their tax-cutting agenda: repeal of the estate tax. But nine months later, in June 2006, they again moved for total abolition of this 'death tax', as they called it. Inherited estates of under $4 million per married couple (already rising to $7m in 2009) were already exempt from the tax, so it was safe to say that this was an issue of direct concern only to very well-off families. It was difficult if not impossible to find real examples of the hardship cases – family farms or small business having to be sold – that featured in the narratives of repeal's proponents. The Senate leadership needed 60 votes to overcome a Democrat filibuster, and fell short by three votes, including two Republicans, but the White House and Congressional leadership vowed to keep trying. They would also continue to push a measure to make Bush's signature tax cuts, set to expire in stages between 2009 and 2011, permanent.

This continuing agenda of tax cuts favouring mainly the wealthy underlined the strange disconnect between wartime rhetoric and the politics of normality. In no way could it be suggested that US society was mobilised for war – either the so-called 'war on terror' or the real war in Iraq. The war did, however, increase national polarisation. Though Bush was generally unpopular – with approval ratings generally trending downwards towards 30% – he was extremely unpopular with Democrats and independents while maintaining fairly high levels of approval from Republicans. Such a sharp differentiation by party was unusual.

It evidently remained the calculation of Karl Rove, Bush's political strategist, that pleasing the Republican base was more important politically than reaching out to independents or Democrats. Rove spoke often of a long-term political realignment favouring the Republicans, on the basis that the United States was an inherently conservative country. This did not actually seem to be the case, judging by public opinion surveys, when it came to the most salient domestic issues, such as tax policy, social security or abortion rights. It may be true, however, in terms of what might be called national temperament: the nationalistic edge of a country that has been fighting one war or another for much of the past 70 years.

It was not easy to make clear judgements about America's political evolution. On both sides of the political spectrum there was remarkable political fluidity. The Democrats were animated by evidence that the American public was fed up with the performance of both the president and the Republican Congress, and ready for a change. The Democrats were also animated by dread – expressed daily through countless Internet blogs – that they were fully capable of flubbing the opportunity. The presumed frontrunner for the 2008 presidential nomination was Hillary Clinton, supported by her ever-popular husband, the former president, and already showing incredible fundraising prowess. But there was a concern among many Democrats that she was a polarising figure. (Rarely was any concern expressed about the historical oddity of a sequence of President Bush, followed by Clinton, followed by Bush's son, followed by Clinton's wife.) Another leading contender, though he said he was unlikely to run, was former Vice President Al Gore, who had the distinction of having won the popular vote count against Bush in 2000, and having had to concede a bitter legal battle decided, in the end, on a 5–4 vote by the US Supreme Court. Many Democrats were convinced that Gore had actually won the Florida electoral votes that carried Bush into the White House. Gore had a passionate base of grassroots Democratic support for two other reasons as well. First, he was a military hawk who nonetheless had argued strenuously against the Iraq War (unlike Hillary Clinton and other leading Democrats, who still supported the war in principle while attacking the administration's execution of it). Secondly, Gore became something of a star in early 2006 with an unlikely film hit, 'An Inconvenient Truth', which was a documentary about his decades-long preoccupation with the threat from global warming.

On the Republican side there were aspects of a political meltdown. The House Republican leader Tom DeLay was forced by criminal indictment in Texas to resign from Congress. DeLay was a ruthless partisan whose 'K-Street Project' was unashamedly designed to make the Washington lobbying industry an arm of the Republican Party, through such measures as openly punishing lobbying firms that hired Democrats. He was also relentless in efforts to force redistricting to solidify safe Republican seats, and efforts to funnel money into Texas Statehouse races for this purpose were what brought the indictments for money-laundering. The K-Street Project is epitomised by the funding efforts of lobbyist Jack Abramoff, whose complicated schemes involving work for Indian casino groups brought his own criminal indictment, and implicated a number of Republican politicians.

Beyond corruption scandals, the Republican Party was demoralised by a deep division over immigration. This issue causes a natural tension in the party between business interests that depend on cheap immigrant labour and a more populist grassroots. Bush, who had enjoyed considerable Hispanic support when governor of Texas and hoped on a national basis to lure more Hispanics away from their traditional home in the Democratic Party, favoured a relatively liberal approach. The US Senate considered a bill that combined stricter enforcement of penalties with a provision of amnesty for illegal immigrants already in the United States who agreed to pay back taxes. The amnesty provision was anathema among Republicans in the House of Representatives, which passed a much more puni-tive bill without the amnesty. In the midst of this debate, in spring 2006, legal and illegal immigrants across the country took to the streets in a series of large demon-strations to assert their place in American society. There seemed no way that this division could do anything but further damage Republican cohesion.

It also suggested that if there was going to be a more permanent Republican majority, it might have to be led from the centre. This lent greater plausibility to the continuing ambitions of McCain to win the Republican nomination. McCain was a Vietnam war hero who had defied his party leadership in a way that endeared him to many on the left. He had fought fiercely for campaign finance reform, to limit the amount of so-called 'soft money' that could be given to candidates. He opposed efforts to enact an amendment to the constitution banning marriage for gay couples. He opposed Bush's tax cuts, calling them an unfair benefit to the rich. And he was a strong advocate of tougher emissions controls to combat global warming.

McCain also had a reputation of being forthright and unwilling to bend for politics, which made it somewhat awkward for him now to court the Republican right wing. It was easy enough to support the war in Iraq, but somewhat embarrassing for him to say that, though he'd opposed the tax cuts, he now favoured making them permanent, since their expiration in 2009 constituted a 'tax rise'.

Faith and doubt

First McCain would have to get past the religious right, which provided the bedrock of support to Bush and had been suspicious of McCain even before his fight for the 2000 Republican nomination, during which he attacked one of its leaders, Jerry Falwell, as an 'agent of intolerance'. This was a fair enough criticism of a Christian zealot who a year later was inspired by the 11 September attacks to endorse part of Osama bin Laden's theology. America's turning away from God, Falwell said,

> possibly has caused God to lift the veil of protection which has allowed no one to attack America on our soil since 1812 … I really believe that the pagans, and the abortionists, and the feminists, and the gays and the lesbians who are actively trying to make that an alternative lifestyle, the ACLU, People for the American Way, all of them who have tried to secularize America. I point the finger in their face and say 'you helped this happen'.

Nonetheless, in May 2006 McCain followed the pilgrimage of most Republican candidates for president, travelling to Falwell's Liberty University in Lynchburg, Virginia to deliver a speech that was a masterpiece of conciliation without pandering. McCain, in fact, addressed none of the religious right's key concerns, in a speech that was almost identical to an address delivered the same month at the New School for Social Research, a bastion of New York liberalism. He spoke of patriotism, offering a hard-line view of the threat from 'Islamic extremists' who had 'disdain for the rights of Man, [and] … contempt for innocent human life'. But he also sounded convincing themes of national reconciliation, with the affecting anecdote of his life-long friendship with an anti-Vietnam War protester who died some years ago of cancer. These speeches suggested that McCain was aiming for a neat trick if he could pull it off: getting on the right side of conservative religious voters while maintaining his appeal to independents, and indeed, many Democrats, of the moderate centre. It was far from clear that he *could* pull it off, however. Although he led in early Republican preference polls, there was a real question about whether the Republican nomination was attainable for someone who had built his reputation as a maverick against conservative Republican orthodoxies.

Yet perhaps something was happening in evangelical America, the stirrings of complication if not an awakening of moderation. On the one hand, the Bush administration was under attack for not being conservative enough. The hard religious right was clearly disillusioned with Bush and the Republican establishment for, in effect, taking them for granted. The fury came out in reaction to the nomination of Bush's White House lawyer to the Supreme Court. Court nominations were one area where Bush's religious backers expected results: with the retirement of Justice Sandra Day O'Connor and the death of Chief Justice William Rehnquist, politically organised conservatives expected and demanded that Bush appoint confirmed judicial conservatives who could be counted on, above all, to overturn the 1973 *Roe vs Wade* ruling that had legalised abortion in the United States. In his initial nomination on 20 July 2005 of John Roberts to replace O'Connor, they seemed to get what they wanted, despite Roberts's moderate demeanour. Following Rehnquist's death, Roberts was nominated as chief justice. To fill his place, Bush on 3 October nominated his former private lawyer and White House chief lawyer Harriet Miers. A firestorm erupted on the right. Miers had no bench experience, and an unformed judicial philosophy that gave no clue how she might rule on issues of key concern to conservatives. Eventually she was forced to withdraw her name from Senate consideration, to be replaced by the more experienced, and more reliably conservative, Samuel Alito. Bush courted similar anger on the religious right by seeming to go through the motions of pushing for a constitutional amendment to ban gay marriage – but only during election years when his party was in trouble. Thus, having dropped the idea after his re-election, he started campaigning for it again in 2006 as Republicans were becoming increasingly gloomy about the polls. The amendment had no chance of passing the Senate, where it required 60 votes; Republican Senators such as McCain were sure to join Democrats in opposition to rewriting the constitution for the purpose of denying fundamental rights to a specific group of people. (Only one state, Massachusetts, recognised gay marriages, and a law passed in the Clinton administration relieved states of any assumption that they had to recognise same-sex marriages performed in another state).

On the other hand, there were signs of a more complicated attitude of evangelicals and religious conservatives to politics, and even a mellowing of their hard-right allegiances. It was a modest shift, one that might easily move back the other way, but discernible in such events as the June 2006 election of the Reverend Frank Page as president of the Southern Baptist Convention. Page was hardly a liberal, but he was supported by some more moderate Baptist groups against the convention's very conservative leadership. 'I believe in the word of God', said Page. 'I'm just not mad about it'. Elsewhere, religious leaders such as Rich Cizik, vice president for governmental affairs of the National Association of Evangelicals, led a campaign to make a strategy against global warming a central part of religious politics. Others pushed evangelicals to concentrate more on such issues as poverty in the Third World and human trafficking. In the Bush administration, a leading evangelical was speechwriter Michael Gerson, who helped push the administration into comparatively generous funding for the fight against AIDS in Africa. And in the conservative rural town of Dover, Pennsylvania, voters in November 2005 turned out of office all eight members of the School Board, who had introduced the teaching of 'intelligent design' (ID) in the science curriculum, making claims for it as an alternative to evolutionary science. A US district judge, in a case argued before the election, ruled on 20 December that the law mandating the teaching of ID was an unconstitutional establishment of religion.

The role of religion in the United States remained huge. But nowhere was it written that religious faith must be reactionary in its impact. It was after all the 'Social Gospel' of the late nineteenth century that supplied fervour to the Progressive-era reforms of the early twentieth. The civil-rights movement of the 1950s and 1960s was in large measure a church movement. This is not to suggest that the early twenty-first century would see the rise of an organised 'religious left' in America, only that the religious narrative was shared by politicians on the left, who could use it to defuse some of the divisiveness that faith has wrought on American society. Hillary Clinton is a devout, life-long Methodist. Her husband, whose very public saga of sin and redemption was a big part of the national drama in the late 1990s, summarised the situation aptly in a 2006 speech:

> For people in America who are a part of my political tradition, our great sin has often been ignoring religion or denying its power or refusing to engage it because it seemed hostile to us … For … the so-called Christian right and its allies, their great sin has been believing they were in full possession of the truth.

Yet the belief that one is in full possession of the truth is driven by the implacable certainties of revealed religion. If American religiosity was going to be a powerful factor of the twenty-first century, it was likely to cause misunderstandings with America's European allies, and a hardened confrontation with Islam. The devotion of so-called 'Christian Zionists' to support for an Israel covering the full West Bank and Gaza is but one example of how faith can be radicalising and damaging in its consequences for US foreign policy.

Bush was another example. He was obviously devoted to the cause of religious toleration, and his rhetoric since 11 September has been full of care to convey respect for people of other faiths, including Muslims, and including non-believers. Gerson crafted for him scriptural allusions of simplicity, eloquence and compassion. Yet there can be little doubt that the face of America seen by the rest of the world for the past few years has been a face of Manichean nationalism. The angry reaction of much of the world is not really surprising: nobody likes a self-righteous superpower.

Yet the faith of Bush, with his very specific personal story, may be more *sui generis* in American terms than is often assumed. Even in a hawkish conservative such as John McCain, the assumptions of American exceptionalism were softer. Abu Ghraib and other outrages had given Americans some cause to remember that the key Christian doctrine of original sin is a foundation-stone of their democracy: in the knowledge that power is corrupting, it requires legal limits that apply to presidents and even superpowers.

The administration as a whole still resisted accepting such limits in principle. In practice, however, it had taken steps to adjust its foreign policy to the palpable decline in US power and prestige. In the run-up and aftermath to the Iraq invasion, America's allies and partners had to adjust to the assertive nationalism of Cheney, Rumsfeld and then Under Secretary of State John Bolton. These men remained important, and their philosophy still strongly influenced US foreign policy. By 2006, however, their role was balanced by the more conciliatory diplomacy of Rice and Under Secretary of State for Political Affairs Nicholas Burns, who seemed determined to fit US foreign policy to the requirements of the world as it is. The final two years of any administration are constrained by a certain 'lame-duck' status, as attention focuses on the coming campaign to replace it. This precluded any very dramatic changes in direction. While the Bush doctrine of radical US leadership was not going to be repudiated in those final two years, however, there was reason to expect a bit more of the 'humility' in the exercise of a superpower's might that Bush promised when he first ran for president in the year 2000.

Canada: Renewed Emphasis on Hard Power

A general election in January 2006 produced a remarkable turn in Canadian federal politics, as a rejuvenated Conservative Party led by Stephen Harper defeated the Liberal Party and formed a minority government. The Liberals had had a large majority for over a decade, but in 2004 were forced to form a minority government headed by Paul Martin after an unexpected election setback as a result of a 'sponsorship' kickback scandal in Quebec.

The Conservatives' more controlled management style has focused on a small number of policy priorities. National security and defence policy, and Canada's overall strategic posture, had hardened after the 2001 terrorist attacks on the United States, and have now hardened further. In the 1990s, Canadian policy discussions had centred on 'soft power' and a 'human security' agenda. The 11 September attacks prompted Canada to pay attention to its own homeland and to participate in the coalition military action in Afghanistan. This led, in turn, to a growing impetus to 'transform' the military for such missions. This trend has been reinforced by the election of the Conservatives, but is likely continue whichever party wins the next election.

The 11 September attacks, which killed at least 25 Canadian citizens, raised the spectre of an attack on Canadian territory. Tighter US border protection measures threatened to disrupt the flow of US–Canadian trade, valued at US$1.3 billion per day. Canada responded immediately with the 2001 Smart Border Declaration (including a 30-point plan to mitigate mutual concerns over border security) and stringent new anti-terrorism legislation. A new 'super department', Public Safety and Emergency Preparedness Canada, was set up in 2003, and a national security adviser to the prime minister was appointed in 2004. The government then published Canada's first 'national security policy' with a clear emphasis on the terrorist threat.

The Conservative government is likely to continue implementing homeland security measures to assuage American concerns over the security of the US northern border and to maintain the flow of cross-border trade vital for Canadian economic security. Harper's first meeting with President George W. Bush at Cancun in March 2006 included discussion of a controversial US plan to introduce mandatory identity cards for all cross-border travellers – which, according to critics, could slow trade while producing only marginal gains in security. Ottawa also intends to expand intelligence capabilities through the creation of a Foreign Intelligence Agency, and to improve coastal and Great Lakes security with a revitalised Coast Guard and Port Police. Other promised measures include the appointment of a new Commissioner of National Security with a coordinating role, and the formation of a National Security Review Committee to increase accountability and transparency.

Canadian troops seem set to continue regular deployments to Afghanistan, the country's largest military commitment since the Cold War. Canada's initial military response to 11 September, the despatch of a naval interdiction task force as part of the US-led *Operation Enduring Freedom*, was at first seen as a temporary measure. In early 2002, however, Canada deployed an infantry contingent and Joint Task Force 2 counter-terrorism units to Afghanistan, both of which worked closely with American counterparts in combat operations. Following their withdrawal, 2,000 Canadian military personnel were deployed to Kabul in mid-2003 as part of the NATO International Security Assistance Force (ISAF); Canada meanwhile made no military commitment in Iraq. This force was reduced to 750 troops in August 2004, and expanded in late 2005 with the deployment of over 2,000 troops to Kandahar as part of ISAF's expansion into southern Afghanistan. These troops were to provide a military component for a Provincial Reconstruction Team (PRT) in this 'hot' zone, and to undertake combat operations against the resurgent Taliban. The need for further Canadian military commitments is due to be reassessed in early 2007.

The formation of a PRT for the troubled Kandahar region, involving not only military personnel but also diplomats, civilian police and aid workers, highlights what Canada has termed its '3-D' approach – the coordination and integration of 'defence, diplomacy and development' efforts to maximise impact. Canada has suffered casualties, prompting public debate on the rationale for Canadian involvement. The Conservative government, while grudgingly allowing this matter to be discussed (but not voted on) by Parliament, appears intent on maintaining Canada's military commitment for the foreseeable future.

The development of the 3-D approach in Afghanistan led to a coordinated policy review, resulting in an overarching 2005 'International Policy Statement' (IPS). This incorporated a 'responsibility to protect' doctrine as a key rationale for a rejuvenated Canadian internationalist role. The humanitarian element was explicitly twinned with equal emphasis on the national security imperative to deal with failed states like Afghanistan. A combination of value and interest would guide Canadian international security policy.

The Defence Policy Statement (DPS) was an especially noteworthy component of the IPS. It recognised the declining state of Canada's military, and the need to reinvest in power-projection capabilities for expeditionary operations. General Rick Hillier, who was appointed chief of defence staff in February 2005, has initiated an incipient military 'transformation'. He has extensive operational experience in Bosnia and later as commander of ISAF in Afghanistan. His vision of the Canadian military – lean, lethal and deployable – is reflected in the DPS proposal for a Special Operations Task Force and a Standing Contingency Task Force with sufficient strategic and tactical lift capability for operations on the scale of the Afghanistan commitment. The DPS streamlined the command structure to consist of a Special Operations Command, an Expeditionary Force Command, a Canada Command and an Operational Support Command. The DPS was supported by the 2005 budget promise of a C$12.8bn boost in defence spending over five years, which would increase the defence budget to nearly C$19bn by 2010 (compared with the 2004 budget of C$13.2bn). Defence spending has traditionally seen only very modest budget increases and this would represent the largest overall increase in two decades.

The Canada Command, which was stood up on 31 January 2006, is intended to enhance crisis-management capabilities so as to secure the Canadian homeland

and to mitigate North America's continental vulnerability. Canada rejected official participation in the American missile defence system in February 2005, but also quietly made the important decision to allow information collected by North American Aerospace Defence Command (NORAD) to be used for American ground-based interceptors. As NORAD is a binational organisation, which closely integrates US and Canadian military personnel, Canada would have a technical role in the early-warning and attack-assessment phase of any missile-defence interception. An increased missile-defence role, to include overt political support and command-and-control responsibilities, is possible in the future.

Canada and the United States also recently agreed to the renewal of the NORAD Treaty. The new deal commits both parties to an indefinite extension of the treaty and expansion of NORAD's area of responsibility to include maritime surveillance. Defence integration might be further expanded in the near future, as both countries are examining the recommendations of the Binational Planning Group's (BPG) final report, released in April 2006. The BPG, composed of senior military officers from both countries, was formed in 2002 and recommends the eventual signing of a 'Comprehensive Defense and Security Agreement'. This could consist of either further expansion of NORAD's responsibilities, possibly including all-domain surveillance and control, or the formation of a new binational defence arrangement.

The Conservative government has expanded on the Liberal Party's emphasis on military transformation with its own 'Canada First' policy, which focuses on enhancing Canada's ability to protect its sovereignty, citizens and strategic interests. An increased Arctic presence is a key component of this defence platform, as there are concerns that Canadian territorial claims over its northern Arctic region will be challenged in the years ahead. The Northwest Passage, for example, could become a major shipping route due to climate change. Canada claims this waterway to be internal, reflected in the recent renaming of this area as 'Canadian Internal Waters', but the United States claims it to be an international strait. To renew its presence in this sparsely populated region, Canada plans to increase its overhead surveillance capabilities, undertake periodic sovereignty patrols, and develop a more visible capability to traverse the region.

In the 2006 budget, the Conservative government has pledged an additional C$5.3bn on top of the Liberals' five-year C$12.8bn defence budget increase, to help pay for improved capabilities for Arctic sovereignty; homeland defence and expeditionary missions; acquisition of such items as large strategic lift aircraft and armed naval heavy ice breakers; the restoration of Canada's paratroop forces; and the recruitment of an additional 15,000 personnel. There may be some conflict in procurement priorities; the Conservatives have emphasised Arctic sovereignty capabilities that could come at the expense of Hillier's expeditionary focus. There remains, however, significant consensus on the need for a general reinvestment in Canada's military assets.

Questions about whether this transformation will be successful and long-lasting remain. Promises of funding for military reinvestment made by a minority government may still face hurdles. However, there is a growing consensus in Ottawa that Canada's international role had suffered as a result of a haphazard approach to the hard-power foundations of its security and defence policy. The return of the Conservatives to government has resulted in a higher priority being placed on defence, and in particular on hard power.

Latin America: Swing to the Left

Left-leaning populist leaders have risen to power in a wave of elections in Latin America as voters have sought an alternative to the more conservative governments that dominated the region's politics over the previous two decades. In several countries, failure to translate economic growth into poverty alleviation led to widespread discontent, fuelling the political rebalancing. This trend has been particularly evident in 2006, a year in which presidential election campaigns have been under way in Mexico, Peru, Nicaragua, Colombia, Ecuador, Brazil and Venezuela (see Strategic Geography, pp. XXIV–XV).

The swing to the left has been occurring while the currents of the world economy have been flowing very much in Latin America's favour. Strong Chinese demand has contributed to high commodity prices and export growth, boosting countries' trade surpluses and foreign exchange reserves, and giving regional leaders more room to increase social spending. These trends have reinforced Latin America's emergence from the chronic economic and financial problems that had plagued the region since the 1982 debt crisis. However, those problems, and the conditions for assistance imposed by international financial institutions, nurtured deep popular animosity towards Washington. US–Latin American relations have reached their lowest level since the Cold War, exemplified by what from the American viewpoint was a public-relations disaster at the November 2005 Summit of the Americas, where US President George W. Bush was met in Argentina by anti-American crowds, and US-led trade negotiations came to a virtual standstill.

This state of affairs is partly the result of the strident anti-American rhetoric of Venezuelan President Hugo Chávez, who has been engaged on a populist crusade to isolate the United States, forging close ties with Cuba and seeking to goad other regional leaders into a similar posture. Chávez found a new potential ally in Bolivia when former coca union leader Evo Morales won an overwhelming victory in presidential elections in December 2005. However, it is far from clear that Venezuela's campaign is succeeding in causing rifts between other large Latin American nations and the United States. In fact, efforts to influence elections in other countries in the region have led to friction. At an Organisation of American States (OAS) meeting in June 2006, then US Deputy Secretary of State Robert Zoellick said: 'It is encouraging that the democracies of Latin American that feel that Venezuela has been infringing on their own democratic process are speaking up on their own.'

The new wave of Latin American leftists is, in the main, markedly different from the armed revolutionaries of the Cold War and the traditional populists whose expansionary policies pushed Latin America into the debt crisis of the 1980s and the painful adjustments of the 1990s. While employing populist rhetoric, many leaders have pragmatically sought to implement popularly palatable versions of free-market policies. Moreover, the leftist shift is neither uniform nor comprehensive. Colombia, for example, has a popular conservative government, led by President Alvaro Uribe, an unapologetic ally of Washington. Its constitution has been amended to permit re-election for a second four-year term, and Uribe on 28 May 2006 won a new mandate by a comfortable margin.

The regional influence of the United States has declined while its focus has been on the Middle East and the 'war on terror'. However, Washington has recently sought to reverse this trend by dedicating high-level attention to engaging the moderate left, about which it had previously been unenthusiastic. The election campaigns in several countries indicate that the real political struggle in the region is not between left and right or between Chávez and the United States, but instead is a conflict within the Latin American left about its future path. The degree to which more moderate leftists can address social exclusion and economic inequalities – and thus forge a path between US-encouraged free markets and Venezuela's radical populism – will determine the outcome of Chávez's attempts to polarise and dominate the region.

Venezuela: from nuisance to threat?

Chávez, having consolidated power politically and economically and facing a fractured opposition, is likely to win another six-year term in December 2006. The strongest threat to him comes not from Venezuela's traditional elites or conservative elements, but from the centre-left platform of Teodoro Petkoff, who has revolutionary credentials as a former Marxist guerrilla and has been a senator and planning minister. Petkoff denounces Chávez as the 'great disintegrator of the region', and pledges to reunite the country.

A former army colonel who led an unsuccessful coup attempt in 1992, Chávez came to power with a decisive victory in the 1998 presidential elections. Denouncing the economic and political elite, he stepped into the vacuum left by the collapse of Venezuela's traditional political parties. Though the country was once seen as a model of Latin American democracy, the seeming stability of its rigid two-party system masked oil-dependent clientelist structures that bred weak institutions and failed to address festering problems of inequality and political exclusion. Having squandered over $250 billion in oil wealth since 1958, Venezuela's political parties were discredited when sharply falling oil revenues in the 1980s left 80% of the country in poverty. As a result, a majority of Venezuelans supported Chávez's moves to replace Venezuela's dysfunctional democratic system with what he called the 'Bolivarian Revolution', which combines anti-imperialism and national-ism with popular democratic participation, economic self-sufficiency and equity in oil-revenue distribution. Chávez's supporters argue that this new system is a 'popular democracy' that is addressing the country's socio-economic problems, but the fractured political opposition counters that Chávez has consolidated his power at the expense of civil liberties.

During the first four years of his presidency, Chávez's Bolivarian Revolution lacked an economic plan beyond distribution of oil revenues, and as the economic crisis deepened so did the poverty of over one million Venezuelans. The presi-dent's approval rating fell from 70% to 30%. Demonstrating political resilience and acumen, Chávez survived a coup attempt in April 2002, nationwide strikes in 2002–03, and a national referendum on his recall in August 2004. He appeared to be facing defeat in the referendum, with 64% of Venezuelans reporting in late 2003 that they would vote to remove him. But windfall oil revenues enabled the president to increase social spending, which in turn contributed to unprecedented growth in 2004. Chávez won the referendum with 59% of the vote.

Endowed with this new mandate, Chávez's Bolivarian Revolution could no longer claim the decimated domestic opposition as a convincing target of revolt. He increasingly directed his attention to the international arena, proclaiming rebellion against US hegemony in Latin America and its imposition of global capitalism. He sought to isolate the United States in the region, forging close ties with Cuba and seeking to goad other regional leaders into a similar posture. The Bush administration's muted response to the coup attempt against him in April 2002 was used by Chávez to bolster his contention that the United States had long sought to dominate Latin America. He has employed aggressive diplo-macy and Venezuela's financial resources to challenge US influence. Chávez's campaign has struck a chord in countries hungry for an alternative to the market economics promoted by the United States.

Purchasing support

Venezuela's oil wealth has been used to court allies and marginalise US influ-ence. The Center for Economic Investigations, a Caracas-based consulting firm, estimates that Chávez has spent up to $25bn in support in more than 30 coun-tries, mostly in Latin America, since he became president in 1999. Even the lower figure of $16bn cited by First Justice, the leading opposition party in Venezuela, on the basis of Chávez's own declarations exceeds the $13bn the United States spent on Latin America during the period.

The closeness of Venezuela's relationship with Cuba has been particularly noteworthy. Chávez and Fidel Castro, Cuba's communist leader, have developed a strong personal relationship. The two have been accused jointly of interfering in elections in other countries, for example in Nicaragua and Bolivia. Chávez has breathed new life into Cuba's economy through subsidised oil supplies. Cuba has provided Venezuela with many doctors as well as security and intelligence officers. Hundreds of Cuban doctors, undoubtedly financed by Venezuela, are also practising in Bolivia. Venezuela has also provided support to leftist governments in Ecuador, Argentina and Bolivia. Methods include preferential oil deals or offers to assume foreign debt – even though the rates that Venezuela charges are sometimes higher than those of the international financial institutions. In Nicaragua, as well, Chávez publicly supported Sandinista Daniel Ortega's bid for the presidency and made preferential oil agreements with Sandinista mayors – a move denounced by the Nicaraguan government as illegal foreign funding of the Sandinista campaign. The Chávez administration brought Nicaraguans to Venezuela for free eye surgery, hosted a retreat for 80 mayors backing Ortega, sent fertiliser to favoured mayors, and bankrolled Cuban gifts of literacy aid and televisions to mayors. Ortega claimed that Chávez also promised to use some of the revenues from oil sales to Nicaragua to fund a Nicaraguan development bank. Similarly in El Salvador, Chávez made preferential oil supply agreements with Salvadorian leftist mayors in the hope of removing the country's conservative government.

In June 2005 Chávez formed Petrocaribe, a regional energy agreement to provide discount oil to Caribbean countries. In the Andes, Chávez is pursuing the creation of a similar accord. Venezuela has even used oil subsidies in the United States: in the winter of 2005–06 Venezuela's national oil company, PDVSA, used its Houston-based subsidiary Citgo to provide discounted heating oil to some 181,000 households and hundreds of homeless shelters across the northeastern United States.

Chávez's campaign for regional power has entailed opposition to the US-backed Free Trade Agreement of the Americas, and the promotion of trade agreements among Latin American countries as well as a region-wide 'Bolivarian Alternative for the Americas'. In April 2006, Chávez announced his decision to withdraw from the Andean Community of Nations, which also includes Bolivia, Colombia, Ecuador and Peru. He argued that this decision, now awaiting formal approval by Venezuelan authorities, was justified by Colombian and Peruvian pursuit of free-trade agreements with the United States. Chávez declared: 'We are a united community or we are not. There is not a way to align oneself with North American imperialism and at the same time want regional unity.' Then, in May, Chávez pulled out of the Group of Three (G3), a trade agreement with Colombia and Mexico, insisting that the G3 'is hurting Venezuela and only benefits a handful of large corporations'. Venezuela would instead concentrate on Mercosur, the

Southern Cone customs union of which Argentina, Brazil, Paraguay and Uruguay are members and Bolivia, Chile, Colombia, Ecuador, Peru and Venezuela are associate members. In May 2006, Venezuela signed a protocol with the Mercosur members that put it on a track towards full membership, subject to ratification and Venezuela's adoption of common external tariffs over the next four years, as well as other integrating measures. Chávez's intent was clear: he viewed Mercosur as a means to 'convert South America into a power' and to counter US hegemony. Mercosur did not impose the conditions of US free trade agreements. Chávez spoke of being protected from an influx of American products by a 'Mercosur wall'. Further afield, Chávez has strengthened ties with China, Russia and Iran, and encouraged the rest of Latin America to do so as well.

Unease about the Chávez crusade

It is not clear that Venezuela's extensive use of oil-derived cash will succeed in purchasing the level of international support that Chávez is seeking. His attempt to polarise Latin America into *chavistas* and *imperialistas* has been divisive, and he has lost favour among some regional leaders because he has been perceived as meddling in their domestic affairs. Chávez is often less well received in private than he is in public by democratic leftist leaders such as Brazil's Luis Inácio da Silva ('Lula') and Argentina's Nestor Kirchner. Because Chávez's tough stance against the United States is popular, Latin American leaders feel the need to express public solidarity. Behind the scenes, however, they distance themselves from what they consider to be needless provocation of the United States.

Chávez's endorsement of leftist candidates in Peru and Mexico actually appeared to damage their political prospects. Relations between Venezuela and Peru became hostile when outgoing Peruvian president Alejandro Toledo chastised Chávez for his criticism of Peruvian and Colombian trade negotiations with the United States, which is the main customer for Venezuelan oil. 'Mr Chávez, learn to govern democratically', Toledo admonished. 'Learn to work with us. Our arms are open to integrate Latin America, but not for you to destabilise us with your checkbook.' Chávez's denunciation of Alan García, former president and then a presidential candidate, and endorsement of front-running nationalist candidate Ollanta Humala, appeared to elevate García in the polls. When García won the election on 4 June 2006, he said his victory was a defeat for Chávez's 'expansionist efforts'.

Mexico's relations with Venezuela deteriorated in 2005 when President Vicente Fox expelled Venezuela's ambassador due to Chávez's attempts to influence Mexican elections by funding 'Bolivarian circles' in Mexican universities to disseminate radical leftist views. In the campaign for the presidential election held on 2 July 2006, television advertisements by conservative candidate Felipe Calderón, a member of Fox's National Action Party, compared the populist candidate Andres Manuel López Obrador to Chávez. Obrador's three-year lead in opinion polls was subsequently erased. Calderón claimed there was evidence of attempts by Chávez to sway the vote and called for a full investigation and legal action against the Venezuelan president. Meanwhile, Obrador sought to distance himself from Chávez.

Chávez has also riled moderate-left leaders. Bolivia's Venezuela-backed moves on 1 May 2006 to nationalise its energy sector dealt a blow to Brazil and Argentina, which have heavily invested in – and are dependent upon – Bolivian natural gas. Chávez further inserted himself into ensuing negotiations among Bolivia, Brazil and Argentina. Brazilian President da Silva denounced Chávez's 'precipitate decisions to interfere in the internal affairs of Bolivia, Peru, and by extension, those of Brazil'. More broadly, the tension between Lula and Chávez exemplifies the struggle between the moderate liberal reformers and the radical populists of Latin America's new left. Chávez portrays the region's choices as strictly between domination by the United States or the Bolivarian Revolution, in effect rejecting more moderate alternatives. But leaders like Lula and Michelle Bachelet, elected president of Chile on 15 January 2006, are seeking avenues between the two extremes. Nevertheless, Chávez has demonstrated that he can at times influence events and win allegiances just as Washington has long been able to do in its strategic and economic backyard.

Washington's tougher approach

The Chávez government and the Bush administration have engaged in volleys of accusations, but until late 2005 the confrontation had remained largely rhetorical in deference to the symbiotic oil relationship between Venezuela and the United States. In September 2005, however, Washington began to adopt a tougher stance. Disputes over drug trafficking led to President Bush 'decertifying' Venezuela for unsatisfactory cooperation in the war on drugs – a move that can lead to economic sanctions. (Myanmar was the only other country so designated in 2005.) This followed Chávez's suspension of cooperation with the US Drug Enforcement Agency over alleged spying. The new US National Security Strategy, published in March 2006, listed Venezuela as one of the world's 'regional challenges', calling Chávez a demagogue who was 'undermining democracy and seeking to destabilise the region'.

In May 2006, the Bush administration banned US arms sales to Caracas, citing lack of cooperation in the 'war on terror'. The State Department objected to Venezuela's close relationship to Iran and Cuba, both of which it has declared state sponsors of terror, as well as voicing concerns over ties to Colombia's leftist groups, which are designated foreign terrorist organisations, and over the Chávez administration's public praise of the Iraqi insurgency. Venezuela has been turning to Russia for arms purchases, including 100,000 AK-47 assault rifles and 15 Mi-17 helicopters, of which three were delivered in April 2006. Chávez has claimed to be on the point of buying *Sukhoi* fighters and of selling Venezuela's 21 US-made F-16s to Iran. Although direct US arms sales to Venezuela have recently been small, at about $30m a year, Washington has sought to block a $2bn sale by Spain of eight patrol boats, 10 transport aircraft and two maritime patrol aircraft on the grounds that these contained US-made parts. Spain has proceeded with the sale, saying it will replace those parts with others, though it is not clear whether it can do so. Washington has succeeded in blocking sales of Brazilian Embraer *Super Tucano* trainer/light attack aircraft.

The United States has accused Venezuela of an arms build-up that threatens regional stability. Chávez's response is that he is replacing old weaponry and bolstering security, which he says is threatened both by an insecure border with Colombia and possibile US invasion. Chávez has sworn to fend off his purported assailants – the United States – with a 100-year war. This is the pretext for a redefinition of Venezuela's military posture to enable it to wage a long-term guerrilla war against large-scale foreign incursions. Chávez has called for volunteers to expand reserve forces from the 2004 level of 30,000 to 2m – they had reached 150,000 by April 2006 – and in November 2005 the legislature passed a law placing military reserves directly under the president rather than the military command structure. Neighbourhood-based militias are also being organised into a Territorial Guard, also under the president's direct control.

Such moves away from a professional army, influenced by US military-to-military contacts with senior officers, to a 'people's army' can be seen as a form of regime security: they build loyalty to the president personally and make him less vulnerable to any disaffection within the 100,000-strong army. A day's training earns $7.45 and meals in a country where one-fifth of households earn less than $2 a day. The Territorial Guard encompasses remnants of Chávez's neighbourhood Bolivarian Circles, which in the president's less popular days mobilised his local support. The Guard, in addition to training for asymmetrical war with the United States, receives training in quelling public disturbances. Chávez has also increased military wages by 50–80%. The president's critics say the true purpose of these new forces is to suppress political dissent.

Social issues: little progress

Chávez has consolidated his power further by extending his control over Venezuela's governing institutions. The National Assembly packed the Supreme Court in the president's favour by adding 12 *chavistas* to its membership and replacing opposition justices. By the December 2005 legislative elections, Chávez had also taken over the National Electoral Council, as well as the ombudsman and audit office. As a result, opposition parties boycotted the elections, and Chávez allies won all 167 seats in the National Assembly – albeit with a 75–80%

abstention rate. This has allowed Chávez to pass laws curtailing press freedoms and restraining public demonstrations and anti-government speeches. Pro-government officials also hold 21 of 23 governorships as well as the influential position of Caracas's mayor.

Oil revenues have bankrolled Chávez's populist social spending, providing him with approval ratings of around 70%. However, expenditures have mostly been on redistributive 'quick fixes' – costing $17bn over the past year – rather than policies to address social problems for the longer term. Chávez has failed to make significant inroads against poverty, inequality, unemployment and inadequate housing. While the National Statistical Institute reported that poverty had declined to 37% by the end of 2005, the figure was unreliable because it was forced to change its 'methodology' after reporting an apparently unsatisfactory poverty level of 53% in 2004. Private estimates indicate that about 67% of the 26m Venezuelans live in poverty while around 35% suffer extreme poverty. Some 1.2m families lack proper housing, and about 1.2m people are unemployed. Chávez's political opponents have seized upon his failure to achieve socio-economic goals in spite of about $50bn of yearly oil revenues. Petkoff, the leading opposition candidate in the election due in December 2006, has said: 'The great success of Chávez has been to introduce social issues into the national debate. Paradoxically, however, seven years later poverty is still the biggest national drama.' Centre-right presidential hopeful Julio Borges claimed Chávez had allotted $4bn for 2006 social programmes while allocating $16bn to court support for his '21st Century Socialism' abroad.

Venezuela's crime rate has grown. According to the United Nations, it has the highest rate of gun-related violence in the world, with nearly 10,000 homicides a year since Chávez took office. High-profile murders, coupled with a justice system seen as inefficient and corrupt, have prompted many street protests, and criminality and corruption have led citizens to arm themselves. Although the government has promised to reform the police and institute a gun buyback programme, the Chávez administration has blamed violence and corruption on the evil influence of capitalism. This theme – which diverts popular attention from domestic failures by fomenting anti-Americanism – is likely to predominate in the campaign for the presidency. Given the weak and fractured nature of the opposition, Chávez's populist rhetoric could well hold sway, even if meeting increasing scepticism both at home and abroad.

Persistent constraints

Venezuela is essentially a rentier state, dependent on oil and the revenues it brings. At the same time, oil gives Chávez considerable governmental autonomy as long as the price remains high. Nevertheless, the United States and Venezuela have a symbiotic oil-based relationship: it is mainly US refineries that can handle heavy Venezuelan crude, which the United States in turn needs to meet energy needs. Chávez is seeking to break the dyad by courting other strategic/economic patrons (China, in particular). But his dismantling of the PDVSA has made him more dependent on 'Big Oil' (including US-based multinationals), which limits his freedom of action. Similarly, while the United States deplores Chávez's politics, its need for Venezuela's oil curtails its options. Accordingly, despite the increase in mutual antagonism in 2005 and 2006, in the medium term both countries are likely to continue policies that, in substance if not rhetorically, adhere more or less to the status quo.

Brazil: Latin America's Third Way

Luis Inácio da Silva, Brazil's first working-class president, known as Lula, entered office in January 2003 with the promise that 'fighting corruption and upholding ethics in the public sphere will be central and permanent objectives of my government'. This promise began to ring hollow in the ears of many Brazilians as a corruption scandal involving Lula's Workers Party (PT) unfolded in May 2005. The *mensalão* (literally 'monthly payment'), as the scandal is dubbed, implicated the PT in illegal use of government monies to finance election campaigns and purchase congressional votes. Four legislators resigned and another three were expelled from Congress. The PT's leadership toppled en masse, bringing down with it several government officials, including Finance Minister Antonio Palocci. By the end of 2005 the scandal had dragged Lula's approval rating down to a low of 47%, raising doubts as to whether he would seek a second term in the October 2006 elections. Falling unemployment and reductions in poverty have, however, buoyed Brazilians' support of their president, and by March 2006 Lula's approval ratings had climbed back up to 53.5%. On 29 March 2006, a congressional investigative committee exonerated the president from direct responsibility in the *mensalão*.

Lula's ability to weather the country's worst corruption scandal in a dozen years appeared to rest on his achievements in economic stabilisation and poverty reduction. Economic growth has been slow but steady during the Lula administration, averaging 2.5% annually. The currency has been strong and inflation dropped from 12.5% in 2002 to an all-time low of 5.5% in 2005. Brazil's risk rating improved in 2005, and the stock market rose sharply. Exports rose 33% to $118bn, creating a trade surplus of $45bn, and boosting foreign exchange reserves to over $55bn. Brazil reduced its debt obligations from 61.7% of GDP in 2003 to 51.6% in 2005, and the government projects that this figure will fall below 50% by the close of 2006. Between 2003 and 2005, 3.5m jobs were created in the formal sector and unemployment was reduced from 13% in 2003 to 9.9% in the first quarter of 2006. Poverty has fallen from 27.3% of Brazil's population of 186 million to 25%. Lula's *Bolsa Familia* (family fund), a cash-transfer programme, has reached 8.7m families. While the *mensalão* diminished the president's support among middle-class and wealthy Brazilians, his strides against poverty and inequality have secured his popularity among the poor.

Brazil's strong economic performance allowed it to pursue greater international financial independence. On 13 December 2005, the Finance Ministry announced it would repay its entire $15.5bn debt to the International Monetary Fund early, saving Brazil $900m in interest payments over the next two years. Meanwhile, Brazil strengthened ties with China and expects to more than double bilateral trade to $35bn by 2010. Brazil was the first large country to grant 'market economy' status to China, and Argentina and Chile soon followed. Chinese demand has helped increase the price of Brazilian export commodities. State-owned Chinese companies have become increasingly involved in Brazilian mining ventures, providing an important source of investment and strengthening what Lula calls the 'strategic partnership' between the two countries. Lula also pursued closer ties with Russia, with bilateral trade increasing by 69.6% in 2005 to $2.9bn, and targeted to reach $10bn by 2010. Brazil has courted other countries in Asia, Africa and the Middle East in the hopes of establishing economic partnerships and boosting its international stature, helping to counter what Lula calls US 'hegemony in international relations'.

With the 21 April 2006 inauguration of the Petrobras-50 (P-50) oil rig off Brazil's Atlantic coast, Brazil declared itself independent in the energy sector, with average production of 1.9m barrels per day (b/d) surpassing average consumption of 1.85m b/d in 2006. Brazil aims to boost production to 2.3m b/d and become a net oil exporter by 2010. Brazil's energy independence is also a result of its diverse resources. Ethanol production has reduced vulnerability to oil price shocks and uranium deposits have allowed Brazil to become Latin America's leading producer of nuclear energy. Plans for seven new nuclear power plants are under way. However, the government was concerned by the May 2006 announcement of Bolivia's nationalisation of its gas industry, in which Petrobras has invested $1.5bn since 1996 and which supplies 40% of Brazil's natural gas. As of summer 2006, it appeared that Petrobras would have to renegotiate its Bolivian contracts at a less profitable rate but would avoid seizure of its assets or interruption of supply.

There remain impediments to Brazil's economic growth. Real interest rates and taxes are high, and the country has an inefficient, opaque bureaucracy. On taking office, Lula embarked upon a 'rescue' of the public service, creating six new ministries and 120,000 new government jobs. There are 20,000 political posts at the executive's disposal in the bureaucracy and state-owned companies. The removal of Finance Minister Palocci in March 2006 made it less likely that Lula would vigorously pursue reforms needed to stimulate growth. Public-sector pensions and the bankruptcy law have been reformed, but overhauls affecting central-bank autonomy and labour laws have stalled. Reform is hindered by a fragmented party system that makes alliance-building difficult. More generally, the *mensalão* threatened to exacerbate the fractious nature of Brazilian party politics and damaged the PT, one of the few strong parties.

Land disputes have also provoked discontent, and disillusionment has persisted among those (largely on the political left) frustrated by the limited extent and pace of social reforms under Lula. Indigenous struggles against territorial encroachment by various economic interests have emerged across Brazil. While the country's indigenous population is comparatively small, at around 700,000, 40% of this population lives apart from the bulk of indigenously held land on crowded reserves which are frequently expropriated by land-hungry neighbours. In 2005, the Supreme Court overrode federal agreements and suspended a reserve at Marangatu, displacing 700 Guarani Indians. Thirty-eight Indians were murdered in 2005, a ten-year high. Indigenous groups within Brazil have, however, increased their retaliation, and in January 2006, 500 Indians invaded eight farms in the northeastern state of Bahia, reclaiming their traditional lands. Land disputes have, more generally, elicited the strongest responses among the various areas of popular dissatisfaction with social reform under the Lula administration. Land distribution in Brazil is the world's third most unequal, reflected by the fact that the country's largest 37 landowners own more land than the 2.5m smallest. The Movement of Landless Rural Workers (MST), which helped elect Lula, has been the most prominent representative of the 4m landless rural families.

Lula promised to seize land deemed unproductive and distribute it, along with other federal lands, to poor families. His administration, however, has only settled an average of 59,000 families per year, well below the annual average of 66,000 under the previous government. The Pastoral Land Commission (CPT) issued a report in April 2006 revealing that 38 social leaders were murdered in 2005 in the land struggle and that 64 other persons died in rural Brazil due to problems related to landlessness, such as starvation and overwork on sugarcane plantations. According to the CPT, there are 11.4m disputed hectares in Brazil, and 1,881 land-related conflicts erupted in 2005. In these conflicts, 4,366 families were driven off their land, 25,618 evicted, 2,189 houses destroyed and 16,995 crimes perpetuated by hired henchmen. Meanwhile, the CPT reports, prosecution against the planners and perpetrators of these crimes stalled during 2005. In response to continued rural inequality and repression, the MST has invaded properties it deemed unproductive across Brazil. In March 2006, the MST launched a new round of protests with the occupation of 30 properties. These renewed actions are representative of more widespread frustration with the slow pace of reform under the Lula administration.

Despite such disappointment among Lula's poor, leftist base, the president remained in good standing for the October 2006 presidential elections, though his performance was likely to depend in large part upon his ability to stimulate economic growth as well as his gestures of social reform. Polls in March 2006 predicted that, if he stood, he would garner 43% in a first-round vote, up from 32% in December and well ahead of the 20% likely to be captured by contender Geraldo Alckmin. Alckmin, governor of São Paulo, was chosen in March to be the candidate for the Brazilian Social Democratic Party. The fragmented Brazilian Democratic Movement Party is unlikely to run a presidential candidate due to the Supreme Court's March 2006 ruling that electoral alliances at the state and local level, also having elections in October 2006, must be reflected in alliances at the national level. While Alckmin and Lula appeared far apart on the political spectrum, whether there would be substantive differences in their platforms was unclear as this chapter was being written. Lula has billed himself as the bridge between the two worlds of economic growth and macroeconomic responsibility, on the one hand, and the needs of the Brazilian poor majority, on the other. This broad swath leaves little unclaimed territory in Brazilian politics. Although Lula remained likely to prevail in the election, his political lustre has been diminished by a spate of political scandals. His tepid response to Evo Morales's decision in May 2006 to nationalise the Bolivian gas industry was widely seen in Brazil as weak and ill considered. Brazil has considerable investment in Bolivia's gas industry and Lula appeared to be more interested in not offending Morales than in standing up for his country's core economic interests.

On the international scene, Lula has played a bridge-building role in hemispheric relations. Commanding Latin America's largest economy, the president has attempted to lead efforts towards regional economic integration by promoting participation in and expansion of Mercosur as well as forging bilateral trade agreements with nearly all countries of the hemisphere. Brazil has also led efforts to negotiate agreements for hemispheric security cooperation. Courted by the United States as well as Venezuela, Lula is attempting to facilitate dialogue between those contentious countries. While Lula's ability to bridge the gap between Hugo Chávez and the Bush administration remains doubtful, his stance nevertheless presents a prime example of a moderate leftist administration not beholden to either Chávez's radical rhetoric or the United States' oppositional posturing. In a situation in which neither side is wholly attractive to most Latin Americans, Lula's conciliatory sensibilities appear to provide an important third way.

Argentina's shaky foundation
Once Washington's poster-child for free-market reforms, Argentina is now taking advantage of its remarkable recovery from collapse in 2001–02 in order to rebel against those very policies and restore government economic involvement. The Argentine economy has grown by one-quarter since its collapse, finally surpassing its pre-crisis peak in 2005 with 9.1% growth. In its third consecutive year of growth at or above 9%, the economy was fuelled by record exports and President Nestor Kirchner's pre-electoral spending spree ahead of the October 2005 midterm elections.

Kirchner completed restructuring Argentina's $81bn debt in February 2006, successfully insisting that international bondholders accept 30 cents on the dollar. Kirchner also, by presidential decree, pre-paid Argentina's $9.8bn debt to the IMF, which he announced would 'generate freedom for national decisions'. Like many of the Kirchner administration's economic policies, this early repayment was primarily a political manoeuvre. Argentina will likely end up paying higher interest rates to other lenders, such as Venezuela, but the move was nevertheless popular with a citizenry that faults the IMF for its former crisis and relishes the notion of freedom from the harmful policies of international financial institutions.

While the Argentine economy has regained its former size, the way in which it has recovered has altered the economy's structure, leaving the country more unequal and many Argentines worse off than before the crisis. It is true that June 2002 peaks of 25% unemployment and 56% poverty have declined to 13% and 40% respectively. The formal sector, however, remains roughly the same size, as job expansion has occurred primarily in the informal sector, which now constitutes 41% of the workforce. Real wages remain one-quarter below their pre-crisis levels and have become increasingly unequal, with the wealthiest 10% of workers earning 33 times the poorest 10%. Meanwhile, the purchasing power of the Argentine workforce was further threatened when, after two years of average annual inflation rates below 5%, prices jumped 12.3% in 2005 and an additional 1.3% in January 2006. The inflation spike was precipitated in part by the Kirchner administration's 22% increase in government spending ahead of the midterm elections as well as the president's refusal to allow the peso to appreciate in an effort to protect Argentine exports.

While acknowledging the problems with the Argentine economy, Kirchner remained primarily concerned with maintaining his own popularity and thus refrained from longer-term economic policy planning. Kirchner has paid steadfast attention to bolstering his popular support after winning the presidency by default with only 23% of the vote in May 2003 after former president Carlos Menem withdrew from the second round. Kirchner's oft-repeated position that the IMF was 'the promoter and vehicle of policies which provoked poverty and pain in the Argentine people' drives his populist reinsertion of the state into the country's economy and his insistence that an 'unorthodox' approach is the only viable solution to Argentina's current economic difficulties. Kirchner's expansionary monetary policy, hard line with foreign investors, reestablishment of state-owned companies in various sectors, and ability to emancipate Argentina from IMF influence has won the president a remarkable approval rating of 75%.

Along with his turn away from the IMF and Washington-backed free-market economics, Kirchner has increasingly strengthened relations with Venezuelan President Hugo Chávez. Chávez, who bought $1bn in Argentine bonds, praised the country's repayment of the IMF, proclaiming that 'if additional help is needed to help Argentina finally free itself from the claws of the International Monetary Fund, Argentina can count on us'. The two presidents penned several agreements in November 2005, including one securing a Venezuelan supply of 5m barrels of oil per year and another to explore the possibility of a gas pipeline between the two countries. The agreements solidified what Chávez has referred to as 'a Caracas–Buenos Aires axis'. Relations with Venezuela have become a priority to Kirchner, as Argentina faces an energy crisis in which its oil reserves have fallen by 12% in the last four years, oil production is down by 14% and supplies from Bolivia are increasingly unreliable due to the nationalisation of its gas resources. Venezuela, in turn, welcomes any opportunity to aid anti-IMF sentiment and seeks stronger alliances with Latin America's leaders as it attempts to counter US dominance in the hemisphere. Furthermore, Chávez wants to buy a nuclear reactor from Argentina, much to Washington's aggravation.

Kirchner appears well positioned ahead of the April 2007 presidential elections, provided that the economy remains strong. The president shored up his political control during the October 2005 midterm elections in which his candidates won 40% of the seats, giving Kirchner a majority in the Senate and 107 of 257 seats in the House of Deputies. The opposition, meanwhile, remains in disarray as it is unable to take advantage of rifts within Kirchner's Peronist party. In order to address Argentina's socio-economic problems, however, Kirchner will need more than reliance on pre-election spending binges and alliances with the region's leftist leaders. The primary threat to his re-election will be social discontent and challenges from the left. A successful Kirchner second term would have to avoid destabilisation by social protests, requiring the president to look beyond short-term concerns for his popularity and focus instead on reforms necessary for Argentina's long-term growth and poverty reduction.

Chile's economic orthodoxy

Socialist Party leader Michelle Bachelet became Chile's first female president on 11 March 2006, inheriting Latin America's strongest economy. Bachelet's government is the fourth successive administration of the centre-left Concertación coalition, which has governed Chile since the end of General Augusto Pinochet's military dictatorship. Combining the successful free-market economic policies of Pinochet with more transparent democratic governance and greater attention to social policy, the Concertación oversaw annual average growth of 7% during the 1990s as the rest of the region averaged a sluggish 2.7%. Following economic slowdown from 1999 to 2003, the Concertación's macroeconomically responsible policies aided Chile's rebound to 6.1% growth in 2004. The country's growth was also fuelled by record global commodity demand and high prices for copper, which constitutes 45% of exports; Chile is the world's largest copper producer.

Outgoing President Ricardo Lagos's counter-cyclical fiscal policy also sustained Chile's economic achievements and paved the way for current expansion. Lagos initiated legislation requiring the government to run a fiscal surplus of a 1% of GDP during times of sustainable growth and stable copper prices, both of which were determined by independent commissions. Strict fiscal policy helped Chile achieve Latin America's best credit rating, the region's highest GDP per capita, low public debt of 12% of GDP, and a universally envied ability to weather recession. Lagos's economic successes resulted in a 70% approval rating at the end of his presidency.

Bachelet, a 54-year-old former paediatrician and single mother of three who was arrested and tortured along with her family during Pinochet's dictatorship, won the presidency with 53.5% of the vote in a 15 January 2006 run-off with conservative businessman Sebastian Piñera. Both campaigns pledged adherence to the Lagos administration's successful economic policies while also emphasising much-needed social reforms. The lack of significant differences in the candidates' platforms increased the importance of their personalities and histories. Piñera's wealth and relative social conservatism repelled many poor Chileans, while many others were enticed by Bachelet's compelling background and her inherently radical nature as a long-separated single mother in a socially conservative country that legalised divorce only in 2004. Bachelet's experience under the largely popular Lagos administration, initially as health minister and then as the first female minister of defence, and her position as Lagos's hand-picked successor, further increased her appeal among voters.

While Bachelet's election has been interpreted by some as further consolidation of Latin America's leftward shift, Bachelet's pragmatic socialism is a far cry from the '21st Century Socialism' of Chávez. Her presidential campaign was devoid of anti-US or anti-'neoliberal' elements, which would have repelled a Chilean citizenry that strongly supports the country's adherence to orthodox economic policies. Rather than employing the rhetoric of radical populism, Bachelet promised 'social inclusion' in a more open government, reflecting Chilean desires to stay the course on the economic front while also appealing to widespread desire for greater political, economic and social equality. Chile's income inequality remains among the highest in the world, and nearly one-fifth of the population lives below the poverty line. Chile's poor are further plagued by the country's traditionally conservative social arena, which has hampered their upward mobility. Despite macroeconomic successes, Chileans remain in need of effective social services, including education and health care. Reforms are needed in areas including the labour code, which restricts organised labour and has helped keep unemployment at 8%, and the pension system.

In addition to addressing Chile's general socio-economic situation, the Bachelet administration will be faced more specifically with the demands of Chile's indigenous peoples. The Mapuche, Chile's main ethnic minority, wages a continuing struggle for territorial, cultural and economic rights. Territorial encroachment pushed many Mapuche from the land-based lifestyles they have led for centuries into cities where low wages, discrimination and dissolution of community structures forces them into extreme poverty. Indigenous resistance and retaliation has been met with the harsh imposition of Pinochet-era anti-terrorism laws, which have dictated long sentences for acts of property destruction and increased prejudice in the general populace by facilitating the characterisation of Indians as terrorists. This draconian use of anti-terrorism laws to suppress domestic social movements has elicited UN reproach of the Lagos administration.

Indigenous attempts to channel demands through Chile's democratic institutions have been repeatedly thwarted. Attempts of an indigenous candidate, who most certainly would not have had much effect on the race, to participate in the 2005 presidential elections were barred by electoral council claims of invalid petition signatures, stimulating international scorn. Chile currently has no indigenous lawmakers, even though its indigenous peoples comprise between 7% and 10% of the population, and only one person of indigenous descent has ever been elected to Congress. Thus, in January 2006, a bill for constitutional recognition of Chile's indigenous peoples could not even be voted upon because not enough Chilean lawmakers bothered to show up, preventing a quorum in the Chamber of Deputies. In February 2006, indigenous leaders announced plans to forge Chile's first political party, 'Wallmapuwen', representing Mapuche interests. If attempts to engage democratic channels of representation continue to be denied Chilean indigenous peoples, the country will face increased extra-institutional, and inevitably sometimes violent, forms of resistance.

While indigenous peoples in Chile do not wield the degree of power they do elsewhere in Latin America because they make up a relatively small proportion of the population, they could make alliances with other discontented elements down the road and thus acquire more substantial power. There is hope, however, that Bachelet will address indigenous struggles better than her predecessor, given her platform of increasing equality and reducing discrimination in Chile. Bachelet has, significantly, promised to push through ratification of international agreements guaranteeing indigenous rights as well as constitutional recognition of indigenous cultures. Furthermore, in light of her personal experience with the Pinochet government's repression, Bachelet is unlikely to continue Lagos's employment of anti-terrorism laws and rhetoric against indigenous movements.

Another significant challenge facing the new president is the need to secure reliable sources of energy for Chile, which imports two-thirds of its energy requirements. Bachelet indicated the high priority this matter would have under her administration by requesting an assessment from the National Energy Commission as soon as she took office. The president announced the discovery of natural-gas reserves in the Lake Mercedes basin in southern Chile, which could supply the area for the next two decades. There has been little other reassuring news, however, as complex diplomatic relations among Chile, Bolivia, Argentina and Peru hinder resolution of the country's energy deficit.

Plans for a gas pipeline through Chile were instrumental in toppling former Bolivian president Gonzalo Sánchez de Lozada, due to widespread anger over Chile's seizure of Bolivian territory in the 1879 War of the Pacific, resulting in the loss of Bolivia's coast. Though insisting that gas exports to Chile are dependent upon Bolivian sea access, Evo Morales has indicated his openness to negotiating a resolution to the impasse. In mid-March, Chile proposed granting Bolivia a section of territory north of Arica. Such a plan, however, would require Peruvian approval. Already tense relations between Chile and Peru have been exacerbated by pending decisions on whether to extradite Peruvian ex-president Alberto Fujimori as well as Peru's renewal of a maritime border dispute in October 2005. Bachelet has had more success in Argentina, where a 21 March 2006 visit secured guarantees of access to Argentine gas supplies. Argentina's ability to provide gas to Chile, however, depends upon Bolivia, upon which Argentine supplies are reliant.

In June 2003 Chile became the first Latin American country to sign a bilateral free-trade agreement with the United States. Chile is also, however, a member of Mercosur and would like to strengthen its regional economic alliances and expand trade. Thus, Bachelet's primary foreign-policy challenge will be to forge closer alliances with Latin American leaders while maintaining Chile's unique relationship with Washington.

Radical populism in the Andes

Persistent social exclusion and inequality juxtaposed with the region's economic growth has led to radical populism in the Andes, where the politics of ethnic identity have increasingly been employed to provide leaders with nationalist legitimacy and appeal to indigenous movements, whose influence has steadily been growing. While Hugo Chávez has set the tone for the radical populist movement, personalised it, and exported it, the movement has taken root in other Andean countries in which ethnic-identity politics are more pronounced than they are in Venezuela.

Bolivia

In Bolivia, former coca-grower Evo Morales rode to presidential victory on a wave of radical populist rhetoric following the failure of successive Bolivian governments to adequately economically, socially, or politically address popular demands. Despite possessing Latin America's second-largest natural-gas reserves, Bolivia remains South America's poorest country, with over two-thirds of its population mired in extreme poverty. Its indigenous majority of 70% bears the brunt of this poverty, as indigenous communities watch 20% of their children die before their first birthday while 90% of the country's wealth remains in the hands of 3% of the population.

On 6 June 2005 Carlos Mesa, whose administration was racked by increasingly violent protests, became Bolivia's second president in 20 months to be toppled by social protest movements, as he warned that Bolivia was 'on the verge of civil war'. Protests prevented the constitutionally mandated presidential succession of the unpopular Senate president. Morales was elected in December 2005 with 53.73% of the vote, giving him the strongest mandate of any president since Bolivia's return to democracy in the mid-1980s. Morales's Movement Towards Socialism party won a majority of the seats in the legislature's lower house and fell just short of a majority in the Senate.

Morales is Bolivia's first president of indigenous descent, and his indigenist rhetoric, a relatively recent addition in his decade-long rise to power, has made him popular among long-excluded and increasingly mobilised indigenous peoples both domestically and internationally. While portraying himself as an indigenous leader, in reality Morales represents the interests specifically of the coca-growing Chapare. His 'multicultural' agenda for Bolivia is markedly more conciliatory than indigenous movement leader Felipe Quispe's demands for 'decolonisation'. Morales included several indigenous persons in his 16-member 'cabinet of change', including the country's first indigenous foreign minister, yet the president's primary concerns lie with Bolivia's *cocaleros*.

Appointing a coca grower to head Bolivia's anti-drug efforts, Morales has proclaimed a policy of 'zero cocaine, but not zero coca', pledging an end to US-backed eradication efforts and instead targeting drug traffickers. Forced eradication efforts in the coca-growing Chapare region largely ceased in October 2004 due to protests led by Morales. The president awaits conclusion of a European Union study of domestic demand for coca for legal uses, intending to increase the number of hectares dedicated to legal coca crops. Furthermore, Morales is pushing the United Nations to decriminalise the coca plant. Morales has insisted that the United States' eradication efforts have failed to curb drug trafficking in Bolivia, calling the drug war 'a pretext for the US government to install military bases'.

During his campaign, Morales proclaimed he would be the United States' 'worst nightmare', but, like Lula, he toned down his rhetoric upon assuming office. Signalling a general shift in Washington's approach to Latin America, the Bush administration initially took a conciliatory approach with Morales. Attempting to forge positive relations with the new administration, both Secretary of State Condoleezza Rice and Assistant Secretary of State for the Western Hemisphere Thomas Shannon visited Morales. These diplomatic gestures were indicative of US efforts to engage the region's leftist leaders proactively rather than leaving them to the sole influence of Chávez. But the Bush administration's tone soon hardened. Rice accused Morales of 'demagoguery' when, in early May 2006, he ordered the military occupation of Bolivia's natural-gas fields as he declared the nationalisation of the country's gas and gave foreign oil companies 180 days to renegotiate their contracts or leave the country.

The seizure was unlikely to change the outcome of contract renegotiations that were already underway, and was thus largely a grand political gesture to boost Morales' declining domestic support. Even so, it signalled Morales's further shift toward Chávez and Castro and away from the United States. Indeed, Morales has strengthened alliances with Venezuela and Cuba, creating what Chávez refers to as the 'Axis of Good', as Cuba has pledged to send doctors and educators to Bolivia and Venezuela has offered to exchange oil for agricultural products in addition to granting the Morales administration $30m for start-up capital for its social reforms. Morales appeared to be attempting to consolidate power over Bolivia's domestic institutions in much the same way Chávez has exerted authoritarian control in Venezuela. Promising to 'refound' the nation, Morales called for a constituent assembly which he claimed would increase indigenous participation in government but which could simply usurp Bolivia's democratic institutions.

Morales has already gone to battle with the judiciary, accusing it of hampering his anti-corruption efforts, and the resignation of four Supreme Court justices has allowed the president to extend his control to all three branches of government. Ultimately, Morales's survival will depend on his ability to live up to the high expectations he has created among Bolivia's populace for greater political and economic equality. Unless he delivers substantive results, Morales will face the same destabilising social protests that he once led against previous presidents.

Ecuador
In April 2005, Lucio Gutiérrez became Ecuador's third democratically elected president in nine years to be ousted by social protests. Gutiérrez's candidacy was backed by an alliance of Ecuador's left-wing parties and the country's powerful indigenous movement, marking the first time in Ecuadorian history that indigenous groups had entered into a governing coalition. But upon assuming office, following Lula's pattern, the president's populist campaign promises gave way to orthodox economic policies and led to the dissolution of his governing alliance. A political outsider with no party backing of his own, Gutiérrez hung onto power with shifting ad hoc alliances. The beginning of the end for his tenure arrived in November 2004 when Ecuador's conservative Social Christian Party (PSC) moved into the opposition and launched efforts to impeach the president. Gutiérrez responded by aligning himself with the populist parties of former president Abdalá Bucaram and presidential hopeful Alvaro Noboa. Attempting to appease his new allies, Gutiérrez sacked the PSC-dominated Supreme Court

in March 2005, packing it with justices sympathetic to his new alliance and spark-ing an outpouring of public discontent.

The president's governing coalition fell apart when the new court absolved Bucaram (commonly referred to as 'El Loco') of corruption charges, facilitating his return from exile in Panama. Bucaram had been removed from office in 1997 after only six months, when Congress declared the president 'mentally incom-petent' and thus unfit to rule in response to corruption scandals and popular unrest. Bucaram returned to Ecuador on 2 April 2005 with the proclamation that he was 'older and crazier than ever', vowing to reclaim the presidency and lead a Chávez-style 'revolution of the poor'.

Outrage over Bucaram's pardon prompted Gutiérrez to announce on 15 April 2005, flanked by military commanders, his decision to dissolve the Supreme Court yet again and decree a state of emergency in Quito. Thousands of protest-ers took to the streets demanding Gutiérrez's removal, and the military's quiet refusal to implement the state of emergency forced the president to rescind the order. As protests grew in size and violence, the legislature finally heeded public demands in a congressional coup much like the one that removed Bucaram. In proceedings held outside congressional chambers and with none of Gutiérrez's supporters present, 60 of 100 legislators approved a resolution declaring that the president had 'abandoned his post' and was therefore to be replaced by Vice-President Alfredo Palacio. Accusations of abandonment aside, Gutiérrez refused to voluntarily relinquish the presidency, finally having to be escorted out of the presidential palace by the army.

Lacking a legitimate electoral mandate, Palacio's initial popularity rapidly evaporated, dropping from 64% to 28% by the close of 2005 and forcing him to call elections for October 2006. Departing from Gutiérrez's fiscal austerity, Palacio embarked upon populist government spending of Ecuador's oil revenues. While Gutiérrez's economic policies were highly unpopular, it was his failure to provide democratic channels for socially excluded sectors which led them to take to the streets and his authoritarian seizure of the courts that sparked his overthrow. Thus, Gutiérrez's ouster was due primarily to political, rather than economic, failings. In its first year, the Palacio administration faced 52 strikes and protesters in the oil-rich provinces of Orellana and Sucumbios have repeatedly shut down oil production. Palacio responded by declaring states of emergency and deploy-ing security forces against demonstrators. Ironically, attempting to protect the oil revenues Palacio deemed necessary for his populist spending, he repressed social protests and thus exacerbated the very discontent his distributionary poli-cies sought to contain.

Palacio's credibility has been further undermined by his attempts to usurp the democratic process in order to push through a referendum on the con-stitution and constituent assembly. In October 2005, Palacio responded to congressional and judicial rejection of his reform efforts, which lack popular support, by ordering the military to prepare to defend his plans to refound the constitution. The Ecuadorian Congress requested OAS protection of its democracy, and Palacio eventually abandoned his plans in December. Indigenous protests against free-trade negotiations with the United States have increased as the indigenous movement has tried to restore the influence it wielded before being fractured by involvement in Gutiérrez's government. As of mid-2006, Ecuador's October 2006 presidential race remained wide open. The Ecuadorian economy has benefited from high oil prices as well as more stable macroeconomic performance following its decision to dollarise its economy in 2000. Former economy minister Rafael Correa appeared to be the most likely Chávez-esque candidate. Any successor to Palacio will need to deal with highly mobilised indigenous political and social movements and parties that in recent years have been extremely effective at stonewalling and even ousting politicians they find to be antithetical to their interests. Muddling through rather than outright polarisation has been Ecuador's political trademark, and this appeared likely to continue for several years.

Peru

Radical nationalist Ollanta Humala emerged onto the scene of Peru's presidential campaign in November 2005, quickly rising in popularity and scoring a first-round victory with 31% of the vote in April 2006. Humala, a former army officer who staged a short-lived coup in 2000, thus joined the ranks of Andean radical populists with his promises to govern Peru with a 'nationalist' economic policy that will curb foreign investments and reclaim Peruvian resources. While Humala drew the support of Chávez and Morales, his principal competition, former president Alan García, was also a populist. García's presidency (1985–90) led to disastrous hyperinflation, economic collapse and guerrilla insurgency. But President Alejandro Toledo's ineptitude allowed both of these improbable candidates to gain political traction. In a run-off vote in June 2006, García prevailed by 52.5% to Humala's 47.5% – in part because much of the electorate considered Humala dangerous to democracy. Indeed, Peruvians resented Chávez's interference in their domestic affairs, and each government withdrew its ambassador from the other's capital. While Humala's Union for Peru (UP) party prevailed in Congress, winning 45 seats against 36 for García's party, in June 2006 UP split on account of dissent over the perceived destabilising effects of Humala's policies.

Populist resurgence in Peru reflects the failure of macroeconomic gains to translate into benefits for the majority. The economy grew by an impressive rate of 6.7% in 2005 on the heels of four years of 5% average growth. Inflation is low, at 1.5% in 2005; the fiscal deficit has fallen to 0.6% of GDP; external debt has been reduced to 41.8% of GDP; and increases in exports and mining sector growth brought foreign reserves to a record high of $13.7bn. Toledo, however, funnelled only 1% of GDP into poverty alleviation programmes that have been highly ineffective and remain in great need of reform. Peruvian poverty has continued to be persistently high, affecting 51% of the population, 24% of whom suffer extreme poverty. Underemployment and unemployment levels total 54.7%. The discontent of Peru's poor majority was exacerbated by Toledo's cheerful proclamations of economic growth.

The Toledo administration, furthermore, squandered opportunities to implement key democratic reforms. Failure to strengthen the judiciary hindered prosecution of crimes committed under the dictatorial and corrupt regime of Alberto Fujimori, impeded the pursuit of justice for human-rights victims of the civil war with the Shining Path Maoist guerrilla organisation, and prevented establishment of the rule of law necessary for democratic consolidation. Accordingly, Toledo was the region's most unpopular president, with approval ratings hovering between 8% and 14%. His administration was plagued by corruption scandals implicating the president's top advisers, government ministers and Toledo's family. A July 2005 poll reported that 56% of Peruvians considered corruption the country's most serious problem. Furthermore, scandals have tainted the few reform attempts the president made. For example, efforts to address the country's racial and ethnic divides were discredited when the National Commission on Andean, Amazonian and Afro-Peruvians, founded by Toledo, collapsed under corruption allegations and led to investigations of Toledo's wife, who directed the programme.

Meanwhile, the security achievements of the last decade were eroded as remnants of the Shining Path became more active, financed by their increasing involvement in the drug trade. Increases in Peruvian coca cultivation, therefore, not only frustrate the United States' efforts in the war on drugs, but threaten to boost the income of insurgent groups. The nature of the incoming García administration was unclear, though it is likely to be less harmful than the radical ethno-nationalism of Humala. García turned the run-off into a referendum on Chávez, casting Humala as a kindred renegade who would imperil Peru's relationship with the United States. Thus, it seemed likely that García's hemispheric approach would at least be more moderate than Humala's would have been, perhaps more in line with Lula than with Chávez. In June 2006, for example, García announced plans to triple foreign investment, particularly in the energy sector.

Colombia

While many countries in the region are flirting with a political and economic framework outside of Washington's orbit, Colombia remains a staunch ally of the United States, and the Bush administration in particular. President Alvaro Uribe won a second term after a constitutional amendment allowing for immediate presidential re-election. The successes of Uribe's Democratic Security Strategy had given him unprecedented popularity ratings of 70–80% over the course of his first term, and he won the 28 May 2006 election in a landslide, with 62% of the vote. In March 2006 legislative elections, Uribe supporters won two-thirds of the Senate seats and a clear majority in the lower house. The administration's policymaking and reform efforts would therefore face fewer difficulties.

Under Uribe, the security of the Colombian citizenry has improved, with marked declines in kidnappings, murders and guerrilla attacks. While the Marxist Revolutionary Armed Forces of Colombia (FARC) continue to launch attacks, they have been pushed out of Bogotá, and forced to retreat to Colombia's southern jungles due to Uribe's 'Plan Patriota', the military's largest offensive against the guerrillas during the 40-year conflict. FARC, however, launched a vicious counter-offensive in 2005, and attacks increased ahead of the elections. On 27 December 2005 FARC killed 29 government troops in the deadliest attack since Uribe took office, and in April 2006 a spate of bombings threatened to move the conflict back into Bogotá. More broadly, the civil conflict has made Colombia second only to Sudan in the number of internally displaced persons. The government has long neglected these 2.5–3m of its citizens (approximately 5% of the population), often denying them access to social services. In 2004, Colombia's Constitutional Court held that such neglect constituted a violation of human rights, and the court threatened prosecution of four government ministers when it found the administration's response inadequate in September 2005. The Uribe administration responded with the November announcement of a fivefold increase in aid to displaced persons, though it remains to be seen how effective this aid will be.

Pro-state paramilitary violence continued to plague the Colombian people despite the supposed April 2006 demobilisation of the United Self-Defense Forces (AUC), the brutal pro-state paramilitary group, once 30,000 strong. The paramilitaries, responsible for the majority of civilian deaths in the conflict, were granted amnesty in a controversial peace agreement with the Uribe administration; yet there were doubts as to whether they would actually disband and fears that some would simply return to illicit activities. The Colombian military is accused of maintaining links to the AUC, which has long provided defence against FARC in areas where government presence has been lacking, and Colombia's security forces may not have the capacity to replace the paramilitaries. Furthermore, the AUC retains strong influence within the government, boasting of effectively controlling 30% of Congress at the start of 2006.

Plan Colombia, the US-backed counter-narcotics and counter-insurgency programme, after five years and $7.5bn in American aid, has purportedly achieved its goal of diminishing the area of Columbia's coca crops by 50%. There is doubt, however, about the accuracy of this statistic, and a December 2005 US Government Accountability Office report admitted that 'estimates could be widely off the mark'. The White House's Office of National Drug Control Policy claimed a small victory in November, announcing that the price of cocaine rose in 2005 by 19%, and that its average purity had declined by 15%. Drug-war victories remain elusive, however, as crop eradication in Colombia has led to coca cultivation increases in Bolivia and Peru. The Bush administration requested $734.5m in 2006 to fund the Andean Counter-Drug Initiative, indicating its continued commitment to provide military and economic aid to Colombia, though the administration has not yet announced a long-term plan to replace Plan Colombia, which expired in 2005. But it is clear that the Bush administration identifies with Uribe's struggle against leftist insurgencies and political violence in general and will continue to play a key role in efforts (especially military ones) to shore up Colombia's democracy.

US attention needed

In Latin America, the greatest challenge to the emergent moderate left represented by the Brazilian and Chilean governments has come not from the right but from the radical populism of the region's other leftist leaders. Many Latin Americans, particularly those who believe their country's endowments of natural resources should ameliorate their hardships, are dissatisfied with the slow pace of reform under moderate liberal leaders. These electorates have tilted towards the radical dictates of seemingly messianic leaders like Chávez and Morales. The United States obviously remains the hemisphere's ranking power, yet it has been overstretched and distracted by strategic challenges elsewhere and consequently has found managing hemispheric relationships unprecedentedly difficult. That said, US domestic politics have always played a disproportionately large role in US policies in the Western Hemisphere, and still do.

US immigration policy, in particular, could undermine Washington's conciliatory efforts in the hemisphere, increasing Chávez's prospects for realising his desires for geopolitical power and the hemispheric isolation of the Bush administration. If the US Congress decides that strong enforcement action must be taken against the United States' estimated 12m illegal immigrants – the vast majority of whom are from Latin America – already prevalent anti-US sentiments throughout the region will almost inevitably increase. Mexican President Vicente Fox was one of the United States' strongest allies in the region, but Mexicans feel they have gained little from their 'special relationship' with Washington; any large-scale expulsion of the roughly 6m illegal Mexican immigrants in the United States will only amplify such feelings.

Given the apparent incoherence of US hemispheric policy, it is not clear that the Bush administration has formulated an effective strategy to counter Chávez's apparent gains in the region. What is more certain is that Washington has learned the hard way that public overreaction to Chávez's bluster merely provides more colourful copy for Chávez to exploit in his ongoing anti-American campaign. The Bush administration will likely increase the frequency and dedication of its private bilateral and multilateral discussions (including intelligence sharing) with countries such as Brazil and even Argentina to come to a better understanding over the oft-debated question of what Chávez is really up to in Latin America – and what to do about it.

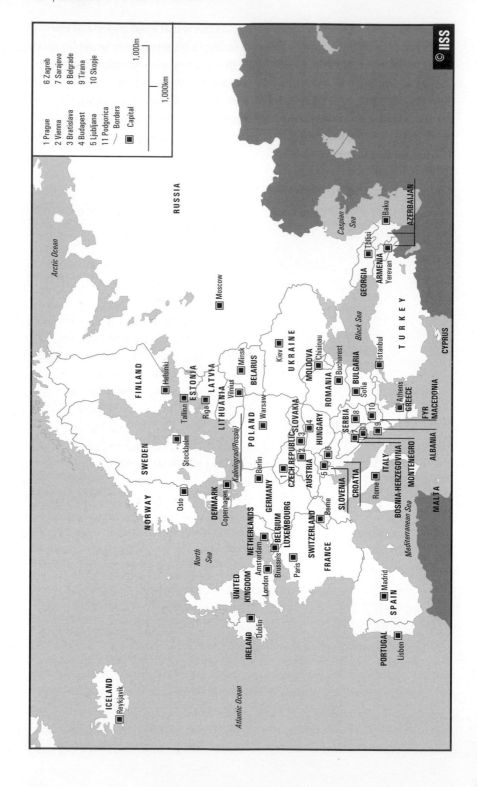

1 Prague
2 Vienna
3 Bratislava
4 Budapest
5 Ljubljana
11 Podgorica

6 Zagreb
7 Sarajevo
8 Belgrade
9 Tirana
10 Skopje

Borders
Capital

1,000m

1,000km

© IISS

4 | Europe

The European Union did not, as some expected, plunge into existential crisis as a result of the rejection of the European Union's proposed constitutional treaty on 29 May 2005 by French voters and on 1 June 2005 by Dutch voters. The rejections did, however, appear to consign the treaty, at least in the form and structure in which it had been drafted, to history. They raised questions – unlikely to be answered for some time – about the future evolution of the Union, with the vision of ever-closer across-the-board integration, long cherished by some, perhaps fatally damaged (see essay, pages 67–80). However, governments of the main European countries preferred to shelve the issue of Europe's future, because they were preoccupied by domestic difficulties.

That European countries needed urgently to confront new threats together was brought home by Europe's first suicide bombings, which killed 52 people and injured some 700 in London's morning rush hour on 7 July 2005, followed by an apparent 'copycat' series of unsuccessful attacks on 21 July. The attacks drove home the problem of home-grown, self-recruiting and self-radicalised terrorists, who are very difficult for law-enforcement agencies to detect before they strike.

Governments of all three of the largest European countries faced domestic problems. With the 29 May vote having already indicated that leaders were increasingly out of touch with voters, France was hit by two weeks of riots in October and November. When two men were electrocuted after climbing into an electricity substation while being pursued by police, disaffection of youths from immigrant families quickly broke to the surface. Violence was, however, mainly restricted to the torching of thousands of cars.

In Britain, in spite of the re-election of Tony Blair's Labour Party for a third term on 5 May 2005, the government continued to be dogged by arguments over Iraq; by speculation about when Blair would step down and allow the ruling party to choose a new leader, expected to be Chancellor of the Exchequer (finance minister) Gordon Brown; and by the scandals and mis-steps that inevitably tarnish governments holding office for long periods.

German disaffection with Gerhard Schröder led his Social Democrats to lose the seats necessary to corral a coalition in a general election on 18 September 2005. The poll led to protracted negotiations producing a grand coalition of Christian Democrats and Social Democrats in November. Angela Merkel, the new chancellor, quickly re-established Germany as a bridge-builder within the European Union, helping to broker a budget compromise at the December 2005 EU summit. Merkel also moved to improve relations with Washington. However, painful domestic policy decisions had yet to be made.

Developments in Italy were also dominated by domestic politics: the 9–10 April 2006 election produced a dead heat between the centre-right and centre-left camps, led respectively by then Prime Minister Silvio Berlusconi and his challenger Romano Prodi, who emerged as the new prime minister.

Immediately following the French and Dutch referendums, Britain assumed the rotating six-month presidency of the European Union; this was seen as an opportunity to foster discussion within the organisation about new directions. Blair began with an ambitious, visionary speech that was widely welcomed across Europe, but this was not followed up. The two main decisions of the presidency were the admission of Turkey to formal talks on membership, likely to last many years and to face further political hurdles; and a scrambled December compromise on the EU budget.

Finally, transatlantic relations benefited from newfound pragmatism after the deep divisions caused by the 2003 US-led invasion of Iraq. In February 2005, George W. Bush became the first US president to visit the European Commission and the European Council in Brussels. While largely symbolic, the gesture was well received across the EU. Continued instability and high levels of violence in Iraq, together with growing concerns about Iran's nuclear programme, instilled a sense of urgency into efforts to improve relations. Irritants nonetheless remained. For example, EU plans to lift an arms embargo on China, put in place after the 1989 Tiananmen Square massacre, ran into strong US opposition and were eventually dropped.

France: Domestic Troubles

The final period of his presidency has not been happy for Jacques Chirac. A combination of social crises and political scandal appear to have seriously weakened the chances of his hand-picked prime minister and long-time confidant,

Dominique de Villepin, successfully contesting the spring 2007 presidential election and succeeding him in the Elysée Palace. The same events have strengthened the prospect of Nicolas Sarkozy, the interior minister and rival of the Chirac–de Villepin camp, leading the right into next year's presidential election, against a revitalised, though fragmented, left.

Chirac's presidency has been in the doldrums ever since France voted 'No' to the European Union's draft constitutional treaty in a referendum on 29 May 2005 (see essay, pages 67–80). The vote, comparable in its impact to the 1954 defeat of the European Defence Community project in the French parliament, effectively killed off the draft constitution – also rejected by Dutch voters a few days later. The referendum verdict made French policy more defensive, if anything, about EU initiatives, more hostile to further enlargement of the EU and more protectionist towards foreign companies.

However, this increased prickliness did not manifest itself on a wider stage – for example, in further clashes with the United States. Indeed in 2005–06 Paris – though still strongly opposed to US policy in Iraq – maintained its participation in US-led operations in Afghanistan, joined Washington in pressuring Syria out of Lebanon, and followed a policy towards Iran that was increasingly aligned with that of the United States.

Falling out of love with Europe
The referendum verdict, with a 55% 'No' vote, marked the end of France's long love affair with the European Union. In truth, though, disenchantment had set in as long ago as the late 1980s, when farm subsidies first became an issue in the EU's trade negotiations with the rest of the world, and France began to realise that the EU was as much a transmission belt for free-trade pressures as a bulwark against liberalisation. This same anxiety about Brussels negotiating away France's agricultural advantages flared up in autumn 2005. Paris demanded a special EU ministers' meeting to force Peter Mandelson, the EU trade commissioner, to withdraw concessions made a week earlier in the World Trade Organisation Doha negotiating round. At the meeting on 18 October, France failed to get sufficient support for its claim that Mandelson had exceeded his mandate, and the EU trade offer was left on the table. But the event was a warning that the Doha round may face further problems from France in the year to come.

France has been experiencing similar disenchantment with internal EU policies as the European Commission implements the Treaty of Rome's restraints on state subsidies and monopolies and its free-market rules, such as the free flow of capital and investment. Paris appeared to infringe the spirit, if not the letter, of EU law in March 2006, when de Villepin announced that Gaz de France would merge with Suez to prevent the latter becoming a takeover target of Enel, Italy's leading electricity company. Other EU governments, notably Spain, took action in the energy field to promote 'national champion' companies over foreign ones. But de Villepin was particularly open about his role and about what he called 'economic patriotism'.

Another EU irritation for France in 2005–06 was the Commission's proposed 'services directive', designed to free up the cross-border provision of services. This proposal, although it had nothing to do with the constitutional treaty, figured prominently in the French 'No' campaign, which chose to demonise the 'Polish plumber' as the prime example of a low-cost service provider threatening to invade France and put French jobs at risk.

Partly because of the spectre of the Polish plumber, the incorporation of no fewer than eight eastern and central European countries into the Union on 1 May 2004 was also a factor in the French 'No' vote; many saw it as a form of 'regional globalisation' forced upon them. On assuming office, de Villepin was quick to call for a freeze on further enlargement, echoed by Nicolas Sarkozy, the interior minister and president of the ruling Union pour un Mouvement Populaire (UMP) party. Almost alone amongst France's political elite, Chirac is a supporter of Turkey's entry into the EU, so France did not seek to block the formal start of accession talks on 3 October 2005. But Paris made it clear in Autumn 2005 that it would not countenance any new candidates for the foreseeable future. This will affect countries in the western Balkans, though not countries like Bulgaria or Romania that have already negotiated entry.

The prospect of a big inflow of labour from new EU states is more imagined than real; the evidence from past enlargements is that migrants return home as the prosperity of their home country increases. Nonetheless, it is made all the more sensitive as an issue by France's persistently high unemployment rate of around 10% nationally, but 20% among young job-seekers and as high as 40% among young members of France's ethnic communities. So it was natural that de Villepin made job creation and labour-market reform his top priority when Chirac named him as prime minister to replace Jean-Pierre Raffarin on 31 May 2005, immediately after the referendum vote. The chronically high jobless rate had undoubtedly helped sour the electorate's mood and contributed to the constitution's defeat. De Villepin's first act in government was to introduce limited contract flexibility in small companies. However, his March 2006 move to extend this to all contracts for young people entering the job market for the first time – the *Contrat Première Embauche* (CPE) or 'First Job Contract' – sparked widespread protests.

Social crises at home

Legislation to introduce the CPE passed parliament quickly – arguably too quickly, because if de Villepin had not used a guillotine measure to cut off debate on opposition amendments, he would have had to spend more time explaining the law's benefits, an effort that would have paid off. As it was, he only offered to consult student and union leaders on the measure after the latter had started to mobilise in the streets. Held on successive Tuesdays, these demonstrations built up to over 1m protesters across the country by early April. Eventually Chirac cracked, as he had done before in the face of student protests; first, he ordered the law suspended and replaced with a diluted version and then, on 10 April, scrapped it entirely in favour of a return to the French state's bad old habit of trying to subsidise French youth into jobs. The main beneficiary of this political climb-down was the left, not least the socialist politician, Ségolène Royal, who took an early lead in opinion polls for the 2007 presidential contest. On the right, the effect of the climb-down was to virtually knock de Villepin out of contention for the Elysée in favour of Sarkozy, who appeared to suffer only limited damage to his presidential hopes. As a result, no serious labour-market or welfare reform is expected until after the 2007 election.

Massive though the job-contract protests were, they were at least more peaceful than the disturbances a few months earlier in the depressed suburbs of Paris and other cities. Indeed part of de Villepin's motive for labour reform was to improve the dismal employment record among France's ethnic minority communities, a record which had contributed to one of the country's biggest social explosions since 1968, triggered by the accidental deaths on 27 October 2005 of two teenagers electrocuted while hiding from police in an electricity substation in a Paris suburb. There followed three weeks of rioting by ethnic-minority youths in dozens of communities around the country. The rioters' favourite tactic was burning cars, and at the peak over 1,400 vehicles went up in flames in one night. The riots produced no recognised leaders. Few demands were clearly formulated by the rioters, so few were met by the authorities, though some new efforts are being made to reduce racial discrimination in the job market. The religious leaders of France's five-million-strong Muslim community seemed almost as surprised as the Paris authorities by the outburst.

The protests shattered any smugness France might have felt about the superiority of its model of integration over those of the United States or Britain. As interior minister, Sarkozy preached the necessity for the practice of Islam in France to adapt to local mores, and expelled several foreign-born Muslim clerics whose extremism he judged incompatible with French values. By the same logic, however, French political parties ought to adapt by encouraging more minority representation within their ranks. The need for this was underlined in the 2002 parliamentary elections. Out of 8,424 candidates, only 123 were of ethnic-minority background, and almost all of them stood as independents rather than for the mainstream political parties.

Toning down foreign policy

Other events during 2005–06 highlighted tension between Europe and its Arab neighbours. France, with its large Maghrebin community, had more reason than most EU states to be disappointed by the failure of the EuroMed summit in Barcelona in November. This was supposed to celebrate ten years of the so-called 'Barcelona Process' between the EU and ten of its largely Arab neighbours on the southern and eastern shores of the Mediterranean. But despite the fact the EU gives €1 billion a year in aid to its EuroMed partners, only two of the latter's leaders (the Turkish prime minister and the Palestinian president) attended the Barcelona summit; most Arab leaders evidently did not want EU states lecturing them about lack of democracy and human rights in their countries.

If this incident underlined the failure of the civilisations, or at least the political establishments, on either side of the Mediterranean to engage, the 'Mohammed cartoons' affair triggered a real clash. What was for Europeans an issue of free speech was taken as deliberate blasphemy by their Arab neighbours. The affair actually started in September 2005 when a Danish newspaper, *Jyllands-Posten*, invited its readers to draw cartoons of the prophet Mohammed, which it then printed. But critical Muslim reaction was on a slow burn until the cartoons were reprinted on 1 February 2006 by *France Soir*, the first major newspaper in a country with a big Arab ethnic community to do so. A day later *France Soir* sacked its managing editor, saying that while he had the right to publish the cartoons, the decision to actually do so was ill judged. As the affair snowballed, the French and other Europeans who had published the cartoons found themselves in the unusual position of being criticised by US politicians for insensitivity towards Muslims and Arabs.

In any event, Paris found itself in 2005–06 far less at odds than in previous years with Washington over Middle East policy. This did not mean that France was suddenly in agreement with the United States over Iraq or Israel – merely that it saw no mileage in highlighting US problems in Iraq, and had every reason to welcome the one major development affecting the Palestinians: Israel's withdrawal from Gaza. But Paris and Washington worked as one to put diplomatic pressure on Syria over its presence, and interference, in Lebanon. President Chirac was perhaps angrier than Washington about the February 2005 assassination of Lebanon's former prime minister, Rafik Hariri, who had been a personal friend. The killing was widely suspected to be the work of the Syrians, and France joined the United States in sponsoring UN Security Council resolutions to force Syria to pull its forces out of Lebanon and to submit to a UN investigation of the assassination.

While France stayed out of Iraq, it did maintain its presence in Afghanistan and deployed special forces in the east of the country to help the United States hunt down al-Qaeda and the Taliban.

Besides Lebanon, the other area of active French diplomatic involvement in the Middle East has been the attempt, as part of the E3 (along with Britain and Germany), to broker a non-proliferation agreement with Iran. In spring 2005 the

Bush administration and the E3 agreed that the former would let the latter try to reach a negotiated deal, but if that failed the E3 would support the US in taking Iran before the Security Council. France has stuck to its side of the bargain. In the face of Iranian prevarication, Chirac publicly warned Tehran in a 29 August speech to French ambassadors that unless Iran 're-establishes cooperation and confidence, the Security Council would have no other choice but to take up the matter'. After further Iranian prevarication, Philippe Douste-Blazy, France's foreign minister, was ready to say on 16 February 2006 that 'today it is very simple: no civil nuclear programme can explain Iran's nuclear programme. So it is a clandestine military nuclear programme.'

At the same time, France has shifted ground to take advantage of nuclear-policy changes by other countries, notably the United States. Chirac visited India just before President Bush in March 2006, partly to persuade the Indians that Paris could match anything that Washington might provide under its new nuclear-technology agreement with Delhi. France also intends to follow up the US–UK achievement in getting Libya to renounce its nuclear-bomb-making effort by reaching a civil-nuclear-power accord with Tripoli.

Operating as part of an EU troika on a major world diplomatic issue clearly sits well with France's conception of its proper role. Indeed, one of the few ideas about the EU's future to fill the vacuum left by the defeat of the constitutional treaty has been Sarkozy's proposal that the EU should be run by a directorate of its six biggest members – France, Germany, Britain, Italy, Spain and Poland. This is not very practical politics. Sarkozy may have been lulled by his ministerial experience in internal security matters, where smaller EU states do not mind their bigger brethren caucusing by themselves on issues like counter-terrorism, into falsely thinking small states would acquiesce in the 'Big Six' taking the lead on general EU business. Nevertheless, the Sarkozy proposal, with its emphasis on national governments as distinct from EU institutions, is revealing of the French desire for a big EU role in foreign policy and defence in which national governments prevail.

A believer in defence

France remains a big proponent of EU defence, both in policy and deployment – the 2003 EU peacekeeping mission to the DRC, which the French led, for example, or the new European Gendarmerie Force that France and several other continental countries with militarised police forces have set up for peacekeeping purposes – and in industry. Paris has pushed hardest for the European Defence Industry (EDA) to be given a sizeable research and development (R&D) budget and involvement in new Europe-wide projects such as UAVs or tanker aircraft. By contrast, the UK, which together with France accounts for 70% of all European defence R&D, sees the EDA more as a referee to ensure the opening of cross-border defence procurement. Nonetheless, even if the two countries do not see eye to eye on the EDA, they reached an important collaborative agreement in March 2006 on building new aircraft carriers. France agreed to pay the UK up to £100m for design work already done on UK carriers that it plans to use for a new French vessel.

The landmark event in French defence in 2005–06 was Chirac's 19 January statement on France's nuclear-weapons posture, in a speech at the country's main submarine base. Such statements only come every few years; this constituted the first real update of French nuclear doctrine in the post-11 September era. The president recognised, as he had before, that nuclear weapons could not be relied on to deter 'fanatical terrorists' ready to die in any case, but argued they could make states using, or aiding and abetting, terrorists think twice. 'Leaders of states which use terrorist means against us, just like those envisaging the use of weapons of mass destruction, should understand they lay themselves open to a firm and adapted response from us', he said. France is known to have adapted its weapons to give them greater accuracy (partly by reducing the number of warheads on some of its submarine-launched missiles), and to allow destruction of an enemy's communications – and therefore command and control – through electromagnetic pulses produced by exploding weapons above ground. These changes are intended to permit a more flexible and limited response; Chirac recognised that it would be simply incredible, therefore useless, for France's only potential riposte to be total annihilation. At the same time, he was at pains to stress France's traditional view of nuclear weapons as weapons of last resort, not battlefield use.

Chirac also defined the sort of vital interests that might be defended by France's nuclear deterrent more widely than in the past. He suggested that 'safeguarding our strategic supplies or the defence of allied countries are, among others, interests that must be protected'. A French president might have to act to counter 'an unbearable act of aggression, threat or blackmail perpetrated against these interests'. He maintained the French deterrent was affordable (now less than 10% of the defence budget) and necessary (because no anti-ballistic missile defence could be relied on to be 100% effective). Chirac claimed the French deterrent was already a factor in European security, as EU states grew closer together. However, judging by the reaction to the Chirac speech in Germany, France's neighbours rate it as either a small or even unwelcome element in their security.

Smears, scandal and political consequences

As the president entered his final year in the Elysée, his government found itself engulfed in a scandal that went under the name of Clearstream, a Luxembourg financial institution, but which involved the government's two leading members, de Villepin and Sarkozy. The scandal had its roots in a company official's private investigation of what he believed to be suspicious Russian transactions in shares of EADS, the Franco-German defence group. This investigation turned up a list, later proved false, of transactions in the name of various people, including

Sarkozy. The scandal turned not on the list itself, but on de Villepin's alleged use of it to tarnish Sarkozy's image when the company official approached the prime minister for help in carrying the investigation further.

Even though de Villepin denied any impropriety, the effect of Clearstream was to weaken his position further – on 17 May only half the ruling UMP deputies turned up at the National Assembly to help the prime minister face down a censure vote – and strengthen that of Sarkozy, the UMP's president. More generally, the scandal boosted the standing of the opposition socialists. There are, however, also serious splits on the left, so the 2007 election is expected to be close.

Germany: New Era?

On 22 November 2005 Angela Merkel was sworn in as chancellor of Germany – the first East German, and the first woman, in that office. The election campaign had been nasty, the outcome of the 18 September vote ambiguous, the coalition negotiations messy. When the uncertainty was finally over, the relief in Germany and elsewhere was palpable. But even with a new government in place, questions remained about the coalition's likely effectiveness and durability, its ability to carry out reforms, and the foreign policy that it would adopt. It was not yet clear that this was the beginning of a new era for Germany.

There seemed plenty of scope for improvement in Germany's foreign relations after the seven-year tenure of Gerhard Schröder. Among the achievements of his coalition of Social Democrats and Greens was breaking Germany's postwar taboo against the use of military force for purposes other than self-defence. He sent the Bundeswehr (Armed Forces) into Kosovo and Afghanistan. But his unconditional refusal to take part in the Iraq War of 2003, while highly popular with German voters, badly damaged relations with Washington.

An uncertain mandate

The mandate handed to Merkel in the 18 September election was less than conclusive. Her centre-right Christian Democratic Party (CDU) won 226 of the 614 seats in the Bundestag, only four more than the 222 of the centre-left Social Democratic Party (SPD), with the liberal Free Democratic Party (FDP) winning 61, the left-wing Linkspartei 54 and the Greens 51. The CDU won, at 35.2 %, just over one percentage point more of the electoral vote than the SPD, and their combined share, at 69.4%, was their worst showing since 1949.

As a result, some questioned whether Merkel had been given a mandate. Schröder, pointing to her loss of a 12-point poll lead over the course of the campaign, initially felt emboldened enough to suggest that he lead the new government himself, but this proved unpopular even within his own party. In the weeks that followed, several permutations of possible coalitions were debated: a 'traffic light' coalition of SPD (red), FDP (yellow) and Greens; a 'Jamaica' coalition with the CDU (black), Greens and the FDP; a minority government (SPD and Greens, or CDU and FDP) tolerated by the opposition. In the end, the CDU and SDU reluctantly turned towards each other and formed a grand coalition for the second time in 36 years. Their nearly 200-page 'coalition contract' contained U-turns for both partners: the CDU toned down its radical labour-market reform plans while the SPD relinquished its growth-boosting spending programme in favour of rigorous fiscal conservatism. The cabinet reflected the near-parity of the election outcome. The powerful post of vice chancellor and labour minister went to the SPD's Franz Müntefering. The CDU claimed the head of the Chancellery (Thomas de Maizière), as well as the ministries for the interior, economics, defence, education, family and agriculture. The SPD supplied the foreign minister, Frank-Walter Steinmeier, as well as the justice, health, transport and development portfolios. By the time the Bundestag, which elects the chancellor, finally voted on 22 November, relations between the two parties had turned from frosty to cordial. Merkel won 397 of the 448 coalition votes.

Germany's first female chancellor was also, at 51, its youngest. A physicist born in Hamburg, the daughter of a Protestant pastor, she spent her first 35 years in Communist East Germany. After the fall of the Berlin Wall, she became a political disciple of Chancellor Helmut Kohl. Yet during the 1999 CDU party finance scandal, she outraged him by calling for his resignation as honorary chairman of the CDU. In a party that emphasises marriage and family, Merkel is childless, divorced and remarried. By the standards of Germany's traditionally corporatist, hierarchical and deferential culture, she ascended with remarkable speed, having been in politics for only 16 years. Her critics contend that she has few friends in her own party, is distrustful, indecisive and a diffident public speaker. Her admirers counter that she is a fast learner with a near-photographic memory, calculating and tenacious, and impatient to modernise the economy and political system.

Foreign policy: pragmatism and principles
In Germany's foreign policy, Merkel the strategist was soon very much in evidence. The foreign-policy chapter of the 11 November coalition agreement offered a broad promise of continuity and few specifics – not surprising against the backdrop of sharp disagreements between the CDU and SPD on most other issues of economic and domestic reform. The two parties' ideological differences over Turkey's EU membership bid were papered over, with the pact merely acknowledging that the negotiations with Ankara were to be 'open-ended'. Another element of continuity with the previous government was seemingly provided by Steinmeier, who had been Schröder's chief of staff and coordinator

of intelligence services in the Chancellery. Steinmeier, like Merkel, is a level-headed pragmatist, and the two have displayed mutual confidence, though with the chancellor clearly setting the foreign-policy agenda.

From her first foreign trip onwards, Merkel deliberately and systematically readjusted Germany's bilateral relationships – demonstrating an acute understanding of political symbolism. She flew to Paris less than 24 hours after her accession, paying homage, like all her predecessors, to the special relationship with France. She pointedly referred – in implied criticism of Schröder – to the need to respect the interests of Germany's eastern neighbours. Visiting Brussels on the same day, she went first to NATO headquarters to pledge her support for the Alliance as the premier body for transatlantic consultation, but added that Berlin would send no soldiers to Iraq. Only then did she go on to visit the European Commission. On the following day in London, Merkel noted that the Franco-German relationship would 'not work against Britain', and emphasised a common interest in EU budget reform. She later gave the UK's EU presidency a much-needed boost by brokering a last-minute budget deal that gave Poland an unexpected windfall. The chancellor also calmed relations with Poland, which had become strained because of Polish protests against a planned information centre on post-war deportations, and a deal on a €4bn oil pipeline through the Baltic Sea, signed by Schröder and Russia's Vladimir Putin in the former's last week in office. Merkel instituted a German–Polish working group on the pipeline.

Looking further east, Merkel firmly rejected Iran's nuclear ambitions, compared Iranian president Mahmoud Ahmadinejad to Adolf Hitler and attacked his anti-Semitic remarks. In Israel, she made it clear that there would be no 'equidistancing' under her leadership – a position warmly welcomed by Tel Aviv. Merkel met with Putin and with Russian NGOs in Moscow; in Berlin, she received Russia's Foreign Minister Sergei Lavrov on the same day as Belarus's opposition leader Alexander Milinkiewicz. In Beijing, she lobbied for support of a UN resolution on Iran, but also publicly criticised China's human-rights record. Her first trip to Washington was a resounding success – not least because she had silenced domestic critics of US foreign policy by demanding, on the eve of her departure, that the Guantanamo Bay detention facility be shut down. After her second visit to meet Bush in May, during which the US president praised her as 'a fascinating person with a unique perspective', there was euphoria on both sides about the new closeness of the relationship between Washington and Berlin.

Merkel's extraordinary success in quickly establishing herself as a leader to be reckoned with internationally is partly to be explained by a combination of unassuming civility and unflinching directness on matters of substance. She believes in more rather than less European integration; greater respect for the needs and interests of smaller European neighbours, without necessarily favouring additional bids for EU membership; a much-improved transatlantic relationship, without exploitation of anti-American public feeling; support for both NATO and the ESDP, with an expanded presence in NATO's Afghan operation and German command of an EU military mission to stabilise elections due to be held in July 2006 in the DRC; a relationship with Russia that is not excessively close, but involves pragmatism on issues such as energy; and a more deliberate pursuit of national interests, though preferably within multilateral frameworks and on the basis of a strong regard for international law.

Nevertheless, Germany's new strength is partly a function of the recent weaknesses of key partners. Berlin's foreign-policy options remain constrained and Merkel's balanced strategy will face further challenges. NATO's Riga Summit in November could expose transatlantic disagreements about enlargement and globalisation of NATO, which the United States favours but of which Germany is sceptical. Berlin has sought to dampen expectations of its presidency of the G8 in 2007 and of the EU in the first half of that year. A new European *Ostpolitik*, which some Berlin policymakers think should be Germany's main focus for 2007, might include an upgraded neighbourhood policy; a more strategic approach to energy security; a review of EU attitudes towards opposition movements, for example in Belarus; and a rethinking of the EU–Russian relationship, in which Berlin's special rapport with Moscow will be an important factor.

Germany's defence-policy debate acquired new momentum by mid-2006, with Minister of Defence Franz Josef Jung (CDU), supported by Minister of the Interior Wolfgang Schäuble (CDU), pushing to remove the constitutional barrier between foreign and homeland security so as to allow Germany's armed forces (the Bundeswehr) to take on more responsibilities at home. The Ministry of Defence argued that terrorist threats made the protection of population and critical infrastructure on German territory more important. Article 87a of the Basic Law (*Grundgesetz*) restricts the use of the Bundeswehr for such purposes. The Social Democrats have so far rejected amending the Basic Law to this effect. This division in the governing coalition was likely to come to a head with cabinet discussions about a new White Paper on Defence (the first since 1994), a draft of which was leaked in April. The White Paper, the final version of which is expected to be published during the second half of 2006, is likely to reassert the primacy of NATO in German security and defence policy. The draft referred to the Alliance as Germany's 'strongest anchor' in this realm and promised a return to security-policy discussion through NATO bodies.

After initial wavering, Germany's decision to lead the EU's military mission to the Democratic Republic of the Congo, to be launched in June, demonstrated that the government was willing to take on new responsibilities in Africa. At the same time, the domestic debate about the deployment again laid bare the fragile consensus on deployment of German soldiers on international missions. There was considerable uncertainty about the rationale for and the tasks of the force among the general population as well as members of the armed forces. The White Paper, coupled with Germany's growing international responsibilities, seemed likely to provoke an overdue public debate about security and defence policy.

Domestic reform challenges

While these foreign-policy changes have captured international attention, Merkel has a pressing agenda of domestic reforms and economic stimulation. The priorities include an overhaul of Germany's federal structure, taxation, labour market, health care, education and immigration. On the economic front, the government faced unemployment of 5m, or nearly 12%, and the need to cut public spending. Economic growth was at an annual rate of just 0.4 % in the first quarter of 2006. The general election revealed that the country was not united on the need for economic reform, but subsequent elections at the state level on 26 March strengthened Merkel's hand, reinforcing the CDU's power relative to the SPD. Her coalition partner has weakened considerably, losing two party chairmen in eight months and supplying only five of the 16 states with premiers. Its opinion-poll support and membership have both fallen.

Merkel's challenge is to translate this strength into effective reform. A tax-reform package in May, including a rise in value-added tax from 16% to 19%, a mostly symbolic 'wealth tax' and cuts in some tax allowances, was widely denounced as certain to dampen growth, and for avoiding spending cuts. The chancellor's high approval rating began to slip and it was clear that more work was required to retain the loyalty of key party officials in the states. Domestic-policy reform that stimulates faster, sustainable economic growth is essential if Germany is to retain its position as a leader within Europe and more broadly. Germany remains Europe's largest economy and the third-largest contributor to the UN budget. The ability of Merkel's coalition to agree and implement domestic changes will thus be a key determinant of her authority in pressing forward with her ambitious programme of foreign-policy renewal.

United Kingdom: Politics and Terrorism

'I have listened and I have learned', said Tony Blair after winning a third consecutive term as British prime minister in a general election held on 5 May 2005. The election saw Labour's parliamentary majority fall from 167 seats to 66 after campaign sparring that, though lacking clear central themes, contained plenty of vitriol about Britain's role in Iraq. His promise to pay more attention to the electorate was an attempt to leave this argument behind: 'I know that Iraq has been a deeply divisive issue in this country. That has been very, very clear. But I also know and believe that after this election people want to move on.'

While Iraq was indeed tending to recede as a dominant issue during the first half of 2006, the Blair government was unable to shake off the *fin-de-siècle* atmosphere that Iraq had helped to induce. Blair's entire nine-year tenure as prime minister since 1997 had been dogged by incessant media speculation, fostered by politicians, about when he would stand down and allow – presumably – Gordon Brown, chancellor of the exchequer (finance minister), to take over the leadership. During mid-2006 this speculation reached unprecedented levels: British journalists accompanying the prime minister on a visit to Australia and New Zealand in March wrote almost exclusively about the timing of Blair's departure from office. His declining command over Labour Party loyalty was further undermined as several ministers ran into personal and political problems. In May 2006, Blair was forced into an extensive reshuffle of his cabinet, but failed to reassert personal authority over the government; indeed, he found it necessary to sack or demote senior 'Blairite' loyalists. Worse for Blair, the changes utterly failed to quash the factional struggle. Brown was apparently very reluctant to accept a further delay to his accession, while Blair's supporters desperately accused their rivals of mounting a 'left-wing coup'. It was by no means clear that Blair could cling to office until the ten-year anniversary of his premiership in May 2007, which appeared to be the target he had set for himself.

Blair's tremendous success had been to make the Labour party electable after 17 years in opposition, by abandoning socialist trade-union-led dogma while at the same time investing heavily in upgrading publicly owned schools and the state health-care system. Blair and Brown's economic policies, pursuing a steady, prudent fiscal stance with relatively low borrowing while allowing the Bank of England to set monetary policy independently, brought an unprecedented period of steady economic growth with low inflation. Blair also had an instinctive ability to capture the public mood.

This was of no use when he decided that it was strategically essential for Britain to stand alongside the United States come what may, and therefore subscribed to Bush's extension of the US 'global war on terrorism' to embrace Iraq. There was strong public opposition to the war from well before its start. Blair's calculation that UN Security Council authorisation for the Iraqi adventure would, if it had been achieved, have satisfied enough of the British public was perhaps correct – but it also revealed his tendency towards wishful thinking. The domestic British political case for invading Iraq was built on Baghdad's weapons of mass destruction programmes and the risk of such weapons falling into the hands of terrorists. As none were found in Iraq, the subsequent low level of public trust in Blair was such that he was believed by many Britons to have deliberately deceived the public about Iraq's capabilities. The flawed political and bureaucratic processes that went into making the public case for war – and the faulty intelligence itself – were the subject of two lengthy inquiry reports. Small wonder that Blair wanted to leave the issue behind in his third term.

Blair has led a government whose political acumen has never developed fully, partly because it enjoyed the cushion of a large parliamentary majority for its first two terms. Among Labour MPs, his non-socialist 'New Labour' approach had always been embraced only half-heartedly by some and not at all by others. Therefore, his drive for public-service reform with elements of market-driven competition found increasing numbers of Labour MPs forming, in effect, the opposition – in fact, a package of educational legislation in 2006 was passed with the support of the Conservatives. It was partly because of Labour MPs' belief that he had throughout been too 'presidential' that his control over them, including many who had been ministers in his government, was draining away in mid-2006.

The shock of domestically generated terrorism

Even in a country long accustomed to Irish terrorism, the 7 July 2005 bombings in London caused profound national shock. Three bombs were detonated simultaneously on London underground trains in the morning rush hour, and a fourth on a bus an hour later – the original target for that bomb may also have been a train. The attacks killed 52 people and injured 700. The suicide bombings were carried out by three men born in northern England of Pakistani origin and one man born in Jamaica who had been brought up in northern England since infancy. While many had expected a terrorist attack on the UK, and the threat from a small minority of UK-based Muslims was well understood, there was still widespread national consternation that the attacks had been domestically generated. The bombings immediately aroused discussion about Britain's 'multicultural' approach to absorbing immigrant communities, about intelligence capabilities and about the tolerable level of intrusiveness of counter-terrorist measures.

Much remains unknown about the 7 July attacks. Even less is known about an unsuccessful set of 'copycat' attacks two weeks later, because these remained *sub judice*: at the time of writing, the suspects were in custody, awaiting trial. In the 21 July attacks, three London Underground trains and a bus were again targeted, but the bombs did not go off. There was no evidence of a link between the two groups of bombers. The next day, an innocent Brazilian man was shot dead on a London underground train by police who wrongly believed he was a suicide bomber about to mount an attack.

A narrative report about the 7 July attacks, published by the government in May 2006, recorded what was known so far about the events and the backgrounds of the four attackers: no other person was identified as being involved in the plot. The apparent ringleader was Mohammad Sidique Khan, who was 30 at the time of his death, and was married with a daughter. He had been employed for three years until autumn 2004 in a local primary school, working with children with special needs and language or behavioural problems. He was talented in this work, and a role model for children. Shehzad Tanweer, 22 at his death, had studied sports science at university, was a keen cricketer, and was working in his father's fish and chip shop. Hasib Hussain, 18, had left school at 16 but completed a college business course in June 2005. All these three were born of parents who had migrated from Pakistan. They grew up in the Beeston area of the city of Leeds, Britain's third most populous metropolitan area: the population, at around 700,000, is about one-tenth that of Greater London. The fourth bomber, Jermaine Lindsay, 19 at the time of his death and married with one child, was born in Jamaica but grew up in Huddersfield, a town not far from Leeds. He had converted to Islam in adolescence, learned Arabic and memorised passages of the Koran. The three men from Beeston frequented mosques, gyms, youth clubs and an Islamic bookshop – all part of the social life for young men in the town. The narrative report said: 'It seems likely that Khan used the opportunities these places afforded at least to identify candidates for indoctrination, even if the indoctrination itself took place more privately to avoid detection.'

Like many thousands of British people of Pakistani origin, Khan and Tanweer had visited Pakistan. The report said it was likely they had contact with al-Qaeda figures there, but no details had been established. The only real clue to the bombers' motivation came in a video statement made by Khan, shown on al-Jazeera television on 1 September. In it, he said: 'Your democratically elected governments continuously perpetuate atrocities against my people all over the world. And your support of them makes you directly responsible, just as I am directly responsible for protecting and avenging my Muslim brothers and sisters. Until we feel security, you will be our targets. And until you stop the bombing, gassing, imprisonment and torture of my people we will not stop this fight. We are at war and I am a soldier.' Khan also left a will, which focused on martyrdom. According to the government report, it drew upon a will written by a British man who was killed in the US bombing of Tora Bora, Afghanistan, in 2001.

The 7 July and 21 July bombers were not the only British Muslims to have attempted terrorist attacks. Richard Reid, who was born and brought up in suburban London, attempted to bomb an aircraft by detonating explosives hidden in his shoe on 22 December 2001. He had converted to Islam while in prison for robberies and was subsequently radicalised. After being caught as he attempted to ignite the explosives, he was convicted and jailed in the United States. Saajid Badat, who grew up in Gloucester, western England, was arrested in 2003 and admitted that he had been asked in 2001 to carry out a shoe bombing like Reid's, but did not go through with it. Bomb materials were found in his house, and he was sent to prison for 13 years. In 2003 Asif Hanif and Omar Sharif, both

British, attacked a bar in Tel Aviv, killing three people. Hanif died in the attack but Sharif's bomb failed to detonate and he was later found dead in the sea.

Trials of other people have revealed more details of terrorist activity, and more legal proceedings are expected. During 2006, seven men from towns around London were on trial for conspiring to cause explosions. The government and police have also targeted British-based radical clerics suspected of stirring extremism, such as Omar Bakri Mohammad, Abu Qatada and Abu Hamza al-Masri, a former Imam at the Finsbury Park mosque in London who was jailed for seven years in 2006 for inciting murder and racial hatred. However, efforts to convict eight men for a plot to spread the deadly toxin ricin in London collapsed in 2005. The only man to be convicted for the plot, Kamel Bourgass, an Algerian, had also been jailed for murdering a policeman who was trying to arrest him. Materials and instructions for ricin manufacture were found, but no ricin. Hundreds more people have been arrested over the past few years on suspicion of involvement in terrorism.

These events, as well as legal problems surrounding the detention in the UK of foreign terrorist suspects, prompted intense discussion on several issues. The first was whether the bombings threw into question Britain's 'multicultural' approach to the integration of immigrants into British society. Under this approach, different cultures, customs and languages of ethnic groups are respected, or even actively encouraged, and the groups make up a diverse entity that forms the nation. The opposite method, termed 'assimilation', is best exemplified by France's policy, which is intended to create an integrated nation by emphasis on French customs and the French language: differences between cultures and customs are discouraged with the aim of maintaining a single nationhood. These are policy choices for governments, and the multicultural approach has been fully embraced by the Labour government since 1997. However, they also reflect more fundamental differences between societies. Britain's laissez-faire capitalism, though with heavy state participation in health and education, lends itself to a multicultural live-and-let-live philosophy in which all comers are nevertheless intended to have equal civil rights and access to education, health care and opportunities. France's more statist approach naturally tends towards greater intervention in the lives of all, whether immigrants or not, and to definitive state-led ideas on what it means to be French. It was suggested after the London bombings, and after the October 2005 violence in France among disadvantaged, ghetto-inhabiting immigrant communities, that both of these European models had failed. The third model is that of the United States, which has drawn elements from both sides of the debate. Cultural differences and languages are respected, but a distinctively American culture evokes a strong sense of American values. A highly dynamic, mobile economy combined with a far less extensive government-provided safety net creates strong incentives for success that, in turn, foster loyalty and belief in the 'American way'.

Even before the London bombings, a discussion was under way in Britain about whether multiculturalism had been taken too far. In 2004, the government-appointed head of the Commission for Racial Equality, Trevor Phillips, argued that there was a danger that multiculturalism risked making a 'fetish of our historical differences' to the extent that it could become a form of benign neglect or even exclusion of communities. Equally, he rejected assimilation, which he described as the 'destruction of difference, an essential ingredient that enriches and strengthens our society'. Phillips argued: 'We need to be more radical and ambitious, not less. We need to pull the rug from under the extremists and remind people that we are all equally British, regardless of race and religion. Our claim for equality in an integrated society is founded on the certainty of our citizenship – on what we have in common, not our differences.'

Londoners arguably live in a successfully multicultural city in which ethnic differences enrich a diverse community; while there are problems and a tendency towards self-isolation in some individual ethnic communities, the pressures and opportunities in a vast metropolis tend to work towards integration. However, it may also be the case that the model has not worked as well in some cities in the Midlands and northern England with large, even predominant Asian communities. Higher-than-average unemployment and crime rates among young men of Pakistani origin, for example, suggest that some ethnic communities are disadvantaged and marginalised and more susceptible to feelings of alienation. The fact that four men brought up in northern England turned to violence renewed the debate about multiculturalism and added a sharp security dimension to it. In particular, Khan's reference to 'my people' in his suicide video – identifying himself with Muslims worldwide rather than with Britons or family – prompted thought about Phillips' call for a change in government policy.

The second issue raised by the bombings was the capacity of Britain's intelligence services. The Intelligence and Security Committee of Parliament conducted an inquiry into – among other aspects – whether there had been an intelligence failure. Khan and Tanweer had previously come to the attention of MI5, the domestic intelligence service, on the periphery of other investigations. Surveillance data showed that the two were among a number of previously unidentified men who had been at meetings with people under investigation in 2004. MI5 also had on record a telephone number that turned out to be Lindsay's, and a number registered to Khan. However, none of these contacts led to further investigation: there was no evidence to suggest they were planning an attack, and MI5 lacked the resources to follow up such contacts at a time when it had other pressing priorities. While the committee said it was understandable that greater priority had not been given to following up the contacts, it commented: 'We have been struck by the sheer scale of the problem that our intelligence and securities agencies face and their comparatively small capacity to cover it.' Three further plots had been thwarted since July 2005, and the number of 'primary investigative targets' in the UK under MI5 investigation had risen from 250 in 2001 to over 500 in July 2004, to about 800 a year later. Not all of these could be covered, and 'the degree of coverage on the most essential subjects was far from complete'. This was in spite of additional resources being provided to the intelligence services: the annual allocation rose from £1.31bn in 2004 to £1.48bn in 2006, with most of the extra money going to MI5. The committee said: 'We remain concerned that across the whole of the counter-terrorism community the development of the home-grown threat and the radicalisation of British citizens were not fully understood or applied to strategic thinking.'

The third issue, and the one creating the most difficult political issues, was the difficulty of reconciling tougher security measures with civil liberties. This involved not only terrorism but also broader issues such as treatment of asylum seekers and prevention of other violent crimes, especially by previous offenders. By mid-2006, the government itself was questioning whether its previous legislative measures had placed too great an emphasis on human rights of suspects or offenders at the cost of public safety. Its counter-terrorist measures had already stirred heated debate, even though Britons are not troubled by some measures viewed as controversial elsewhere, such as the extensive use of surveillance cameras in public places. Identity cards are being introduced in spite of wide opposition. The government's attempt to lengthen the period of detention without charge from 14 days only won parliamentary approval when the proposed length was cut from 90 days to 28. Among other controversial legislation was that covering detention of detainees whom the government wished to deport, but could not do so because of the risk that they would be tortured if they returned to their home countries. The government was forced for legal reasons to repeal its 2001 legislation on this, to release nine men from prison and to introduce a new law, the Prevention of Terrorism Act 2005, including a system of Control Orders. Further legislation in 2006 provoked discussion because it made – in addition to encouraging or training terrorists – 'glorification' of terrorism a criminal offence.

British foreign policy re-launched

If Blair's hoped-for legacy within Britain will be public services – especially health and education – improved beyond recognition, he would perhaps wish to be remembered internationally for defining and performing an activist, intervention-ist role. He sought to carve out a strong post-colonial, post-Cold War role for the UK, playing an important role in addressing the world's challenges as they presented themselves – the rise of al-Qaeda, persecution in the Balkans, poverty in Africa, the many problems of the Middle East. Rightly or wrongly, events in Iraq are seen as having tarnished his record in this regard. So Blair, perhaps with an eye to his portrayal in the history books, sought in 2006 to re-state UK foreign policy in a series of speeches. He picked up the themes of his April 1999 Chicago speech, in which he called for much greater international cooperation to address financial, economic, environmental, trade and security issues – a so-called 'doctrine of international community'. In an increasingly interdependent world, engagement rather than isolation was essential. This, he said in Chicago (NATO's Kosovo campaign was under way at the time), should be backed up by a willingness to intervene militarily to right wrongs, provided the case was strong; diplomatic options had been exhausted; there were sensible and prudent military options; the commitment was long term; and national interests were at stake.

In March 2006 Blair, while admitting that mistakes had been made, robustly defended his interventionist policy. However, he was less than convincing as he sought to cast choices about intervention as between 'benign inactivity' – hope that international problems would work themselves out – or action to confront extremist and reactionary views, defeat terrorism, and promote democracy and progress. This, for British commentators, was to continue to accept and parrot Bush's conflation of complex and separate issues into a 'global war on terrorism', and to subsume UK interests into this – an argument that has never been persuasive in Britain. As a result, Blair's call for extremist ideology and propaganda to be tackled head-on, without excessive sensitivity, did not get the attention that, in light of the London bombings, it might have done: 'I mean telling [extremists] that their attitude to America is absurd; their concept of governance pre-feudal; their positions on women and other faiths, reactionary and regressive.'

The strong emphasis placed on countering terrorism was reflected in a re-statement of UK foreign policy, published in March 2006 as a White Paper entitled 'Active Diplomacy for a Changing World: the UK's International Priorities'. Number one on the list of strategic priorities was 'making the world safer from global terrorism and weapons of mass destruction', followed by 'reducing the harm to the UK from international crime, including drug trafficking, people smuggling and money laundering'. These two priorities appeared to bring together a wide range of separate policies. The European Union was described as 'the UK's single most important multilateral commitment', while the 'single most important bilateral relationship' was that with the United States. Otherwise, the paper put fresh emphasis on the growth of China and India, and issues such as climate change.

Britain's role in Europe, always contentious both between and within UK political parties, receded over the past year in terms of its ability to contort domestic politics. Though Blair still claimed to be a fervent pro-European, he had settled into a compromise in which British membership of the euro was postponed indefinitely, but the UK actively promoted and participated in the EU's expanding defence identity. The relative comfort of this position was threatened by a referendum on the EU constitutional treaty, in which the government would probably have suffered a humiliating defeat. French and Dutch rejection of the treaty removed the obligation to hold a referendum. With the Union's entire future nature and scope now having to be reconsidered across Europe, the whole subject lost, at least temporarily, some of its domestic political edge.

The UK, holding the rotating presidency of the EU from July to December 2005, judged it was not yet the time to attempt a new post-constitution European compact, and nor was it realistic for Britain to do so – the weakness of governments in France and Germany was another reason to hold back, not to mention Blair's increasingly tetchy personal relationship with Chirac. Therefore, Blair launched the presidency by sketching out broad lines for the EU's future in a widely welcomed speech to the European parliament, but left it at that. The presidency focused mostly on low-profile issues, though it did culminate in the beginning of Turkish accession talks and a deal on the hotly contested EU budget. In his 23 June 2005 Strasbourg speech, Blair emphasised his belief that Europe was a political and not just an economic project, but said the EU had lost touch with voters and needed to address issues important to them, such as unemployment: hence there was a need for a new social model, economic reforms, lower subsidies for farmers and more effective Europe-wide counter-terrorist action.

New relationships
Whoever is Britain's next leader – it is possible that another Labour politician could challenge Brown's succession – he will have the opportunity to forge new relationships with European partners and the EU as a whole. The extent to which he will have to strike a new partnership with Bush will depend on the timing of Blair's handover. The Iraq War is identified in Britain so personally with Blair that the next leader, even if a member of the same party, will be able to leave an enormous amount of domestic political baggage behind. The effect that this could have on the Washington–London axis is unclear. One issue that could become a touchstone for the future relationship is Britain's demand for adequate transfer of technology for the F-35 Joint Strike Fighter, to which it has contributed substantial funding as a joint project.

What is surprising both to the UK electorate and to Britain's international partners is how little they know about Gordon Brown. In nine years of office, he has held only the finance and economy portfolio, and his views on subjects beyond this brief have not been expressed eloquently – his expressions of support for the Iraq War, for example, have been terse. Not surprisingly, he and Blair have wanted to play down the factional struggle in which they have been engaged, mostly through proxies. They insist in public that they have worked together on a common agenda. Even less is known about Brown's likely rival at the next election, David Cameron, who was elected leader of the Conservative Party in December 2005 at the age of 39, after only four years in parliament. He has cast himself as a dynamic moderniser, arguing that after three election defeats the party needed to shed some of the dogma of its former leader, Margaret Thatcher. However, the substance and direction of the new Tory party will not become clear until nearer the next general election, which must be held by May 2010 but is more likely to be in 2009, barring earlier disintegration of the Labour government.

Any changes at the top are unlikely to bring wrenching alteration of Britain's approach to the most immediately pressing security issues: support for the Iraqi government will remain a high priority, though with a steady reduction of the number of UK troops deployed; so too will the search for a diplomatic solution to the confrontation with Iran, in partnership with France and Germany; Afghanistan will pose a severe challenge to British troops, their numbers swelled as NATO takes on new responsibilities in the south, and any important setbacks there are likely to lead to the deployment being questioned at home; meanwhile international terrorism, whether generated in the UK or elsewhere, will remain a present danger.

The Balkans: Steps to Stability

The past year for the western Balkans has been a year of waiting. After positive developments in all the countries of the region in 2005 – especially in developing closer relations with the European Union – a number of important decisions were due in 2006. The last year also witnessed the passing of two key figures in the disintegration of Yugoslavia. In January 2006 Ibrahim Rugova, president of Kosovo, died, followed in March by Slobodan Milosevic, the former Serbian leader whose four-year trial at the United Nations' International Criminal Tribunal for the Former Yugoslavia (ICTY) in The Hague had been drawing to an end. At the time of his death two key issues left over from the disintegration of Yugoslavia still remained to be resolved: Montenegro and Kosovo.

Montenegro votes for independence

On 21 May 2006 Montenegrins voted in a referendum to end their loose federation with Serbia, known as the 'State Union'. Unlike Kosovo, which was a province of Serbia, Montenegro was one of the six original Yugoslav republics. When the others seceded in the early 1990s, Montenegro opted to stay with Serbia. However, as opposition began to mount against Milosevic, Milo Djukanovic, the republic's then president who is now premier, began to distance himself from the Serbian leader and gradually adopted a pro-independence stance.

After the fall of Milosevic in October 2000, Djukanovic agreed to stay in a loose federation with Serbia. Under an accord that came into force in February

2003, either republic could hold a referendum on independence after three years. Djukanovic agreed to this delay under intense pressure from Javier Solana, the EU foreign-policy chief, who wanted to forestall demands from Kosovo for independence. While Montenegro has a population of 672,000, Kosovo's is about 2m, more than 90% of whom are ethnic Albanians who have long demanded independence from Serbia. The UN Security Council's announcement in October 2005 that talks on Kosovo's future would soon begin meant that Solana's reason for trying to keep Montenegro in union with Serbia had formally lapsed.

Over the three years of the State Union, the pro-independence authorities in Montenegro made sure that it was as dysfunctional as possible, while working hard to build support for independence. They also pointed out that it was difficult to make a union work well because Serbia, with a population of 7.5m and an economy 17 times larger, found it hard to accept Montenegro as an equal partner.

Solana continued to play an important role in Montenegro's future. Following the announcement of a referendum, it quickly became clear that those in favour of independence and those in favour of union differed on the terms under which the poll should be held – in particular the voting threshold that would determine the outcome. Each side wanted terms that would assure victory. Fearing a boycott of the referendum by unionists would rob it of credibility, Solana appointed Miroslav Lajcak, political director of the Slovak Foreign Ministry, to broker a deal. He suggested that approval of independence should require 55% of the vote. In the event 55.5% voted in favour, with a turnout of 86.3%, meaning that the republic's future was decided by a respectable margin. Solana made another shrewd choice in appointing the Slovak diplomat Frantisek Lipka to head the referendum commission. Both Lajcak and Lipka spoke Serbian and could draw on their own experience of separation from Prague – and are examples of what new member countries can bring to the EU.

The mechanics of separation were not expected to be difficult: the union was in any case loose and most assets, including the military, had already been long divided. The new Montenegro plans a small army of 2,000–3,000 and a coastguard, while Serbia plans a professional military of some 30,000. Montenegro will have to seek international recognition as a new state, while Serbia will inherit the legal identity of the previous union.

Serbia faces realities

Vojislav Kostunica, Serbia's prime minister, initially reacted with apparent disbelief to the Montenegrin vote. Nor was this his only miscalculation. He had become premier after the December 2003 election in which he defeated the Democratic Party previously led by Prime Minister Zoran Djindjic, who had been assassinated in March 2003. In the wake of the murder thousands of arrests were made as the authorities tried to stamp out organised crime, which was believed to have played a key role in the killing. Kostunica began by seeking to undo reforms made by Djindjic since the fall of Milosevic. But by late 2004 he had apparently had a change of heart, and reforms stalled since Djindjic's murder resumed. In the economic field the driving force was coalition partner G17 Plus, a party that included economists such as Miroljub Labus, who became deputy premier, and Mladjan Dinkic, who became finance minister. From late 2004, foreign investment began to flow into the country, attracted in particular by privatisations, although a year later this had slowed.

In October 2005 Serbia and Montenegro were deemed to have made enough progress to begin talks with the EU on a Stabilisation and Association Agreement (SAA), the first step towards eventual EU membership. These began well, but on 3 May 2006 they were suspended by Olli Rehn, the EU Enlargement Commissioner, because of Serbia's failure to apprehend General Ratko Mladic, the Bosnian Serb wartime commander. A condition for continuing the talks was Serbia's cooperation with the ICTY, including the arrest of Mladic, who has been indicted for genocide including his role in the 1995 murder of some 8,000 Bosnian Muslim men and boys at Srebrenica. Kostunica promised Rehn and Carla Del Ponte, the tribunal's chief prosecutor, that Mladic would be arrested. Rehn was then compelled to suspend the talks when Kostunica failed to deliver. At this point, in a severe blow to the government's international credibility, Deputy Premier Labus resigned. Montenegro was soon scheduled to restart negotiations while Serbia would now have to wait.

The Montenegro and Mladic affairs were signs that Kostunica's government had slipped out of touch with reality. It was possible that the prime minister believed Mladic would surrender himself or be found, but he remained at large. Kostunica, because he did not expect Montenegro to break from Serbia, had made no plans to restructure the government in Belgrade – for example, it now needed its own ministers of foreign affairs and defence. At mid-2006, there was a danger that Kostunica had failed to prepare Serbs for the biggest shock of all: the impending loss of Kosovo. For, while he had said he did not believe Kosovo would be independent, none of the international actors involved appeared to concur.

Talks on Kosovo

When riots engulfed Kosovo in March 2004 the members of the Contact Group – Britain, France, Germany, Italy, Russia and the United States – decided the situation was no longer tenable. Meeting in Pristina in April 2004, the group said the violence was 'a severe setback to the vision that we have for the future of Kosovo ... a multi-ethnic Kosovo where all its citizens live in peace and security'. The Contact Group declared its intention to step up its engagement, remaining committed to a 'standards before status' approach but noting that critical standards had been 'trampled upon'. In May 2005 Kai Eide, Norway's ambassador to NATO, was appointed to produce a report for the UN on whether talks on the final or future status of the province should begin. In a frank 16-page assessment, presented to Kofi Annan, the UN secretary-general, in October, Eide said progress in implementing a series of standards devised by the UN was 'uneven'. He concluded: 'There will not be any good moment for addressing Kosovo's future status … nevertheless an overall assessment leads to the conclusion that the time has come to commence this process'.

Martti Ahtisaari, the former Finnish president with considerable Balkan experience, was appointed by the Security Council to lead the talks, which began in Vienna on 20 February 2006 and took the form of rounds devoted to different subjects. The Kosovo Albanians were relatively flexible on everything bar their demand for independence. Serbia's position more or less mirrored this, being prepared to allow Kosovo enhanced autonomy falling short of independence. Under the Serbian formula, sovereignty would remain with Serbia, but Kosovo would be entirely self-governing. It would not send representatives to the Serbian parliament, and would not have a seat at the UN. NATO-led troops would remain in Kosovo to ensure security, and the issue would be revisited after 20 years. This was rejected by the Kosovo Albanians.

Kosovo itself remained calm, with an 18,500-strong NATO force maintaining security. There were occasional inter-ethnic incidents, and in autumn 2005 armed men reportedly calling themselves 'The Army for Kosovo's Independence' appeared briefly on roads in the west of the province and threatened UN officials with death and kidnapping if they acted in such a way as to prevent Kosovo's independence. They vanished almost as mysteriously as they had appeared, but they served as a reminder that an otherwise peaceful situation could change overnight. Diplomats repeatedly warned Albanian leaders of the need for good behaviour by their supporters so as not to jeopardise hopes of speedy moves towards independence.

By contrast, early summer 2006 saw tensions rising in the Serb-inhabited north of the province. A murder, which Serbs claimed was ethnically motivated, prompted Serbian leaders there to declare a 'state of emergency'. This was followed by the announcement that the UN had begun to deploy 500 extra international police to the region and KFOR, the NATO-led peacekeeping mission, announced it was re-opening a former base in the area. Whether this was an overture to a final spasm of violence and ethnic cleansing in Kosovo remained to be seen.

The talks on Kosovo's status were clearly heading in the direction of independence. The 100,000 Kosovo Serbs – two-thirds of whom live in enclaves across the centre and south, with the remainder in a compact area abutting Serbia – were shocked in February when John Sawers, political director of the UK Foreign and Commonwealth Office, told their representatives that the Contact Group had decided on Kosovo's independence. The UN High Commissioner for Refugees began to prepare for a mass flight. Serbian negotiators predicted that if Kosovo became independent against their government's will, the Serbs in northern Kosovo would hold a referendum on secession from Kosovo. This could provoke violence from Kosovo Albanian extremists.

For the Contact Group, the paramount issue was to deal correctly with the Kosovo Serbs. Given that its members had in effect decided that Kosovo must have independence, as far as they were concerned the talks were principally about the status of the Serbs within Kosovo rather than the status of Kosovo itself.

Though the Kosovo Albanians were confident things were going their way, they suffered domestic upheavals. In March 2005 Ramush Haradinaj, the Kosovo prime minister, resigned after being indicted by the ICTY. His replacement, Bajram Kosumi was seen as weak as he had neither an effective party machine nor a Kosovo Liberation Army (KLA) guerrilla background to enhance his authority. In March 2006 he was replaced by Agim Ceku, the former head of the Kosovo Protection Corps (KPC), a supposed civil emergency force that had grown out of the KLA, the military wing of which Ceku had led during the latter stages of the war. Although he quickly reached out to the Serbian and minority communities, Serbian leaders continued to boycott Kosovo's institutions, including parliament and government. Kosovo's government had become tainted with scandal and corruption, but an expected clean-up following the death of Ibrahim Rugova and replacement of Kosumi did not occur. Though Rugova himself was never regarded as corrupt, many of his ministers were. The transition following his death went remarkably smoothly, with the presidency passing to Famir Sejdiu, a party loyalist and lawyer.

Ahtisaari is expected to propose to the Security Council in Autumn 2006 that Kosovo should become independent, albeit with some limitations on its sovereignty. For example, it would not be permitted to have an army, but the KPC might be given the status of a gendarmerie answering to a ministry of defence. Russia and China are not expected to oppose this. Serbia has argued that this cannot be done without its agreement, since Kosovo is part of its territory and cannot be recognised as another state. However, the Security Council could simply invite UN member states to recognise the new state and pass a new resolution to supersede the current one giving it jurisdiction in Kosovo. Diplomats of Western countries have argued that Kosovo is a unique case and has no ramifications elsewhere, but others are less sure. Russian diplomats, for example, argue that recognition of Kosovo would give Moscow leverage over Georgia because it would suggest that the breakaway provinces of Abkhazia and South Ossetia could follow Kosovo's example.

The loss of Kosovo, if it occurs, seems likely to have a big effect on politics within Serbia, as Serbs regard Kosovo as the cradle of their civilisation. The extreme nationalist Serbian Radical Party looks set to benefit. Though nominally the party is led by Vojislav Seselj, now in detention at the ICTY, real power is in the hands of Tomislav Nikolic, its leader in Belgrade. The party is the largest in the Serbian parliament, but is not in government, though its support helps to keep Kostunica's minority government in power. The Radicals have repositioned themselves: while retaining their belief in a Greater Serbia, they now say they would not go to war to reclaim lost territory and have concentrated on social issues. While Serbia's general economic trends have been good, these have not yet translated into a better standard of living for most Serbians. The official unemployment rate is 32.6%, although the real figure is certainly much less than this. Although no elections are necessary in Serbia until 2007, it is unclear whether the Kostunica government could last until then. An electoral win for the Radical Party would seem likely to return Serbia to international isolation, though coalition politicking could again bar it from appointing a prime minister.

Progress in Bosnia

Bosnia also remained very calm as the ten year anniversary passed of the Srebrenica massacre, the Dayton peace agreement and the deployment of 60,000 NATO troops to Bosnia – all of which occurred in 1995. Since the December 1995 deployment, no foreign peacekeeper has been killed by hostile action. Security is now overseen by a 6,000-strong European Union force, by far the largest EU mission so far, with 200–300 NATO personnel remaining to assist with defence reform and counter-terrorism – watching for Islamic extremists – as well as with finding indicted war criminals.

While the Dayton accord successfully ended Bosnia's war, it is widely felt that the arrangements it set in train need adjustment as the country enters a transitional phase that it hopes will lead to EU membership. With a weak central government, two second tier 'entities' (Republika Srpska and the Croat–Bosniak Federation) and an autonomous zone (Brcko), the administration of Bosnia's 3.5m people is far from efficient. After the US State Department assisted the Bosnians on possible reforms, seven major parties agreed on a package of changes, but on 26 April 2006 this failed to muster enough support in the Bosnian parliament. This left them in limbo, with elections due on 1 October.

Amidst this uncertainty, a change of UN high representative marked a shift to a more hands-off international approach towards Bosnia. In January 2006 Paddy Ashdown retired after four years in the post and was replaced by Christian Schwarz-Schilling. Ashdown, former leader of the UK Liberal Democrat Party, had made liberal use of the Bonn Powers which gave him the right to remove even the highest elected officials from office. His activist interpretation of his mandate helped to ensure that Bosnia fulfilled the 16 conditions laid down by the EU in November 2003 – ranging from police reform to restructuring of the energy sector – for the country to embark on negotiations for an SAA. Talks began in November 1995, leading Ashdown to declare that he was ready to go, having led Bosnia 'from Dayton to Brussels'.

Schwarz-Schilling, a 75-year-old former German minister and businessman with considerable experience of Bosnia, came to the post with a different philosophy. He said he would only use the Bonn Powers in case of a threat to the peace, or in relation to men indicted by the ICTY. He believed it was time for Bosnians to take responsibility for their own future, even if this meant mistakes being made. He is due to be the last high representative, as he expects the Bonn Powers to be abolished in spring 2007. Schwarz-Schilling is likely to remain as EU special representative.

The previous decade's tensions have, however, not completely dissipated. Two developments have revived wartime antipathies. Bosnia's constitutional court ruled on 31 March 2006 that both entities had to change their national symbols, which were deemed anti-constitutional. While the Federation agreed, leaders of Republika Srpska refused to drop the Serbian flag and crest. Meanwhile, between February and May the International Court of Justice in The Hague heard testimony concerning Bosnia's claim, lodged in 1993, that Serbia and Montenegro were committing genocide in the country. A ruling that Bosnia was subjected to genocide could be used politically to question the future existence of the Republika Srpska.

Other Balkan states

Croatia removed an important obstacle to EU membership when information apparently supplied by its intelligence services led to the arrest in Tenerife on 7 December 2005 of General Ante Gotovina, wanted by the ICTY since 2001. In March 2005 the EU had postponed the launch of accession talks until Gotovina's arrest, but talks began in October when Carla Del Ponte informed the EU that Croatia was now fully cooperating with the court. The arrest then followed.

As Croatia thus moved from candidate status to accession talks, the European Council decided on 17 December 2005 to award Macedonia candidate status – recognition of the progress made by Macedonian and ethnic Albanian politicians following the 2001 crisis which brought the country to the brink of civil war. In neighbouring Albania, elections in July 2005 brought back to power Sali Berisha, who had fallen following the collapse of the state into anarchy in 1997. Albania signed an SAA in February 2006. While trafficking and organised crime continue to be problems, progress has been made, particularly in combating the trafficking of illegal migrants and smuggled goods across the Adriatic.

The pull of the EU

Western strategy in the region is based on the pull factor of the EU. Using the Stabilisation and Association process, the EU is seeking to enhance state-building, modernisation and reform, much as it did in the former communist states of eastern and central Europe. On 9 November 2005, the European Commission noted in a new enlargement strategy that for the states of the western Balkans, 'a convincing political perspective for eventual integration into the EU is crucial to keep their reforms on track'. A European Commission statement of 27 January 2006 laid out a series of practical measures the western Balkans needed to follow, especially in the field of regional integration and promoting trade. In spite of this coherent policy, there is increasing worry in the region that the promise of eventual membership given to the western Balkan states by the EU in 2003 may be beginning to dim. Following the rejection of the European constitutional treaty by French and Dutch voters, politicians such as Sarkozy in France and Edmund Stoiber and Angela Merkel in Germany have questioned whether full membership, as opposed to some form of 'privileged' or 'strategic' partnership, should still be on offer for the western Balkans. Such suggestions could undermine Balkan governments' drive to undertake painful reforms. There is also a fear that the Balkan states could suffer collateral damage from other disputes – for example, the EU's 'absorption capacity' could be being used as a convenient excuse by those whose real target is stopping Turkish accession. However, those who remember the Balkan turmoil of the 1990s will wish to ensure that Balkan states are given the necessary incentives to make further strides towards security and prosperity. It is unclear how the EU or other actors could devise such incentives.

Turkey: Loss of Momentum

In mid-2006, three-and-a-half years after it swept to power in the Turkish general elections of November 2002, the moderate Islamist Justice and Development Party (JDP) appeared to have lost direction. The confidence and optimism that it had displayed in its early months of office had been replaced by indecision, inertia and a defiant defensiveness.

Government officials repeatedly defended their record in office, noting that Turkey had been enjoying one of its longest-ever periods of rapid economic growth, accompanied by unprecedented inflows of foreign investment and single digit inflation for the first time in more than 25 years. In October 2005, the government scored a notable success when the European Union began negotiations on Turkey's accession to membership, 18 years after it first applied. The negotiations will continue for some years.

The country's economic success was not a panacea. The JDP had been elected on a pledge to create jobs, but by May 2006 unemployment was higher than it had been when it took office, and the rate seemed set to rise further. While gross national product grew 7.6% in 2005, growth was expected to slow sharply in 2006. Even during the boom of 2002–05, wages had remained static. However, many Turks had gambled on a future increase by taking out consumer loans or shifting purchases from cash to credit cards: the effect was that in 2006 the volume of unpaid credit card bills and bad consumer loans began to climb steeply. It seemed unlikely that there would be an economic collapse similar to the one in 2001 that had helped propel the JDP into power. But the strain on many Turks was spilling over into other areas: an increase in crime and social tensions could be detected, and there was increasing frustration at the government's failure to find a solution for longstanding problems such as the rights of the country's Kurdish minority and the role of Islam in public life. In spite of its EU success, Turkey appeared in 2006 to be in something of a retreat towards a bruised and recalcitrant nationalism.

Foreign relations: lonely present, uncertain future

On 17 December 2004, EU leaders announced that full accession negotiations with Ankara would begin on 3 October 2005 with a view to Turkey becoming the Union's first predominantly Muslim member in around 2014. The understanding was that, by the time the talks began, Turkey would have continued to push ahead with democratic reforms to bring the country closer to EU norms, and would have extended its customs union agreement with the EU to include the ten new members that had joined in May 2004 — among whom was the Republic of Cyprus, which Ankara still refused to recognise.

But by early summer 2005 the atmosphere in the EU had changed, with French and Dutch voters rejecting the proposed EU constitutional treaty. As governments and EU officials scrambled to head off what threatened to be the most serious crisis in the Union's history, opinion polls suggested that the public in most member states was opposed not only to the constitution but to further expansion, and particularly to Turkish membership.

In Turkey, it was not until 29 July 2005 that the government finally signed a protocol extending its customs union to the new EU member states. However, it still refused to recognise Cyprus. Turkey was also lagging on other steps that would smooth its path towards EU membership. The democratisation process had stalled. By late September 2005 there had been no substantive legislative reforms for over a year, and there were problems with implementation of many of the reforms that had reached the statute book. Indeed, there appeared to be little awareness of how much still needed to change. During the first nine months of 2005, plans by a handful of Turkish intellectuals to hold the first-ever international conference in the country on the treatment of the Armenians in the late Ottoman Empire were twice blocked by the courts. The conference was finally held on 24–25 September 2005 as the government realised that banning it again could jeopardise the opening of EU accession negotiations.

As a result, far from being a formality, the meeting of EU foreign ministers in Brussels on 3 October 2005 turned into a protracted struggle as representatives of countries such as France and Austria, in which a majority of the public opposed Turkish membership, sought to delay the opening of accession negotiations. It was not until the early hours of 4 October than an agreement was finally reached and negotiations formally inaugurated. Prime Minister Tayyip Erdogan proclaimed that Turkey had passed a critical test with flying colours, but few were convinced. In fact, the EU had made it clear that the real tests were still to come; Turkey needed not only further democratisation but also to normalise its relations with Cyprus.

There were other signals of trouble ahead. Despite repeated warnings from Brussels, Turkey still refused to open its ports and airports to Greek Cypriot ships and planes, arguing that the customs union agreement applied only to goods not services. Privately, EU officials warned that the accession process could not move forward unless the ports and airports were opened. Meanwhile, in November 2005 the JDP began to lobby the Danish government to close down Roj TV, a Kurdish-language satellite television channel based in Denmark, on the grounds that it was a mouthpiece for the Kurdistan Workers' Party (PKK). Turkey based its argument on the fact that the PKK was included on the EU's list of proscribed terrorist organisations. But the Danish government insisted that court action to close Roj TV needed evidence of a direct link with the PKK. The dispute was continuing when, on 6 February 2006, Austria, which held the rotating EU presidency, announced that Turkey had agreed to align itself with the EU's common position on terrorism, including the list of proscribed terrorist organisations. But on 16 February 2006, Turkey invited Hamas leader Khaled Meshal to Ankara, where he held a series of meetings with leading members of the JDP, including Foreign Minister Abdullah Gul. Hamas was on the same EU list of proscribed terrorist organisations as the PKK.

It soon emerged that Meshal's visit had been the brainchild of Ahmet Davutoglu, a former academic who now served as Erdogan's chief foreign-policy adviser, and had taken place despite vigorous opposition from the Turkish Ministry of Foreign Affairs. Not surprisingly, the visit severely strained Ankara's already troubled relations with Israel, dealing an apparently fatal blow to what had been touted in the late 1990s as an emerging regional alliance. To make matters worse, Meshal flew from Ankara to Tehran where he publicly re-stated Hamas's commitment to violence and its refusal to recognise the state of Israel.

Washington's public reaction was restrained. Privately, US officials appeared more bewildered than angry. Washington's muted approach appeared to sum up the state of US–Turkish relations: long gone was the warmth of the months following the 11 September 2001 terrorist attacks on the United States, when Washington had frequently cited Turkey as a model for other Muslim nations to follow. Following tensions over the US-led intervention in Iraq in 2003, when Turkey refused to allow a northern arm of the invasion to be launched from its territory, this was replaced by pragmatism and a realisation in Ankara that Turkey needed good relations with the United States more than it wanted them. An official visit to Washington by Erdogan in June 2005 was followed by a string of visits by US officials to Ankara in late 2005 and early 2006. Publicly, both countries were keen to reiterate the importance of the bilateral ties, but privately US officials expressed frustration at the low level of intelligence cooperation, particularly on organisations providing logistical support for transnational militant Islamist groups. On the Turkish side, wounded pride at what was seen as exclusion from consideration during the formulation of US policies towards the region was compounded by opposition to the policies themselves, particularly the US military occupation of Iraq. Tensions were exacerbated by Washington's failure either to move against PKK camps in the mountains of northern Iraq or to allow Turkey to launch a unilateral military operation. Turkish officials raised the issue of the PKK at each meeting with their US counterparts but received little but expressions of sympathy in return. Privately, US officials admitted that they did not have sufficient available military resources to launch an operation in extremely difficult terrain and were wary of antagonising the Iraqi Kurds, who were reluctant either to confront the PKK or to tolerate Turkish forces in their territory.

Washington's refusal to move against the PKK further fuelled anti-Americanism amongst the Turkish public, which blamed Washington for the violence in Iraq and by early 2006 feared that the United States was preparing a military strike against Iran. The depth of anti-American sentiment was demonstrated by the release in February 2006 of the film 'Valley of the Wolves in Iraq'. Based on a popular television series about the Turkish underworld, the film portrayed a fictional response to the real-life detention of Turkish special forces by US troops in northern Iraq in July 2003. Virulently anti-American and anti-Semitic in tone, the film proved a huge success and broke Turkish box office records. Erdogan and half of his cabinet attended the premiere and gave enthusiastic reviews to journalists outside.

The 'Valley of the Wolves in Iraq' owed some of its success to its explicit nostalgia for the Ottoman Empire. It reflected a widespread, though rarely publicly expressed, resentment at what many Turks, particularly on the religious right, see as the usurpation by the United States of Turkey's role as the natural imperial power in the Middle East. The Iraq War not only distanced Ankara from Washington politically but brought the US physically into the region through the occupation of Iraq. The American presence on Turkey's border has severely limited Ankara's options in northern Iraq, the border area about which it is most concerned. Turkish nationalists still harbour recidivist hopes of reasserting formal or informal control over the oilfields of Kirkuk. They also fear that the emergence of a Kurdish political entity in northern Iraq could serve both as an inspiration for Turkey's own Kurdish minority and as a platform for PKK attacks into Turkey. Yet throughout late 2005 and the first half of 2006, Turkish officials privately admitted that the risk of a US military response had severely reduced their ability to exert pressure on the Iraqi Kurds, either to prevent the gradual emergence of a Iraqi Kurdish state or to persuade them to give concessions to Turkish oil companies around Kirkuk. It had also made it virtually impossible for Turkey to launch unilateral military operations against PKK camps in northern Iraq.

This constraint on Turkey's ability to exert influence in the region has also forced it to explore alternative forms of leverage, for example by strengthening ties with Syria and Iran, both of whom have Kurdish minorities and have no wish to see an independent Kurdish state on their borders. An upsurge in ethnic unrest in Iran in late 2005 and the first half of 2006 conversely gave Tehran a reason to forge a closer relationship with Turkey, not least because one of the main Iranian Kurdish militant groups, the Party of Free Life of Kurdistan (PJAK), has very close ties with the PKK.

Iran has long been an anathema to the secularist Turkish military. However, Turkish military officials admitted that in late 2005 and early 2006 there was a marked contrast between the respective willingness of Tehran and Washington to take action against the PKK. Official contacts between Turkey and Iran expanded and there was also a substantial increase in unofficial meetings, including between the two countries' militaries. In late April 2006, Iran attacked PJAK/PKK units in the mountains of southwest Iran and, almost simultaneously, the Turkish military launched its largest anti-PKK military operation in a decade, as over 200,000 troops were deployed through southeast Turkey. Although Turkish military officials denied that the two operations were coordinated, privately they acknowledged that they had received prior notification from Iran and that one reason for the timing of their operation was to cut off PJAK/PKK militants fleeing the Iranian army and attempting to transit Turkey en route to camps in northern Iraq.

In early 2006, the threat of international isolation as the result of US-led pressure to suspend its uranium-enrichment programme gave Iran another reason to bolster its ties with Turkey. Ankara has repeatedly defended Iran's right to nuclear energy, not least because Turkey plans to build five nuclear-power plants. Yet Turkish officials have also made clear their opposition to Iran acquiring a nuclear-weapon capability. Ankara has said it would abide by any decisions taken by the UN, including the imposition of sanctions against Tehran. However, in practice much would depend on the nature of possible sanctions. In 2005 bilateral trade between Iran and Turkey grew by 57.1% to $4.4bn. By 2007, Iran is expected to account for 25% of Turkey's imports of natural gas. Shutting off the gas supply would damage Turkish industry and leave many homes without heating, and would also, under take-or-pay provisions in its contract with Tehran, leave Turkey with a bill of approximately $1bn per year. These economic considerations, combined with high levels of anti-Americanism in Turkey, would also make it difficult for Ankara to support any US-led military initiative against Iran.

Domestic politics: old problems unresolved

For most Turks, EU membership has always been as much about status and psychological reassurance as about shared values. It was a chance to number themselves as part of what they regard as an elite of nations, regardless of their reservations about EU policies. This view has helped domestic proponents of greater democratisation, freedom of speech and human rights to use the EU process to counter both the authoritarian reflexes of the Turkish establishment and the conservative instincts of the mass of the population. Successive governments have tried to strike the right balance between making too few concessions to the demands of EU candidacy, which could have antagonised Brussels, and making too many, which could have alienated nationalist sentiments at home. Yet even the most enthusiastic proponents of accession have often expressed doubts about whether a union of Christian nations would ever accept a Muslim country, regardless of whether it met all the criteria for membership.

These doubts were reinforced by the wrangling in Brussels in October 2005. Over the months that followed, the government did little to move the accession process forward – nor was there any public pressure for it to do so. By March 2006 only 58% of Turks still supported EU accession, down from over 70% a year earlier. EU membership had slipped out of the headlines and public attention had turned to the two issues that have dominated the country's domestic agenda for more than a decade: the Turkish establishment's interpretation of the principle of secularism, and the Kurdish issue.

On 12 August 2005 Erdogan travelled to Diyarbakir, the largest city in the predominantly Kurdish southeast of the country, where he explicitly acknowledged the existence of a distinct Kurdish identity, albeit within a unified Turkish state and nation. But neither then nor over the months that followed did he give any indication of what this acknowledgement would mean. By May 2006 there was still no sign that the government would formulate a strategy to address the web of social, economic, political and cultural issues that constitute what is commonly referred to as the 'Kurdish problem'. The only area in which there had been discernible progress was broadcasting. In March 2006, two privately owned local television channels were allowed to begin broadcasting in Kurdish. But bureaucratic obstacles and strict controls on content, format and time meant that by May 2006 they were restricted to two 45-minute programmes a week on cultural issues. Radio stations playing Kurdish songs continued to have their licenses suspended or revoked if they broadcast anything deemed to encourage separatist sentiments.

Under pressure from the EU, the Turkish authorities had allowed private language schools to offer Kurdish courses in March 2004. But by May 2006 all the courses had closed down as a result of either bureaucratic harassment or lack of demand in the most impoverished region of the country. Turkey still refused to allow Kurdish in the state-controlled education system, either as a foreign language or as a medium of instruction.

It was not clear what the country's Kurds wanted, beyond improvements in economic and social conditions in southeast Turkey. Public opinion polls and academic studies in the region leave researchers vulnerable to prosecution for encouraging separatist sentiment. Formation of an explicitly Kurdish political party or non-governmental organisation (NGO) remains forbidden by law. Political parties and NGOs primarily run by Kurds have traditionally been caught between persecution and the threat of closure by the state, on the one hand, and pressure from the PKK, which is reluctant to allow any organisation to usurp its self-proclaimed role as the sole representative of the country's Kurds, on the other.

After abandoning its unilateral five-year cease-fire in June 2004, the PKK stepped up its armed campaign through 2005, combining a rural insurgency in the mountains of southeast Turkey with an urban bombing campaign in the west that primarily targeted the tourism industry, Turkey's largest source of foreign currency. No reliable figures were available, but approximately 100 members of the Turkish forces and 400–500 PKK militants were believed to have been killed in southeast Turkey in 2005. Poor training and limited tradecraft combined with high levels of penetration by Turkish intelligence reduced the effectiveness of the urban bombing campaign. Nevertheless, eight people were killed by PKK bombs in western Turkey in 2005; five of these, including two foreign tourists, died in an explosion on a minibus in the Aegean resort of Kusadasi on 16 July 2005.

The PKK's use of urban terrorism and the tactics it adopted in rural areas – where it focused primarily on mines, ambushes and long-range harassing fire – demonstrated its military weakness compared with the early 1990s when it was able to control large swathes of the countryside after dark. Although it retained around 5,000 militants under arms, the PKK also seemed to have only limited access to more sophisticated weaponry, such as shoulder-launched surface-to-air-missiles. But it nevertheless appeared to have sufficient resources to maintain its armed campaign at its current level almost indefinitely. Under the prevailing circumstances, giving in to the PKK's only clearly articulated goal – the release of its leader Abdullah Ocalan, serving a life sentence on the prison island of Imrali – would be political suicide for any Turkish government.

After the lull during the winter, when most of the mountain passes in southeast Turkey are blocked by snow, the PKK resumed its insurgency in spring 2006. In late March 2006, the funerals of 14 PKK militants killed in a firefight with the Turkish security forces triggered a week of rioting in ten different cities, in which 17 people were killed and over 300 injured. Alarmingly, there were also clashes between PKK supporters and groups of Turkish ultra-nationalists in the shantytowns of Istanbul which, as a result of migration from the countryside, now has the largest Kurdish population of any city in the world.

The Turkish army then launched its largest anti-PKK military operation in a decade as over 200,000 troops were deployed to sweep the southeast for PKK units and disrupt the organisation's supply lines from its main camps in the mountains of northern Iraq. Turkish Chief of Staff General Hilmi Ozkok announced that, despite warnings from both the Iraqi Kurds and the US, Turkey would launch cross-border operations against the PKK camps in Iraq if the need arose. In May 2006 Turkish intelligence reports indicated that the PKK was planning an urban terrorism campaign in western Turkey during the summer.

The upsurge in PKK-related violence through 2005 and early 2006 weakened public morale in Turkey and brought the Turkish military back onto the political stage at a time when the government was coming under increasing pressure to ease restrictions inherent in the Turkish establishment's interpretation of secularism.

Although it has consistently rejected the label, ever since its establishment in 2001 the JDP has been regarded as an Islamist party by both opponents and supporters. Even if its 2002 election victory was partly attributable to disenchantment with all of the older political parties, there is also little doubt that many conservative Turks voted for the JDP because they believed that it would increase access to religious education and relax the ban on women wearing Islamic headscarves in public institutions. This prohibition effectively bars women wishing to wear headscarves from working as civil servants or studying at university.

During its first year in office the JDP tentatively tried both to increase the number of religious schools and to relax the headscarf ban. However, it retreated each time in the face of opposition from the secular establishment, led by the Turkish military. Initially, the JDP appeared prepared to bide its time, calculating that the EU process would both reduce the political influence of the military and allow it to relax the traditional interpretation of secularism in Turkey under the EU's apparent commitment to guaranteeing freedom of religion. As a result, during the early years of the JDP's term in office its more religiously committed supporters were often amongst the most enthusiastic advocates of the EU accession process.

However, doubts that had begun in March 2004, when head-coverings were prohibited in French schools, were reinforced in November 2005 when the European Court of Human Rights upheld the headscarf ban in Turkish universities. The court rejected an appeal by Leyla Sahin, a Turkish student who had been excluded from classes for refusing to uncover her head. No longer able to use the EU accession process as an excuse for prevarication – and with fresh elections due by the beginning of November 2007 at the latest – by May 2006 the JDP leadership was coming under increasing pressure from its conservative supporters.

Any move to increase the number of religious schools or ease the headscarf ban would be certain to provoke a response from the Turkish military. Under Ozkok, the military had adopted a relatively low public profile, intervening to apply pressure on politicians only as a last resort. Ozkok knew that being too assertive could jeopardise the prospect of EU accession negotiations. But by mid-2006, no such constraints applied. Ozkok was due to retire in August 2006 and all his potential successors were known hardliners. Many in the higher echelons of the Turkish General Staff were privately scathing about what they regarded as Ozkok's passivity. Several broke with Turkish military tradition by issuing public statements critical of the government without clearing them with Ozkok.

There were also signs that nationalist and secularist elements in the Turkish judiciary were becoming more assertive. On 16 December 2005, Orhan Pamuk, Turkey's best-known novelist, appeared in court accused of 'insulting Turkishness' – a charge carrying a maximum sentence of three years in prison – after telling a Swiss newspaper that 1m Armenians had been massacred in the final years of the Ottoman Empire. After an initial hearing, the case against Pamuk was quietly dropped on 22 January 2006. But prosecutions of less prominent intellectuals followed. By May 2006 more than 50 writers and journalists were facing charges related to freedom of expression.

The judiciary also began to apply pressure to the JDP. On 24 April 2006 a local JDP mayor was arrested for chewing gum while laying a wreath at a statue of Mustafa Kemal Ataturk (1881–1938), the staunchly secularist founder of the modern Turkish republic. On 10 May 2006, Erdogan walked out of a ceremony to mark the anniversary of the Turkish Supreme Court of Appeal after the court's president launched a thinly veiled attack on the JDP government and warned that the republic was under threat from separatism and religious fundamentalism.

On 17 May 2006, Alparslan Aslan, a 28-year-old lawyer with ultranationalist and Islamist sympathies, walked into the Council of State building in Ankara, shot dead one of the judges, Mustafa Yucel Ozbilgin, and wounded four others. When he was arrested, Aslan told police that he had carried out the assassination in protest at the Council of State's rejection of an appeal against the headscarf ban. The attack brought the long-running tensions in Turkish society between Islamists and secularists out into the open. Secularists claimed that Aslan was acting on behalf of all those who opposed the headscarf ban; Islamists, including the JDP government, declared that Aslan's ultranationalist sympathies were proof of a larger conspiracy involving elements within the military. In fact, police investigations suggested that the attack had been at Aslan's initiative and that any conspiracy involved less than half-a-dozen like-minded acquaintances with varying degrees of knowledge of his plans.

Nevertheless, Ozbilgin's funeral turned into a secularist and anti-JDP rally. It was attended by all military personnel stationed in the capital, including the top commanders who walked through the streets to the ceremony to the cheers of secularist mourners. Erdogan did not attend.

The JDP's uncertain prospects

During its first years in office the JDP's reluctance to tackle potentially contentious issues, such as the Kurdish problem or the role of religion in public life, had
appeared to be an asset. After a decade of short-lived, fractious coalitions, the
election in November 2002 of a single-party government with a comfortable parliamentary majority had brought the country much-needed stability at a time when
the economy was beginning to recover from recession. Nor did the JDP appear
to need to set its own agenda: the previous government had initiated a domestic reform programme to enable Turkey to begin accession negotiations with the
EU and had agreed an economic stabilisation programme with the International
Monetary Fund in 2001. But by mid-2006, the JDP appeared to have no strategy for
what to do next. Strong economic growth had been based on investor confidence,
an overvalued Turkish lira – which reduced the cost of the imported industrial
inputs – and a credit-fuelled consumer boom. Since this mixture had also produced
a high trade deficit, the prospect of a devaluation of the lira threatened to increase
the cost of imports, reduce economic growth and increase unemployment.

The run-up to the opening of EU accession negotiations had provided the
JDP with a degree of protection against the secular establishment, particularly
the military. Provided that it did not attempt anything too radical, the JDP knew
that the military would not risk jeopardising Turkey's relations with the EU by
being too assertive. But by May 2006, as the prospect of EU membership began to
slip off the public agenda, so too did the protection it had provided the JDP.

In the aftermath of the attack on the Council of State on 17 May 2006, the
various elements in the Turkish judicial system issued a joint statement calling
on all institutions 'responsible for protecting secularism' to 'do their duty' – a
clear reference to the military. With parliament due to appoint a new president in
April 2007, and with the JDP known to be keen to choose somebody from within
its own ranks, tensions between secularists and Islamists are expected to rise still
further through late 2006 and early 2007. In the absence of an effective parliamentary opposition, the secularists are likely to turn to the Turkish military, not
to oust the JDP or to seize power, but to be more assertive in applying pressure
on the government and constraining its policies.

Developments in European Defence

EU and NATO: deployment capabilities increased

Both the European Union and NATO continued to adjust their roles in 2005. The
EU expanded the scope and reach of its crisis-management operations, launching a number of mainly civilian missions. At the same time, efforts to strengthen

European military capabilities through cooperation within the framework of European Security and Defence Policy (ESDP) made progress, with plans for 1,500-strong rapid-reaction 'battlegroups' proceeding and the European Defence Agency (EDA) up and running and fully staffed. ESDP had outgrown the focus on Europe and Balkan-style peacekeeping envisioned at its creation in 1999.

NATO meanwhile pursued a complex agenda. The NATO Response Force (NRF), due to be fully operational by November 2006, undertook its first missions, and the Alliance's footprint in Afghanistan expanded significantly. Efforts to strengthen the political dialogue among allies characterised the meetings of NATO foreign ministers in Vilnius on 20–21 April 2005 and defence ministers in Berlin on 13–14 September 2005, as NATO leaders tried to reach a common understanding of what a transformed Alliance should be able to do. Beyond this very broad issue, three particular areas of discussion between members were noteworthy. First, an important issue still under debate is common funding for operations, which if agreed would change the incentive structure for NATO countries to participate. As it is, NATO missions are paid for almost exclusively under the 'costs lie where they fall' principle, which means that those allies who contribute to the effort and accept the risks also have to pay for most of the operational costs. Secondly, a new initiative is under way for NATO to create a framework for structured cooperation with states beyond the Euro-Atlantic realm such as Australia, Japan, New Zealand and South Korea, as well as to expand cooperation with Finland and Sweden, which both remain militarily non-aligned, although they joined NATO's Partnership for Peace initiative in 1994. Thirdly, NATO continued its efforts to develop partnerships in the Gulf region.

EU missions grow

As of April 2006, the EU was running no less than 11 missions, following the completion of the 'rule of law' mission *Operation Themis* in Georgia in July 2005, and the police mission *Operation Proxima* in Macedonia in December. *Operation Althea* in Bosnia and Herzegovina, a mission the EU took over from NATO's Stabilisation Force (SFOR) in December 2004, continued to be by far the largest EU mission, with some 6,200 troops deployed. This operation, carried out under the so-called 'Berlin Plus' arrangement in coordination with NATO, has revealed persistent difficulties in NATO–EU cooperation: although military cooperation is working to a satisfactory degree, the political bodies find it difficult to strengthen their strategic dialogue. Delays in decision-making because of diverging views in NATO and EU bodies in relation to *Operation Althea* have been reported. A similar pattern seemed to emerge in relation to EU and NATO support for the African Union's mission AMIS II in Sudan. Although the EU uses the European Airlift Centre (EAC) in Eindhoven, and NATO employs the Air Movement Coordination Cell (AMCC) at Supreme Headquarters Allied Powers Europe

(SHAPE), contact between the staffs is close and constant. However, the political discussion leading to the establishment of two distinct support operations was marred by bickering. Except for matters of operational planning, the EU–NATO partnership remains limited.

In 2005, the EU launched nine civilian crisis-management missions under the ESDP umbrella.

- Since April 2005, a police mission in Kinshasa, Democratic Republic of the Congo (DRC), EUPOL Kinshasa, has monitored, mentored and advised local police.
- This mission is complemented by EUSEC Congo, launched in June 2005 with a 12-month mandate, which assists and advises Congolese security sector officials in an attempt to build capacity in accordance with international standards and with respect to the rule of law.
- EUJUST LEX, launched in July 2005, trains Iraqi judicial officials outside Iraq. Participating EU member states aim to complete 21 training courses, including senior management courses, by June 2006.
- Through AMIS II, the EU has since July 2005 supported the African Union in Darfur with airlift capabilities provided by France, Germany and Greece and coordinated through the EAC in Eindhoven, which processes AU demands.
- Since September 2005, the EU has run the Aceh Monitoring Mission (AMM), which monitors the implementation of the peace agreement between the government of Indonesia and the Free Aceh Movement (GAM). Several ASEAN countries as well as Norway and Switzerland participate. AMM assists with the demobilisation of GAM, and the decommissioning and destruction of weapons. At its height, the mission involved some 225 civilian observers; it runs 11 dispersed district offices as well as four mobile decommissioning teams.
- In late 2005 the EU also became involved in the Palestinian Territories. A monitoring mission at the Rafah border crossing between Gaza and Egypt, EU BAM Rafah, has been operational since 30 November 2005. The mission has a 12-month mandate and is some 70 strong. The EU monitors and verifies the performance of the Palestinian Authority (PA) but does not undertake substitution tasks.
- Since 1 January 2006, the EU has also run EUPOL COPPS, a capacity-building police mission in the Palestinian Territories. Headquartered in the Palestinian Interior Ministry and with a field presence, the mission consists of some 33 unarmed personnel. It helps the PA establish effective policing according to international standards and is scheduled to last for three years.

- In December 2005, the EU launched a 69-strong border-monitoring mission at the Ukrainian and Moldovan border, EU BAM Moldova and Ukraine. The mission has a two-year mandate, is headquartered in Odessa and has five field offices. It includes border police and customs officials in an effort to prevent smuggling, trafficking and customs fraud while building capacity in both Ukraine and Moldova.
- As a follow-on from *Operation Proxima*, the EU launched a policy advisory team mission, EUPAT, in FYROM on 15 December 2005. Some 30 advisers mentor local forces and work on the implementation of police reform.

The EU approved a military mission to help secure the elections in the DRC scheduled for 30 July 2006. The mission came at the request of the UN on 27 December 2005 and was to be conducted to support the MONUC mission already in place. The EU mission was planned to have an overall strength of some 2,000 troops, of which only a part would be on the ground in the DRC. A battalion-sized, over-the-horizon force would act as rapid-reaction reinforcement. The deployment was planned to begin some 50 days before the polls opened and would last for four months. With Germany to act as lead nation, the German parliament approved the mission on 1 June. The European Council was scheduled to formally launch the mission in mid-June. France and Germany had pledged some 750–800 troops each and at least 16 other states would contribute, including about 100 troops each from Spain and Portugal and 50 each from Belgium and Sweden.

Parallel to the operational activities, the EU has expanded its exercise programme. From 22 November to 1 December 2005, the EU conducted its first-ever military exercise, *Milex 05*, which tested parallel planning of two headquarters, a French Operations Headquarters and a German Force Headquarters, using a fictional scenario. On 5 April 2006, the EU furthermore conducted *Evac 06*, an exercise which simulated the launch and conduct of an EU operation to evacuate thousands of EU citizens and others from a country outside the EU in which levels of internal violence had escalated.

Although EU activity has been widely spread geographically, some missions have been of a rather symbolic character. Most importantly, a coherent strategy seems to be missing, with EU member states exploiting some opportunities but limiting their engagement in others. The comparative advantage of the EU in crisis management is likely to be its comprehensiveness: the combination of simultaneous military and civilian activities. The emphasis so far has been on civilian missions, but experience shows that simple sequencing of military and civilian missions is inadequate, and that the ability to run parallel and coherent missions is critical. Nonetheless, as the EU continues to build up both civilian and military capabilities and its member states and institutions accumulate experience, the EU will potentially command an impressive set of crisis-management tools.

An illustration of such capabilities is the European Gendarmerie Force, based in Italy, which will be operational from January 2006. Gendarmeries, or para-military police forces, combine policing expertise with the capacity for robust action and can be very useful in stabilisation, in particular in circumstances in which there is a transition from military to civilian missions. France, Italy, the Netherlands, Portugal and Spain have together made commitments to an 800-strong force that can be deployed globally within 30 days.

NATO: new deployments

The NRF, which is to provide a force of up to 25,000 troops globally deploy-able at five days' notice for a wide range of missions, is due to become fully operational by November 2006. Made up almost entirely of European military personnel, the NRF is a crucial element of the Alliance's transformation efforts. NATO member states pledge troops to NRF rotation cycles. Directly before the multinational NRF units are put on operational standby for six months, they undergo a six-month joint training period, after which they are evaluated. SHAPE certifies whether the units brought together by the member states are combat ready. The training and standby phase, usually followed by a six-month refitting phase, make up a full NRF cycle. Most forces participating in the NRF are 'double-' or even 'triple-hatted', the latter meaning that they, in principle, are available for NATO, EU and national missions. So far, rotation schedules have been drawn up that deconflict the NRF and EU battlegroups. No units will be assigned to both forces at the same time. Troops pledged by contributing states should thus be available even during parallel deployments of the NRF and EU battlegroups. However, whether the same holds true for critical enablers such as airlift remains to be seen. There remained doubts in mid-2006 over whether the NRF would meet the November deadline; General James L. Jones, Supreme Allied Commander Europe, indicated in February that about 25% of the force was still not committed. Slight improvements had been made before NRF-7, the force that is to achieve Full Operation Capability in November, assumed its oper-ational standby period on 1 July. However, by mid-May the NRF was still 18% short of its required strength, with the gaps being mainly in the areas of logistics, combat support and combat service support.

The first NRF deployments occurred in 2005, in relief operations in the United States and Pakistan. In the wake of Hurricane Katrina, which devastated coastal areas of Louisiana and Mississippi on 29 August, the US government requested food as well as medical and logistical supplies. Following the 8 October 2005 earthquake in Pakistan, the NRF undertook a relief mission lasting until 1 February 2006 and involving up to 1,000 troops. NATO forces delivered about

3,500 tonnes of relief supplies on 160 flights, moved more than 7,600 people affected by the disaster, and treated more than 8,000 patients.

An important milestone was due with a live exercise, *Steadfast Jaguar 06*, to be conducted on the Cap Verde islands between 1 June and 12 July 2006, with the main active phase scheduled for 15–28 June. Some 7,000 NRF troops were to be deployed – less than the originally planned 8,000 due to budgetary problems. In the run up to the exercise, NATO found it difficult to assemble an adequate number of helicopters, a problem that had already plagued the Alliance in Afghanistan.

The expansion of the International Security Assistance Force (ISAF) in Afghanistan is NATO's most important and ambitious venture in 2006. On 8 December 2005, NATO foreign ministers endorsed the expansion under which an additional 6,000 troops would be deployed, bringing the potential total to more than 15,000. In this Stage 3 of ISAF's expansion, NATO would deploy to six additional provinces (Day Kundi; Helmand; Kandahar; Nimroz; Uruzgan; Zabul) in southern Afghanistan.

Four additional Provincial Reconstruction Teams would be established in Helmand, Kandahar, Uruzgan and Zabul. While ISAF and the US-led coalition operation *Operation Enduring Freedom* would continue to have separate mandates, ISAF was expanding into parts of Afghanistan in which the distinction between stabilisation and security missions on the one hand and counter-terrorism operations on the other was blurred. The southern provinces of Afghanistan suffer from higher levels of violence and insurgency activity than the areas where NATO had been active so far (see Afghanistan section, pages 327–336).

Aside from Afghanistan, NATO continues its KFOR mission in Kosovo, with 18,500 troops deployed (see Balkans section, pages 150–157). It has also been engaged in Darfur, where the Alliance supports the AU mission AMIS II. NATO has trained AU troops in strategic planning and operational procedures, airlifted about 5,000 African peacekeepers between July and October 2005 and is undertaking another airlift phase related to troop rotation between February and May 2006. No NATO troops were deployed to Darfur. At the request of the UN secretary-general, NATO, as of 29 March 2006, has agreed to study options for continued support for AU missions and also possible UN follow-on missions. However, neither a leading role for NATO nor a NATO ground force is under discussion (see Sudan section, pages 251–259).

Matching capabilities to political will

A persistent problem facing European governments is how to match military capabilities to political commitments. The divergence between what leaders sign up to in collective frameworks such as NATO or the EU and their readiness to provide the necessary forces to meet such commitments has become a significant obstacle to force generation and undermines the credibility of coalition operations. Within NATO, the debate about the deployment of some 1,400 Dutch soldiers planned for the Stage 3 expansion of ISAF highlighted these issues. When the Dutch government announced its intention in December 2005, it ran into considerable domestic opposition. A leaked Dutch military intelligence report warned of the increased risk to the deployed forces in the southern provinces of Afghanistan. In addition, some parts of the political spectrum in the Netherlands were disillusioned with US policy in the region and hence reluctant to increase Dutch commitments. While parliament on 2 February 2006 approved the deployment with a clear majority, an eight-week-long debate had undermined NATO credibility, complicated the planning processes of other major contributors, notably Canada and the United Kingdom, and undermined the cohesion of the ruling coalition in the Netherlands. Though such debates will be different in each country, due to different national strategic cultures and foreign-policy traditions, they could become more intense as multinational operations become more demanding and dangerous.

Within the EU, discussions surrounding the planned mission in support of the UN in the DRC demonstrated further uncertainty. Three months passed between the 27 December 2005 UN secretary-general's request for support and the 23 March 2006 Council of the European Union decision to launch planning efforts for the mission. EU member states then found it difficult to use the tools at their disposal. Although the planned EU battlegroups were not yet fully operational, Initial Operational Capability in 2006 was to be provided by Franco-German battlegroups with Belgian support. The new German government nonetheless proved reluctant to accept the responsibility due to several domestic concerns, including the lack of training and equipment of the Bundeswehr, the German armed forces, for such a deployment. Minister of Defence Franz Josef Jung (CDU) in February 2006 rejected a German lead role, but changed his mind in early March 2006 on the condition that other EU member states would share the burden and that there would be a precise UN mandate, limiting the duration and scope of the deployment.

Work on the improvement of capabilities has proceeded with mixed results. Within the EU, the EDA has seen its workload expand considerably after becoming fully operational in 2005. Its most visible initiative to date has been the establishment of a voluntary code of conduct for defence procurement, which was due to come into effect on 1 July 2006. Under Article 296 of the Treaty on European Union, defence procurement is exempted from the rules of the internal market. The code of conduct requires those governments who choose to abide by it to open contracts worth more than €1 million to EU-wide competition and publicise them through a single online portal, as well as defining transparent criteria for selecting the successful bidder. The code has been criticised for being non-binding and non-enforceable. Furthermore, some exemptions will remain, such as nuclear-weapons-related items and propulsion systems, as well as cryptographic equipment. The EDA will monitor member states' performance, but will essentially have to rely on peer pressure and collective shaming to have any sanctioning effect on defectors.

There are further examples that suggest that the EDA could play a role as a catalyst for the development of European capabilities if member states were to allow it to do so. On 13 October 2005, for example, ten member states agreed at an informal EDA steering board meeting to set up a working group to address the shortfall in air-to-air refuelling. At the informal EU defence ministers' meeting on 6–7 March 2006, member states in principle agreed to pursue a joint research and technology (R&T) initiative through the EDA. Difficulties remain with the two biggest R&T spenders in the EU, France and the UK, at opposing ends of the spectrum. Whereas France favours an R&T programme to be run by the EDA, the UK prefers to fund ad hoc projects. Nonetheless, new impulses are clearly visible.

The EU battlegroup initiative, begun in November 2004, also made progress. During 2005 the EU organised two Battle Group Coordination Conferences, leading to further pledges bringing the total to 18 battlegroups. It is envisioned that a maximum of two of these battlegroups would be deployable simultaneously. Battlegroups are on standby for six-month periods, and all slots up to 2010 have been filled. The initiative has begun to influence national defence debates, particularly in smaller EU member states. In Sweden, for example, the government made clear that it viewed its responsibility as lead nation for a battlegroup to become operational in 2008 as a crucial driver of programmes in transport and command and control. In Ireland, there was a continuing discussion about amending legislation which has been interpreted by the government as preventing Irish participation in the initiative. The 18 battlegroups are scheduled to become operational between 2005 and 2012.

According to the EU Presidency Report on ESDP published in December 2005, EU members had finalised the so-called 'Requirements Catalogue 05', identifying what military capabilities were needed in order to fulfil the roles the EU wanted to take on. The Requirements Catalogue, based on a range of illustrative scenarios, details the military units necessary to deliver the capabilities needed. This was an important step as the EU worked towards its Headline Goal 2010, adopted in 2004. The EU measures its progress on closing existing capabilities shortfalls in six-monthly reports, the Capabilities Improvement Charts. Of a list of 64 originally identified shortfalls, no less than 52 still existed unmitigated by May 2006 – though some could not be fixed quickly. However, the fact that projects had been initiated in 30 of the 52 areas suggested that gradual progress was being made.

At the national level, the signals continue to be mixed. Italy's defence budget was cut in both 2005 and 2006. Whereas in 2005 cuts focused heavily on investment, severely delaying several programmes, in 2006 funding for running costs was cut as well. The reductions put into jeopardy the reform effort that the Italian armed forces were undertaking and also raised questions over whether Italy's growing international deployments were sustainable. Over the previous three years Italy was second only to the UK in the EU with regards to its provision of troops to international peacekeeping missions, continuously deploying some 8,000–10,000 troops. Similarly, budget cuts scheduled for 2006–08 have slowed Czech reform efforts, and in Sweden the 2005–07 defence bill introduced cuts that would see the defence budget slip below 1.5% of GDP. Such reductions make it difficult for armed forces to take on an increasing number of challenging deployments while trying to reform.

The logic for pooling resources and cooperating in various ways is therefore strong. For example, France, which already has similar bilateral arrangements with Germany and the UK, created a permanent bilateral defence council with Spain on 10 November 2005. There is also a range of specific initiatives. In May 2005, France, Sweden and the UK agreed to pool €60m worth of technological demonstration programme funding to collaborate on a future land-combat missile system known as the European Modular Missile. Germany, Italy and Spain also voiced interest in this project. The Franco-British aircraft carrier cooperation programme advanced, with France to use a British design for its new vessel. The two countries also announced on 24 January 2006 that they would in future aim to better use their research budgets by undertaking joint work, for example, on lightweight radars for missiles and unmanned aerial vehicles (UAVs).

The Asian tsunami of December 2004, Hurricane Katrina of August 2005 and the earthquake in Pakistan of October 2005 – not to mention the deployments in Iraq and Afghanistan – were reminders of the importance of airlift. In the case of the Pakistan earthquake, countries willing to provide relief supplies engaged in a bidding war for leasing privately owned aircraft, with NATO allies reportedly bidding against each other to secure capacity. Since then, the Strategic Airlift Interim Solution (SALIS) has become operational: NATO allies on 23 January 2006 signed a contract with the Leipzig-based Ruslan SALIS corporation to charter up to six AN124-100 large transport planes, each able to carry up to 120 tonnes of cargo. Under the three-year contract renewable annually until 2012, NATO allies are committed to 2,000 flying hours a year at a cost of approximately €38m. Available since early February 2006, two aircraft are at the full-time disposal of both NATO and the EU, an additional two at six days' notice and the final two at nine days' notice. Significant portions have been taken by Germany (750 hours per year) and France (450 hours per year). The SALIS agreement fills an important gap, since the Airbus A400M transport plane is not expected to be available before 2009.

Additional steps forward in European security and defence capabilities are occurring less visibly in national, bilateral, multilateral and NATO and EU arenas. It will be some years before there is a significant increase in Europe's force-projection capabilities. However, in spite of setbacks and political uncertainties, the elements appear to be falling into place. Increasing experience of EU and NATO missions will help further clarify the need for enhanced capabilities and focus defence-policy debates in European capitals. The development of EU battle-groups and the NRF reaching full operational capability will mean that, from 2007, permanent high-readiness forces will be available within both frameworks for deployment, including combat missions. Both forces, however, are limited in that they are essentially initial-entry forces, self-sustainable for 30 days for the NRF or up to 120 days for the EU battlegroups. With a restricted but clearly visible military dimension, as well as crisis-management decision-making structures, the EU will become increasingly able to exploit the advantage of having a comprehensive set of tools at its disposal. This will also open up the prospect of complementary NATO–EU operations, especially given that truly demanding military operations will continue to require NATO and US involvement. However, even slow and patchy advancements in the field of European capabilities will be fruitless if member governments do not find the will the use them.

Strategic Geography

2006

Legend

—————— subject country
international boundaries

——————— other international boundaries

·················· province or state boundaries

ANBAR   province or state

▣ capital cities

● state or province capital cities

◉ cities/ towns/ villages

 shooting(s)/ attack(s)/ incident(s)
and skirmishes

GLOBAL ISSUES: World refugees and IDPs

In June 2006, the United Nations High Commission for Refugees (UNHCR) released its latest set of data concerning the number of refugees and Internally Displaced Persons (IDPs), among other key data sets. The information revealed that the number of the world's refugees was at its lowest level

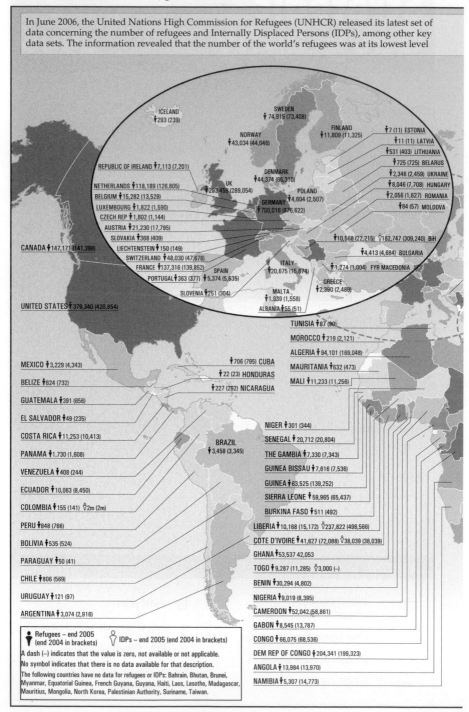

ICELAND ♀293 (239)

SWEDEN ♀74,915 (73,408)

NORWAY ♀43,034 (44,046)

FINLAND ♀11,809 (11,325)

♀7 (11) ESTONIA
♀11 (11) LATVIA
♀531 (403) LITHUANIA
♀725 (725) BELARUS
♀2,346 (2,459) UKRAINE
♀8,046 (7,708) HUNGARY
♀2,056 (1,627) ROMANIA
♀84 (57) MOLDOVA

REPUBLIC OF IRELAND ♀7,113 (7,201)
DENMARK ♀44,374 (65,310)
NETHERLANDS ♀118,189 (126,805)
UK ♀293,459 (289,054)
BELGIUM ♀15,282 (13,529)
POLAND ♀4,604 (2,507)
LUXEMBOURG ♀1,822 (1,590)
GERMANY ♀700,016 (876,622)
CZECH REP ♀1,802 (1,144)
AUSTRIA ♀21,230 (17,795)
SLOVAKIA ♀368 (409)
LIECHTENSTEIN ♀150 (149)
♀10,568 (22,215) ♂182,747 (309,240) BiH
CANADA ♀147,171 (141,398)
SWITZERLAND ♀48,030 (47,678)
♀4,413 (4,684) BULGARIA
FRANCE ♀137,316 (139,852)
ITALY ♀20,675 (15,674)
♀1,274 (1,004) FYR MACEDONIA
SPAIN
PORTUGAL ♀363 (377) ♀5,374 (5,635)
GREECE ♀2,390 (2,489)
SLOVENIA ♀251 (304)
MALTA ♀1,939 (1,558)
UNITED STATES ♀379,340 (420,854)
ALBANIA ♀55 (51)

TUNISIA ♀87 (90)
MOROCCO ♀219 (2,121)
ALGERIA ♀94,101 (169,048)
MEXICO ♀3,229 (4,343)
♀706 (795) CUBA
MAURITANIA ♀632 (473)
♀22 (23) HONDURAS
MALI ♀11,233 (11,256)
BELIZE ♀624 (732)
♀227 (292) NICARAGUA
GUATEMALA ♀391 (656)
EL SALVADOR ♀49 (235)
NIGER ♀301 (344)
COSTA RICA ♀11,253 (10,413)
BRAZIL
SENEGAL ♀20,712 (20,804)
♀3,458 (3,345)
PANAMA ♀1,730 (1,608)
THE GAMBIA ♀7,330 (7,343)
GUINEA BISSAU ♀7,616 (7,536)
VENEZUELA ♀408 (244)
GUINEA ♀63,525 (139,252)
ECUADOR ♀10,063 (8,450)
SIERRA LEONE ♀59,965 (65,437)
COLOMBIA ♀155 (141) ♂2m (2m)
BURKINA FASO ♀511 (492)
PERU ♀848 (766)
LIBERIA ♀10,168 (15,172) ♂237,822 (498,566)
COTE D'IVOIRE ♀41,627 (72,088) ♂38,039 (38,039)
BOLIVIA ♀535 (524)
GHANA ♀53,537 42,053
PARAGUAY ♀50 (41)
TOGO ♀9,287 (11,285) ♂3,000 (–)
CHILE ♀806 (569)
BENIN ♀30,294 (4,802)
URUGUAY ♀121 (97)
NIGERIA ♀9,019 (8,395)
ARGENTINA ♀3,074 (2,916)
CAMEROON ♀52,042 (58,861)
GABON ♀8,545 (13,787)

♀ Refugees – end 2005 (end 2004 in brackets)   ♂ IDPs – end 2005 (end 2004 in brackets)

CONGO ♀66,075 (68,536)

A dash (–) indicates that the value is zero, not available or not applicable.

DEM REP OF CONGO ♀204,341 (199,323)

No symbol indicates that there is no data available for that description.

ANGOLA ♀13,984 (13,970)

The following countries have no data for refugees or IDPs: Bahrain, Bhutan, Brunei, Myanmar, Equatorial Guinea, French Guyana, Guyana, Haiti, Laos, Lesotho, Madagascar, Mauritius, Mongolia, North Korea, Palestinian Authority, Suriname, Taiwan.

NAMIBIA ♀5,307 (14,773)

since 1980 – at 8,394,373 – while numbers of IDPs, as reported by UNHCR offices worldwide, were 22% up on the previous year, at 6,616,791. According to the UNHCR, this 'primarily reflects the newly reported IDP situations in Iraq (1.2 million) and Somalia (400,000)'.

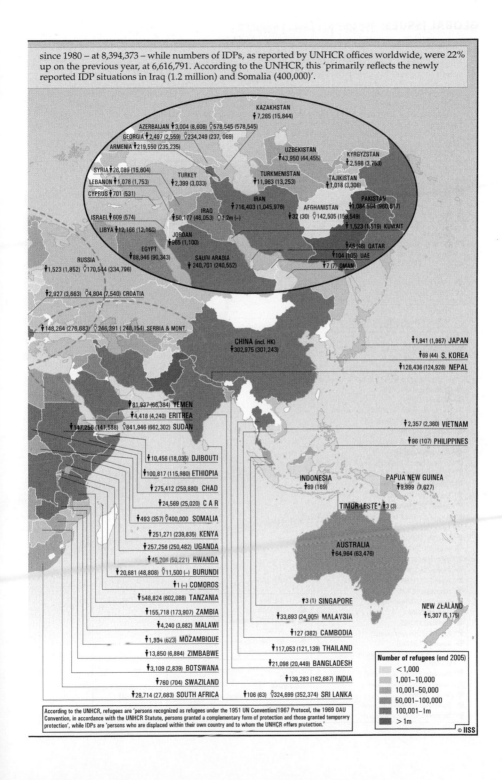

According to the UNHCR, refugees are 'persons recognized as refugees under the 1951 UN Convention/1967 Protocol, the 1969 OAU Convention, in accordance with the UNHCR Statute, persons granted a complementary form of protection and those granted temporary protection', while IDPs are 'persons who are displaced within their own country and to whom the UNHCR offers protection.'

© IISS

GLOBAL ISSUES: The spread of avian influenza

Medical experts and governments across the world remain concerned by the spread of strains of avian influenza which, according to the World Health Organization, is 'a contagious disease of animals caused by viruses that normally infect only birds and, less commonly, pigs'. While 'Influenza A viruses have 16 H and 9 N subtypes […] only viruses of the H5 and H7 subtypes are known to cause the highly pathogenic form of the disease. However, not all viruses of the H5 and H7 subtypes are highly pathogenic and not all will cause severe disease in poultry.' The H5N1 virus is causing greatest concern because, of those avian influenza viruses that have infected humans, it has caused the greatest number of cases of severe disease and death. A further concern is that the virus could change into a highly infectious form easily transmissible between humans. The accompanying map shows data on avian and first human instances up to early May 2006. Up to then, it was believed that, although there had been 228 human cases, with 130 fatal, human-to-human transmission had not occurred.

Germany
- 14/2/06: Wild swans
- 28/2/06: Dead domestic cat
- 8/3/06: Kills 2 cats   9/3/06: Stone marten
- 5/4/06: H5N1 outbreak in poultry

Belgium
- 22/10/04: Cases confirmed in 2 eagles, illegally imported from Thailand.

Austria
- 14/2/06: Wild swans
- 7/3/06: Confirmed in 3 cats

France
- 19/2/06: Wild duck   25/2/06: Farmed turkeys

Egypt
- 17/2/06: Domestic poultry   1 20/3/06
- TOTAL: 14 6

UK
- 23/10/05: Confirmed in dead imported parrot (in quarantine).
- 6/4/06: Confirmed in whooper swan

Sweden
- 15/3/06: Wild ducks
- 27/3/06: Detected in a mink.

Kazakhstan
- 2/8/05: Outbreak in poultry in areas adjacent to Siberia. Dead migratory birds are found in the vicinity.

Other instances of H5N1* avian influenza
- Afghanistan: 16/3/06
- Albania: 7/3/06
- Bosnia-Herzegovina: 25/2/06 (wild swans)
- Bulgaria: 11/2/06 (wild swans)
- Burkina Faso: 4/4/06
- Cameroon: 12/3/06 (domestic duck)
- Côte d'Ivoire: 5/5/06
- Croatia: 26/10/05 (wild birds)
- Czech Republic: 28/3/06 (wild swan)
- Denmark: 15/3/06 (wild bird)
- Georgia: 27/2/06 (wild swan)
- Greece: 11/2/06 (wild swans)
- Hungary: 21/2/06 (wild swans)
- India: 18/2/06 (domestic poultry)
- Iran: 14/2/06 (wild swans)
- Israel: 17/3/06
- Italy: 11/2/06 (wild swans)
- Jordan: 24/3/06
- Kuwait: 11/11/05 (migratory flamingo)
- Myanmar: 12/3/06
- Niger: 27/2/06 (wild swans)
- Nigeria: 8/2/06
- Pakistan: 21/3/06
- Poland: 5/3/06 (wild swans)
- Romania: 15/10/05
- Serbia & Montenegro: 2/3/06 H5 found in a wild swan
- Slovakia: 21/2/06 (wild swans)
- Slovenia: 12/2/06 (wild swan)
- Sudan: 2/5/06
- Switzerland: 1/3/06 (wild duck)
- Ukraine: 5/12/05 (domestic birds)

* Unless stated otherwise

Turkey
- 13/10/05
- 27/12/05: Outbreak in Igdir province
- 2   5/1/06
- 23/1/06: Outbreaks in 11 out of 81 provinces
- TOTAL: 12 4

Iraq
- 1 30/1/06
- 2/2/06: Outbreak in backyard flocks in same province as human case
- TOTAL: 2 2

Djibouti
- 1 12/5/06
- TOTAL: 1 0

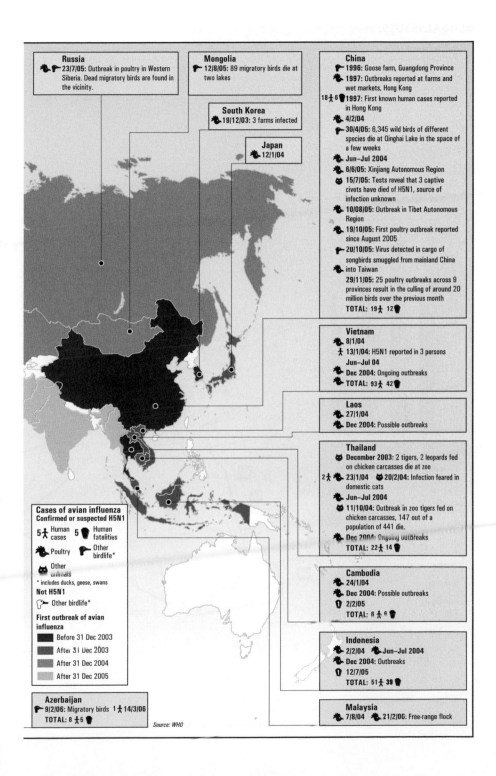

Russia
23/7/05: Outbreak in poultry in Western Siberia. Dead migratory birds are found in the vicinity.

Mongolia
12/8/05: 89 migratory birds die at two lakes

South Korea
19/12/03: 3 farms infected

Japan
12/1/04

China
1996: Goose farm, Guangdong Province
1997: Outbreaks reported at farms and wet markets, Hong Kong
18 6 1997: First known human cases reported in Hong Kong
4/2/04
30/4/05: 6,345 wild birds of different species die at Qinghai Lake in the space of a few weeks
Jun–Jul 2004
6/6/05: Xinjiang Autonomous Region
15/7/05: Tests reveal that 3 captive civets have died of H5N1, source of infection unknown
10/08/05: Outbreak in Tibet Autonomous Region
19/10/05: First poultry outbreak reported since August 2005
20/10/05: Virus detected in cargo of songbirds smuggled from mainland China into Taiwan
29/11/05: 25 poultry outbreaks across 9 provinces result in the culling of around 20 million birds over the previous month
TOTAL: 19 12

Vietnam
8/1/04
13/1/04: H5N1 reported in 3 persons
Jun–Jul 04
Dec 2004: Ongoing outbreaks
TOTAL: 93 42

Laos
27/1/04
Dec 2004: Possible outbreaks

Thailand
December 2003: 2 tigers, 2 leopards fed on chicken carcasses die at zoo
2 23/1/04 20/2/04: Infection feared in domestic cats
Jun–Jul 2004
11/10/04: Outbreak in zoo tigers fed on chicken carcasses, 147 out of a population of 441 die.
Dec 2004: Ongoing outbreaks
TOTAL: 22 14

Cambodia
24/1/04
Dec 2004: Possible outbreaks
2/2/05
TOTAL: 6 6

Indonesia
2/2/04 Jun–Jul 2004
Dec 2004: Outbreaks
12/7/05
TOTAL: 51 39

Cases of avian influenza
Confirmed or suspected H5N1
5 Human cases   5 Human fatalities
Poultry   Other birdlife*
Other animals
* includes ducks, geese, swans
Not H5N1
Other birdlife*
First outbreak of avian influenza
Before 31 Dec 2003
After 31 Dec 2003
After 31 Dec 2004
After 31 Dec 2005

Azerbaijan
9/2/06: Migratory birds 1 14/3/06
TOTAL: 8 5

Malaysia
7/8/04 21/2/06: Free-range flock

Source: WHO

GLOBAL ISSUES: Selected energy supply issues – Europe

The tightness and insecurity of oil markets is a further incentive to countries that were already looking to increase use of natural gas in key sectors like electricity generation and manufacturing. Delivering more natural gas to major centres of demand will require massive investment in the construction of expensive pipelines and liquefied natural gas (LNG) facilities.

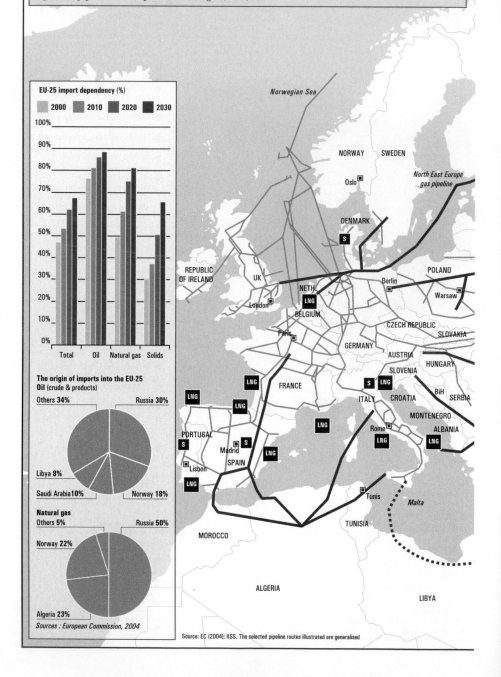

EU-25 import dependency (%)

2000 2010 2020 2030

The origin of imports into the EU-25
Oil (crude & products)

Others 34%   Russia 30%

Libya 8%

Saudi Arabia 10%   Norway 18%

Natural gas
Others 5%   Russia 50%

Norway 22%

Algeria 23%

Sources : European Commission, 2004

Source: EC (2004); IISS. The selected pipeline routes illustrated are generalised

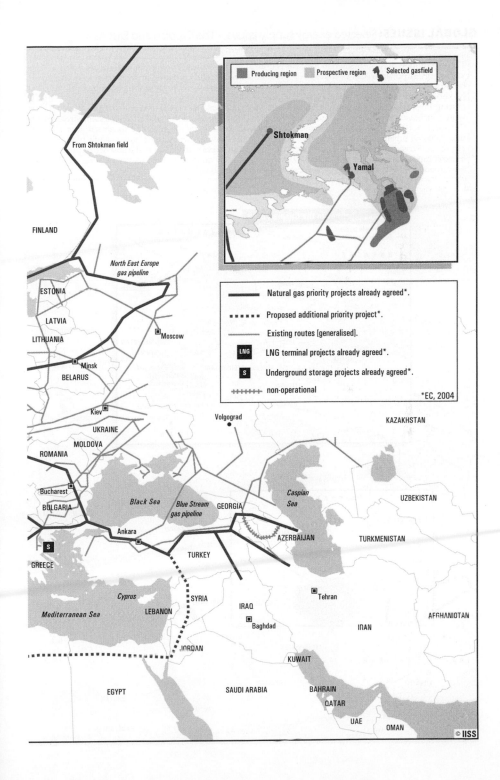

Producing region   Prospective region   Selected gasfield

Shtokman

Yamal

From Shtokman field

FINLAND

North East Europe
gas pipeline

ESTONIA

LATVIA

LITHUANIA
Moscow

Minsk
BELARUS

Kiev

UKRAINE

MOLDOVA

ROMANIA

Bucharest

BULGARIA

GREECE

S

Volgograd

Black Sea   Blue Stream
gas pipeline   GEORGIA

Ankara

TURKEY

Cyprus

Mediterranean Sea   LEBANON   SYRIA

JORDAN

EGYPT

Caspian
Sea

AZERBAIJAN

SAUDI ARABIA

KAZAKHSTAN

UZBEKISTAN

TURKMENISTAN

Tehran

IRAQ

Baghdad   IRAN

KUWAIT

BAHRAIN

QATAR

UAE

OMAN

AFGHANISTAN

Natural gas priority projects already agreed*.

Proposed additional priority project*.

Existing routes [generalised].

LNG   LNG terminal projects already agreed*.

S   Underground storage projects already agreed*.

non-operational

*EC, 2004

© IISS

GLOBAL ISSUES: Selected energy supply issues – The Caspian and East Asia

The exploration of eastern Siberian deposits is crucial for Russia to realise its ambition of becoming a key energy supplier to Asia as well as Europe. Russia needs significant foreign investment to support construction of a Pacific oil pipeline that could take Russian energy exports to the eastern port of Nakhodka and onwards to Japan, Asia and possibly North America.

During President Putin's visit to China on 21–22 March 2006 a deal was agreed under which Russia would increase gas exports to China. Gazprom and China's state-controlled China National Petroleum Corporation (CNPC) signed an agreement on supply of Russian gas to China and construction of a new 3,000km pipeline, Altai, estimated to cost about $10bn, which will connect Russia and China. However, Russia 'will have little spare capacity to expand exports to China: in the absence of progress in exploration of eastern Siberian deposits, Russia has to rely on exports from western Siberia which are already committed to Europe, the CIS and domestic consumption.'

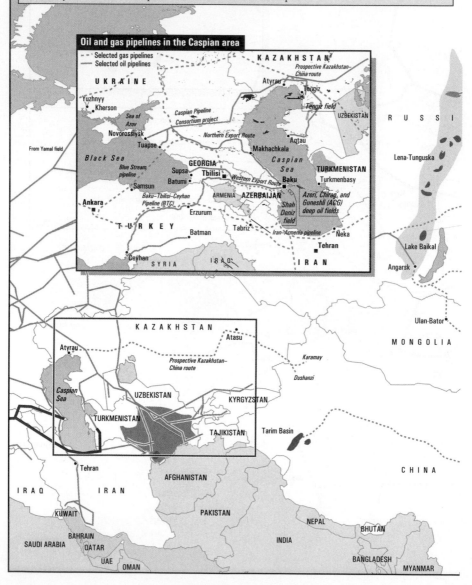

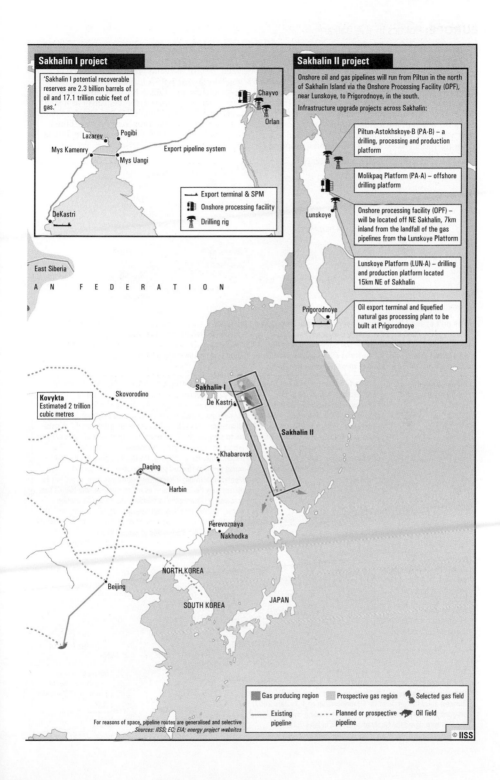

Sakhalin I project

'Sakhalin I potential recoverable reserves are 2.3 billion barrels of oil and 17.1 trillion cubic feet of gas.'

Chayvo

Orlan

Lazarev   Pogibi

Mys Kamenry

Mys Uangi   Export pipeline system

DeKastri

- Export terminal & SPM
- Onshore processing facility
- Drilling rig

East Siberia

A   N   F   E   D   E   R   A   T   I   O   N

Sakhalin II project

Onshore oil and gas pipelines will run from Piltun in the north of Sakhalin Island via the Onshore Processing Facility (OPF), near Lunskoye, to Prigorodnoye, in the south.

Infrastructure upgrade projects across Sakhalin:

Piltun-Astokhskoye-B (PA-B) – a drilling, processing and production platform

Molikpaq Platform (PA-A) – offshore drilling platform

Lunskoye

Onshore processing facility (OPF) – will be located off NE Sakhalin, 7km inland from the landfall of the gas pipelines from the Lunskoye Platform

Lunskoye Platform (LUN-A) – drilling and production platform located 15km NE of Sakhalin

Prigorodnoye

Oil export terminal and liquefied natural gas processing plant to be built at Prigorodnoye

Kovykta Estimated 2 trillion cubic metres

Skovorodino

Sakhalin I

De Kastri

Sakhalin II

Khabarovsk

Daqing

Harbin

Perevoznaya
Nakhodka

NORTH KOREA

Beijing

SOUTH KOREA   JAPAN

- ▪ Gas producing region
- ▪ Prospective gas region
- Selected gas field
- —— Existing pipeline
- ---- Planned or prospective pipeline
- Oil field

For reasons of space, pipeline routes are generalised and selective
Sources: IISS; EC; EIA; energy project websites

© IISS

EUROPE: Politics in the Balkans

On 21 May 2006 the citizens of Montenegro voted, in a referendum, to leave the 'State Union' which had joined them to Serbia since 2003. For a result to be valid, 55% of the valid votes cast had to be in favour of the referendum question. In the event 55.5% voted in favour, with a turnout of 86.3%, meaning that the republic's future was decided by a respectable margin. Olli Rehn, EU Commissioner for Enlargement, said after the result that 'The European perspective is open to Montenegro – as it is to Serbia once it fulfils the various criteria, in particular […] cooperation with the ICTY. Pending the final confirmation of the results the European Commission will now prepare two proposals for the Council of Ministers: a proposal for a new Stabilisation and Association Agreement (SAA) negotiating mandate for the independent Montenegro and a proposal for a modified SAA mandate for Serbia, as successor state of the State Union.'

The pull of the EU: Western strategy in the region is based on the pull factor of the EU. Using the Stabilisation and Association process, the EU is seeking to enhance state-building, modernisation and reform, much as it did in the former communist states of eastern and central Europe. On 9 November 2005, the European Commission noted in a new enlargement strategy that for the states of the western Balkans, 'a convincing political perspective for eventual integration into the EU is crucial to keep their reforms on track'.

Slovenia joined the EU in the 2004 enlargement round.

Croatia has moved from candidate status to accession talks. This followed the earlier postponement, in March 2005, of the launch of accession talks until the arrest of General Ante Gotovina. The 'talks began in October when Carla del Ponte informed the EU that Croatia was now fully cooperating with' the ICTY.

Serbia and Montenegro: On 3 May 2006, Olli Rehn, the EU Enlargement Commissioner, called off the negotiating round on a Stabilisation and Association Agreement with Serbia and Montenegro, scheduled for 11 May, regretting 'that Serbia and Montenegro was still not fully cooperating with the ICTY' in its bid to bring fugitive ICTY indictees – taken to refer particularly to former Bosnian Serb army commander Ratko Mladic – to The Hague. However, on 15 May, the Council 'reiterated its firm commitment to the European perspective of Serbia and Montenegro. In this context, the Council indicated its support to resume negotiations as soon as full cooperation with the ICTY is achieved'. Following the referendum, the EU and its member states 'decided that they will develop [...] their relations with the Republic of Montenegro as a sovereign, independent State', while the Council noted that the Republic of Serbia had been defined by the Parliament of Serbia as the continuing State of the State Union.

In November 2005, **Bosnia-Herzegovina** began talks on a Stabilisation and Association Agreement .

Albania signed a Stabilisation and Association Agreement in February 2006.

Macedonia was awarded candidate status on 17 December 2005.

Bulgaria and Romania: 'The Commission considers that Bulgaria and Romania should be prepared for EU membership on 1 January 2007, provided that they address a number of outstanding issues.' Bulgaria and Romania signed the treaty of accession in April 2005.

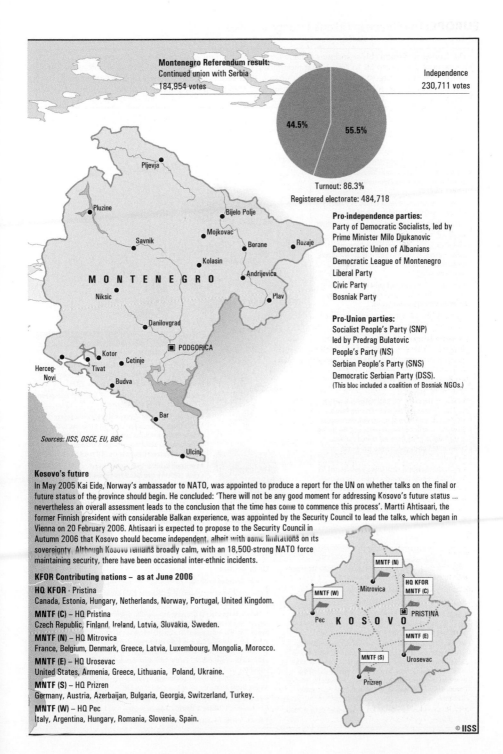

Montenegro Referendum result:
Continued union with Serbia
184,954 votes

Independence
230,711 votes

44.5% 55.5%

Turnout: 86.3%
Registered electorate: 484,718

Pro-independence parties:
Party of Democratic Socialists, led by
Prime Minister Milo Djukanovic
Democratic Union of Albanians
Democratic League of Montenegro
Liberal Party
Civic Party
Bosniak Party

Pro-Union parties:
Socialist People's Party (SNP)
led by Predrag Bulatovic
People's Party (NS)
Serbian People's Party (SNS)
Democratic Serbian Party (DSS).
(This bloc included a coalition of Bosniak NGOs.)

Sources: IISS, OSCE, EU, BBC

Kosovo's future
In May 2005 Kai Eide, Norway's ambassador to NATO, was appointed to produce a report for the UN on whether talks on the final or future status of the province should begin. He concluded: 'There will not be any good moment for addressing Kosovo's future status ... nevertheless an overall assessment leads to the conclusion that the time has come to commence this process'. Martti Ahtisaari, the former Finnish president with considerable Balkan experience, was appointed by the Security Council to lead the talks, which began in Vienna on 20 February 2006. Ahtisaari is expected to propose to the Security Council in Autumn 2006 that Kosovo should become independent, albeit with some limitations on its sovereignty. Although Kosovo remains broadly calm, with an 18,500-strong NATO force maintaining security, there have been occasional inter-ethnic incidents.

KFOR Contributing nations – as at June 2006

HQ KFOR - Pristina
Canada, Estonia, Hungary, Netherlands, Norway, Portugal, United Kingdom.

MNTF (C) – HQ Pristina
Czech Republic, Finland, Ireland, Latvia, Slovakia, Sweden.

MNTF (N) – HQ Mitrovica
France, Belgium, Denmark, Greece, Latvia, Luxembourg, Mongolia, Morocco.

MNTF (E) – HQ Urosevac
United States, Armenia, Greece, Lithuania, Poland, Ukraine.

MNTF (S) – HQ Prizren
Germany, Austria, Azerbaijan, Bulgaria, Georgia, Switzerland, Turkey.

MNTF (W) – HQ Pec
Italy, Argentina, Hungary, Romania, Slovenia, Spain.

© IISS

EUROPE: The European Union's security activities

The European Union (EU) continues to increase the number and range of its security missions. The major new mission so far in 2006 is that monitoring the election process in the Democratic Republic of Congo. The EU's largest mission remains that in Bosnia-Herzegovina, where it took over from the NATO force in December 2004 and where around 6,000 troops participate in its *Althea* operation. (See page XIV.)

Palestinian territories

EU police mission in the Palestinian territories (EUPOL COPPS)

• Dates: The operational phase started on 1 January 2006 and will have an initial duration of 3 years.

• Mandate: Council Joint Action of 14 November 2005.

• Context: 'The EU Police Mission for the Palestinian Territories ... has a long term reform focus and provides enhanced support to the Palestinian Authority in establishing sustainable and effective policing arrangements.'

• Personnel: 'When fully deployed EUPOL-COPPS will include approximately 33 unarmed personnel mainly seconded from EU Member States.'

• Costs: €6.1m is allocated for mission expenditure until the end of 2006.

EU Border Assistance Mission at Rafah Crossing Point in the Palestinian Territories (EU BAM Rafah)

• Dates: The operational phase of the Mission began on 30 November 2005 and will last for 12 months.

• Mandate: Council Joint Action of 12 December 2005.

• Context: 'The aim of "EU BAM Rafah" is to provide a third party presence at the Rafah Crossing Point in order to contribute, in co-operation with the European Community's institution-building efforts, to the opening of the Rafah Crossing Point and to build confidence between the Government of Israel and the Palestinian Authority.'

• Personnel: During the initial phase, approximately 55 police officers from 15 Member States were deployed. In the full deployment phase this number was scheduled to increase to 75 to facilitate 24-hour operations.

• Costs: Scheduled mission-related expenditures will be €11,475,200.

Darfur

EU support to AMIS II

• Dates: The EU announced additional measures to support AMIS II (African Union Mission to Darfur) at the International Pledging Conference in Addis Ababa in May 2005.

• Mandate: Council Joint Action of 18 July 2005 in response to a request from the African Union.

• Context: This military and police assistance to the African Union mission is part of the EU's response to the crisis in Darfur, which has included financial disbursements for humanitarian assistance, in support of the political process and as contributions to the CFC and AMIS.

• Personnel includes: 16 EU police officers to reinforce AMIS civilian police; 19 operational and logistic planners 'deployed to the Darfur Integrated Task Force in Addis Ababa, Mission HQ in Khartoum and the Joint Logistic Operations Centre in El-Fasher.' Personnel have also been allocated to support strategic and tactical airlift and general transportation duties as tasked. Furthermore, 11 monitors were scheduled for deployment in Darfur.

Democratic Republic of Congo

EUSEC-DR Congo (EU advisory and assistance mission for security reform in the Democratic Republic of Congo)

• Dates: Launched on 8 June 2005 for 12 months.

• Mandate: Council Joint Action of 2 May 2005.

• Context: 'Following an official request by the DRC government, the EU decided to establish an EU advisory and assistance mission for security reform in the Democratic Republic of Congo.'

• Personnel: In 2005, the mission was envisaged as comprising eight experts who will be seconded by the member states and by EU institutions. Experts were to be assigned to: the private office of the Minister of Defence; general military staff, including the Integrated Military Structure; staff of the land forces; the National Commission for Disarmament, Demobilisation and Re-assignment (CONADER); and the Joint Operational Committee.

• Costs: €1m allocated in 2005; €4.75m allocated so far in 2006.

EUPOL-Kinshasa

• Dates: Launched on 30 April 2005.

• Mandate: Council Joint Action of 9 December 2004 and an October 2003 request from Kinshasa.

• Context: In response to a request from the DRC government, EUPOL is in place to support the creation of an Integrated Police Unit (IPU) and monitor, mentor and advise. The 'IPU is the subject of a project whose aim is to train 1,008 Congolese police. The IPU's objective is to scale up the neutral force currently made available by MONUC (the UN force in the DRC) to guarantee the security of the government and transitional institutions.' Furthermore, since January 2006, EUPOL has formed part of the 'think tank' on the reform and reorganisation of the Congolese National Police Force (PNC), bringing together policing experts from the EU, MONUC, France, Angola, South Africa, the UK and members of the PNC.

• Personnel: In March 2006, EUPOL consisted of 28 international staff: 11 French, 6 Portuguese, 4 Italians, 2 Dutch, 2 Belgians and two from Canada and Turkey.

• Costs: Around €4.5m in 2005; €3.5m allocated to date in 2006.

Moldova–Ukraine Border Mission

• Dates: The EU Border Assistance Mission to Moldova and Ukraine became operational on 1 December 2005. The mission is in response to a 'joint letter of the presidents of Moldova and Ukraine dating from 2 June 2005 calling for additional EU support in overall capacity building for border management, including customs, on the whole Moldova-Ukraine border.' The mission has a two-year mandate, which can be extended. • Mandate: Council Joint Action of 7 November 2005 • Context: 'This Mission helps to prevent smuggling, trafficking, and customs fraud, by providing advice and training to improve the capacity of the Moldovan and Ukrainian border and customs services.' • Personnel: border police and customs officials from 16 EU Member States, with 69 experts seconded from EU Member States, as well as some 50 local support staff. • Costs: Around €8m

FYR Macedonia

EU Police Advisory Team

• Dates: The operational phase of EUPAT began on 15 December 2005, with a scheduled duration of six months. • Mandate: Council Joint Action of 24 November 2005 • Context: ' EUPAT will further support the development of an efficient and professional police service based on European standards of policing.' 'Under the guidance of the EU Special Representative and in partnership with the host Government authorities, EU police experts monitor and mentor the country's police on priority issues in the field of border police, public peace and order and accountability, the fight against corruption and organised crime.' The launch of EUPAT follows the termination on 14 December 2005 of the mandate of the EU Police Mission PROXIMA.

• Personnel: EUPAT consists of about 30 police advisers, headquartered in Skopje, with one 'central co-location unit at the Ministry of Interior level', and 'mobile units co-located within the country at appropriate levels'. • Costs: €1.5m is allocated for EUPAT expenses.

Iraq

EU Integrated Rule of Law Mission for Iraq (EUJUST LEX)

• Dates: The mission became operational on 1 July 2005. • Mandate: Council Joint Action of 7 March 2005. • Context: The establishment of this mission followed an invitation from Iraq's Transitional Government. EUJUST-LEX consists of integrated training in management and criminal investigation for 'senior officials from the judiciary, the police and the penitentiary in order to promote an integrated criminal justice system in Iraq'. • Personnel: Although the training is scheduled to take place in EU member states, the mission has a liaison office in Baghdad.
• Costs: €10m has been allocated to cover common mission costs until 31 October 2006.

Indonesia

Aceh Monitoring Mission (AMM)

• Dates: Mission became operational on 15 September 2005. 'On 11 May 2006 in Brussels, favourable consideration was given by the EU to the Government of Indonesia's request for AMM to continue its mandate until the date of the local elections (Pilkada) in Aceh, but no later than 15 September, 2006.'
• Mandate: Memorandum of Understanding between the Government of the Republic of Indonesia and the Free Aceh Movement (GAM), Helsinki, 15 August 2005 and Council Joint Action 9 September 2005. • Context: The mission is designed to monitor the implementation of the peace agreement between the Indonesian government and GAM. The formal process of decommissioning GAM armaments and relocating 'organic military and police forces was completed on 5 January 2006.' • Personnel: 80-strong, nearly two-thirds drawn from the EU, Norway and Switzerland and more than one-third from five ASEAN nations (Brunei, Malaysia, the Philippines, Singapore and Thailand). • Costs: Financing through CFSP budget (€9m) and from EU states and participating nations (€6m). €1.133m allocated to date in 2006.

EUFOR – RD Congo

• Dates: EUFOR-RD Congo was launched on 12 June 2006 and is due to be deployed for up to four months after the first round of the DRC presidential and parliamentary elections.
• Mandate: Council Joint Action of 27 April 2006 and United Nations Security Council Resolution 1671 (2006).
• Context: On 30 July 2006, elections are scheduled for the DRC, The EU's military mission is designed to support MONUC, the UN force in the DRC, during the election period. (The EU is also deploying a 250-strong Election Observation Mission to the DRC.) With its operational headquarters in Potsdam, EUFOR-RD has been tasked with: supporting 'MONUC to stabilise a situation, in case MONUC faces serious difficulties in fulfilling its mandate within its existing capabilities; to contribute to the protection of civilians under imminent threat of physical violence in the areas of its deployment, and without prejudice to the responsibility of the Government of the DRC; to contribute to airport protection in Kinshasa; to ensure the security and freedom of movement of the personnel as well as the protection of the installations of EUFOR RD Congo; [and] to execute operations of limited character in order to extract individuals in danger.'
• Personnel: EUFOR-RD 'will involve the deployment of an advanced element to Kinshasa of circa 400–450 military personnel and the availability of a battalion-size on-call force over the horizon outside the country, but quickly deployable.' Germany and France are to provide the majority of forces: Berlin is due to deploy about 500 soldiers and 280 logistical and medical support staff for a period of four months, with the majority stationed in Gabon as the 'over the horizon' force. France is due to send about 700 troops. At least 16 other states are due to contribute forces.
• Costs: The financial reference amount for the four-month operation is €16.7m.

© IISS

EUROPE: The European Union's security activities

Bosnia-Herzegovina: EUFOR *Althea*
- Dates: Launched on 2 December 2004 • Mandate: Under UNSCR 1575 (2004) and Council Joint Action decision of 12 July 2004. • Context: EUFOR succeeded NATO's SFOR operation. The main objectives of *Althea* are to: 'maintain a safe and secure environment in BiH and to ensure continued compliance with The General Framework Agreement for Peace' and 'to support the International Community's High Representative in BiH and the local authorities, inter alia in the fight against organised crime.' • Costs: 'The common costs of Operation *Althea* are paid through contributions by Member States to a financial mechanism (Athena) based on GDP.' The common costs of the operation are €71.7 million. Personnel and other items are on a 'costs lie where they fall' basis. • Personnel: See table below for November 2005 troops in theatre figures.

Multinational Task Force Northwest (MNTF NW) – under British command
- Headquarters MNTF-NW is located at Banja Luka.
- MNTF-NW has approximately 1,300 personnel.

EU Countries	Country	Number
EU Countries	Austria	8
	United Kingdom	700
	Italy	2
	Netherlands	410
Non-EU Countries	Bulgaria	20
	Switzerland	24
	Norway	12
	Romania	40
Others	Canada	40
	Chile	23
	New Zealand	13

Multinational Task Force North (MNTF N) – under Austrian command
- Headquarters MNTF-N is located at Tuzla.
- MNTF-N has approximately 1,300 personnel. Multinational Task Force North is composed of 14 EU and other participating nations - Austria, Belgium, Czech Republic, Estonia, Finland, Greece, Ireland, Latvia, Poland, Portugal, Slovakia, Slovenia, Sweden and Turkey.

Multinational Task Force Southeast (MNTF SE) –
under German command
Multinational Task Force-South East includes six European and other participating Nations: Italy, Germany, France, Spain, Morocco and Albania.
Troops in MNTF (SE): about 1,500

Integrated Police Unit (IPU) – coverage over whole of BiH
- Headquarters IPU is located at Sarajevo.
- Authorised troop strength: 534.
- IPU comprises a HQ; Mobile Element, that consists of 4 company-sized mobile units; a Specialised Element, that consists of 5 investigation teams and 1 operational support team; and a Logistic Element, that consists of units for logistic supply and maintenance.

EU nations troops in theatre

Austria	221
Belgium	52
Czech Republic	90
Estonia	3
Finland	184
France	463
Germany	1,014
Greece	88
Hungary	142
Ireland	51
Italy	955
Latvia	3
Lithuania	1
Luxembourg	1
The Netherlands	384
Poland	244
Portugal	237
Slovakia	4
Slovenia	90
Spain	492
Sweden	77
United Kingdom	706
Sub total EU nations	**5,502**

Non-EU nations troops in theatre

Albania	71
Argentina	2
Bulgaria	36
Canada	3
Chile	23
Morocco	132
Norway	17
New Zealand	9
Romania	120
Switzerland	23
Turkey	332
Sub total non-EU	**768**
Total number of troops in EUFOR	**6,270**

European Union Police Mission (EUPM)
- Dates: Initially from 1 January 2003–December 2006. 'Following an invitation by the BiH authorities, the EU decided to establish a follow-on Mission to EUPM with a modified mandate and size. The refocused EUPM follow-on mission will have a duration of two years (from 1 January 2006 until the end of 2007). '

- Mandate: Council Joint Action of 11 March 2002; Annex 11 of the Dayton Peace Agreement. The move was also welcomed by the UN under UNSCR 1396.

- Context: Designed to follow on from the UN's International Police Task Force, the 'EUPM operates in line with the general objectives of Annex 11 of the Dayton/Paris Agreement' and is 'supported by the European Community instruments. It aims to establish in BiH a sustainable, professional and multiethnic police service operating in accordance with best European and international standards.'

- Costs: €12m allocated to date.

- Personnel: As of 23 June 2006, numbers allocated were: Austria 5; Belgium 4; Bulgaria 2; Canada 3; Cyprus 2; Czech Rep. 5; Denmark 3; Estonia 2; Finland 6; France 24; Germany 16; Greece 4; Hungary 3; Iceland 0; Ireland 9; Italy 15; Latvia 2; Lithuania 2; Luxembourg 2; Malta 2; Netherlands 11; Norway 5; Poland 7; Portugal 6; Romania 6; Russia 0; Slovakia 4; Slovenia 4; Spain 10; Sweden 5; Switzerland 3; Turkey 7; Ukraine 6; United Kingdom 18; **Total: 203.**

EUPM assistance at the following locations, among others:

Potential operations: Kosovo
The EU is preparing for an enhanced role in Kosovo. In this context, the Council decided on 10 April to establish an EU planning team regarding a possible future EU crisis management operation in the field of rule of law and possible other areas in Kosovo. The legal basis for this activity is Council Joint Action of 10 April 2006 and the Political and Security Committee decision of 2 May 2006.

© IISS

MIDDLE EAST / GULF: Reconstruction activity in Iraq

The progress of reconstruction in Iraq has been severely restricted by the ongoing insurgency, which as well as targeting Iraqi civilians and security forces, foreign reconstruction and aid workers and coalition personnel, has also seen repeated attacks on Iraq's infrastructure. Nonetheless, reconstruction and rehabilitation projects are proceeding across the country. In the US, quarterly reports are produced by the Special Inspector General for Iraq Reconstruction (SGIR); the information below is abstracted from the SGIR's April 2006 Report to Congress.

Status reports on heavy construction sectors

Completed   Ongoing   Not started

Transportation and communication projects

330 | 64 | 22

Subsector	Number of projects	Cost of projects
Roads and Bridges	330	$83m
Communications	3	$67m
Expressways	3	$43m
Airports	15	$34m
Railroad Stations	85	$32m
Ports	9	$26m
Misc. Facilities	1	$3m
Postal Facilities	24	$2m

Water projects

427 | 238 | 11

Subsector	Number of projects	Cost of projects
Water Treatment	59	$505m
Potable Water	470	$335m
Sewerage	117	$181m
Irrigation & Drainage Systems	8	$92m
Miscellaneous	2	$39m
Other Solid Waste Mgmt	2	$20m
Conservation	18	$20m

Electricity projects

268 | 277 | 58

Subsector	Number of projects	Cost of projects
Generation	27	$1,306m
Distribution	526	$921m
Transmission	44	$527m
Miscellaneous	6	$73

Oil and gas projects

13 | 42 | 5

Subsector	Number of projects	Cost of projects
LPG/LNG Plant Refurb	6	$131m
Miscellaneous	30	$96m
Water Injection Pump Stations	18	$60m
Dedicated Power	6	$34m

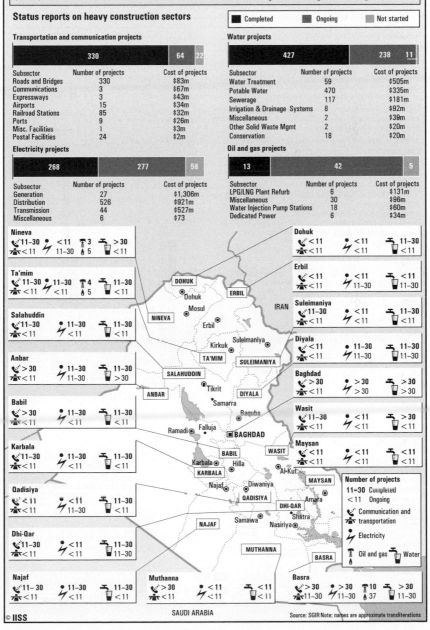

Number of projects
11–30 Completed
<11 Ongoing
Communication and transportation
Electricity
Oil and gas   Water

© IISS

SAUDI ARABIA

Source: SGIR Note: names are approximate transliterations

ASIA: Indonesia's earthquake and other security problems in Southeast Asia

On 27 May 2006, an earthquake measuring 6.3 on the Richter scale struck the southern coast of Java, Indonesia – approximately 37 km south of Yogyakarta – at 05:54 local time, at a depth of 17 km. By early June, casualty figures had passed over 6,000 dead, with estimated 97,000 injured. Some 150,000 houses were destroyed, with a further 260,000 damaged. This was in an area which also saw increased volcanic activity on Mount Merapi – by 9 June it was estimated by media sources that 19,000 people had been evacuated from the slopes of the mountain. In the aftermath of the earthquake, regional and international states offered assistance – both financial and material – towards a relief effort that will overall, according to comments attributed to UN officials, last six months and cost more than $100m.

The regional and international response: selected activities

28 May: 35-member Singapore Armed Forces (SAF) medical team deployed at TNI Field Hospital in Plered, Bantul.

From 28 May, 43 members of the Singapore Civil Defence Force (SCDF) also participated in search and rescue, medical and relief operations in the Bantul area. On 30 May this SCDF contingent relocated to Pleret – about 16 km from Adi Sutjipto Airport, where a temporary Operations Base was first set up.

On 29 May, China dispatched a 44-strong 'Chinese International Rescue Team'. Thailand sent a medical team of about 50 personnel to Indonesia. The Philippines also sent a humanitarian response team, as did Brunei, while Australia sent a team over 60 strong.

31 May: 19-member SAF-SCDF medical team deployed at Bantul District Hospital (8 SAF doctors and 11 SCDF medical personnel).

(The Republic of Singapore Air Force flew nine C-130 flights and two Fokker 50 flights in support of relief efforts, while Singapore facilitated 23 US KC-130 flights through Paya Lebar airbase to support relief operations.)

165 US service personnel, mainly from a marine corps surgical company, were deployed to Java. As at 6 June, supporting US aircrew completed 42 missions , involving five C-17 flights, six C-130 missions and 31 KC-130 tanker/transport flights. US forces included personnel drawn from 3rd Marine Expeditionary Force based in Okinawa, Japan, US Pacific Air Forces units in Guam, as well as USNS *Mercy*, which was at the time located in the Philippines.

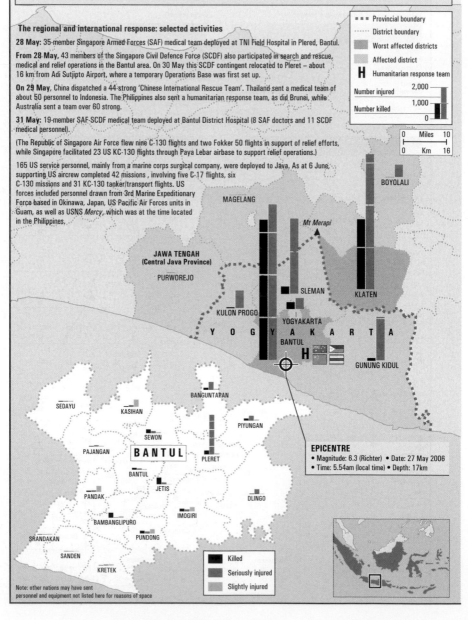

Legend:
- Provincial boundary
- District boundary
- Worst affected districts
- Affected district
- H Humanitarian response team
- Number injured — 2,000
- Number killed — 1,000 / 0

0 Miles 10
0 Km 16

EPICENTRE
- Magnitude: 6.3 (Richter) • Date: 27 May 2006
- Time: 5.54am (local time) • Depth: 17km

- Killed
- Seriously injured
- Slightly injured

Note: other nations may have sent personnel and equipment not listed here for reasons of space

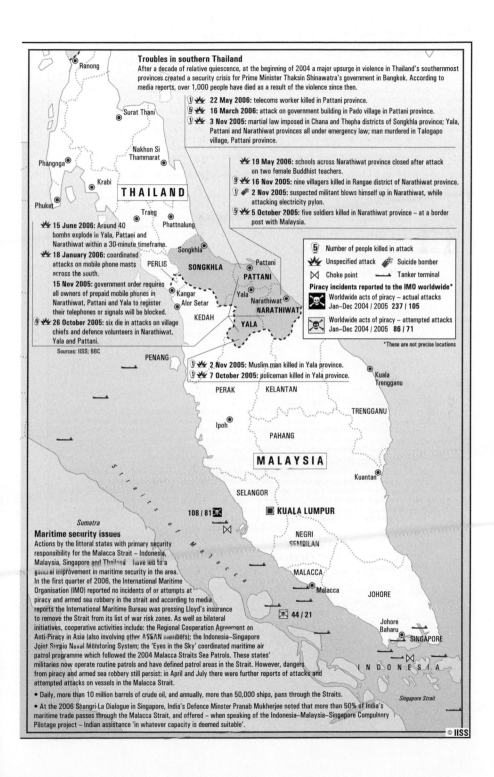

Troubles in southern Thailand

After a decade of relative quiescence, at the beginning of 2004 a major upsurge in violence in Thailand's southernmost provinces created a security crisis for Prime Minister Thaksin Shinawatra's government in Bangkok. According to media reports, over 1,000 people have died as a result of the violence since then.

① 💥 **22 May 2006:** telecoms worker killed in Pattani province.

⑤ 💥 **16 March 2006:** attack on government building in Pado village in Pattani province.

① 💥 **3 Nov 2005:** martial law imposed in Chana and Thepha districts of Songkhla province; Yala, Pattani and Narathiwat provinces all under emergency law; man murdered in Talogapo village, Pattani province.

💥 **19 May 2006:** schools across Narathiwat province closed after attack on two female Buddhist teachers.

⑨ 💥 **16 Nov 2005:** nine villagers killed in Rangae district of Narathiwat province.

① 💣 **2 Nov 2005:** suspected militant blows himself up in Narathiwat, while attacking electricity pylon.

⑤ 💥 **5 October 2005:** five soldiers killed in Narathiwat province – at a border post with Malaysia.

💥 **15 June 2006:** Around 40 bombs explode in Yala, Pattani and Narathiwat within a 30-minute timeframe.

💥 **18 January 2006:** coordinated attacks on mobile phone masts across the south.

15 Nov 2005: government order requires all owners of prepaid mobile phones in Narathiwat, Pattani and Yala to register their telephones or signals will be blocked.

⑥ 💥 **26 October 2005:** six die in attacks on village chiefs and defence volunteers in Narathiwat, Yala and Pattani.

Sources: IISS; BBC

① 💥 **2 Nov 2005:** Muslim man killed in Yala province.

① 💥 **7 October 2005:** policeman killed in Yala province.

⑤	Number of people killed in attack		
💥	Unspecified attack	💣	Suicide bomber
⋈	Choke point	⟞	Tanker terminal

Piracy incidents reported to the IMO worldwide*

☠ Worldwide acts of piracy – actual attacks
Jan–Dec 2004 / 2005 **237 / 105**

☠ Worldwide acts of piracy – attempted attacks
Jan–Dec 2004 / 2005 **86 / 71**

*These are not precise locations

RANONG, Ranong, Surat Thani, Nakhon Si Thammarat, Phangnga, Krabi, **THAILAND**, Phuket, Trang, Phattnalung, Songkhla, **PERLIS**, **SONGKHLA**, Pattani, **PATTANI**, Kangar, Alor Setar, Yala, Narathiwat, **KEDAH**, **NARATHIWAT**, **YALA**, **PENANG**, Kuala Trengganu, **PERAK**, **KELANTAN**, Ipoh, **TRENGGANU**, **PAHANG**, **MALAYSIA**, Kuantan, **SELANGOR**, Sumatra, **■ KUALA LUMPUR**, **NEGRI SEMBILAN**, 108 / 81 ⋈, **MALACCA**, Malacca, **JOHORE**, 44 / 21, Johore Baharu, ★ **SINGAPORE**, ⋈, **INDONESIA**, Singapore Strait

Maritime security issues

Actions by the littoral states with primary security responsibility for the Malacca Strait – Indonesia, Malaysia, Singapore and Thailand – have led to a general improvement in maritime security in the area. In the first quarter of 2006, the International Maritime Organisation (IMO) reported no incidents of or attempts at piracy and armed sea robbery in the strait and according to media reports the International Maritime Bureau was pressing Lloyd's insurance to remove the Strait from its list of war risk zones. As well as bilateral initiatives, cooperative activities include: the Regional Cooperation Agreement on Anti-Piracy in Asia (also involving other ASEAN members); the Indonesia–Singapore Joint Surpio Naval Monitoring System; the 'Eyes in the Sky' coordinated maritime air patrol programme which followed the 2004 Malacca Straits Sea Patrols. These states' militaries now operate routine patrols and have defined patrol areas in the Strait. However, dangers from piracy and armed sea robbery still persist: in April and July there were further reports of attacks and attempted attacks on vessels in the Malacca Strait.

• Daily, more than 10 million barrels of crude oil, and annually, more than 50,000 ships, pass through the Straits.

• At the 2006 Shangri-La Dialogue in Singapore, India's Defence Minster Pranab Mukherjee noted that more than 50% of India's maritime trade passes through the Malacca Strait, and offered – when speaking of the Indonesia–Malaysia–Singapore Compulsory Pilotage project – Indian assistance 'in whatever capacity is deemed suitable'.

© IISS

ASIA: Indonesia's earthquake and other security problems in Southeast Asia

Turmoil in Timor Leste...

One year after the UNTAET peacekeepers departed, international peacekeeping troops have returned to Timor Leste. This followed unrest resulting from the dismissal of an estimated one-third of its army in March, after these troops protested against the government and made allegations reported to concern 'nepotism and injustice'. Rioting and clashes, mainly between security forces and the former soldiers, but which according to media reports has also involved gangs, has since April 2006 led to much disorder in Timor Leste and the displacement of substantial sections of the country's population, particularly from Dili.

In late May, Australia, New Zealand, Malaysia and Portugal began deploying security personnel and troops in response to a request from José Ramos Horta, Timor Leste's foreign minister. Australia started its deployment on 24 May, negotiating terms and conditions of the deployment a day later. About 2,600 personnel from the four countries deployed to Timor Leste. Ships as well as air assets were also employed. New Zealand dispatched around 150 personnel, including military police; Malaysia sent one vessel and over 300 paratroopers and commandos; while Portugal sent a 120-strong gendarmerie force. On 30 May, President Xanana Gusmão took control of national security matters in a bid to defuse tension and re-establish public order. This was followed by the sacking of the defence and interior ministers and the appointment on 2 June of José Ramos Horta as defence minister. 14 June saw the first limited weapons surrender by one of the dissident groups: Australian troops were due to receive these weapons at Maubisse, south of Dili and at Gleno. On 26 June, Mari Alkatiri resigned as Timor Leste's prime minister. This did not halt violence however and late June saw more disturbances in Dili.

4 June: fighting breaks out between gangs close to Dili airport.

12 ⚔ 25 May: 12 policemen killed, a number wounded in Dili.

5 ⚔ 28 April: five killed, around 20 injured, during protests in Dili.

26 April: police disperse rally by sacked soldiers and supporters in Dili.

24 May: marine officer wounded, likely in Dili.

2 ⚔ 23 May: two killed, five wounded in and around Dili.

⚔ 8 June: Provincial office of Fretilin burned in Gleno; party official's house targeted in Ermera (40km SW of Dili).

1 ⚔ 8 May: Policeman killed and two injured in Gleno (30km SW of Dili).

Australian forces supporting operations:
- HMAS *Tobruk* • HMAS *Kanimbla*
- HMAS *Tarakan* • HMAS *Manoora*
- HMAS *Labuan* • C-130 airbridge
- Bde Comd elm • 3 RAR Gp • 4 RAR (Cdo)
- 8 x S70A *Blackhawk* helicopters

Malaysia dispatched the KD *Mahawangsa* and over 300 troops

On 26 May **New Zealand** dispatched a RNZAF Boeing 757 and a C-130 to Darwin to assist operations; 150 personnel also moved to Timor Leste

Portugal sent 120 paramilitary police.

...and instability in the Solomon Islands

In 2003, long-standing ethnic tensions in the Solomon Islands spilled over into serious challenges to law and order that, at one stage, led the then-prime minister to evacuate Honiara. In response, an Australian-led intervention force deployed in a bid to restore order; following stabilisation, the Regional Assistance Mission to the Solomon Islands (RAMSI) was established, comprising personnel from Australia, New Zealand, Fiji, Tonga, Papua New Guinea, The Cook Islands, Kiribati, Samoa, Vanuatu and Nauru. While RAMSI assists Honiara in 'nation building' initiatives, it also contributes to security in the Islands through its Participating Police Force (drawing personnel from RAMSI nations) and its military component. (RAMSI's military presence comprises forces from Australia, New Zealand, Tonga and Papua New Guinea.)

Elections in April 2006, which passed off without major incident, led the country's MPs to elect Snyder Rini as prime minister. This appointment aroused serious opposition, with demonstrators marching on parliament and rioting breaking out in Honiara, with the ethnic Chinese community a particular target. On 19 April, one day after six Australian police personnel were injured, Canberra augmented its RAMSI contingent – a move that was followed by Papua New Guinea; New Zealand rotated its army contingent in early May. (RAMSI coordinator James Batley also thanked Tonga for its assistance, as its police contingent rotated in early April.) On 26 April, Snyder Rini resigned as prime minister, being replaced in early May by opposition leader Manasseh Sogavare.

- At the height of Australia's deployment, there were about 400 ADF personnel reinforcing RAMSI, including troops from 1 RAR, 3RAR and RAAF Field Defence Guards. Following the drawdown of Australia's enhanced presence in the Solomon Islands, Australian forces comprised about 140 personnel.

- Australia deployed the vessels HMAS *Bathurst*, *Armidale* and *Townsville* in the period following the April riots and utilised 707 and C-130 aircraft to support deployments. Two UH-1 helicopters supported movements in-theatre.

- 20 April 2006 Papua New Guinea dispatched – with aviation support from the New Zealand military – 20 officers from its Police Tactical Response Unit.

© IISS

ASIA: Sri Lanka's ongoing conflict

The December 2002 ceasefire agreement between the Sri Lankan government and the Liberation Tigers of Tamil Eelam (LTTE) has come under severe strain in 2006. A series of attacks on civilians, and clashes between the LTTE and Sri Lankan military forces, have left scores dead, while the responsibility for some attacks remains disputed. Meanwhile, the Norwegian-sponsored peace talks, on-off since 2002, have also suffered, with the LTTE reportedly refusing to attend a round of talks in Oslo scheduled for June 2006. In May 2006, the EU added the LTTE to its list of banned terrorist organisations.

Reported incidents: January–June 2006

13 May: Tamils killed.

11 May: 'Dozens' reported dead after sea battle – one Sri Lanka navy vessel and unconfirmed numbers of LTTE vessels sunk.

4 May: Army reports seven killed in attack on army post.

2 May: 2 killed, 2 injured at Tamil language newspaper offices.

19 April: Tamils killed near Puttur.

10 April: five Sri Lankan soldiers; two civilians die in attack at Mirusuvil.

16 Jan: three women killed; one man killed in separate incident.

6 June: Two Tamils killed – one reported to be former member of the EPDP anti-LTTE political group.

17 June: Attack on church, 1 dead; more than 30 die in naval clashes between LTTE and Sri Lankan forces.

12 Jan: at least nine sailors killed.

8 June: Family of four killed.

12 June: one soldier killed, three civilians wounded.

6 June: Two policemen and one civilian killed.

24 April: Sinhalese guards killed.

23 April: Farmers killed.

27 May: Sri Lankan tourists.

5 May: Sri Lankan navy reports destruction of LTTE boat nr Kalpitiya.

15 June: mine attack on bus leaves 64 dead and 80 wounded.

26 June: Army Deputy Chief of Staff and two others.

6 June: two people hurt in bomb attack blamed on Tamil rebels outside Welisara naval base.

25 April: 27 reported injured, army HQ; army chief seriously injured. Sri Lankan military attacks targets in the north-east.

25 March: LTTE personnel die after their vessel detonates close to navy patrol boat – also destroyed; eight sailors reported missing. LTTE disputes account. Colombo subsequently re-imposes offshore fishing ban.

16 June: Rebel positions and suspected airfield.

15 June: LTTE positions.

21 April: three security personnel; one civilian dies in subsequent violence.

12 April: Market and police patrol; rioting follows.

21 / 30 March: Naval clash.

24 Jan: Tamil civilians, including a journalist.

7 Jan: LTTE attack on naval vessel.

2 Jan: Tamils killed; defence ministry later reported to have announced investigation.

6 June: Two Tamils shot.

1 May: Mine attack; Navy reports LTTE attack.

26 April: Sri Lankan military forces engage reported LTTE targets in the area, citing attacks on naval vessels.

11 April: Navy bus hits mine near Trincomalee.

7 April: Tamil activist killed.

15 June: LTTE positions.

7 June: Tamils.

30 April: Fighting between LTTE and breakaway Karuna faction

17 June: renegade rebel commander Karuna threatens to attack LTTE positions – his group have an office in Batticaloa.

4 June: eight LTTE personnel escape from prison.

22 May: reported senior LTTE official killed.

30 April: Suspected Tamil rebels.

2 March: LTTE personnel.

26 Jan: LTTE senior staff member.

16 Jan: Tamils killed.

14 Jan: SLMM offices.

Number of IDPs (conflict, at 30 April 2006)

- 50,000 to 80,138
- 25,000 to 40,000
- 11,000 to 25,000
- 5,000 to 10,000
- 1 to 5,000

5 Number of people killed
Shooting
Unspecified attack
Air attack
Naval attack
Mine attack
Suicide attack
Suicide boat attack

8 June: Two-day talks in Oslo, to discuss the security situation and role of the Sri Lanka Monitoring Mission (SLMM) break down; neither side actually meets. • **22 April:** attempt to convene renewed peace talks in Geneva on 24–25 April unsuccessful. • **10 April:** Canada lists LTTE as terrorist group. • **22-23 February:** both sides meet in Geneva. Statement released includes: 'The GOSL and the LTTE are committed to respecting and upholding the Ceasefire Agreement, and reconfirmed their commitment to fully cooperate with and respect the rulings of the Sri Lanka Monitoring Mission (SLMM).'

Sources: IISS, BBC, HIC Sri Lanka, EU

© IISS

ASIA: The South Asia earthquake

On 8 October 2005 a 7.6 magnitutde earthquake struck near Muzaffarabad in South Asia's Kashmir region, hitting populations on both side of the disputed Line of Control. Estimated to have killed 73,000 people in Pakistan/Pakistan-administered Kashmir alone, and an estimated 1,400 in Indian-administered Kashmir, the earthquake left hundreds of thousands more without adequate food or shelter before winter.

According to Islamabad, the 'region is home to a scattered population of some 5.7m people, nearly half of whom are under the age of 15. Eighty-eight percent of the population lives in hilly, mountainous rural settlements, which range in size from two households to more than 300. The earthquake destroyed 203,579 housing units, damaged another 196,574 and left an estimated 2.5m people in need [of] shelter.' A substantial international aid effort, with the involvement of the UN and international and national NGOs mobilised assistance, while in mid-November, some $5.4bn was pledged to Pakistan at an international donors conference in Islamabad. Domestic and international military, civil defence and crisis response forces also reacted, while NATO sent equipment and personnel from its NATO Response Force.

Selected elements of the international civil and military response:

Most affected area

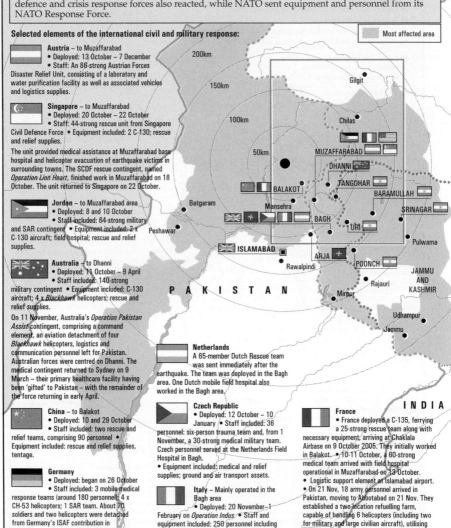

Austria – to Muzaffarabad
• Deployed: 13 October – 7 December
• Staff: An 86-strong Austrian Forces Disaster Relief Unit, consisting of a laboratory and water purification facility as well as associated vehicles and logistics supplies.

Singapore – to Muzaffarabad
• Deployed: 20 October – 22 October
• Staff: 44-strong rescue unit from Singapore Civil Defence Force • Equipment included: 2 C-130; rescue and relief supplies.

The unit provided medical assistance at Muzaffarabad base hospital and helicopter evacuation of earthquake victims in surrounding towns. The SCDF rescue contingent, named *Operation Lion Heart*, finished work in Muzaffarabad on 18 October. The unit returned to Singapore on 22 October.

Jordan – to Muzaffarabad area
• Deployed: 8 and 10 October
• Staff included: 64-strong military and SAR contingent • Equipment included: 2 x C-130 aircraft; field hospital; rescue and relief supplies.

Australia – to Dhanni
• Deployed: 11 October – 9 April
• Staff included: 140-strong military contingent • Equipment included: C-130 aircraft; 4 x *Blackhawk* helicopters; rescue and relief supplies.

On 11 November, Australia's *Operation Pakistan Assist* contingent, comprising a command element, an aviation detachment of four *Blackhawk* helicopters, logistics and communication personnel left for Pakistan. Australian forces were centred on Dhanni. The medical contingent returned to Sydney on 9 March – their primary healthcare facility having been 'gifted' to Pakistan – with the remainder of the force returning in early April.

China – to Balakot
• Deployed: 10 and 29 October
• Staff included: two rescue and relief teams, comprising 90 personnel • Equipment included: rescue and relief supplies, tentage.

Germany
• Deployed: began on 26 October
• Staff included: 3 mobile medical response teams (around 180 personnel; 4 x CH-53 helicopters; 1 SAR team. About 70 soldiers and two helicopters were detached from Germany's ISAF contribution in Afghanistan. After the NATO mission ended, Berlin offered to keep its air component operational for a limited period.

Netherlands
A 65-member Dutch Rescue team was sent immediately after the earthquake. The team was deployed in the Bagh area. One Dutch mobile field hospital also worked in the Bagh area.

Czech Republic
• Deployed: 12 October – 10 January • Staff included: 36 personnel: six-person trauma team and, from 1 November, a 30-strong medical military team. Czech personnel served at the Netherlands Field Hospital in Bagh.
• Equipment included: medical and relief supplies; ground and air transport assets.

Italy – Mainly operated in the Bagh area
• Deployed: 20 November–1 February on *Operation Indus* • Staff and equipment included: 250 personnel including specialist engineering and logistics personnel; over 140 vehicles; and two C-130s for the NATO air bridge.

France
• France deployed a C-135, ferrying a 25-strong rescue team along with necessary equipment, arriving at Chaklala Airbase on 9 October 2005. They initially worked in Balakot. • 10-11 October, a 60-strong medical team arrived with field hospital operational in Muzaffarabad on 13 October.
• Logistic support element at Islamabad airport. • On 21 Nov, 18 army personnel arrived in Pakistan, moving to Abbotabad on 21 Nov. They established a two-location refuelling farm, capable of handling 6 helicopters (including two for military and large civilian aircraft), utilising 3x300,000 tanks. France was asked to keep the fuel farm operational beyond the NATO operation end-date. • C-130 allocation to NATO airbridge.

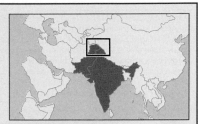

UK
On 13 October a UK officer arrived in Islamabad as part of NATO's Operational Liaison Reconnaissance Team. The UK contribution to *Operation Maturin* included the following bilateral assistance: 3 CH-47 *Chinook*, with 81 personnel; six-person Operational Liaison and Reconnaissance Team arrived in Islamabad on 19 October; two-person Mobile Air Operations team deployed to Chaklala airbase on 29-30 October for FOB reconnaissance, four logistics planners to Islamabad on 26 October to assist UN Joint Logistics Centre; four-person Joint Media Operations Team; 4 x C-17 flights; C-130 flights from Afghanistan. • Assistance offered through NATO included: 4 x C-130 with six crews deployed to assist NATO airbridge with 91 personnel in total (84 Incirlik, 7 Baku); Four-strong RAF Mobile Medical Team • 8 December: 86 members of 59 Ind Cdo Sqn RE deploy to Bagh to construct shelters – also work in Chittra Topi, Gahl Chhaprian, Dhirkot, Dhal Khazian. The Cdo Engineers returned to the UK on 2 February.

India – India's military response to an earthquake that also claimed lives on its side of the Line of Control was termed *Operation Imdad*. The Indian army established medical camps at Uri and Poonch and provided assistance in Rampur, Naogaon, Poonch and other areas.
• The Indian army deployed 50 columns, with approximately 2,500 personnel, for rescue efforts • Indian army established relief camps at: Uri, Tanghdhar, Kupwara, Baramullah • Baramullah district: 22 army columns • Kupwara district: 16 columns • Poonch district: 2 columns, 1 surgical team; eight columns with medical teams to outlying areas; two engineer columns to Poonch town • Additional army forces were placed on notice to move to Srinagar. • As at 13 October, the Indian Air Force had flown: 96 Mi-17 sorties; 17 *Chetak* sorties; 81 AN-32 sorties; 198 *Chetak* sorties; 2 B-737 sorties; 2 Dornier sorties; and 26 Il-76 flights.

Pakistan
Substantial sections of Pakistan's military forces were devoted to immediate rescue and relief efforts, after the earthquake claimed the lives of many service personnel. Brigades and battalions were dispatched to reach outlying towns and villages across Pakistan-administered Kashmir, with – in more remote and mountainous areas, – animal transport being used to move supplies where roads had been destroyed. *Chinook*, Mi-17 and Bell helicopters were much used in transport and evacuation efforts – up to 12 November, 6,076 sorties had been flown by Pakistan's army and air force. Reconstruction and rehabilitation efforts continue.

US
US rescue teams were in Pakistan on 10 October and the last US forces completed their missions on 31 March. At the peak of initial US efforts, 'more than 1,200 personnel and 25 helicopters provided vital transport, logistics and medical and engineering support in the affected areas'.
• On 16 February, US forces handed over to Pakistan the 84-bed 212 Mobile Army Surgical Hospital, which had been operational since 25 October in Muzaffarabad. • The US also deployed a 60-bed hospital to Shinkiari, staffed by the medical company from the Okinawa-based 3rd Marine Logistics Group. • Mobile Construction Battalion 74 (Seabees) deployed to Muzaffarabad. • 25 helicopters (including a number of CH-46); C-130s; C-5s; and C-17s were flown in support of US operations • Assets from the 212th Rescue Squadron, 818th Contingency Response Group and 24th Air Expeditionary Group • Landing Ship Dock *USS Pearl Harbor* and Landing Platform Dock *USS Cleveland* also made a number of stops in Karachi in support of the relief effort.

NATO – On 11 October, in response to a request from Pakistan, NATO launched an operation to assist in the urgent relief effort. NATO activated its NATO Response Force, which dispatched a number of nations' contributions to Pakistan under NATO control – the first units of engineers and medical units arrived on 29 October. Some nations also sent bilateral contributions, as well as those dedicated to NATO.
The NATO Land Component in Pakistan was led by the Spanish, headquartered in Arja and included: • Two light engineer units in the Bagh district (one Spanish and one Polish); • An Italian engineer unit with heavy construction equipment; • A unit of British engineers specialised in high-altitude relief work;
• A multi-national team of medics operating the NATO field hospital, including staff for inpatient and outpatient care, as well as mobile medical teams in the Bagh area – led by the Dutch Army and including Czech, French, Portuguese and British personnel;
• Four Water Purification teams (one Spanish, three Lithuanian) • Two civil-military cooperation teams from Slovenia and France.
'The NATO Air Component in Pakistan came from the French Air Defence and Operation Command and included: • A German helicopter detachment; • A Luxembourg rescue helicopter; • A French ground handling team; • A fuel farm operated by a French unit at Abbottabad.'
NATO's HQ in Pakistan comprised personnel from NATO's Joint Force Command, Lisbon, augmented by staff from (SHAPE). In total, some 1,000 NATO engineers and supporting staff, as well as 200 medical personnel, worked in Pakistan during the operation.

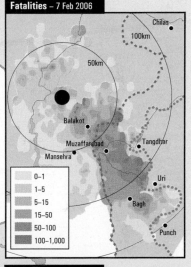

Fatalities – 7 Feb 2006

Chilas
100km
50km
Balakot
Muzaffarabad   Tangdhar
Mansehra
Uri
Bagh
Punch

0–1
1–5
5–15
15–50
50–100
100–1,000

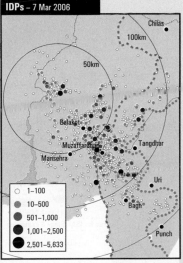

IDPs – 7 Mar 2006

Chilas
100km
50km
Balakot
Muzaffarabad   Tangdhar
Mansehra
Uri
Bagh
Punch

○ 1–100
10–500
501–1,000
1,001–2,500
2,501–5,633

Note: the nations listed above, and others not listed for reasons of space, provided other assistance packages, while non-governmental organisations – as well as the United Nations – provided substantial monetary, practical and long-term relief and reconstruction assistance to earthquake victims
Sources: national defence and government websites; NATO; IISS

Miles	50
Km	80

ASIA: Afghanistan: NATO's expansion

On 4 May 2006, NATO's Headquarters Allied Rapid Reaction Corps (ARRC) took over the leadership of the International Security Assistance Force (ISAF), from the Italian-commanded NATO Rapid Deployable Corps. ISAF is expanding its mission into Afghanistan's southern provinces where, in the main, Coalition forces have hitherto been operating. The US is expected to reduce its military presence there by some 2–3,000, while NATO will increase its forces from 9,000 to around 15,000. The NATO expansion is described in terms of stages, with the latest being Stage 3. A Stage 4 expansion is also being discussed, with a possible move into the areas currently hosting operations by Coalition forces.

ISAF Provincial Reconstruction Team (PRT)

ISAF Forward Supporting Base (FSB)

ISAF PRT being established

Currently Non-ISAF / NATO PRT

NATO HQ

Stage 1
Stage 2 } to 2005

Stage 3 (2006)

OEF (not incl US PRTs)
US forces – Dec 2005
    US Army – 15,400
    Navy – 400
    Marines – 1,200
    Air force – 3,400

Coalition: €4,000 (April 2006)

NATO-ISAF (36 nations*): > 15,000

Estimated contributions of NATO ISAF nations

Albania	**37	Germany	2,800	Norway	433
Austria	**4	Greece	157	Poland	3
Australia	400	Hungary	187	Portugal	**162
Belgium	301	Iceland	*nk	Romania	550
Bulgaria	100	Ireland	7	Slovakia	40
Canada	2,300	Italy	**1,370	Slovenia	58
Croatia	**150	Latvia	**57	Spain	572
Czech Republic	**150	Lithuania	120	Sweden	**210
Denmark	106	Luxembourg	10	Switzerland	4
Estonia	150	FYROM	257	Turkey	825
Finland	**101	Netherlands	**1,400	UK	5,700
France	500+	New Zealand	106		

*crisis response unit (non-military)
** June 2006 figures; remainder April 2006

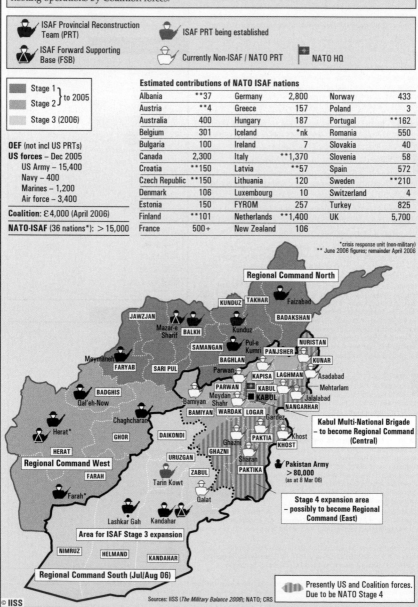

Regional Command North

Regional Command West

Regional Command South (Jul/Aug 06)

Kabul Multi-National Brigade – to become Regional Command (Central)

Pakistan Army > 80,000 (as at 8 Mar 06)

Stage 4 expansion area – possibly to become Regional Command (East)

Area for ISAF Stage 3 expansion

Presently US and Coalition forces. Due to be NATO Stage 4

© IISS

Sources: IISS (*The Military Balance 2006*); NATO; CRS

ASIA: Afghanistan: ISAF's move south

ISAF's Stage 3 expansion has led to the deployment of British forces in Helmand province, Dutch forces to Uruzgan and Canadian forces to Kandahar, sometimes with attached forces from other nations. But Afghanistan's south faces continuing problems: as well as the impact of poppy growing, in 2006, a resurgence of Taliban strength was being reported, and newly deployed British troops in the south were already becoming involved in clashes in June. The Taliban were reported to be massing in large numbers in some rural areas, operating checkpoints and harassing villagers.

Afghanistan's south – the opium problem:
Uncertainty remains over the role that ISAF Stage 3 forces in Afghanistan will have in addressing poppy cultivation. That the problem remains substantial is beyond doubt: in early 2006 the UN Office on Drugs and Crime (UNODC) released its Opium Rapid Assessment Survey. The report states that in Helmand, Badakhshan, Zabul, Ghor and Uruzgan, 'a sharp increase in cultivation is expected'. While the UNODC reported that in Helmand traffickers and smugglers were in some cases paying villagers to grow poppy, villagers across the country cited unemployment, lack of government assistance and the wish to obtain disposable income as factors contribuing to poppy cultivation; the UNODC also noted that 'opium poppy farmers earn up to 10 times more per hectare cultivated than cereal farmers'.

UK assets: In February, the UK began the dispatch of 850 men (starting with troops from 39 Regt RE and A Coy 42 Cdo, along with 3 CH-47 from 18 (B) Sqn RAF) to construct facilities in Helmand province. The main body of UK forces, which will constitute a new Provincial Reconstruction Team in Helmand, was due to be operational by July, consisting of:
3 PARA; elm 9 Regt AAC (8 AH-64 *Apache*, 4 *Lynx*); elm 27 sqn RAF (6 CH-47); elm Household Cavalry Regt (incl *Scimitar* and *Spartan* vehs); 7 Para RHA (L118 Light Gun bty); elm 32 Regt RHA (*Desert Hawk* UAV bty); 13 Air Aslt Regt; 29 Regt RLC; 7 Bn REME; 16 Close Spt Med Regt; 4 C-130; various elements of the reserve forces. On 15 June, the UK defence secretary announced the deployment of 34 Sqn RAF Regiment to Kandahar airfield.

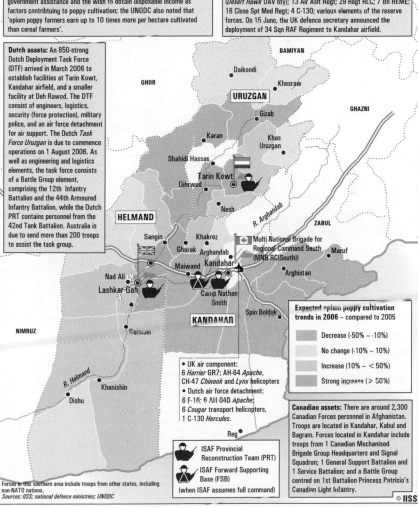

Dutch assets: An 850-strong Dutch Deployment Task Force (DTF) arrived in March 2006 to establish facilities at Tarin Kowt, Kandahar airfield, and a smaller facility at Deh Rawod. The DTF consist of engineers, logistics, security (force protection), military police, and an air force detachment for air support. The Dutch *Task Force Uruzgan* is due to commence operations on 1 August 2006. As well as engineering and logistics elements, the task force consists of a Battle Group element, comprising the 12th Infantry Battalion and the 44th Armoured Infantry Battalion, while the Dutch PRT contains personnel from the 42nd Tank Battalion. Australia is due to send more than 200 troops to assist the task group.

Canadian assets: There are around 2,300 Canadian Forces personnel in Afghanistan. Troops are located in Kandahar, Kabul and Bagram. Forces located in Kandahar include troops from 1 Canadian Mechanised Brigade Group Headquarters and Signal Squadron; 1 General Support Battalion and 1 Service Battalion; and a Battle Group centred on 1st Battalion Princess Patricia's Canadian Light Infantry.

Expected opium poppy cultivation trends in 2006 – compared to 2005
- Decrease (-50% – -10%)
- No change (-10% – 10%)
- Increase (10% – < 50%)
- Strong increase (> 50%)

- UK air component: 6 *Harrier* GR7; AH-64 *Apache*, CH-47 *Chinook* and *Lynx* helicopters
- Dutch air force detachment: 6 F-16; 6 AH-04D *Apache*; 6 *Cougar* transport helicopters, 1 C-130 *Hercules*.

ISAF Provincial Reconstruction Team (PRT)
ISAF Forward Supporting Base (FSB) (when ISAF assumes full command)

Forces in this southern area include troops from other states, including non-NATO nations.
Sources: IISS; national defence ministries; UNODC

© IISS

AMERICAS: Latin America's year of elections

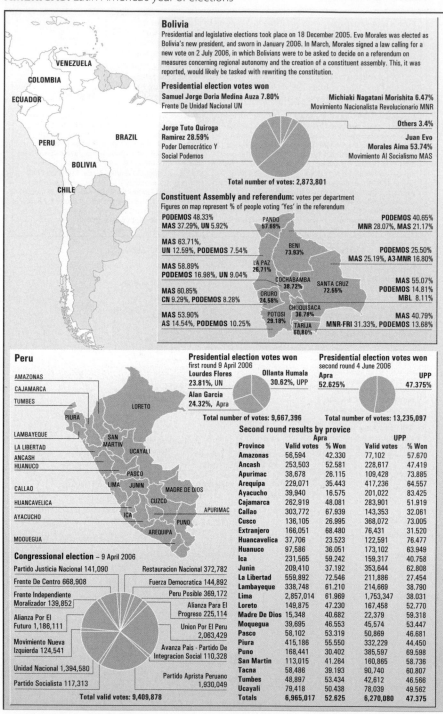

Bolivia

Presidential and legislative elections took place on 18 December 2005. Evo Morales was elected as Bolivia's new president, and sworn in January 2006. In March, Morales signed a law calling for a new vote on 2 July 2006, in which Bolivians were to be asked to decide on a referendum on measures concerning regional autonomy and the creation of a constituent assembly. This, it was reported, would likely be tasked with rewriting the constitution.

Presidential election votes won

Samuel Jorge Doria Medina Auza 7.80%
Frente De Unidad Nacional UN

Michiaki Nagatani Morishita 6.47%
Movimiento Nacionalista Revolucionario MNR

Jorge Tuto Quiroga Ramirez 28.59%
Poder Democrático Y Social Podemos

Others 3.4%

Juan Evo Morales Aima 53.74%
Movimiento Al Socialismo MAS

Total number of votes: 2,873,801

Constituent Assembly and referendum: votes per department
Figures on map represent % of people voting 'Yes' in the referendum

PODEMOS 48.33%
MAS 37.29%, UN 5.92%

PANDO 57.69%

PODEMOS 40.65%
MNR 28.07%, MAS 21.17%

MAS 63.71%,
UN 12.59%, PODEMOS 7.54%

BENI 73.93%

PODEMOS 25.50%
MAS 25.19%, A3-MNR 16.80%

MAS 58.89%
PODEMOS 16.98%, UN 9.04%

LA PAZ 26.71%

COCHABAMBA 38.72%

SANTA CRUZ 72.55%

MAS 55.07%
PODEMOS 14.81%
MBL 8.11%

MAS 60.85%
CN 9.29%, PODEMOS 8.28%

ORURO 24.58%

CHUQUISACA 36.78%

MAS 53.90%
AS 14.54%, PODEMOS 10.25%

POTOSI 29.18%

TARIJA 60.80%

MAS 40.79%
MNR-FRI 31.33%, PODEMOS 13.68%

Peru

AMAZONAS
CAJAMARCA
TUMBES
LORETO
PIURA
LAMBAYEQUE
LA LIBERTAD
ANCASH
HUANUCO
CALLAO
HUANCAVELICA
AYACUCHO
MOQUEGUA
SAN MARTIN
UCAYALI
PASCO
LIMA JUNIN
MADRE DE DIOS
CUZCO
ICA
APURIMAC
PUNO
AREQUIPA

Presidential election votes won
first round 9 April 2006

Lourdes Flores 23.81%, UN

Ollanta Humala 30.62%, UPP

Alan Garcia 24.32%, Apra

Total number of votes: 9,667,396

Presidential election votes won
second round 4 June 2006

Apra 52.625%

UPP 47.375%

Total number of votes: 13,235,097

Second round results by provice

Province	Apra		UPP	
	Valid votes	% Won	Valid votes	% Won
Amazonas	56,594	42.330	77,102	57.670
Ancash	253,503	52.581	228,617	47.419
Apurimac	38,678	26.115	109,428	73.885
Arequipa	229,071	35.443	417,236	64.557
Ayacucho	39,940	16.575	201,022	83.425
Cajamarca	262,919	48.081	283,901	51.919
Callao	303,772	67.939	143,353	32.061
Cusco	136,105	26.995	368,072	73.005
Extranjero	166,051	68.480	76,431	31.520
Huancavelica	37,706	23.523	122,591	76.477
Huanuco	97,586	36.051	173,102	63.949
Ica	231,565	59.242	159,317	40.758
Junin	209,410	37.192	353,644	62.808
La Libertad	559,892	72.546	211,886	27.454
Lambayeque	338,748	61.210	214,669	38.790
Lima	2,857,014	61.969	1,753,347	38.031
Loreto	149,875	47.230	167,458	52.770
Madre De Dios	15,348	40.682	22,379	59.318
Moquegua	39,695	46.553	45,574	53.447
Pasco	58,102	53.319	50,869	46.681
Piura	415,186	55.550	332,229	44.450
Puno	168,441	30.402	385,597	69.598
San Martin	113,015	41.264	160,865	58.736
Tacna	58,486	39.193	90,740	60.807
Tumbes	48,897	53.434	42,612	46.566
Ucayali	79,418	50.438	78,039	49.562
Totals	6,965,017	52.625	6,270,080	47.375

Congressional election – 9 April 2006

Partido Justicia Nacional 141,090

Frente De Centro 668,908

Frente Independiente Moralizador 139,852

Alianza Por El Futuro 1,186,111

Movimiento Nueva Izquierda 124,541

Unidad Nacional 1,394,580

Partido Socialista 117,313

Restauracion Nacional 372,782

Fuerza Democratica 144,892

Peru Posible 369,172

Alianza Para El Progreso 225,114

Union Por El Peru 2,063,429

Avanza Pais - Partido De Integracion Social 110,328

Partido Aprista Peruano 1,930,049

Total valid votes: 9,409,878

Chile

Presidential election – first round 11 December 2005
Second round run-off – 15 January 2006

Sebastián Piñera	Michelle Bachelet
3,227,658 votes,	3,712,902 votes,
46.50%	53.49%

Total valid votes: 6,940,560

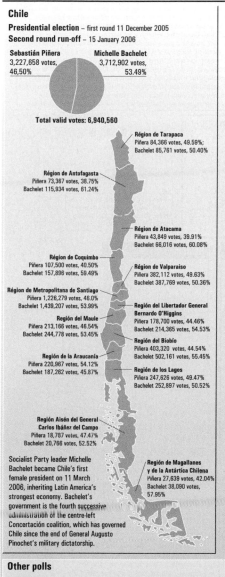

Région de Tarapaca
Piñera 84,366 votes, 49.59%;
Bachelet 85,761 votes, 50.40%

Région de Antofagasta
Piñera 73,367 votes, 38.75%
Bachelet 115,934 votes, 61.24%

Région de Atacama
Piñera 43,849 votes, 39.91%
Bachelet 66,016 votes, 60.08%

Région de Coquimbo
Piñera 107,500 votes, 40.50%
Bachelet 157,896 votes, 59.49%

Région de Valparaiso
Piñera 382,112 votes, 49.63%
Bachelet 387,769 votes, 50.36%

Région de Metropolitana de Santiago
Piñera 1,226,279 votes, 46.0%
Bachelet 1,439,207 votes, 53.99%

**Región del Libertador General
Bernardo O'Higgins**
Piñera 178,700 votes, 44.46%
Bachelet 214,365 votes, 54.53%

Región del Maule
Piñera 213,166 votes, 46.54%
Bachelet 244,778 votes, 53.45%

Región del Biobío
Piñera 403,320 votes, 44.54%
Bachelet 502,161 votes, 55.45%

Región de la Araucanía
Piñera 220,967 votes, 54.12%
Bachelet 187,262 votes, 45.87%

Región de los Lagos
Piñera 247,626 votes, 49.47%
Bachelet 252,897 votes, 50.52%

**Región Aisén del General
Carlos Ibáñez del Campo**
Piñera 18,787 votes, 47.47%
Bachelet 20,766 votes, 52.52%

**Región de Magallanes
y de la Antártica Chilena**
Piñera 27,639 votes, 42.04%
Bachelet 38,090 votes,
57.95%

Socialist Party leader Michelle Bachelet became Chile's first female president on 11 March 2006, inheriting Latin America's strongest economy. Bachelet's government is the fourth successive administration of the centre-left Concertación coalition, which has governed Chile since the end of General Augusto Pinochet's military dictatorship.

Colombia

Legislative elections were held on 12 March 2006, resulting in victory for parties in the governing coalition of President Alvaro Uribe. He also secured re-election in the presidential polls of 28 May.

Senate election votes won, % – 28 May 2006

Alvaro Leyva Duran
Movimiento Nacional De Reconciliacion
18,263 votes, 0.15%

Carlos Gaviria Diaz
Polo Democratico Alternativo
2,613,157 votes, 22.02%

**Carlos Arturo
Rincon Barreto**
Movimiento Comunal Y
Comunitario De Colombia
15,388 votes, 0.12%

Horacio Serpa Uribe
Partido Liberal Colombiano
1,404,235 votes, 11.83%

Enrique Parejo Gonzalez
Movimiento Reconstruccion
Democratica Nacional
42,652 votes, 0.35%

**Antanas Mockus
Sivickas**
Movimiento Alianza
Social Indigena
146,583 votes, 1.23%

Alvaro Uribe Velez
Primero Colombia
7,397,835 votes, 62.35%

Regional election results, % votes won by Alvaro Uribe Velez

1. Amazonas	41.75%
2. Antioquia	70.87%
3. Arauca	66.42%
4. Atlantico	42.00%
5. Bolivar	59.26%
6. Bogota D.C.	63.91%
7. Boyaca	63.03%
8. Caldas	69.28%
9. Caqueta	62.75%
10. Casanare	81.64%
11. Cauca	40.53%
12. Cesar	66.70%
13. Choco	49.45%
14. Cordoba	58.25%
15. Cundinamarca	70.85%
16. Guainia	53.89%
17. Guaviare	62.80%
18. Huila	70.76%
19. La Guajira	
Carlos Gaviria Diaz	43.42%
Alvaro Uribe Velez	39.86%
20. Magdalena	56.08%
21. Meta	71.71%
22. Nariño	
Carlos Gaviria Diaz	43.40%
Alvaro Uribe Velez	41.09%

23. Norte De Santander	67.11%
24. Putumayo	43.36%
25. Quindio	69.28%
26. Risaralda	72.42%
27. San Andres Y Providencia	54.03%
28. Santander	50.89%
29. Sucre	51.60%
30. Tolima	65.05%
31. Valle	59.97%
32. Vaupes	58.65%
33. Vichada	65.74%

Other polls

Brazil
Presidential election – 1 October (1st round); 29 October (2nd round).

Ecuador
Presidential election – 15 October (1st round); 26 November (2nd round).

Mexico
Presidential and legislative elections – 2 July.

Venezuela
Presidential elections are due in December 2006.

© IISS

AFRICA: Problems in East Africa and the Horn

Ongoing security problems in East Africa and the Horn of Africa are receiving increasing international attention. The peace deal in southern Sudan, the ongoing conflicts in Sudan's Darfur province and in Somalia, as well as the unresolved border dispute between Ethiopia and Eritrea remain key areas of concern. Issues of food security are compounding problems for the region's inhabitants: although rains in early- to mid-2006 have improved the situation somewhat, the legacy of past droughts – when allied with security issues – has hampered the effective distribution of foodstuffs and humanitarian assistance to needy populations.

Darfur: The conflict-related problems of Sudan's Darfur region have again been compounded this year. Both sides at times blocked aid and supplies to displaced persons, who numbered over two million and have spilled into neighbouring Chad. As of October 2005, the Darfur conflict had produced between 63,000 and 143,000 Sudanese fatalities, according to the US State Department, although other sources estimate as many as 400,000 deaths. In May 2006 the African Union (AU) brokered a peace deal which, though it was not signed by all rebel groups, has been viewed as easing the possible introduction of a UN peacekeeping force. In early June, media sources reported that the AU intended to boost its force in Darfur from 7,000 to 10,000, while personnel from the UN were in discussions with Khartoum over the possible replacement of the AU force by one from the UN. The crisis in Darfur contributed to an escalation of war in Chad, with Khartoum giving active support to rebel forces opposed to the government of President Idris Déby. In December 2005, the government of Chad announced that 'a state of war' existed along its border with Sudan. In April 2006, a large group of attackers invaded N'Djamena, Chad's capital, where they were thwarted by government troops in violence that killed 350 people.

See insets below

KHARTOUM

S U D A N

There has been growing unrest in the Nubian heartland in the east, with public discontent over the Hamdab (Merowe) dam culminating in unrest.

Security incidents reported by location – Jan–March 2006

NORTH DARFUR

EAST DARFUR

SOUTH DARFUR

○ 1–3
● 4–9
● 10–19
● 20–41

Rainfall – Jan–May 2006

Cumulated actual rainfall (mm)
☐ 0–50
51–100
101–200
201–400
401–600
601–800
> 800

U G A N D A

DEMOCRATIC REPUBLIC OF CONGO

IDPs – 19 March 2005

NORTH DARFUR

Kulbus 156,759

El Geneina 369,123
Zalingei 116,664
Jebel Marra 329,234

Habila 111,283
Sheiria 95,332

Wadi Salih 145,441
Kass 93,180
Nyala 303,654

WEST DARFUR
Ed el Fursan 10,976
Mukjar 54,487
Tullus 4,000
Adila 13,895

Rahad el Berdi 0
SOUTH DARFUR
Buram 99,898
El Daein 54,169

○ 518–10,000
● 10,001–20,000
● 20,000–30,000
● 30,000–50,000
● 50,001–142,125

Sudan In January 2005, a Comprehensive Peace Agreement (CPA) – which included power sharing arrangements – was signed to end a long war between north and south. But by mid-2006, Sudan was facing problems on many fronts. The CPA was proving difficult to implement and the National Petroleum Commission was slow in addressing the north–south division of oil revenues. Meanwhile, in the south, inadequate implementation of the CPA has created dissatisfaction, while there has been continued activity by the Lord's Resistance Army, who have shifted their area of operation from south of Juba west towards the border with the DRC. In the west, conflict continued in Darfur, in spite of efforts to ameliorate the situation.

TANZANIA

© IISS

Ethiopia and Eritrea
The decision of the Ethiopia–Eritrea Border Commission on resolution of the border dispute between the two states has still to be implemented. Meanwhile, the UN Mission in Ethiopia and Eritrea is due to be scaled down, although the force's mandate has been extended by four months. Although tensions rose in late 2005, hostilities did not resume and the border issues, as well as a long-standing dispute over access by land-locked Ethiopia to the sea, remain unresolved. Meanwhile, the Ethiopian elections saw irregularities such that it is not possible to say who won. 'Whoever actually won, the margin appears to have been slim. The election was therefore a political defeat for the regime: despite having pre-secured 72 constituencies, and notwithstanding a recent military victory, it could not credibly point to an unequivocal popular mandate.'

Somalia: In May 2006, the 'Islamic Courts Militia' gained control of Mogadishu, having driven out the warlords who previously largely controlled the city. Media sources then reported forces associated with the group moving towards Jowhar and Baidoa. Their level of control outside these centres is as yet uncertain, as are the future prospects of civilians again displaced by the fighting.
Meanwhile, WFP and UNICEF representatives in June pointed to concern that continued fighting, together with the impact of last season's severe drought, could create the 'bleakest malnutrition situation in years'. 'Current malnutrition rates are acute. At 23 percent they are well above the 15 percent that signals an emergency.'

ERITREA

ASMARA

DJIBOUTI

Piracy incidents reported
Jan 05 – Mar 06
Hijacked   Attempted boarding

Food security
Generally food secure
Chronically food insecure
Acute food and livelihood crisis
Humanitarian emergency

ADDIS ABABA

E T H I O P I A

S O M A L I A

MARSABIT

MOYALE

TRANS-
NZOIA   SAMBURU

BARINGO

LAIKIPIA

K E N Y A

MOGADISHU

*Sources: UNOSAT; WFP; USAID;
MO Seriat; IISS; IFRC; EC JRC*

NAIROBI

Northern Kenya
In April 2006, the IFRC reported deaths from clashes between pastoral communities in northern Kenya. Some analysts are positing that moderately improved rainfall, which could lead to greater animal survival, and in turn potentially less rustling of animals to restock herds, could lead to a reduction in violence. Nonetheless, there are fears that their escalation may spread into other districts and cause further complications'.

Horn of Africa
Estimates of vulnerable population in drought-affected countries (m)

■ Population at risk
(chronic and acute)
Total: 15.75m

■ Of which: acute
(relief) current drought
emergency (as of
early April 2006)
Total: 7.88m

10

3.5 3.5

2.6*

2.1

1.7

0.08 0.15

Djibouti Somalia Kenya Ethiopia

*Of which 1.7 million in south-eastern pastoral areas

Offshore Horn of Africa
The international community remains concerned by the incidents of piracy and armed sea robbery that continue to occur off the Horn of Africa. While multinational naval forces have had an impact and continue operations, and a new regional anti-piracy centre was recently opened in Mombasa, continued piracy and sea robbery has a negative impact on the optimum provision of supplies to needy populations both in Somalia and further inland in the Horn of Africa.

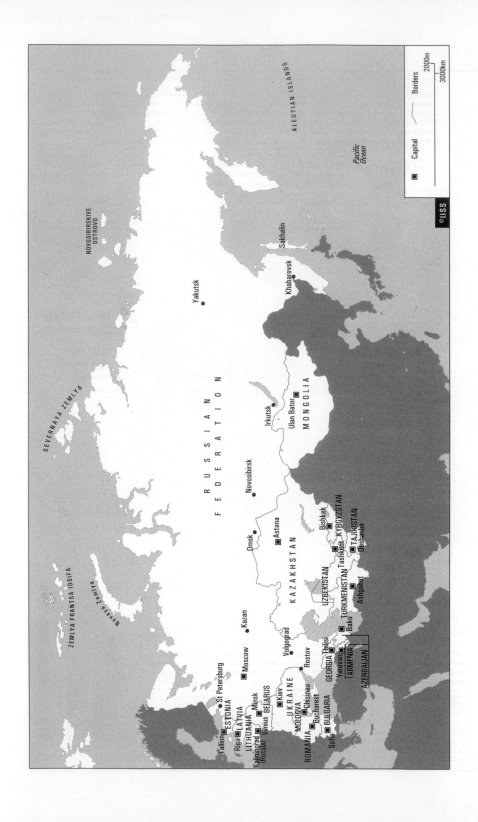

5 | **Russia and Eurasia**

Russia: An Emerging Energy Superpower?

The year to mid-2006 saw the emergence of a more confident, more assertive and more powerful Russia – though over-dependent on oil and gas exports and facing domestic social challenges as well as continuing insecurity in the North Caucasus.

Russia was as stable, prosperous and independent as it had ever been in the post-Soviet era, and even in several decades preceding the collapse of the Soviet Union. No major terrorist attacks on the scale of the 2002 Moscow theatre siege and 2004 Beslan hostage crisis took place in the year to mid-2006. Driven by the rise in world energy prices, Russia's economy has continued to grow, bringing an increasing sense of wealth and power to the Russian political elite. This new domestic stability, combined with Moscow's presidency of the G8 and its role in addressing Iran's nuclear programme, have enhanced Russia's role in international affairs. Russia engaged in active global diplomacy, seeking to restore ties to Middle Eastern states, including Syria and Egypt, and to develop closer ties with China, India and Southeast Asia. Russian business interests, often used in support of its foreign-policy agenda, are increasingly visible in world markets, with companies such as Gazprom, Russia's main natural gas producer, acquiring assets in Europe and declaring their intention to expand their European presence.

However, Russia's growing dependence on revenue from oil and gas exports risks stalling growth of other sectors of the economy: plans to diversify the economy have run into the sand. There is insufficient investment in the exploitation of the country's very large oil and gas reserves, indicating that production will tend to fall in the near future. In addition, there is growing political uncertainty leading up to the 2008 presidential elections, when President Vladimir Putin is barred by the constitution from seeking a third term. Although Putin's approval rating remained high in 2005–06, there was growing dissatisfaction with endemic corruption, an increasing gap between rich and poor, and lack of investment in social reforms, in modernisation of aged infrastructure and in resolution of demographic challenges. Domestic security problems continued in the North Caucasus, where instability was spreading from the decade-long conflict in Chechnya to engulf the entire region. Other domestic security challenges included proliferation of radical nationalist and neo-fascist groups, which carried out regular attacks against ethnic minorities and foreign migrants throughout Russia, particularly in Moscow and St Petersburg.

A perception that Russia was moving away from democratic reforms led to a further deterioration in relations with the United States and Europe. These relationships could no longer be cast as strategic partnerships, and were increasingly characterised by mutual mistrust, divergent interests and a limited agenda for practical cooperation. In 2005 Eurasia emerged as an important source of tension between Russia and Europe, as well as between Russia and the United States. Russian and Western interests clashed over elections in Ukraine and Belarus, over approaches to the resolution of conflicts in Georgia and Moldova, over routes for transport of Central Asian and Caspian oil and gas resources, over the stationing of US and coalition troops in Central Asia, and over prospects for NATO membership for Ukraine and Georgia.

The poorly conceived and badly executed decision temporarily to stop natural gas supplies to Ukraine in January 2006 over a price dispute undermined confidence in Russia as Europe's key strategic energy supplier and cast a shadow on preparations for the G8 summit in St Petersburg in July 2006. It prompted the European Union to take steps to lessen long-term dependency on imports from Russia. Europe was seeking to increase imports of Caspian and Central Asian energy resources, bypassing Russian territory and triggering new geopolitical rivalries with Moscow.

The likelihood that NATO would offer Ukraine and Georgia Membership Action Plans (MAPs) at the Riga Summit in November 2006 also generated tension. Expanding European and American engagement with the South Caucasus and newly independent states such as Ukraine and Moldova also provoked suspicion and resentment in Moscow. The departure of German Chancellor Gerhard Schröder and Italian Prime Minister Silvio Berlusconi, who had both been close allies of Putin, had a significant impact on European policies towards Russia, making it difficult for Moscow to prevent convergence of European policies towards Russia – even if most EU states tend to pursue primarily national policies towards it.

Economic successes

When Putin came to power in 2000 he inherited a country in deep economic crisis, suffering from domestic insecurity and under threat of further disintegration. US President George W. Bush, who entered office months after Putin, asserted in his campaign that Russia should no longer be treated as a major power and that American interest lay in safeguarding Russian nuclear materials in the face of domestic chaos and insecurity. Putin's commitment to restore law and order and to project Russian power abroad sounded unrealistic. Yet in 2006 Russia is stable and prosperous at home and increasingly assertive in its foreign policy. Putin's supporters argue this is due to his policies; his personal approval ratings remain above 70%. Critics say most of the economic achievements came in spite of Putin's policies, which failed to develop and implement badly needed reforms.

Putin has indeed been lucky to enjoy a continuous increase in oil and natural gas prices, bringing Russia unprecedented revenues. Russia remains the biggest oil producer outside the Organisation of Petroleum Exporting Countries. In the first quarter of 2006 Russia extracted on average 9.04 million barrels of oil per day (b/d), about as much as Saudi Arabia's 9.39m b/d. Russia extracted around 116.3m tonnes of oil in the first quarter of 2006, 1.8% more than in the first quarter of 2005, of which 61m tonnes (52.5%) was exported. Oil constituted 49.9% of Russia's overall energy exports (including oil, natural gas and petroleum products). Russia's natural gas production rose 2.5% in the first five months of 2006 compared with the same period a year ago, reaching 283.9 billion cubic metres, of which state-controlled Gazprom produced 233.8bn cubic metres, or 88% of total Russian gas production.

According to the Russian Federal Statistics Service, Russia's trade surplus in 2005 rose 40% year-on-year to $120bn, with exports increasing by 33.9% to $245bn and imports rising 28.5% to $125bn; over the same period the price of Urals crude increased by 50% and natural-gas prices increased by 26%. Europe remained the main market for Russian oil and gas. In January–April 2006 the EU accounted for 54.8% ($68.23bn) of Russian trade, up from 53.2% in the same period in 2005, while energy exports increased from 64% to 71.4% of total exports outside the Commonwealth of Independent States (CIS).

The impact is obvious. In 2005 Russia experienced its seventh straight year of economic growth, over the whole period Russia's GDP increased by over 50%, with 6.4% growth in 2005 alone. Russian foreign exchange reserves, the fourth largest in the world, increased from $12bn in 2000 to $217bn in April 2006 – the increase in 2005 was 46%. Russia has paid off most of its foreign debt, which stood at $154bn in 1998 and $22bn in 2006, and has completed negotiations over early retirement of its remaining debt to the Paris Club. At the beginning of 2006 Russia's budget surplus stood at 7.5% of GDP, the seventh straight year in the black. The stabilisation fund set up to harvest windfall oil revenues over $27 per barrel exceeded $66bn in April 2006. In the first quarter of 2006 Russia attracted over $8.8bn in foreign investment, 46% more than the same period in 2005. By March 2006 total accumulated foreign investment in Russia reached $113.8bn, 33% higher than a year before.

Living standards have risen. Average income and pensions are increasing and there is greater distribution of wealth across Russia, particularly in commodity-producing regions. Consumption is increasing, attracting foreign investment in the consumer sector. Russians continue to travel to Europe and worldwide, constituting the fastest-growing outbound travel market in Europe and the third fastest worldwide. The number of Russian tourists rose by a further 18.6% in 2005 after a 66.7% increase in 2004. Russia now enjoys its highest levels of prosperity and stability for several decades.

Economic success has transformed the Russian leadership's view of the country's role in world affairs. Moscow's new foreign-policy doctrine relies to a large extent on projecting Russia's role as an energy superpower upon which Europe and China are increasingly dependent. Revenue from energy exports provides Russia with new resources to support domestic and international policies. Moreover, Russia's economic independence, in stark contrast to the 1990s when it relied heavily on Western loans and advice, has transformed it into an increasingly assertive and unilateralist power with global ambitions. This has led to increasing problems in relations with Europe and the United States, which, according to Russian decision-makers, refuse to recognise and accept Moscow's new international role.

Energy wealth: sustainability in question

Russia's slide towards the model of a classic 'petroleum state' has implications which, if not addressed, could lead it towards a new crisis. Amidst Russia's economic boom, economists and policymakers increasingly question the sustainability of its commodity-induced economic growth. Not only does dependence on oil and gas exports have a deleterious effect on the rest of the economy, but it is doubtful whether Russia can maintain its present levels of output.

Russia's drift towards becoming a petroleum state has undermined incentives to pursue badly needed structural, administrative and other economic reforms that could increase industrial production and stimulate technological innovation. Russia is experiencing growing inflation as well as the 'Dutch disease', in which high resource revenues cause appreciation of the rouble, making the manufacturing sector less competitive. Instead of implementing structural reforms, the government is increasingly engaged in redistribution of oil and gas revenues. At the same time, the gap between rich and poor is nearing a factor of 15: in 2005 the richest 10% of the population received 29.8% of the income, whereas the poorest 10% received only 2%. The World Trade Organisation views a factor of 14.2 as enough to create a real danger of social unrest in a country, a line that Russia crossed in 2003.

A further effect of dependence on oil and gas income is declining competitiveness. Russia is witnessing endemic and growing corruption, even at the highest level of government; increasing centralisation, declining efficiency and slow restructuring of state institutions; excessive state intervention in and control of energy companies; a continuing monopoly over transport infrastructure; limited scope for introducing private-sector management experience and technological innovation in the energy sector; and growing pressure to limit foreign (and private) ownership of major mineral resources. Russia has made little progress in enhancing the rule of law; reducing bureaucratic controls over the economy; improving corporate governance, particularly in the energy sector; establishing guarantees for private property rights; and encouraging domestic investment.

As a result, economic growth has been slowing, from 7.3% in 2003 to 7.2% in 2004 and 6.4% in 2005. This level of GDP growth, although high compared with the United States and Europe, puts Russia ninth among the 12 states of the former Soviet Union. The decline in growth is taking place in spite of record energy export earnings, and is likely to continue in the coming years in the absence of structural reforms and faster investment. Slowing growth will affect living standards and foreign investment, and will hamper development of the non-commodities sector, which displays signs of healthy market-driven transformation. It will present a major challenge to Putin's successor, who may have to implement economic reforms in a much less favourable economic environment. The economy is also vulnerable to external shocks such as a drop in oil prices.

The position becomes even more worrying when a flattening of oil and gas production and failure to invest sufficiently in unexploited reserves are taken into account. Experts predict that oil and gas production will decline gradually over the next decade. According to the European Bank for Reconstruction and Development (EBRD), 70% of the production of Gazprom comes from fields with declining output.

Although Russia still has large undeveloped oil and gas deposits, its companies lack sufficient funds to initiate and sustain exploration and production, particularly in eastern Siberia, where resources are increasingly costly to develop. The EBRD estimates that the Russian energy sector needs investment of around $700bn over the next 20 years. However, new Russian policies impede foreign investment in the energy sector. The government has made clear that only those foreign investors who accept the new rules will be allowed significant stakes in new exploration projects. Favour is likely to be shown to those foreign companies that would help Gazprom, which controls the Russian gas pipeline system, gain access to European energy-distribution assets. In April 2006 the German company BASF became the first beneficiary of the new rules. It signed a comprehensive deal with Gazprom under which its Wintershall unit would acquire 34.9% of Severneftegazprom, the company that owns the licence to develop the Yuzhno-Russkoye gas field in western Siberia. For its part Gazprom would increase its share in Wingas, a joint venture with BASF's Wintershall unit, from 35% to 49.9%, and Wingas would concentrate on selling and marketing natural gas in Germany. Gazprom and BASF would each take a 50% share in Wingas Europe, a joint venture that would concentrate on distributing gas outside Germany. In June 2006 President Putin and Italian Prime Minister Romano Prodi announced an agreement under which Italian companies will be allowed to bid for production contacts in exchange for Russian companies gaining access to Italian energy markets.

Such deals, even if signed, are still likely to run up against obstacles. A case in point is the giant Kovykta field, estimated to contain 2 trillion cubic metres of natural gas, where the BP–TNK joint venture holds a licence for exploration, but has so far been unable to develop deposits that could play a key role in expanding Russian gas exports to China. Another major project, the $20bn development of the Shtokman gas field in the Barents Sea, estimated to contain 3.2 trillion cubic metres of gas and 31m tonnes of gas condensate, has attracted attention from foreign investors including ConocoPhillips and Chevron, as well as the Norwegian companies Statoil and Hydro and the French company Total. But Gazprom has postponed a decision on foreign participation in the project.

The exploration of eastern Siberian deposits is crucial for Russia to realise its ambition of becoming a key energy supplier to Asia as well as Europe. Russia needs significant foreign investment to support construction of a Pacific oil pipeline that could take Russian energy exports to the eastern port of Nakhodka and onwards to Japan, Asia and possibly North America. Investors are reluctant to commit significant funds while Moscow maintains a state monopoly over the ownership of transport infrastructure (through Transneft) and remains reluctant to offer a significant stake in exploration and production projects to foreign investors. Russia has therefore given priority, at least in the short term, to the construction of a gas pipeline to China. During Putin's visit to China on 21–22 March 2006 a deal was agreed under which Russia would increase gas exports to China. Gazprom and China's state-controlled China National Petroleum Corporation (CNPC) signed an agreement on supply of Russian gas to China and construction of a new 3,000km pipeline, Altai, estimated to cost about $10bn, which will connect Russia and China. According to Putin, Russia planned to supply up to 80bn cubic metres of gas per year starting in 2011. In addition, Russia's state-controlled Transneft and CNPC signed an agreement to conduct a feasibility study on the East Siberia–Pacific Ocean pipeline to China, and CNPC and Rosneft signed a joint-venture agreement that could allow the Chinese company to take part in exploration and extraction of oil in Russia.

Moscow's decision to expand its oil and gas exports to China came on the back of increasingly strained relations between Russia and Europe following the temporary cut-off of Russian gas deliveries to Ukraine in January 2006. This resulted from a price dispute: Gazprom was seeking to reduce the degree to which it subsidised gas supplies to Ukraine. The cut-off had the effect of reducing supplies to other European countries at the peak period of demand. Within four days, however, the two countries had resolved their price dispute by agreeing that Ukraine would purchase gas from Russia at $230 per 1,000 cubic metres and from Turkmenistan at $65, against a former price of $50; Russian and Turkmen gas would be blended and supplied to Ukraine by the Russian–Ukrainian joint venture RosUkrEnergo at $95. The parties also agreed to raise the transit tariff from $1.09 to $1.60 per 1,000 cubic metres per 100km for both transit of Russian gas to Europe and Turkmen gas through Russia to Ukraine. The deal was criticised in the West for a lack of transparency and for the alleged involvement of organised crime groups in RosUkrEnergo – which denies any such involvement. Gazprom also announced its intention to raise the price to Belarus from $46.68 to $200 per 1,000 cubic metres after the controversial re-election of President Alexander Lukashenko in March 2006. The price increases are hard for Ukraine and Belarus to handle, but they are unable to diversify their sources.

Europeans became concerned over Russia's potential use of gas exports as a political tool, fearing that it might resort to future supply cuts if relations deteriorated. Moscow retorted that concerns over its reliability as a supplier were unfounded because neither Russia nor the Soviet Union had ever cut off gas supplies to Europe, with the exception of Ukraine, which had refused to accept market prices. Alexei Miller, Gazprom chairman, warned European ambassadors that if Europe continued to criticise Russia, challenge its reliability and restrict Gazprom's investments and acquisitions on political grounds, Russia had the option to re-orient its energy exports from Europe to Asia. Russia, however, will be unable in the short to medium term to meet increasing demand for gas from Europe, which is expected to depend on imports for over 80% of its gas by 2030. And it will have little spare capacity to expand exports to China: in the absence of progress in exploration of eastern Siberian deposits, Russia has to rely on exports from western Siberia which are already committed to Europe, the CIS and domestic consumption.

Gazprom has compensated for declining production by importing cheap gas from Turkmenistan, using its virtual monopoly over pipeline options for Turkmenistan's exports northwards into both Russia and Ukraine. However, this monopoly will not last forever. In 2005 the United States renewed attempts to convince Turkmenistan to send gas via the Caspian Sea to join the Baku–Tbilisi–Erzurum pipeline, which opens in 2006. Although prospects for a trans-Caspian gas pipeline remain remote, it has not been ruled out. In April 2006 Turkmenistan and China signed an agreement to construct a pipeline eastwards from Turkmenistan to China. The pipeline was expected to be constructed by 2009, and China agreed to buy 30bn cubic metres of gas annually from Turkmenistan. Judging from the pace of construction of the 998km Kazakhstan–China (Atasau–Alashankou) oil pipeline, built in a year and completed at the end of 2005, few financial and logistical obstacles stand in the way of the Turkmenistan–China pipeline. If any of these projects materialise – driven by increasing frustration in Turkmenistan about Russia's use of its monopoly to pay low prices for Turkmen gas – Gazprom will have difficulty coping with export obligations and domestic commitments. This explains its push to raise prices for exports to the CIS, on the grounds that it can no longer afford to continue to subsidise exports and must either raise prices or redirect gas to customers who pay more. This has meant raising prices not only for Ukraine, Georgia and Moldova, all of which have had difficult relations with Moscow, but also for Armenia and Belarus, both close strategic partners for Moscow.

Stagnation of Russian oil and gas production is bound to have important implications for Russia's domestic development and relations with its neighbours. It further reinforces concerns among importers of Russian oil and gas, who increasingly place energy security at the top of their policy agendas, about the reliability of Russia's long-term supply commitments.

Domestic political prospects

The political succession remains a key source of concern and anxiety for Russia's political elite and the international community. Recent Russian history suggests that in the absence of functioning democratic institutions – a real multi-party system, independent parliament and strong civil society – the personality of the leader plays a decisive role in defining the direction of domestic and foreign policy. The real leadership contest takes place behind closed doors in the Kremlin, balancing the interests of different power groups. As in the transition from Boris Yeltsin to Putin, a candidate will eventually be nominated by Putin and put forward for approval in the general election, likely to take place in March 2008, perhaps combined with parliamentary elections. The Kremlin candidate is unlikely to face any significant challenge, either from liberal parties on the right or communist parties on the left, since the opposition remains weak and lacks popular support. The pro-government United Russia Party is likely to shift towards nationalist sentiment as it struggles to maintain unity under pressure from two groups within the party, one supporting greater state control and intervention, the other emphasising globalisation and the market economy. Within the government, however, liberal reformers who constituted a significant power bloc in the first Putin administration have been virtually deprived of influence in strategic policy decisions, particularly after their reservations over the Yukos affair in which the company's chairman, Mikhail Khodorkovsky, then the most powerful of Russia's business oligarchs, was detained in 2003 on tax evasion charges and sentenced in 2005 to nine years in prison.

Questions remain over the identity of Putin's successor and what role Putin will himself play after 2008. In 2005 two front runners for the succession emerged, who are likely to be selected either jointly – as a president–prime-minister combination – or separately. Dmitry Medvedev was the head of Putin's presidential administration and was promoted in November 2005 to first deputy prime minister. Sergei Ivanov, the minister of defence, was simultaneously appointed deputy prime minister. Neither enjoys popular support, with ratings ranging between 6 and 9%, yet Putin's backing, combined with the use of administrative and media resources controlled by the state, is likely to ensure victory for whoever is eventually selected. It is possible that another candidate might emerge before 2008 as a result of the continuous power struggle within the Kremlin. Leading up to 2008 the succession issue will dominate Russian politics, limiting prospects for domestic reforms and affecting relations with the outside world.

Russia asserts power

Russia has struggled to translate its status as an energy power into long-sought recognition of Great Power status. Russia's chairmanship of the Group of Eight (G8) industrialised countries, combined with its active diplomacy in Europe, Iran and the Middle East, presented opportunities for increasing its international profile. But assertive and threatening approaches towards some of its neighbours – including the cut-off of gas to Ukraine – combined with increasingly anti-Western political rhetoric at home, has led to a gradual deterioration in Russian–Western relations. In spite of Moscow's protestations to the contrary, pressure on Ukraine over gas supplies was perceived by the outside world as political. Europe and the United States agree that developments in Russia – both domestic and in regard to its policies in Eurasia – are a source of concern. However, dependence on Russian energy and the need to keep Russia on board in addressing the Iranian nuclear issue meant that they have mostly exercised caution in criticising Putin's policies. Russian–Western relations have shifted from strategic partnership towards a partnership of convenience.

An exception to the West's caution was criticism of Russia's policies towards its neighbours by US Vice-President Dick Cheney in a speech in Vilnius, Lithuania on 4 May 2006. He said: 'No legitimate interest is served when oil and gas become tools of intimidation or blackmail ... and no one can justify actions that undermine the territorial integrity of a neighbour or interfere with democratic movements.' Russia's response was angry but restrained, dismissing the remarks as geopolitically motivated, inherently anti-Russian and a sign of Cold-War era thinking. Anti-Western rhetoric increased among mainstream Russian policymakers and analysts, who assert that Western policies in Eurasia are directed against Russian interests and seek to push Russia out of its traditional sphere of influence. Russia's policies, combining increased investment and economic assistance with support for existing regimes, have increased its influence in many parts of Eurasia, particularly Central Asia, where fear of Western-supported revolutions and unmet expectations about Western investment compel regional leaders to seek renewed strategic partnership with Moscow.

Russia has developed a more independent and assertive foreign policy relying on three principles. First, it seeks to promote its economic interests as part of its foreign-policy agenda (for example in relations with Germany, China, India and Eurasian states) or to use economic power in support of foreign-policy objectives. Secondly, it seeks to exploit weaknesses and mistakes of Western policy. It has positioned itself as a mediator in relations between the West and the Muslim world by developing closer ties with, for example, Syria, the Hamas-controlled Palestinian Authority, and Egypt. While the image of the United States and Europe is declining in Muslim communities, Russia's has been rising, following several years of anti-Russian sentiment stemming from its war in Chechnya. Russia has also attempted to play a mediating role in relations between Iran and the West, and is expanding military ties with Venezuela, China and Iran. The third principle is the restoration of its presence in Eurasia, particularly in Central Asia, where Russian influence has increased dramatically over the past year because of growing concerns among regional authoritarian leaders over the spread of Western-supported uprisings such as occurred with Ukraine's 'Orange Revolution'. At the same time, America's regional role and influence declined as it failed to meet expectations of economic benefits and political support in regional states in exchange for their cooperation in the Afghanistan war and the US 'war on terror'.

In contrast to the 1990s and Putin's first term, Russia no longer intends to follow the Western policy line, nor does it seek closer integration with Western institutions.

This shift is a result of annoyance in Moscow over growing Western criticism of Russia's domestic affairs, including what the West sees as Russia's drift away from the path of democratic development. Russian officials and analysts say Moscow is frustrated with what it sees as Western unwillingness to acknowledge and reciprocate Russia's goodwill gestures or concessions towards the West during Putin's first term, particularly after the 11 September attacks. Many in Moscow are also frustrated by a Western policy of democracy promotion and regime change in Eurasia: they see a Western conspiracy to initiate and finance the wave of democratic movements in Ukraine, Georgia and Kyrgyzstan.

Europe and the United States, on the other hand, criticise Russia for intervening in the domestic affairs of its neighbours and supporting undemocratic rulers such as President Lukashenko of Belarus. The West refused to recognise the 2006 elections in Belarus, alleging fraud and intimidation, while Putin was quick to congratulate his ally with 'winning in a free and fair election'. As the G8 Summit in St Petersburg approached while this chapter of *Strategic Survey* was being written, it was difficult to envision what could prompt a new rapprochement between Russia and the West. It seemed more likely that relations would continue to deteriorate under the weight of mutual mistrust and disagreement over respective approaches to Eurasia.

New regional groupings exclude Russia

As Russia becomes more assertive both within and beyond its immediate vicinity, Ukraine, Georgia and Moldova are seeking to develop new post-Soviet identities and closer ties with Europe – particularly the new EU and NATO members in Central Europe who share their fears and concerns over Russian policy. Democracy promotion, prospects for diversification of energy transportation routes, and principles for resolution of conflict are the main areas of disagreement between Russia and the Western-oriented states of Eurasia.

The new pro-Western states in Eurasia have sought to build new groupings and institutions to bring them closer to the West. In August 2005 Georgia and Ukraine initiated the Community of Democratic Choice, including countries ready to embrace and support democratic reforms, with the support of the United States and many European states. The first meeting on 2 December 2005 in Kiev was attended by the presidents of Ukraine, Georgia, Lithuania, Latvia, Estonia, Romania, Moldova, Slovenia and Macedonia. The Community established links between countries in the Baltic and Black Sea regions seeking to distance themselves from Russian domination, share experiences in domestic reforms and come closer to Europe.

In May 2006 another loose grouping of states – GUAM, after its members Georgia, Ukraine, Azerbaijan and Moldova –was formalised into the GUAM Organisation for Democracy and Economic Development. The aim was to develop closer ties among Eurasian states wanting to reduce their dependence on Russia and pursue closer integration with the West. Among the key priorities of the new organisation were free trade and economic integration, particularly in regard to energy transportation, and plans for joint peacekeeping forces to address regional conflicts.

Russia views these bodies them with suspicion as having inherently anti-Russian agenda to create an alternative to Russo-centric regional groupings such as the CIS. Statements from Georgia and Ukraine that they intend to review their CIS membership have reinforced the prospects for further fragmentation of Eurasia and the emergence of parallel regional alliances pursuing either the Russian or the Western policy agenda.

Ukraine: Tensions with Russia

Following the 2004 'Orange Revolution' (see *Strategic Survey 2004/5*, pp. 156–7) President Victor Yushchenko saw his domestic popularity decline, his political coalition all but fall apart, and Ukraine's economy decline. Ukraine continued to enjoy support from NATO and the EU – including its Central European neighbours – but relations with Russia remained tense, triggering a number of crises, most importantly over gas prices.

The crisis over Russian gas supplies and divisions between members of the Orange coalition, particularly the president and former prime minister Yulia Tymoshenko, led to poor results in the 26 March 2006 parliamentary elections for the presidential Our Ukraine party, which received only 13.95% of the vote. Yushchenko's rival and pro-Moscow candidate Victor Yanukovich and his Regions party won the highest number of votes at 32.14%. Tymoshenko's bloc finished with 22.29% and the Socialist Party, also part of the 2004 Orange Coalition, won 5.69%. Following the elections, the three parties of the former Orange Coalition tried to form a new coalition in parliament, and reached agreement on 22 June: Tymoshenko's faction received the post of prime minister and several key ministerial posts; Yushchenko's Our Ukraine party received the post of speaker of the parliament. Yushchenko had appointed Petro Poroshenko, one of Ukraine's leading oligarchs, to this post. Given the history of open confrontation between Tymoshenko and Poroshenko, the new coalition government might not last.

Yushchenko identified membership of the EU as one of his key priorities, but has so far not received a clear signal from the EU about its prospects. Relations are guided by the EU–Ukraine European Neighbourhood Policy (ENP) Action Plan, adopted by the European Council and Ukrainian parliament in February 2005. ENP offers some elements of integration, but no clear commitment to membership. The EU is unlikely to consider Ukrainian membership until it has absorbed the ten newest members and prospective members Bulgaria and Romania, as well as developing greater consensus regarding Turkey's accession and resolving the deadlock over internal reform following the failure of the constitutional treaty. Ukrainian membership of the EU is therefore unlikely for many years. However, membership of NATO is still under active discussion.

Ukraine's NATO prospects

In April 2005 Ukraine and NATO launched an intensified dialogue. Kiev could be offered a Membership Action Plan at the NATO summit in Riga on 28–29 November 2006, possibly leading to full membership as early as 2008. The majority of NATO member states strongly support Ukrainian membership. From Washington's perspective, it would be an important legacy for President George W. Bush. For Europeans, Ukraine's armed forces, experienced in multinational operations in the

Balkans and Iraq, could make an important contribution to an alliance that is short of deployable troops for commitments in Afghanistan and elsewhere.

However, NATO membership is a complicated issue for Ukraine and a source of new tension with Russia. While the Ukrainian leadership strongly supports NATO membership, opinion polls show the public is much more sceptical, with less than 50% in favour: it would be difficult for the government to win a referendum. In Crimea and eastern parts of the country, many people strongly oppose NATO membership. In June 2006 small but vocal protests in Crimea, combined with parliament's refusal to authorise the temporary presence of foreign troops on Ukrainian soil, led to the postponement of the annual Ukraine–NATO *Sea Breeze* exercises in the Black Sea. Ukrainian officials blamed Russia for masterminding the demonstrations and banned entry to several nationalist Russian MPs.

Russian concerns over potential Ukrainian NATO membership run deep and are unlikely to be alleviated in the near future. Russian Foreign Minister Sergei Lavrov stated that NATO enlargement to embrace Ukraine and Georgia would be a 'colossal geo-political shift', and that Russia was 'trying to foresee the consequences of this move, primarily from the viewpoint of Russia's national security and economic interests and relations with these countries'.

Moscow's concerns are based on a number of factors. First, in spite of expanding cooperation in the framework of the NATO–Russia Council, many in Russia continue to view NATO with suspicion as an 'anti-Russian organisation' and a potential threat. A US announcement about potential deployment of a missile defence system in Central Europe provoked a sharp negative reaction from Moscow, which saw it as directed primarily at Russia's nuclear deterrent and threatened to withdraw from the 1999 Adapted Conventional Forces in Europe Treaty.

A second factor relates to the extensive defence-industrial ties between Russia and Ukraine. Russian officials made clear that these ties would be suspended if Ukraine joined NATO. This could be costly for both countries. According to Russian Defence Minister Sergei Ivanov, co-production arrangements and easy-terms arms trade involved 1,330 Russian and Ukrainian enterprises in 2005. Russian–Ukrainian defence-related trade involves up to 8,000 items. Russia accounted for 22.8% of Ukrainian defence imports in 2005, and 50–60% of Ukrainian exports went to Russia. Some 95% of Russian helicopters are fitted with engines from Ukraine's Motor-Sich Factory in Zaporozhye, which also turns out engines for the Beriyev Be-200 Amphibious Multi-Role Twinjet Aircraft and the Yak-130 *Mitten* combat trainer. Ukraine produces warship and hovercraft propulsion units for Russia. Ukraine's Kremenchug automotive factory produces KRAZ trucks for S-300 surface-to-air missile systems, a Novokramatorsk plant makes S-300 radars, and a Lvov factory produces electronic units. Kiev has delivered avionics and weapons for Russian Sukhoi Su-30-MKI and Su-30-MKK *Super Flanker* fighters, exported to India and China, but its participation in these projects has been reduced in recent years. In June 2006 Ivanov declared that Russia would pull out of the joint Ukrainian–Russian Antonov AN-70 transport aircraft project.

A third issue is the stationing of the Russian Black Sea Fleet at Sevastopol in Crimea. In 1997 Kiev and Moscow reached an agreement under which Russia had the right to station its fleet at Sevastopol, under lease, until 2017. The agreement, however, left points unresolved. Ukraine and Russia continue to disagree over ownership of the navigation and hydrographic infrastructure serving the Crimean coast. After the break-up of the Soviet Union Russia assumed control of this infrastructure, but Ukraine, which now has a fleet of its own, and military ties with other Black Sea and NATO states, wants to take it over. When Russia raised the price of gas exports to Ukraine, Kiev reciprocated by demanding an increase in the $97m annual rent that Russia pays for basing its fleet. While Ukraine has indicated it is unlikely to agree to extend the lease beyond 2017, Russia intends to re-open negotiations on the terms of the 1997 agreement. There is little prospect of amicable resolution of tensions mounting between the Russian and Ukrainian fleets.

Russia has few options for relocating the fleet. Its short Black Sea coastline includes Novorossiysk, Russia's largest commercial port, built for shipping large quantities of oil. But it would require very large investment to house the naval fleet. Some NATO officials have suggested that Ukrainian membership of NATO would be incompatible with fulfilment of its 1997 agreement with Russia, since Ukraine would become the first NATO member with a non-NATO state's base on its territory. Russian concerns go beyond the basing issue: it objects to the prospect of greater NATO involvement in the Black Sea.

A further outstanding issue is a long-standing border dispute over the status of the Sea of Azov, which has busy shipping routes, rich fishing grounds and prospective oil fields. Russia wants to keep the sea as a common-use area between the two states, while Ukraine wants to demarcate a border. The argument escalated in 2003 when Russia started building a dike from the Russian mainland toward Ukraine's Tuzla Island in the Kerch Strait, which connects the Sea of Azov with the Black Sea. Ukraine sent troops to the island, and Russia stopped construction after tense high-level talks. Following perhaps the most dangerous crisis in post-Soviet Russian–Ukrainian relations, the two sides agreed to share the Sea of Azov as common property and to determine the countries' border in the Kerch Strait. In 2006, Ukrainian Deputy Foreign Minister Anton Buteiko said Kiev wanted to revise the agreement to change the status of the sea, but Russia refused to negotiate. It is unlikely that the two sides can reach a compromise on the matter given Ukraine's prospective NATO membership.

The issue of Ukraine's NATO membership comes on top of two other recent crises between Ukraine and Russia: the Orange Revolution and Russia's decision in January 2006 to stop gas supplies to Ukraine in the pricing dispute referred to above. For Ukraine the agreement that ended the dispute meant that it had to accept higher gas prices at a time when its economy was experiencing a severe decline. The new price was not guaranteed, and is likely to increase when Turkmenistan increases its prices. In addition, Yushchenko, who initially hailed the deal, agreed under international pressure to conduct investigations into RosUkrEnergo. He has not signed an agreement cementing the January terms, but has stopped short of re-opening negotiations.

The South Caucasus: Conflicts Cloud Prospects

The South Caucasus – Armenia, Azerbaijan and Georgia – has seen growing interest and engagement from both the West and Russia. The region's importance has increased following EU enlargement and with the growing strategic importance of the Black Sea. In 2005 the EU began to consider the deployment of peacekeeping forces should Armenia and Azerbaijan reach agreement over the Nagorno-Karabakh conflict. The EU has been negotiating ENP Action Plans, expected to be finalised during 2006, with all three states. In February 2006 the EU appointed a new special representative, Peter Semneby, whose mandate was expanded to support resolution of regional conflicts. The United States has also been expanding high-level contacts and military and economic ties in the South Caucasus. Since 2005 the United States has actively promoted the resolution of frozen conflicts in the region.

These conflicts – Georgia–Abkhazia, Georgia–South Ossetia and Nagorno-Karabakh – are the main reason for increased European and US engagement in the South Caucasus. The second half of 2005 and the first half of 2006 brought new hopes – so far frustrated – for conflict resolution in Nagorno-Karabakh, the only major inter-state conflict in Eurasia, unresolved since the end of violence in 1994. Armenia occupies Nagorno-Karabakh and seven adjacent territories recognised by the international community as parts of Azerbaijan. However, the Nagorno-Karabakh Republic now exists as a de facto entity, populated by ethnic Armenians who claim it as their historic land. The prospects of Nagorno-Karabakh returning to Azerbaijan appear slim, although the territory's status must eventually be resolved by a referendum. The conflict has been frozen for over ten years without foreign peacekeeping forces, but Armenia and Azerbaijan remain in a state of war and are engaged in an arms race. While Armenia continues to receive assistance from Russia, which has military bases on its territory, Azerbaijan is able to redirect its rapidly increasing revenues from oil exports into defence spending. The growing number of clashes between Azerbaijani and Armenian forces, as well as concerns about future instability in Iran, which borders both states, reinforced concerns about future escalation, which would have devastating consequences for both states. Negotiators saw 2006, a year in which elections were due in both nations, as offering potential for a break-through, but this has not yet occurred.

International mediators represented by the Minsk Group, which has Russian, US and French co-chairmen, sought to create conditions for beginning the settle-ment process by encouraging Armenia to return to Azerbaijan all or part of the occupied territories around Nagorno-Karabakh, to allow refugees to return and to agree on a timetable for holding a referendum on the status the territory. The proposed plan envisaged deployment of international peacekeepers, most likely by the EU. The Russian defence minister expressed readiness to deploy peace-keepers to the conflict zone should an agreement be reached, although both sides were reluctant to endorse this. Components of the plan were discussed during the so-called Prague process meetings between the Armenian and Azerbaijani foreign ministers throughout 2005. The two presidents met on 10–11 February 2006 at Rambouillet in France for direct talks, but these yielded no results. Follow-up talks in Washington in March 2006 and in Romania in June similarly ended without a breakthrough.

No significant progress has been achieved in resolving two other frozen con-flicts, involving Abkhazia and South Ossetia, which seek independence from Georgia following bloody conflicts in the early 1990s. Although no escalation took place in 2005–06, the environment for bringing about political resolu-tion of these conflicts became more complex. The success of the referendum in Montenegro (see pp. 150–152) and expectations of independence for Kosovo raised hopes that the two entities could also gain recognition. Both counted on Russia for support. Speaking against the background of deteriorating Georgian–Russian relations, President Putin called for application of universal criteria to the future of Kosovo, Abkhazia and South Ossetia. The Russian Foreign Ministry questioned Georgia's territorial integrity, calling it virtual and aspirational rather than real. During a June 2006 summit between the Russian and Georgian presi-dents, Putin softened his tone, saying Russia did not intend to take over any Georgian lands; however, he reiterated the need for a referendum to determine the future status of Abkhazia and South Ossetia.

Moscow's statements angered Georgia, which has long accused Russia of wanting to take over the two territories. Russia extended citizenship to the major-ity of residents in Abkhazia and South Ossetia and provided extensive economic assistance and political support to the de facto authorities, some of them former Russian civilian and security officials. Georgia claimed that Russia now consti-tuted not an impartial mediator but a party to both conflicts, and the Georgian parliament demanded the withdrawal of Russian peacekeepers from South Ossetia and Abkhazia, to be replaced by international forces. Georgia has so far been unable to find replacement forces, with both the UN and the Organisation for Security and Cooperation in Europe unable to provide sufficient troops. Moreover, the de facto regimes that control the two regions view Russia as their security guarantor and refuse to admit external peacekeeping forces. Progress appeared to depend on the state of Georgian–Russian relations, which remained perhaps the most tense among all post-Soviet states. Although on 31 March 2006 Georgia and Russia signed a final agreement on the timetable for withdrawal of Russian military bases from Georgia by 2008, Russia followed by increasing support for the de facto states, introducing an embargo on imports of Georgian wine and mineral water, and raising concerns over potential Georgian membership of NATO.

Following its 2003 Rose Revolution, Georgia enjoys widespread support in the West. It wants to obtain a NATO Membership Action Plan at the Riga summit in November 2006 and hopes to win membership of NATO in the near future. This aspiration is supported by the United States, but is opposed by some important Western European countries. Georgia's case is more complicated than Ukraine's. On the positive side is the remarkable success of its defence reforms. It has implemented an Individual Partnership Action Plan agreed in 2004 and has increased its defence budget from \$20m in 2002 to \$31m in 2003 and \$90m in 2004. Georgia has troops in Iraq, the Balkans and Afghanistan: its 850 troops in Iraq represent the largest per capita deployment of any member of the coalition. On the negative side, Georgia still has the unresolved Abkhazia and South Ossetia conflicts, which involve a stand-off with Russia. Concerns remain that Georgia has not excluded the use of force to resolve these conflicts. It refused to sign an agreement not to resume hostilities, and over the past year there have been instances when the conflict in South Ossetia threatened to escalate. NATO therefore risks being dragged into Georgia's internal conflicts, which might include confrontation with Russia.

The South Caucasus is also of note because it borders Iran. Any prospective military action against Iran would have to use facilities in the South Caucasus, just as Central Asian facilities were used during operations in Afghanistan. The United States has been developing close military cooperation with both Azerbaijan and Georgia. Washington and Baku have reportedly discussed potential US use of military facilities in Azerbaijan, including airfields. Azerbaijani airfields have been used by US aircraft operating in Afghanistan. In 2005 the United States signed an agreement on operating two radars in Azerbaijan which are likely to be used for monitoring Iran. In April 2006 Azerbaijani President Ilkham Aliev visited the United States, where he was given a very warm reception despite reservations about the conduct of the November 2005 elections in Azerbaijan, when international observers recorded election fraud and intimidation of the opposition. The new relationship is underpinned by US concerns over Iran's nuclear programme. For Azerbaijan, however, the issue is sensitive: there are three times more Azeris in northern Iran than in Azerbaijan itself. Baku traditionally has close relations with Tehran and any destabilisation in Iran is likely to have severe effects within Azerbaijan. Days after returning from Washington, Aliev hosted a visit by the Iranian president.

Central Asia: Developing Relationships Eastwards

Central Asia has seen a decline in US and European influence and growing engagement from Russia, China, India and other Asian neighbours, which are interested in the region because of its energy resources, geographic proximity and the threat of Islamic radicalisation. For land-locked and energy-rich Central Asian states, cooperation with Asian neighbours is essential to develop transport routes.

Most states, though they hold elections and have opposition parties, retain authoritarian governments. The only pluralist society is Kyrgyzstan, where the March 2005 'Tulip Revolution' attempted to repeat the examples of Georgia and Ukraine by removing the corrupt President Askar Akaiev through peaceful, popular discontent. A year later, Kyrgyzstan remained pluralist and pro-Western, hosting a large US and coalition military base at Manas, but was also economically undeveloped, criminalised, unstable and dominated by traditional and regional clans at the expense of its 'revolutionary' leaders. Little progress had been made towards real democracy.

The United States has sought to promote its own vision for Central Asia. During her trip to the region in October 2005, US Secretary of State Condoleezza Rice proposed a new concept of 'Greater Central Asia' as a framework for long-term integration as well as stabilisation in Afghanistan. However, this vision has not been supported by Central Asian states, which seek to distance themselves from what they view as increasing instability and the growing influence of radical Islamic groups in Afghanistan.

The establishment of US and coalition military bases for the 2001 invasion of Afghanistan failed to deliver expected economic benefits. Uzbekistan offered the most extensive and immediate cooperation with the United States, but later found its regime threatened by the prospect of popular revolution coupled with a rise of radical Islamist sentiment. Violence in Andijan in May 2005, when security and police forces clashed with Islamic militants and civilian demonstrators, resulting in the reported deaths of hundreds of people, provoked a crisis in Uzbekistan's relations with the US and EU. Washington and Brussels requested an independent international inquiry, but were refused. Uzbekistan notified the United States that the agreement on basing rights would not be renewed, forcing the US to close its bases by the end of 2005. The EU imposed sanctions, leading to an almost complete freeze in diplomatic relations and a loss of European leverage. The majority of European- and US-funded NGOs have been closed. Uzbekistan moved towards rapprochement with Russia, agreeing mutual security guarantees, conducting bilateral military exercises and joining the Eurasian Economic Community. It also developed closer cooperation with East and South Asian neighbours and improved relations with Kazakhstan and Tajikistan.

Kazakhstan, the most oil-rich state in Central Asia, has developed close strategic relations with Russia, the United States and China. Previously dependent on Russia for transit of its oil to world markets, it completed in 2005 a 1,000km oil pipeline to China and signed an agreement with Azerbaijan to ship its oil westward through the Baku–Tbilisi–Ceyhan pipeline, also completed in 2005. These steps were taken without undermining relations with Russia. Kazakhstan has emerged as a regional leader, playing an important role in regional organisations such as the Eurasian Economic Community, the Collective Security Treaty Organisation and the Shanghai Cooperation Organisation (SCO), while at the same time becoming the first Central Asian state to conclude an Individual Partnership Action Plan with NATO and pursuing close military ties with the United States.

The SCO has become the most influential organisation in Central Asia, with a growing role in the wider Asian region. It was established in 2001 following more than five years of an informal confidence-building process known as the 'Shanghai Five', involving multilateral consultations over the demarcation of China's border with Tajikistan, Kyrgyzstan and Kazakhstan. Founding members were China, Russia, Tajikistan, Kazakhstan, Kyrgyzstan and Uzbekistan. In 2005, India, Pakistan, Iran and Mongolia were admitted as observers: all have expressed interest in full membership. On 14–15 June 2006 the fifth anniversary summit of the SCO in Shanghai was attended by the heads of state of all SCO members and observers except India. Afghan President Hamid Karzai also took part. The SCO has established a regional anti-terrorist centre in Uzbekistan and has conducted joint exercises, which are expected to increase in scale and number. It is also an economic organisation, focusing on regional cooperation including infrastructure projects, and investment and credit for development schemes. Cooperation on energy issues is expected to become a major area of SCO activity, one particularly attractive to countries like India and China. However, the SCO is viewed with suspicion in the West, particularly in the United States, which portrays it as an anti-Western bloc dominated by Russia and China that seeks to exclude Washington from playing a role in Central Asia. It is also criticised as a 'club of dictators', given that the majority of members are not democracies, and that it does not seek to promote democratic or other political reforms in member states. This view may be alarmist: as an Asian organisation, rather like the Association of Southeast Asian Nations, the SCO does not address domestic political issues of its members. A number of its members and observers maintain close relations with the United States.

However the future of the SCO remains uncertain, with two competing visions. One, favoured by Russia and some Central Asian states, sees it as a regional security organisation, with close cooperation between militaries and in fighting terrorism, separatism and extremism in Central Asia. This school of thought views the SCO as a geopolitical actor balancing the involvement of non-regional powers, keeping up pressure for the withdrawal of US and coalition bases from the region. Another view, supported primarily by China and India, would make the SCO primarily an economic organisation focusing on developing preferential ties in the energy field and introducing a free-trade area. The latter idea is opposed by Central Asian states and Russia, which fear they could not compete with China. Beijing, on the other hand, is adamant that the SCO will never become a NATO-type military bloc. Given these tensions, it is likely that the SCO will continue to combine security and economic dimensions. There could be room for dialogue and, at some point, cooperation with the United States, Europe and Japan.

Conclusion: Russia's Regional Power Curbed

In spite of its new economic clout and assertiveness, Russia is being forced to come to terms with the fact that its previously dominant regional power can no longer be taken for granted. It is having to accept greater pluralism, and growing presence and engagement of Europe, the United States, China and other Asian powers. Nevertheless, the region's future development and stability still depend to a large extent on Russia's future prospects, as well as its ability to find a pragmatic *modus vivendi* with newly influential states in Eurasia. Russia's new identity as an energy power, which increasingly underpins its foreign policy, particular in regard to neighbouring states, is likely to reinforce rather than mitigate geopolitical rivalries and to complicate the resolution of Eurasian challenges.

6 | Middle East / Gulf

The region's multiple tensions continued to threaten the world's security over the past year. Amidst persistent violence and insecurity, Iraq struggled to regain domestic stability. Though the milestone of a representative elected government was reached, daily life for Iraqis continued to pose many challenges. American and coalition military forces were gradually handing over responsibility for security to Iraqis, but the withdrawal of 130,000 American troops was likely to be a slow process. The attention of Washington and other capitals was increasingly focused on Iran, where newly elected President Mahmoud Ahmadinejad adopted a more combative stance towards the West and Israel. A sudden stepping up of Iranian nuclear-development activities prompted intense diplomatic activity, as the permanent members of the United Nations Security Council united behind efforts to obtain Tehran's agreement to a halt. The West was surprised by the election victory of Hamas in Palestine, which made the continued foreign funding of the Palestinian Authority highly problematic. With Israeli politics also in uncharted waters following the illness of Ariel Sharon, his replacement as prime minister by Ehud Olmert and the marginalisation of the Likud party in elections, the future course of the Israel–Palestine dispute hung very much in the balance.

Iraq: Instability Mars Political Advances

Iraq today is undermined by two interlinked problems, which primarily account for the profound insecurity and violence that dominate the country. The first and overriding cause of instability is the complete collapse of state capacity in the aftermath of regime change in April 2003. The three weeks of looting that erupted in the wake of the liberation of Baghdad destroyed the institutions of the state, gutting 17 of the 23 ministry buildings in the capital. The result is that Iraqi society continues to live in a profound security vacuum. The opportunities provided by the collapse of the state and the disbanding of the Iraqi army were seized upon by a myriad of groups deploying violence for their own gain. Organised crime continues to be the dominant source of insecurity in the everyday lives of ordinary Iraqis. For coalition and Iraqi security forces, it is the diffuse groups carrying on an insurgency in the name of Iraqi nationalism, increasingly fused with a militant Islamism, that have caused the highest loss of life. In early 2006 a new crisis arose with even greater potential for destabilisation: the spectre of civil war. The explosion that destroyed the al-Askariyya Mosque in the Iraqi city of Samarra on 22 February 2006 triggered mounting sectarian violence and large-scale population transfers. The numbers displaced by ethnic cleansing have become the primary indicator that Iraq, following the collapse of state authority, could be heading towards civil war.

The second problem that has dominated the politics of the country since the fall of Saddam Hussein is the question of who should rule – how to find Iraqis who after 35 years of dictatorship had both the technical capacity and national legitimacy to rule over a country of 26 million people. Throughout 2005 and the early months of 2006, there was a struggle to build a representative government that could act as a rallying point for the country, allowing the population to invest hope and legitimacy in a new ruling elite that could stabilise the nation and move towards rebuilding the state. This process saw in January 2005 a transitional election for a government to serve for 12 months, in October a constitutional referendum and in December a parliamentary election for a full-term four-year government. For Iraq to become a stable country and for regime change to be judged a success, sustained progress will have to be made in both of these interlinked processes: the building of country-wide state capacity and the growth of a legitimate and competent governing elite.

Politics in Iraq

The task of creating a stable and legitimate post-regime-change political order has been hampered by the two dominant facts of Iraqi politics today. The first and major problem is the legacy left by 35 years of Ba'athist rule. Before the imposition of sanctions in 1990, Saddam Hussein used Iraq's oil wealth and high levels of state violence to break any organising capacity within Iraqi society. Those who were active in anti-regime politics were either murdered, imprisoned and tortured, or driven into exile. Those who stayed in the country increasingly came to realise that survival and economic well-being were directly linked to complete political passivity. As a result, civil society simply did not exist in any measurable form before the US military reached Baghdad in April 2003. Iraqi politics had to start from scratch in 2003. The politicians and the parties they run have either been involved in active politics for three years or, more commonly, have been long absent from the country and have battled with hostility and suspicion since their return. The second concern for the new political system has been its establishment under US occupation. Those active in constitutional politics initially had to make an accommodation with the US occupation, in the form of the Coalition Provisional Authority. Since the de jure handover of sovereignty to an Iraqi government in June 2004, politicians have continued to operate in a country heavily financed by the American taxpayer and patrolled by over 100,000 US troops. The intense political process of 2005 was meant to overcome these two hurdles by creating a new political elite chosen by the Iraqi people and drafting a constitution under which they could rule.

This 12-month process was inaugurated by the elections of 30 January 2005. Given the lack of government and order in the country, it was decided to organ-

Map 6.1 **Iraq's constitutional referendum**

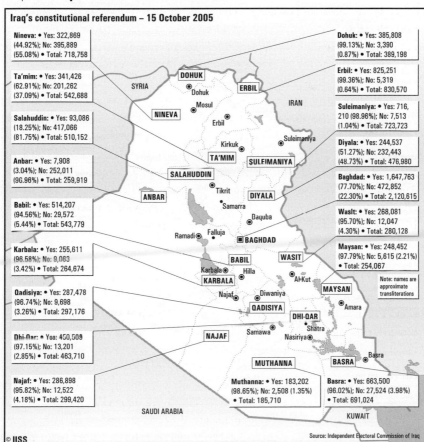

Iraq's constitutional referendum – 15 October 2005

Nineva: • Yes: 322,869 (44.92%); No: 395,889 (55.08%) • Total: 718,758

Dohuk: • Yes: 385,808 (99.13%); No: 3,390 (0.87%) • Total: 389,198

Ta'mim: • Yes: 341,426 (62.91%); No: 201,262 (37.09%) • Total: 542,688

Erbil: • Yes: 825,251 (99.36%); No: 5,319 (0.64%) • Total: 830,570

Salahuddin: • Yes: 93,086 (18.25%); No: 417,066 (81.75%) • Total: 510,152

Suleimaniya: • Yes: 716, 210 (98.96%); No: 7,513 (1.04%) • Total: 723,723

Anbar: • Yes: 7,908 (3.04%); No: 252,011 (96.96%) • Total: 259,919

Diyala: • Yes: 244,537 (51.27%); No: 232,443 (48.73%) • Total: 476,980

Baghdad: • Yes: 1,647,763 (77.70%); No: 472,852 (22.30%) • Total: 2,120,615

Babil: • Yes: 514,207 (94.56%); No: 29,572 (5.44%) • Total: 543,779

Wasit: • Yes: 268,081 (95.70%); No: 12,047 (4.30%) • Total: 280,128

Karbala: • Yes: 255,611 (96.58%); No: 9,063 (3.42%) • Total: 264,674

Maysan: • Yes: 248,452 (97.79%); No: 5,615 (2.21%) • Total: 254,067

Note: names are approximate transliterations

Qadisiya: • Yes: 287,478 (96.74%); No: 9,698 (3.26%) • Total: 297,176

Dhi-Qar: • Yes: 450,509 (97.15%); No: 13,201 (2.85%) • Total: 463,710

Najaf: • Yes: 286,898 (95.82%); No: 12,522 (4.18%) • Total: 299,420

Muthanna: • Yes: 183,202 (98.65%); No: 2,508 (1.35%) • Total: 185,710

Basra: • Yes: 663,500 (96.02%); No: 27,524 (3.98%) • Total: 691,024

SYRIA

DOHUK
Dohuk

ERBIL

Mosul

IRAN

NINEVA
Erbil

Kirkuk

Suleimaniya

TA'MIM

SULFIMANIYA

SALAHUDDIN

ANBAR
Tikrit

DIYALA

Samarra

Daquba

Ramadi
Falluja

■ BAGHDAD

BABIL

WASIT

Karbala
Hilla

KARBALA

Al-Kut

Najaf
Diwaniya

MAYSAN

QADISIYA

Amara

DHI-QAR

Samawa
Shatra

NAJAF
Nasiriya

MUTHANNA

BASRA

Basra

SAUDI ARABIA

KUWAIT

© IISS

Source: Independent Electoral Commission of Iraq

Map 6.2 **Iraq's Council of Representatives election**

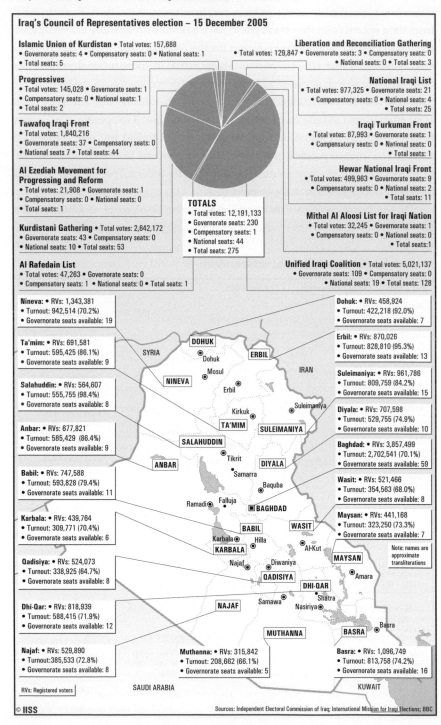

Iraq's Council of Representatives election – 15 December 2005

Islamic Union of Kurdistan • Total votes: 157,688
• Governorate seats: 4 • Compensatory seats: 0 • National seats: 1
• Total seats: 5

Liberation and Reconciliation Gathering
• Total votes: 129,847 • Governorate seats: 3 • Compensatory seats: 0
• National seats: 0 • Total seats: 3

Progressives
• Total votes: 145,028 • Governorate seats: 1
• Compensatory seats: 0 • National seats: 1
• Total seats: 2

National Iraqi List
• Total votes: 977,325 • Governorate seats: 21
• Compensatory seats: 0 • National seats: 4
• Total seats: 25

Tawafoq Iraqi Front
• Total votes: 1,840,216
• Governorate seats: 37 • Compensatory seats: 0
• National seats 7 • Total seats: 44

Iraqi Turkuman Front
• Total votes: 87,993 • Governorate seats: 1
• Compensatory seats: 0 • National seats: 0
• Total seats: 1

Al Ezediah Movement for Progressing and Reform
• Total votes: 21,908 • Governorate seats: 1
• Compensatory seats: 0 • National seats: 0
• Total seats: 1

Hewar National Iraqi Front
• Total votes: 499,963 • Governorate seats: 9
• Compensatory seats: 0 • National seats: 2
• Total seats: 11

Kurdistani Gathering • Total votes: 2,642,172
• Governorate seats: 43 • Compensatory seats: 0
• National seats: 10 • Total seats: 53

TOTALS
• Total votes: 12,191,133
• Governorate seats: 230
• Compensatory seats: 1
• National seats: 44
• Total seats: 275

Mithal Al Aloosi List for Iraqi Nation
• Total votes: 32,245 • Governorate seats: 1
• Compensatory seats: 0 • National seats: 0
• Total seats:1

Al Rafedain List
• Total votes: 47,263 • Governorate seats: 0
• Compensatory seats: 1 • National seats: 0 • Total seats: 1

Unified Iraqi Coalition • Total votes: 5,021,137
• Governorate seats: 109 • Compensatory seats: 0
• National seats: 19 • Total seats: 128

Nineva: • RVs: 1,343,381
• Turnout: 942,514 (70.2%)
• Governorate seats available: 19

Dohuk: • RVs: 458,924
• Turnout: 422,218 (92.0%)
• Governorate seats available: 7

Ta'mim: • RVs: 691,581
• Turnout: 595,425 (86.1%)
• Governorate seats available: 9

Erbil: • RVs: 870,026
• Turnout: 828,810 (95.3%)
• Governorate seats available: 13

Salahuddin: • RVs: 564,607
• Turnout: 555,755 (98.4%)
• Governorate seats available: 8

Suleimaniya: • RVs: 961,786
• Turnout: 809,759 (84.2%)
• Governorate seats available: 15

Anbar: • RVs: 677,821
• Turnout: 585,429 (86.4%)
• Governorate seats available: 9

Diyala: • RVs: 707,598
• Turnout: 529,755 (74.9%)
• Governorate seats available: 10

Baghdad: • RVs: 3,857,499
• Turnout: 2,702,541 (70.1%)
• Governorate seats available: 59

Babil: • RVs: 747,588
• Turnout: 593,828 (79.4%)
• Governorate seats available: 11

Wasit: • RVs: 521,466
• Turnout: 354,563 (68.0%)
• Governorate seats available: 8

Karbala: • RVs: 439,764
• Turnout: 309,771 (70.4%)
• Governorate seats available: 6

Maysan: • RVs: 441,168
• Turnout: 323,250 (73.3%)
• Governorate seats available: 7

Note: names are approximate transliterations

Qadisiya: • RVs: 524,073
• Turnout: 338,925 (64.7%)
• Governorate seats available: 8

Dhi-Qar: • RVs: 818,939
• Turnout: 588,415 (71.9%)
• Governorate seats available: 12

Najaf: • RVs: 529,890
• Turnout:385,533 (72.8%)
• Governorate seats available: 8

Muthanna: • RVs: 315,842
• Turnout: 208,662 (66.1%)
• Governorate seats available: 5

Basra: • RVs: 1,096,749
• Turnout: 813,758 (74.2%)
• Governorate seats available: 16

RVs: Registered voters

SYRIA
DOHUK
Dohuk
ERBIL
Mosul
IRAN
NINEVA
Erbil
Kirkuk
Suleimaniya
TA'MIM
SULEIMANIYA
SALAHUDDIN
Tikrit
DIYALA
ANBAR
Samarra
Baquba
Falluja
Ramadi
■BAGHDAD
BABIL
WASIT
Karbala
Hilla
Al-Kut
KARBALA
MAYSAN
Najaf
Diwaniya
Amara
QADISIYA
DHI-QAR
Samawa
Shatra
NAJAF
Nasiriya
Basra
MUTHANNA
BASRA
SAUDI ARABIA
KUWAIT

© IISS

Sources: Independent Electoral Commission of Iraq; International Mission for Iraqi Elections; BBC

ise the vote around a single nationwide constituency. As well as reducing the preparations needed for the election, it was hoped that this would encourage the formation of cross-communal coalitions in the search for maximum votes. Sadly, the opposite occurred. The imposition of one constituency meant the elimination of local issues or personalities in campaigning. The majority of politicians deployed ethno-sectarian campaign material in an attempt to appeal to the widest number of people. This process was heralded in October 2004 by the head of the Shia religious establishment in Iraq, Grand Ayatollah Ali al-Sistani, who encouraged the formation of a 'Shia List' for the elections. Parties and individuals could join this list if they agreed to vote as a bloc in the new parliament, uphold the 'Islamic character' of the Iraqi people and refuse to back any legislation that ran counter to sharia law. In effect, al-Sistani had lent his considerable moral weight to the creation of an electoral machine for mobilising specifically Shia voters. The Kurdish Democratic Party (KDP) and the Patriotic Union of Kurdistan (PUK), dominant in the north of Iraq, followed suit and formed a 'Kurdish List' designed to maximise the Kurdish vote and hence their influence over the drafting of the new constitution. It was left to the incumbent Prime Minister Ayad Allawi and his 'Iraqi List' to try to rally the secular middle-class vote on the basis of law, order and Iraqi nationalism.

The Sunni community, lacking the hierarchal religious organisation of Shia Islam or the two dominant parties of the Kurdish community, found it difficult to organise. In the end it was a coalition of mosques, the Association of Muslim Scholars (AMS) who first emerged to give voice to their fears and post-regime-change insecurities. The AMS managed to give coherence to the widespread outrage against the US military assault on the town of Falluja in April 2004. It was joined by the more moderate Iraqi Islamic Party, which after the Falluja assault felt unable to participate in the elections.

In the event, 8.5m Iraqis, or 58% of those eligible, voted. The election took place despite as many as nine suicide bombings in Baghdad and insurgent attacks across the country. However, turnout varied dramatically across the country and amongst Iraq's different ethnic and religious communities. In the northern areas dominated by the Kurdish population, turnout was between 82% and 92%. In the southern districts, where the majority of the population is Shia, between 61% and 71% voted. In Anbar province, an area of north-western Iraq with a high concentration of Sunnis, only 2% voted. The United Iraqi Alliance (UIA), the 'Shia List' anointed by Ayatollah Sistani, won 48% of the vote and 140 seats in the 275-member assembly. The Kurdish Alliance won 27% and 77 seats. However Allawi and his 'Iraqi List', damaged by his decision to authorise the attack on Falluja, only managed to secure 14.5% of the votes and 40 seats. The ethno-sectarian basis of voting and the success of the boycott led to low Sunni representation in the parliament.

It was not until the first week of April 2005 that the newly elected assembly finally managed to select a president for the country, the veteran Kurdish leader

Jalal Talabani, and two deputies, the Shia ex-minister for finance, Adel Abdul al-Mahdi, and the former American-appointed president, Ghazi al-Yawer. The head of the Dawa Party, Ibrahim al-Jaafari, was elected by the assembly to be prime minister. However the three months that this process took and the rancour surrounding the choice of a Sunni speaker of parliament highlighted the inexperience of those elected and the deep divisions amongst them.

The assembly's main task was to oversee the drafting of Iraq's new permanent constitution, with a 15 August deadline. The successful boycott of the December elections meant that 15 unelected Sunni politicians had to be co-opted onto the parliamentary committee mandated to do the work. This however, increased the acrimony and sectarian nature of arguments that dogged the committee. After being operational for one month, it was circumvented and the process taken over by an ad hoc group of party leaders. During early August it was this 'leadership council' that did the main bulk of the drafting. Consisting of Prime Minister al-Jaafari, the leader of the other main Shia party, Abdul Aziz al Hakim, and the two Kurdish leaders, President Talabani and the head of the KDP, Masoud Barzani, this small group not only marginalised parliament's role but also excluded other politicians with differing perceptions of what the constitution should contain.

The document was voted on in a national referendum on 15 October 2005. Turnout at 63% was higher than for the transitional election, with 78.4% voting for the constitution. In addition, the political violence that has dogged the country since the removal of Saddam Hussein temporarily abated to allow the vote to take place in comparative calm. However, the Transitional Administrative Law that governed the plebiscite stipulated that the constitution would not pass if two-thirds of the voters of any three of Iraq's 18 provinces voted against it. This gave those opposed to the constitution the incentive to build an electoral coalition against the document. In the event the constitution passed. However, given the three-provinces rule it was a close run thing, with 96.6% of voters in Anbar province and 81.75% of those in Salahuddin rejecting the document and 55.8% of Nineva also voting against. Anbar, Salahuddin and Nineva are thought to have large Sunni majorities, highlighting the sectarian dynamics shaping both attitudes to the constitution and voting in the referendum. This impression was bolstered by high majorities in favour in the Kurdish areas of Dhouk and Erbil and across the Shia south of the country.

Once the constitution had been passed, a second nationwide ballot for a full-term government could take place. The vote, held on 15 December, was generally perceived to have been a success, with voter turnout reaching 76%. The elections were dominated by three broad coalitions. The most important of these remained the UIA, which won 46.5% of the vote, with 128 of its list elected to parliament. The UIA was still dominated by the Iranian-backed Supreme Council for the Islamic Revolution in Iraq (SCIRI) and the Islamic Dawa Party. However, it widened its appeal by joining forces with the radical nationalist, Moqtada al-Sadr, whose Mahdi Army has twice led uprisings against the American occupation. The second coalition fighting the elections, the Kurdish Alliance, won 19.27% and 53 seats. However, the increased voter turnout indicated the widespread participation of the Sunni section of the electorate. The coalition that succeeded in gaining the majority of this vote was the Accord Front, which took 16% of the vote and 44 seats in parliament. A more radical Sunni grouping, the Iraqi Dialogue Front, took another 4% and 11 seats. Once again the main losers of the election were those attempting to rally a secular nationalist vote. This time Allawi built an even wider coalition to form the National Iraqi List, but the list only managed to secure 9.09% of the vote and 25 seats in parliament.

Although the elections themselves were a success, it took five months of talks in their aftermath for Iraq's newly elected governing elite to reach an agreement on the cabinet. A large part of this delay was caused by disputes within the victorious UIA about who should become prime minister. In the wake of the January elections, al-Jaafari had been elected prime minister. As head of the Islamic Dawa Party, one of the two main parties in the UIA, al-Jaafari had good reason to assume that he would be reappointed to the post in December. However, during his year as premier, al-Jaafari had alienated a number of key Iraqi politicians as well as the British and American governments. He was considered to lack the personal dynamism and diplomacy needed to weld the disparate political factions that dominate Iraqi politics into a coherent coalition government. Both London and Washington began to look favourably on SCIRI's deputy leader Adel Abdul al-Mahdi as a more suitable candidate. However, neither al-Jaafari nor al-Mahdi could gain a decisive majority within the UIA. In the end it took the extended application of diplomatic pressure, including a visit to Baghdad by US Secretary of State Condoleezza Rice and then-UK Foreign Secretary Jack Straw to force a compromise. On 21 April 2006 the UIA nominated al-Jaafari's deputy Nouri al-Maliki as a compromise candidate. After four months of discord other members of the UIA, the Kurdish parties and the main Sunni political bloc agreed on al-Maliki as a candidate they could all work with. The 50-year-old al-Maliki was perceived to be a far more skilled politician than al-Jaafari. During 2005 he took on the role of the UIA's chief spokesman and led the detailed and often bitter negotiations on the constitution. However, like many of the politicians resident in Baghdad's heavily guarded Green Zone, he had been long absent from the country. After being driven into exile by Saddam Hussein's regime in 1980, he fled first to Tehran and later to the Syrian capital, Damascus.

It was testament to al-Maliki's skill that, once appointed in late April, he took less than a month to cobble together the majority of the cabinet. Constitutionally the office of prime minister is a weak one. Real political power is vested in the parties, with electoral success rewarded by dividing up the spoils of government, cabinet portfolios and the jobs and resources they bring. Al-Maliki's task was to build a government of national unity, carefully rewarding the main coalitions while also seeking to balance electoral achievement with the identity politics that the main parties claim to personify. In addition, al-Maliki had to move ministers who had either proved to be inefficient, scandal ridden or controversial during the previous year. The result was a cabinet that sought to balance electoral outcomes with the needs of a population traumatised by the collapse of the state in 2003, a crime wave and the spectre of civil war.

The acceptance of sectarian politics was seen in the reappointment of Talabani as president. This not only placed a Kurdish politician at the geographical centre of politics in Baghdad, but also allowed Talabani's long time rival, Masoud Barazani, to dominate the politics of the Kurdish regional government in the north of the country. Communalist mathematics were furthered by the appointment of a Sunni and a Shia, Tareq al-Hashemi and Adel Abdul Mahdi, as vice presidents and a Kurd and a Sunni, Barham Salih and Salam al-Zobaie, as deputy prime ministers.

One of al-Maliki's early successes was the appointment of Dr Hussein Shahristani as the new minister of oil. Shahristani is a key member of the UIA, but refused to join any of the parties that make up the coalition. Amongst the new ruling elite his reputation for moral probity is unrivalled. Shahristani trained as a nuclear scientist but fell foul of the old regime for refusing to help further its nuclear ambitions. After imprisonment and torture he escaped into exile amidst the chaos of the 1991 uprisings. By putting Shahristani in charge of the oil ministry, the prime minister acknowledged the need for a non-partisan figure to oversee the country's major source of wealth. He also moved to staunch a wave of complaints about the high levels of corruption and mismanagement within Iraq's oil sector. The reappointment of Hoshiyar Zebari as foreign minister was also positively received. A Kurd, he represented the multi-cultural make up of the new Iraq. He is also a redoubtable diplomat, cementing strong ties in Europe and at the United Nations whilst performing well in negotiations with both Iraq's Arab and non-Arab neighbours.

The limitations placed upon the prime minister's powers of appointment were highlighted by his choice of other cabinet ministers. Bayan Jabor's appointment as minister of finance is a case in point. He is a key member of SCIRI and a former commander in its militia, the Badr Brigade. As interior minister in the last government, he was the focus of sustained criticism for sacking large numbers of staff and replacing them with many of his old comrades from the Badr Brigade. Under his leadership the ministry's special commandos were accused of hastening Iraq's descent into civil war by their use of death-squad tactics. Although al-Maliki succeeded in moving Jabor from the interior minister post, the politics of coalition government meant that he still had to be given a central post. The demands of UIA politics also meant that members of al-Sadr's organisation, twice involved in extended and bloody rebellions against the US Army, took charge of education and health.

The main political opposition to al-Maliki's government developed within parliament. The presentation of the cabinet to parliament was marked by protest, as 15 parliamentarians walked out of the chamber. The protest was led by the head of the smaller Sunni coalition, Salih Mutlak of the National Dialogue Front. Mutlak damned the new government for being divisive, sectarian and unfocused on the three areas – security, disorder and services – that cause most problems for ordinary Iraqis. In the aftermath of the elections the unity of the UIA itself was damaged when one of its members, Fadila or the Virtue Party, walked out of the coalition, taking 16 members of parliament with it. This left al-Maliki's own alliance with 112 of the 275 seats in parliament, severely constraining his government and forcing it to build a new voting bloc for each successive piece of legislation. With the prime minister devoting so much of his time to this task, the government reverted to business as usual, with each minister dominating his or her own ministry. The result was highly variable governance, with some ministers running their institutions to the best of their ability but others carving out fiefdoms for personal or factional benefit, disengaged from the pressing need to build state capacity and to extend it across the geographical extent of the country.

The most immediate problem that the new government faced was the redrafting of the constitution, which had produced a highly decentralised federal system. On the eve of the October referendum, US Ambassador Zalmay Khalilzad brokered a deal that secured Sunni political participation in the plebiscite. This mandated a committee of the Iraqi parliament to review and possibly redraft the constitution's most divisive aspects. However, the balance of power within the parliament will tend to limit substantial constitutional change. Although the constitutional committee is the focus of intense and acrimonious debate, it will not deliver political compromise, creating instead renewed resentment amongst the Sunni population, the majority of whom voted against the constitution in 2005.

The selection of al-Maliki as prime minister and his formation of a new government, represented the end of an intense political process. The danger for Iraq in the aftermath of successful elections is that politicians locked away within the fortified Green Zone will quickly become removed from the everyday concerns of the population. If the new government follows the path of its predecessor and becomes mired in the incestuous politics of zero-sum party competition, then it may well hasten Iraq's descent into inter-communal strife and collapse.

Continued violence and instability

Apparent success on the political front during 2005 has not been matched by increased security. If anything, as the political process moved forward the level and nature of the violence grew worse. The inability of the Iraqi security services to impose order on the south and centre of the country has given rise to three distinct groups perpetrating violence beyond the control of the state. The first group is the 'industrial strength' criminal gangs who operate mainly in Iraq's cities like Basra, Baghdad and Mosul. The second, posing the greatest threat to the future stability of the new Iraqi government, is the insurgency. In the aftermath of regime change, the insurgency was born in a reactive and highly localised fashion, as the US military's inability to control Iraq became apparent. This process saw the creation of a number of small fighting groups built around personal ties of trust, cemented by family, locality or many years of friendship. Disparate groups formed to rid the country of US forces were estimated to consist of between 50 and 74 separate, autonomous units, with between 20,000 and 50,000 fighters in their ranks. Over the past three years they have been innovative in the technology they deploy and the tactics they use.

Over 2005, however, the insurgency to a large degree consolidated around four or five main groups. These organisations include the Islamic Army in Iraq, the Partisans of the Sunna Army, the Mujahidin's Army, Muhammad's Army and the Islamic Resistance Movement in Iraq. As their names suggest, political violence has been increasingly justified on religious terms. These groups have found ideological coherence by fusing a powerful appeal to Iraqi nationalism with an austere and extreme Sunni Salafism. The attraction of the Salafist doctrine for the insurgents is that it allows a distinction to be drawn between those involved in the jihad or struggle (the true believers), and those who are not. Under Salafism those not backing the struggle can be branded non-believers and, as such, killed. This Salafist approach has also lent itself to the increased use of sectarian violence. Shias can be murdered both because they do not follow the 'true path of Islam' and because they form the majority of those staffing the security forces against whom the violence is directed.

The numbers and role played by Arabs from neighbouring countries, and the organising capacity of 'al-Qaeda in Mesopotamia', have slowly increased over the last year, now estimated by the US military to be between 5% and 10% of the total. US and Iraqi forces achieved an important breakthrough on 7 June 2006 when Abu Musab al-Zarqawi, the Jordanian who had led al-Qaeda in Mesopotamia and was believed responsible for many murders, was killed by an American air strike on a house near Baquba, 65km north of Baghdad. The likely impact on the organisation and on the insurgency was difficult to judge: a successor was named but his true name and identity remained unclear. Foreign fighters have played a disproportionately large role in the insurgency's increased ideological coherence. Al-Qaeda in Mesopotamia has led the rising influence of Salafist doctrine and has claimed responsibility or has been blamed for most of the violence that has increased sectarian tensions in the country. This dynamic reached a peak with the destruction of the al-Askariyya Mosque in Samarra on 22 February 2006. Although the city of Samarra has long been dominated by the insurgency, the destruction of the mosque, one of Shia Islam's most important shrines, was calculated to outrage Shia opinion. In the aftermath of the destruction Sunni mosques across Baghdad were targeted, with an estimated 220–550 civilians killed. But of greater concern was the movement of the population triggered by intimidation and the threat of sectarian violence. The Iraqi government has estimated the number of displaced people to be as high as 65,000, with the majority coming from in and around Baghdad.

The violence that erupted following the Samarra bombing saw the insurgency combine with a third group deploying violence, the militias formed by political parties. These militias, estimated to hold as many as 140,000 fighters in their ranks, are organised and legitimised along sectarian lines. They have increased their power and visibility on the streets of Iraq's major towns and cities. Although these militias enjoy little popular support, their existence is testament to the inability of the Iraqi government to guarantee the personal safety of its citizens. The militias can be divided into three broad groups, depending on their organisational coherence and relationship to national politics. The first consists of the two Kurdish militias of the KDP and PUK. These two separate forces together number between 80,000 and 100,000 fighters. The second set are those created in exile and brought back to Iraq in the wake of Saddam's fall. The most powerful of these is the Badr Brigade, the military arm of SCIRI. Estimated to have 10,000 fighters, the Badr Brigade, along with SCIRI itself, was set up as a foreign-policy vehicle for the Iranian government. Indeed the Badr Brigade was trained and officered by the Iranian Revolutionary Guard, at least until its return to Iraq. It is the Badr Brigade's integration into the security forces, especially the police and paramilitary units associated with the Ministry of Interior, that has done so much to de-legitimise the state-controlled forces of law and order. The third group of militias are those created in Iraq since regime change. They vary in size, organisation and discipline, from a few thugs with guns to militias capable of running whole towns. The largest and most coherent is the 10,000-strong Mahdi Army, set up by al-Sadr. The Mahdi Army was blamed for the majority of violence in and around Baghdad following the destruction of the al-Askariyya shrine.

If civil war develops in Iraq, the combination of the insurgency and the militia fighters will have been a key factor. Although formed as an instrumental response to the security vacuum, they have attempted to legitimise themselves by the deployment of hybrid ideologies: sectarian, religious and nationalist.

Faced with increasing violence and an inability to make significant reductions in their own casualty figures, the countries that make up the US-led coalition are primarily focused on indigenisation. In the words of President George W. Bush, 'US troops will stand down as Iraqi troops stand up'. To this end the Multinational Security Transition Command embarked on a $5.7 billion plan to train 270,000 Iraqi troops and paramilitary police units by summer 2006. The plan, initially developed by retired US Army General David H. Luck, envisioned a speedy transfer of responsibility from US to Iraqi forces, who would take on patrolling duties and hence bear the brunt of casualties. However by the middle of 2005, senior US military commanders in Iraq realised that simply focusing on troop numbers ran the danger of neglecting the capacity of the force they were building. To counter this problem they instigated a four-tier assessment process. Level one represented the goal for the whole of the Iraqi security services; units fully capable of planning and conducting counter-insurgency operations. In the summer of 2005 only three of Iraq's then 115 police and army battalions had reach this gold standard and by September, US Army General George Casey was forced to reduce this number to one.

In spite of the lack of indigenous military capacity, coalition policy in Iraq is still primarily focused on returning responsibility back to Iraqi troops as quickly as possible. In May 2006, the US military estimated that Iraqi forces controlled half of the 'battle space' across the country. However, its target was to turn all of the battle space over to Iraqi forces by the end of the year, allowing American forces to be reduced to 100,000 and British troops to 6,000. This highly ambitious timetable faces major problems, since the Iraqi armed forces are poorly equipped and lack the command-and-control capacity to plan and execute medium-to-large-scale operations.

If the Iraqi military is still a work in progress, then the police force is an even graver cause for concern. As with the new army, police training has been extremely hurried: cadets are trained to march in a straight line, fire 200 rounds at a static target and attend a course on human rights and Iraqi law. There are concerns that the loyalty of the Iraqi police force to the Iraqi state is open to doubt. Across Iraq, and particularly in the south, there is strong evidence to suggest that the political militias have targeted the police force, infiltrating their members into its ranks and placing their own senior commanders in regional management positions. In May 2005 this state of affairs led the police chief of Basra, General Hassab al-Sade, to state that he had lost control of 75% of his force. Criminals, militias and political parties have been able to impose their will on the police and the population of Basra beyond. The extent of the problem was highlighted in September 2005, when two British undercover soldiers were seized by members of the Basra police force. The British army were forced to deploy a tank to rescue them from a police barracks when intelligence suggested that a militia faction within the police, the 'Jamaet', were planning to move them to another location.

The Ministry of Interior in Baghdad has also become the focus of a series of scandals. In November 2005 the US military raided a detention facility run by the Ministry of Interior in a Baghdad suburb. Inside they found 170 illegally held detainees, a number of whom were malnourished and had been tortured. Of even greater concern were the actions of the special commando forces directly recruited, trained and managed by the Interior Ministry. John Pace, upon his retirement as head of the Human Rights Office of the United Nations Assistance Mission in Iraq, accused the ministry in February 2006 of 'acting as a rogue elephant within the government'. The central focus of his concern were the ministry's counter-insurgency special commando units who have been repeatedly blamed for sectarian-motivated killings in Sunni areas of Baghdad.

The weakness of both the Iraqi army and police thus requires US forces to maintain responsibility for counter-insurgency at the very least until the end of 2006. The apparent inability of the US military's overwhelming technological superiority to defeat the insurgency triggered a policy rethink in Washington. Previously US Army tactics had been dominated by offensive action, focused on destroying the insurgency, capturing its key leaders and striking at its supply lines and sanctuaries. This overly kinetic or muscular approach failed to produce sustained success in the first three years of its application. The publication of US government's *National Strategy for Victory in Iraq* in November 2005 signalled a change in counter-insurgency policy. Conventional doctrine stresses that success can only be achieved by fully integrating the deployment of military force into an overall strategy with distinctly political goals. The deployment of kinetic force can be highly counterproductive unless it serves to deliver wider political aims. Counter-insurgency operations can exacerbate the situation and alienate the population, becoming a recruiting sergeant for the very organisations they seek to defeat. With this in mind the US military's approach shifted from a policy of targeting the insurgency across the country to one of 'clear, hold and build'. Offensive action is now focused on clearing specifically targeted areas of insurgent activity and holding those areas while government capacity and legitimacy can be built. It is too early to speculate on whether this policy will bear dividends. But it does recognise the major problem facing the Iraqi government: its inability to build legitimacy by delivering regularised services to its population. By combining its counter-insurgency tactics in Iraq with a policy specifically designed to tie the population to the state, the US military is returning much more fully to what has generally been considered best practice.

Conclusions

Iraq is a country desperately in need of a state. To halt its descent into civil war its governing institutions – bureaucratic, military and political – have to be rebuilt from the ground up across the entire country. Ultimately the sustainability of state capacity depends on the extent to which its actions are judged to be legitimate in the eyes of its citizens. This is not primarily an issue of ethnic identity; the evolution of state power is intimately linked to the ability of state institutions to penetrate society in a regularised fashion and become central to the population's daily strategies of survival. The collapse of the Iraqi state in the aftermath of regime change forced the population in the south and centre of the country to survive as best they could. The lack of government control and the resultant security vacuum allowed informal groupings, personified by politically motivated militias, to dominate the lives of the majority of Iraqis. These militias have legitimised themselves in terms of ethnic and religious identity. Once the insurgency adopted highly sectarian attitudes the stage was set for state collapse to degenerate into civil war. The capacity of the US-dominated coalition to avoid this outcome is not primarily focused on its counter-insurgency campaigns. Instead the institutional capacity of the new Iraqi state needs to be speedily enhanced. The elections of December 2005 may have been a milestone on the way to this goal. A government of national unity has been formed with parliamentary backing and a national mandate. However, if this government, like its predecessor, indulges in inter-party bickering and sectarian one-upmanship instead of state-building, then it will hasten Iraq's journey towards a very destructive civil war.

Iran: Turbulence Within and Without

Iran's hotly contested June 2005 presidential election, resulting in the somewhat surprising victory of Mahmoud Ahmadinejad, led to a volatile year for Iran's domestic politics and foreign relations. Although his victory ostensibly consolidated the conservative clerical establishment's grip on political power, domestic infighting has yet to subside because extreme tension remains between Iran's factional elites and its disaffected population. In an effort to contain domestic, factional, regional and international crises, the regime has struggled to maintain the equilibrium between its domestic and foreign policy, often using one to bolster the other. The one issue on which Iran's people appear to broadly support the government, however, is Iran's national right to master the nuclear fuel cycle. Its assertion of that right alarms most of the rest of the world.

Moderates in decline

Ahmadinejad's election has dramatically changed the domestic and international dynamic. He not only forced a run-off election but also defeated the favourite – the politically reborn moderate ex-president Hashemi Rafsanjani. Some 22m people voted in the run-off poll – a turnout of 60%, slightly lower than the 63% that voted in the first round. Ahmadinejad won 62% and Rafsanjani 36% of the run-off vote, suggesting that the electorate ultimately regarded the latter as too slippery a politician for comfort. Mehdi Karroubi, third-place candidate and former speaker of the Majlis el-Shurah (parliament), placed third in the first round. He had seized on the economic imperatives of the population, offering if elected to give every Iranian $60 a month. He accused the Guardian Council and members of the Revolutionary Guard of voting irregularities. Ahmadinejad, 49, mayor of Tehran since 2003, adopted a conservative Islamic platform, seeking to revive the late Ayatollah Ruhollah Khomeini's revolutionary creed by rooting out corruption and the rising Western decadence that many Iranians perceive as poisoning Iranian society. He brought considerable credibility to this stance. Ahmadinejad fought in the Iran–Iraq war as a member of the Revolutionary Guard, and was reported to have been involved in covert operations.

Overall, the presidential contest revealed the success of the conservative establishment in polarising the reformist movement. The conservatives exposed the fragility of a movement that had failed, critically, to complement democracy and human rights with economic performance. Ahmadinejad, though, will now require the country's oil resources to meet his populist pledges, and those resources are not a permanent solution. As oil prices hovered at around $70 a barrel, Ahmadinejad aired ambitions to disperse Iran's oil wealth to the *mostasafin* – the dispossessed members of society. Additionally, he promised to provide assistance to Iran's youthful population – 70% of Iranians are under the age of 30 – by creating a 'love fund' that would draw on oil revenues to help provide young married couples with jobs and housing. Yet Ahmadinejad has not met his campaign promises. Plans for the fund were quickly withdrawn. The priorities of the $217bn budget he submitted in February were 'justice, kindness, public service, and national development'. But its dependence on oil revenues and the president's redistributive inclinations were criticised not only by the press, but also by cabinet members and parliamentarians. In particular, conservative member Mohammad Reza Mirtajedini castigated the government for increasing reliance on oil almost fourfold.

Factional politics

In spite of the conservative resurgence within the theocratic republic, factional unity has yet to be achieved. Within the Majlis, in which Ahmadinejad's Abadgaran party has a majority, the president faced significant obstacles in obtaining the approval of four of his cabinet ministries, including the oil ministry. Many of his 21 cabinet nominees appeared to be political choices with little governmental or technical experience. The emergence of this new group signalled the coalescence of a new elite from the stronghold of the Revolutionary Guard Corps. Manuchehr Mottaki was selected as foreign minister. He joined the Foreign Ministry in 1984 and held ambassadorships in Turkey and Japan. Mottaki served in parliament as a member of the conservative Abadgaran coalition. He leads the legislature's National Security and Foreign Policy Committee, and he has used this platform to force greater parliamentary involvement in Iran's nuclear negotiations. Mustafa Mohammad Najjar is minister of defence and armed forces logistics. A committed member of the Islamic Revolutionary Guard Corps since its creation in May 1979, he participated in the suppression of a Kurdish insurgency in 1978–79. He is closely allied with the president, and was one of those responsible for 'exporting the revolution' to Lebanon, Palestine and the Persian Gulf. The appointment of Hojatoleslam Mustafa Purmohammadi as interior minister has also been controversial. Purmohammadi has served as a revolutionary prosecutor and head of foreign intelligence. Accountability in internal security is likely to diminish during his tenure.

Attempts by Supreme Leader Ayatollah Sayyid Ali Khamenei to mitigate factional disputes have only heightened tensions. While rhetorically supporting the new president, Khamenei – who enjoys Iran's ultimate constitutional authority – granted the unelected Expediency Council, headed by Rafsanjani, supervisory powers over the elected executive, legislative and judiciary branches. The idea was apparently to encourage Ahmadinejad to remedy the lack of governmental unity. The strong conservative coalition of the Abadgaran party, however, may be difficult to control. Increasingly dominant since the 2003 municipal elections, this group has mounted a steady challenge for power as they outmanoeuvred reformists in the domestic political arena. Abadgaran adherents, many of whom have served as commanders in Iran's Revolutionary Guard, believe that generational change is needed to safeguard the Islamic revolution. Most are relatively unknown politicians, with little or no public record. Ironically, this group – in view of its solidarity with the Revolutionary Guard, as well as the involvement of hardliners within the political and security establishments, and a significant number of religiously inclined members of Iran's lower and middle classes – was initially supported by Khamenei against the reformists. This strategy backfired, however, as Abadgaran has become powerful enough to challenge the Supreme Leader.

The Assembly of Experts elections scheduled for October 2006 are critical for Khamenei, as the Abadgaran party could pose a challenge to his rule as Supreme Leader. The last elections occurred in 1998, when the body reconfirmed Khamenei as Supreme Leader. The Council of Guardians has the authority to vet candidates for the 86 clerical positions; the population votes on the candidates; and the assembly thus elected then chooses the supreme leader from its own ranks. There is considerable debate and speculation within the group as to the future of the position of Supreme Leader, including some talk of devolving his power into a decentralised system of shared authority among a number of clerics. In this connection, it is important to note that the concept of the *velayat-e-faqih* (guardianship of the jurist) – as created by Ayatollah Khomeini – has not been accepted universally by the Shi'ite community. Indeed, many consider this concept to be antithetical to Shia Islam. This doctrinal reality, alongside Khamenei's relative deficit of Shi'ite theological credentials, makes change in the power of the Supreme Leader position a real possibility.

At the same time, Khamenei has defused the immediate challenges to his constitutional power through tactical manoeuvring. The arrival of Ahmadinejad and Abadgaran has necessitated an alliance between Khamenei and his former challenger Rafsanjani. Rafsanjani's roles as deputy chairman of the Assembly of Experts as well as his elevated powers on the Expediency Council are not a coincidence. As a disciple of Ayatollah Mohammad Taqi Mesbah-Yazdi, Ahmadinejad, among others, hopes to see Mesbah-Yazdi himself as the next supreme leader. Mesbah-Yazdi is a hard-line cleric who espouses radical ideology and complete isolation from the West. A number of his former students at the Haqqani seminary currently hold cabinet positions. This group and its adherents are enjoying a revival. They retain a messianic vision of Islam, believing that the Twelfth Imam, having gone into occultation in the ninth century, will return and restore justice to the world. While Khamenei himself is a conservative cleric, since the emergence of Ahmadinejad he has appeared a pragmatist by comparison. The tense international environment has led some politicians to suggest that the Assembly of Experts election be delayed to coincide with the 2008 parliamentary election cycle. Such a postponement, however, is unlikely, as popular support is paramount for maintaining theocratic legitimacy in the Iranian system.

Discomfiture on the fringes

Iran has experienced ongoing ethnic unrest, primarily in the Arab-dominated southwest Khuzestan province and in the northwest Kurdish region. Iran's ethnic minorities include Arabs, Azeris, Baluchis, Kurds and Turkmen. These irredentist groups have never embraced the Islamic revolution and have been neglected by the government's more urban-based development initiatives. The strong Persian-dominated culture and language has also perpetuated an overarching sense of discrimination. Historically, minorities' low voter participation has indicated their alienation and dissatisfaction with the direction of the theocratic republic.

Since summer 2005, Kurds have increasingly agitated in the hope that more attention will be brought to local development and political representation. In southwestern Ahvaz, rioting, violence and, in October 2005, bombings led to arrests and clashes with Iranian security forces. Two Kurds were executed in early 2006 for their purported participation in an uprising. The Sunni minority in the Sistan and Baluchestan province near the Pakistan border has also agitated against the government, forming a group known as *Jundallah*, or God's Soldiers. In January 2006 they held several Iranian border guards hostage, demanding the release of their own 16 jailed group members in exchange. The group claims that the regime has killed over 400 of its members and committed political, economic and human-rights violations in the decades since the revolution.

Especially threatening for the conservative elite was the February 2006 bus drivers' strike in Tehran. The drivers united in protest against a political ban on trade unions, accusing their managers of corrupt practices. Their demands included better salaries and working conditions. Ahmadinejad had promised to deal with the corruption of the entrenched regime, but knew that any such move would only increase his factional challenges on the domestic front. Many of the strikers were arrested. Comparable conduct by former President Mohammad Khatami produced public disenchantment. During his term, however, the Iranian population was not only more politically active and optimistic but also aware and tolerant of a reformist president's more substantial constitutional and factional constraints. In the new political environment, a population that elevates economic mandates over political ones may well be less acquiescent. This possibility could reinforce the new government's tendency to suppress domestic complaints by way of an aggressive foreign policy. And that tendency is entirely consistent with the clerical elite's preoccupation with bolstering Iran's political influence in the Middle East through regional and international posturing.

Aggressive external stance

Iran appears to have abandoned détente in favour of a more aggressive stance both on the nuclear and regional front. Not accidentally, this development has coincided with the United States' intensifying military involvement in the region by way of Iraq. Washington and Tehran have converging interests in the Middle East. Both, for instance, could gain from cooperation on regional security issues – particularly in Iraq and Afghanistan. But the United States has continued to accuse Iran of being the 'central banker of terrorism', and Iran has used a mixture of military and religious influence to cultivate ties with insurgent groups and militias in Iraq. Iran's links with most of Iraq's current Shi'ite elite are longstanding and to an extent defensible, as many sought refuge and support from the theocracy during Saddam Hussein's reign of terror, directed by his Sunni Ba'athist regime against Shi'ites and Kurds. Tehran has maintained that its Iraq policy is premised on democracy and religious solidarity, and not designed to export its theocratic model. It has, however, funnelled millions of dollars through its charity network to revitalise Shi'ite mosques and communities. Tehran's apparent hope is that Iraq remains in a state of 'controlled chaos', which is useful for both bogging down US military assets and instilling fear of civil unrest into Iran's own domestic population so as to keep it tame.

Ahmadinejad has also stated that 'Israel should be wiped off the map', that 'if the Europeans claim that the Zionists were suppressed during the Second World War, they can place a part of Europe at their disposal', and that 'they have created a myth today and they call it the massacre of the Jews'. These antagonistic assertions are most likely part of the president's strategy of rallying nationalists to sideline factional squabbles. Regionally, he has tried to position himself as the champion of the Arab street. His rhetoric was well received among Iran's regional strategic allies – in particular, Khaled Mishaal, the leader of Hamas. Following its stunning victory in the January 2006 Palestinian elections and a withholding of funds from the Hamas-dominated Palestinian Authority government by Israel, the United States and the EU, Tehran gave $50m to the group. Iran has also provided financial and other support for Hamas's terrorist operations. In recent visits to Tehran, Hamas leaders guaranteed that any potential attacks on Iran due to its threatening nuclear programme would be reciprocated by attacks on Israel.

Tehran is well situated to threaten American and other interests not only in Iraq and Palestine but also in Lebanon, Syria and the wider Persian Gulf. Hizbullah, while tilting significantly towards non-violent democratic politics in Lebanon, has not renounced its militant identity. The group's principal outside benefactor has been and remains Iran. Syria, Hizbullah's other key state supporter, signed a mutual-defence pact with Iran last spring. Indeed, each of these diplomatically isolated countries continues to lend broad political support to the other. Iran's regional alignment seeks mainly to protect the Islamic Republic in the event of possible pre-emptive military action by Israel and the United States. Surprisingly, this prospect prompted Arab governments, as the nuclear problem matured into crisis, to voice sympathy for Tehran. Foreign Minister Saud al Faisal of Saudi Arabia – Iran's principal regional geopolitical and sectarian rival – suggested that 'the West is partly to blame for the current nuclear stand-off with Iran because it allowed Israel to develop nuclear weapons', while Egypt's foreign minister Ahmad Aboul Gheit, called for a continuation of dialogue. That said, Gulf Co-operation Council (GCC) statements by mid-2006 were beginning to take a more robust line, partly as the council presidency was taken up by the United Arab Emirates, which has a territorial dispute with Iran. Additionally, Russian and Chinese reluctance to chastise the clerical regime signified converging commercial and strategic synergies that, in their view, overrode the importance of the nuclear issue. There were signs by spring 2006, however, of some Russian and Chinese frustration with Iran's refusal to negotiate in good faith.

Nuclear negotiations

France, Germany and the UK (the E3, later joined by EU High Representative Javier Solana) made it clear from the start of negotiations in 2003 that their long-term goal was an end to enrichment and reprocessing programmes in Iran that, while ostensibly for civil nuclear-energy purposes, could also produce fissile material for nuclear weapons. Iran made it equally clear throughout that it would never abandon these programmes. Faced with these incompatible bottom lines, the E3 fell back on tactics to suspend the enrichment programmes, however temporarily, realising that stringing together a series of temporary suspensions might be the best that could be achieved until such time as conditions became conducive to a long-term agreement. Iran agreed to a suspension in October 2003, in the so-called Tehran Agreement. That deal soon fell apart, but Iran again avoided being referred to the UN Security Council by striking a new deal with the E3/EU in Paris in November 2004, in which it agreed, 'on a voluntary basis', to suspend all enrichment-related and reprocessing activities, including, inter alia, 'all tests or production at any uranium conversion installation'. It was also agreed that 'sustaining the enrichment … will be essential for the continuation of the overall process' – meaning that the suspension was essential for the negotiations and the EU process of engagement. The agreement also called for negotiations, which began in December 2004, on long-term arrangements that would provide 'objective guarantees' that Iran's nuclear programme was exclusively for peaceful purposes. In March 2005, in the context of a US announcement to support the E3's diplomacy with Iran, the E3/EU stated publicly that if Iran did not maintain the suspension, they would support referring Iran's nuclear programme to the UN Security Council.

Notwithstanding the Paris Agreement, in May 2005 Iran announced it had decided to resume uranium conversion at the Esfahan uranium conversion facility, on grounds that it had received very little from the negotiations. In response, the E3 foreign ministers said any break in the agreement would result in referral to the Security Council but offered to meet in Geneva with Council for National Security Secretary Hassan Rowhani on 25 May to try to avert a crisis. Rowhani floated a deal whereby Iran would be allowed to produce uranium hexafluoride but send the product to Russia for enrichment and fabrication into fuel elements for Bushehr. In any case, Iran would resume the uranium conversion work. When the E3 held firm, Rowhani agreed to postpone the decision on uranium conversion until the Europeans presented comprehensive proposals for long-term arrangements, which they undertook to do in late July or early August.

Waiting until Ahmadinejad took office, the E3/EU made their proposal on 5 August. The 31-page document included substantive incentives for Iran in the areas of: political and security cooperation, including committing to work with Iran on regional security arrangements; support for Iran's civil nuclear programme, including committing to support further Russian nuclear power reactors in Iran, relax export controls, cooperate with Iran in radioisotope research, and develop with Iran a framework to assure supply of nuclear fuel for its reactors; and economic and technical cooperation, including work toward early conclusion of an EU–Iran Trade and Cooperation Agreement and practical cooperation in oil and gas technology.

Ahmadinejad's response was an immediate and derisive rejection. The linchpin of the proposed agreement was the call for a binding commitment by Iran not to pursue fuel-cycle activities other than the construction and operation of light-water power and research reactors. Iran saw this as a denial of its right to enrichment, even though the proposed framework agreement made it clear that this commitment would be reviewed after ten years. Iran regarded the incentives in the proposal as too little and too vague. Most would require the explicit support of the United States to lift investment sanctions, approve export licences and provide the only security assurances that matter to Iran.

Even before receiving the E3 proposal, Iran notified the International Atomic Energy Agency (IAEA) that it would resume the uranium-conversion work, spurring an extraordinary session of the IAEA Board of Governors. Although uranium conversion, which began on 8 August, was a clear violation of the Paris Agreement, the E3 judged that other board members would need time for deliberation, so board action was deferred to the regular September meeting. At the September meeting, the board decided, by a vote of 22–1 and 12 abstentions, to find Iran in non-compliance with its safeguards obligations and to further find that Iran's history of concealment and the resulting lack of confidence that its nuclear programme is for peaceful purposes raised questions within the competence of the Security Council as the body responsible for threats to international peace and security. The two findings thus provided a dual basis for reporting Iran to the Security Council. The board decided to defer actual reporting, however, due to opposition by Russia and China, both of which abstained on the vote. Most of the other non-aligned members of the board also abstained, although notably India voted yes. Venezuela voiced the lone 'no' vote.

Resumption of enrichment

In the autumn, as a way out of the crisis, Russia proposed a joint venture to use Iran's uranium hexafluoride to produce enriched uranium fuel on Russian soil. Conceding that uranium conversion could continue in Iran, the United States and EU gave support to the Russian proposal. Iran's leaders said they were willing to accept the joint venture proposal, with one change: the production venue would also have to include uranium enrichment in Iran – a condition that obviated the whole point of the proposal. Russia and Iran continued to talk about the joint venture, but it now had no purpose, and the two sides could not agree on the central issue. From the American point of view, Iran was engaged in stalling tactics, dragging out negotiations with Russia in order to avoid sanctions while incrementally moving toward acquisition of a nuclear-weapons capability.

On 10 January 2006, two weeks after it had stirred hopes for a compromise by saying it would 'seriously consider' Russia's face-saving proposal, Iran ratcheted up the crisis by removing IAEA seals at Natanz and other facilities and resuming research and development work on its uranium-enrichment programme. Iran claimed that the intended enrichment work would only involve small-scale research and development, and that it would all continue to be covered by IAEA inspections. The transatlantic allies argued that enrichment at any level was unacceptable. By enriching uranium in even one centrifuge, Iran could learn the difficult art of balancing the spinning machine. Spinning a score of centrifuges in a cascade allowed Iran to test its domestically manufactured parts before it began making more. Once Iran mastered the enrichment technology, it could replicate cascades in covert facilities and gain experience in how to minimise the chance of detection.

Meeting in London on 30 January, the foreign ministers of the permanent members of the Security Council plus Germany came to an agreement that Iran's non-compliance should be reported to the Security Council when the IAEA Board next met in extraordinary session. In a concession to Russia, however, and to give further time for negotiation, it was agreed that the Security Council would take no action until after the regular March board meeting (when, not coincidentally, the United States would no longer act as the rotating Security Council president). A 4 February board resolution duly instructed the IAEA director-general to report to the Security Council all IAEA reports and resolutions relating to the Iran issue, and laid out explicit steps required of Iran: to fully suspend all enrichment-related and reprocessing activities; to reconsider the construction of a heavy-water moderated research reactor (because of its potential use for plutonium weapons); to ratify and implement the Additional Protocol and act in accordance with its provisions pending ratification; and to implement transparency measures requested by the director-general, including access to individuals, documentation, dual-use equipment and certain military-owned workshops. With Russian and Chinese support along with half of the non-aligned members of the board, the resolution passed 27–3 (the three 'no' votes being Venezuela and new board members Cuba and Syria), with five abstentions.

When the board met again on 6–8 March, Iran had met none of the board's conditions, save for allowing a few more transparency visits by the IAEA. Director-General Mohammed ElBaradei's report to that board meeting also provided the strongest evidence yet of a 'smoking gun'. Referring to a 15-page document Iran had received from Pakistani nuclear scientist A.Q. Khan's black-market network (shown to IAEA inspectors but not turned over to them) describing procedures for the re-conversion and casting of uranium metal into hemispheres, ElBaradei characterised it as 'related to the fabrication of nuclear weapons components'. The report also detailed discussions with Iran about information that the agency had received (from Western intelligence briefings) about Iranian alleged undeclared activities, known as the Green Salt Project, concerning the conversion of uranium dioxide into uranium tetrafluoride (known as 'green salt' because of its colour and texture), as well as tests related to high explosives and the design of a missile re-entry vehicle, all of which he said appeared to have administrative interconnections. While not confirming the information, which reportedly was contained in hundreds of documents on a laptop computer turned over by an Iranian defector, IAEA Deputy Director General for Safeguards Olli Heinonen briefed IAEA members on 31 January that the Green Salt Project 'could have a military nuclear dimension'.

The Security Council began deliberations in the second week of March, and three weeks later issued a statement by the Security Council president (an action requiring consensus of all 15 members), noting with serious concern the director-general's report of issues 'which could have a military nuclear dimension', and calling on Iran to take the steps required by the IAEA Board's February resolution, giving Iran 30 days to comply. Missing from the statement was any reference to the Security Council's responsibility for the 'maintenance of international peace and security'. Russia and China had abstained on the September IAEA Board resolution that included this phrase and would not accept it in the Security Council presidential statement, seeing it as tripwire to authorising military action.

Iran responded to each step in the UN process by taking escalatory steps of its own. After the February IAEA Board resolution, Iran stopped implementing the Additional Protocol and all other non-legally binding specifications of cooperation with the IAEA. Iran said it henceforth would accede to inspections only in accordance with full-scope safeguards agreement required under the NPT. On 11 February, Iran started enrichment tests by feeding uranium hexafluoride into a single P-1 centrifuge, and soon thereafter, into 10-and later 20-centrifuge cascades. By early April, Iran was already introducing gasified uranium into a cascade of 164 centrifuges – cutting six weeks off what experts expected was the earliest possible timeline. Skipping many of the intermediate steps of testing smaller cascades for longer periods of time, first with inert gas and then with the highly corrosive uranium hexafluoride, the Iranians seemed to be in an almost reckless hurry. It was clear that they wanted to establish new facts on the ground, to show that they already had an enrichment capability and could not be persuaded to give up the knowledge.

To great fanfare, Iran on 13 April announced that an enrichment level of 3.6% had been achieved from a 164-machine cascade, a level that IAEA samples confirmed. In addition, by April, the Uranium Conversion Facility at Esfahan had produced 110 tonnes of uranium hexafluoride – enough, when enriched, for fissile material for at least 15 weapons. When the Security Council's 30-day deadline was up, ElBaradei could report no progress on any of the steps required of Iran. Ahmadinejad declared Iran 'did not give a damn' about UN resolutions. ElBaradei's report was replete with further instances of Iranian refusals to turn over documents or answer many of the questions about concerns that have a military nuclear dimension. He could only say that Iran was prepared to provide a timetable for cooperation to resolve the remaining outstanding issues provided that Iran's nuclear dossier came off the Security Council agenda.

Iran also announced that by March 2007, it would operate a 3,000-centrifuge complex. This would be the first stage in the 54,000-centrifuge underground commercial fuel production facility at Natanz. Having 3,000 centrifuges operating would give Iran a significant breakout capability. Although the cascade will be configured for fuel production and monitored by the IAEA, the Iranians could reconfigure the facility for weapons-grade enrichment if it broke out of Iran's Nuclear Non-Proliferation Treaty commitment. They could then produce enough enriched uranium for a nuclear weapon within nine to eleven months. If Iran's boast is true, the earliest timeline for a nuclear weapon is thus the end of 2007. The boast lends cogency to the worst-case scenario, and with the IAEA access to Iran's nuclear programme now strictly limited to the safeguards agreement, the international community has fewer means of gauging Iran's progress. It is highly unlikely, however, that Iran could assemble a 3,000-machine complex in just a year's time. Iran does have enough components on hand for that many centrifuges. Taking into account the time it takes to build the centrifuges, assemble them in a connected series, and complete all tests that Iran finessed in its race to demonstrate an enrichment capability, however, the 3,000-unit complex is not likely to be running until 2009. Accordingly, it would probably be late 2009 before Iran could have a nuclear weapon. This timetable provides room for diplomacy.

The US government has insisted that it is focused on a diplomatic solution, but has also made it clear that no other options are off the table. Concern about potential military measures was heightened by American investigative reporter Seymour Hersh's claim in the April edition of *The New Yorker* magazine that US military planners, on orders from political leaders, were considering a tactical nuclear weapon among the possible means for destroying underground nuclear facilities in Iran. The article produced a flurry of comment and debate on both sides of the Atlantic, mostly disparaging the notion on grounds of both necessity (conventional bunker-busters probably could penetrate the underground facility at Natanz) and horrific consequences. Hersh seemed to have confused operational planning, which suggests ripening intentions, with contingency planning, which remains essentially theoretical. Some analysts speculated that the idea of a nuclear bunker-buster was a part of a psychological operations plan to sow doubt in Iranian leaders' minds about US intentions, and extend the deterrent effect of the US nuclear arsenal. If so, there were no signs that it produced the desired effect. Iranian leaders, seeing America bogged down in Iraq, and confident of their own ability to strike back, discounted America's ability and willingness to employ any military option. In the United States, meanwhile, there was a growing realisation that any military action to destroy Iran's nuclear facilities would not remain 'surgical' or limited, given the likelihood of asymmetric responses by Iran and the escalation that would ensue. If diplomatic efforts do not stop the programme before Iran nears the worst-case timeline for acquiring enough highly enriched uranium for a nuclear weapon, however, the military option is likely to be considered in earnest.

Buoyed by their technological success, the Iranians have shown no sign that they would ever agree to forego uranium enrichment entirely. Having endured

27 years of US sanctions and weathered isolation when the rest of the world supported Iraq in the Iran–Iraq War, Iran is apparently ready for whatever sanctions the Security Council metes out. Few Iranians believed the sanctions would be too severe or, as evidenced by US acceptance of India's nuclear status, too long lasting.

The West, however, is quite unified in its vehement opposition to Iran's emergence as a nuclear power. The end of two-and-a-half years of negotiations between Iran and the E3 set the stage for the long-held US goal of using the enforcement power of the Security Council to put pressure on Iran. Washington had been generally sceptical that the European negotiation process would be successful in stopping Iran's march toward a nuclear-weapons capability. Whether the Security Council option would do any better was an open question. The permanent members of the Council were stalemated over what measures the Security Council should bring to bear. The United States, UK and France were seeking to impose under Chapter VII of the UN Charter a mandatory obligation on Iran to stop all enrichment activity and fully cooperate with the investigations by the IAEA. This could pave the way for a second resolution authorising sanctions should Iran fail to comply, starting with political and legal sanctions that would isolate and stigmatise Iran. As of May 2006, however, Russia and China had refused to go along with any steps that could lead to Security Council sanctions, claiming they would only exacerbate Iran's belligerent defiance and potentially lead down a path of escalation possibly culminating in war, in a replay of the Iraq situation a few years earlier. If Russia and China block Security Council action, concerned countries could take actions on their own, including through the EU, to impose costs on Iran such as by restricting its access to trade credits and foreign investment. Already, financial measures the US has used effectively to restrict North Korea's access to the international banking system are being employed against Iran as well. It was against this background that the five permanent members of the Security Council plus Germany put a new package of incentives to Iran in another attempt to resolve the crisis. At mid-2006, Tehran was considering its response.

It was unlikely that Iran's expansionist aspirations and visions of regional integration would be fulfilled as long as the US adamantly opposed them. The Bush administration had not engaged the regime directly, had not pursued the option of a grand bargain, and believed that it had gone a considerable distance to cooperate through the E3 negotiation process. At the same time, the Bush administration and Tony Blair's government have drawn a sharp distinction between Iran's government and its people, seeking to impose sanctions and other measures that would impact only the theocratic government. The US State Department has gone so far as to request $75m from Congress for promoting democracy in Iran, which the clerical establishment and the Iranian government construes as an attempt at regime change. Against this backdrop of extreme contentiousness between Iran and major Western powers, a growing moderate consensus was calling for full US engagement – arguably the only strategic option that has yet to be tried. In December 2005, the United States did seek direct talks with Iran in Baghdad, limited to security issues in Iraq. Iran, seeing itself in a position of strength, declined. In private, however, Iranians not tied to the Ahmadinejad camp sent out signals and emissaries indicating their interest in engagement with the United States. In March, when Iraqi Shi'ite cleric Abdul Aziz al-Hakim called for US–Iran talks, this gave the Iranian leadership an excuse for saying yes. However, talks had to be delayed until Iraq formed a new government, and did not get underway. The Iranian president took the step of sending a letter on 8 May 2006 to President Bush. The Bush administration initially did not take the letter seriously, but also did not preclude more vigorous engagement.

US direct engagement, whether bilaterally or, more palatable to administration hardliners, in a multilateral context, could conceivably address the range of obstacles to bilateral relations, including Iran's support for groups employing terrorism, its antipathy to Israel and hindrance to the Middle East peace process, its human-rights violations and its pursuit of sensitive nuclear technologies. On Iran's side of the ledger, the concerns underlying the rhetoric in Ahmadinejad's scolding 8 May letter to Bush, including respect for the Islamic revolution, lifting of sanctions and, above all, freedom from foreign interference. Given the decades of animosity between Iran and the United States, however, and the heavy historical baggage of past failed attempts at reconciliation, it is hard to believe that direct talks could produce the 'grand bargain' that could conceivably come out of direct talks. A sustained suspension of enrichment activity balanced by explicit US support for EU economic incentives is a steep enough goal for the first step.

Israel/Palestine: Future in the Balance

The Israeli impulse to construct settlements in the territories it occupied during combat operations in June 1967 was finally reversed in the past year. The settlement of the West Bank and Gaza had been the result of a haphazard combination of perceived military necessity, religious zeal and political expediency. It was not the result of a coherent decision-making process. Indeed, there was little agreement on what to do with the West Bank in the immediate aftermath of the war, in contrast to plans for the use of the Golan Heights and Gaza Strip as bargaining chips with Syria and Egypt.

Israel had been unprepared for the 1967 war, a 'nebechdiker Shimshoyn', in the Yiddish of then prime minister Levi Eshkol, a 'pathetic Samson', a country with an effective military capability wringing its hands over the threat of extinction. The rapid move to war had not allowed the fractious and anxiety-stricken cabinet to think through, let alone agree upon, the implications of Jordanian withdrawal from the West Bank and a subsequent Israeli occupation. A concept did ultimately emerge, the Allon plan, according to which an autonomous Palestinian entity would take shape within an Israeli ring of frontier settlements and army installations. This, however, was neither a strategy nor a stable policy. Successive governments disowned it, in favour of a maximal objective in the case of Menahem Begin, or the opposite in the case of Yitzhak Rabin's Oslo plan. A disciplined settler movement took skilful advantage of this policy incoherence, popular nostalgia for bygone days of Zionist pioneering and the peculiar structure of Israeli politics to expand its infrastructure throughout the northern and southern West Bank. By creating 'facts on the ground', the movement severely constrained the space for negotiation with Palestinians, while undermining the possibility of a sustainable Palestinian economy.

The defeat of Labour Prime Minister Ehud Barak by Ariel Sharon in 2000 and the eruption of the al-Aqsa intifada that summer set in motion events that would lead to seismic change. Sharon's reputation as a hardliner was well deserved, but many observers missed the pragmatic side of his thinking. He wanted the greatest possible area of the West Bank and Gaza under Israeli administration and open to Jewish settlement. The emphasis in his thinking, however, was on the word 'possible'. In his view, the increasing ungovernability of Palestinian areas combined with demographic realities had sharply reduced the scope of the possible. Yet the make up of the Likud party leadership was not conducive to bold steps. While the party rank-and-file reflected a wide array of views on territorial issues, from a rejection of negotiation over a biblical legacy to consideration of concessions deemed consistent with Israel's security requirements, the Central Committee of Likud disproportionately represented the right end of this spectrum. Since it was the Central Committee's role to select candidates for the Likud electoral list, the right wing was in a position to shape the party's Knesset representation in a way that would prevent Sharon from garnering the votes he would need to make territorial concessions. Sharon had made no secret of his evolving strategic views. In 2003 and 2004 he gave successive speeches outlining his vision at the annual Herzliya policy conference in Israel. In the first, he stated that he endorsed 'a democratic Palestinian state with territorial contiguity in Judea and Samaria and economic viability, which would conduct normal relations of tranquility, security and peace with Israel'. He went on to say, 'However, if in a few months the Palestinians still continue to disregard their part in implementing the road map – then Israel will initiate the unilateral security step of disengagement from the Palestinians.' The term he used for disengagement suggested a complete severing of the connection between Israel and an emergent Palestine. In 2004, just prior to the Knesset vote on the withdrawal plan for Gaza, Sharon sounded like a Labour politician might have five years earlier: 'Disengagement recognises the demo-graphic reality on the ground specifically, bravely and honestly. Of course it is clear to everyone that we will not be in the Gaza Strip in the final agreement. This recognition, that we will not be in Gaza, and that, even now, we have no reason to be there … is uniting the people. It is uniting us in … maintaining Israel's char-acter as a Jewish state – rather than goals where it is clear to all of us that they will not be realised, and that most of the public is not ready, justifiably, to sacrifice so much for.' The frank acknowledgement of the demographic dilemma identi-fied after the 1967 war by Israel's first prime minister, David Ben Gurion – that an Israeli state ruling the West Bank and Gaza could not be both democratic and Jewish – signified the end of expansionist Zionism. That the death knell for the dream was rung by Ariel Sharon was a necessary irony.

The withdrawal from Gaza proceeded more smoothly than had been expected. In a rapid redeployment, 1,530 families (about 8,500 settlers) were extracted from 12 settlements, all of which were razed to spare the Palestinian government the need to decide how to allocate these suburban developments – which, in any case, were not needed in densely populated Gaza. Although there was a show of civil disobedience and scattered use of non-lethal booby-traps, the settler popu-lation left without too much of a fuss: compensation offered by the government, as well as awareness of their unpopularity among the majority of Israelis, prob-ably contributed to the settlers' decision to leave quietly.

Israel's initiative left the United States and Palestinians in a quandary, prima-rily because it was carried out unilaterally, albeit with a modicum of coordination with both parties: coordination is not the same thing as negotiated collabora-tion. The Palestinian leadership was seen by its own electorate as ineffectual, unable to influence either Washington or Jerusalem – a perception that would return to haunt all three parties. Both Washington and Ramallah were concerned by the possibility that 'Gaza first' would turn out to be 'Gaza last'. Sharon did specify in his initial withdrawal plan that four small settlements situated deep in the northern West Bank would also be evacuated. Yet the legacy of Sharon's past maximalism, superimposed on a belief that the Gaza withdrawal would be so traumatic that the government would be unwilling to go further, generated much anxiety in capitals. Moreover, it was widely believed, for good reason, that the West Bank would be more tenaciously defended by the settlers and that public opinion, muted in the case of Gaza, might be mobilised when the issue devolved to historical Israel.

Sharon, however, intended to proceed with a significant pullback from the West Bank if the politics of the proposal within his own party could be untan-gled. The Gordian knot was unexpectedly cut as a result of an upheaval within the Labour party. A leadership struggle dislodged Shimon Peres, the octogenar-ian statesman and perennial electoral loser, and brought to power Amir Peretz, a youngish trade-union official. Peretz's elevation carried important implications. In its own right, it signified a change in Israeli priorities, wherein social and economic issues were elevated above security issues. For decades, Israel's party leaders, with the large exceptions of Golda Meir and Menahem Begin, had been drawn from the ranks of senior military officers or, like Benjamin Netanyahu, had served in the military beyond the obligation of basic national service. Yitzhak Shamir's career had been in the Mossad and Shimon Peres had been the architect of Israel's nuclear-weapons programme. All ran on security-related platforms. Peretz, in contrast, had been a draftee and reservist and could claim no special military expertise or command experience. His campaign was resolutely confined to closing the gap between rich and poor in Israeli society.

Peretz is also the first *mizrahi*, or so-called 'oriental Jew', to lead the Labour party. He was born in Morocco and shared with other *mizrahiim* the history of immigration, settlement in dismal development towns and discrimination that had resulted in political and economic marginalisation. The exclusion of this ethnic group from the elite of the Labour party apparatus led to their wholesale defection to Likud in 1977, a sea change that brought 30 years of Labour dominance to an end.

Perhaps it was fitting that Likud economic policy, under the aegis of Netanyahu, who served as Sharon's finance minister, reinvigorated Labour and propelled Peretz into the top slot. Netanyahu's approach, which entailed getting deficits and inflation under control and spurring economic growth, worked well. Between 2004 and 2005 GDP rose 5.2%, the current account turned from deficit into a small surplus and a more inviting investment environment developed. These impressive gains, however, widened the already unhealthy gap between rich and poor. Four out of ten Israeli children live below the poverty line, a 50% increase from 1996 and a disturbing fact in a country with socialist roots. Netanyahu slashed the budgets for social services, health care, public assistance and education. Those at the lower end of the income ladder flocked to Labour and saw in Peretz a man who understood them and would fight for their access to the country's new wealth. That he had few military credentials and had not focused on security issues made no difference.

The first thing Peretz did upon his selection as party leader was to pull Labour out of Sharon's grand coalition. Peres had brought Labour into the coalition to ensure that the withdrawal from Gaza was carried out; Sharon had invited Labour in to diffuse responsibility for a major initiative that threatened to result in civil discord within Israel and anarchy in Gaza. In any case, Peres had pledged to pull Labour out when the withdrawal was complete, but never followed through. With Peretz's defection, Sharon no longer commanded a majority in the Knesset and was compelled to call for new elections.

At this point, Sharon confirmed rumours that had swirled for months about his intention to bolt from Likud and lead a new political party into elections.

For Likud, this was a devastating development. From Labour, he picked up representatives of the Ashkenazi elite, such as Haim Ramon, who had been displaced by the Sephardi revolt in the party. Sharon called his creation 'The National Responsibility Party', which soon acquired the rubric of 'Kadima', or 'Forward!' Its appeal to voters lay in its platform of action by Israel in its own interest without waiting for a Palestinian partner, while on the other hand not catering to the messianic inclinations of settlers.

The Israeli campaign season, which would culminate on 26 March 2006, was complicated by momentous political events on the Palestinian scene. After postponing elections to the Palestine Legislative Council (PLC), Palestine's parliament, from July 2005 until 25 January 2006, Palestinian Authority President Mahmoud Abbas presided over an election that stripped Fateh of its majority in the parliament and its control over the government. Hamas did better than expected, winning 74 seats in the 132-seat parliament. Fateh won only 45, partly because party discipline eroded as the vote neared, resulting in many of its candidates standing as independents, and partly because the mixed Palestinian electoral system split seats between a national list based on proportional representation and local individual candidates in a 'first past the post' majority system. This left Fateh at a disadvantage in local precincts. Hamas's expectations had in any case been high, given widespread disappointment in the quality of Fateh's governance, declining living standards and endemic corruption. Abbas's inability to command Israel's attention and respect as a counterpart in the run-up to the withdrawal from Gaza weakened the standing of the party, and reinforced a growing perception of it as feckless and ineffective. Hamas had cultivated a contrasting image of squeaky-clean reformers motivated by principle rather than pursuit of power. It ran a clever campaign in which the movement's emphasis on the Islamisation of society was downplayed, reassuring voters who were not enthusiastic about a religious agenda. Of Hamas's 74 members of parliament, nine were in Israeli prisons, giving it de facto 65 votes – allowing Fateh President Abbas some room for manoeuvre to propose or veto legislation.

The election returns reflected a fundamental shift in Palestinian society. For the first time, the political culture of the Palestinians who returned with Arafat from Tunis – where they had sheltered between expulsion from Lebanon in 1982 and the Oslo agreement of 1993 – had been challenged. Hamas itself was in the midst of yet another reincarnation. Having started in 1987 in Gaza to deepen popular religious commitment through the provision of social services and schooling, Hamas had evolved into a clandestine military organisation and sponsor of terrorist attacks against Israeli civilians. The organisation's decision to participate in national elections was certain to spur yet another stage in its evolution. Pending the next development cycle, however, Palestine now had a government that rejected the concept of negotiation with Israel over a two-state solution to their conflict.

Fateh took measures to hobble the incoming Hamas government and to retain as many powers as possible for itself. In February 2006, just before the new parliament began, the Fateh majority created a special constitutional court, appointed by the president without consent of parliament, empowered to strike down laws it deemed inconsistent with Palestine's Basic Law. They also created two new parliamentary positions, a secretary-general and deputy who could control resources on which the Hamas speaker and parliamentary secretary would depend. In addition, Abbas took control of the official media and promoted or installed Fateh members to senior positions in key ministries. In expectation of a large Hamas majority, the PLC had already transferred control of major police and security services from parliament to the president.

Abbas also acted in the diplomatic arena. For Fateh, it was imperative that Hamas be starved of the funds it would need to deliver services and make good on its pledge to improve everyday life for the Palestinian population. This stratagem meshed well with Washington's objective, which was to ensure that a Hamas government failed within months. For the US administration, the Hamas victory not only made the possibility of lower tensions between Israelis and Palestinians quite remote, just when the White House was looking for some respite in the region as the situation in Iraq worsened, but it presaged yet another enduring unfriendly Islamist regime. From the US perspective, such regimes were impossible to dislodge once they established themselves in power. Hamas's record of terrorism and its association with Syria and Iran only added to these concerns. Hence the convergence of American and Fateh views on how best to proceed to hamstring Hamas quickly and decisively.

European governments, thanks to Hamas's rhetoric, had no choice but to join in this approach. The United States asserted three conditions for the continuation of aid and suspension of American unilateral economic sanctions against the Hamas government. Hamas had to recognise Israel, forswear terrorism and abide by agreements that the previous government had undertaken. The US rationale was that although these conditions might well be difficult for Hamas to swallow – particularly recognition of Israel – agreement by Hamas would amount to a watershed in the 50-year conflict. If Hamas refused, then its recalcitrance would be exposed and it would have to suffer the consequences. Although this logic did not fully take into account the fact that Palestinian citizens would likely blame the US and Europe, not Hamas, for the resulting hardship, the argument was strong enough to keep the United States and EU synchronised.

As the Palestinians were preparing for their momentous election in January, Ariel Sharon was felled by a series of strokes that left him comatose. His sudden disappearance from the political stage, where he had played such a pivotal role, was disorienting but not disabling, for his new party or the country as a whole. On 4 January 2006 he was replaced – at first in an acting capacity – by Deputy Prime Minister Ehud Olmert, a wealthy lawyer, Likud member of the Knesset, and former mayor of Jerusalem, who had been plucked from a lowly place on the party list by Sharon to serve as his second-in-command. Like his opposite number in the Labour party, Olmert had no significant military experience. As further evidence of a shift in Israeli popular priorities, his own constituency seemed unfazed by this lacuna in his career. His own family is of a left-ish temperament (his son is a conscientious objector) and it is thought that he was influenced by the need to manage the contending emotions and demands of the many communities that make up Jerusalem's population. Olmert made clear during the election campaign precisely what he would do if elected. Since Israeli campaigns have tended to revolve around vague proposals and inscrutable slogans, this in itself was unusual. More important was the content. The security barrier, he said, would become the de facto border between Israel and Palestine. The 60,000 Israelis who occupy territory to the east of the barrier would be compelled to return to the other side of the barrier. The barrier would encompass approximately 8% of West Bank land. Presumably, if negotiations were to ensue, this area might shrink somewhat, perhaps down to 5%, the point President Bill Clinton reached with the parties in 2000. According to Olmert, this would happen with or without Palestinian input within 6–8 months. The plan was dubbed 'Convergence', but the Hebrew root connotes a concept that is somewhat more warm and fuzzy, akin to 'ingathering'. The realism of this timetable was not addressed. Nor was the disposition of the Israeli army, leaving open the possibility that it would remain in the West Bank or Jordan valley after the settlements were dismantled. The source of funds to pay the cost of relocating 60,000 settlers was also not addressed.

The results of the elections held on 28 March 2006 were clearly an endorsement for Olmert's Convergence plan. They eviscerated Likud as an effective party, reduced the right-wing religious representation by 19 seats and awarded the centre-left 70 seats, a clear majority within the 120-seat Knesset. The fact that ten of these seats belonged to Arab parties meant that as a practical matter the government had only 60 usable votes for withdrawal – the ruling coalition will be unwilling to rely on Arab votes to facilitate the surrender of land deemed to be part of historical Israel.

With victory in hand, Olmert left for Washington in the hope of getting Bush's blessing for unilateral withdrawal. Despite the invitation to speak before a joint session of Congress, a relatively rare honour for a foreign visitor, and talk of a good personal rapport with Bush, the visit was awkward. With the US position in the Middle East deteriorating, largely as the result of the intervention in

Iraq, the White House was not eager to associate Washington with a concept that might look like convergence to Israelis, but would likely be regarded as a land grab by Palestinians and in wider regional opinion. From the administration's point of view, the United States would have no attractive options in the event that Olmert got as far as implementing the plan, or even got as far as turning what was essentially an idea into a plan that could be carried out. If Washington declared the withdrawal to the barrier as fulfilling UN Security Council Resolutions 242 and 338 – which called for withdrawal of Israeli forces from occupied territories under a 'land for peace' formula – it would be isolated. On the other hand, if it could not go quite that far, it would have to take a position that would not make the United States appear to oppose the relocation of settlers to communities that lay outside the 1967 borders, but within the barrier line. Presumably, Washington would have to obtain a commitment from Israel to negotiate at some stage in the future with a Palestinian government, to which it would offer territorial compensation for land occupied by the settlement blocs behind the barrier. This, however, presupposed a degree of diplomatic engagement that the administration has avoided until now and for which it would scarcely have the energy or incentive at the start of a election campaign at home and while coping with a persistent insurgency in Iraq.

While the new Israeli government solidified, it appeared that the Palestinian administration was becoming unglued. The armed forces and police were beginning to split into Hamas and Fateh factions, which have since engaged in running gunfights in Gaza and the West Bank. Fateh loyalists asserted that they would not maintain public order on behalf of Hamas. The Palestinian Authority had gone on a hiring spree in the security sector beginning in late 2005 to boost the size of services that were beholden to Fateh and controlled under the new dispensation by the office of the president, as opposed to the Hamas prime minister. The increasing number of armed units loyal to competing parties heightened the risk of civil conflict. Fateh was in a weak position, divided between a discredited old guard and a young guard sidelined by the election results, for which they held the old guard responsible. The younger elements were also divided. Few Fateh activists could summon the credibility and respect that their more disciplined Hamas counterparts enjoyed. Nevertheless, there were also fissures within Hamas. On the one side were pragmatists who would subordinate the armed conflict to facilitate Israel's withdrawal from the West Bank and Gaza and gain breathing space for the creation of an Islamic state in Palestine. But not all are prepared to take this approach.

The humanitarian situation worsened considerably after Western donors stopped providing aid in the wake of Hamas's accession to power and its highly vocal gestures of commitment to the armed struggle with Israel. The Palestinian Authority employs 40% of workers in Gaza. The loss of income was difficult to manage in a territory already in the midst of a serious economic decline that began with the outbreak of the al-Aqsa intifada. Gross domestic product is about half what it was during the summer of 2000, foreign investment is at a standstill, unemployment hovers between 40 and 60%, public health is worsening, water is running out and the rate of population growth is dangerously high.

This has put intense pressure on the Quartet (the United Nations, United States, European Union and Russian Federation) to devise a way to get money flowing again without somehow empowering Hamas. Because governments failed to anticipate the election results and, in the case of the United States, inadvertently helped bring them about, diplomats had no chance to address this earlier. As a result, it was not until 17 June 2006 that the Quartet announced a proposal 'for channeling aid directly to the Palestinian people' via a 'temporary international mechanism' that would be reviewed after three months. Under the arrangement, donors could provide essential equipment, supplies and support for health services, support for the uninterrupted supply of fuel and utilities, and basic needs allowances to poor Palestinians. This stopgap is unlikely to avert a humanitarian crisis over the medium term, if a political solution is not found. This, however, is unlikely. Qassam rocket attacks launched from Gaza against the Israeli city of Sderot have been intense, triggering Israeli artillery and air strikes, as well as targeted killings, within Gaza. The rocket attacks were having a larger political effect within Israel, where people were wondering whether the same threat would emerge from the West Bank after 'convergence'. Hamas has taken the position that it will abide by the tacit truce it has made with Israel, but that other groups, including al-Aqsa Martyr Brigades and Islamic Jihad, still have the right to carry out attacks against Israelis. This too raised doubts in Israel about Olmert's wisdom. As *Strategic Survey* was going to press, international concern deepened as Israel launched a military offensive in Gaza aimed at retrieving a captured Israeli soldier. The tense stand-off indicated the fragility of positions on both sides of the Israel–Palestine dispute, and presaged an uncertain future.

Lebanon: After the Cedar Revolution

In 2005, the non-violent 'Cedar Revolution' in Lebanon ushered in the return of a sovereign, democratic polity after almost three decades of Syrian occupation, though it did not end Syria's strong influence over the country.

The car bomb that killed Rafik Hariri, the former Lebanese prime minister, on 14 February 2005 triggered massive protests against Syria, which was believed to have masterminded the assassination. The protests led to the withdrawal of all Syrian troops from a country that it had dominated since 1976, when Syria had sent 40,000 troops to intervene in the Lebanese civil war. By 2004 some Lebanese leaders who had hitherto collaborated with Syria sought change, and the opportunity came with the impending elections. When Syria insisted on amending the Lebanese constitution to extend the term of President Emile Lahoud for three years, leaders including prime minister Hariri and exiled General Michel 'Awn won the support of France and the United States for UN Security Council Resolution 1559, passed in September 2004, calling for free elections, withdrawal of foreign troops and dissolution of militias. However, Hariri resigned when parliament voted for the constitutional change.

Hundreds of thousands attended Hariri's funeral. The pro-Syrian Hizbullah organised a counter rally in support of Syria, with an estimated half a million people, on 8 March 2005. In response, the Lebanese opposition called a rally in Beirut, estimated to have drawn 1.5m people, on 14 March. This marked the culmination of the Cedar Revolution, which had the support of most Lebanese people, including Christians, Druze and Sunni, though Shi'ite participation was limited because of Hizbullah's dominance of Shi'ite regions of southern Lebanon, northern Biqa' and the southern suburbs of Beirut. Syria, under intense pressure from the United States and France to comply with Resolution 1559, completed its withdrawal of troops and intelligence services on 26 April 2005.

However, the withdrawal did not mean that Syria's influence in Lebanon was ended. This was evident when the Maronite Patriarch Nasrallah Sfair called for the adoption of a 1960 electoral law that would divide Lebanon into smaller constituencies and result in a more representative parliament. The speaker of the Chamber of Deputies, Nabih Birri – seen as a Syrian proxy – prevented the convening of a session to adopt the 1960 law, thus keeping in force a 2000 law devised by Syria to favour Birri's Amal organisation and Hizbullah and to marginalise voters in Christian regions. Nevertheless, parliamentary elections held in May–June 2005 maintained the momentum of the Cedar Revolution: political parties and movements that formed its backbone won 93 seats, while the pro-Syrian Hizbullah, Amal and allies won the remaining 35. Prime Minister Fouad Siniora, a former banker and finance minister, and a close associate of Hariri, formed a 24-member cabinet on 30 June 2005 –but it included five ministers representing Amal and Hizbullah because of the Lebanese system of consociational democracy under which all cabinets are equally divided between Christians and Muslims, and all religious communities are represented.

Syria continued its terrorist campaign in Lebanon. On 2 June 2005, Samir Qasir, a prominent figure of the Cedar Revolution and a columnist on the daily newspaper *al-Nahar*, was assassinated. A former secretary-general of the Lebanese Communist Party was killed on 21 June 2005. Minister of Defence

Elias al-Murr (Lahoud's son-in-law, previously seen as an ally of Syria) survived an assassination attempt on 12 July 2005, having refused to obey Syrian orders. On 25 September 2005, May Chidyak, a television journalist who had hosted guests critical of Syria's role in Lebanon, was badly injured by a bomb placed in her car. On 12 December 2005 Jubran Tueni, publisher of *al-Nahar*, member of parliament and a leader of the Cedar Revolution, was assassinated.

On 7 April 2005, the UN Security Council established a commission to investigate the Hariri's murder, headed by German prosecutor Detlev Mehlis. Preliminary investigation led to the suspicion that four Lebanese security chiefs headed by the director of public security, General Jamil al-Sayyid, who worked closely with the Syrians, were involved. The Lebanese public prosecutor was asked to arrest them, and did so on 14 September 2005. The Mehlis report, issued on 22 October 2005, said there was 'converging evidence pointing at both Lebanese and Syrian involvement in this terrorist act ... Given the infiltration of Lebanese institutions and society by the Syrian and Lebanese intelligence services working in tandem, it would be difficult to envisage a scenario whereby such a complex assassination plot could have been carried out without their knowledge.'

Following internal political discussions and agreements between groupings, a national dialogue was convened in the parliament building in Beirut on 2 March 2006, with 14 major participants representing political parties and personalities of the Cedar Revolution as well as pro-Syrian leaders of Amal and Hizbullah. Agreement was reached on establishing diplomatic relations between Lebanon and Syria, and demarcating Lebanon's border with Syria. Issues such as Lahoud's replacement and disarmament of Hizbullah went unresolved. UN Security Council Resolution 1644, passed on 12 December 2005, stated that 'the Syrian Government has yet to provide the Commission with the full and unconditional cooperation'. Syrian President Bashar al-Assad was interviewed by the new head of the UN commission, Belgian investigative judge Serge Brammertz, on 25 April 2006.

Saudi Arabia and the Gulf: Slow Pace of Change

The past year has been one of measured change in the Gulf region. An increasingly sharp strategic rivalry was developing between an ascendant and defiant Iran and its Arab neighbours. Three Gulf leaders died: King Fahd bin Abdul Aziz Al Saud of Saudi Arabia, Shaikh Jabir al-Ahmad Al Sabah of Kuwait and Shaikh Makhtoum bin Rashid Al Makhtoum of Dubai. With the American-led military presence in Iraq entering its fourth year, Gulf rulers were wary of the American call for democracy in the Arab world because of the danger that swift socio-political changes could translate into a loss of power. Few Arab leaders, from the Atlantic to the Indian Ocean, welcomed Washington's importuning even if none objected vehemently. While most leaders encouraged reforms, they preferred gradual approaches rather than rapid steps that could erode their authority: they routinely chanted the tune of 'political reform' while carefully ensuring their survival. Nevertheless, fundamental socio-economic changes were under way throughout the region.

Gulf rulers remained alarmed by largely unemployed young men who turned to religious radicalism to vent their frustration with corruption. In his inaugural address, Saudi King Abdullah bin Abdul Aziz Al Saud identified poverty and religious inequalities as core concerns. He welcomed calls for reform but, like his fellow Gulf rulers, wished to proceed at a gradual pace. This perspective was shared by the new Kuwaiti ruler, Shaikh Sabah al-Ahmad Al Sabah, as well as King Hamad bin Isa Al Khalifah in Bahrain. Even Shaikh Hamad bin Khalifah Al Thani, the ruler of Qatar, endorsed this overall outlook, as Doha held a series of human rights and democracy conferences. Virtually every ruler in the region tried to project an image of tolerance.

Saudi Arabia: measured change inside and out

Abdullah bin Abdulaziz Al Saud, 11th son of Ibn Saud, succeeded his brother Fahd as ruler on 1 August 2005, at the age of 83. Crown prince for 23 years, Abdullah was regent after Fahd was left largely incapacitated by a stroke in 1995, and effectively ruled the kingdom thereafter. While some fondly remembered Fahd as a reformer, the late monarch heightened radicalism when he invited Western powers to defend Saudi Arabia from Saddam Hussein in 1990. Whether the presence of so many 'infidels' saved the House of Saud from an imminent Iraqi invasion was debatable, but one of its spillover effects – the mobilisation of distraught youths against the regime – was not. Abdullah thus inherited from his brother a significant regime-threatening burden.

As expected, the new monarch appointed his brother Sultan bin Abdulaziz Al Saud, the world's longest-serving defence minister, as his new heir apparent. Sultan became the new leader of the Sudayri faction after Fahd's demise and was automatically elevated to the position of deputy prime minister. Despite past rivalries between the monarch and his heir, with Sultan now firmly assured of succession and of continued influence given the advancement of his sons Khaled (to deputy defence minister) and Bandar (to head of a newly established national security council), the relationship between the two senior Al Sauds should be less stormy.

Abdullah was aided during his first year in power by a healthy and growing government treasury. With major new investments in the oil sector, Riyadh regarded its unemployment and poverty problems – priorities identified by the new monarch in his inaugural address – as containable threats to long-term internal stability, even if the economy needed to create several million new jobs over the next two decades. He was also fortunate that the Saudi public turned against terrorists spreading havoc throughout the kingdom. As several hundred people had been killed in Saudi Arabia since 2003, Saudis looked to the state to enforce the country's stringent anti-terrorism laws, rallying behind the House of Saud even though its methods were drastic and overbearing. Arguments advanced by liberal reformers were overwhelmed by conservative pressure to impose law and order. Abdullah successfully put pressure on establishment clergymen, forcing thousands into re-education camps, cajoling others to tone down inflammatory rhetoric and to set clear examples for acceptable behaviour.

This last issue was particularly irritating to many clergymen who believed they had near-divine mandates to impose a particular interpretation of Muslim dogma. True to his long-standing preference to incorporate a far more tolerant religious environment, Abdullah did not mince words, nor did he limit his actions against Wahhabi clergymen. An estimated 1,000 were summarily dismissed on 11 June 2003 and many more were made to recant deviant teachings. This was followed by several meetings with Shi'ite clergymen, many of whom pledged their *ba'yah* (oath of allegiance) in public. In August 2005, Hassan al-Saffar, the putative leader of the Saudi Shi'ite community since the late 1970s, committed his loyalty to the Saudi nation. This was followed in mid-September by a rare meeting with five Ismaili leaders from Najran, who underlined the king's pledge to seek 'prayer and advice' from them, and to instil 'the principles of justice and equality among [Saudis] without distinguishing between them'. This rapprochement between the two Muslim sects is considered heretical by Wahhabi leaders, and has irked them.

In fact, of all the strategic challenges to Abdullah, the potential clash between Sunnis and Shi'ites loomed as the most dangerous. Unlike his brother, the late King Faisal, Abdullah did not enjoy the licence to discuss religious matters with theologians – that is, *ijazah*. Nevertheless, he needed to persuade powerful clergymen to allow serious social reforms. Abdullah's exemplary private life is of benefit in this regard, but he still needs to extend accountability to the clergymen themselves and to further rally the public, especially young Saudis, to back him. In a sense, the ruler needs to compete with Osama bin Laden for the hearts and minds of the less privileged. Whether Abdullah can persuade the clergy not to back Saudi jihadists who return home from Iraq with the aim of overthrowing the establishment, and whether he can further cajole them into allowing reforms in their educational fiefdoms, will determine his success.

These challenges notwithstanding, Abdullah has already accelerated the transformation process. Nowhere was this more evident than in the reappraisal of textbooks in the kingdom's education system. Clerics who thrived on intolerant rhetoric saw their work purged, with more broadminded texts replacing xenophobic ones. The ruler further widened the scope of representative government by empowering, albeit on a limited basis, the Majlis al-Shurah – the country's principal legislative body – to debate historically sensitive topics like the budget. Abdullah welcomed a discussion of the country's finances, including those pertaining to the ruling family itself, and sowed a culture of tolerance by holding five 'National Dialogues' on important subjects. He also pardoned prominent dissidents and declared the kingdom's National Day – 23 September – a public holiday. This decision introduced a whiff of nationalism into a tribal society that had inhibited young Saudis from developing a sense of pride in their country. Perhaps his most symbolic change was a blanket ban on kissing his hand, because he viewed such subservient formality as demeaning and un-Islamic.

There remained two procedural complications stemming from the succession. First, King Abdullah and Crown Prince Sultan retained all of their previous portfolios. Many Saudis wondered why a ruler still needed to head the National Guard and why an heir apparent still needed to remain defence minister. Others questioned whether these fiefdoms were ultimate refuges for weak leaders. Secondly, the monarch delayed naming a second deputy prime minister, a position that traditionally designated the heir to the heir apparent. Under normal circumstances, he would quickly have settled on a deputy in order to aid stability. But because of a possible contest for the post between Interior Minister Nayif bin Abdulaziz and Riyadh Governor Salman bin Abdulaziz, the monarch chose to procrastinate – possibly to signal his discomfort over the prospect of power passing to the interior minister after Sultan. Abdullah stripped Nayif of national security responsibilities when Bandar bin Sultan, the former ambassador to Washington, was appointed head of the newly created National Security Council. This was a clear indication that the monarch contemplated long-term stability, and institutionalisation of decision-making, within the ruling family. Future monarchs could thereby rely on professional advice before reaching critical judgements, minimising the intrigue and caprice that Abdullah and his allies deplored. The monarch consolidated his hold by appointing several allies to critical positions: Muqrin bin Abdulaziz as head of intelligence and Turki al-Faisal bin Abdulaziz as ambassador to the United States.

Domestic politics

On 15 May 2004, a Saudi religious court sentenced three prominent liberals – Ali al-Dumayni, Abdullah al-Hamad and Matruk al-Faleh – to between six and nine years in jail. The three men, a poet and two university professors, were among 13 arrested a few months earlier after they called for the establishment of a constitutional monarchy in Saudi Arabia. They were the vanguard of a larger liberal movement pushing senior House of Saud officials to introduce lasting political reforms. Ten of the original group were eventually released after they pledged to respect a written oath to stop making demands or speaking with foreign journalists. One of the original defendants, Abdul Rahman al-Laham (who also became the three remaining defendants' attorney), broke his pledge and was promptly rearrested. The three intellectuals rejected settlement terms and vowed to 'defend themselves in court'. Extraordinarily, the first session of the trial was public, but public outcry and mayhem moved the presiding judge to rule that future sessions would be held in camera and without any of the defence team's most vocal members. The justices were discomfited by the defendants' assertions that Wahhabi ideology was too thoroughly embedded in the kingdom's educational system and that the combination fuelled extremism. The justices also noted that the accused breached the country's traditional codes not to vent in public or directly challenge established authority. Supported by the interior minister, the court further reminded the three men that their calls to stir masses were contrary to the country's interests. Human-rights advocates quickly decried the closed trials.

King Abdullah granted royal pardons to the three men on 8 August 2005. The monarch reasoned that this strengthened the House of Saud's political hand, in that the family stood for both authority and mercy, and because he concluded that the country's intellectuals were assets in the long-term fight against terrorism. The ruler also commuted the jail sentence imposed on Said Mubarak al-Zuair, a commentator who had criticised the House of Saud on al-Jazeera television in April 2004.

The pardons reflected a keen awareness that the intelligentsia needed to be mobilised against jihadists determined to bring the government down. Despite substantial counter-terrorism efforts that resulted in the killing or capture of hundreds of potential terrorists, religious radicalism continued to attract Saudi recruits, including several hundred that 'served' in Iraq. An undetermined number died in 'martyrdom' operations in both Iraq and Saudi Arabia. Abdullah worried that extremists were acting beyond the control of the al-Qaeda leadership and were consequently more dangerous. Much like their European counterparts, Saudi authorities concluded that upstart terrorists – not bin Laden – were largely responsible for the dozen or so acts mounted inside the kingdom. Between May 2003 and May 2006, more than 500 people were killed by terrorists in Saudi Arabia. Riyadh responded robustly. In June 2005, Prince Nayif reported that the internal security forces were gaining the upper hand, having killed at least 92 suspected terrorists. On 31 March 2006, Nayif told the pan-Arab *al-Hayat* daily that Saudi Arabia had foiled about 90% of planned attacks, without providing details. Nor did he give specific figures on several hundred suspects who had been arrested. Confessions led to further arrests, but casualties among security forces were also high. In an address to the Majlis al-Shurah on 31 March 2006, King Abdullah stated that there was 'no room ... for extremism' in the kingdom, as he vowed to crush the 'misguided group of terrorists and murderers'. The Saudi public, even if wary of the ruling House of Saud, rallied behind the family as many concluded that these senior leaders were as capable as any of ridding the country of the scourge of violence. A nervous public tolerated frequent checkpoints and armed guards at most public venues even as they dismissed optimistic predictions like the one uttered by Crown Prince Sultan who, on 20 November 2005, declared: 'I can assure you that with the vigilance of security forces, intelligence agents and especially the Saudi people we might be able to end terrorism, God willing, within the next two years.' The Saudi public welcomed stricter controls on Islamic charities operating in the country and, most importantly, few objected when preachers were publicly warned to curb vitriolic speeches that passed for religious discourse.

Municipal elections

In early February 2005, Saudi Arabia held in its first municipal council elections, albeit for only half of the available seats. Although women were barred from the exercise, and a mere one-third of eligible men bothered to register and vote, the drill was a useful learning process. To be sure, few Saudis perceived these elections as genuine 'democracy', but many were enthusiastic about their potential. In Riyadh alone, close to 700 candidates competed for seven open seats; several candidates disbursed large sums on fledgling campaigns with Kuwait-style neighbourhood tents. 'Constituents' raised pertinent questions at these gatherings, which were thoroughly covered by local media outlets. A few technically savvy operations set up web pages or used text messages on cellular telephones. Organisers highlighted elections as a permanent new feature of public life, pointing out how local issues such as safer neighbourhoods, hygiene and traffic could be usefully addressed.

By late April 2005, when the last municipal elections were held in the western and northern regions of the kingdom, 592 officials had been elected to 178 new bodies. Another 608 men were appointed for the remaining seats. While Riyadh was concerned that Islamist candidates swept most available posts, four out of seven men chosen in the capital were Western educated and five held doctorates. While traditionally isolated parts of the kingdom were expected to elect conservative contenders, Islamists also won on both coasts, including in relatively liberal Jeddah and Dammam. Still, the House of Saud was worried by serious sectarian cleavages (all five seats in Qatif and five out of six in Ahsah were won by Shi'ite candidates). In fact, popular preachers ensured that their preferred representatives were victorious, with Shi'ite clerics in particular exhorting their constituents to be worthy of their co-religionists in Iraq, where many risked their lives to participate in the January 2005 plebiscite. Most obliged, enduring scorching heat while waiting to cast their ballots.

These results delighted Abdullah, as the ruling family strengthened the notion that the House of Saud represented an indispensable glue that held this multifaceted society together. Its leaders argued that their record as protectors of Islam's holiest shrines, as well as the country's oil resources, justified popular confidence in their intrinsic abilities to introduce reforms. Still, Riyadh was agitated by some of the consequences of the April 2005 elections, which witnessed the rise of popular preachers who were not part of the controlled Wahhabi establishment. These successful Islamist candidates opposed the state orthodoxy premised on the 1744 alliance between the House of Saud, which wielded the political power, and the al-Shaikh, which fulfilled the regime's social and religious responsibilities. Thus, Riyadh was faced with a fresh populist vision.

National Dialogues

Abdullah was eager to move faster to address thorny social questions. He continued to promote the National Dialogues, which first convened in Riyadh in July 2003. At the time, assembled learned Saudis engaged in a free overview session that identified critical issues facing the nation. Most were happy to gather and exchange views, even though little was actually accomplished. Others dismissed the forum as a venting session, but the second dialogue in Mecca in December 2003 addressed intellectual dialogue and terrorism – an issue at the heart of Saudi society after 11 September. A third conference was summoned in June 2004 in the holy city of Medinah to discuss the question of women in the segregated society. This was followed by a December 2004 meeting on the role of youth held in the Eastern Province, where unemployment among young Shi'ites topped 40%. But while these sessions empowered many to speak out, few Saudis were conscious of the deliberations or, more important, the substance of the recommendations presented to the government.

As a remedy, the King Abdulaziz Centre for National Dialogue, which had organised the conferences, arranged for television broadcasts of the 17 December 2005 Abhah session on the premise that 'internal differences are a source of strength as [Saudis] moved to a more prominent position in the international arena'. The Abhah forum, entitled 'We and the Others', discussed intellectual exchanges with other world cultures and the best methods for Saudis to engage outsiders politically, economically and culturally. The dialogues put an institutional process in place, with hundreds of participants voicing distinct opinions in the hope that their suggestions would eventually be implemented.

A fluctuating but stable economy

As was stressed in the fourth National Dialogue, the primary strategic concern facing Saudi Arabia was unemployment, especially among male university graduates. Although the state officially acknowledged a 10% rate, independent estimates asserted that 30% of young men – and nine out of ten young women – did not earn regular wages. With the population expected to grow from 23m in 2005 to 33m in 2020, and with 50% of the population now under the age of 20, the kingdom will see a continuing sharp rise in jobseekers. The state has failed to encourage indigenous employment. Expatriate workers continue to make up the overwhelming bulk of the workforce, and the foreign population of the kingdom stood at 8.8m in August 2004. Private entrepreneurs prefer to hire foreign labourers rather than more expensive Saudis who insist on job security and higher pay. The 2005 'Saudisation' law required a level of indigenous employees of 75%, but this is difficult to implement.

Nevertheless, in 2006 economic reforms sought to generate a sustained rise in living standards as well as a more equitable distribution of wealth. Riyadh recorded a 7% rise in GDP for 2005, along with a 50% surge in oil exports that added over $160bn to the treasury. Although much of this expansion was directly linked to higher oil prices, there was also significant growth in non-oil sectors, including finance, manufacturing and tourism. Under the guidance of Prince Sultan bin Salman, the kingdom's astronaut-turned-economic-tsar, tourism reached new heights. A new proposal to issue tourist visas – albeit for pre-screened groups – on arrival at major entry ports was under consideration, with a decision anticipated by the end of 2006.

In 2005, the stock market performed impressively, though it then fell sharply in the first half of 2006. The Tadawul All-Share Index (TASI) leaped 100% in value on surging investor confidence in the economy. By January 2006, an estimated 3m Saudis held local equities or had invested in other Gulf markets. But after reaching a peak in February, the index fell sharply in the following months, losing nearly $400bn, or half its market capitalisation. Analysts recommended that the state slowly dispose of its near-monopoly share in several corporations that were heavily traded on TASI, on the argument that this would enable the state to settle most of its estimated $180bn debt, accumulated in the 1980s and 1990s, and that it would distance the government from any bailouts of major investors.

With its accession to the World Trade Organisation on 11 December 2005, Saudi Arabia updated its commercial laws, scrapped regulations that discouraged entrepreneurship, and entered a new era. New regulatory bodies for capital markets and telecoms and various standards were quickly introduced for additional transparency, and the patent office was revamped. Reduced taxes and repatriation rights were aimed at attracting foreign investment, and trade was encouraged with a zero customs duty on most items for GCC countries and 5% for the rest of the world.

Oil and diplomacy
Saudi Arabia stepped up oil production in 2005 and invested significant amounts of money in protecting its oil facilities from terrorist attack; one such attack on

the processing centre at Abqaiq was foiled in February 2006. Production in 2005 averaged a record 11m barrels per day, and in 2006, with the oil price exceeding $70 a barrel, net revenue is likely to be around $160bn.

Many Saudis were delighted to see oil prices soar, anticipating a $100-per-barrel level before 2008. But senior Saudi officials, including Oil Minister Ali Naimi, insisted that the kingdom's optimal and 'fair' price would hover between $32 and $34 a barrel. On 14 February 2005, Naimi called for a massive expansion of new production fields: between 55 and 77 new rigs would be added by the end of 2006. However, Saudi Arabia's long-standing willingness to be a reliable producer could be questioned by a younger generation that dislikes the demonisation of their country in the West and is less inclined to accommodate every request for increased output. Though some experts have argued that Saudi oilfields may have reached their peak, Naimi has expressed confidence that new fields would replace those that have been the big producers for many years. The International Energy Agency (IEA)'s *World Energy Outlook* also expects Saudi Arabia to be able to increase its production significantly.

Saudi leaders are keenly aware of Western interests in other oil producing countries in Central Asia, Africa and Latin America. Riyadh has followed with particular alarm Kurdish designs on Iraq's northern fields, worried that secessionist movements might gain the upper hand and further destabilise the country. Riyadh further wonders whether Washington might abandon, or drastically alter its long relationship with the kingdom. Yet given dwindling American oil resources and the United States' appetite for oil, it is unlikely that the US will become energy independent in the foreseeable future, so long as it relies on fossil fuels. Consequently, Washington's regional policies, coupled with Asian designs on the Gulf, have prompted Saudi officials to engage in a new courtship.

Saud al-Faisal, the foreign minister, set the overall tone in Beijing, when he declared that China was 'one of the most important markets for oil', and that Saudi oil was 'one of the most important sources of energy for China'. King Abdullah's first official foreign visit was to China on 24 January 2006, and the warm welcome he received from Chinese President Hu Jintao stood in contrast to the difficult reception he got from President George W. Bush in Crawford, Texas in April 2005. Abdullah extended an even warmer reception to Hu when the latter stopped in Saudi Arabia after a difficult April 2006 US visit. The Chinese president signed several accords with the Saudis to ensure that Beijing's oil imports (17% of total purchases) would continue to grow. Omar Bahlaiwah, the secretary-general for the Committee for International Trade, a branch of the Saudi Chambers of Commerce, employed a telling metaphor to characterise the changes under way: 'We are in a Catholic marriage with America', he concluded, emphasising that divorce was unthinkable. 'But we are also Muslims – we can have more than one wife'.

The US–Saudi relationship has been clouded by Saudi frustration over US visa requirements. In Crawford, the two countries agreed to establish a high-level joint committee, headed by the Saudi foreign minister and the US secretary of state, to deal with strategic issues of vital importance to the two countries. Both sides acknowledged that expanded 'dialogue, understanding, and interactions between citizens' were necessary. To that end, they foresaw new 'programs designed to increase the number of young Saudi students to travel and study in the United States; increase military exchange programmes so that more Saudi officers visit the United States for military education and training; and increase the number of Americans travelling to work and study in the Kingdom'. However, these objectives failed to remove the many obstacles that Saudi businessmen and students face when they wished to enter the United States.

Saudi Arabia also sought to maintain relationships in Europe. On 21 December 2005 Riyadh reached an agreement with the UK under which it would place a $10bn order believed to be for 48 Eurofighter *Typhoon* jets (with an option for a further 24), to replace the kingdom's *Tornado* fighter fleet. The two countries also signed a new framework accord on closer aerospace and defence links between the two countries.

When French President Jacques Chirac ended a three-day visit to Riyadh on 6 March 2006, he attempted to secure a separate deal for up to 72 *Rafale* fighters, as well as a border-monitoring system. Although the French oil company Total signed a contract to build a refinery in Saudi Arabia, nothing concrete was agreed to on the military aircraft. More significant was the unprecedented opportunity granted Chirac when he became the first foreign leader to address the Majlis al-Shurah. Advocating tolerance and mutual respect, the president declared that France 'always condemned a clash of civilisations', which he interpreted as a 'clash of ignorance'. Saudis were impressed by the Frenchman's directness and his implicit confirmation that France was a valuable alternative to both the United States and Britain.

Pressing issues

In 2005–06, Saudi Arabia prepared to reconsider how to tackle internal reforms and, equally important, how to respond to the persistent pressure of a Bush administration cognisant of the mutual dependence between the United States and Saudi Arabia but inclined to view Riyadh as corrupt and, through its reliance on Wahhabism for legitimacy, indirectly complicit in Islamist terrorism. Much depends on developments in Iraq and whether Baghdad develops an effective federal democracy. While higher oil prices and counter-terrorism measures may have stabilised US–Saudi relations, American-led military activity in Iraq as well as the Israeli–Palestinian conflict remain major sources of antagonism for Muslims and spurs to jihadist recruitment. This phenomenon, in turn, could ultimately increase terrorism in Saudi Arabia through Saudi returnees from Iraq.

Two basic factors govern Saudi Arabia's strategic position: Iraq and oil. Iraq raises worries of a rising Shi'ite crescent, as Iraq could become a Shi'ite power backed by Iran. High oil demand and correspondingly high oil prices provide Saudi Arabia with the current and prospective revenues needed to cushion the political repercussions of its demographic 'youth bulge' and to provide political leeway for incremental reform. The result is an ongoing dependency on the United States tinged by wariness that dictates the tentative cultivation of other strategic options. Change in Saudi Arabia on both the domestic and the international fronts is thus likely to be both gradual and reversible.

Gulf states: reforms advance slowly

The smaller countries of the GCC are changing, each at its own pace. Many in these states believe reforms must strike a delicate balance between what the outside world wants and what the internal dynamics of these fragile states can sustain while maintaining a stable order. Despite this difficult balancing act, the past year has seen modest moves towards political liberalisation in almost all the small GCC states, especially in the area of women's rights: in 2006, women were voting and could stand for parliament for the first time in Kuwait.

They were able to exercise this right sooner than expected, after the emir, Shaikh Sabah al-Ahmad Al Sabah, disbanded parliament because of a dispute over election laws and districts between pro-government parliamentarians and some 29 opposition members, and brought forward elections originally due to be held on 29 June 2006. 32 women stood as candidates. The emir had himself been in office for only four months when the dispute erupted. Shaikh Jabir al-Ahmad Al Sabah died on 15 January and was succeeded by Shaikh Saad Al-Abdullah Al-Salim Al-Sabah, the 76-year-old crown prince, who was ill. On 24 January he was voted out of office by parliament and replaced by the prime minister, Shaikh Sabah.

Women have also won the right to vote and to stand for election in Bahrain. However, sectarian issues continued to pose a threat to internal stability, with the Shia majority unlikely to remain quiet if international tensions surrounding Iran's nuclear programme escalate – the US Naval Forces Central Command and Fifth Fleet are based in the kingdom. Bahrain, the smallest GCC member, has always felt under pressure to accommodate Iranian demands in order to avoid Shia riots. But it is also under pressure from Saudi Arabia, which was upset when in January 2006 Bahrain signed a free-trade agreement with the US without its knowledge. Following the first parliamentary elections in 2002 and the enfranchisement of women, expectations of further reform in Bahrain, a constitutional monarchy headed by King Hamad bin Isa Al Khalifah, are tempered by these pressures.

Qatar is due to hold its first legislative elections in early 2007, following approval of a constitution by referendum in 2003. The constitution stipulates a legislative body with 30 members elected by direct voting and 15 appointed by the emir. However, the current Qatari Council is entirely appointed by the emir and has a limited advisory role, with fewer powers than those of its counterpart in Saudi Arabia. According to the constitution, the future legislature will have powers to approve the national budget; to assess ministers' performance; and to exercise a vote of no confidence in the government. Qatar has opened up in the area of women's rights, but remains governed by the parameters of the Wahhabi doctrine that governs social life, except in zones frequented by Westerners. On a regional level Qatar has problems with Iran over a disputed gas field. There is also rising tension with Saudi Arabia over a Saudi decision not to allow Qatari gas through its territory to reach Kuwait: this is played out in a war of words via satellite television channels: Qatar owns al-Jazeera and Saudi Arabia its competitor al-Arabiya.

Oman has extended voting rights to every citizen over 21, including women, since November 2002. The process of democratisation has been gradual, beginning with the creation in 1991 of a 59-member consultative council appointed by the sultan – expanded to 83 members in 1993. In 2000, the first direct elections were held to choose members of the consultative council, with about 25% of the population eligible to vote. In addition to the consultative council, the sultan created an appointed 57-member upper house, the state council, with eight women members. In spite of these steps, some Omanis oppose the sultan's regime: in April 2005, the government arrested 31 men accused of conspiring to overthrow the regime.

Gulf Co-operation Council: security issues unresolved

In 2006, the GCC marked 25 years since its establishment on 25 May 1981. During that time, it has made advances in the field of security but remains, as a region, vulnerable. The degree to which member states have been able to furnish security indigenously has failed to meet their security needs; this particularly applies to the smaller states. The United States, Britain and France still play important roles in the provision of regional security. The shortfall in regional security, as well as in cooperation between and among GCC states on security, has come particularly into focus as the Gulf has confronted a series of major problems: the growth of Islamic extremism and terrorism; the US-led invasion of Iraq and its aftermath; and growing concerns both inside and outside the region about Iran's nuclear ambitions and about the potential consequences for Gulf states of an escalation of the confrontation with Iran. US calls for Arab assistance in the stabilisation of Iraq posed awkward dilemmas for Gulf governments, particularly given the negative depiction of the Iraq War in the Arab media. However, the Gulf states feared the impact of radicalisation fomented by the Iraq conflict, and in particular the possible return of nationals who had gone to assist the insurgency in Iraq. They remained wary of genuine cooperation, preferring to strike

individual defence agreements with the United States, which remained their ultimate security guarantor. Efforts in various forums, such as the annual Regional
Security Summit (the Gulf Dialogue) organised in Bahrain by The International
Institute for Strategic Studies, sought to overcome such barriers, but progress
seemed likely to remain tentative.

The restraint was partly a function of the very different political dynamics
influencing each GCC member – in spite of the things that bind them, including
deep religious and cultural ties, as well as common values and characteristics,
geographic proximity, close interaction and strong family relations among citizens. At one end of the spectrum, Kuwait enjoys vibrant political debate that
includes the aggressive demands for reform of the electoral system and redistricting that led to the dissolution of parliament in May 2006. At the other end is
the quietist politics of Oman and the United Arab Emirates. Although movement
towards reform is taking place in both countries, it is done from the top and
without fanfare: in the UAE, some citizens seem more interested in economic
reforms. When Shaikh Khalifa bin Zayed, the president, suggested a new parliament that would be half elected and half appointed, influential members of the
mercantile class of Dubai rejected the idea. In their view, Dubai was developing
because of the absence of politics, and the introduction of politics would undermine economic success. Therefore, while the enfranchisement of Kuwaiti women
and other reforms there may be a sign of gradual reform, it would be a mistake to
believe that all GCC states would follow the Kuwaiti model, since it is the individual culture of each state and its demographic make up that will determine
both the shape and pace of change.

7 | Africa

A Boost from the G8, China and Oil

Events appear at last to be moving in the right direction for the world's poorest continent, even though many countries remain beset by chronic poverty, conflict and disease. Fuelled by a global commodity boom, African economic growth was 5.1% in 2004, and was estimated at 5% in 2005 and 4.7% in 2006, the best performance for many years. In July 2005, the leaders of the G8 agreed at the Gleneagles Summit in Scotland to increase development aid by $50 billion by 2010, of which half would go to Africa – thereby doubling aid to the continent. This was followed in May 2006 by a commitment from the 25 member states of the European Union to double annual development aid to $80bn by 2010. In September 2005, 15 members of the United Nations committed themselves to increasing aid to the long-standing UN target of 0.7% of gross domestic product, met so far by only a handful of countries. There was also agreement to cancel $55bn of debt to 18 countries, 14 of which were in Africa. These commitments were made in the spirit of British Prime Minister Tony Blair's Commission for Africa, a group of prominent Africans and others, launched in 2004, that produced recommendations before the Gleneagles Summit.

To be fulfilled, the industrialised world's expanded aid commitments must be answered by improvements in African governance. The New Partnership for Africa's Development (NEPAD) is Africa's part of that bargain. During 2005, a number of countries, notably Ghana, South Africa, Rwanda and Kenya, undertook their NEPAD peer review process, designed to encourage higher governance standards.

However, African leaders were also the targets of aggressive investment approaches from China, which made no such political demands. With oil import needs expected to double in the next 15 years, China has invested in particular in

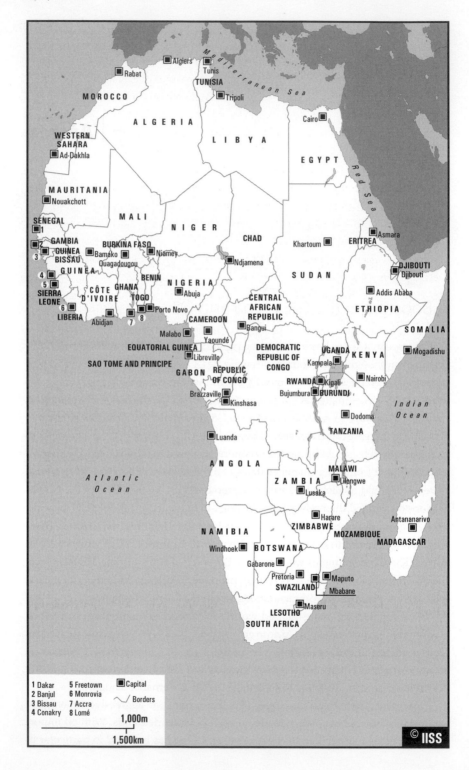

Algiers
Rabat
Tunis
TUNISIA
Tripoli
MOROCCO
Cairo
ALGERIA
LIBYA
WESTERN
SAHARA
EGYPT
Ad-Dakhla
MAURITANIA
Nouakchott
MALI
NIGER
CHAD
Khartoum
ERITREA
Asmara
SENEGAL
1
GAMBIA
BURKINA FASO
Niamey
Ndjamena
SUDAN
DJIBOUTI
2
GUINEA
Bamako
Djibouti
3
BISSAU
Ouagadougou
BENIN
NIGERIA
CENTRAL
Addis Ababa
GUINEA
4
GHANA
Abuja
AFRICAN
ETHIOPIA
5
TOGO
REPUBLIC
SIERRA
CÔTE
Porto Novo
SOMALIA
LEONE
D'IVOIRE
6
7
8
CAMEROON
Bangui
LIBERIA
Abidjan
Malabo
Mogadishu
Yaoundé
EQUATORIAL GUINEA
DEMOCRATIC
UGANDA
KENYA
Libreville
REPUBLIC OF
Kampala
SAO TOME AND PRINCIPE
CONGO
Nairobi
GABON
REPUBLIC
RWANDA
Kigali
OF CONGO
Brazzaville
Bujumbura
BURUNDI
Kinshasa
Dodoma
Indian
Ocean
Luanda
TANZANIA
ANGOLA
MALAWI
ZAMBIA
Lilongwe
Lusaka
Atlantic
Ocean
Harare
Antananarivo
NAMIBIA
ZIMBABWE
MOZAMBIQUE
MADAGASCAR
Windhoek
BOTSWANA
Gabarone
Pretoria
Maputo
SWAZILAND
Mbabane
Maseru
LESOTHO
SOUTH AFRICA

1 Dakar   5 Freetown   ■ Capital
2 Banjul   6 Monrovia
3 Bissau   7 Accra   / Borders
4 Conakry 8 Lomé

1,000m

1,500km

© IISS

Sudan, Angola and Nigeria. China National Petroleum Corporation is the largest investor in Sudan, with stakes in oilfields producing 350,000 barrels per day as well others about to come on stream, a pipeline to the Red Sea, and a tanker terminal. China is also investing in other sectors: forestry in Equatorial Guinea, retailing in Sierra Leone, construction in Botswana, mobile phones in Zimbabwe and pharmaceuticals in Ethiopia. Large numbers of Chinese people and companies are accompanying the money. In 2005, Angola's energy minister reportedly said as many as three million Chinese could move there during the next five years, a substantial amount compared to Angola' s 14m population.

Africa's oil boom is likely to see established and small producers sharply increasing their output, and new countries such as Tanzania, Kenya, Uganda, Mozambique and Madagascar emerging as producers. However, this boom carries risks. There are fears that China will swamp Africa with cheap manufactured goods: in 2004, China's exports to Africa rose 35% to $14bn. This could limit African companies' ability to develop their own products, given the scale and productivity advantages of Chinese competitors. In turn, economies could fail to diversify sufficiently away from dependence on oil and commodities, maintaining their vulnerability to market slumps. Most worrying from the perspective of the Western emphasis on governance standards and democratisation is China's lack of interest in these issues as it pursues its investments.

Those pursuing the NEPAD framework are well aware in any case that plentiful experience shows that the politics of African countries can prevent good advice from being taken up. Continuing political impasses in countries such as Côte d'Ivoire and Zimbabwe illustrate the limits on the role of external actors. African nations are increasingly differentiated, demanding a variety of internal and external solutions, but the determinants of economic success are primarily domestic. In the most pivotal states and regions over the past year democratisation, security-sector reform and political succession were dominant themes.

Risks to democracy in Congo

The link between governance and economic performance is nowhere more evident than in the Democratic Republic of the Congo (DRC). The country has enormous potential in terms of mineral deposits and hydroelectric power from the Congo River. But little of this potential has been realised: there are only 500km of paved roads, and no bridges span the Congo. Over the past year, the country moved hesitantly toward its first democratic elections in four decades. The process was marred by delays, lack of political will, opposition boycotts, slow security-sector reform and violence.

An interim government was established in 2003 under the terms of the Lusaka Peace Process to unify the country, create a national army and conduct democratic elections. Presidential and parliamentary elections were set for 30 June 2005, but the government invoked a provision enabling a one-year postponement following parliamentary delays in setting up the independent electoral commission and drafting the new constitution and electoral law. President Joseph Kabila, who came to power in 2001 at the age of 29 following the assassination of his father, was a candidate. The logistics of the ballot were daunting: the electoral commission had 64 liaison offices, 9,000 voter-registration centres and 53,000 booths; some 25.6m voters were registered; in April 2006, the commission approved a list of 33 presidential candidates and 9,500 legislative candidates. The commission succeeded in mobilising women as candidates and voters. In December 2005 voters adopted a new constitution in a national referendum, enshrining the decentralisation of power in 25 provinces, power-sharing between a president and prime minister, and executive term limits.

There remained serious threats to the elections due to be held on 30 July 2006, including violence between government security forces and two opposition groups – the Congolese Rally for Democracy, previously one of the main rebel groups, and the Union for Democracy and Social Progress (UDPS) headed by former prime minister Etienne Tshisekedi. The run-up to the poll was marked by escalating violence, repression of opposition rallies, arbitrary detentions, media intimidation and displacement of large population groups in the volatile east. Opposition parties claimed the poll date was illegal since it came after the stipulated one-year extension period. The UDPS initially boycotted the elections, then sought an extension of the voter registration period to ensure its supporters could sign up. The commission did not grant its petition.

Most worrisome was the security situation. Most of the 39,000-strong police force tasked with election security received just six days of training and were no match for the country's battle-tested militias. Security-sector reform has been slow, with more spent on demobilising combatants than on training and paying the newly integrated national army. Substantial numbers of Congolese were killed in 2006 in low-intensity conflicts throughout the country. Even if the balloting process proceeded as planned in July, the credibility of the new government and the political allegiance of the new security forces were likely to remain very much in doubt.

On 12 June, the European Union launched a 2,000-strong military operation, EUFOR RD Congo, to provide support for the UN's 16,000-strong peacekeeping force during the election. The force included an advance element in Kinshasa of several hundred personnel and a battalion-size rapid reaction force located in neighbouring Gabon. The EU force was to be deployed for up to four months after the date of the first round of the presidential and parliamentary elections.

Mixed progress in West Africa

In West Africa, some previously intractable conflicts are yielding to democracy, reconciliation and indications of better economic management.

Sierra Leone has made steady process in post-conflict reconstruction: publishing the report of its Truth and Reconciliation Process, entrenching the rule of law, establishing state institutions and preparing for elections in 2007. A special international criminal court has indicted 11 alleged war criminals. More than half of 112 planned new police stations have been set up, an anti-corruption commission has issued indictments and the government has begun to gain control over essential state services and mining-sector activities. Inflation was projected to fall to single digits and economic growth to climb to 6.5% by 2007. But there were still formidable problems: pre-election violence had begun to flare by mid-2006; security-sector reform was inhibited by shortages of resources; there was high unemployment among the demobilised youth.

Neighbouring Liberia elected Africa's first woman head of state, Ellen Johnson-Sirleaf, in January 2006, and a large portion of combatants were disarmed and demobilised. Most significantly, Johnson-Sirleaf took the bold step of requesting that Nigeria surrender Charles Taylor, and an agreement by the United Kingdom to imprison him if convicted paved the way in June for the former dictator and warlord to be tried at The Hague. The UN in June proposed lifting sanctions on timber exports and weapons imports to enable new revenue flows and arming of the new police force. Johnson-Sirleaf, however, put an embargo on new timber concessions pending the introduction of market regulations that would ensure timber sales benefited the Liberian people. Meanwhile, judicial reform remained a critical priority after 14 years of civil war.

Nearly a year after a military coup on 3 August 2005, Mauritania showed encouraging signs. A constitutional referendum was scheduled for 26 June 2006 and a schedule for municipal, legislative and presidential elections was set. Since taking power, the military junta – which gave assurances that none of its members would stand for office – has consulted with political parties, taken tentative anti-corruption measures, and introduced regulations to govern oil resources and fisheries. The country began producing oil in February 2006; the European Union resumed aid in June; and the country has signed the World Bank's Extractive Industries Transparency Initiative (EITI). Two-thirds of the 3m population, however, still live in extreme poverty on less than $2 per day.

Elsewhere in West Africa, there were less encouraging signs. Absence of border controls remained a key challenge across the region, most particularly between the three interlocking conflicts of Sierra Leone, Liberia and Côte d'Ivoire, but also across the Sahelian states, facilitating the easy movement of small arms, fighters, Islamists, child soldiers, narcotics, organised crime and disease. Only half the states in the region have signed the UN Firearms Protocol, and a regional moratorium on the import, export and manufacture of small arms has met slow compliance.

The United States, and in particular the US Navy, was paying special attention to the Gulf of Guinea, having identified this region as an area of strategic interest principally because of its role as an important source of oil to the United States, and its perceived vulnerability to radicalisation. The region is expected to produce one-quarter of the oil consumed annually in the US by 2015 and has rich, poorly protected marine fisheries. Piracy is rife, and has contributed to the weapons trade and money laundering. In 2005, an estimated 200,000–300,000 barrels of oil were stolen daily. The International Maritime Organisation has launched a port-security programme. The rapid and competitive increase in oil infrastructure investment, with China, India and the United States all jockeying for position, will raise the attractiveness of oil installations as potential terrorist targets. Admiral Harry Ulrich, commander of US Naval Forces Europe, has been working closely with West African leaders on enhancing maritime safety and security.

Much of the progress made in recent years toward stabilising West Africa remained threatened by unrest in Côte d'Ivoire, which was caught in a stalemate between the government-controlled south and the rebel-held north. A cessation of fighting has held for the past three years, but movements towards peace have been stuttering at best. Failure to implement the April 2005 Pretoria peace accord – which followed an earlier peace agreement in 2003 – resulted in cancellation of planned elections in October 2005. After the African Union (AU) called for a one-year extension to the peace process, some progress was made: in November 2005 Charles Konan Banny filled a new UN-backed office of prime minister, and three months later he succeeded in convening the first face-to-face dialogue between the factions on Ivorian soil. Elections are due to be held in October 2006. But key problems that remained unresolved included disarmament, demobilisation, disputes about the basis of Ivorian citizenship, and the absence of a functioning judicial system. There remained considerable potential for violence to break out.

In Nigeria, the Senate in May 2006 blocked an attempt by President Olusegun Obasanjo to change the constitution in order to seek a third term in power in the 2007 presidential election. While this decision removed one possible trigger of sectarian problems, Nigeria still faced the challenges of Muslim–Christian tensions in the north and a violent insurgency in the oil-producing Niger Delta. A critical question is whether Nigeria can manage the windfall of rising oil prices to stabilise its fragile democracy and improve living standards.

Since coming to power as only the second civilian president in 1999, Obasanjo, a southern Christian, has overseen considerable progress, introducing greater prudence and transparency to fiscal management. He attempted to stem corruption and signed Nigeria up to the EITI so that the country's hydrocarbon income could be audited. As a result, it was able to reach a deal with official creditors on a substantial debt reduction. Inflation has fallen into single digits and economic growth has risen above 5%. Obasanjo has begun reforms of state-owned enterprises, the civil service and procurement.

In the north, the confluence of large criminal syndicates and radical Islamist groups has made Nigeria a country of concern with regard to transnational terrorism. In 2003 Osama bin Laden, the al-Qaeda leader, urged his followers to focus on Nigeria. Smuggling and human traffic across the Sahel and northern Nigeria exacerbates security problems. In February, the Danish cartoon incident stoked violent clashes between Muslims and Christians across the northern states where sharia law is practised.

Meanwhile, violence in the Niger Delta has steadily escalated. During the first six months of 2006, there were repeated attacks on foreign oil workers and installations by a group called the Movement for the Emancipation of the Niger Delta. Production was cut by more than 20%, contributing to higher world prices. Obasanjo created the Niger Delta Peace and Security Strategy to foster security and development and has launched programmes to demobilise and reintegrate former combatants. Those initiatives were undermined, however, by the lack of jobs. Elections in 2003 stoked violence and there is a strong possibility that the 2007 elections will have the same effect.

War and Peace in Sudan

The January 2005 signing of a Comprehensive Peace Agreement (CPA), which introduced power-sharing arrangements to end a long war between north and south, did not bring an end to Sudan's travails. Indeed, by mid-2006 the war-torn country was facing problems on many fronts. The CPA was inevitably proving difficult to implement; in particular, the National Petroleum Commission (NPC) was slow to address the crucial issue of the north–south division of oil revenues; in the west, fighting continued in Darfur in spite of efforts to ameliorate a grave situation, as the UN sought to take over the peacekeeping role from the AU after a partial peace agreement was signed by the government and one rebel faction on 5 May 2006; the plight of Darfur was contributing to increased hostilities across the border with Chad; in the south, inadequate implementation of the CPA created dissatisfaction, and there was continued activity by the Lord's Resistance Army (LRA); in the east, there was growing unrest; in the Nubian heartland, public discontent over the Hamdab (Merowe) Dam culminated in violence. There was a danger that the international community's focus on Darfur could distract attention from the lengthy and detailed process of implementing the CPA.

The death of Garang and the SPLM succession
Large crowds gathered to greet long-time Sudan People's Liberation Movement/ Sudan People's Liberation Army (SPLM/A) leader John Garang's inauguration as

first vice-president of the Government of National Unity (GONU) in Khartoum on 9 July 2005, reflecting his status as a national figure. His death in a helicopter accident on 30 July came as a profound shock, not just to the south but to the country as a whole. Subsequent riots in Khartoum and Juba demonstrated both the depth of this disappointment and the precariousness of the unity temporarily forged by the peace agreement.

Under the CPA, Sudan was committed to unity for an interim period of six years, but the Southern Sudanese, whose leader Garang had been, may then vote to end that unity. Southern Sudan was to have an autonomous government.

The SPLM/A quickly confirmed Garang's deputy, Salva Kiir Mayardit, as the new head of the movement, and he took over Garang's positions as president of the Government of Southern Sudan (GOSS) and first vice-president in the GONU. There were concerns that he might lack the charisma and national stature of Garang, or the strength to keep the south together and hold his own against the National Congress Party (NCP). But while Garang's death during this crucial transition period undoubtedly was a setback, Kiir's accession also opened up new opportunities for the SPLM and the south.

Kiir has a long military background. A veteran of the guerrilla movement of the first civil war, he was absorbed into the national army in 1972 and served in military intelligence. He was one of the original founders of the SPLM/A in 1983 and brought considerable organisational and military skills to the movement. As SPLA chief of staff in later years, he forged a strong base in the army. He was one of the few SPLA commanders to support the grassroots peace movement that attempted to heal the rift in the south following the 1991 SPLA split, and was the guarantor of the 1999 Wunlit peace conference between the Nuer of Western Upper Nile and the Dinka of Bahr el-Ghazal (his home region). He was also the head of the SPLM delegation at the Machakos talks in 2002 and negotiated the south's right to self-determination, for which he was later branded a 'separatist'. He also had differences with Garang over the democratic deficits in the movement and Garang's reluctance to engage in a 'South–South' dialogue before concluding a peace agreement with Khartoum. These disagreements came to a head at a leadership meeting in Rumbek in November 2004, where he accused Garang of carrying the movement 'in his own briefcase'. Many outside the SPLM hoped that Kiir would replace Garang as head of the SPLM/A, but in the end Kiir refused to split the movement, and the leadership supported his insistence on greater collective accountability.

As president of the GOSS Kiir had the opportunity to replace Garang's patronage with his own in the appointment not only of his cabinet, but of the Southern assembly and state governments as well. Instead, he maintained a balance by retaining many Garang loyalists in high positions and also instituted a more representative nomination system for the lower levels of government. His greatest achievement so far was in making good on his earlier commitment to reconcile

Map 7.1 **Sudan**

with the SPLM's southern critics – in particular, bringing Paulino Matip and the majority of the South Sudan Defence Force (SSDF) into the SPLA, and co-opting civilian critics.

Implementation of the CPA

The main activities of the six-month pre-interim period following the signing of the CPA in January 2005 were the drafting of an interim constitution, preparations for the deployment of the United Nations Monitoring Mission (UNMIS) peacekeeping force, and the formation of the Abyei Boundaries Commission (ABC). The Interim National Constitution (INC) was signed into law on 9 July, and the commission reported to the tripartite presidency on 14 July, but the SPLA's preparations for receiving UNMIS were well behind schedule.

Garang's death delayed the formation of both the GONU and the GOSS. The distribution of ministries between the NCP and SPLM was the first showdown between Kiir and the two other members of the presidency, President Umar al-Bashir and Second Vice-President Ali Uthman Muhammad Taha. The NCP retained control of the most important economic ministries, including finance and energy, leaving Kiir looking weak in the face of NCP intransigence. The GONU was finally appointed in September, and the GOSS and the southern state governments followed in October. Six of the nine national commissions of the CPA (Assessment and Evaluation; Petroleum; Cease-fire Political; Fiscal and Financial Allocation and Monitoring; Judicial Service; and the Technical Ad Hoc Border Committee) were appointed in November 2005, but the remaining three (Human Rights, Civil Service, Land), and the six Southern commissions (Land; Civil Service; Human Rights; Anti-Corruption; Relief and Rehabilitation; Disarmament, Demobilization and Reintegration) were delayed. The National Constitutional Review Commission had not been convened by April 2006, causing a postponement of reviewing legislation to be brought in line with the INC. The old penal code, with its Islamic provisions, remained in force.

Most other state governments in the north, where power is shared between the NCP and SPLM, have been formed, but a deadlock over the constitution of Khartoum State was not resolved until May 2006, when the draft constitution was brought in line with the INC and the CPA at the SPLM's insistence.

There has been confusion over oil revenue transfers to the GOSS, the main element of the wealth-sharing protocol of the CPA. Half of the oil revenues from southern Sudan were supposed to go to the GOSS after 2% was paid to the government of the state in which the oil was produced. The GOSS doubted whether it was receiving its share, but had no means of verifying this. The GONU claimed to have transferred more than $700m of 2005 revenues and more than $200m to cover the first quarter of 2006. There were continuing disagreements between the governments over boundaries of oil-producing areas, oil-production figures and the status of oil contracts. The NPC, set up under the CPA to oversee and regulate the oil business, had been slow to convene – by May 2006 it had met just twice – and to pass relevant information on these issues to the GOSS.

Security arrangements are also sensitive. The Juba Declaration of 8 January 2006 announced the integration of the majority of the SSDF into the SPLA, leaving only a small number of southern militias aligned with the northern-based government's Sudan Armed Forces (SAF) that have traditionally opposed the SPLA. The transfer of these units has not gone smoothly, with reports of government forces attacking units of the SPLA-aligned militias. There was also strong evidence that SAF continued to arm and supply anti-SPLA militias, who have been involved in attacks on civilians in Jonglei and Upper Nile states. The threat to rural security that these militias posed meant that many communities were unwilling to give up their weapons and resisted SPLA attempts to disarm them.

A further threat to security was the continued presence of Joseph Kony's LRA in Southern Sudan, having shifted their area of operation from south of Juba westwards towards the border with the DRC. There were reports of continued support for the LRA by elements of the SAF and Sudanese security personnel stationed in the south. Kiir and President Yoweri Museveni of Uganda announced a joint initiative in May 2006 to try to persuade Kony to negotiate an end to his insurgency.

The withdrawal of SPLM and SAF forces from contested areas, their reduction in size and the demobilisation of soldiers have also been proceeding slower than scheduled, and the formation of Joint Integrated Units for deployment in the south, Blue Nile, Southern Kordofan and Abyei was delayed. UNMIS's ability to monitor force redeployments was hampered by restrictions placed by Khartoum. Anxiety over security was reflected in the Southern Assembly's allocation of $536m – 40% of the South's first budget – to support of the SPLA.

The biggest long-term challenge for the GOSS will be adopting and implementing effective social and economic policies, especially regarding the repatriation of an estimated 4m refugees and internally displaced persons. In a country devastated by 22 years of war, with very little of the pre-war infrastructure left in place and almost no investment outside the oil industry, there are too many challenges to address at once. The southern government is suffering from the SPLM's failure to draft a comprehensive reconstruction and development plan during the two-year period of peace negotiations.

Quite apart from the challenges posed by the south, there was further uncertainty over the future of the three areas covered by protocols in the CPA. Abyei, straddling the Kordofan–Bahr el-Ghazal borderland and inhabited by the Ngok Dinka tribe, is supposed to come under the authority of the presidency throughout the interim period and is to vote in 2011 whether to remain in Kordofan or join the south. The territory included in the Abyei area was defined by the ABC, whose decision was to be 'final and binding' and implemented with immediate effect. However, the NCP has refused to accept the ABC's report, because it recognised Ngok claims to territory that includes most of the area's major oil fields. No civil authority has been appointed, Khartoum has restricted the movement of UNMIS forces in Abyei, and the NCP has tried to mobilise local opposition to the boundary decision. The assistant president, NCP hard-liner Nafi Ali Nafi, has been quoted as pledging that the Abyei Protocol will never be implemented.

Another difficult issue in CPA implementation was the fate of the Nuba Mountains, which were re-incorporated into Southern Kordofan State, whose boundaries include all of former Southern Kordofan Province – thus assuring the Nuba Mountains a continued minority status. The SPLM and NCP have failed to agree on a state constitution, the main disagreement being over land issues. A caretaker government was established by the presidency in March 2006. There was a growing feeling among the Nuba people that they had been betrayed by the CPA. The formation of Blue Nile State in December 2005 was less problematic. But refugees returning from Ethiopian refugee camps were reportedly dismayed to learn that Blue Nile State was not part of Southern Sudan, and one SPLM state official warned that if the CPA was not implemented fairly, the Blue Nile state assembly would vote to join the south. The disputes over Abyei, the oil fields and Southern Kordofan raised the prospect of bitter disputes over the boundaries of Southern Sudan, affecting who would have the right to vote in the self-determination referendum of 2011, what oil fields the south possessed and whether agricultural schemes currently annexed to neighbouring northern states would be returned to the south. These boundaries will probably be hotly contested.

International engagement

International backing for the CPA received a boost from the Oslo donors' conference in April 2005, at which \$4.5bn was pledged for reconstruction. There was disappointment in the south, however, when it transpired early in 2006 that many of those funds were being diverted to the crisis in Darfur in western Sudan. Nevertheless, international agencies have begun to work with the GOSS on reconstruction and development. The World Bank and the US Agency for International Development are collaborating on a Core Fiduciary Systems Support Programme. National and Southern Multi-Donor Trust Funds became operational in June 2005. The UN Development Programme is involved in a major town-planning project in the south and numerous NGOs are involved in both relief and development projects. While this activity demonstrates the intention of the international community to be fully engaged in securing peace through results on the ground, it has yet to produce those results. Donors have been tardy in honouring their commitments, the Multi-Donor Trust Funds are subject to cumbersome World Bank bureaucratic procedures, and there has been a lack of tangible reconstruction.

The formal declaration of peace opened the way for major new private investments, many of which will have political implications. Members of the Arab League are being encouraged to invest in the south, in order to help persuade southerners to vote for unity in 2011. Not all are supportive of the NCP, however. Kuwait has announced large-scale investment in Juba, possibly in recognition of the public backing southerners gave Kuwait during the Gulf War, in which Khartoum supported Iraq. By far the most visible new investors in the South are Ugandan, Kenyan and South African merchants and businessmen, and these economic ties with African countries are set to grow.

The oil industry will attract the most substantial investment, as further oil blocks in the south become safe for exploitation. Confusion still exists over oil concessions granted prior to the signing of the CPA. Both the SPLM and the SSDF claim to have extended concessions to different oil companies for rights Khartoum had granted to France's Total. But China is the main international player in Sudan's oil and will remain so for some time.

Darfur

Once the CPA was signed, international diplomatic attention switched to Darfur. Tensions over water, grazing and access rights between non-Arab farmers and Arab herdsmen in Darfur prompted an armed insurrection by two non-Arab groups – the Justice and Equality Movement (JEM) and the Sudan Liberation Movement/Army (SLM/A) – in February 2003. The Sudanese government supported the Arabs with air power and proxy Arab militias known as the Janjaweed. As of October 2005, the Darfur conflict had produced between 63,000 and 143,000 Sudanese deaths, according to the US State Department, although other sources estimate as many as 400,000 deaths. Each side attacked non-combatants on the basis of ethnicity. But the Janjaweed, with government air support, quickly gained the upper hand and undertook a programme of ethnic cleansing against the non-Arab civilian population. Rebel forces also continued to target civilians. Both sides at times blocked aid and supplies to displaced persons, who numbered over 2m and have spilled into neighbouring Chad.

A cease-fire was established in April 2004, but has been routinely violated. In June 2004, the fledgling AU, eager to surpass the predecessor Organisation of African Unity in providing African solutions to African problems, dispatched one-third of an authorised 7,000 peacekeepers, mainly Nigerians and Rwandans, to Darfur. By mid-2005, the force was almost at full authorised strength. NATO, the US and the EU have provided support to the AU force. So far, however, the force has not been equal to the task of stabilisation. The government of Sudan has repeatedly broken promises to suspend hostilities. Although violence in Darfur abated over summer 2005, it increased in the autumn, during which the first peacekeepers were killed, hundreds of Sudanese died and another 10,000 Sudanese were forced to flee.

In July 2005, a Declaration of Principles, providing the framework for an agreement, was signed by the Sudanese government, the SLM/A and the JEM at the end of the fifth round of AU-sponsored peace talks in Abuja. Two further rounds were convened in 2005 against the background of continued cease-fire violations. Fragmentation of the Darfur rebels has been one factor hampering negotiations, with the largest movement, the SLM/A, split into two. But while cease-fire breaches by the SLA seem to have been committed largely by semi-autonomous commanders beyond the control of their political leaders, violations by Khartoum have been systematic, with the same coordinated use of airpower and ground militia that has characterised the war since 2003. A major government offensive in southern Darfur began in April 2006, coinciding with the AU's latest deadline at the Abuja talks.

With some 7,000 men to patrol an area the size of France, under-equipped, under-funded and short on petrol, the inadequacy of the AU Mission in Sudan (AMIS) force in Darfur was painfully evident by the end of 2005. The consensus in both the AU and the UN moved towards transferring the responsibility of peacekeeping to the UN, with NATO support. Khartoum, however, has resisted this course, casting it as foreign interference in Sudan's domestic affairs. The war in Darfur has hurt Sudan diplomatically, costing it the presidency of AU. Sudan is not, however, completely isolated, and the convergence between Sudan's and China's economic interests and the ambiguity of US foreign policy seem to have emboldened Khartoum to resist new international efforts. China, Russia and Qatar have blocked stronger resolutions from the UN.

While former US Secretary of State Colin Powell labelled the conduct of Khartoum and the Janjaweed in Darfur 'genocide' in June 2004 Senate testimony, wavering US policy has contributed to international uncertainty surrounding the Darfur crisis. US action on Darfur has consisted basically of air-logistical and economic support for AU forces, either directly or through NATO, coupled with relatively low-key diplomatic pressure through the UN and the AU. In April 2006, though, the Bush administration raised the possibility of sending several hundred NATO military 'advisers' to bolster AU efforts in Darfur – and also argued for the UN to take over control from the AU. Though the United States has denounced continuing violence in Darfur, privately it regards some of the architects of Sudan's war in Darfur, most notably Vice President Ali Uthman Muhammad Taha and Intelligence Director Salah Abdallah Gosh, as useful allies in the 'war on terror'. Washington, which appeared still to be obtaining counter-terrorism cooperation from Sudan, seemed unlikely to undertake direct military action, whether overt or covert, because this could risk derailing the north–south agreement and cause that cooperation to flag. Thus the United States, while publicly chastising the UN for its weakness over Darfur, also worked to water down a UN sanctions resolution. Both the United States and Britain were instrumental in removing Taha's and Gosh's names from the original list, tendered by the UN to the International Criminal Court, of persons to be sanctioned by the UN for war crimes in Darfur.

Perhaps because decisive UN or other multilateral action seemed unlikely, there was strong international support for what the AU declared were the final negotiations in Abuja. The UN, EU, Arab League, US and Canada all supported a peace plan tabled by the AU mediators, with a 30 April 2006 deadline for acceptance. Khartoum expressed a willingness to sign, but the SLM/A and JEM were particularly unhappy with the security and power-sharing provisions. Nevertheless, the government and one faction of the SLM/A signed a peace accord on 5 May 2006. The agreement called for a cease-fire, disarmament of government-linked militias, integration of thousands of rebel fighters into Sudan's armed forces and a protection force for civilians in the immediate aftermath of the war. Even though the other SLM/A faction and the JEM held out, the agreement was viewed as easing the possible introduction of a UN peacekeeping force.

The crisis in Darfur contributed to an escalation of war in Chad, with Khartoum giving active support to rebel forces opposed to the government of President Idriss Déby. In December 2005, the government of Chad announced that 'a state of war' existed along its border with Sudan. In April 2006, a large group of attackers invaded N'Djamena, Chad's capital, where they were thwarted by government troops in violence that killed 350 people. An AU investigation found that many of the captured attackers had Sudanese or Central African Republic identification and had been conscripted by Sudan. Déby told the *Washington Post*: 'Sudan mercenaries are what they are. There is not a rebellion in Chad. This is an invasion by Sudan.' However, the situation continued to be complex, with each country providing support to rebel groups in the other. With Janjaweed attacks across the border into Chad continuing after a temporary February peace agreement between Sudan and Chad, the outlook for some 200,000 Sudanese refugees from Darfur in eastern Chad remained bleak.

Problems elsewhere

The Kassala and Red Sea states of eastern Sudan, with SPLA forces active in the region, were part of the larger war brought to an end by the CPA. But no provision was made to address the east's grievances. Two groups formerly part of the National Democratic Alliance (NDA), the Beja Congress and the Rashaida Free Lions, merged to form the Eastern Front in January 2005 and, along with a branch of the JEM, continued low-level military activity. The aim seems to have been less to raise the level of the insurgency than to bring about negotiations, but the international community did not rise to the challenge, and after a brief foray by UNMIS in 2005, no mediating forum has been established.

The NDA, who were excluded from the CPA negotiations, agreed to participate in the GONU, and appointments were made to the cabinet, the National Assembly and Council of States in November 2005. Sadiq al-Mahdi's wing of the Umma Party and Hassan al-Turabi's Popular National Party (PNP) both remain outside the GONU but plan to contest elections during the interim period. There has also been dissatisfaction within the NCP over the terms of the CPA, as some feel that it concedes far too much to the SPLM. One such critic is the NCP's deputy chairman, Nafi Ali Nafi, who has been elevated to the position of assistant president, a post not established by the CPA. Osama bin Laden's April 2006 call rallying jihadists against the CPA and international intervention in Darfur is not likely to influence events in Sudan significantly, but it echoes the sentiments of many in the NCP and quite possibly the PNP.

Political grievances arising from social, political and economic marginalisation are spreading beyond Darfur and the east. In Nubia, the Hamdab (Merowe) Dam was generating grassroots opposition. The dam is being constructed without an environmental impact assessment and the central government has ignored local land rights in the appropriation of land for the project in favour of the interests of Arab and Chinese investors and European companies. In April 2006, police attacked local protesters, killing three, wounding some 50 others and arresting several more. Such conduct in the northern heartland reprises policies that contributed to the outbreak of war in Blue Nile, the Nuba Mountains, Darfur, the east and the oil fields, where local land rights were overridden by 'national' projects that privileged private and foreign investors.

A highly uncertain future

The CPA has not yet led to the emergence of a less repressive regime in Khartoum. The international community (the United States and the UK in particular) appears to be inhibited by fear of creating a political vacuum in Sudan if the NCP implodes or falls. This has given the NCP some diplomatic space to 'tough it out' over Darfur. The international community's preoccupation with Darfur has deflected it from more robust support for implementation of the CPA, allowing the NCP to ignore the Abyei Protocol, imposing restrictions on the UNMIS force or violating the cease-fire by attacking Southern militias joining the SPLA. In the long run, compartmentalisation of the CPA and Darfur may turn out to have been unwise. If the international community fails to establish an implementing authority for a peace agreement in Darfur, just as it failed to do for the CPA, there will be little guarantee that any Darfur agreement will hold.

The challenge to external actors now is to see Sudan in the round, to recognise that separate regional grievances are part of a wider national problem, and to follow through on making peace take hold throughout the country.

Political Dysfunction in the Horn of Africa

Following a series of civil and international wars since the mid-1990s, the Horn of Africa has been relatively calm during 2005–06. The emphasis of the international community has been on attempts at gradual democratisation and institutional reconstruction aimed at curbing the spread of Islamist terrorism in the region. This tepid policy produced varied and not altogether successful results.

Somalia's elusive quest for government

In Somalia, after over a decade-and-a-half of warlord and clan rule and no national government, the Transitional Federal Government (TFG) was established in October 2004 by clan delegates who had been meeting at Mbagathi in Kenya over the preceding two years. General Abdullahi Yusuf Ahmed was picked as first president, with strong Ethiopian support. He is a veteran politician from the Majerteen clan who began his career organising a coup against President Mohammed Siad Barre in 1978; for many years he led an Ethiopia-based guerrilla movement against the dictator. Already president of the de facto independent entity of Puntland in the northeast, Yusuf has a forceful political style, backed by the willingness to use violence. In December 2004, he picked as his prime minister Ali Mohamed Gedi, a little-known Hawiye/Abgal technocrat with a reputation for honesty and efficiency.

Selection of a cabinet was a major hurdle, as it had to be done according to the pre-set 'four-and-a-half' formula, with an equal number of representatives for the four main clan families (Darod, Hawiye, Dir and Digil-Mirifle) and a half share for the smaller clans. This formula reflected neither the demographic nor political realities of the country. For example, the Darod make up 50% of the population, so it is their sub-clans and not their clans which are significant; Hawiye sub-clans – especially the Abgal and the Habr Gedir in Mogadishu – are bitterly opposed to each other; Dir clans live in breakaway Somaliland, which wants nothing to do with a 'Somalia' government. As a result, the TFG was more symbolic than real, and was in any case immediately beset by political problems, both internal and external. The president and prime minister were far from united, and Assembly Speaker Sharif Hassan Sheikh Aden soon set himself up as leader of the organised opposition to the president. Several TFG ministers, while refusing to resign from the cabinet, joined a rival quasi-governmental grouping, the so-called Somali Rehabilitation and Redemption Council (SRRC). Thus, from the outset, the TFG appeared so divided as to be impotent. Split between two different locations, Baidoa and Jowhar, the new government was not even able to safely enter Somalia's putative capital, Mogadishu, where the warlords of the SRRC still held sway. When Gedi tried to visit Mogadishu in November 2005, he was the object of an assassination attempt in which one of his bodyguards was killed.

The TFG sought to play up is its 'anti-terrorist' credentials. The United States has a substantial military presence in the Horn of Africa, both in Djibouti and in eastern Ethiopia, for purposes of anti-terrorist monitoring and operations. Although less alarmed about the prospect that Somalia could turn into a haven for Islamist terrorists than it was immediately after al-Qaeda and the Taliban were ousted from power in Afghanistan, Washington has not dismissed the possibility, and has consequently been willing to support those proclaiming their

Map 7.2 **Somalia**

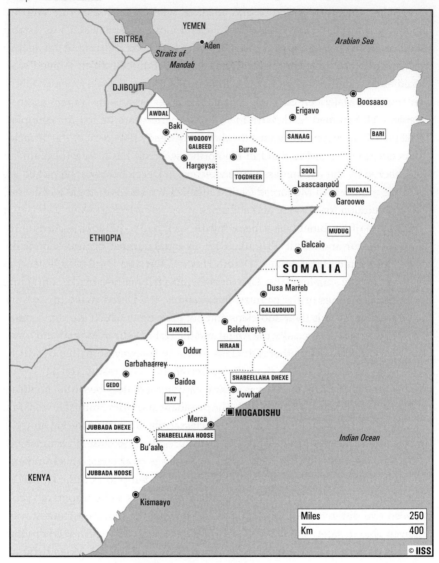

animosity towards terrorism or militancy. Yusuf is known as a strongly secular politician and so are many in his cabinet. Yet the TFG did not manage to capitalise on this potential asset. Part of the problem was Washington's chronic misperceptions of Somali politics and society.

American officials tended, for instance, to equate the so-called Islamic Courts movement with militant Islamist fundamentalism. In fact, the Islamic Courts movement involved a motley assortment of warlords, Muslim clerics and businessmen who have been attempting to marshal Islamic law to enforce contracts in a stateless society with no civil law infrastructure to speak of. When a number of alleged al-Qaeda operatives surfaced in Somalia in late 2005, the CIA sent five well-funded agents from Kenya to track them down and neutralise them. Instead of dealing with the TFG they chose to approach the SRRC, which was only too happy to help and immediately created a 'new' coalition under the name 'Coalition against Terror and for the Restoration of Peace'. The SRRC viewed the Islamic Courts movement with extreme suspicion because it feared the movement would ally with the TFG and provide a viable alternative to the SRRC's mercenary activities. The first move of the new CIA-sponsored organisation was to attack the Islamic Courts militias in February 2006, leading to successive bouts of violent fighting in Mogadishu that killed hundreds of civilians but failed to net any al-Qaeda militants. Moreover, the assault was perceived as anti-Islamic, and actually boosted the appeal of the small Somali radical Islamist movement led by Colonel Hassan Dawer Aweys, enabling it to side with the Islamic Courts militias and drape itself in the flag of anti-US Somali nationalism. In June 2006, the CIA move – which had attracted strong criticism from within the State Department – appeared to have backfired badly. The Islamic Courts militias took control of Mogadishu in an apparent victory over the warlords. The streets of the capital were reported to be unusually peaceful. Leaders of the movement sought to portray it as wanting 'a friendly relationship with the international community' in spite of the movement's reported adherence to sharia law. The TFG was reported to have welcomed the militias' victory and to be seeking talks with them.

The breakaway Republic of Somaliland, which has been independent de facto since May 1991, has kept aloof from the confusion and mayhem in the south. Grounded on a sensible foundation (the Borama *shir*, or constitutional assembly, of 1993), legitimised by a referendum in which 97% of the voters chose independence, and by several peaceful democratic legislative and presidential elections, Somaliland has escaped the fate of its southern neighbour. It is violently disliked by Somali nationalists, who consider it as a living insult to the pan-Somali vision. This, and the opposition of both the Arab League and the AU which fear that a 'contagion effect' of separatism would result if they were to recognise the breakaway state – has prevented Somaliland from receiving official international recognition. Although the AU's position seems to have softened of late, recognition still appears distant. In spite of several Islamist attempts at destabilisation, Somaliland's present prospects (including the next presidential election) are quite peaceful. But its economic life is dire and made worse by an almost complete absence of foreign aid, as well as by recurrent Saudi import bans on its only exportable commodity, cattle.

Ethiopia and Eritrea: failed normalisation

Since the end of the war between Ethiopia and Eritrea in 2000, the international community has taken a dual approach to the two countries. First, continued efforts have been made to implement border changes agreed by both parties during the 2000 Algiers cease-fire. The areas at issue are of no strategic or economic interest, but the two governments find it difficult to compromise, in spite of their shared roots in liberation fronts that fought together against the dictatorship of Colonel Mengistu Haile Mariam. Their leaders remain politically insecure, more sensitive to internal Tigrean criticism than to broad national concerns or international pressures. The result is an almost complete lack of flexibility. There has also been pressure for democratisation – though far more on Ethiopia than on Eritrea.

The end of hostilities in June 2000 was followed in September by UN Security Council Resolution 1320, which defined the mandate of the UN Mission in Ethiopia and Eritrea (UNMEE), outlined the creation of a 25-kilometre deep Temporary Safety Zone on the Eritrean side of the 1,800km border and made provision for a five-member Boundary Commission (EEBC). UNMEE comprised about 3,800 military personnel and about 200 observers, provided by 44 countries. The EEBC set to work in late 2000, using old colonial documents and 'applicable international law' rather than any measurements or information gathered on the ground. The EEBC's mandate did not allow it to revise existing borders even where they were disputed, but simply to arbitrate the contradictory claims of the parties. In April 2002, the EEBC awarded much of the disputed Zala Ambessa and Irob territories to Ethiopia, but the town of Badme to Eritrea. Since Badme had been administered by Ethiopia before the war and was one of the major battlefields during the conflict, this was a bitter pill for Addis Ababa to swallow. Given the delicate political position of the Ethiopian regime – accused by ultra nationalists of being pro-Eritrean – it was all the more difficult for Prime Minister Meles Zenawi to accept the judgment. For two years, Ethiopia refused to do so, but under international pressure Zenawi announced on 25 November 2004 that Ethiopia accepted the ruling 'in principle'. This, however, did not lead to action.

On 5 October 2005 the Eritrean government, suddenly and without warning, banned all flights by UNMEE helicopters in Eritrean airspace, causing the international mission to lose 50% of its border-monitoring capacity and rendering it unable to carry out its mandate. On 23 November 2005 the Security Council passed Resolution 1640, which noted 'with deep concern the high concentration of troops on both sides of the Temporary Security Zone', demanding that Eritrea lift the ban and that Ethiopia implement the EEBC's demarcation decisions. Eritrea's response was to ask personnel from 18 of the 44 UNMEE contributing countries to leave forthwith. The personnel expelled numbered 180 and the countries targeted were all North American or European. This prompted immediate concern about renewed war. However, hostilities did not resume and the border issues, as well as a long-standing dispute over access by land-locked Ethiopia to the sea, remain unresolved.

Within Ethiopia there was more palpable progress, but it was no less fraught. Despite intimidation and arrests during the pre-election period, the Ethiopian elections on 15 May 2005 were, according to the National Electoral Board, 'the first free and fair elections the country had ever known'. With 85% of the voting-age population on the electoral lists, turnout was very high. The elections were supervised by international monitors whose presence was greater in easily accessible urban areas than in distant rural regions, but even before the votes were counted, the government and the opposition started to make contradictory claims. When it became obvious that the regime's previous 'victories' of 1995 and 2000 were not going to be repeated, the situation became contentious.

In urban areas, where the counting was rapid, the opposition made big gains, carrying every city or large town, including all 23 Addis Ababa constituencies. Apart from Zenawi, every government minister running for a parliamentary seat was defeated. It looked as though the political landscape had changed: in 1995 the opposition had decided to boycott the polls and in 2000 it had had been allowed to 'win' a mere 12 constituencies. This was, of course, more a protest vote against a widely disliked regime than an affirmation for the opposition; the challenging parties had been organised only a few months before the polls, with largely ignored platforms. The government was shocked by its urban defeats and feared the worst, even though it had tipped the scales by not allowing any opposition candidates to run in Tigray (33 seats), the Afar region (eight seats) or the Somali region (31 seats) . The government then delayed proclaiming results, began to harass opposition MPs and voters, and started to tamper with ballots. The nine opposition parties (grouped in two coalitions) lodged 140 complaints with the Complaints Investigation Panels while the government coalition lodged 23. The panels rejected 96% of the opposition complaints and only 30% of the government's. As a result, 31 re-runs were held, most of them resulting in Ethiopian People's Revolutionary Democratic Front (EPRDF) governmental coalition victories; many were boycotted by the opposition parties. On 16 May, the opposition claimed to have won at least 185 seats while the EPRDF claimed over 300 seats, enough to give it a majority of the 547 constituencies.

As a result of these irregularities, it is not possible to say who won. The European Union Electoral Report, issued nine months after the vote, did not offer reliable figures. Whoever won, the margin appears to have been slim. The election was therefore a political defeat for the regime: despite having pre-secured 72 constituencies, and notwithstanding a recent military victory, it could not credibly point to an unequivocal popular mandate. This led to an overall loss of legitimacy. Demonstrations in July and November 2005 resulted in a number of deaths. The EU, for its part, suspended $375m of direct budgetary aid – a serious financial blow for the government – and demanded an open trial for 131 detained opposition leaders accused of high treason, which can carry the death penalty. However, the government postponed the trial indefinitely. Sporadic agitation has since developed in the provinces, where repressive measures continue to be used, particularly in the Oromiya region, where the government most fears an armed insurgency.

Little change likely

The major powers are likely to pursue a status-quo policy in the Horn. Although Ethiopia's government, for instance, appears increasingly repressive, Ethiopian cooperation with the United States in the 'war on terror' has yielded the Zenawi government $800m a year in aid from the Bush administration and international financial institutions. The United States will continue to maintain a 1,200-strong contingent of special-operations forces in Djibouti for deterrent purposes, to heighten regional awareness of threats and to facilitate a quick armed response to any emergent terrorist enclaves or activities. But it probably will not do much else, politically or militarily. France maintains a base with 2,850 troops in Djibouti.

Considerable lip-service has been paid to the heightened post-11 September need to save failed states like Somalia and improve poor governance in countries like Ethiopia to discourage popular discord that might lead to religious radicalism. However, the strategic preoccupations of major powers with problems such as Iraq, Iran and North Korea have distracted them from deep engagement with the problems of the Horn of Africa. Yet those problems have proved too profound for local actors to handle. Furthermore, if any regional concern is likely to attract substantial international attention, it is the Darfur crisis in Sudan, rather than the difficulties in Ethiopia, Eritrea and Somalia. The focal point for powerful external actors remains counter-terrorism rather than more ambitious tasks like conflict resolution, good governance and state-building. Terrorism has indeed gathered momentum in the Horn of Africa. The Ethiopian and Eritrean governments and the most powerful of the Somali clans, however decadent they may be politically, are basically aligned with the West on that score.

8 | Asia

While Asia's rising powers substantially deepened their engagement with the rest of the world over the past year, the region's many problems and tensions persisted. Many countries viewed China's rapid emergence with a blend of caution and self-interest, and Beijing adopted a similar stance towards the outside world. India and the United States moved forward in their quest for a strategic relationship. However, long-standing bilateral tensions among East Asian nations were much in evidence, and the impasse on North Korea's nuclear programme continued. In Afghanistan, an expanded NATO mission was under pressure from Taliban fighters. There was little progress in resolving the India–Pakistan dispute, and the conflict in Sri Lanka worsened. In Southeast Asia, there was significant progress in resolving the Aceh conflict in Indonesia, but Timor Leste slipped back into violence.

China: Rapid Emergence

China's foreign policy, presence and pertinence have all become more global. The tempo and breadth of its dealings with established and emerging centres of strategic gravity – the United States, Europe, Russia and India – have grown impressively. Contacts with neighbouring powers in Asia are, by and large, thickening; even where relations are politically indifferent (as with Japan) or militarily antagonistic (as with Taiwan), economic interests are proving highly magnetic. Beijing has cultivated regions and powers that lay outside its traditional diplomatic contemplations: in the Middle East, Latin America and Africa,

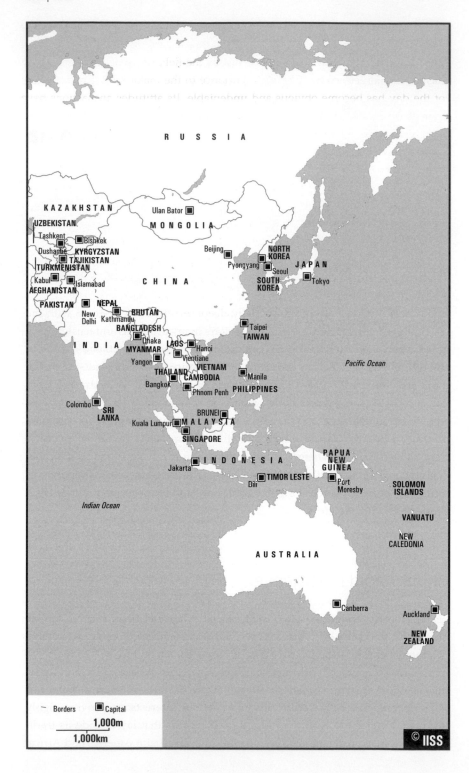

relationships underpinned by economic, political and security interests – albeit with the balance among these varying from case to case – are being formed and partnerships have been pronounced. Just as the field of its diplomatic activity has been enlarged, so too China's importance to the major strategic challenges of the day has become obvious and undeniable. Its attitudes and actions have a great – and, to some degree, decisive – bearing on whether the international community will be able satisfactorily to resolve the disputes arising from the nuclear-weapon aspirations of North Korea and Iran, or whether future problems of energy security can be adequately anticipated and addressed. The stability and governance of the international financial and trade regimes, as well as global environmental and health matters, are other, broader areas in which China's views and behaviour count for much.

So rapid has China's emergence been that the process has elicited a variety of responses. In one strand of thinking, China's foreign-policy extroversion is seen as functionally determined by its expanding international trade flows. This new strategic cosmopolitanism is regarded as somewhat paradoxical, in the sense that Beijing – historically and instinctively introspective – is hugely preoccupied by domestic political and social frailties that can, however, only be properly tackled by seeking out new markets and natural resources abroad. While this might bring China into association with other states whose internal and international behaviour is problematic, and while China may in pursuit of its national interests occasionally demonstrate rude indifference towards the priorities and values of other major powers, Beijing in essence hopes for a quiet strategic life – and, in due course, a modicum of respect as a generally responsible international power.

Another strand of thought, however, argues that a more troublesome pattern is discernible in China's outreach. Here, Beijing is seen as seated in the cockpit of a collection of illiberal states: working to expand a zone of political influence and developing exclusionary policies towards other powers; actively resisting international democratic change and fostering peculiarly cordial ties with autocratic regimes responsible for egregious human-rights violations; building commercial and aid relationships with developing countries that pay little heed to, or undermine, governance and conditionality strategies carefully crafted by international agencies and Western powers; proving tolerant towards Iran and North Korea in their nuclear antics; and all the while developing its military capabilities at great expense and in circumstances of calculated opacity.

The debate between these two narratives – one positing a China that is essentially not disruptive, the other arguing the opposite – has yet to be resolved; there is, in fact, enough ambiguity in China's foreign policy and behaviour to provide an arguable evidential basis for either perspective. It is unsurprising, then, that many countries have, to varying degrees, prudentially responded to

China's rise by trying to incorporate, or at least remain sensitive to, both messages. Encapsulated in the term 'hedged integration', this posture acknowledges the desirability of engaging China in the interests of economic benefit and in the hope that China will be become attuned to the norms and conventions of the international community. At the same time, however, it calls for vigilance and regard to the possibility of alternative, less benign outcomes, and recognises that China's ultimate strategic designs and trajectory, to the extent that they are not still evolving, are unknown. The challenge for countries that choose this approach is how most efficiently to balance hedge and integration: too explicit a hedge would preclude broad integration; too weak a hedge would leave only unconditional engagement. The challenge for China is to pursue its perceived national interests while minimising hedging activity directed against it.

It seems reasonable to assume that these strategic calibrations will take years to play out, barring more immediate crises and contingencies that could expose stark divisions between China and other powers, and that might lead to overt confrontation. Developments in China's immediate Asian vicinity, where its national-security interests are most deeply engaged, are crucial in this regard. In the last year, there was much to unsettle China, but a number of compensating diplomatic advances were also recorded. Relations with the United States have, notwithstanding the increase in official contacts at all levels, proved generally troublesome and subject to many points of disagreement. The North Korean nuclear dispute remained unresolved and apparently irresolvable under the current dispensation. American irritation at China's reluctance to pursue a more forceful diplomatic approach towards Pyongyang in view of its continuing intransigence and provocations provided a source of bilateral friction, but in general terms China could through much of the year feel satisfied that tensions on the peninsula were vaguely contained and that its attitude was shared by other participants in the Six-Party Talks, notably South Korea (whose alliance with the United States remained somewhat fraught). Beijing observed with some discomfort the closer alignment of India and the United States. China's relations with Japan worsened steadily throughout the year, with historical and maritime disputes typically to the fore and official bilateral dialogue faltering. The deepening of defence ties between Japan and the United States also continued to fuel broader, long-held Chinese concerns about a prospective 'strategic encirclement'. China sought some relief and to augment its own strategic heft by cementing its defence ties with Russia, with which it mounted an ambitious military exercise that seemed designed to advertise Chinese capabilities. Beijing's political reach and influence in Central Asia continued to expand in the last year, and it attempted, with varying degrees of success, to build on progress in fashioning sound working relations with the member states and institution of the Association of Southeast Asian Nations (ASEAN). Perhaps most importantly as far as Beijing was concerned, there were grounds for satisfaction with the course of developments in Taiwan. Here, its policy of isolating and sitting out the government of President Chen Shui-bian, who at the very least favours a distinct international identity for the island, while actively engaging his friendlier domestic political opponents and dangling economic temptations before the island's business community, seemed to have the desired effect of unsettling Chen – although his attempts to wrest back the political initiative produced moments of alarm in Beijing.

Further afield, China in the last year worked with some success to invest its still-maturing relationships in the Middle East, Africa and Latin America with greater strategic content. Relations with the European Union – formally a 'strategic partner' – remained generally sound but more sober in tone than in previous years, as member states and EU institutions reflected at greater length than they have before on the challenges and opportunities posed by China's emergence.

Relations with the United States
While China has taken great care to diversify its portfolio of diplomatic relationships, the United States remains uniquely important to Beijing. That China has assumed unprecedented importance in US strategic calculations also seems clear, albeit not for entirely encouraging reasons. It is now widely recognised that the framework of Sino-American relations that came into being following the 11 September 2001 terrorist attacks on the United States has dissolved. In this framework, the United States and China, having identified themselves as collaborators in the 'war on terror' – albeit informal and rather episodic ones – found the occasion to set aside the disputes that had preoccupied them to a worrying extent in the months preceding the attacks, and to focus energies on other agendas (counter-terrorism, Afghanistan and then Iraq for Washington; domestic developments for Beijing) rather than on each other. The approach combined artificial stimulants and suppressants: rhetoric about the supposed health of the bilateral relationship reached improbable heights, while long-standing disagreements were wilfully downplayed.

This arrangement was mutually convenient but not likely to last. On the one hand, Chinese assessments of the evolving situation grew rather bleak. Beijing objected to what it saw as the increasing militarisation of US foreign policy, the Bush administration's apparent attachment to pre-emption and regime change, and its seeming lack of tolerance for ambiguous threats – all of which, in Beijing's view, predisposed Washington to rash and geopolitically unsettling action. Beijing worried about the regionally destabilising consequences of the Iraq intervention, not least because of potential effects on energy markets and because of the reaction the invasion seemed to have elicited from Iran. It was further troubled by the Bush administration's growing determination to advance democracy wherever it could and by many means. China disapproved of American efforts to enhance and adjust its military alliances in Northeast Asia, including the giving of encouragement to South Korea and in particular Japan in their efforts to elaborate a more forward-leaning and internationally activist defence posture that featured support of US operations in Afghanistan and Iraq. China also worried about a stronger US military presence in both Southeast and Central Asia.

On the other hand, many strategists in the United States came to the view that Beijing had sensed a certain moment of geopolitical opportunity in America's preoccupation with Iraq and the wider Middle East. In this view, Beijing was seeking to exploit a generalised decline in US international standing and fill diplomatic vacuums in Asia, Europe and elsewhere. With the United States unable to fully concentrate on the quarrel over North Korea's nuclear activities, and having become reliant on China's mediation there, it seemed to many in Washington that Beijing was working very tightly to its own interests in the Six-Party Talks rather than responding to the wishes of the United States. Indications that China's exertions in building up its military were making good progress, and the sense that Beijing was recording diplomatic advances across the board at some expense to the United States, meshed with concerns about Chinese trade practices to generally sour the American mood.

Although the past year produced many areas of dispute and sources of tension, there remained more than enough mutual interest in the relationship to make any significant breakdown appear unlikely. Acrimony over economic issues did, however, require especially sensitive handling. In response to congressional charges that China was manipulating its currency for mercantilist reasons, and in view of pressure from the Bush administration for China to take steps that would ostensibly help to correct America's ballooning bilateral trade deficit, the People's Bank of China on 21 July allowed, in a policy departure, the renminbi to appreciate by around 2%. It also announced that henceforth the renminbi would be pegged to a basket of currencies, not just the dollar, and would be permitted to trade in a marginally wider fluctuation band. Impatience for a much higher revaluation led to continuing threats from sections of Congress to impose a blanket 27.5% tariff on Chinese goods imports, an eventuality that has been avoided. Just as contentious was the $18.5 billion bid by the state-linked China National Offshore Oil Corporation (CNOOC) to acquire Unocal Corporation; the bid was withdrawn in August 2005 following a not particularly edifying debate in the United States concerning the commercial and strategic wisdom of Chinese ownership of American corporations.

An impressive amount of diplomatic energy has thus been required to keep the relationship roughly in balance. In July 2005, US Secretary of State Condoleezza Rice travelled to Beijing for consultations as part of a wider Asian tour. Bush and Chinese President Hu Jintao were both present at the July 2005 Gleneagles Summit of the G8. Hu's scheduled visit to the United States – which was to have been the first since his assumption of all of the key state, party and military offices in China – had to be rescheduled in early September 2005 as Bush was forced to focus on the aftermath of Hurricane Katrina, but the two leaders were able to meet later that month at the UN General Assembly in New York. Directly after attending the Asia Pacific Economic Cooperation (APEC) leaders' summit in Busan, South Korea, Bush and Hu met again in Beijing in late November 2005. Hu's postponed trip to the United States eventually took place in early April 2006.

Such presidential exchanges have proved publicly cordial but, from a policy perspective, somewhat banal. Few of the meetings resulted in notable initiatives. Instead, they served instead as occasions on which established agenda items could again be rehearsed – somewhat routinely, and not to any particular effect. Indeed, China's apparent desire for meetings that were more ceremonial than substantive revealed itself in the months leading up to Hu Jintao's April 2006 visit, as American and Chinese diplomats became increasingly bogged down in circular discussions about presentational and procedural details. Beijing, apparently preoccupied by the domestic political requirement for Hu to be received with maximum pomp and dignity, pushed hard for the trip to be formally designated a 'state visit'. This rubbed up against Washington's stated preference for a more business-like encounter. Agreement could not be reached and the two powers ultimately chose their own designations. The American suggestion that Hu be received by Bush at his Crawford, Texas, ranch – typically taken by world leaders as signalling political confidence and familial intimacy – was rebuffed by an apparently puzzled Beijing on grounds of its unusual informality. In view of this attention to *amour propre* it was therefore somewhat ironic that the summit came to be overshadowed by a variety of indignities and faux pas – Hu being formally introduced as the president of the Republic of China (the official designation for Taiwan), Bush at one point tugging somewhat too forcefully at the elbow of a surprised Hu, and a known Falun Gong protester by-passing security arrangements to noisily disturb the two presidents' press event.

In truth, much in the way of serious bilateral diplomatic engagement and thinking took place at a more functional level during the last year. On the American side, then-Deputy Secretary of State Robert Zoellick proved particularly active in sustaining a 'Senior Dialogue' with his Chinese counterparts, especially Executive Vice Foreign Minister Dai Bingguo. This dialogue was launched in China in August 2005 with the aim of reviewing a broad range of international issues, and a second meeting took place in Washington in December that year. While tightening his grip on the China portfolio with the strong backing of Rice, Zoellick also took the lead in publicly articulating a framework for US policy towards Beijing. Speaking on 21 September 2005 to the National Committee on US–China Relations in New York, he noted that China had now achieved membership of the international system but had yet to emerge as a fully 'responsible stakeholder' in it. He criticised China's ties to 'troublesome states' such as Sudan, its military modernisation, 'signs of mercantilism' in its economic policy, its abuse of intellectual property rights, and a seeming wish to 'lock up' global energy supplies. He identified the scope for China to do more to help resolve the North Korean and Iranian nuclear disputes. US policy, he said, would be directed at working cooperatively with China to change the terms of trade of its engagement with the international system. The theme of encouraging China to become a 'responsible stakeholder' has become a mantra in US pronouncements on China. It featured again in the US National Security Strategy published by the White House on 16 March 2006.

Beijing no doubt rejects the premises of Zoellick's analysis, to the extent that it is understood (sinologues point to difficulties in translating 'responsible stakeholder'). But, perhaps because it seems rhetorically milder than previous American characterisations of China as a 'strategic competitor', Beijing has chosen not to issue public criticisms. Indeed, other recent US official pronouncements on China have been rougher. The release of the National Security Strategy was preceded on 6 February by the Pentagon's publication of the 2006 Quadrennial Defense Review (QDR), which cited China as a power that stood at a 'strategic cross-roads', and discussed the need for the United States to take steps to 'shape' China's choices. Perhaps understandably in view of its departmental provenance, the QDR pays more attention to the 'hedge' than the 'integration' aspects of US policy. It states that 'China has the greatest potential to compete militarily with the United States and field disruptive military technologies that could over time offset traditional US military advantages'. It calls among other things for a strengthening and broadening of US military capabilities in Asia and the adjustment of its alliances – with South Korea, Japan, Australia and others – to reflect uncertainties about China's future behaviour. From a planning perspective, the QDR also underlines the need for the United States to preserve a balance between capabilities that allow it to tackle the challenges of 'irregular' warfare of the kind being pursued in Iraq and those capabilities required to deal with more traditional, conventional inter-state contingencies.

Indeed, American concerns about China's military modernisation were voiced with increasing force and frequency in the last year. Speaking at the 4th annual IISS Asia Security Summit, the 'Shangri-La Dialogue', in June 2005, US Secretary of Defense Donald Rumsfeld berated the People's Liberation Army (PLA) for the lack of transparency surrounding its efforts to develop military capabilities, and for concealing the full extent of its defence expenditure. He implied that China's exertions were inconsistent with its strategic circumstances and credible security concerns. These themes were developed more fully in the Pentagon's 2005 'Report to Congress on the Military Power of the People's Republic of China'. Interagency differences had contributed to a delay by some months in the release of this document, as National Security Council and State Department officials apparently sought to caveat and qualify the Pentagon's initially bleak – and, by some accounts, determinist – assessment of the implications of China's rise and the resultant scope for Sino-American military contingencies, especially as regards Taiwan. Whatever the adjustments, the unclassified version of the report still noted China's apparent penchant for 'strategic deception', described its military modernisation as undermining the delicate status quo in the Taiwan Strait, discerned increasing efforts by China to acquire anti-access and area-denial capabilities aimed at the United States, and concluded that China was in fact pursuing military means 'that go beyond [the requirements of] a Taiwan scenario'. Regional military balances, the report argued, had been put at risk by China's activities, which now could potentially pose 'a credible threat to modern militaries operating in the region'. Such views were reinforced by the well-publicised comments on 15 July 2005 of Major General Zhu Chenghu, the dean of China's National Defence University. Zhu was reported to have said that in the event that the United States used precision-guided munitions and missiles in a contingency with China, 'war logic' would dictate that China would have to respond with nuclear weapons. Zhu was quick to underline the private nature of his views, which were disowned by Chinese officials, but the remarks were nevertheless studied with concern by US officials. They were cited in the Pentagon's 2006 report to Congress, published in May, in the context of a discussion of whether China might be moving away from a doctrinal nuclear posture of 'no first use' towards a more ambiguous stance intended – in tandem with a reported programme of vigorous technical modernisation – to strengthen the credibility and survivability of its deterrent. It was significant, therefore, that Bush and Hu were reported to have agreed in April 2006 to commence a bilateral nuclear dialogue in which concerns of this kind could be addressed. On matters of conventional forces, meanwhile, the Pentagon report again emphasised that China was rapidly developing and procuring capabilities – ballistic and cruise missiles, combat aircraft, surface combatants and modern submarines – that could be used in wider regional contingencies 'such as conflicts over resources or territory'. Such statements have been rebuffed by China, which customarily draws attention to the comparative modesty of its defence capabilities and outlays as against those of the United States.

In these circumstances, it was somewhat reassuring that exchanges between Chinese and American defence leaders were stepped up in the last year. In July 2005, Admiral William Fallon, the commander of the US Pacific Command, voiced his desire for closer military contacts with the PLA, and in September 2005 he visited China's Guangzhou Military Region. On 18–20 October, Rumsfeld made his first visit to China since assuming his post, holding talks with Hu and Chinese Defence Minister General Cao Gangchuan, and making an unprecedented visit to facilities of the 2nd Artillery (China's strategic rocket forces). Regular US–China

Defense Consultative Talks also proceeded. In January 2006, Cao noted that China was ready to work towards greater contacts between Chinese and American militaries, a theme that was taken up again during Fallon's visit to China in May 2006. At that time, press reports suggested that Beijing and Washington were considering setting up a 'hotline', although some US defence officials privately expressed doubts about what this would mean in practical terms. While bilateral defence exchanges of this kind constitute a useful channel of communication, and while there now seems to be an appetite to expand their scope on both sides, it is far from apparent that a sufficient degree of confidence has been established to allow for detailed, technical discussions of military postures and plans. Predictably, mutual suspicions about intentions towards Taiwan are at the root of this.

Taiwan's trajectory

Since spring 2005, when Beijing decided to receive sequentially Lien Chan and James Soong – the leaders, respectively, of Taiwan's main opposition Kuomintang (KMT) and People First Party (PFP) – a clear Chinese strategy towards the island has become apparent. This approach is still heavily skewed towards military deterrence as a means of averting any formal declaration of independence by Taipei, but it now also entails a much more overt outreach to political forces on Taiwan that are wary of, or directly opposed to, Taiwan President Chen Shui-bian's efforts to establish a distinct identity for the island (albeit one that stops short, for the time being at least, of formal independence). Economic interests animated by the need to take advantage of China's boom have also been engaged, with trade and investment concessions being extensively offered by Beijing. These have been targeted with some precision at Chen's own political constituencies. In this approach, Chen's administration is to be isolated and ignored, and represented as the only barrier to political reconciliation and healthier economic exchanges between Taipei and Beijing. The 2008 presidential elections, China hopes, will bring the defeat of Chen's Democratic Progressive Party (DPP). To the extent that this approach has indeed both irritated Chen and bolstered his opponents, China has had cause for some satisfaction.

Events in Taiwan seemed, to Beijing's mind at least, to be developing further to China's advantage with the election on 16 July 2005 of Taipei Mayor Ma Ying-jeou as the new head of the KMT. Indeed, his election elicited a message of congratulation from Hu. Ma, widely seen as an attractive candidate for the 2008 presidential elections, has been quick to call for reconciliation between China and Taiwan and the establishment of direct transport links through which trade would be enlivened. While he has not articulated a precise roadmap for how reconciliation might be achieved, nor detailed exactly what manner of negotiations with Beijing he might be willing to enter into, the tonal shift has been marked: Ma has underlined the importance of arriving at a modus vivendi with China by avoiding unilateral or provocative steps that would unsettle the status quo. He has stressed that the KMT remains wedded to eventual reunification with China, albeit to no specific timetable and with due regard to be given to the wishes of the people of Taiwan. Beijing has been disconcerted by the latter qualification, to the extent that such wishes might run counter to the goal of reunification. Still, it has welcomed his endorsement of the awkwardly phrased 'four noes and one without' commitments that Chen elaborated at the start of his administration, but with which he has appeared to become much less comfortable as his term has progressed – that is, no declaration of independence; no change to Taiwan's formal designation of the Republic of China; no amendments to the constitution that imply statehood; no referendums on unification or independence; and no abolition of the National Unification Council or the National Unification guidelines. To these, Ma has added his 'five do's', which are to involve pushing for cross-Strait dialogue, setting out a framework for engagement, boosting economic ties, talking with Beijing about Taiwan's entry into international bodies, and promoting cultural and economic exchanges.

Faced with a more coherent Chinese strategy and a revitalised domestic political opposition, and with his DPP having suffered a setback in the December 2005 local elections, Chen's response was to attempt to seize back the initiative and to galvanise his core supporters. He portrayed the KMT and its leader Ma as instruments of Beijing's will who risked sacrificing Taiwan's interests in a foolhardy rush to embrace China. In a bid to underline this message of Chinese hostility and also to appeal to American sensibilities, he committed his administration to raising defence spending to 3% of GDP. Most significantly, however, on 29 January 2006 he announced his intention to abolish the National Unification Council – which is notionally charged with promoting unification but has been dormant under Chen – and associated National Unification guidelines. This was intended as a clear signal to Beijing and Chen's grassroots supporters that there was no requirement for these as Taiwan carved out a status separate from China. Because this step was in direct contravention to earlier commitments given to Beijing – and, by extension, to Washington – the reaction in both capitals was predictably severe. The matter became the subject of secret but reported discussions: Dennis Wilder, the acting senior director for Asia at the US National Security Council, flew with the State Department's Clifford Hart to Taiwan on 12 February to urge Chen to change course. In a compromise that embodied all the semantic nuances common to the lexicon of cross-Strait diplomacy, Chen on 27 February announced that the National Unification Council and the guidelines had 'ceased to function' – a formulation that did not preclude their continuing existence.

Although Rice noted in March 2006 that Chen's behaviour had been 'problematic', the Bush administration has not entirely allowed itself to be persuaded by Beijing that Chen is the lone 'troublemaker'. Washington has been critical of Beijing's refusal to talk directly to Chen, and any irritation with the Taiwanese leader has not been so great as to prevent Bush from stressing Chen's legitimacy as a democratically elected interlocutor (during a November 2005 speech in Tokyo, Bush heaped voluble praise on Taiwan's democracy and held it up as a model for China). Yet it is also true that Washington could live with a Taiwanese leader less inclined to embark on diplomatic white-knuckle rides. This sense was reflected in the cordial welcome extended to Ma on his visit to Washington in late March, when he met with, among others, Zoellick and Deputy National Security Adviser J.D. Crouch; Ma deftly used these occasions to broadcast soothing noises. This stood in marked contrast to Washington's refusal to grant Chen the transit rights he sought while en route to Latin America; instead of a stopover in New York, he was offered one in Alaska.

Chen's political embarrassments had deepened severely by late June: a scandal surrounding alleged financial improprieties by Chen's wife and son produced measures of some desperation by Chen to secure his political survival, including the devolution of some powers onto his respected prime minister and an extensive and placatory reshuffle of senior advisers. The KMT, meanwhile, mobilised to push through a parliamentary resolution to remove Chen amid plummeting poll ratings and public protests. Although the resolution failed to secure the required two-thirds majority support on 27 June, the imbroglio means that Chen's ability to carry forward anything other than a debilitated lame-duck administration is highly circumscribed.

North Korean impasse

The North Korean nuclear dispute remains the second major source of instability on China's periphery, and Beijing defines its national interest in commensurately precise terms. Its strong preference is for a North Korea without a nuclear capability. This is not least because of the famous unpredictability and acute sense of threat that Pyongyang so worryingly combines. It is also because North Korea's activities provide continuing grounds for a US regional military presence, of which China generally disapproves, as well as a rationale for Japan to develop defence doctrines and capabilities that, in Beijing's reasoning, might as much be turned on China as on North Korea one day. Yet China sees greater risks in approaching the nuclear dispute in ways that might destabilise, perhaps fatally, the North Korean regime. Its strategy is to avoid such a collapse, and it is willing to provide sufficient assistance to Pyongyang to ensure this. Beijing has also, though without notable success, encouraged a process of economic reform within North Korea that would reduce the precariousness of its current circumstances and future prospects. Diplomatically, Beijing's objective is to find ways of fending off coercive measures by the United States, while making certain that North Korea does not behave in ways that would invite a forceful US response or undermine the case for engagement of Pyongyang. The Six-Party Talks, convened by Beijing, are the process through which these goals are pursued. They are seen as more than worth sustaining, even in the absence of any likelihood of substantive progress. Indeed, although China has invested considerable energies into the talks over the last year, principally in trying to keep Pyongyang at the negotiating table, there has been little to show for the effort.

Interactions between Pyongyang and Beijing have been conducted frequently and at a senior level. Following trilateral talks in Beijing on 8 July 2005 that included US Assistant Secretary of State for East Asian and Pacific Affairs Christopher Hill and his North Korean counterpart Kim Gye Gwan, Chinese State Councillor Tang Jiaxuan travelled to Pyongyang on 12–14 July, where he met North Korean leader Kim Jong Il. This helped to pave the way for the fourth round of Six-Party Talks to commence on 20 July. It proved to be a session of unprecedented length, breaking up only on 7 August after China had failed to gain agreement on four separate drafts of a joint statement of principles that would provide a framework for future discussions. Wu Dawei, the Chinese vice foreign minister for Asia and head of the Chinese delegation to the talks, then travelled to Pyongyang on 27–29 August to urge on North Korean Foreign Minister Paek Nam Sun a resumption of talks. The delegations reconvened on 13 September, and ultimately produced a Joint Statement on 19 September. Its heralding as a major breakthrough proved highly premature (see Korea section, pp. 289–304). A masterpiece of diplomatic drafting, the document was faulty as a work of diplomacy. It quickly became apparent that the Joint Statement had been acceptable to all only because it could be interpreted by each as preserving positions that were, in fact, mutually contradictory. On 20 September, North Korea in essence disavowed the joint statement as interpreted by the United States.

There followed further efforts to draw Pyongyang back to the table, including a visit on 8–10 October by Chinese Vice Premier Wu Yi to Pyongyang, where she met with Kim Jong Il and celebrated – presumably through somewhat clenched teeth – the 60th anniversary of the ruling Korean Workers Party. The ostensible cordiality of official relations was underlined in a telegram sent to Kim by Hu, published by Pyongyang on 15 October. Two weeks later, on 28–30 October, Hu travelled to Pyongyang, where he was received with antique totalitarian paraphernalia and ceremony. Although Hu's visit produced no breakthroughs – in retrospect, it seems unlikely that this had been the purpose, which was probably more to comfort than to cajole Pyongyang – it did prove possible to convene a fifth round of Six-Party Talks on 9–11 November. No headway was made, however, and by mid-December Pyongyang announced that it was indefinitely suspending its participation in the talks. It did so in protest at a number of financial sanctions imposed by the United States on the basis of Pyongyang's extensive involvement in currency counterfeiting and other illicit activities. From China's perspective, the financial sanctions were ill advised. Beijing's concern about their impact on the stability of North Korea, and their potential to encourage retaliatory sabre-rattling by Pyongyang, was shared in Seoul. Indeed, the sense of a gradual alignment of priorities and preferences on North Korea policy between Seoul and Beijing, as against those of the United States and to some extent Japan, has become increasingly concrete over the last year. Hu's state visit to Seoul in mid-November 2005 provided an opportunity for consultations on this basis, and it again underlined the deftness with which China has been able to extend its influence in both Korean capitals.

Even as it has applied financial sanctions, the US government has looked carefully for signs that China and South Korea might be forthcoming with compensating forms of largesse that eased the effect of those measures on Pyongyang. Certainly, Beijing's contacts with North Korea have been stepped up in recent months. On 10–18 January 2006, Kim Jong Il made a secret visit – or at least, one that according to the established pattern was only formally acknowledged once it had concluded – to Beijing and Southern China, where he was able to inspect the benefits of the economic reforms that the Chinese government has urged him to emulate. During Kim's visit, Chinese negotiator Wu Dawei was dispatched to Pyongyang for further talks with his counterpart. This was followed on 18 January by a trilateral meeting in Beijing of the American, Chinese and North Korean heads of delegation to the Six-Party Talks. However, it proved impossible to agree a resumption of those talks. There followed a lull punctuated by North Korean objections to the critical terms in which it was described in the February and March 2006 releases of the US QDR and National Security Strategy, respectively. However, on 8 March, Li Gun, the deputy head of the North Korean delegation to the Six-Party Talks, came to New York to be briefed by US Treasury officials on the financial measures imposed by Washington. Although this was generally taken as an encouraging development, the talks proved unsatisfactory: the North Korean side approached them as an opportunity to negotiate, whereas American officials stressed the mandatory nature of the actions they had taken under US law. Presumably as an act of reassurance by Beijing, Cao in early April travelled to Pyongyang for leadership meetings that had no noticeable outcome. Indications in May of activity at the test site for North Korea's *Taepo-dong* missile were widely taken as reflecting increasing North Korean irritation and a desire to remind the outside world of Pyongyang's disruptive potential.

Differences between China and the United States over how to proceed towards North Korea seemed likely to increase irrespective of whether Pyongyang ultimately decided to test-launch its intercontinental ballistic missile as it attempted unsuccessfully to do on 5 July 2006. Further signs of intransigence or provocative behaviour by Pyongyang will presumably generate calls by Washington for Beijing to apply pressure on North Korea; Beijing's reply, and that of Seoul, might then be that it is US pressure on Pyongyang that is preventing a resumption of the Six-Party Talks. Washington, in turn, will argue that the talks are of little value if North Korea is not made to approach them in a spirit of compromise. At root, Washington and Pyongyang are each convinced of the hostility and insincerity of the other, and the basis for an agreement between them does not seem to be present. At the same time, however, both must for their own tactical reasons continue to posture and appeal to other participants in the Six-Party Talks, and this fact alone might augur for further rounds. China will continue to be stuck uncomfortably in the middle, but this is the position that it has chosen for itself.

Elsewhere in Asia ... and beyond

If the North Korean nuclear dispute settled into a more fractious stalemate over the last year, China's dealings with Japan were more definitely set on a downward trend. It is the central paradox of Sino-Japanese relations that increasingly vibrant economic exchanges go hand-in-hand with a growing capacity for suspicion, rancour and argument. The most immediate and sensitive source of grievance has been Prime Minister Junichiro Koizumi's persistent visits to the Yasukuni shrine, which contains among others the remains of 14 class-A war criminals. On 17 October 2005, Koizumi made his fifth visit to the shrine in the face of shrill protests from Beijing, which the following day announced that an all-too-rare visit to Japan by Foreign Minister Li Zhaoxing, scheduled for the following week, would be cancelled in protest. Indeed, the almost complete absence of sustained, high-level political dialogue between the leaders of two of Asia's leading powers has become as glaring as it is disconcerting. The grievances are not all on the Chinese side: many in Japan regard Beijing's obsessive attention to Koizumi's visits as indicative of the same uncouth nationalism and anti-Japanese sentiment that marked protests held, with the initial acquiescence of the Chinese authorities, against Tokyo's bid for a permanent seat on the United Nations Security Council. There is a general sense in Tokyo that China's leadership exploits anti-Japanese feeling to confirm its own domestic legitimacy, and it is not understood how speeches of the kind given by Hu on 3 September 2005 to celebrate China's victory in the last century over Japanese aggression and fascism helps to draw the two powers closer together now. A suspicion has also developed that constant reference to Japan's past misdeeds is intended for regional as much as domestic consumption. It is seen as a device intended to counter and delegitimate Japan's wish to play a greater role in the provision of regional and international security.

Issues of history and nationalism also vitally infuse the running dispute between China and Japan regarding disputed maritime boundaries in the East China Sea and the associated issue of resource-exploration rights. Both countries have, over the last year, been to some extent probing the boundaries – even dispatching naval forces – and both have been capable of what the other side sees as unilateral action in pursuit of their claims (including pipe-laying and surveys in the case of China, and formulation of legislation governing exploration in the case of Japan). Dialogue on these issues was carried out over the last year, but a compromise agreement has proved elusive.

For China, apprehension about the evolution of a more extrovert and forward-leaning Japanese defence and foreign-policy posture, largely encouraged by the United States, is a broad contextual concern. Primarily at issue is what this might imply for Tokyo's prospective involvement in any contingency over Taiwan, particularly in view of a formal pronouncement by Japan and the United States that developments between China and Taiwan impinge on their national interests. China has in this regard also monitored closely the trilateral exchanges convened in the last year among the United States, Japan and Australia. Such a meeting in Tokyo on 24 October 2005 had as its ostensible focus developments in Iraq, Afghanistan and North Korea; a second meeting in Australia on 18 March was understood to have concentrated largely on matters regarding China.

Japan has been careful to characterise recent alterations in its posture as inspired by the 'war on terror' – Japan has ground troops in Iraq involved in reconstruction activities, and has maritime forces in South Asia in support of coalition forces in Afghanistan – and North Korea, but it is clear that China's military build-up is a consideration that looms large. It underlies much of the attractiveness to Japan of the development of ballistic missile defences; in October 2005, Tokyo and Washington agreed to strengthen cooperation towards the 'development stage' in 2006.

It is unclear whether Koizumi's planned departure from office in September 2006 will produce a lasting thaw in bilateral relations. This will depend on whether his successor discontinues visits to the Yasukuni shrine. There will be temptations to do so in the interests of reversing the precipitous deterioration in relations; influential power-brokers within the ruling Liberal Democratic Party, like former premier Yoshiro Mori, have urged this course. But there might also be domestic political risks in appearing to make too quick and large a concession to China. Chief Cabinet Secretary Shinzo Abe, who as of May 2006 was seen as the front-runner to replace Koizumi, and who is generally antipathetic towards China, stated on 29 May that it was his intention to continue to visit the Yasukuni shrine. More broadly, Abe has argued that Japan's foreign policy should prioritise strategic dialogues with the democratic powers of the United States, India and Australia, in the expectation that this will give Tokyo greater leverage in its dealings with China.

Such potential geopolitical alignments have been sensed by China for some years, and it has taken steps to prevent constellations of this kind from coming into being. Its engagement of India in recent years has been particularly notable in this regard. Traditionally, Chinese attitudes towards India were somewhat remote and, as seen from Delhi, condescending. An intended function of China's support for Pakistan was the de facto confinement of India in strategic affairs to the sub-continent. However, new thinking in Beijing has been prompted by India's emergence in 1998 as a declared nuclear power (and one that voiced concerns about China as a motivation for conducting its nuclear tests), its increasing appetite for influence in East Asia and beyond, its importance to energy security, and, most notably, its stunning rapprochement with the United States and then Japan. A particular concern was whether, as many in Washington speculated and hoped, India might under American tutelage emerge as a counterweight to China. Sensing such apprehensions, Delhi was quick to exploit China's desire for a strategic dialogue, through which it has been possible to resolve some of the long-standing disputes over territory and sovereignty: India now recognises Chinese sovereignty over Tibet, and China recognises Indian sovereignty over the former princely state of Sikkim. However, neither Delhi nor Beijing have set aside suspicions of each other. Many in India's foreign policy establishment are concerned by China's military build-up, and there is a sense that China is pursuing a policy of 'strategic encirclement' through its links to Pakistan to the west, Bangladesh and Myanmar to the east, and, increasingly, the Himalayan states to the north. Beijing, for its part, senses a continuing policy by India of excluding China from South Asia.

Beijing might have taken some reassurance from its increasingly busy bilateral contacts with Delhi, which suggested a high degree of policy independence from the United States. Yet any such sense will have been dented by the proposal for civilian nuclear energy cooperation between the United States and India announced on 18 July 2005 by Bush and Prime Minister Manmohan Singh – subject to the agreement of the US Congress, Indian parliament and members of the 44-strong Nuclear Suppliers Group (NSG), and in return for India's commitment to separate its military and civilian nuclear facilities and put the latter under International Atomic Energy Agency (IAEA) safeguards. The agreement was received in Beijing as consistent with the Bush administration's desire to facilitate India's rise as a great power at the implicit expense of China. Such official views were not publicly advertised; like other governments around the world, Beijing confined itself to criticising the agreement on the grounds that it undermined the international non-proliferation regime and robbed the United States of much credibility in its attempts to persuade North Korea and Iran to relinquish their nuclear programmes. Beijing was presumably discomfited by being torn between its fundamental objections to the agreement on the one hand, and its desire not to antagonise India on the other. Speculation thus developed that Beijing would acquiesce to the deal within the NSG if that body were also to grant exemption from full-scope safeguards standards to Chinese nuclear cooperation with Pakistan.

By and large, Chinese concerns about India's emergence as an American bulwark seem overdone. India has a strong sense of its particular national interests, and has traditionally exhibited a disinclination to be used in an instrumental manner by other powers. Yet it seems safe to assume that, for their own reasons, China and India will continue to regard each other with some caution.

A notable feature of China's diplomacy in Southeast Asia over the course of the last year, outside of customary economic and other dialogues, has been the emphasis placed on improving bilateral defence ties. Thailand, which is designated a Major Non-NATO Ally of the United States, has been a particular target of Chinese overtures. In July 2005, Cao underlined that the PLA hoped for closer links to the Thai armed forces. The theme was taken up by General Xu Caihou, vice-chairman of China's Central Military Committee, in September of that year, and again by Cao in January 2006. The following month, a 70-strong delegation from Thailand's Defence College was reported to have held a three-day exchange in Beijing with Chinese counterparts. Similar attention has been paid to Malaysia – whose defence minister, Najib Tun Razak, met with Cao in September 2005 – and Singapore, where Cao held meetings in April 2006 with Defence Minister Teo Chee Hean. Meanwhile, the 'strategic partnership' between Indonesia and China that was announced during President Susilo Bambang Yudhoyono's state visit to Beijing in July 2005 featured a commitment by China to assist Jakarta's efforts to develop indigenous missiles with ranges of up to 150km. China did not favour Philippine Foreign Affairs Secretary Alberto Romulo's August 2005 call for claimants to disputed territories in the South China Sea to elaborate a formal Code of Conduct to replace the loose arrangement favoured by Beijing. But such disagreements did not preclude tighter defence collaboration with the Philippines, another Major Non-NATO Ally of the United States: in January 2006 it was reported that China had donated military equipment to Manila, apparently to assist its armed forces in tackling rebel insurgents.

In contrast to this extensive bilateral activity, China continued to decline opportunities to participate at a senior level in multilateral defence-diplomatic forums in the region. It did, however, have a strong hand in the convening, on 14 December 2005, of the first East Asia Summit in Kuala Lumpur, which brought Northeast Asian and Southeast Asian states together with Australia, New Zealand and India. Championed by China as a constructive exercise in building a regional community, Beijing's strong preference for participation to be restricted to the ten members of ASEAN, Japan, South Korea and itself was read in the United States as an exclusionary policy. Tokyo and, less publicly, Singapore shared the sense that such a limited membership base would increase China's preponderance within the forum. ASEAN's requirement, stipulated in April 2005, that participants be signatories to its Treaty of Amity and Cooperation (TAC) allowed for the participation of India and New Zealand. Australia on the eve of the summit decided despite considerable reservations to accede to the TAC too, but this was a price that the United States declined to pay for its own inclusion; Washington judged that the TAC would place restrictions on its military posture in Asia and conflicted with its obligations to defence allies.

Washington's approach was also prudential in a wider sense: it was far from clear, as the summit approached, that it would prove substantively interesting. As things transpired, the summit produced only the blandest of communiqués and left uncertainty as to how often the forum might be reconvened. Yet the episode confirmed the sense in Washington that China was attempting to edge the United States out of strategically important regions. Indeed, running in parallel to the frictions over the East Asia Summit were growing tensions between Washington and both Moscow and Beijing concerning America's military presence in Central Asia, which Russia sees as a traditional sphere of influence and China regards as of increasing importance to its energy needs. Although China and Russia had acquiesced to this presence as a practical necessity of the Afghan intervention, both had grown uneasy about the combination of an apparent entrenchment of American forces in the region and Washington's overt support for the democratic 'colour' revolutions that have swept Eurasia since late 2003. This latter issue was also a matter of concern to Uzbekistan's President Islam Karimov, who had been incensed at American criticism of the violent suppression of demonstrations in Andijan in May 2005. The 5 July 2005 Astana summit of the Shanghai Cooperation Organisation, which was immediately preceded by a summit in Moscow between Hu and Russian President Vladimir Putin, issued a declaration calling for the withdrawal of US troops from Central Asia. This elicited a diplomatic counter-offensive from Washington, which on 25 July dispatched Rumsfeld to Bishkek, Kyrgyzstan, and Dushanbe, Tajikistan, to shore up defence ties. On 29 July, however, Karimov informed the US Embassy in Tashkent that he was terminating America's military presence at the Karshi-Khanabad airbase.

The precise details of China's involvement in these developments remain somewhat opaque, but the American impression that China and Russia collaborated strongly to produce this outcome is now fairly well established. This is seen as part of a broader politico-security convergence especially evident in the military sphere, where Russia continues to supply China with the advanced military technologies – fighter-bombers, surface combatants, submarines – that it cannot produce for itself, and which pose an increasingly credible challenge to US forces in the event of any contingency over Taiwan. However, Russian military assistance now extends beyond the provision of hardware. On 18–25 August 2005, some 2,000 Russian troops participated with 8,000 Chinese troops in their first joint exercise, euphemistically designated *Peace Mission 2005*. Held in the Shandong Peninsula in northeastern China, the exercise was ostensibly aimed at simulating an intervention in a territory threatened by terrorists and suffering from political turmoil, but the multi-service exercise seemed to many observers better configured for more conventional contingencies. Given that China has little experience of joint operations, and in view of the combinations of air, land and sea forces a contingency over Taiwan would call for, the exercise is likely to have been instructive.

The strength and durability of the Sino-Russian relationship over the longer term remains a matter of speculation. Moscow is ill at ease with the growth in its economic dependence on China and suspects that the balance of power in the relationship is migrating rapidly towards China. Beijing, for its part, senses this apprehension and consequently doubts the reliability of Russia. The two powers are for the time being more yoked together by necessity and lack of alternatives than blissfully wedded.

Further afield

With its relations with Washington in flux, China has continued to attach considerable importance to the European Union (EU). The eighth EU–China summit was held in Beijing on 5 September 2005, and the 30th anniversary of the establishment of diplomatic relations was celebrated. The Joint Statement issued at the conclusion of the summit encapsulated the extraordinary breadth of collaborative programmes between the two sides, ranging from culture and education to trade, health, the environment, energy and security. There followed in November 2005 state visits by Hu to Britain, Germany and Spain. Beijing continued to lobby hard for the repeal of the EU arms embargo on China, but to little avail. Although the formal position of the EU remains to work towards an early repeal, political realities have moved on. The Franco-German motor has stalled on this matter: since the rejection of the EU constitutional treaty by the French electorate, President Jacques Chirac has been politically weakened and distracted by far more immediate matters of domestic and EU policy; Gerhard Schröder has meanwhile been replaced by the more atlanticist and, on security issues at least, somewhat more Sino-sceptical German Chancellor Angela Merkel. While it is still possible that China may be willing to make concessions – on human rights observances, for example – to recreate momentum towards a repeal, this seems unlikely for the foreseeable future – not least in view of the very high benchmark set by US expectations.

Implausible though it would have seemed even a year ago, when Washington and Europe were still embroiled in the furious debate concerning the proposed repeal of the arms embargo on China, there is now a greater degree of convergence in American and European perspectives towards China as an actor in global security affairs. This has not least been a result of the inauguration of a regular, official transatlantic Strategic Dialogue on China. It has also been a product of a debate on China largely initiated under the British presidency of the EU in the second half of 2005.

It has been remarked that whereas the United States seems concerned about the implications of China's success, Europe has been more preoccupied by the consequences that would flow from its failure. Certainly, in the traditional European view, China was seen as a large developing country beset by internal problems that threatened to ripen into international ones and thus required attention and help. It was also seen through a narrow economic lens: member states jockeyed for commercial advantage in their dealing with Beijing, while, at the EU level, the Commission dealt overwhelmingly with trade and investment issues – not being functionally equipped to address anything else. There was patchy familiarity with security issues regarding China and little interest in or understanding of America's attachment to Taiwan. Detachment from such issues in some quarters, and resentment in others about a perceived US effort to exclude Europe strategically from Asia, mingled confusingly with a degree of relief about the free-rider opportunities that strong American regional engagement in Asia offered.

There has been, and still is, great receptivity in Europe to notions of China's 'peaceful rise' propounded by Chinese intellectuals, although of late more regard has been given to the possibility that such doctrines simply articulate a Chinese strategy for acquiring great power rank, rather than promising anything meaningful about China's long-term intentions. Finally, there has been a tendency to regard American assessments of China as too shrill and conspiratorial; certainly US claims about rapid advances in Chinese military capabilities tended to be seen in that light.

If Europeans have not exactly undergone a conversion to the American point of view about China, insofar as there is a single view, then at least there have been notable adjustments. This process was precipitated by the dispute over the EU arms embargo, which cast a spotlight on many issues of Chinese behaviour and forced European governments and EU institutions to develop and defend policy positions. In this process, it became apparent that the foundations of the 'strategic partnership' that China and the EU espouse were not as firm as had been imagined or pretended in Brussels and Beijing. China's proliferation practices, its opposition to the democratisation agenda, and its perceived subversion of good-governance programmes in Africa came more sharply into view, just as Europe found itself last year being lectured by China's neighbours about its apparent indifference to their concerns about the PLA. Most recently, the sense has grown that China might pose an economic threat as much as an economic opportunity to Europe.

Europe therefore has seemed privately to be moving towards a more rounded view of China – a view that is unlikely to be identical to Washington's, but will provide a broader basis for cooperation in handling relations with Beijing. There will in particular be a willingness to hedge against as well as to engage China, provided that the hedge is not too blatant. Europe will be more inclined to introduce the principle of reciprocity into its dealings with China; this will mark a departure from the previous habit of making symbolic gestures in order to come into good standing with Beijing, while asking for nothing directly in return. Greater regard will also be given to the fact that Asia is a region of several large powers, not one, and that there are risks for Europe in appearing to place all its eggs into the Chinese basket. Europe shows increasing awareness that India and Japan will assess their relations with the EU to a large degree in the light of how Brussels conducts its relations with Beijing. Europe has an increasing incentive to signal to China that it understands these regional dynamics.

It seems likely that China's attitudes in the crisis over Iran's nuclear ambitions will be highly influential in shaping European as well as American views of Beijing as a strategic actor. China wishes to avoid a nuclear-armed Iran, since this would increase instability in a region vital to China's growing long-term energy needs, and it does not wish to sacrifice its relations with the United States and Europe over this issue, yet it is averse to coercive measures against Tehran – diplomatic or military – that too could produce a regional crisis while jeopardising China's extensive oil and gas supply contracts with Iran, which are worth in the region of $70bn. Having preferred to keep the matter of Iran's nuclear transgressions within the counsels of the IAEA, Beijing and Moscow ultimately acquiesced to Iran's referral to the UN Security Council, where the two powers have to date resisted attempts by the United States and the E3 (Britain, France and Germany) to agree a Chapter 7 Resolution demanding that Iran come into compliance with its obligations and holding out the possibility of a resort to sanctions or force if Tehran does not comply. A continuing rejection by Iran of incentive packages, including assistance with civilian nuclear energy programmes proffered by Europe, and further advances in Iran's uranium-enrichment capacity in the face of international disapproval, will presumably weaken the diplomatic ground on which Russia and China currently stand. As of May 2006, the broad expectation was that Russia might be willing to concede on the point of a Chapter 7 Resolution, and that China would fall into line. Beijing was clearly hoping not to be confronted with such a stark choice, and that calculations inside both the United States and Iran would argue for direct bilateral contact to avert an escalation of the crisis.

The challenge for China will be how to balance its narrower national interests with both the expectations of the transatlantic alliance and the sensibilities of Arab Gulf states. Particularly significant in this regard are the views of the Kingdom of Saudi Arabia, with which China has sought much closer ties and, intriguingly, a history of military cooperation. In January 2006, King Abdullah bin Abdul Aziz visited China for discussions on energy and security issues, during which it was decided to increase annual Saudi oil exports to China by about 40%; in April Hu made a three-day visit to Saudi Arabia and addressed its Consultative Council. It is reported that Saudi supplies are of importance to Chinese efforts to establish a Strategic Petroleum Reserve that would provide a degree of energy security and insulation from fluctuations in prices. In view of their collective disagreements with Iran, the Arab Gulf states will follow China's contribution to Iranian nuclear diplomacy in some detail. Li's tour in late May 2006 of Bahrain, the United Arab

Emirates and Qatar provided scope for consultations, but it seems in China's continuing tactical interest to adopt the lowest profile on this matter.

And yet, as the pursuit of energy supplies draws China into closer associations with Latin American and African states that pursue controversial internal and regional policies, scrutiny of its diplomacy is clearly growing. Although Beijing's critics would argue that there have been no instances in which China has allowed concerns about international opinion to override its national interest calculations – witness, for example, its continuing attachment to the governments of Sudan and Zimbabwe – there are at least indications of growing discomfort and defensiveness on the Chinese side. Chinese strategists often argue that they have little choice but to engage states the West views as rogueish, since China has been shut out by the United States elsewhere. Beijing's unease arises to some extent out of the general international perception that China has responsibility for the errant behaviour of states with which it deals, but increasingly by the tendency of some of those states to brandish their connections with China as something that provides protection from Western criticism and punishment. Tehran's tendency to take China's support of its position for granted in public pronouncements, or Venezuelan President Hugo Chávez's characterisation of his country's relations with Beijing as being aimed at circumscribing US influence in Latin America, are sources of considerable embarrassment. That said, a strategic shift in the diplomatic attitudes of a Chinese government overwhelmingly preoccupied with its own survival is not to be expected soon.

Korean Peninsula: Tensions Deepen

The stand-off over North Korea's nuclear programme deepened in 2005 and the first half of 2006, notwithstanding the first tangible success of the Chinese-hosted Six-Party Talks that began in 2003. On 19 September 2005, the parties to the talks agreed to a Joint Statement of Principles, in which North Korea – the Democratic Peoples Republic of Korea (DPRK) – agreed to abandon its nuclear programmes in exchange for concessions in principle by the other parties, mainly the United States. Deep divisions between the United States and North Korea, however, quickly ended the promise of progress produced by the joint statement.

In repeatedly putting off and setting conditions for resuming the talks, North Korea has shown that it thinks the Bush administration will never provide incentives sufficiently attractive to compensate for giving up the regime's nuclear weapons deterrent. That judgement is surely correct: Washington sees greater prospect for success in increasing the pressure on Pyongyang. One consequence of that pressure, however, has been to weaken the consensus among the other five parties to the talks, a consensus that so far has been the only real value of the talks for Washington. The talks will stumble on, so that China's chairmanship should not be seen to end in failure, but they appear to be in a state of semi-permanent stalemate with small chance of significant change before the end of the Bush administration.

In a South Korea – the Republic of Korea (ROK) – buoyed by steady economic growth and a stable democracy, the generational shift away from voters who experienced the Korean War, and the resultant ideological swing to the left, continued to generate growing feelings of national identity, distrust of the United States, and excuse of North Korea's failings. President Roh Moo-Hyun's governing Uri Party sought to reshape South Korean thinking, to put South Korea on equal footing with the United States and to put primary foreign-policy emphasis on promoting peace with North Korea and maintaining peninsular stability. Concerns about Japanese re-militarisation played the foil to rising nationalism. The ruling party's massive losses in local elections 31 May 2006 reflected a national lack of trust in Roh's leadership, but it is too early to predict a conservative pendulum swing in national elections at the end of 2007.

Resumption of Six-Party Talks

In July 2005, after months of cajoling North Korea to return to the table, China hosted the fourth round of the Six-Party Talks, 13 months after the previous session. In the second half of 2004, North Korea had postponed the talks, first in pique over US adoption of the North Korean Human Rights Act, and then because it decided to await the outcome of the US presidential election – which did not produce the result for which it was hoping. In early 2005, North Korea justified staying home on grounds of US hostility, exemplified by Secretary of State-designate Condoleezza Rice, in her confirmation hearing, characterising North Korea as an 'outpost of tyranny'. Pyongyang did not get the apology it demanded, but Washington did modulate its tone. Rice, in April, referred to US acknowledgement of North Korean sovereignty. President Bush, in a June 2005 summit with South Korean President Roh, politely referred to North Korea's leader as 'Mister' Kim Jong Il, and State Department officials were allowed to meet with North Korean mission officials in New York and to convey that the new tone represented US policy.

A new tone of pragmatism also characterised the US position in the talks themselves, which for the first time became actual negotiations on matters of substance. Christopher Hill, Assistant Secretary of State for East Asia, reached out to his counterpart, Vice-Minister Kim Gye Gwan, to arrange a private meeting before the talks began, and moved quickly from the six-party format to a series of substantive bilateral discussions as he drove toward agreement on a statement of principles. That the six parties agreed to such a statement when talks resumed in September 2005 after a five-week recess was a surprising testimony to US flexibility.

The sticking point was North Korea's insistence on its right to nuclear energy. For North Korea, a light-water reactor (LWR) remained the holy grail. Agreement on provision of LWR technology was the most important US concession in the 1994 Agreed Framework, and has additional significance as a legacy of founding father Kim Il Sung and a visible assurance of US good will. In the fourth round of the Six-Party Talks, Washington started with the position that North Korea, having violated the Nuclear Non-Proliferation Treaty (NPT), had no right to any nuclear programme, civilian or otherwise. Seeing itself isolated, even from Japan, the United States begrudgingly accepted North Korea's right, in principle, to nuclear energy after it had fully dismantled its weapons programme and returned in good standing to the NPT. But actually providing a nuclear reactor was a different matter, and out of the question. The Bush administration was unalterably opposed to repeating what it saw as former President Bill Clinton's futile concession.

As the fourth round of talks reached a climax, however, the United States still found itself in a minority of one on the LWR issue. China, which Washington had long been pressing to take leadership in the negotiations, did just that, but not by putting pressure on North Korea as Washington had hoped. Instead, Washington itself was presented with an ultimatum: to accept China's final rewrite of the joint statement of principles or be seen as the party responsible for scuttling the talks. Washington ultimately agreed on the key concession: provision of a LWR would be discussed 'at an appropriate time'. In exchange for that and other concessions, North Korea committed itself to 'abandoning all nuclear weapons and its existing nuclear programmes', to return to the NPT and to accept the return of IAEA inspectors.

North Korea's pledge to 'abandon' its nuclear programmes fell short of the US demand that they be 'dismantled' – one of the ambiguities that will need to be clarified in any future agreement. The pledge to return to the NPT carries no weight until all Pyongyang's nuclear weapons and the facilities to make them are dismantled, so that the North can re-accede to the treaty as a non-nuclear weapons state. More important for now is North Korea's agreement to accept IAEA inspectors, who will need to play a central role in any verification process and whose expulsion by Pyongyang in December 2002 sharply accelerated the current long-drawn-out crisis.

Additional US concessions included a willingness to join the other four parties in providing energy assistance to North Korea. The Bush administration had previously resisted any such commitment, which sounded too much like the 1994 Agreed Framework. This time, however, the energy assistance would largely come from South Korea, which in July 2005 offered to provide 2 million kilowatts of electric power to the North as an alternative to the two LWRs that no longer will be built under the defunct 1994 agreement.

As a security assurance, the undertakings expressed in the 19 September Joint Statement included an explicit US affirmation that 'it has no intention to attack or invade the DPRK with nuclear or conventional weapons', and a statement that 'the DPRK and the United States undertook to respect each other's sovereignty, exist peacefully together, and take steps to normalise their relations'. The actual US security assurances to North Korea flowing from these undertakings, in the form of a letter (not a treaty), were not further specified and will have to be worked out later, as part of the envisioned process leading to the actual dismantling of North Korea's nuclear programmes.

The Joint Statement had other gaps. Missing was any restraint on North Korea's continued production and reprocessing of plutonium or any mention of its uranium enrichment programme – the cause of the current crisis – except implicitly, by saying the 1992 North–South Denuclearisation Declaration (which forbade enrichment and reprocessing anywhere in the Korean Peninsula) should be observed and implemented. The statement also masked deep divisions over sequencing, by saying simply that the six parties agreed to take 'coordinated steps' to implement the accord 'in a phased manner in line with the principle of "commitment for commitment, action for action".'

Disagreement over sequencing erupted almost immediately, when the United States, as the result of an internal debate over the compromise on LWRs, issued a statement interpreting the 'appropriate time' for discussion on LWRs to mean the time at which North Korea complied with the NPT and 'has demonstrated a sustained commitment to cooperation and transparency' – a subjective criterion of which the US would be the judge. The next day, North Korea announced that it would implement the joint statement as soon as the US provided LWRs but not before.

Sequencing, along with other key issues of verification, scope, compensation details and the missing elements of the 19 September statement, were to be taken up in subsequent rounds of the Six-Party Talks. Mutual antagonism and mistrust, however, re-emerged to prevent the talks from coming to grips with the substantive issues. In Washington, the limited flexibility that Hill was able to deploy in his first half-year on the job was clipped by hardliners who saw the 19 September statement as having gone too far. Hill was told not to travel to Pyongyang for a preview session unless the North shut down the nuclear work at Yongbyon in a unilateral concession. North Korea, not surprisingly, demanded compensation for any resumed freeze. More seriously, the Bush administration implemented a series of steps to curb North Korean illicit activities, and Pyongyang seized upon this action to again postpone the talks.

Financial sanctions

In October 2005, the US Treasury Department formally accused North Korea of producing high-quality counterfeit $100 bills, known as 'supernotes', and under the US Patriot Act placed sanctions on Macao-based Banco Delta Asia for money-laundering North Korea's black market dealings. (In 2006, the bank said it had terminated its business with North Korean entities and was implementing new procedures to prevent money-laundering.) The same month, the US Treasury Department, under a separate, recently promulgated authority, designated eight North Korean companies as having been involved in the proliferation of weapons of mass destruction (WMD) and their delivery vehicles. The latter action, first applied to three North Korean companies (and five others in Iran and Syria) in June, froze any assets the companies had under US jurisdiction and prohibited US persons from doing business with them. Although it is unlikely any of the North Korean companies had any assets in the United States, the action was designed to limit the companies' access to the international banking system by threatening to target otherwise innocent foreign entities that aided the proliferating companies.

North Korea labelled the financial sanctions an embodiment of hostile intent and used the fifth round of the Six-Party Talks on 9–11 November 2005 for little more than an acrimonious response. Then in December North Korea said talks could not proceed until the sanctions were lifted. North Korea was particularly incensed by the action against Banco Delta Asia, which caused a run on the bank and resulted in the freezing of 30 North Korean accounts upon which the leadership had relied. According to the US Congressional Research Service, North Korea earned as much as $15–25 million a year from counterfeit notes. Since 1989, US officials have seized $50m of the supernotes globally, mostly during 2001–04. Under pressure from the United States, other banks around the world restricted business with North Korea, so as not to run afoul of US Treasury sanctions themselves. North Korean businessmen were forced to carry cash and to rely more on Chinese financial assistance. Notwithstanding the windfall to China's drive for regional dominance, delighted American officials saw these measures as the perfect sanction, targeting North Korea's leaders but not its general public – although the impact of reduced foreign exchange is spreading throughout the economy. US Ambassador to South Korea Alexander Vershbow added insult to injury in December when he labelled Pyongyang a 'criminal regime' and accused Kim Jong Il of being the first national leader to be involved in counterfeiting since Hitler.

American officials insisted that the action against Banco Delta Asia had nothing to do with the Six-Party Talks, and was a purely a defensive law-enforcement measure to protect US financial institutions. The financial measures were indeed divorced from the Six-Party Talks in the sense that they were carried out without heed for the impact on the talks. The Bush administration, divided as before on how to handle North Korea, was following bifurcated policy tracks. Hardliners, including officials in Vice-President Dick Cheney's office and the Pentagon, saw little purpose in the negotiations and little chance of success, believing that Kim would never give up his nuclear weapons or follow through with dismantling his nuclear facilities unless the future of his regime were at stake. Opposed to offering any incentives, because they would prop up the regime, the hardliners saw financial sanctions as a means of putting pressure on it instead.

Amidst the deterioration of US–North Korea relations, the few other avenues of bilateral interaction also closed. In January 2006, the Korean Peninsula Energy Development Organisation (KEDO) pulled the last remaining personnel out of the LWR reactor site at Kumho (as the US and South Korea continued to disagree over who will be responsible for the considerable liquidation costs). The US military programme to recover the remains of US war dead in North Korea ended in mid-2005, in frustration over North Korean interference and corruption and Pentagon concerns that US personnel could become hostage if tensions rose. International food aid officials left by year's end after North Korea demanded that they either depart or convert emergency aid programmes to developmental initiatives. The World Food Programme, whose annual food aid fell to one-tenth of the 500,000–700,000 tonnes previously supplied, in March 2006 agreed to go along with Pyongyang's demands, with little change to the content of the aid package but a likely restriction in the monitoring parameters.

In spring 2006, North Korea showed signs of seeking to overcome the impasse over the US Treasury's measures. After an internal debate in Washington over the level at which Pyongyang could be enjoined on the issue, Li Gun, the deputy head of the North Korean delegation to the Six-Party Talks came to New York in March for a Treasury briefing on the sanctions and steps the North could make to have them removed. The United States, insisting the briefing was not a negotiation, rejected Li's proposal to set up a joint committee to exchange information on financial matters, including steps to cope with illicit activities and assist in international efforts against money laundering. In early April 2006, when all the principal negotiators for the Six-Party Talks showed up in Tokyo for a 'Track II' academic conference, US negotiator Hill would not meet bilaterally with his North Korean counterpart. In May, when China sent a senior envoy to try to coax North Korea back to the talks, Kim Jong Il repeated that the United States must first lift sanctions on Banco Delta Asia, thereby hardening North Korea's stance by putting it in his name.

Meanwhile US officials hinted that further law enforcement actions may be in store to stem North Korean illicit activity such as counterfeiting of cigarettes and pharmaceuticals, narcotics trafficking, and smuggling of endangered species and other sanctioned items.

In late March, the Treasury Department for the first time extended application of the new authority to a company outside the proliferating states. Swiss industrial wholesale company Kohas AG and its president had all their assets within the US frozen, and US companies were barred from doing business with the firm. According to the US Treasury, Kohas is half-owned by a North Korean firm that was designated in October, and has procured goods for Pyongyang with weapons-related applications. Most recently, in a measure to go into effect 8 May, Washington further turned up the heat by banning US citizens and US-based companies, including their subsidiaries, from owning, leasing, operating or insuring any North Korean-registered ship. One other policy in play is to persuade other countries to take measures similar to those already enacted by the United States. The overall strategy is simple: 'squeeze them'. However, it will be tricky to coordinate this strategy with North Korea's neighbours, who have very different priorities.

Mixed results for containment strategy

The US policy of isolation and pressure was also designed to contain North Korea. The Proliferation Security Initiative (PSI), launched in May 2003, now boasts 70 countries committed to strengthening the collective means to stop international transit of cargo deemed to be related to weapons of mass destruction. In the absence of any known PSI-related interdiction of a WMD-laden North Korean ship, it is hard to substantiate the success of PSI in this regard, although undoubtedly there has been a deterrent effect. To try to halt North Korean missile exports to Iran, in particular, Washington sought to persuade China and several Central Asian nations to tighten their border controls and to deny air-transit rights to suspect North Korean planes. According to press reports, the defensive measures to deny overflight rights came after an Iranian cargo plane was tracked landing in North Korea, presumably to pick up missile components. Combined with steps to stop North Korea's illicit activity, PSI is also a display of muscle that can give leverage to diplomacy – and demonstrate that Washington has more options at its disposal than simply negotiations or military action.

US satisfaction over the pressure North Korea was feeling on the financial front could not conceal a basic flaw in Washington's policy. North Korea might be contained – albeit imperfectly, given the reports of continued North Korea–Iran missile cooperation – but it continued to build up its nuclear arsenal. North Korea announced in early 2005 that it indeed had nuclear weapons and sought to be dealt with accordingly. In early April 2005, North Korea shut down its 5MWe reactor in Yongbyon and declared that the spent fuel would be extracted to increase the nation's 'nuclear deterrent'. By September, North Korea completed reprocessing that spent fuel, producing enough plutonium for another 1–2 nuclear bombs. North Korea is now assessed to have enough reprocessed plutonium for 5–11 weapons, compared to the 1–2 weapons worth of plutonium in North Korea's hands in 2001 at the start of the Bush administration. The nuclear arsenal could grow by one bomb a year if the 5MWe reactor continued to operate at capacity.

If North Korea is able to complete the construction of a larger, 50MWe reactor, the arsenal could grow much faster. North Korea told visitors in August 2005 it was resuming construction of the two power reactors on which work had been halted under the 1994 Agreed Framework. The larger of those two planned power reactors, rated at 200MWe, is many years away from completion and would cost more to complete than if the North started anew. The 50MWe reactor at Yongbyon, however, could conceivably be completed in 3–4 years, at which time it would be able to produce 56kg of plutonium a year, enough for another 5–10 nuclear weapons, significantly adding to what must already be considered a nuclear deterrent.

North Korea also continued its development of intermediate- and long-range missiles that potentially could carry nuclear weapons. According to March 2006 Congressional testimony by the commander of the US Forces Korea, General Burwell B. Bell III, North Korea appeared ready to field and test intermediate-range missiles that could reach as far as Alaska. North Korea's capability to make a nuclear weapon small enough for its missiles is a matter of conjecture, although Pyongyang's own announcements have reinforced the threat perception. In March 2006, North Korea repeated that it had atomic weapons to counter the US nuclear threat, and claimed it had the ability to launch a pre-emptive attack on the United States. Until 5 July 2006, it continued to abide by the voluntary moratorium on medium- and long-range missile tests it undertook after its 1998 test of a 2,000km-range *Taepo-dong* missile with a trajectory toward Japan. But on that day, Pyongyang launched seven ballistic missiles, the first tests since its self-imposed moratorium. The tests included a *Taepo-dong* 2, with a presumed range of 6–10,000km, but since it failed within a minute after launch, the actual range remains unknown. Press reports in May–June 2005 of preparations of a tunnel for a nuclear test proved false – a worst-case analysis of apparently benign tunnel construction activity.

Hitting closer to the truth were extensive press reports about continued North Korean assistance to Iran's expanding ballistic missile programme. Owing to US pressure, Libya, Egypt, Pakistan, Yemen and other countries have stopped buying North Korean missile technology. Iran remains one of the North's few remaining customers, and in recent years has reportedly purchased North Korean missile technology to improve both the range and accuracy of its strike capacity.

Political developments in South Korea

In the southern half of the Korean Peninsula, the Republic of Korea registered impressive gains in almost every field. The economy in 2005 registered a second year of 4% real growth and per capita GDP rose to over $19,000. South Korean industry became known for cutting-edge information technology, telecommunications and biotechnology – although the latter lost lustre in December 2005 when world-renowned cloning expert Hwang Woo-suk's research turned out to be fabricated. South Korean popular culture – TV dramas, movies and pop music – continued to ride a boom of popularity in the rest of East and Southeast Asia. South Korea's democracy continued to mature. President Roh Moo-Hyun's administration remained stable, despite consistently low rankings in public opinion polling. Corruption replaced human rights as the primary social concern, but government prosecutors and the media pursued zealous campaigns to root out cosy ties between big business and elected officials. Prime Minister Lee Hae-chan had to leave office in March 2006 because he went golfing during a national railway strike, but his real sin was the chequered past of his golfing partners. His replacement, Han Myun-sook, came from a dissident background that would have been unthinkable only a few years earlier; her husband spent 15 years in prison for his role as head of a pro-Pyongyang political party.

Charting the generational shifts in South Korea will be key to domestic politics and to Seoul's relations with the US and North Korea. The generational change that saw the coming to power of former college radicals and the sharply diminished threat perception of North Korea on the part of most South Koreans began to take a new turn, however, with the emergence of a new generation of voters who aspire most of all to the enjoyment of South Korea's new affluence. Courted by both the leftist governing Uri party and the right-leaning Grand National Party, these swing voters could spark a new political alignment as potential candidates jockey to replace President Roh when his single five-year term expires in February 2008. Signs of change were apparent in the Uri Party's devastating loss in local elections on 31 May 2006. It won only one of 16 of the big-city mayors and provincial governorships and only 10% of lower level positions. Polls confirmed that the results reflected more a lack of confidence in President Roh and his party, seen as incompetent and arrogant, than a groundswell of support for the conservative opposition Grand National Party. It would therefore probably be incorrect to put too much emphasis on the results. Although Roh now must be considered a lame duck, the Uri Party, with a near majority of seats in the National Assembly, is likely to continue to exercise dominance in national politics. Korean politics are nothing if not volatile, and it is far too early to predict a conservative win in the parliamentary elections scheduled for December 2007 and the presidential election in February 2008. Splits in both major parties could occur before then as competitors jockey for power. Though conservatives have qualms about unrequited assistance being showered on North Korea, there is a nearly universal consensus in South Korea on the merits of engagement.

President Roh walked a tightrope in trying to satisfy his leftist core constituents while not alienating the new right. A row over an attempt by Uri Party ideologues to exert government control over private schools emerged as a classic confrontation with the establishment, as Roh promoted a compromise with the opposition. In national security policy, Roh sought to work out the complicated mechanics of the oxymoronic 'cooperative independent self defense', taking halting steps to support a realignment of US forces away from the Demilitarized Zone, while telling left-wing constituents he was not giving in to American demands. On foreign policy, Roh sustained the US alliance by supporting the financial sanctions on North Korean counterfeiting, working toward a Free Trade Agreement, and cooperating on flexible US troop deployments. But to placate his left, he abjured criticism of North Korea, particularly on human-rights violations – a rallying cry that passed from the left to the right of the political spectrum when the focus of concern moved from South to North Korea. Criticism of Japan, on the other hand, appealed to all parts of the body politic, and Japan's some-times tone-deaf policies gave Koreans on both sides of the 38th parallel ample scope for criticism. Nationalist outrage in South Korea rose to fever pitch over moves by a prefectural government in Japan to press claims over the disputed Tokdo/Takeshima islands.

South Korea and the United States: differing perceptions

The hardening of US attitudes toward North Korea exacerbated strains between the United States and South Korea, whose governments have an increasingly divergent set of threat perceptions and security priorities. The totalitarian, aggressive failed state in the northern half of the peninsula is antithetic to the democratic, free-market values and national interests of both South Korea and the United States. Yet where Americans see an increasingly dangerous and repressive evil regime, South Koreans see a pitiable renegade brother, estranged by an accident of history in which America was culpable. South Koreans do not believe the North Koreans would use their nuclear weapons unless they were forced to do so for regime survival. South Koreans are thus more afraid of a US policy of regime change that could provoke North Korea. Under President Roh and his predecessor, Kim Dae Jung, South Korea's priorities have been regional peace, regional prosperity, engagement and eventual long-term unification with the North. In contrast, the Bush administration's priorities are to counter the dual threat of terrorism and proliferation and to promote democracy.

Many South Koreans see the US promotion of human rights in North Korea as a cynical means of promoting American supremacy in northeast Asia. US human-rights envoy to North Korea Jay Lefkowitz, in a December speech in Seoul, bluntly called on the South Korean government to confront Pyongyang over its record and criticised Seoul for abstaining on a UN resolution that condemned the North's human-rights abuses. South Korean officials said the speech, and another by Ambassador Vershbow the same month, stepped across a line: they asked that Washington coordinate with Seoul before taking actions such as the sanctions against Banco Delta Asia. In January 2006, Roh bluntly warned of potential friction between Seoul and Washington, saying 'the South Korean government does not agree with some forces in the United States that raise issues about North Korea's regime, put pressure on it and apparently desire to see its collapse'. His government made clear that maintaining stability on the Korean Peninsula was a higher priority than North Korean human rights. Seoul feared that speaking out on the latter would jeopardise its engagement strategy. By contrast, in June 2005, Bush welcomed a prominent North Korean defector to the White House, and in spring 2006 the US began to give asylum to groups of defectors.

South Korea's increasing eagerness to invest in and trade with its northern neighbour conflicts with Washington's policy of applying financial pressure on North Korea. Trade between the two Koreas exceeded $1 billion in 2005, up from $700m in 2004 and spurred by the joint North–South Korean industrial park in Kaesong just north of the Demilitarized Zone, set to house 100 factories by the end of 2006. South Korea's motivations are not purely commercial. Watching Beijing's energetic economic efforts to woo North Korea, Seoul realises that if it does not keep pace, it will lose out in the race to control the Korean peninsula. In Seoul's view the future of the peninsula is as a united country along the South Korean free-market model. Knowing that China has no interest in seeing a Western-oriented, united Korea on its border, Seoul fears that a dominant Chinese influence in the North could keep the peninsula divided. Seoul is not keen to be enlisted in America's drive to build up strategic alliances vis-à-vis China. Former head of the Presidential Committee on Northeast Asian Cooperation Moon Jung-in voiced the consensus South Korean view when he said in March 2006 that the alliance 'should not be a tool to alienate North Korea, China and Russia but a step on the way toward a multinational regional security pact.'

'Strategic flexibility'
In an effort to stem the growing divergence and to broaden the scope of the bilateral relationship, South Korea and the United States launched a ministerial-level strategic consultative process in January 2006. The communiqué from this first meeting of the US–ROK Strategic Consultation for Allied Partnership emphasised cooperation on Iraq, Afghanistan, democratic institutions and human rights worldwide, counter terrorism, proliferation and pandemic disease. Most importantly, it dealt with the Pentagon's controversial push for 'strategic flexibility' of US forces in South Korea. The communiqué confirmed that 'the ROK, as an ally, fully understands the rationale for the transformation of the US global military strategy, and respects the necessity for strategic flexibility of the US forces in the ROK. In the implementation of strategic flexibility, the US respects the ROK position that it shall not be involved in a regional conflict in Northeast Asia against the will of the Korean people.' In other words, South Korea understood that it could not prevent the United States from using its forces elsewhere and Washington understood that South Korea did not want to be drawn into a conflict with China. According to US officials, 'strategic flexibility' was not aimed at China, but at enhancing effi-

ciency in dealing with the unknown threats of the future. As a practical matter, US ground forces in Korea do not have the naval and marine components that would be needed to deal with a crisis over Taiwan. Nevertheless, fear of being entangled in a dispute with China is a persistent element of the South Korean approach, and a reason why the strategic flexibility concept will likely remain a source of misunderstanding and mistrust in the US–South Korea relationship.

The United States and South Korea also took other steps to rejuvenate the alliance. After repeatedly rebuffing US requests to join the Proliferation Security Initiative, South Korea in late 2005 agreed to attend PSI exercises and briefings as an observer – a half step toward full participation in what is not in any case a membership organisation. South Korea also agreed that joint US–Korea military exercises would include drills on the interdiction of suspected shipments relating to weapons of mass destruction. In February 2006, South Korea and the United States agreed to open negotiations on a Free Trade Agreement, with an ambitious goal of completing it by March 2007. Requiring liberalisation and restructuring of many sectors of the Korean economy – not an easy sell in South Korea's fractious political system – the FTA promises to revitalise the economic relationship while boosting South Korea's economy and to provide a stronger basis for overall bilateral relations that for too long have been dominated by the security dimension. South Korean officials may have overstated the case in claiming that a Free Trade Agreement would help ease the risks related to North Korea: it will not provide leverage to induce US concessions on North Korea, but will give greater ballast to an alliance in need of attention.

Chinese influence on the North Korean economy

Americans have long believed that the solution to resolving the North Korean problem lies in China's willingness to exercise the enormous economic leverage it presumably wields over the North. When China interrupted the oil pipeline to North Korea for three days in 2003, it was seen as a hopeful sign of stronger pressure to come. Whatever the truth behind that incident, China has taken a decidedly more subtle approach to influencing North Korean behaviour. Beijing fundamentally opposes sanctions, which it fears would be successful only in damaging the fledgling process of market reforms. President Hu Jintao listened politely to US concerns about North Korea when he visited Washington in April 2006, but showed no interest of putting pressure on the North. Looking beyond the Six-Party Talks goal of denuclearising the peninsula, Beijing has taken a longer-term approach to influencing Pyongyang through trade and economic reforms. There is no mistaking the deep and extensive nature of the relationship between the two countries. Chinese annual investment and trade with North Korea rose to $2bn in 2005, revitalising ports, building factories and modernising the energy sector. China now accounts for 40% of North Korea's foreign trade. President Hu visited Pyongyang in October 2005 and hosted Kim Jong Il in January 2006, both times pressing the message of managed reform along the Chinese model. Kim apparently got the point. Following his visit, which included visits to Shenzhen and other southern cities famous for their export-led wealth, the North Korean news agency for the first time gave an unreserved favourable commentary on China's opening and reform.

The market reforms and economic restructuring that Kim Jong Il unveiled in 2002 continued in 2005, but with significant deviations. His pursuit of reform is reflected in North Korea's encouragement of Chinese and South Korean investment, including in the Kaesong industrial park, where the impact of economic openness cannot easily be walled off from the rest of North Korea. His caution, on the other hand, is reflected in the measures the leadership took in late 2005 that suggested a return to the command economy. Pyongyang restricted private grain sales, revived food rationing to revitalise the public distribution system and reportedly seized harvests. Rather than a reversal of market reforms, however, these steps seemed likely to be a temporary measure, deemed necessary to stem the tide of worker absenteeism from state-sector jobs and combat spreading corruption. However, the crackdown was unlikely to be effective as long as there were profits to be made and food to be had in the informal sector. The underlying problem could not be solved without the infusion of foreign capital to allow factories to run properly. By providing that capital, China gains ever more influence over the long run, although its ability to persuade North Korea is still limited.

Questions of leadership succession also cast a potential shadow on the long-term efficacy of economic reforms in North Korea. By age 63, Kim Il Sung had already designated his son as his chosen successor. Kim Jong Il celebrated his 64th birthday on 16 February 2006 without any sign of a similar designation, raising speculation that he was unsure who to pick or faced a power struggle behind the scenes. A smooth succession is key to North Korea's future, to the continued reform of the economy and, indeed, to the survival of the regime. Presumably, no other issue is a greater source of palace intrigue in Pyongyang and of jockeying among the three sons considered the most likely candidates for the hereditary leadership. For all the outside world knows, and for all the North Koreans know, Kim Jong Il might already have decided on a successor, but left the announcement until later. Whoever it is will need a significant period of grooming for the position, so it is natural that the unveiling may take time. Yet if Kim's reported failing health should lead to an abrupt death before he publicly names a successor, political chaos would ensue.

Tensions between Japan and the Koreas

Japan and North Korea held bilateral talks in Beijing from 4 to 8 February 2006 on the issue of North Korea's admitted past abduction of Japanese nationals, normalisation of ties and security problems, including the nuclear and missile issues. If North Korea had played its hand differently, it might have been able to drive a wedge between Tokyo and Washington by playing on Japan's national preoccupation with the kidnapping issue. That is to say, North Korea could have tried to fan Japanese citizens' impatience with the lack of progress in the Six-Party Talks, to which Japanese officials have given diplomatic priority. Prime Minister Jinichiro Koizumi had sought normalisation of relations with North Korea – predicated on resolution of the kidnapping issue – as his legacy. As he approached the fulfillment of his his pledge to leave office by September 2006, however, time was running out, and the February talks represented a step backwards. North Korea's response to Japan's request for a return of surviving abductees and a thorough investigation was to demand in turn that Japan turn over seven Japanese citizens who had assisted North Koreans to defect. The predictable reaction on the part of the Japanese public was to call for further pressure on North Korea. The ruling Japanese Liberal Democratic Party in spring 2006 began parliamentary action on a bill to impose sanctions on North Korea if it failed to make progress in addressing its human-rights abuses, including the abduction issue. Tokyo already has several pressure points it can apply, including invoking recent laws enabling the control of North Korean ships entering Japanese ports and halting remittances by North Korean sympathisers in Japan. Far from harbouring concerns that Tokyo will cut its own deal with Pyongyang, Washington can now look to Tokyo for further pressure on North Korea akin to the US illicit-activities initiative.

Other bilateral relationships among the parties to the Six-Party Talks also came under pressure in 2005. Koizumi's visits to the Yasukuni Shrine (see pp. 360–363) and moves by right-wing groups in Japan to recast history textbooks led to rows with both China and South Korea. A June 2005 summit between Koizumi and Roh was dominated by discussion of history. A debate flared between South Korea and China over the historical classification of the ancient Korean kingdom of Koguryo. Trade issues over garlic, kimchi, fish and mobile phones also entangled China and South Korea. Meanwhile territorial disputes between South Korea and Japan over Dokdo/Takeshima Island and among Japan, China and Taiwan over the Senkaku/Diaoyu islands continued to simmer.

Prospects

Under Chinese pressure, North Korea is likely to return to the Six-Party Talks, if only to please its benefactor and to prevent the United States from abandoning its half-hearted engagement strategy altogether. Given the 13 months that elapsed between rounds three and four, round six may not begin before 2007. If and when talks do resume, they are unlikely to produce much of consequence. At best, to preserve the alliance with South Korea, Washington might be willing to make concessions to secure another freeze on plutonium-related activities at Yongbyon (the 5MWe reactor, reprocessing campaigns and construction of the larger reactors). In line with the principle enshrined in the 19 September Joint Statement of 'action for action', a freeze would require compensation, most likely in the form of energy assistance from South Korea and US willingness to work out a deal on the financial sanctions.

If the Six-Party Talks were to move ahead, they would quickly head into the difficult territory of verification. The United States would demand intrusive inspections that would go against the very grain of North Korea's secretive society: American-led teams having the right to go anywhere at any time, necessary because the United States does not know where the uranium enrichment facilities are located. Verification measures would be even more difficult than they were between the United States and Soviet Union in the Cold War, when verification was two sided. The first verification clash would come over the declaration North Korea would be asked to make as the first stage of the verification process. If that declaration failed to include the uranium enrichment equipment North Korea procured from Pakistan-based Abdul Qadeer Khan and from other black market sellers, the United States would claim deceit.

More fundamentally, the two protagonists have no willingness to offer fundamental compromises. North Korea will not give up its nuclear deterrent without a tangible, irreversible assurance of 'no hostile intent', and the only tangible assurance it seems willing to settle for is a light-water reactor. The Bush administration simply will not be party to providing a nuclear reactor. It believes North Korea will not give up its nuclear weapons for any inducement, unless the survival of the regime is at stake. Hence, pressure through financial measures is deemed useful not only for containing North Korea but as part of a longer-term strategy of destabilisation.

North Korea has pressure points of its own. It can threaten to sell nuclear material or test a nuclear weapon, although actually doing so would be suicidal. North Korea can test the *Taepo-dong* missile again, particularly if it thinks this pressure would improve its bargaining position with Japan, but this would also entail consequences including the application of Japanese financial sanctions. In the end, North Korea's best card is to continue to sow division among the Six-Party Talks partners, pulling South Korea and China further from the United States and Japan.

All parties to the Six-Party Talks officially agree on the ultimate goal of a denuclearised peninsula. But in the short to medium term, their aims are decidedly different. The United States has the greatest interest in dismantling North Korea's nuclear programme. Seeing little prospect for reaching that goal, however, and having no desire to offer concessions that would sustain Kim Jong Il, Washington's tactics emphasise containment of and pressure on the North Korean regime. In a mirror image of the US perspective, North Korea sees no hope for the talks leading to a solution it could accept. Pyongyang might find a tactical reason to resume talks, but for any real negotiations it will wait out the Bush administration. Japan supports the United States, but its own short-term emphasis is the fate of its abducted citizens. South Korea places greatest emphasis on just keeping the talks alive, as a confidence-building measure and to defuse tension, both for domestic political reasons and in line with its long-term vision of peaceful reunification. Russia wants the talks to resume so it can continue to have a role. China has a long-term interest in stopping the regional proliferation of nuclear weapons, but it is equally interested in preserving a stable, independent client state on its border. Meanwhile, as chairman and host, China has an immediate interest in shepherding a successful outcome from the talks. As of early summer 2006, just getting all parties back to the table would be success enough for China, but even that small step looked distant.

South Asia: New Possibilities, Old Problems

In a year during which the rise of India as an economic power attracted increasing attention, Indian Prime Minister Manmohan Singh and US President George W. Bush continued efforts to forge a new strategic partnership between the two countries. They struck a controversial nuclear deal – still awaiting approval – with profound implications not only for India, but also for its neighbours and for the international non-proliferation regime.

India–Pakistan relations made only slow progress. Although the leaders of the two countries deemed their peace process 'irreversible' in April 2005, it was clear at mid-2006 that it was slowing down. Mutual mistrust persisted amidst mixed results from the ongoing bilateral dialogue and confidence-building measures (CBM), and in the absence of substantive cooperation in the aftermath of the Kashmir earthquake, which killed nearly 75,000 people in October 2005. While Pakistan stressed the urgency of resolving the Kashmir dispute, India was loth to move forward in the absence of an end to militancy and violence, which escalated with a series of bombings in New Delhi.

Meanwhile, the rest of the region was in flux. 'People power' in Nepal brought a dramatic regime change, though prospects for stability and security remained uncertain. Sri Lanka experienced a surge in its low-intensity war. In Bangladesh, the rise of Islamic extremism continued to be a source of concern.

Nuclear deal dominates India–US relations

A major transformation of relations with the United States was under way, with a landmark bilateral nuclear deal to provide previously denied civil nuclear technology and supplies to India in return for separation of civil and military nuclear facilities and acceptance of international safeguards on civil facilities. Having previously declared that it would help India become a major world power in the twenty-first century, the Bush administration agreed to push for full civil nuclear cooperation despite Delhi's refusal to sign the Nuclear Non-proliferation Treaty (NPT) and the provisions of UNSC resolution 1172, passed after the nuclear tests of 1998. For Bush, India – with its economic emergence, democratic political system and strategic importance – was a country with which the United States shared common values and interests and which could be a potential counter-weight to a rising China. Bush was keen to make the strategic relationship with India a foreign-policy success.

In India, with a high growth rate of 8.3% and plans to further accelerate the economy, but with dwindling domestic oil resources accounting for only one-fifth of total consumption, nuclear energy is seen as key to future economic growth. The removal of 30-year-old nuclear and dual-use export controls by the United States, imposed after India's first nuclear test in 1974, would end India's nuclear isolation and remove a major irritation. Prospects for a partial recognition of India's nuclear-weapons status, a key political goal of India's foreign policy, were also a key determinant. For Singh, the nuclear-related technology trade restrictions were the last remaining hurdle for the transformation of bilateral ties to a strategic level.

Singh and Bush sealed the deal in a far-reaching 18 July 2005 joint statement in Washington, in which Bush agreed to push for 'full civil nuclear energy cooperation' with India, despite its refusal to sign the NPT or give up nuclear arms. Terming India a 'responsible state with advanced nuclear technology', Bush said he would seek agreement from Congress to amend US laws and work with friends and allies to adjust the international non-proliferation regime.

In return, India agreed to identify and separate its civilian and military nuclear facilities and programmes in a phased process. It agreed to continue its unilateral moratorium on nuclear testing, refrain from transferring nuclear technology and materials to non-nuclear states, work with the United States on the Fissile Material Cut-Off Treaty, strengthen export control guidelines and adhere to Missile Technology Control Regime and Nuclear Supplier Group (NSG) guidelines. In fact, India, in a key precondition for the 18 July statement, had already brought its export control laws into conformity with the global non-proliferation regime through the promulgation of a law on Weapons of Mass Destruction and their Delivery Systems (Prohibition of Unlawful Activities), which passed both houses of parliament in May 2005 and entered into force on 6 June 2005.

Before the deal could be consummated, it needed approval from the US Congress and the members of the 45-member NSG, which operates by consensus. The Bush administration insisted that India's separation plan be credible, transparent and defensible from a non-proliferation standpoint. For India, separating its deeply entwined civilian and nuclear facilities posed challenges. The

Indian government struggled to ensure that influential sections of the nuclear scientific community agreed to the separation plan. A key difference hinged on the status of the fast breeder reactor programme. The programme, in its present R&D phase, comprises a 40MWth fast-breeder test reactor and an upcoming 500MWe prototype fast-breeder reactor at Kalpakkam, which will process spent fuel from existing heavy-water reactors to recycle the nuclear fuel but which will also produce plutonium that could be used for nuclear weapons.

In a newspaper interview on 12 August 2005, the chairman of the Indian Atomic Energy Commission, Dr Anil Kakodkar, argued that R&D programmes such as the fast-breeder reactor programme should not be placed under International Atomic Energy Agency (IAEA) safeguards. In a riposte two months later, the Indian foreign secretary stated that it made no sense to deliberately keep some of India's civilian facilities out of its declaration for safeguards purposes. Nonetheless, pre-empting Bush's early March 2006 visit to India by three days, Singh bowed to pressure from the nuclear scientific community and informed parliament that 'we will offer to place under safeguards only those facilities that can be identified as civilian without damaging our deterrence potential or restricting our R&D effort ...We will ensure that no impediments are put in the way of our research and development activities. We have made it clear that we cannot accept safeguards on our indigenous Fast Breeder Programme'.

Following last-minute negotiations during the Bush visit, agreement was reached on a separation plan for India on 2 March 2006. Of India's 22 nuclear reactors (15 operational and seven under various stages of construction), 14 would be irreversibly classified as civilian. This would increase the extent of nuclear reactors under safeguards from the current four, accounting for 19% of total installed thermal nuclear power capacity, to 65%. In 2010 India would also shut down the Canadian-built Cirus research reactor, which had been used to produce plutonium for India's nuclear weapons, and shift the French-sourced fuel core of the Apsara reactor outside the sensitive Bhabha Atomic Research Centre and place it under safeguards. Although India would place all future civilian thermal-power reactors and fast-breeder reactors under safeguards, the classification of these reactors as civilian was to be determined by the Indian government. In addition, India would seek to negotiate an India-specific safeguards plan for its civilian reactors with the IAEA, as it was formally neither a nuclear-weapons state nor a non-nuclear weapons state. This safeguard plan would apply in 'perpetuity' (meeting a critical US condition), but only as long as foreign fuel supplies remained uninterrupted.

The separation plan did not cover eight Indian reactors, operational or under construction, which would not be placed under international safeguards. Reprocessing and enrichment capabilities and other facilities associated with the fuel cycle for India's nuclear-weapons programme were also kept out. In his statement to parliament on 7 March, Singh forcefully reiterated that the 'separation plan will not adversely affect our strategic programme ... there will be no capping of our strategic programme'.

Although the landmark nuclear deal was welcomed by IAEA Director-General Mohamed ElBaradei, it was severely criticised in both India and the United States. In India, the opposition Bharatiya Janata Party (BJP) argued that the deal capped India's nuclear deterrent, the physical separation of civilian and military nuclear facilities would be impossible to implement, the India-specific IAEA safeguards agreement would be intrusive and fraught with dangers and that there was no need for haste in securing the deal. Had India waited, it was implied, it would have got a better deal. Leftist parties claimed that the nuclear deal amounted to a foreign-policy alignment with the United States that violated the government's non-aligned policy.

In the US, criticism came from the influential non-proliferation lobby in Washington and from Congressional Democrats. This focused on six arguments: that the deal would erode the NPT and weaken the global nuclear non-proliferation regime; it would undermine non-proliferation efforts vis-à-vis Iran and North Korea; it would enable India to rapidly expand its nuclear arsenal, which could trigger an arms race in the region; it would demonstrate US 'double standards' by rewarding India with civil nuclear technology and supplies despite its nuclear-weapon programme and refusal to sign the NPT; it would reverse a 30-year US policy without extraction of concessions from India on its nuclear-weapons programme or other foreign-policy issues (including relations with Iran and as a potential counter-weight to China); and it would encourage China to provide nuclear technology to Pakistan.

In response, the US administration and the Indian government argued that India's position in the past had been untenable, and as a rising global power and a democracy with nuclear weapons it should be brought more closely into the nuclear non-proliferation regime; the nuclear deal would strengthen the global nuclear non-proliferation regime, as India had not, and was unlikely in future ever to provide nuclear technology and supplies to non-nuclear-weapons states; India had exercised restraint in its nuclear arsenal, and the civil nuclear cooperation deal with India would not trigger an arms race; India was unlikely ever to sign the NPT or to dismantle its nuclear weapons; and India could not be compared to Iran or North Korea.

Following agreement on the separation plan, the focus shifted to ensuring its acceptance by the US Congress and the international nuclear regime. This required four major steps to be taken – amendment of the Atomic Energy Act of 1954 by the US Congress with an India-specific waiver; Congressional approval of a bilateral civil nuclear cooperation agreement; an additional protocol between India and the IAEA on India-specific nuclear safeguards; and consensus on the supply of nuclear fuel and technology to India by the NSG. Each of these steps was complicated.

Although the Bush administration introduced legislation in Congress to amend the Atomic Energy Act, the timetable to consider the legislation remained the prerogative of Congress. On the prospective bilateral India–US civil nuclear cooperation agreement, differences appeared over whether the Indian moratorium on nuclear testing should remain voluntary and unilateral or whether it should be a bilateral undertaking with the United States, with the proviso that the nuclear deal would end if India were ever to carry out a test. Differences over the synchronisation of this four-stage process have also emerged between the Indian and US governments.

Moreover, with regard to the IAEA additional protocol, there were concerns in the Indian nuclear scientific establishment over the prospect of intrusive inspections. With regard to the NSG, although the United States, UK, France and Russia have welcomed the nuclear deal, Ireland, Sweden, Norway and Austria have asked difficult questions. Others are still considering it or unwilling to express a view until the situation is clearer. Most important to achieving the necessary consensus is China, whose response remains uncertain. So far, Beijing has only said that the deal 'must conform with provisions of the international non-proliferation regime'.

At the end of June 2006, versions of the legislation had been approved in committee in both houses, although it was unclear whether Congress had time to complete action before adjournment in October. The legislation required two separate votes, with the second coming after a formal US–India peaceful nuclear cooperation agreement is negotiated and after India and the IAEA agree on the India-specific safeguards. Although many members of Congress wanted India to cap its production of fissile material, there was recognition that adding such a condition would be a 'deal breaker' and that the opportunity for achieving this long-held non-proliferation goal was lost when Bush and Singh agreed the outline of the deal in July 2005. Members of Congress also recognised that if the deal was not approved, the momentum of the prospective bilateral strategic relationship would be lost, affecting India–US relations more broadly. There could also be severe domestic repercussions within the Indian government.

Rejection of the nuclear cooperation deal would overshadow other areas of growing US–India cooperation. Just after the July 2005 Singh–Bush joint statement, Indian Defence Minister Pranab Mukherjee and US Secretary of Defense Donald Rumsfeld signed a ten-year framework on India–US defence cooperation that could lead to joint weapons production and cooperation in defence R&D. For the first time, New Delhi agreed to cooperate with Washington on combined multinational military operations in the absence of a UN mandate or UN forces command. This was a key policy shift given India's decision the previous year not to send troops to Iraq. Following expanded defence cooperation, including joint naval and air exercises, both countries subsequently also agreed to substantively enhance security cooperation on maritime issues.

Kashmir and India–Pakistan relations

The earthquake

Kashmir was the focal point for India–Pakistan diplomacy, due largely to the devastating earthquake that struck on 8 October 2005. Measuring 7.6 on the Richter scale, its epicentre was near Muzaffarabad, the capital of Pakistan-administered Kashmir, where over 73,000 people died and over three million became homeless. The impact of the earthquake in Indian-administered Kashmir was far smaller, with some 1,400 deaths. The earthquake triggered a massive international relief operation, including the first troop deployment of the rapid-reaction NATO Response Force (see Strategic Geography, pp. XX–XXI).

As the extent of devastation became clear, Singh offered India's help to President Pervez Musharraf. A telephone hotline was immediately activated between the nations' foreign secretaries. On 12 October, the first Indian Air Force aircraft bringing relief supplies landed in Islamabad. Two other consignments of relief supplies, including tents, were sent by train. On 19 October, India and Pakistan announced the setting up of four telecommunication facilitation centres at Srinagar, Jammu, Uri and Tangdhar to enable divided families in Kashmir to communicate with relatives across the Line of Control (LoC). On the Indian side, however, the use of mobile-phone services was prohibited. India also offered $25m in relief assistance to Pakistan at the international donors' conference in Islamabad in November.

Cooperation in humanitarian relief and assistance across the LoC, however, remained restricted and mired in political one-upmanship and acrimony. Within two days of the earthquake, India proposed joint relief operations with the use of Indian paramilitary and military forces in areas of Pakistan-administered Kashmir that were closer to Indian-administered Kashmir than Islamabad. While this may have reflected standard Indian operating procedures in the wake of major natural disasters, in view of the existing level of mistrust between the countries it was perceived as provocative by Islamabad, which promptly ruled it out. Instead, Pakistan offered its help to Indian-administered Kashmir, but was ignored by India. To India's subsequent offer to send helicopters to assist in rescue and relief operations, Pakistan responded that it would be acceptable only if they flew without Indian pilots, which India rejected. There were also inaccurate press reports of Indian forces helping repair Pakistani military bunkers across the LoC, which led to a series of denials and counter-denials between the two countries.

Much of the public diplomacy on the LoC centred on the opening of new crossing points and relief centres to enable Kashmiris to cross over for humanitarian and relief purposes. In a surprise move on 18 October, Musharraf, speaking from the virtually destroyed city of Muzaffarabad, offered to open the LoC to 'any amount of people' to facilitate free movement for earthquake-hit families to assist with reconstruction. While this was later understood to be applicable only to Kashmiris,

Musharraf urged India to agree to the plan. Three days later, Pakistan's foreign minister said he would like this to become a permanent feature of the LoC.

India received the proposal with considerable unease as it was loth to open the LoC to allow militants in the guise of relatives or rescue workers to cross into Indian-administered Kashmir. When the proposal was formally put to India on 22 October, New Delhi demurred. Instead, it offered to set up three rehabilitation centres on the LoC in Uri, Titwal and Chakan-da-Bagh to help the people of Pakistan-administered Kashmir during the day, with the understanding that they would return at night. After talks in Islamabad on 29 October, the sides finally agreed to open five crossing points and relief centres along the LoC – at Poonch–Rawalkot, Uri–Chakoti, Titwal–Nauseri, Mendher–Tattapani and Uri–Hajipur – for divided families and relief and reconstruction efforts. While the first crossing point was opened in Poonch-Rawalkot on 7 November, the fifth opened on 16 November, marking the first multiple crossing points across the LoC in nearly 60 years.

Continuing violence

Notwithstanding the announcement of a temporary suspension of operations by Syed Salahuddin, chairman of the United Jihad Council, an amalgamation of a dozen jihadi militant groups, attacks in Indian-administered Kashmir continued without respite. Five days after the earthquake the first suicide bomb attack by a woman took place. Five days later, the provincial minister of state for education was killed in Srinagar. On 26 October, a car bomb exploded at an army camp. Militants allegedly continued to infiltrate into Indian-administered Kashmir, their passage made easier by ongoing rescue and relief operations and severe damage in places to the border fence. Initial reports indicating vast damage to militant infrastructure in Pakistan-administered Kashmir soon began to be discounted in New Delhi. Indeed, there were concerns that the swift rescue-and-relief response by militant groups, especially members of the Jamaat-ud-Dawa – the parent outfit of the banned Pakistan-based militant jihadist outfit, Lashkar-e-Toiba (LeT) – in accessing remote areas where the Pakistan military had yet to reach, would add to their support base.

Although cross-border infiltration into Indian-administered Kashmir decreased in the winter months, violence continued amidst Indian allegations that militant infrastructure in Pakistan-administered Kashmir had not been destroyed, despite Pakistan's assurances. Nonetheless, in February 2006, the Indian defence minister stated that an additional 5,000 troops had been moved out of the region due to the improved security situation. Later that month, the Indian home minister informed parliament that infiltration had nearly halved and terrorist killings had decreased by a fifth in the previous year.

In summer 2006, however, violence and cross-border infiltration into Indian-administered Kashmir appeared to be increasing. On 30 April 2006, militants killed 32 Hindu villagers in two separate attacks in the Doda and Udhampur districts in Indian-administered Kashmir. The following month, attacks took place against tourists, a Youth Congress rally in Srinagar, and a patrol of the paramilitary Border Security Force (BSF). The latter was targeted by a suicide bomber on the eve of Singh's second roundtable conference in Srinagar on 24 May. On 25 June the Indian defence minister ruled out any further reduction of troops in Indian-administered Kashmir for the time being due to the increase in violence.

However, the cease-fire along the LoC and in Siachen continued successfully into its third year. At the expert-level meeting on conventional CBMs on 8 August 2005 the sides significantly agreed, for the first time, 'to reaffirm their commitment to uphold the ongoing ceasefire', an affirmation Islamabad had been reluctant to provide lest it be perceived as a legitimisation of the LoC. The statement was reiterated at the meeting of the foreign secretaries on 1 September. The two sides also agreed to upgrade the existing hotline between the respective chiefs of military operations, not to develop any new posts and defence works along the LoC and to hold monthly flag meetings between local commanders at four places along the LoC. At the next round of talks in late April 2006, they agreed that new border ground rules be framed, as the existing agreement (signed in 1960) was outdated. At the same time, India rejected a Pakistani proposal to remove all heavy weapons from Kashmir.

The prospect of an internal cease-fire with militants in Indian-administered Kashmir also appeared unlikely before violence had ended. At the same time, there was growing concern in India over the spread of violence beyond Indian-administered Kashmir to the capital, New Delhi, and southern India, allegedly carried out by LeT. On 29 October, a series of bombings took place in New Delhi, amidst preparations for the Hindu festival of Diwali. Two bombs exploded almost simultaneously in crowded commercial markets in Paharganj and Sarojni Nagar, and a third exploded on a bus in Govindpuri, killing 62 people and injuring 210. Fears that this would force India to pull out of the peace process with Pakistan did not materialise, but Singh made it clear to Musharraf that India was 'disturbed' over indications of 'external linkages'. On 28 December, an attack took place in Bangalore at the prestigious Indian Institute of Science, killing a senior scientist and injuring others.

A series of bomb attacks on Hindu and Muslim religious sites was seen as an attempt to provoke communal violence in a country where stability is determined by the harmony of relations between the majority Hindu and minority Muslim communities. On 5 July 2005, an attempt was made to storm the makeshift Lord Rama temple at the disputed religious complex in Ayodhya, the scene of considerable national communal tension in December 1992. The six militants shot dead by security personnel were allegedly members of LeT. This was followed by three bomb blasts on 7 March 2006 at the Hindu Sankatmochan temple and the railway station in the Hindu holy city of Varanasi in northern India. Twenty people were killed and over 50 others injured. Seven bombs were later defused. This was allegedly carried out by Bangladeshi nationals linked to the militant group Harkat-ul-Jihad-al-Islami of Bangladesh, at the behest of Pakistan-based militant groups. On 14 April 2006, two crude bombs also exploded in Delhi's Jama Masjid (Grand Mosque), one of the largest and most influential Muslim holy sites in India, soon after Friday prayers, injuring 13 worshippers.

Proposals and counterproposals

Amidst these developments, the India–Pakistan peace process seemed to be slowing down. There was little appetite in New Delhi to move forward on several of Musharraf's proposals on the resolution of the Kashmir conflict. These focused on building further on his October 2004 three-stage 'proposal' for the future of Kashmir, which had already been rejected by Singh.

Addressing a conference in Islamabad in May 2005, Musharraf said a compromise on the stated Indian and Pakistani positions – that boundaries could not be redrawn and that the LoC could not be made a permanent border – was needed. This would be to make the borders 'irrelevant'. Ruling out any solution on the basis of religion, he added that the way forward was to grant maximum possible autonomy to both parts of Kashmir, and open more passenger and trade routes between them. In addition, both sides of Kashmir needed to be 'demilitarised'. Musharraf also indicated that the international community should play a role in guaranteeing these developments.

In September, Musharraf proposed self-governance and the demilitarisation of Kashmir through the withdrawal of Indian forces from three key militancy-prone areas, Baramulla, Kupwara and Srinagar. On 31 October 2005, Musharraf put forward an 'idea' for Kashmir to be divided into regions, each to be demilitarised and then allowed self-governance. The following day, India reacted cautiously to this suggestion by stating that the demilitarisation of Indian-administered Kashmir could not be done unilaterally, with the implication that cross-border infiltration and violence had first to end. Later that month, a more forceful Indian response by an External Affairs Ministry spokesman rejected Pakistan's idea of 'so-called self-governance' in Kashmir, on the basis that the province already enjoyed autonomy and popular democratic rights, adding that this was not the case for Pakistan-administered Kashmir. Nonetheless, President Musharraf continued to reiterate his proposals for demilitarisation and self-governance, stating that an ultimate solution would make the LoC irrelevant and require neither the redrawing of borders nor making the LoC permanent. On 23 June 2006, Musharraf further proposed demilitarisation as a 'final resolution' of the dispute, following which the people of Kashmir were to be given self-governance with a joint management arrangement.

In response to these proposals, on the occasion of the inaugural Amritsar–Nankana Sahib bus service on 24 March 2006, Singh suddenly offered Pakistan a 'Treaty of Peace, Security and Friendship', as the culmination of the ongoing peace process. He also said 'meaningful agreement' was possible on issues like Siachen, Sir Creek and Baglihar, but 'it would be a mistake to link normalisation of other relations with finding a solution to Jammu & Kashmir'. He added that while borders between the two sides could not be redrawn, they could be made 'irrelevant' – as just lines on a map. While Islamabad welcomed this offer, it cautiously responded that attempts to delink the Kashmir dispute from an overall settlement were unrealistic.

Although parallels may be drawn between Musharraf's and Singh's ideas for making the LoC 'irrelevant', they appear to differ markedly. Musharraf's focus rests on the division of Kashmir into regions, followed by demilitarisation and self-governance. The 'irrelevance' of the borders appears to be an important CBM, but simply as a means to demilitarisation and self-governance. 'Self-governance', however, has not been clearly defined: would it be independence, autonomy or something else? In marked contrast, Singh talked of the 'irrelevance' of the LoC over time, largely alluding to the growing network of transportation and economic links within Kashmir. He appeared to focus on the 'softening' of the LoC, but this idea, too, is not clearly defined.

Notwithstanding these differences, a key focus for the future of India–Pakistan relations appears to be on making the LoC 'irrelevant', a desire expressed by both leaders. This would include a substantive expansion of cross-LoC people-to-people movement, increased focus on trade links starting with the truck service in July 2006, and initiating tourism and business links among key stakeholders in Kashmir.

Talks with Kashmiri leaders

Singh began to actively engage with the political leadership in Kashmir, albeit with little success with regard to the moderate faction of the separatist All Party Hurriyat Conference (APHC). In a significant development, Singh permitted a Hurriyat delegation led by its chairman Mirwaiz Omar Farooq, along with the chief of the Jammu Kashmir Liberation Front, Yasin Malik, to travel to Muzaffarabad in June 2005 on the recently opened cross-LoC bus service. This was the first visit of the Hurriyat leadership to Pakistan-administered Kashmir, subsequently extended to Pakistan, although the latter visit was frowned upon by New Delhi. The Kashmiri delegation had meetings with Musharraf and senior leaders of Pakistan and Pakistan-administered Kashmir.

Just over two months later, Singh met the APHC delegation in New Delhi for the first time, over a year-and-a-half after their last meeting with the previous government's deputy prime minister, L.K. Advani. At the meeting on 5

September, a few days prior to Singh's meeting with Musharraf in New York, Singh offered to cut the number of troops in Indian-administered Kashmir, but only if there was an end to infiltration and violence. Later that month, in a sign of renewed confidence, India announced the replacement of the last of the BSF's 9,000-strong force in Srinagar with the Central Reserve Police Force.

In an attempt to bolster the dialogue with Kashmiri leaders, Singh organised his first official roundtable conference on Kashmir in New Delhi on 25 February. This comprised some 70 delegates, including Kashmiri leaders and government officials, but the Hurriyat rejected the invitation. Singh's second round of talks with the Hurriyat leadership took place on 3 May, partly in an attempt to encourage their participaton at Singh's follow-on Kashmir conference scheduled for Srinagar on 24–25 May. In these talks, Singh and Mirwaiz reportedly agreed to evolve a mechanism and discuss specifics to ensure forward movement on the dialogue process. Notwithstanding early indications that the Hurriyat leadership might participate in the second Kashmir conference, they dismissed the meeting as merely a 'seminar' and did not attend.

At the end of the second two-day roundtable conference in Srinagar on 25 May, Singh announced the establishment of five working groups to discuss various issues relating to Indian-administered Kashmir. The groups, would deal with improving the conditions of those affected by militancy; furthering relations across the LoC; employment generation and sub-regional development; reviewing the cases of detainees and ensuring good governance; and strengthening centre–state relations, including discussions on autonomy and the special status of Indian-administered Kashmir within the Indian Union.

Slow steps in the formal process

Meanwhile, the overall peace process continued into its second year with mixed results from high-level meetings, the composite dialogue on a set of eight disputes and issues, expert- and technical-level talks and a series of CBMs. The most successful CBMs were on transportation and communication links. New cross-Line of Control (LoC) and cross-border road and rail links were established to complement the existing Delhi–Lahore bus service, Atari–Lahore passenger and freight train, and the cross-LoC Srinagar–Muzaffarabad bus service. On 20 January 2006, a bus service between Amritsar and Lahore began for the first time. This was followed on 24 March by an Amritsar–Nankana Sahib bus service linking Sikhism's two holiest sites. Following talks in May 2005 the Poonch–Rawalkot bus service, the second cross-LoC link, was launched on 20 June. In addition, five cross-LoC border points were opened in the aftermath of the Kashmir earthquake in October 2005. On 18 February 2006, the train service between Munabao and Khokrapar was restarted, 40 years after it had been suspended. In mid-July 2006, trade was to resume on the Srinagar–Muzaffarabad road.

A notable achievement of the composite dialogue was a bilateral agreement on pre-notification of flight testing of ballistic missiles. At the third expert-level meeting on nuclear CBMs in August 2005, an understanding on the proposed agreement was reached. Formalised by the Indian and Pakistan foreign secretaries on 1 September 2005, the agreement was signed in the presence of the two foreign ministers in Islamabad on 3 October. It committed the parties to notify each other at least three days in advance of a five-day test-launch window, and to issue appropriate notices to airmen and provide navigational area warnings at sea. Each party was also to ensure that the launch site did not fall within 40km, and the planned impact area not within 70km, of the international border or the LoC. Ballistic missile tests by both parties have since conformed to the agreement.

Parallel to these developments, people-to-people contact continued to grow and cultural ties increased. Cultural troupes were exchanged and two Bollywood films were shown in cinemas in Pakistan in April 2006. Visits of pilgrims to religious shrines increased with better transportation links. On 12 September 2005, the two countries exchanged 600 prisoners languishing in each other's jails.

There was no progress on other key issues of the composite dialogue, nothwitstanding considerable diplomatic activity and press speculation on the demilitarisation of the Siachen glacier. Singh's visit to the base camp at Siachen on 12 June 2005, the first by an Indian prime minister, raised prospects of an agreement in the offing. While Singh announced that he hoped to turn Siachen into a 'mountain of peace', he simultaneously rejected the redrawing of boundaries. There was no breakthrough at the Siachen talks in May 2006. Major differences between the parties remained, encouraged by their militaries. These differences appeared to be on the principle of mutual authentication of military positions on the glacier (which New Delhi insisted on and Islamabad refused, as legitimising India's control of the area) and mechanisms for demilitarisation (with New Delhi being in a more difficult position for access and logistics support). Nonetheless, simultaneous 'back-channel' talks on Siachen between designated special envoys continued.

On the Sir Creek dispute the two nations agreed to carry out a joint survey, but on little else. There was mutual agreement that talks on the Tulbul navigation project/Wular barrage would continue. On the Baglihar power project, India agreed to the appointment of a neutral expert, Swiss hydropower engineer Raymond Lafitte, to examine alleged violations of the 1960 Indus Water Treaty. Pakistan claimed that the design, size and water-storage capacity of the project currently under construction in Indian-administered Kashmir violated the treaty. After visiting the site in October 2005, and hearing technical and legal arguments by both sides, Lafitte is due to submit his report to the World Bank in late 2006.

India

Domestic challenges

Singh's Congress-led United Progressive Alliance (UPA) government completed its second year in office in mid-May 2006, amidst growing criticism from its leftist partners bolstered by gains in recent provincial assembly elections. The opposition Bharatiya Janata Party (BJP), meanwhile, continued to struggle with leadership issues and remained demoralised over the resignation of its chief, L.K. Advani, in June 2005 following a controversial visit to Pakistan.

The leftist parties had attained their strongest-ever political position. They held 60 seats in parliament, were providing key support to the government (without which it could not rule) and fully controlled three provinces. In state assembly elections in April–May 2006, leftists retained control of West Bengal and unseated the Congress-led front in Kerala to form a Left Democratic Front (LDF) government. However, despite their increased influence in the national government, they fell far short of forming a 'third front' in parliament after the UPA and opposition National Democratic Alliance (NDA) coalitions. Although leftist criticism of the central government focused sharply on foreign-policy issues such as the India–US nuclear deal and India's vote against Iran in the IAEA in September 2005, it was in the economic sphere that their influence was greater and prospects for conflict sharper. A case in point was the shelving of the central government's policy to disinvest in key public-sector companies in October 2005 and June 2006. Nonetheless, in January 2006 Singh deftly handled leftist opposition to the privatisation of Delhi and Bombay airports.

The Indian economy grew by 8.3% in 2005, the highest after China and Pakistan. Though it is ambitiously targeted at 10% for 2006, it could decrease to 7.5–8% due to the rise in fuel prices, inflation and interest rates. Following an 80% rise in the Bombay Stock Exchange's Sensitive Index (Sensex) from June 2005, exceeding 12,000 points for the first time in April 2006, a fall was expected. When this came, it demonstrated the volatility of the markets. On 10 May 2006, the Sensex reached a peak of 12,612, but with simultaneous substantial withdrawals from the equity markets by foreign institutional investors and expectations of an interest rate hike in the United States, it fell dramatically by over 2,000 points in ten days, wiping off a fifth of the value of shares. By 2 June, it had slowly recovered to 10,451.

Internal security

With the third-largest Muslim population in the world, after Indonesia and Pakistan, at over 150m people, India prides itself that no Indian Muslim has been identified as a member of an international terrorist organisation. This is due largely to Indian Muslims' lack of support for pan-Islamic ideology, the existence of democratic institutions and historical cultural influences. But, for the first time, there appears to be some unease in sections of the Indian Muslim community over foreign developments. Indian Muslims have registered their concern over the US-led war in Iraq, India's IAEA vote against Iran, atrocities in the Abu Ghraib prison in Iraq, and the caricatures of the Prophet Mohammed in a Danish newspaper. These concerns led to anti-Western and anti-US demonstrations, some during Bush's visit to India.

Long-standing internal problems continued to fester. With Naxalite Maoist rebels stepping up attacks against police stations and transport and communication links, large rural areas of six eastern and central provinces – Andhra Pradesh, Bihar, Chhattisgarh, Jharkhand, Orissa and Uttar Pradesh – remained severely affected. Spurred on by extreme poverty, severe unemployment and an absence of rural development or land reforms, Naxalites attacked civilians, police personnel and political activists and triggered landmine blasts. In more daring operations, over a hundred Naxalites attacked a home-guard training centre in Pachamba, Jharkhand, on 11 November 2005 and looted arms and ammunition; two days later, nearly 200 of their cadres launched simultaneous attacks on the jail, police lines and a paramilitary camp at Jehanabad, Bihar, killing four people and freeing nearly 350 prisoners. In March 2005, the Naxalites captured a train carrying more than a hundred passengers in Jharkhand. Later that month in Udayagiri, Orissa, they attacked a police station, a camp of the state armed police, the local jail and a bank. In April 2006, the Orissa chief minister warned that 16 of the province's 30 districts were affected by Naxalite activities. The most significant rise in Naxalite violence took place in Chhattisgarh. On 3 September 2005, 24 security-force personnel were killed in a landmine blast in the Dantewada district. At least 25 ethnic tribals were killed and 40 others injured in a landmine blast near Eklagoda village at the end of February 2006. These attacks forced the provincial government to introduce new anti-terrorism training for the police and form a controversial anti-Naxalite civil militia called Salwa Judum ('campaign for peace').

With nearly 300 people killed in Naxalite violence in the first four months of 2006, the level of violence exceeded that in Kashmir for the first time. Singh described it in mid-April 2006 as the 'single biggest internal security challenge' for the country. Yet attempts by the central and provincial governments to tackle it appeared to lack focus and priority. While the central government advocates a 'carrot and stick' approach, provincial governments continue to see it largely as a law-and-order problem. Also, inter-provincial security coordination in intelligence and joint operations remain weak, compounded by a lack of intelligence on the ground. In view of reported links between the Nepali and Indian Maoists, the two governments on 3 August 2005 agreed to strengthen border controls and construct four new checkpoints on the border to prevent Maoist infiltration into India.

Elsewhere, the Indian government made progress on cease-fires on several fronts. Following the MoU with the Bru National Liberation Front in Mizoram in April 2005, a cease-fire accord with the National Democratic Front of Bodoland

(NDFB) in Assam took place in May 2005. According to the terms of the agreement, all insurgency and counter-insurgency operations were to be suspended for a year from 1 June 2005. In July 2005, India extended cease-fires with two separatist groups – the Achik National Volunteers Council of Meghalaya and the United People's Democratic Solidarity of Assam – for another year. It also extended the cease-fire with the National Socialist Council of Nagaland-Isak-Muivah to consolidate peace talks and resolve the five-decade-old insurgency in Nagaland.

The main conflict in Assam with the United Liberation Front of Assam (ULFA) continued, however, with little prospect for peace. The first peace talks between Singh and a team negotiating on ULFA's behalf, led by a well-known Assamese writer, took place on 26 October 2005. After two more sets of talks, the Indian government agreed to hold direct talks with ULFA, but differences continued over the issue of sovereignty for Assam as an agenda item in the talks.

The construction of a fence along the Tripura border increased tensions with neighbouring Bangladesh, which claimed that it violated agreements prohibiting such security measures. Nonetheless, India alleged that key militant organisations, the National Liberation Front of Tripura and the All Tripura Tiger Force, had camps in Bangladesh, used for staging attacks in Tripura.

Military developments

India carried out three successful flight tests of its supersonic *BrahMos* cruise missile during 2005–06 – the first naval test with a live warhead at sea on 16 April 2005, the first army test using mobile launchers on 30 November 2005 and a second army test by trained army personnel on 1 June 2006. While the *BrahMos* was being deployed in the Indian Navy, the army was not far behind. Following the two flight tests of its version of the missile, the army has reportedly begun to prepare for its entry into service, with the formation of a new *BrahMos* artillery regiment. Meanwhile, the programme for the development of the air-launched version of the *BrahMos* from the air force's Su-30 aircraft has begun in earnest, with the first air-to-ground flight test scheduled for late 2007. Indian orders for the *BrahMos* missile have reportedly boosted prospects for its sale to Chile, Malaysia and South Africa.

On 11 June 2006, India carried out a user trial of its *Prithvi* I short-range (150–250km) nuclear-capable ballistic missile. The longer-range (250km) *Prithvi* II was tested on 12 May 2005. On 28 December 2005, India also successfully test-fired at sea its 350km-range *Dhanush* missile, the naval version of the *Prithvi*. There remains considerable speculation over the much-delayed maiden flight of India's potentially long-range ballistic missile, the 3,000–3,500km-range *Agni* III. In May 2006, the chief of the Defence Research and Development Organisation publicly stated that the *Agni* III was 'technically ready' for launch, but awaiting a political decision.

India's defence budget for 2006–07 increased by 7.2% to $19.85bn. Capital expenditure, comprising 42% of the budget with major hikes in the past three years, increased to $8.34bn. The rise in defence expenditure is expected to continue in view of India's strategic environment and high annual economic growth rates. Even with defence spending more than doubling in the past six years, it is currently a very manageable 2.29% of GDP. Singh has publicly said that defence expenditure could be set at 3% of GDP if the economy grew at 8% annually in the next few years. This level would be manageable both politically and economically.

India's arms procurement programme continues to gather pace, with prospects for major orders in the next 10 years estimated at $50–60bn. On 6 October 2005, India signed a $3.5bn deal with France to build six advanced *Scorpene* submarines in Mumbai's Mazagon shipyard between 2012 and 2017. The submarines would be armed with 36 SM39 *Exocet* anti-ship missiles. This was the first arms deal in which 30% offsets for goods and services had been mandated, in accordance with the government's new defence offset policy of June 2005. Future arms procurement orders include a $7.5bn deal for 126 medium multi-role combat aircraft for the air force and 60 for the navy, 1,200 howitzers, maritime patrol aircraft, multiple-launch rocket systems, upgrade of Mig-29 combat aircraft, 80 medium-lift helicopters, naval ships and helicopters and air defence systems.

India–China relations

Despite the simultaneous emergence of the two nations as rising global powers, bilateral Sino-Indian relations grew. At the IISS Global Security Review Conference in Geneva in September 2005, India's national security adviser to the prime minister, M.K. Narayanan, stated that 'there is enough space for both societies to continue to grow and simultaneously achieve their aspirations'. This was reflected in trade figures, which shot up to $18bn in 2005. Although bilateral India–US trade was slightly higher, the higher growth rate of Sino-Indian trade could lead to China's emergence as India's largest trading partner in the near future.

In November 2005, at the 13th South Asian Association for Regional Cooperation (SAARC) summit, India agreed that China, along with Japan, be invited as an observer to the eight-member organisation. In a significant development on 6 July, India and China re-opened border trade through the 4,300m-high Himalayan pass of Nathu La after 44 years. The second round of the 'strategic dialogue' at the foreign-secretary level took place in early 2006, and the eighth round of talks between high-level special representatives on the border issue took place at the end of June 2006. These talks are now at the 'second phase of negotiations' as set out during Chinese premier Wen Jiabao's visit to India in April 2005, defined as exploring 'the framework of a boundary settlement'. This followed the Indian defence minister's visit to China in May 2006, when the first bilateral MoU on expanding military ties, by institutionalising military training and holding joint military exercises, was signed.

Pakistan

Internal security

Pakistani security forces have had limited success in their campaign in Waziristan, one of the semi-autonomous Pushtun tribal areas bordering Afghanistan. There have been major clashes with local militants since operations against al-Qaeda and local Taliban forces began four years ago, involving nearly 80,000 Pakistani troops. The most significant clash was over Miranshah, the administrative capital of North Waziristan. In March 2006, hundreds of armed Pushtun tribesmen seized the bazaar and government buildings in the town. The main army base at Miranshah also came under heavy rocket fire. Pakistani security forces mounted a major operation with helicopter gunships and heavy artillery fire, killing over 100 militants and regaining Miranshah

A few days later, Pakistani security forces attacked Khattay Killay village, 10km from Miranshah, to target two Taliban leaders. As a result of Pakistani military operations, Pushtun tribesmen from North and South Waziristan demanded in April 2006 that Pakistan withdraw its forces from the tribal areas. In May 2005, Pakistan arrested a top al-Qaeda terrorist, Abu Faraj Al Libbi, who was thought to be behind two assassination attempts against Musharraf. In April 2006, another senior al-Qaeda operative, Abu Marwan al-Suri, was killed in the Bajaur tribal area bordering Afghanistan.

Nonetheless, there was mounting criticism that Pakistan was not doing enough to neutralise al-Qaeda or Taliban forces in the lawless tribal lands along the Afghan border. On 19 June 2005, then US Ambassador to Afghanistan Zalmay Khalilzad said Taliban chief Mullah Mohammad Omar had been hiding in Pakistan and criticised Islamabad's failure to act against Taliban leaders. US attempts to deal with al-Qaeda leaders on Pakistani territory, however, were severely criticised after a botched missile attack on 13 January 2006. Four US unmanned *Predator* drones fired missiles into Damadola village in the Bajaur tribal area in an attempt to target al-Qaeda's second-in-command, Ayman al-Zawahiri. The US attack killed at least 18 people, mostly women and children, and injured several others, but al-Zawahiri was reportedly not present. The Pakistani government angrily denounced the missile attack. In summer 2006 there was tension with Afghanistan over its official criticism of Pakistan's campaign against the Taliban as 'half hearted'. With British troops now deployed in Afghanistan's neighbouring Helmand province, there is growing concern over the apparent inaction of the Pakistani military against the Taliban in the increasingly lawless tribal areas. Musharraf remains on a tightrope, trying to meet US demands bhile assuaging local resentment.

Attacks on key government offices, transport and communication links, economic infrastructure (especially natural-gas pipelines) and security forces intensified in Baluchistan, Pakistan's largest province bordering Afghanistan and

Iran. Pakistan's military response also intensified, triggered by a rocket attack on a paramilitary base at Kohlu on 13 December 2005, while Musharraf was visiting the nearby town. The Pakistani response on 18 December was swift, with security forces using helicopter gunships and strike aircraft against Baloch rebel forces; over 50 people were reportedly killed and around 100 injured. In January 2006, security forces mounted another major operation, against the town of Kahan in the Marri area. In early February, Baloch rebels carried out a rocket attack on the town of Dera Bugti, targeting communications and civil and paramilitary installations. Later that month, they killed three Chinese engineers, along with their Pakistani driver, in the city of Hub, about 700km south of Quetta, the capital of Baluchistan. On 9 March 2006, an anti-tank landmine exploded in Dera Bugti, killing 26 people.

A month later, the Pakistan government banned the shadowy militant Baluchistan Liberation Army (BLA), suspected to be responsible for these attacks, after declaring it a terrorist organisation. The Pakistani government alleged that the BLA was involved in sabotage activities, including rocket attacks on national installations, the civilian population and security forces. The BLA was also accused of laying landmines in various parts of the province. Baloch militant activities continued: on 11 May, six anti-terrorist police were killed and 13 others injured in five powerful bomb explosions at the firing range of the Police Training College in Quetta. To deal with the worsening situation, Pakistan reportedly deployed some 25,000 security forces in the province, largely paramilitary with elements of the army. Expression of official Indian concern over the deteriorating situation in late December 2005 met with a curt response and allegations that India's foreign intelligence agency was involved in fomenting the unrest.

Outbreaks of religious extremism and sectarian violence continued, with Sunni and Shi'ite armed groups attacking each other's shrines. On 27 May 2005, a suicide bomber exploded a powerful bomb at the Shi'ite Bari Imam shrine in Islamabad, killing 25 people and injuring 100. Three days later, an explosion in the courtyard of a Shia mosque at Gulshan-e-Iqbal in Karachi killed six people, including the bomber. In the riot that followed the next day, four employees of a US fast-food franchise were killed. Sectarian violence also continued in the Gilgit region in the Northern Areas in September 2005, when two people were killed. The following month, Gilgit came under curfew.

On 9 February 2006 a suicide attack on a Muharram Festival procession of Shia Muslims in the Hangu town of the North-West Frontier Province killed 40 people and injured 50. An exchange of gunfire and violence erupted between the Shi'ite and Sunni communities, claiming a further four lives the next day. In one of the worst attacks, at least 57 Sunni Muslims were killed and over 80 injured in a double suicide bomb attack at Nishtar Park in Karachi on 11 April 2006. This attack, on the occasion of the birthday celebrations of the Prophet Mohammad, eliminated the entire top leadership of the Sunni Tehreek, a fundamentalist Sunni organisation.

Following reports that two of the three suicide bombers of Pakistani extraction involved in the 7 July 2005 attacks in London had visited madrassas (religious schools) in Pakistan a few months earlier, Musharraf ordered a country-wide drive against extremism and reiterated his resolve to combat terrorism. Following the arrest of 120 clerics and students at madrassas, he reportedly told Singh that he would rein in the militants in Pakistan-administered Kashmir within a month. In a televised address to the nation on 21 July, Musharraf said the UK and Pakistan urgently needed to take 'serious measures' to eradicate the menace of terrorism rather than blaming each other for the London bombings. He declared that no banned group would be allowed to operate in the country under any name and strict action would be taken against violators, adding that possession and display of unauthorised arms would be strictly prohibited. He also warned that strict action would be taken against those involved in printing, publishing and distributing hate material, including newspapers, magazines, handbills and pamphlets, as well as audio and video material. A special cell would also ensure the registration of all madrassas in the country by December 2005.

On 29 July, Musharraf further said that all foreign nationals studying in madrassas, estimated at over 1,400 from 56 countries, would have to leave the institutions. No new visas were to be issued to non-Pakistanis wishing to pursue religious studies in the country. On 16 August, Musharraf promulgated an ordinance amending the Societies Registration Act, 1860, requiring nearly 12,000 madrassas in the country to register with the government. This drive against extremists and jihadi groups was bolstered on 1 December, when Musharraf promulgated the Societies Registration (second amendment) Ordinance 2005, making it mandatory for every madrassa in Islamabad to audit its accounts and prepare reports on its educational activities. It also prohibited seminaries from promoting militancy, sectarianism and religious hatred.

The drive to register madrassas met with considerable opposition and institutional resistance. Amidst large-scale public demonstrations against the registration of madrassas and the deportation of foreign students, Musharraf strove to stay on course. By 6 December some 8,200 madrassas had registered with the government. On 10 December, the government and the Ittehad-e-Tanzeemat-e-Madaris-e-Deenia, an alliance of five education boards that controlled the majority of madrassas, reached an agreement to allow foreign students to complete their studies. In February 2006, amidst considerable pressure, they finally agreed to register all madrassas associated with them.

Domestic and military developments

Sensing a possible role in the general elections scheduled to be held by late 2007, the two main secular opposition parties, the Pakistan Muslim League–Nawaz (PML-N) and the Pakistan's People Party (PPP), attempted to agree on a common platform. Their leaders, Nawaz Sharif, exiled to Saudi Arabia but in London for medical treatment, and Benazir Bhutto, self-exiled in the UAE and the UK, agreed to make concerted efforts to restore to Pakistan a genuine parliamentary system, in which the army would be kept out of politics. Notwithstanding their enthusiasm, it is unlikely they will play an influential role in general elections in late 2007, with Musharraf and the army expected to continue to rule.

At 8.4%, Pakistan's strong economic growth during 2005–06 was second only to China's, though it was expected to decrease to 6.5% in 2006–07 due to high oil prices. Foreign-exchange reserves rose from $1.56bn in 2000 to $13bn in 2005. In 2006, Pakistan increased its defence budget by 12% to $4.1bn, following a 15% increase the previous year. This accounted for 20% of total government spending.

Notwithstanding post-earthquake reconstruction, Pakistan is embarking on an ambitious arms acquisition programme for its air force and navy, including a $1.14bn order finalised in late June 2006 for a Swedish AWACS system based on a SAAB 2000 aircraft. Having temporarily postponed in November 2005 the acquisition of up to 75 new US-built F-16 combat aircraft for $4bn due to the earthquake, Pakistan reportedly agreed in April 2006 to proceed with a scaled-down package of 18 new and 36 used aircraft (worth $1.8–2bn). Pakistan is also expected to acquire an estimated 36 J-10 fighter aircraft from China ($1.2–1.4bn) and up to 150 JF-17 joint Pakistan–China *Thunder* fighter aircraft ($2bn). These arms purchases were largely intended to counter India's arms acquisition programme and mitigate concerns over the India–US nuclear deal. The Pakistan Navy also struck a $600m deal to acquire four frigates, currently under construction in China. It received eight surplus US P-3C *Orion* maritime patrol aircraft at no cost.

In April 2006, the Pakistan Navy took over command of a multinational naval counter-terrorism task force in the Arabian Sea and the northwest Indian Ocean for a year. The first non-NATO nation to command the 12-nation Task Force-150, Pakistan has provided a destroyer with onboard helicopter and a maritime patrol aircraft since April 2004.

On 11 August 2005 Pakistan test fired its first cruise missile, the *Babur* (*Hatf* VII), with a range of 500km. This came as a surprise to India, though advance notification of the test was not required. The second test of the *Babur* took place on 21 March 2006. On 29 April 2006, Pakistan successfully test-fired its longest-range surface-to-surface nuclear-capable ballistic missile *Hatf* VI (*Shaheen* II), with a range of 2,000–2,500km, for the third time. The *Hatf* VI is a two-stage solid-fuel missile.

Foreign relations

With criticism emerging from Washington on the role of the Pakistani Army in the tribal areas bordering Afghanistan, relations with the United States came under pressure, exacerbated by prospects of a US–India strategic relationship.

Although President Bush, visiting Pakistan in early March 2006, publicly praised Islamabad's role in the global 'war on terror', there appeared to be implied criticism on this issue. Bush refused to concede to Pakistan a deal similar to the one he had just signed with India on civil nuclear cooperation, or indicate an American role in the Kashmir dispute.

Several anti-Bush demonstrations took place prior to the visit, demonstrating the difference between official and public perceptions of the United States, despite its important role in post-earthquake relief and rescue operations. In a reminder of the violence afflicting Pakistan, a US diplomat was killed by a bomb blast in Karachi a day before the Bush visit. In a surprise declaration on 23 August 2005, Musharraf said disgraced Pakistani nuclear scientist A.Q. Khan had provided 'probably a dozen' centrifuges and their designs to North Korea to produce nuclear fuel, but said there was no evidence that he provided a Chinese-origin design to build a nuclear bomb. The Pakistani government subsequently announced the end of Khan's official interrogation, though he remained under house arrest with no access provided to foreign intelligence personnel.

Pakistan's relations with its neighbour China improved. Sino-Pakistan trade reached $4.26 billion in 2005, a 40% increase from the previous year. The newly constructed Gwadar port in Baluchistan, built with Chinese financial assistance, appeared to be the key to greater Sino-Pakistani trade links. Road and rail links between Gwadar and northwest China's Xinjiang Uygur autonomous region are to be considerably improved. In late December 2005, Pakistan started work, with China's help, on the construction of a second 325MW nuclear power station at Chasma in Punjab province, adjacent to a nuclear power station operative since 2000.

Bangladesh

The power struggle between the alliance of the ruling Bangladesh Nationalist Party (BNP) and the fundamentalist Jamaat-e-Islami, on the one hand, and the main opposition party, the Awami League, on the other has resulted in considerable violence and encouraged the growth of Islamic extremism. In May 2005, a senior member of the Awami League, Khorshed Alam, was shot dead in Dhaka. On 17 August 2005 more than 300 minor explosions took place simultaneously in 50 cities and towns across the country, including Dhaka. In each incident, the explosive device was set off in a crowded place, mainly government offices and courts. Two people were killed and more than 100 injured in the explosions reportedly carried out by the banned extremist Islamist group Jama'at-ul-Mujahideen Bangladesh (JMB). On 29 November 2005 the JMB allegedly also carried out two bombings in Gazipur and Chittagong, killing at least seven people. The Gazipur bomb was the first recorded suicide bombing in Bangladesh. Two days later, another bombing took place in Gazipur, killing one person and injuring several others.

Following these attacks, the government mounted a series of raids to appre-hend the perpetrators. This was a departure from the earlier view that the attacks were part of an anti-Bangladesh campaign by foreign nationals and anti-state activists. The presence of potential home-grown suicide bombers also raised concerns within the government. Nearly 400 JMB cadres were arrested, includ-ing Ataur Rahman Sunny, commander of the JMB's military wing. Bangladesh also adopted new legal measures to counter terrorist activities. The growth of Islamic radicalism in Bangladesh remained a key issue.

Sri Lanka

Although the Sri Lankan government and the Liberation Tigers of Tamil Eelam (LTTE) signed an MoU on 24 June 2005 establishing a Post-Tsunami Operational Management Structure for disbursement of $3bn in international assistance, oppo-sition from the government's coalition partner, the Janatha Vimukthi Peramuna (JVP), prevented its implementation. The assassination of Sri Lankan Foreign Minister Lakshman Kadirgamar on 12 August, allegedly by the LTTE, led to a hardening of views. On 17 November, Prime Minister Mahinde Rajapakse won the presidential elections with a little over 50% of the popular vote. A hard-liner on the conflict with the LTTE, Rajapakse repeatedly stated that he would ensure Sri Lanka's territorial integrity and review the current cease-fire agreement. With LTTE leader Velupillai Prabhakaran's annual speech on 27 November, threat-ening to intensify violence unless a 'reasonable political framework' was put forward by the government in 2006, sharp differences emerged.

There was a surge in violence, largely attacks by the LTTE against civilians, security forces and police personnel, and between the LTTE and the militia of LTTE renegade Vinayagamoorthi Muralitharan ('Colonel Karuna'), largely believed to be supported by the security forces. Tamil groups also alleged that disappearances and abductions were simultaneously being carried out by secu-rity personnel or affiliated paramilitary groups. On 25 April 2006 a suicide attack killed eight people and severely injured the army chief and 27 others. The gov-ernment's response was to mount a series of air strikes on the LTTE stronghold in the Sampoor area of Trincomalee, reportedly killing 12 civilians. In the worst attack, at least 64 civilians were killed in a mine attack on a bus in the Sinhalese-majority district of Anuradhapura on 15 June 2006. On 26 June, the deputy chief of the Sri Lankan Army was killed in a suicide bomb attack. Targeted attacks on Sri Lankan naval vessels also continued, in an attempt to assert LTTE rights at sea, denied by both the government and the Norwegian peace facilitators.

Amidst these developments, the LTTE came under intense pressure from the new Canadian government's decision in April 2006 to proscribe the LTTE, and, more importantly, the EU ban the following month on the LTTE as a terrorist organisation. In response, the LTTE demanded that EU members of the five-nation Nordic cease-fire monitoring mission should leave the island. Although peace talks between the government and the LTTE were held for the first time in three years on 21–23 February 2006 in Geneva, follow-on talks scheduled for April and June did not take place, with the LTTE refusing to talk with the Sri Lankan government. Nonetheless, the cease-fire agreement of 2002 formally held, despite the low-intensity conflict that accounted for 700 deaths between January and June 2006.

Nepal

Following a demonstration of 'people power' through three weeks of anti-monarchy and pro-democracy mass protests, the ruling monarch, King Gyanendra, dramatically gave up political power on 24 April 2006. The Maoist rebels, locked in a ten-year armed struggle against the monarchy, equally dramatically agreed to take part in an interim government, though critical issues still remained to be resolved. The trigger for these developments was an agreement between the Seven Political Parties Alliance (SPA) and the Communist Party of Nepal–Maoists. The 12-point agreement of 22 November 2005 essentially provided a road map for resolving concerns over Nepal as a 'failing' state. Critically, it incorporated the Maoists 'firm commitment' to accept a competitive multiparty system, fundamental rights, human rights, and rule of law and democratic principles.

On 19 March the SPA and the Maoists agreed to launch a fresh campaign against King Gyanendra. In mass protests on the streets of Kathmandu and in other parts of the country on 4 April, over 400 protesters and journalists were arrested. Public transport, shops and schools were shut. The following day, three people were killed and over 26 injured in demonstrations. The king's message to the nation on 13 April, calling for a dialogue to activate a multi-party democratic polity, was rejected by the SPA. On 20 April, India's special envoy, Karan Singh, called on the king, urging restraint. The following day, Gyanendra announced that he would hand over political power to the people and accept a new prime minister nominated by the SPA. However, the SPA rejected this as inadequate and the Maoists made it clear they would not accept anything but the formation of a constituent assembly. Bowing to the mass protests, Gyanendra, in a televised address to the nation on 24 April, agreed to restore the House of Representatives (parliament) dissolved in May 2003. While the Maoists rejected this as inadequate, the SPA welcomed it, and nominated Nepali Congress president Girija Prasad Koirala as the new prime minister.

When the reinstated House of Representatives passed proposals for elections to a constituent assembly – the key demand of the Maoists – and deprived the king of control of the army, the Maoists agreed to join an interim government. In talks on 16 June the SPA and the Maoists agreed to an eight-point accord, which included the drafting of an interim constitution, formation of an interim government and dissolution of the existing House of Representatives. They also agreed to seek UN help in monitoring and managing the armies and arms of both the government and the Maoists.

Critical differences remained, though, with prospects for peace and stability uncertain. Despite the cease-fire, violence continued. The government wanted the Maoists to disarm before joining an interim government but they had not agreed to renounce violence. It was not clear when an interim constitution would be formed or a constituent assembly elected, or even how these elections would take place. On the future of the monarchy as well, deep differences remained. While the government would like to retain a constitutional monarch, the Maoists bitterly opposed this. The government and the Maoists continued to lack the level of trust required to work together effectively.

Regional prospects

Although there was some expectation from the international community that India, as the most powerful state in the region, could play a role in the developments in Nepal and Sri Lanka, New Delhi was constrained. Not only do developments in both countries have domestic repercussions in India, but India has also had troublesome relations with both in the past. Following India's military intervention in Sri Lanka in 1987–90, former prime minister Rajiv Gandhi was assassinated in 1991 by a Tamil suicide bomber. In the early 1990s, India mounted an effective blockade of Nepal in response to the kingdom's growing relationship with China. Though India's room for political manoeuvre in the 2006 crisis was limited, it played a discreet role in Nepal, reportedly helping the SPA and the Maoists cobble together an agreement.

While India's neighbours watch with some apprehension the development of New Delhi's relationship with the United States, Washington and other capitals will closely follow the suggestions from both India and Pakistan on reducing the importance of the LoC in Kashmir. This could involve a big expansion of movements across the line, trade and commercial links, tourism, and business links among stakeholders in Kashmir. Both India and Pakistan have an interest in moving forward on this issue.

Afghanistan: Building Slowly

Afghanistan presented a mixed picture during 2005 and the first half of 2006. The increased number of casualties from conflict, the emergence of suicide bombings as a tactic, and the continued trafficking of opium and heroin suggested that the country remained trapped in conflict, extremism and poverty. However, there were also reasons to argue that it was seeing a gradual stabilisation, and that some of its problems were growing pains. There was an increasing focus on developing state capacity, harnessing rapid economic growth into licit activities, and continuing the disbandment of illegal armed formations. However, sustaining progress on these issues in 2006 will hinge to a significant extent on decisions made outside the country: in particular, the willingness of President Pervez Musharraf of Pakistan to curb the export of Taliban violence across the Durand Line which separates the two countries. More generally, Afghanistan's fate remains dependent on the political will of NATO members and other regional actors to invest in a supportive framework conducive to continuing post-conflict reconstruction.

Security poses continuing challenges

Fighting between the *Operation Enduring Freedom* forces of the US-led coalition and Taliban/al-Qaeda militants claimed over 1,500 lives in 2005, more than in any year since the fall of the Taliban regime in late 2001. The upsurge in violence spoke less of the Taliban's increased operational capacity than of the determination of coalition forces to eliminate once and for all militant forces embedded in rural areas to the south and east of the country. The coalition objective was not fully achieved, and there was the usual seasonal upsurge in violence in spring and early summer 2006, as the snows melted and the ranks and supplies of the Taliban were replenished.

During 2005, the changing pattern of violence indicated that the Taliban had largely lost the capacity to mount frequent large-scale operations in many regions of the country. *Operation Enduring Freedom* offensives in Kandahar, Uruzgan and Zabul provinces in June 2005 eliminated several pockets of Taliban fighters. Many of those captured were Pakistanis, confirming intelligence analysis that recruitment was now centred on Pakistani tribal areas as much as in Afghanistan itself. Similarly, the fighters who shot down a US MH-47 *Chinook* helicopter in August 2005 were Arabs located in the eastern Kunar and Nuristan provinces, reliant on supply lines from the Pakistani borderlands. Many such supply chains will be difficult to disrupt because some long-standing foreign fighters have married into families in tribal villages, and therefore can depend upon an additional layer of insulation against intelligence penetration from external agencies. The principal consequences of the Taliban's diminished operational capacity, and increased reliance on non-Afghan operatives, led to a reconfiguration in the pattern of violence from summer 2005. The shift involved an increased number of suicide bombings, particularly of soft civilian targets. The changing pattern of violence suggested a cross-fertilisation of tactics and possibly personnel with terrorists in Iraq, Algeria and Chechnya.

While these attacks have claimed lives among foreign forces and demoralised local communities, they are also indicative of the changing internal dynamics of the Taliban's relationship with recruits and supporters. During summer 2005, payments made to Taliban fighters increased, suggesting that recruitment was becoming more difficult. Moreover, a dozen planned suicide attacks conducted between December 2005 and March 2006 failed due to premature detonation or faulty bomb-making, suggesting that the quality of recruits and technical expertise was lacking. The attempted assassination in March 2006 of Sebghatullah Mojaddedi, head of the Truth and Reconciliation Commission and speaker of the Meshrano Jirga (House of Elders), who had been instrumental in detaching some Afghan Taliban fighters from their commanders, also indicated that Taliban leaders based in Pakistan were concerned that local support was being eroded. The number of Taliban defections was thought to be around 700, and included high-ranking figures such as former Foreign Minister Mawlawi Wakhil Ahmad. Between May 2005 and January 2006, three separate air strikes conducted with CIA-operated *Predator* unmanned aircraft reportedly killed Haitham al-Yemeni, Abu Hamza Rabia and Midhat Mursi al-Sayid 'Umar, all foreign-born al-Qaeda senior explosives experts, as well as al-Qaeda's head of media Abdul Rehman Al-Misri al Maghribi, the Moroccan son-in-law of Ayman al-Zawahiri, Osama bin Laden's deputy.

The 'Stage-3' expansion of NATO's International Security Assistance Force (ISAF) into the southern provinces, which began in early 2006, seemed set to put greater pressure on the Taliban. Destruction of social and infrastructural projects, including attacks on new schools such as one that killed six children and injured 14 others in the eastern city of Asadabad on 11 April 2006, had already served to alienate local communities from the Taliban agenda. Nevertheless, the Taliban was keen to cultivate new tactical alliances, for example with the growing number of illegal armed groups connected to trafficking of narcotics.

In 2006, a resurgence of Taliban strength was being reported, and newly deployed British troops in the south were already becoming involved in clashes in June. The Taliban were reported to be massing in large numbers in some rural areas, operating checkpoints and harassing villagers. However the extent of this build-up, and the degree of the challenge it posed, remained unclear.

The success or otherwise of the Taliban over the next year will continue to depend significantly on the degree of support from within Pakistan – notwithstanding the considerable Pakistani military effort, with some 80,000 troops deployed on the border. Breaking down the mosaic of sanctuaries in tribal border areas such as Waziristan has been an arduous and often frustrating process, hindered by local intransigence and hostility, and the difficulties faced by the Pakistani Army in operating in the tribal areas in which they are deeply unpopular. Local pockets of support are well embedded.

However, the need for cooperation is complicated by a severe deterioration in Afghan–Pakistani relations. President Hamid Karzai has accused Pakistan of interference and stoking violence in Afghanistan, while Pakistan has characterised as 'absurd' allegations that funding and direction are being provided to Taliban/al-Qaeda operatives by the Inter-services Intelligence (ISI), Pakistan's security service. In addition, military-to-military relations across the border have been inadequate to address the security challenges.

Shifts in international forces

US policy in Afghanistan during 2005 and the first half of 2006 has sought to reduce *Operation Enduring Freedom* force commitments as part of a strategy designed eventually to integrate *Operation Enduring Freedom* and NATO forces and provide a single hard and soft security package. Under a proposal by US Secretary of Defense Donald Rumsfeld in December 2005, integration would eliminate confusion on the ground about the separate mandates of two parallel forces, and would ease pressure on the US military. Some 2,500 *Enduring Freedom* troops were withdrawn in December 2005, though this still left more than 20,000 US troops deployed. One consideration for Washington was that the United States lost its military basing facilities in southern Uzbekistan in 2005 and was also at risk of being evicted from Manas air base in Kyrgyzstan, though talks on this were continuing in June 2006.

Some European NATO member states found difficulty in agreeing fully to the US proposal. As a consequence, extensive political work was required within the Alliance before agreement was reached on the terms of the Stage-3 expansion of ISAF announced on 12 December 2005. France and Germany would not support a combat role for their forces within ISAF, and the Dutch government only obtained authority to despatch 1,200 troops after a tense parliamentary session in February 2006. These differences have raised questions of operational flexibility within ISAF, and the ability of national contingents to support each other should that be necessary. However, despite the restrictions on deployment for the forces of some nations, the rules of engagement for the contingents of over 30 nations that make up the NATO force are common to all and are regarded as being relatively robust, allowing the use of pre-emptive force against perceived threats.

Stage-3 involved the extension of ISAF's presence in Kabul to the south of the country, to set up Provincial Reconstruction Teams (PRTs) in Helmand, Kandahar, Uruzgan, Zabul and elsewhere. The ISAF force was being expanded from 9,000 to between 15,000 and 16,000 personnel, of which the UK contributed the largest number of additional personnel. Its commitment of a further 3,300 troops was set to raise the UK deployment in Afghanistan to a maximum of 5,700, with the British Army's 16 Air Assault Brigade assuming control of the PRT for the large, complex and volatile province of Helmand. Britain also took over overall command of ISAF from May 2006.

The expanded British deployment raised questions in the UK about the purpose of the mission and what would constitute its success. John Reid, then defence secretary, said there was a 'fundamental difference' from the US-led *Operation Enduring Freedom* counter-terrorist operation, which he described as a 'search-and-destroy' mission. British troops would be focused on reconstruction efforts, and the protection of these, though they would conduct counter-insurgency operations and would also be involved in training and security for Afghan counter-narcotics forces.

British control of the Helmand PRT brought with it structural and operational challenges. The region is chronically poor and underdeveloped. The *Operation Enduring Freedom* presence in Helmand, both before and after the establishment of the PRT at Lashkar Gah in March 2005, was principally focused on counter-terrorism rather than civil reconstruction. Farmers faced severe poppy eradication measures. The region accounted for a 25% share of national opium production in 2005, up from 19% in 2003. Pacifying Helmand is central to the wider ISAF mission. The complex ethno-linguistic profile of its one million inhabitants has given rise to extensive linkages across the largely unpoliced southern border with Pakistan. Mohammed Daoud, appointed regional governor in January 2006, is a member of the Safi tribe from eastern Afghanistan and is thus less subject than others might be to local tribal pressures. However, he is dependent on ISAF forces to implement policy. In the first months of his governorship, authority appeared increasingly to reside with his deputy, Mullah Amir Mohammed, a local religious leader. British troops thus had the unenviable task of conducting, at the same time, robust counterinsurgency operations, such as that in the northern district of Musa Qala in late May 2006, and more orthodox civilian–military reconstruction programmes of the sort conducted by ISAF PRTs in other regions. This could create the risk that its rules of engagement will be unclear to the local population and that pre-emptive military action may be incompatible with a 'hearts and minds' approach focused on civilian projects.

Crucial to the expansion of the civil–military reconstruction remit of PRTs will be the augmentation of their security capabilities by troops from the Afghan National Army (ANA). With over 33,000 personnel in service or training as at April 2006, the ANA has contributed to the development of state capacity. It was built more or less from scratch with extensive support from, in particular, the United States, UK, France and Canada. The ANA is expected to be fully operational by 2010 with over 60,000 troops. Progress in developing the Afghan National Police (ANP), a task entrusted principally to Germany and the United States, has been less satisfactory. The challenge for German police trainers was to change the organisational culture, since the ANP, numbering around 30,000 officers, had previously existed in rudimentary form. Moreover, the ANP was susceptible to 'street pressures' – bribery, nepotism, community hierarchies – resulting in illegal armed groups connected to the drugs trade being able to operate with relative impunity in many areas.

Political dynamics

Although the security environment has fluctuated during 2005–06, the political process has moved more decisively into a post-conflict phase. The agenda of the Bonn Agreement, the political roadmap formulated immediately after the overthrow of the Taliban in late 2001, was largely fulfilled when parliamentary and provincial elections were conducted on 18 September 2005. A new constitution, political institutions, electoral laws and elected representatives are now all in place. However, significant challenges remain in developing the capacity and texture of political institutions, and weaving them successfully into international reconstruction projects in a manner that will empower ordinary Afghans and their elected representatives.

The September 2005 elections passed off peacefully and, according to international election monitors, were generally representative of the public will, if not entirely free and fair. There were 2,838 candidates standing for election to 239 seats in the Wolesi Jirga (House of the People), the lower house of the Shura-e Milli (National Assembly). A further ten seats were reserved for the nomadic Kuchi community, itself the subject of a controversial amendment to the constitution. The Joint Election Management Board (JEMB), consisting of Afghan and UN representatives, organised the election competently, and the Election Complaints Commission also appeared to fulfil its responsibilities impartially in spite of complaints that it had been appointed entirely by Karzai. The core election staff of over 1,000 Afghans, as well as 100,000 temporary polling station officials, were undeterred by Taliban injunctions to boycott the elections. ISAF, ANA and ANP forces combined to deal with security threats.

Nevertheless, there remained outstanding issues. Almost 3m Afghan refugees in Pakistan, Iran and other states were not given the opportunity to vote. Voter turnout, at a little over 50%, was far lower than in the presidential election of October 2004, suggesting that awareness of the election was limited, or that Afghans were becoming sceptical of the advantages of the process. The European Union Election Observation Mission report released in December 2005 identified an urgent need to develop the mass media and to increase female participation in the political process. With the profiles of political parties weak, the election allowed candidates with substantial financial support to exercise an inordinate influence over the campaign.

A number of additional steps were required to deepen the political process. The Shura-e Milli needed to be endowed with real political content that would allow it to check the powers of the presidency and to initiate policy. The infrastructure of political institutions required rapid development: parliamentary deputies and civil servants have inadequate facilities in which to work as they await the construction of the parliament building for which Manmohan Singh, the Indian prime minister, laid the foundation stone in August 2005 – India having promised funding for the project. A further important element of the deepening of the political process will be closer definition of the powers and functions of the Provincial Councils, elected to administer each of the country's 34 regions. At present, the only functions of those elected are to provide a proportion of the representation in the Meshrano Jirga, the upper house of the National Assembly. While it may be unrealistic to expect significant devolution of authority to the councils over the next year, they could work more effectively with ISAF PRTs in order to legitimise counter-narcotics and human-security-building initiatives. Finally, the third tier of government provided for under the constitution needed to be put in place: District Councils are essential in large and sparsely populated provinces with limited transport and communications infrastructure. The District Council elections had been scheduled for 18 September 2005, but were postponed until late 2006, or even 2007. Too much further slippage risked damaging the development of effective local governance, possibly allowing Taliban forces to wield increasing influence in many areas, including several districts of northern Helmand.

A broader question for the country's political future is the role of political parties. Afghanistan's politics are primarily ethnically based, and politicians have differing views on the value of political parties as vehicles of popular representation. Karzai is known to view them negatively and has chosen not to associate himself with any political party, believing that to do so would be divisive. He may fear that a new Pushtun-based party might emerge, hostile to the government and to the tactical alliances he has concluded with other ethnic groups to keep the government functioning. The two main political blocs that crystallised in 2005 were the National Understanding Front, led by Younous Qanooni, a Tajik who was the main challenger to Karzai in the 2004 presidential election; and the National Democratic Front, a loose coalition of left-wing groups, into which General Abdul Rashid Dostum's Junbish-e Milli-ye Islami (National Islamic Movement) is negotiating entry. Although some of the entities that comprise these blocs have unsavoury pasts, several do reach out across geographical and ethnic boundaries. If Karzai checks the growth of political parties, he risks the possibility that political identity could coalesce around ethno-territorial allegiances.

Counter-narcotics policy

Beyond the hard security agenda, the main policy priority uniting government and international actors is the effective implementation of measures to stem the sharp rise in poppy cultivation since 2002. Some 87% of global opium production is estimated to originate in Afghanistan. A survey conducted in spring 2006 by the Afghan government and the UN Office on Drugs and Crime suggested that cultivation levels had remained stable in 16 provinces, risen in 13, and fallen in only three provinces, and that the total acreage under cultivation had increased from 2005. The opium economy accounted for 40–60% of gross domestic product in 2005, and yielded profits of $2 billion, of which around $500m was received by the farmers. About 2.3m Afghans are involved in, or financially dependent upon, the growing of opium poppies, and farmers can earn at least four times the revenues available from other crops. Eradication is difficult because the risk calculation made by farmers is weighted in favour of continuing to grow poppies. Karzai's objective of completely eradicating the opium economy within ten years will be a tall order.

The government's response has been to work with international agencies to formulate the Counter-Narcotics Implementation Plan (CNIP), which was unveiled in February 2005 under the administration of the newly created Ministry for Counter-Narcotics, which is responsible for policy with the Interior Ministry responsible for execution. The CNIP has four strands: (1) developing legal capacity through improved criminal justice and money-laundering legislation, and the creation of dedicated drug courts with specialist judges and prosecutors to try 'drug lords'; (2) developing enforcement capacity in a new Special Narcotics Force, and a Counter-Narcotics branch in the police force, manned by 750 officers, working with Provincial and District Development Committees on intelligence and eradication measures; (3) reorienting communities away from economic dependency through the Alternative Livelihoods Programme, and physical dependency on opium with addiction treatment programmes; (4) removing drug traffickers with Taliban connections, as was the case with Bay Mohammed, who was extradited in October 2005 to face trial in the United States on terrorism offences.

It is too soon to determine whether this strategy will be effective. Incentives will be as important to farmers as disincentives in the decisions they take about what to grow. Because heroin derived from Afghan opium does not reach the United States in significant quantities, American counter-narcotics policy had been predicated on drug profits being an engine of terrorism and extremism. However, rapid eradication and airborne crop-destruction techniques alienated communities. With the development of a more comprehensive Afghan counter-narcotics strategy within a framework of Afghan government institutions in 2005, the US administration has acknowledged that subsistence farmers are not career criminals and has recognised the value of conducting operations through eradication and interdiction agencies. Its own 'five pillar' plan is broadly analogous with the CNIP: a public information campaign enlisting national and local religious leaders; expansion of the Vertical Prosecution Taskforce, through which US federal prosecutors train local lawyers; increased resourcing of alternative livelihoods programmes including provisioning 'immediate needs' in post-eradication districts; Drug Enforcement Agency support in the form of Foreign Advisory Support Teams for local National Interdiction Unit officers; and support for specific Poppy Elimination Programmes.

There is also scope for creative proposals such as that of the Senlis Council, a French philanthropic NGO which in 2005 advocated licensed cultivation of opium poppies to meet a global shortfall of production for medicinal use, notably in the manufacture of morphine and codeine. It is unclear how much of Afghanistan's opium output this could absorb, but according to the Council current licensed production is only meeting 24% of global morphine requirements. However, there is strong opposition to this proposal within NATO on the grounds that it would not be possible to impose adequate controls on licensing, and that it would lead to parallel markets without any effective curb on unlicensed production.

Economic development

The progress that Afghanistan has made can be measured by comparing the content of the Afghanistan Compact reached at an international conference of donors in London on 31 January 2006 with the Bonn Agreement of December 2001. In Bonn, the focus was on assembling basic political mechanics: it was not clear that the Afghan state was sufficiently cohesive to survive. By contrast, the 2006 Afghanistan Compact, of which the Afghanistan National Development Strategy (ANDS) is the central component, aims to build the dimensions and fabric of the state through three key objectives: enhancing the rule of law, economic and social development, and building the government's capacity to decide on and implement development projects.

Economic growth has been rapid, although from a low base, and with narcotics undoubtedly playing an important role. ANDS, unveiled at an international conference of donors held in London on 31 January 2006, envisaged a rise in average income per capita per year from $200 to $500 within five years.

The emphasis in Kabul is on empowering the government to direct the country's developmental path. Accordingly, 70% of the UK government's development assistance in 2006 will be routed through the Afghan government in 2006, with some money targeted towards the National Solidarity Programme in which 13,000 villages now self-manage development and reconstruction projects. However, development goals have to be set against the reality that 93% of the $4.75bn national budget of 2005 came from international donor assistance. Afghanistan will be unable to fund its security needs for many years. The London conference yielded substantial pledges of aid, notably $4bn from the United States, $900m from the UK and $1bn in grants and low-interest loans over five years from the Asian Development Bank. The problem by mid-2006 was that official aid commitments were not being fulfilled, hampering international reconstruction efforts. The task ahead is daunting: in 2005, the Afghan government took only 5% of GDP in taxation, life expectancy was only 45 years, and up to 40% of the population in rural areas suffered malnutrition. The country has the fourth highest rate of infant mortality and the highest rate of maternal mortality in the world. However, there are also positive signs: the number of children in school has increased fourfold since 2002. Vaccination programmes have all but eradicated measles. Work on dismantling landmines continued to be effective and a Disabled Commission was established in 2005 to assist victims of landmine explosions.

There were also significant improvements during 2005 in the redress available on human-rights issues, with the accession of Afghanistan to many international covenants and conventions on the rights of the child, women and minorities, and Karzai's firm public statements against forced marriages. The government's resolve was, however, tested in March 2006 by the case of Abdul Rahman, a Muslim convert to Christianity who, according to senior clerics and many ordinary Afghans, was guilty of apostasy and should be put to death. Following international pressure, he was released and left the country. This highlighted the dissonance between the government's stated adherence to human-rights treaties and the constitutional stipulation that no law could be made contrary to the tenets of Islam.

The future
The increased number of casualties in the conflict with Taliban/al-Qaeda forces during 2005 and spring 2006 underlined the fact that building security in Afghanistan would be a long and painful process. The deployment of NATO troops to the country's more challenging provinces during 2006 has increased their exposure to attacks and risk of casualties. The shift towards 'Iraqi' tactics by the Taliban may indicate the degree to which it has been marginalised as a result of the demobilisation of militias, development of a political system and the influx of aid to develop state capacity and economic growth. However, the regrouping of the Taliban insurgency, Afghanistan's dependence on foreign actors, its development challenges and the high level of poppy cultivation together mean that the country's future will continue to hang in the balance.

Southeast Asia: Political Crises and Security Challenges

The domestic political instability seen in early 2006 in the Southeast Asian states which were in theory the most democratic in the sub-region – the Philippines, Thailand and Timor Leste (formerly East Timor) – indicated strongly that 'democratisation' is not necessarily an irreversible or sufficient solution to problems of political development, and that more fundamental reforms and safeguards are also needed.

Political disturbances in the Philippines and Thailand
After winning the 2004 elections, Philippine President Gloria Macapagal Arroyo faced opposition from supporters of her vanquished opponent, Fernando Po, Jr,

who claimed that she had rigged votes. In July 2005 Arroyo survived an attempt to impeach her for electoral corruption, but street rallies calling for her removal continued and by early 2006 there was growing support in Congress for a new impeachment bill. Meanwhile, controversy mounted over the Arroyo administration's attempts to amend the constitution, including a shift from a US-style presidential system to parliamentary government. Congressional opponents of this 'Cha-cha' (Charter Change) claimed that, by dissolving Congress, creating an unelected parliament and extending the terms of public officials, Arroyo would maintain her hold on power.

At the same time, military elements became restive. In late February 2006, Arroyo declared a state of emergency after Chief of Staff General Generoso Senga announced that an elite unit's commander had planned to join anti-government protests and had asked military leaders to withdraw support from the administration. Despite this move to counter an apparent coup attempt (the 12th since 1986), disaffected military splinter groups continued to pose a threat to political stability. Though the state of emergency, which allowed for arrest without warrant and dispersal of demonstrations, lasted for only a week, critics voiced fears that it might be a prelude to Arroyo declaring martial law. In late May, military intelligence officers arrested five supporters of former President Joseph Estrada, who were charged with rebellion for their alleged involvement in a plot to assassinate members of Arroyo's cabinet, and National Security Advisor Norberto Gonzalez claimed that the government had uncovered another coup plot.

In Thailand, Thaksin Shinawatra's Thai Rak Thai ('Thais Love Thais', TRT) party won the February 2005 elections with a massive 61% of the vote and 377 out of 500 parliamentary seats. Key to TRT's success were not only a substantial increase in its membership (from 11 to 14 million since 2001) and Thaksin's alluring political persona, but also his government's rural development efforts including million-baht ($26,000) village grants, subsidised health clinics and debt relief for farmers. These schemes fostered Thaksin's image as an indispensable friend of the rural poor, winning him huge support in the countryside. Another policy that proved popular in the short term was the campaign against the illegal trade in methamphetamines, begun in 2003, which resulted in approximately 2,700 alleged drug dealers being killed by police and vigilantes.

Following the 2005 elections, however, Thaksin's rule faced mounting opposition, and by early 2006 political crisis gripped the country. While Thaksin retained his rural support, as well as that of the urban poor and elites who benefited from the TRT government's cronyism, his policies alienated a large part of the better-educated urban middle class. At issue was rising discontent over the way that Thaksin has used his huge popular mandate to subvert constitutional checks and balances to implement self-serving policies. The drug-related killings and the inept clampdown from early 2004 on the renewed Muslim separatist insurgency in the country's deep south constituted targets for the ire of the protest movement, spearheaded by the People's Alliance for Democracy (PAD), a coalition of civil-society groups.

The larger charge of his opponents was that Thaksin had grossly abused his popular mandate by ignoring parliament and compromising state bodies such as the Inland Revenue Department, the Anti-Money-Laundering Commission and the Election Commission by placing his supporters in key positions. Further complaints centred on Thaksin's disregard for media freedom. Anti-government protest crystallised in October 2005 after Thaksin sued a Bangkok newspaper for publishing an article by a controversial but popular monk criticising the prime minister's alleged hunger for power. State television also dropped a talk-show hosted by the newspaper's owner, Sondhi Limthongkul. Fuel was added to the opposition fire in January 2006 when Thaksin's family sold its controlling stake in the large telecommunications company Shin Corporation to Singapore's state investment arm, Temasek Holdings. Because it involved what many saw as the unpatriotic disposal to foreigners of an asset of national importance, this transaction provoked considerable criticism and boosted support for PAD.

In an effort to defuse the political crisis that grew as PAD mounted large-scale anti-government demonstrations in Bangkok and other urban centres, in late February Thaksin called a snap general election for 2 April, three years earlier than necessary. Opposition parties claimed that the election would not resolve the question of Thaksin's probity and, in the hope of creating political paralysis and eventually forcing his resignation, boycotted the election. According to the constitution, all 500 parliamentary seats must be occupied before a government is formed; in seats with a single candidate, to be elected that candidate must win 20% of the vote. In the event, despite the TRT winning about 16m votes against 10m abstentions, 40 seats – mainly in the south, where anti-Thaksin sentiment ran high – were left unfilled. Unable to form a new government, Thaksin stepped aside from the premiership and went on vacation, though he remained 'caretaker prime minister'. By-elections in the unfilled seats were held in late April, but even then 13 seats were left vacant. With the country locked in protracted crisis, in early May the Constitutional Court invalidated the 2 April poll and ordered a new general election.

At mid-2006, Thailand's political future remained uncertain. With new elections likely in October, parliament probably would not sit again until 2007. Thaksin faced lawsuits seeking to prevent him from becoming prime minister again, and further mass demonstrations against him were in prospect. Yet, after seven weeks' absence, in late May Thaksin had resumed formal control of the government and was chairing cabinet meetings. While the celebrations in June of the 60th accession anniversary of Thailand's revered king would dampen political controversy temporarily, tensions seemed likely to rise subsequently.

In both cases these crises distracted governmental and to some extent military attention from the important security problems that both the Philippines and Thailand continued to suffer. But there were significant differences between the Philippine and Thai political crises. Most importantly, whereas President Arroyo's electoral legitimacy has always been questioned, Thaksin has secured greater success at the polls than any other Thai politician and retained huge popularity with the electorate. However, both national examples reinforced the case that it is hard for democracy to produce effective governance that is acceptable across the political spectrum in an environment characterised by major socio-economic inequality and where money politics in various guises holds sway. There was evidently no slick solution to this problem. In the long term, however, sustained economic growth (which is much more apparent in Thailand than the Philippines), poverty reduction programmes, and redoubled efforts to bolster the independence of institutions such as constitutional courts, electoral commissions and anti-corruption agencies were important components of the answer. A second lesson was that, in societies such as the Philippines and Thailand, while the electoral weight of the well-educated urban middle class may not be huge, it may nevertheless hold the key to political stability because of its effective veto power.

Turmoil in Timor Leste

While the Philippine and Thai crises were kept within the bounds of the political process in spite of the deep tensions they revealed, a dispute in early 2006 between the government and renegade security force elements in Timor Leste escalated out of control. In part, the crisis had its roots in a mutiny by troops from the tiny republic's 1,400-man defence force, who went on strike in February in protest against ill-treatment and poor working conditions. There was an important ethnic component in the dispute: most of the mutinous troops came from the country's west and complained that they suffered discrimination in a force dominated by officers from the east, reflecting its origins in the eastern-based, pre-independence anti-Indonesian armed resistance movement, Falintil. However, another explanation may have been opposition within the security forces to the leadership of Prime Minister Mari Alkatiri, who had become increasingly unpopular since independence in 2002 because of his leadership style, widely seen as characterised by arrogance and an unattractive willingness to confront critics such as the Catholic Church. At the same time, large-scale unemployment and grinding poverty have fuelled easily exploited discontent amongst urban youths.

In the absence of the reassuring presence provided from 1999 until mid-2005 by UN peacekeeping troops (notably from Australia), law and order broke down rapidly in 2006. In March almost 600 soldiers were dismissed and subsequently fled the capital, Dili, and camped out in the hills surrounding the town. In April, security forces opened fire on a crowd demonstrating in support of the former soldiers, sparking a riot that left at least five dead and leading to an exodus of more than 20,000 people from Dili. After exchanges of gunfire between the rebel troops and loyal forces in May, Timor Leste's government requested Australia, New Zealand, Malaysia and Portugal to intervene militarily in order to disarm the renegades. On 24 May, defence force troops attacked the national police headquarters, accusing the police of aligning themselves with the rebels; 12 unarmed police officers were killed. Subsequently, the army and police largely disintegrated: 70% of the police force deserted, many joining the rebels; only 400 troops remained loyal to the government. Law and order broke down, with youth gangs loosely allied to the feuding security-force factions engaging in widespread fighting and arson. The first Australian troops landed in Dili on 25 May, and by the end of the following day the full 1,300-strong contingent had been deployed. In total, 2,250 troops from the four contributing countries were in East Timor by the end of May. On 30 May, President Xanana Gusmão announced 30 days of emergency rule and – in his formal capacity as military commander-in-chief – took over responsibility for defence and internal security from the respective ministers in Mari Alkatiri's government. In early June, the president transferred responsibility for the security forces to Foreign Minister José Ramos-Horta. Meanwhile, looting and arson continued despite the presence of foreign troops, whose restrictive rules of engagement apparently constrained them from using lethal force to restore order. The challenge for Australia and other members of the ad hoc coalition providing troops to control the disorder was to help pull Timor Leste back from the brink of becoming a failed state. In early June, speaking at the IISS Shangri-La Dialogue in Singapore, Australian Defence Minister Brendan Nelson called for a broader regional coalition to assist Timor Leste, and it emerged that other Asian states such as Singapore and South Korea might contribute to the international security force there.

Repression in Myanmar

Through the use of repressive force and by exploiting its economic and political links with neighbouring states (China, India and members of the Association of Southeast Asian Nations (ASEAN)), during 2005–06 Myanmar's authoritarian State Peace and Development Council (SPDC) regime maintained its tight grip on power despite the internal upheaval that followed the ousting of the country's relatively pragmatic prime minister and chief of military intelligence, General Khin Nyunt, in October 2004. Myanmar's domestic politics remained deadlocked. In February 2005 the constitutional convention resumed discussions aimed at establishing a framework for the return of participatory politics, but the main opposition and ethnic minority groups were not allowed to participate. The talks ended in January 2006, with no indication of progress. Aung San Suu Kyi, leader of the National League for Democracy (which won the 1990 elections), remained under house arrest; in May 2006 her detention was extended by a further year.

The SPDC administration continued to face significant security challenges. In May 2005, three near-simultaneous explosions in retail districts of Yangon killed at least 23 people. Among subsequent bomb attacks, there were six explosions in Yangon in April 2006 but no casualties. Though some observers suspected the hand of shadowy elements within the regime or the armed forces, the government blamed exiled opposition groups and ethnic minority rebels for the blasts. Whatever the truth of the matter, the regime used the bomb attacks as a justification for mounting a major offensive against the main ethnic minority group still in rebellion – the 'terrorist' Karen National Union (KNU) and its military wing, the 20,000-strong Karen National Liberation Army – during early 2006, causing thousands of Karen refugees to flee to the border with Thailand. More credible explanations for the offensive against the KNU, which had largely respected an informal cease-fire since 2004, included the need to clear areas where the government wanted to build dams, and to secure the hinterland east of Pyinmana, the new site for Myanmar's administrative capital.

The government's move to Pyinmana, 320km from Yangon, began in November 2005 and most ministries were relocated by February 2006. In March 2006, the capital site was renamed Naypyidaw ('Royal City'). The rationale for the move remains unclear: explanations have ranged from the influence of SPDC Chairman Tan Shwe's personal astrologer who allegedly predicted the fall of the regime if it did not move, to the need for a site that would be more defensible if the United States mounted an Iraq-style invasion. While this appeared to be a far-fetched suggestion, the regime faced mounting international pressure during 2005–06, particularly from Washington. In July 2005, under pressure from other members of ASEAN, which feared the potential impact on the grouping's international respectability, the SPDC turned down its opportunity to chair the association during 2006. In December 2006, the United States persuaded the UN Security Council to provide a briefing on Myanmar's human-rights record. After Aung San Suu Kyi's detention was extended in May 2006, UN Secretary-General Kofi Annan called for the SPDC to release her. The United States sought a second briefing for the Security Council and a State Department spokesman speculated that some form of Security Council 'action' might result as well.

Indonesia: breakthrough in Aceh

Internal security challenges have continued to loom large for several Southeast Asian governments, not least Indonesia's. However, in August 2005 Indonesia's government and GAM – the rebel Free Aceh Movement – signed a comprehensive peace agreement that represented a remarkable and unexpected triumph for the small, EU-backed Finnish non-governmental organisation (NGO) that brokered it. Under the supervision of international monitors from Europe and Southeast Asia, in mid-September 2005 GAM members began disarming while the Indonesian government started withdrawing its forces from Aceh. An estimated 12,000 lives had been lost in a war that had flared sporadically since the late 1980s, accompanied by human-rights abuses perpetrated by both sides. If the peace process succeeds and Aceh develops as an autonomous province within Indonesia, there could be significant ramifications not only for Indonesia but also elsewhere in Southeast Asia.

The August 2005 agreement followed two abortive efforts to bring peace to Aceh since the fall of President Suharto's authoritarian New Order in 1998. Both the May 2000 'Humanitarian Pause' and the December 2002 'Cessation of Hostilities Agreement' (brokered by the Geneva-based Henry Dunant Centre) failed due to the absence of detailed provisions beyond mere cease-fires, the lack of effective dispute-resolution mechanisms, the Indonesian military's deep-rooted distrust of GAM, and both sides' reluctance to sacrifice the financial benefits that the protracted conflict had generated from protection rackets, illegal logging and drug smuggling. At the same time, exiled GAM leaders in Sweden appeared to have incomplete control over rebel commanders in Aceh. At the political level, there remained stark disagreement over the rightful status of Aceh, a province with 4.3m people, rainforests covering an area the size of Belgium and still-substantial oil and natural gas deposits.

The 26 December 2004 tsunami was catastrophic for Aceh: it killed more than 130,000 people (mainly on the west coast), including thousands of military and police personnel, and made more than 600,000 homeless. But its political impact was also profound. Even before this natural disaster, it was clear that the conflict had reached stalemate. The tsunami's aftermath forced a profound re-evaluation by both Jakarta and GAM. Under pressure from international donors, whose promised large-scale reconstruction aid – the biggest global response ever to a natural disaster – could not be delivered effectively in the absence of security and stability in Aceh, by the end of January 2005 the two sides in the conflict commenced new peace talks, brokered by Crisis Management Initiative (CMI), the NGO led by Finnish ex-President Martti Ahtisaari, and funded by the European Commission (which had committed $720m to Aceh's reconstruction) and several European states. The intention was to find a comprehensive solution to the conflict within the framework of 'special autonomy'. From the beginning, it was clear that CMI intended any resultant settlement to cover long-term socio-economic development and reconstruction; the government's security arrangements for Aceh; terms for the demobilisation and reintegration of GAM forces; an amnesty for the rebels; elections, justice and human rights; and monitoring of the two sides' undertakings. Even to commence dialogue required significant concessions by both sides. Crucially, GAM relinquished – at least for the purposes of the talks – its cherished objective of independence for Aceh. The Indonesian leadership overrode the objections of those in the TNI officer corps and parliament who feared – following the 'loss' of East Timor in 1999 – that international involvement in the negotiations and potentially in a settlement might presage Aceh's separation.

Over the following six-and-a-half months, four more rounds of talks were held in Helsinki. During the fourth round in May 2005, CMI felt sufficiently confident to invite experts from the European Union Council Secretariat and European Commission to observe the discussion on monitoring arrangements. On 15 August, the talks culminated in a Memorandum of Understanding (MoU) between Indonesia and GAM. According to the MoU, under a new Law on the Governing of Aceh, the province will exercise autonomy in all fields except foreign affairs, external defence, national security, monetary and fiscal matters, justice and the freedom of religion. Local elections to elect the head of Aceh's administration and other provincial officials are to be held during 2006. But crucially, Jakarta agreed to allow, within 18 months, the establishment of Aceh-based political parties, which will be able to contest elections for the province's legislature in 2009. Foreign monitors will be invited to oversee both the 2006 and 2009 elections. The economic dimension to the settlement equates with the terms of a previous 'special autonomy' package offered by Jakarta: 70% of oil and gas revenues will remain in Aceh. But an important new concession by Jakarta was to allow GAM to be represented at all levels in BRR, the commission established for post-tsunami reconstruction.

Under the terms of the MoU, GAM agreed to demobilise all its 3,000 guerrillas (though considerably more rebel combatants subsequently materialised), and decommission its weapons; its total firearms inventory was to be surrendered and destroyed under international supervision in four stages between 15 September and 31 December 2005. On its part, Jakarta agreed to withdraw all 'non-organic' troops and police from Aceh, leaving a garrison of 14,700 TNI personnel, responsible only for external defence, along with 9,100 police responsible for internal law and order. No sudden major troop movements will be allowed within Aceh, and the provincial police will receive special human-rights training. The MoU also obliged Jakarta almost immediately to grant amnesty to all GAM members and supporters, and to release all political prisoners and detainees. Indonesia will allocate farming land and funds to assist the reintegration into society of former combatants, and to compensate pardoned political prisoners and civilians who suffered demonstrable losses in the conflict. Former GAM combatants will be allowed to serve in the local Indonesian police and armed forces. A Commission for Truth and Reconciliation will facilitate justice for past abuses; there will also be a Human Rights Court to hedge against future excesses.

The MoU provided for an Aceh Monitoring Mission (AMM), led by the EU within the framework of the European Security and Defence Policy but including personnel from several Southeast Asian states as well as Norway and Switzerland, to oversee the implementation of these commitments. The AMM's tasks included monitoring GAM's demobilisation and the destruction of its arms, monitoring the withdrawal of non-organic Indonesian forces, monitoring the reintegration of GAM members, monitoring the human-rights situation, and ruling on disputed amnesty cases. A final key role was to act as a mechanism for dealing with any complaints, disputes and violations of the settlement. Though the AMM was 'of a civilian nature', many of its personnel were drawn from contributing states' armed forces. In advance of the settlement, an initial monitoring presence consisting of 80 personnel deployed to Aceh on 15 August 2005; full deployment commenced on 15 September for a period of six months. The AMM included 130 European personnel, and 96 from Brunei, Malaysia, the Philippines, Singapore and Thailand, and monitored the settlement's implementation through 11 district offices across Aceh and four mobile decommissioning teams. In June 2006, the mandate of the AMM was extended until September.

Indonesia's President Susilo Bambang Yudhoyono and Vice-President Jusuf Kalla both invested considerable political capital in the peace process and appeared determined to make it work. Though it appeared initially that the process could be derailed by problems such as continuing GAM criminal activities, or the TNI and its militias using force against GAM supporters, implementation of the settlement was generally smooth. In mid-2006, the main dimension of the settlement remaining to be put into effect was the all-important governance law for the province, which was submitted to the Indonesian parliament in January 2006. After extensive scrutiny by a parliamentary special committee, a working committee and a drafting team, the law was expected to be passed in mid-June 2006.

The unexpected peace dividend for Aceh from the tsunami disaster reinforced the impression that Indonesia has been 'coming right' in political and security terms since Susilo Bambang Yudhoyono became president in October 2004. It might also provide a template for a similar settlement in the province of Papua, where a low-level insurgency against Indonesian rule has continued. During March 2006, two events raised the profile of the Papua issue. The first involved violent clashes by Papuans protesting at highly profitable large-scale copper- and gold-mining by the multinational Freeport-McMoran corporation which allegedly contributed little to local development. Soon afterwards, the Australian government granted asylum to 42 pro-independence Papuans who had landed in northern Queensland in January, prompting Indonesia to temporarily recall its ambassador from Canberra.

Thailand's unstable south

Across the Malacca Strait, the conflict in Thailand's three Muslim-dominated southernmost provinces of Narathiwat, Pattani and Yala intensified during 2005–06. There were no more major incidents on the scale of the 28 April and Tak Bai incidents in 2004, in which more than 180 Muslim militants and demonstrators died. However, during the first half of 2006 shootings and bombings were occurring almost daily, with civilians often being the victims, bringing the total dead to 1,300 since the conflict started in January 2004. The insurgents were reportedly using more sophisticated tactics and weapons apparently imported from Iraq and Afghanistan, such as bombs triggered by mobile phones and roadside improvised explosive devices encased in cement for camouflage and increased lethality.

However, there was no evidence that the Thai insurgency was receiving significant support from outside the country, or was linked to Jemaah Islamiah or other Southeast Asian terrorist groups. Nevertheless, it caused tension between Thailand and neighbouring Malaysia, where Thai Muslims had close social connections. During 2005, bilateral relations soured after 131 Thai Muslims sought refuge in northern Malaysia. The Malaysian government refused to force the asylum-seekers to return. In December, after Malaysia extradited one of the group who was wanted by the Thai authorities in connection with the insurgency, there was a thaw. However, relations remained poor and, in April 2006, the Malaysian government reacted angrily to a Thai newspaper report claiming that 50 Thai Muslim women were being trained in bomb-making and intelligence-gathering in Malaysia to replace insurgents arrested by the security forces.

There was little sign that Thaksin Shinawatra's government in Bangkok would make political compromises with the separatists to defuse the insurgency. Probably because of pressure from Thaksin's administration, in June 2006 the recommendations of the National Reconciliation Commission (NRC) appointed in February 2005 did not include the granting of autonomy for the southernmost provinces. Nevertheless, the NRC's proposals included a new administrative body to give southern residents a greater say in local decision-making. The proposals also emphasised the need to resolve 'structural conflicts' in the areas of justice, human rights, development, employment, planning and natural resource management, and suggested that Islamic law be introduced and that the Malay dialect Yawi should be made the official second language of the region. Caretaker Prime Minister Thaksin ordered the immediate adoption of the proposals, with the exception of those that would require new laws: these would have to wait until a new parliament was elected.

The Philippines: peace for Mindanao?

Internal security also remained an important concern for the government in Manila. During 2005–06, there was no sign that the Philippine government and its armed forces were making significant progress against the New People's Army (NPA), the military wing of the Communist Party of the Philippines. Indeed, though the NPA's strength had fallen from a high of 26,000 armed personnel in 1987 to an estimated 7,000 by 2006, its attacks on government security forces seemed to be occurring more frequently and across wider areas of the country. In May 2005, Secretary of National Defense Avelino Cruz spoke of defeating the communist insurgency over the next 6–10 years but, given the Philippines' beleaguered national leadership, the prevailing poor economic conditions and the military's weak fighting capability, this estimate appeared optimistic.

However, in the southern Philippines, it seemed that an end might be in sight to the Moro insurgency which has pitted Muslim separatist groups in Mindanao and Sulu against the Philippine central government and its armed forces. In April 2005, the Philippine government and the Moro Islamic Liberation Front (MILF) recommenced peace talks in Malaysia brokered by the Organisation of the Islamic Conference (OIC). Crucially, both sides claimed that continuing conflict in Mindanao would not be allowed to derail the peace process. While the renewed cease-fire since July 2003 had effectively ended hostilities between government forces and the MILF, the Armed Forces of the Philippines (AFP) stepped up its operations against other armed groups in the south, including the Jemaah Islamiah (JI) terrorist network and the Abu Sayyaf Group (ASG), an insurgent splinter faction specialising in kidnapping-for-ransom and bombings, as well as a breakaway element of the Moro National Liberation Front (MNLF, which signed a peace agreement with Manila in 1996). Reflecting US government concern that the southern Philippines could become an important haven for international terrorists, Washington backed these AFP operations with military advice, intelligence, training and logistics support. During 2005, the US provided Manila with $31.8m worth of military assistance.

Concerned to maintain the momentum of the peace process and to avoid being labelled by the US as a terrorist organisation, in March 2005 the MILF leadership categorically disavowed links with JI, the ASG and other militant factions such as Rajah Solaiman Group (RSG), and its commanders were told to 'weed out and hold responsible' rogue members providing sanctuary for foreign militants. Though the AFP claimed that it was 'cautious' about mounting operations against terrorists in known MILF areas, it remained a key security objective to neutralise the threat from JI, ASG and RSG, particularly in the wake of coordinated bombings that killed 13 people in Manila's financial district and the southern cities of General Santos and Davao in February 2005. After a Manila prison siege in March left 28 people dead, including three senior ASG figures, ASG operations chief Jainal Antel Sali ('Abu Solaiman') threatened to 'bring the war to Manila'. But while cease-fire violations by both government forces and the MILF were reported, fears that AFP operations might undermine the peace process proved largely misplaced.

After a seventh round of exploratory talks in April 2005, Manila and the MILF agreed that a 'breakthrough' had been achieved on key issues relating to the Moro people's 'ancestral domain'. However, in May 2006 after a further five rounds of talks, the two sides conceded that still further negotiations were needed on the extent of areas to be placed under the proposed Bangsamoro Juridical Entity. Though the government spoke of a final settlement by the end of 2006, how this might be achieved so quickly remained unclear. To hold beyond the short term, any settlement must go much further towards meeting Moro aspirations for both political self-determination and sustainable economic development than Manila's peace agreement with the MNLF, which established an Autonomous Region of Muslim Mindanao as a step towards self-government. From the MILF viewpoint autonomy has failed as a solution, but Moro independence is out of the question for the government as well as the Christians, who now constitute 80% of the total population of Mindanao and Sulu. There is clearly a need for a solution involving some form of political autonomy that builds on steps already taken towards regional self-government while protecting the Christian community's interests. But finding a political format that satisfies all parties will be difficult.

A key obstacle to a settlement is the absence of unity amongst the Moros, and the related fact that the OIC recognises only the MNLF as the legitimate representative of Philippine Muslims. A related problem is that the MNLF is split into two factions. A meeting in April 2005 brought together senior MILF and MNLF figures, but despite OIC efforts to bring the Moro movements closer to each other, unity remained elusive. In May 2006, the MILF rejected an agreement between Manila and the OIC to 'converge' elements of the peace agreement with the MNLF and the continuing negotiations with the MILF. Though constructing a common platform will be difficult given the political divergence between the MILF (which emphasises restoring the Moro people's sovereign rights) and the MNLF (which is oriented towards power-sharing), it seemed unlikely that any new settlement could succeed this happened. The dire possibility remained that hard-line MILF commanders – some of whom have warned that they will not accept a settlement short of Moro independence – might not only revive their rebellion but could coalesce more closely with some or all of ASG, JI, RSG and the MNLF's Nur Misuari faction. Rumours in March 2006 of efforts to unseat the MILF's chairman, Al-Haj Murad Ebrahim, lent additional credibility to such concerns.

A mutating terrorist challenge

Extremist Islamic terrorism has remained a threat, particularly in Southeast Asia's maritime states. The terrorist bombings that killed 23 people, including five foreign tourists, and injured more than 120 on the Indonesian island of Bali on 2 October 2005 should not have come as a surprise. Despite advances in Indonesian counter-terrorism over the last three years and the splintering of the Indonesian-based but pan-regional JI terrorist organisation, a tangible threat persisted. While weaknesses in Indonesian law enforcement are partly to blame, the October 2005 Bali attack highlighted the fact that lawlessness in the southern Philippines has provided JI and other militants with an important sanctuary.

Though JI was never strictly a subsidiary of al-Qaeda, it has certainly been influenced by its ideology and methods, particularly in terms of its willingness to attack targets seen as representing Western interests, and it has been linked to the larger organisation through personalities such as Hambali (arrested in Thailand in August 2003) and by transfers of funds. Since the first terrorist bombings on Bali, which killed more than 200 people in October 2002, substantial international pressure and assistance – particularly from Australia, but also from the United States, the United Kingdom and Singapore – has helped to galvanise Indonesia's counter-terrorism efforts. Though there were subsequently major attacks on the Marriott hotel in Jakarta in August 2003 and against the Australian embassy in September 2004, Indonesian law enforcement against terrorism has become considerably more effective. Crucially, by late 2005 the Indonesian authorities had tried and convicted 36 JI members and associates for their role in the 2002 Bali attacks. Three of the 'Bali bombers' had been sentenced to death. In March 2005, Abu Bakar Bashir, chairman of the Indonesian Mujahideen Council (MMI) and JI's alleged 'amir', was sentenced to 30 months in jail for conspiracy in relation to the first Bali bombings. Widespread revulsion amongst Indonesians at the series of JI bombings – in which many of the victims were local people rather than the Westerners who were supposedly JI's target – has been demonstrated in broad public support for the Jakarta authorities' more assertive counter-terrorist policies since 2002.

The impact of Indonesia's greater earnestness in dealing with terrorism and the turn in public opinion against JI has been reflected in the group's declining strength and unity. Before both the series of arrests that crippled its networks in Malaysia and Singapore during 2001–02 and the first Bali bombings that provoked Indonesia's crackdown, JI comprised four geographical commands; four years later it had contracted to a single command. Whereas JI was formerly well financed, by 2005 it was short of funds; expanding in 2001, JI was subsequently decimated by arrests and finds few new recruits. Crucially, whereas in 2001 JI was dominated by the faction led by Hambali and espousing a jihadist version of Salafi fundamentalist ideology including terrorist bombings as a legitimate tactic, four years later Hambali was in US custody and the pro-bombing faction was marginalised.

From the viewpoint of what might be called 'mainstream' JI thinking, the organisation's proper focus should be on transforming Indonesia into an Islamic state through a process of religious and political campaigning aimed at securing and then expanding a geographical base in which Islamic law would be upheld. Yet a minority of JI militants continued to plan and perpetrate terrorist attacks aimed at causing large-scale loss of life amongst Westerners without serious regard for unfortunate Indonesian bystanders. Prominent amongst these were the infamously elusive Malaysian bomb-makers Noordin Mohammed Top and Dr Azahari Husin, both sought by the Indonesian security forces in connection with the original Bali attacks and the subsequent Marriott and Australian Embassy bombings. These renegades styled themselves the Thoifah Muqatilah (Combat Unit) and recruited suicide bombers and other 'foot-soldiers' from not only the ranks of JI but also other aggressive Indonesian militias, including Abu Bakar Bashir's MMI, offshoots of the Darul Islam movement and groups such as KOMPAK that grew out of Muslim–Christian sectarian conflict in the provinces of Maluku and Central Sulawesi in eastern Indonesia since the late 1990s. Though the international media mainly blamed JI, it seems likely that it was the Thoifah Muqatilah that was responsible for the 2 October bombings.

With support from Western governments, during the months after the 2005 Bali bombings the authorities in Indonesia and other Southeast Asian countries registered significant gains against suspected terrorists. Indonesian police quickly claimed that three suicide bombers died in the attacks, identified Azahari Husin and Noordin Mohammed Top as the probable masterminds, and subsequently mounted a major operation to uncover the network that must have provided planning and logistic support. As in the aftermath of the 2002 attacks, Australia and the UK deployed forensic and other police specialists to Bali in support of Indonesian efforts. In mid-October, several arrests were made in Banten, West Java, and police were reportedly seeking other West Java militants also blamed for the 2004 Australian Embassy bombing and linked to Imam Samudra (on death row for his part in the 2002 Bali attacks).

Bali police commander Inspector-General I Made Mangku Pastika's claim a week after the latest attacks that the October 2005 Bali suicide bombers were 'new players' who had possibly graduated recently from terrorist training camps in the southern Philippines focused attention on the ease with which militants may move in the territories surrounding the Sulawesi Sea. Here, lax border security (particularly in Indonesian waters, but also around the offshore Malaysian islands of Sipidan and Ligatan) has facilitated illicit movement of people and goods between Indonesia's East Kalimantan province, Malaysia's Sabah state and the Philippine island of Mindanao. The Philippine military claimed in June 2006 that it had monitored the presence of some 30 JI members in the southern Philippines. In the immediate aftermath of 2 October, the US government offered bounties of $10m and $1m, respectively, for the capture of Dulmatin and Umar Patek, senior JI members wanted for their alleged roles in the October 2002 Bali attacks, who are thought to have found sanctuary with the ASG in Mindanao. The bounty announcement's timing prompted speculation that Dulmatin and Umar Patek had some part in the latest Bali attacks. Meanwhile, both the Philippine government and the MILF claimed that ASG and JI were jointly planning carbomb attacks in Metro-Manila and on other targets where Westerners might be killed. In February 2006, the Indonesian and Philippine national police forces announced that they would intensify their counter-terrorism cooperation.

Western governments interested in countering international terrorist threats as far from their homelands as possible are concerned that terrorist groups may establish themselves in these relatively lightly governed areas in the southern Philippines, eastern Indonesia and east Malaysia. In addition to US support for Philippine military operations against the ASG, in mid-October 2005 then-Australian Defence Minister Robert Hill announced that Canberra was negotiating a status-of-forces agreement with Manila that would allow Australian troops to support the Philippines' efforts to prevent Indonesian terrorists from securing safe havens in Mindanao.

During late 2005 and early 2006, Southeast Asian governments' efforts to capture terrorist suspects continued apace, and with some success. In November 2005, Indonesian police killed Azahari Husin and two other militants during a raid on their hide-out in Malang, East Java. However, Noordin Mohammed Top narrowly escaped, as he did again in March and April, though several of his accomplices were killed or captured. In December, Philippine security forces captured RSG leader Ahmed Islam Santos in Zamboanga City. In February 2006, Indonesia handed over Singapore's most-wanted terrorist suspect, Mas Selamat Kastari, who had allegedly plotted to hijack an airliner and crash it into the city-state's Changi airport. In April, Philippine police arrested Al-Sharie Amiruddin Mohammed Nur, who they claimed was not only an ASG commander but also a 'hardcore' JI member. In May, Malaysia arrested 12 alleged members of Darul Islam Sabah (DIS) in the Sabahan coastal towns of Sandakan and Tawau. According to Malaysia's police, the role of DIS was to facilitate transit of Indonesian militants to the southern Philippines, smuggle weapons from the southern Philippines to Indonesia, and to obtain military training in the southern Philippines.

Closer security cooperation
Though variations in threat perception and mutual suspicions continue to prevent any rapid intensification of multilateral security links among Southeast Asian states, counter-terrorism was only one of the security spheres in which ASEAN member governments have gradually deepened their collaboration. Since 2004, when user states' concerns and the Pentagon's Regional Maritime Security Initiative (which apparently threatened direct US military intervention) galvanised Southeast Asian states into enhancing and coordinating their responses to the problems of piracy and potential maritime terrorism in the Malacca Strait more closely, the maritime domain has proved a particularly fruitful area for security cooperation. In August 2005, the foreign ministers of Indonesia, Malaysia and Singapore issued the Batam Statement, which reaffirmed the sovereignty of the littoral states over the Straits of Malacca and Singapore, upheld their primary responsibility for maritime security in the straits, acknowledged the interests of user states in the straits, and welcomed closer collaboration with and assistance from user states, international organisations and the shipping community in capacity-building, training and technology transfer.

Within the framework provided by the Batam Statement, the littoral states continued to intensify not just their national responses but also coordinated activities aimed at improving security in the straits. At the national level, the establishment during 2005 of the Malaysian Maritime Enforcement Agency as a national coast guard responsible for maritime security from the 12-mile territorial limit out to the 200-mile Exclusive Economic Zone boundary was a significant indication of the seriousness with which the Malaysian government viewed maritime security threats from non-state actors. Under *Operation Gurita*, Indonesia made efforts to improve coordination in the Malacca Strait between its navy and agencies such as the marine police, coast guard and customs. At the level of sub-regional cooperation, in May 2005 Indonesia and Singapore established the joint surface picture ('Surpic') naval monitoring system, which allows their navies to share a real-time situation picture of the Singapore Strait. Meeting in Kuala Lumpur in August 2005, the defence and naval chiefs of the littoral states added a maritime air patrol element to the trilateral coordinated Malacca Straits Sea Patrols that had begun the previous year. Thailand also indicated its interest in joining both the surface and air patrols. In April 2006, military chiefs from the four countries institutionalised these arrangements by agreeing the terms of reference for the Malacca Strait Patrol Joint Coordinating Committee, along with standard operating procedures for the patrols. By mid-2006 it seemed that cooperation among the littoral states might intensify in the medium term to allow genuine joint patrols and hot pursuit of maritime criminals across international boundaries.

Another important maritime security initiative involving the ASEAN states is ReCAAP (the Regional Cooperation Agreement Against Piracy), initiated by Japan in 2001. When it has been ratified by sufficient states to enter into force, ReCAAP – which also involves China, South Korea, India, Bangladesh and Sri Lanka – will primarily involve intelligence exchange. An Information Sharing Centre (ISC) will be established in Singapore. While the ISC is expected to begin operations by December 2006, in mid-year Indonesia and Malaysia had still not ratified the agreement, probably because of their continuing concerns ReCAAP might constitute a form of internalisation of security in the straits that could impinge on their sovereignty.

During 2005 and the first half of 2006, recorded attacks on vessels in the Malacca Strait declined dramatically. According to International Maritime Bureau statistics, incidents of piracy and sea-robbery in the straits declined from 38 in 2004, to 18 in 2005 and only three during the first five months of 2006. While the impact of the tsunami disaster, the subsequent international naval presence during the Acehnese relief effort, and the Acehnese peace settlement on GAM's maritime activities may have played more important parts in restoring security to the strait, the individual and collective measures implemented by the littoral states must also have contributed.

There was also movement within Southeast Asia towards more broadly based security cooperation. In May 2006 in Kuala Lumpur, ASEAN convened its first defence ministers' meeting (ADMM) as part of its long-term effort to establish an ASEAN Security Community. The involvement of ASEAN monitors in Aceh, and Malaysian Deputy Prime Minister Najib Tun Razak's call at the 2006 Shangri-La Dialogue for ASEAN to take the lead in establishing a regional humanitarian relief coordination centre were also signs that the grouping was moving gradually towards a more active role in regional security, broadly defined. However, there was no sign that ASEAN would in the foreseeable future be able to respond effectively to crises such as that which erupted in East Timor in early 2006, let alone intervene to resolve domestic political problems (as in Myanmar) or bilateral disputes, such as those which continue to plague Singapore–Malaysia relations.

Even after the first, much-trumpeted East Asian Summit, held in Kuala Lumpur in December 2005 and bringing together the heads of government of the 10 ASEAN states, their Northeast Asian counterparts (China, Japan and South Korea) as well as Australia, India and New Zealand, it remained unclear in what way this new pan-regional institution, aimed at intensifying discussion of security-related as well as economic issues, might add value to other regional dialogues' efforts. Malaysian Prime Minister Abdullah Badawi, the chairman, summed up the three-hour-long first meeting in the blandest possible terms, citing the participants' 'productive exchange of views on regional and international political and economic issues' and their agreement that it was in their common interest that 'peace, stability and prosperity' should prevail in the region. Although the summit did issue a separate declaration on preventing, controlling and responding to the threat of avian influenza, the absence of substantive discussion was confirmed by the 'motherhood-and-apple pie' language of the Kuala Lumpur Declaration on the East Asia Summit, which said little of importance beyond confirming that ASEAN would continue to be the summit's driving force and membership gatekeeper, and that in future the summit would be convened 'regularly'.

Simultaneously with these indications of greater interest in security multilateralism, the United States has continued its drive to intensify its bilateral security ties in the sub-region, with a view not only to bolstering key associates in the global struggle against violent extremism but also as part of an unspoken but nevertheless intensifying competition with China for influence in Southeast Asia. Most importantly, in November 2005 Washington restored full defence links with Indonesia, thus allowing Jakarta to purchase US military equipment and to receive US loans or grants for such purposes. Indonesian participation in the May 2006 US-led *Cobra Gold* military exercise in Thailand highlighted the new closeness in bilateral defence relations. The United States also deepened its security relations with the Philippines, establishing a Security Engagement Board as a framework for handling 'non-traditional' security issues such as terrorism, transnational crime, piracy and pandemic diseases which are not covered by the US–Philippine Mutual Defense Treaty. When US Defense Secretary Donald Rumsfeld visited Hanoi in June 2006, he made clear Washington's interest in reinforcing security links with Vietnam as well. The indications are that, given their domestic challenges, intra-regional tensions and latent concerns over the rise of China, Southeast Asian governments will continue to hedge their security options by acquiescing in these US initiatives.

Japan: Evolving Security Policy

Japan's long-term, incremental process of developing a more proactive and glo-bally focused security policy, in train since the mid-1990s, has stepped up a gear following the conclusion of a major security agreement with the United States in May 2006. At the same time, the effort by the government of Prime Minister Junichiro Koizumi to carve out a distinctive, independent set of foreign-policy priorities has run into difficulties, including the failure to secure a permanent seat on the United Nations Security Council and damaging tensions with neigh-bours, in particular China and the two Koreas.

The first, long-overdue signs of economic recovery have helped to give the leadership political breathing space, but there is little to suggest that economic growth has enhanced Japan's ability to assume a leading position either globally or regionally. In the Asia-Pacific region, Japan has often found itself struggling to keep up with its rivals, especially China, either in negotiating free-trade agreements or in developing a prominent voice in the newly emerging East Asian community.

Koizumi, who has done much to redefine both the style, and in some respects, the substance of Japanese politics, was due to retire in September 2006. There were signs in the intra- and inter-party leadership contest to succeed him of forces that were likely to have a significant impact on Japan's future standing and influence in the world.

A new roadmap for US–Japan security cooperation

The defining moment of the past year for Japan's strategic policy was the issuing on 1 May 2006 of the *United States–Japan Roadmap for Realignment Implementation*. An ambitious and wide-ranging agreement, this represents a de facto redefini-tion and expansion of the US–Japanese security relationship, promoting much greater integration and cooperation between US and Japanese military forces not only in defending Japan but also addressing a wide range of security con-tingencies, both regionally in East Asia and globally. It can be seen as the logical culmination of a series of enhancements of the bilateral security partnership dating from the 1997 US–Japan Defense Guidelines. It is consistent with the Bush administration's post-11 September Global Force Posture Review with its stress on 'roles and missions', the promotion of 'coalitions of the willing', a more flexible strategy of smaller lily-pad bases in Asia and an enhanced front-line role for Japanese defence forces in meeting regional security challenges. The roadmap had been foreshadowed by the publication in December 2004 of Japan's National Defense Program Outline and Japan's medium term defence buildup plan for 2005–09, and two key meetings in 2005 of the US–Japan Security Consultative Committee (SCC) – the regular 'two-plus-two' meeting of the US and Japanese foreign and defence ministers. The first of these meetings, in February 2005, advocated the development of 'common strategic initiatives', while the second, in October, involved the publication of an interim report outlining the details of the reforms embodied in the final roadmap.

The roadmap, a six-part set of initiatives, aims to strengthen interoperability between the US military and Japan's Self-Defense Forces (SDF) in areas including contingency planning, intelligence sharing and peacekeeping operations. The reforms include:

- Realignment of US forces on Okinawa. The Okinawa question has long been a sensitive issue in US–Japan relations. With 18,000 marines concentrated in one of the poorest prefectures of Japan, many local residents feel they bear a disproportionate share of the national defence burden and have long been pushing for a reduced US presence. Realignment will involve relocation by 2014 of the Futenma air station from central Okinawa to a more rural area within the prefecture and the construction of two new runways; redeployment of the Third Marine Expeditionary Force, totalling 8,000 troops (plus 9,000 dependents), from Okinawa to Guam by 2014; and drafting of a detailed consolidation plan by 2007 setting out measures for the return of land currently occupied by US bases and the development of shared US–Japan facilities in Okinawa.

- Improving US Army command and control capability through relocating the headquarters of the US Army I Corps from Washington State to Camp Zama in Kanagawa by US FY 2008. This will be complemented in 2012 by the arrival of new Ground SDF Central Readiness Force with rapid-reaction, anti-terrorist capabilities.

- Relocation of Japan's Air SDF Command to the US Yokota Air Base by 2010. This will involve creation of a joint operations and coordination centre to enhance bilateral air-defence and missile-defence coordination – an area of increasing collaboration between the US and Japan since 1999. The new arrangements will also aim to return control over a proportion of the airspace at Yokota to Japanese jurisdiction and the allowing of civilian flights at the base. The intention is to enhance Japan's role in defence arrangements and to promote a more explicitly mutually supportive security partnership.

- Relocation of the US aircraft carrier at Atsugi air base in Kanagawa prefecture to Iwakuni air base in Yamaguchi prefecture by 2014, including the development of facilities to accommodate Maritime SDF squadrons.
- Enhanced missile-defence collaboration, including the deployment in Japan of a new US X-band radar system and, by summer 2006, the deployment of US *Patriot* PAC-3 missile batteries to Japan to meet the growing ballistic-missile challenge from China and North Korea.
- Greater stress on joint training by US and Japanese forces at Japanese SDF facilities throughout Japan and the development of annual bilateral training plans in 2007.

Increasing Japanese security activism

Koizumi's Liberal Democratic Party (LDP) administration has taken a series of decisions that materially strengthen cooperation with the United States and underline Japan's commitment to addressing its national-security interests in a variety of contexts. Revision of the Japan Defense Agency (JDA) Law to enhance joint operations between Japan's Air, Ground and Maritime Self-Defense Forces – the first major reorganisation of the SDF since 1954 – means that, as of 27 March 2006, the once separate branches of the SDF are formally integrated via a new Joint Staff Office commanded by a uniformed Joint Staff Chief who reports directly to the civilian head of the JDA. A July 2005 revised SDF Law simplifies rules governing missile interception and allows the prime minister to authorise the interception of a foreign missile without having to go through the time-consuming process of securing cabinet approval for the mobilisation of the SDF.

The government decided in December 2005 to embark, with the United States, on a major programme to jointly develop and produce a next-generation sea-based interceptor missile. The project is expected to take nine years and cost some $3bn, with Japan shouldering one-third of the overall cost. The government also committed itself to licensed production of PAC-3 missiles, and the US military and the JDA conducted important tests off Hawaii of the *Aegis*-based missile-defence system in November 2005 and March 2006.

The government took measures to enhance the information and analysis capabilities of Japan's armed forces, including establishment within the Ground SDF of a new 600-officer intelligence-gathering unit; and possible establishment with the United States of a new General Security of Military Information Agreement (GSOMIA) to protect sensitive, classified information shared between US and

Japanese forces, modelled on past agreements between the United States and its allies. US defence planners have been especially concerned by the leak of information in early 2006 of the SDF's surface-to-air missile development plans – information which may, inadvertently, have been passed on to groups in Japan sympathetic to North Korea.

Continuing stress on joint training and simulation exercises in anticipation of a broad range of security scenarios in 2005–06 included Maritime SDF participation in multinational drills in August 2005 in Singapore as part of the Proliferation Security Initiative (PSI). While Japan has hosted PSI initiatives in the past, this is the first time Japan's forces have participated overseas in other than an observer capacity, and represents an important symbolic and practical change. Ground SDF bilateral exercises with the US Marine Corps in January 2006 off the coast of San Diego simulated the defence of island territories to the southwest of Japan. A *Keen Edge* simulation in February 2006 involved an integrated operational response by US and Japanese forces to a hypothetical attack on Japan.

Measures to enhance Japan's ability to address a broad range of security contingencies both at home and abroad included establishment of a new, dedicated SDF training centre at Shizuoka to provide training in international peace-keeping operations; the possible creation of a J-Alert nationwide real-time warning system, using communication satellite technology linked to municipal wireless networks, to relay critical information on domestic emergencies; and reinvigoration of the nation's long-term space-development programme following a series of damaging launch failures. As part of a new ten-year space-exploration plan, the government may relax its long-standing restriction of space technology to 'purely peaceful purposes'. According to a plan under consideration by an LDP panel, this may open the door to the development of new reconnaissance satellites and the active sharing of intelligence data with the United States as part of the promotion of missile defence collaboration.

Several factors have created the impetus for these changes: the steady expansion in Chinese military spending; the uncertain situation on the Korean peninsula; the threat of international terrorism; and pressure and encouragement from the United States. An additional critical factor has been the new public and cross-party consensus in favour of a more robust and unambiguous Japanese security posture, as reflected in the continuing debate over constitutional reform.

In autumn 2005, both the LDP and the main opposition Democratic Party of Japan (DPJ) published new, separate draft constitutions calling for a revision of Article IX – the so-called pacifist 'no war' clause of the existing 1947 Constitution – to allow recognition of the country's right to maintain military forces for self-defence. Opinion remains somewhat divided over whether Japan should be free to exercise its right under the United Nations charter to participate in collective security initiatives and in what context – either UN based or in collaboration with the United States. However, there is a broad, emerging public consensus (over 50% support, according to an April 2006 *Yomiuri* poll) that this change is desirable and should be mandated either via a new constitutional provision or through the drafting of new, permanent enabling legislation.

In spite of these examples of a more proactive approach to security issues, in some areas, the Koizumi government has been keen to limit rather than expand Japan's responsibilities. For example, the government decided in June 2005 to extend its ad hoc anti-terrorism law, enabling it to continue to provide logistical 'rear-area' support to US, UK and French forces operating in the Indian Ocean as part of the anti-Taliban and anti-al-Qaeda efforts in Afghanistan. However, it coupled this with a decision to sharply curtail its force presence in the Indian Ocean to one escort ship – leaving only a token presence in the region. Similarly, in May 2006 Koizumi signalled his commitment to pull out some 600 SDF troops from Samawa in southern Iraq once a stable Iraqi national government had been established. Although the withdrawal was likely to be followed by the creation of a residual Japanese provincial reconstruction team as well as maintenance of a small Air SDF logistical team, this would represent a sharp reduction of Japan's presence in Iraq.

Efforts to enhance the preparedness of local authorities in Japan to deal with security crises, under the terms of the Citizens' Protection Law of 2004, have been hampered by lack of trained personnel and expert knowledge at the local level. Such problems have been compounded by limited measures to deal with new security threats, such as the risk of bio-terrorism in Japan, and the lack of adequate facilities to deal with infectious disease. Plans to upgrade the Japan Defense Agency to full ministerial status, although still under consideration, were set back in early 2006 by a damaging bid-rigging scandal involving the Defense Facilities Administration Agency and by further revelations of breaches in national security involving the dissemination of sensitive Maritime SDF information.

Tensions in the Japan–US partnership

The partnership with the United States, while broadly healthy, has been showing unexpected signs of strain over the past year.

The most immediate sign of bilateral tension has been the willingness of senior US officials to express their frustrations in public. US Defense Secretary Donald Rumsfeld and Under Secretary of Defense Richard Lawless have been unusually forthright in expressing their irritation at delays in reaching agreement with the Japanese government on a number of critical security issues. In the case of Lawless, part of the discontent was prompted by repeated delays in reaching an understanding on the Futenma relocation plan. The original bilateral acceptance of the need for relocation dated from the mid 1990s. However, the relocation had failed to happen due to local Okinawan opposition to the US presence and differences between the US and Japanese governments over the appropriate alternative to Futenma, with the US military favouring a floating off-shore facility and the JDA opting for a land-based runway extension. The final, eleventh-hour agreement in March 2006, reached after lengthy and at times contentious discussions, represented a compromise between competing strategic, political and environmental interests.

Intergovernmental tension also surfaced in alliance discussions over the relocation of US Marines from Okinawa to Guam. Here the principal concern was financial, with the United States arguing that Japan, since it had taken the initiative in calling for a reduction in US forces, should shoulder the lion's share of the $10.27bn relocation cost. Rumsfeld, in particular, echoing the burden-sharing arguments that dominated US–Japan relations in the 1970s and 1980s, stressed the numerical discrepancy between Japan and the United States, pointing out that Tokyo spent 0.98% of its gross domestic product on defence compared with Washington's 3.2%. Japanese officials generally preferred to stress the wider context in which Japan had contributed to regional and international security. The solution was a compromise under which Japan assumed 59% of the relocation costs, somewhat more than the 50% it had originally sought but substantially less than the 75% requested by the Americans.

While compromises helped to bridge the divide between the two governments, it was not clear that Japanese public opinion would warm to the new accord. Keiichi Inamine, governor of Okinawa, was ambivalent about the Futenma deal. With a gubernatorial election scheduled for November 2006, local opposition may once again become an issue. Similarly, in a March 2006 plebiscite, 89% of Iwakuni's voters registered their opposition to the Atsugi airbase relocation, raising difficult legal and political issues for the Koizumi administration. In addition, though Japan and the United States agreed in October 2005 to replace the ageing diesel-powered aircraft carrier *Kitty Hawk* with a nuclear-powered carrier, the *George Washington,* public and especially local opinion in Japan remained acutely sensitive to the nuclear issue and was likely to be vocal and active in opposing this agreement.

Implementing the new, enhanced security partnership was also likely to face administrative challenges. The newly integrated operational structure of the SDF will facilitate joint operations between the United States and Japan. However, Japan lacks a joint planning framework to complement the coordinated planning mechanism that has long operated in the United States. Locating US forces at SDF-managed bases in Japan will raise important questions about the application of the US–Japan Status of Forces Agreement (SOFA) and US jurisdiction over US service personnel accused of crimes on Japanese territory.

Cooperation between the United States and Japan in dealing with broad-based territorial threats is complicated by the existence of new, unfamiliar inter-governmental bureaucratic partnerships. America's Department of Homeland Security (DHS) has attempted, for example, to liaise with Japan's Ministry of Education, Sports, Science and Technology – a bureaucratic actor which traditionally has not been involved in security and diplomatic matters and which has appeared, to some US officials, slow to respond to US anti-terrorist initiatives.

Difficulties associated with bilateral security cooperation have been compounded by new political disagreements. Tokyo has been disappointed by Washington's apparent lukewarm support for its efforts to secure a permanent seat on the UN Security Council. Despite Koizumi's efforts and those of the Foreign Ministry to make the Security Council bid into a flagship foreign-policy initiative, the Bush administration was unwilling to endorse the four-power (Germany, Brazil, India and Japan) campaign for enlargement, preferring instead to support only the addition of Japan in isolation – a tokenism that rankled with senior Japanese bureaucrats and politicians. The Bush administration also watched with growing concern the widening rift between China and Japan, prompted in part by historical controversies and Koizumi's decision to visit the controversial Yasukuni shrine in Tokyo, commemorating Japan's war dead. Such was the extent of US concern that then Deputy Secretary of State Robert Zoellick publicly stated during a January 2006 visit to Tokyo the importance of not allowing the history issue to become a negative influence.

Japan's gradual recovery and return to economic health following the long 'Lost Decade' of the 1990s has also meant that economic issues have re-emerged as a source of bilateral friction. With US opinion more exercised by the rising economic challenge of China, such friction remains a pale shadow of the trade conflict of the 1980s and 1990s, but its return after a long absence is noteworthy. Beef has been a source of disagreement: in December 2005 the Koizumi government lifted a long-standing ban on imports of US beef imports, imposed because of food safety concerns, but reimposed it in January 2006 following the discovery of prohibited bone material in American beef shipments. Tokyo cited the risk of bovine spongiform encephalopathy, or 'mad cow disease', associated with US beef. But US producers and officials in the Department of Agriculture were critical of what they saw as an unduly dilatory and possibly disingenuous response by Japan to US efforts to reassure Japan of the safety of US beef. In June 2006, the dispute appeared to have been resolved.

Tokyo has meanwhile shown an uncharacteristic assertiveness on trade issues, imposing 15% tariffs on US steel in September 2005 and joining forces for the first time with the European Union and Canada to challenge successfully, via the World Trade Organisation, US use of countervailing duties and anti-dumping orders under the Byrd Amendment to favour American producers. Some in the US Congress have also been quick to criticise Japan for alleged unfair exchange-rate manipulation and failure of Japanese companies to pay adequate compensation to US prisoners of war and internees forced to work as slave labour.

In spite of these tensions – and of the departure from the Bush administration in December 2005 of seasoned 'Japan hands' such as Michael Green, the president's former special assistant on Asian affairs – the bilateral relationship looks set to remain broadly positive and constructive. Bush's November 2005 visit to Japan was judged to have been a success, while Koizumi's farewell visit to the United States at the end of June 2006 was capped by a visit by the two men to Graceland, Elvis Presley's home in Memphis, Tennessee.

Washington and Tokyo have also worked successfully to address potential flashpoints in the relationship, including the murder of a Japanese woman by a US soldier in early 2006, as well as the beef dispute. The two countries also reached an understanding over how best to tackle a number of critical security threats during 2005–06, including the nuclear proliferation challenge posed by North Korea and Iran. In the latter case, Japan's long-standing commercial interest in promoting a $2bn oil development stake in Azadegan in southwest Iran might have divided Tokyo and Washington. However, by mid-2006 there were tentative signs that Tokyo was willing to place non-proliferation objectives ahead of its economic self-interest and to risk courting the displeasure of Tehran by threatening to impose economic sanctions in an effort to discourage Iran from pursuing a nuclear-weapons programme.

A trilateral security partnership was emerging among Australia, Japan and the United States: following an 18 March 2006 meeting in Canberra among the foreign ministers of the three countries, there were clear signs of interest in developing practical measures and a regular dialogue mechanism to address regional and international security challenges.

Sino-Japanese discord

The past year has been plagued by an acrimonious relationship with China. Irritants have included Koizumi's visits to the Yasukuni shrine, a war memorial dedicated to 2.5m dead, including war criminals; competition over territorial claims and access to natural resources in the East China Sea; unresolved issues linked to Japanese chemical-weapons stockpiles left over in China from the Second World War; Tokyo's decision to end its yen-loan programme to China after 2008; and damaging public revelations regarding a Shanghai-based Japanese diplomat who committed suicide in 2004. While some of these are long-standing problems, they have become more serious against a background in which Japan, the world's second-largest economy, is competing for influence with China, a major regional actor with global aspirations and potential. Bilateral tensions are symptomatic of a fundamental struggle for power and influence, highlighted by China's opposition to Japan's UN Security Council bid, as well as Beijing's efforts to dominate the newly emerging East Asian community, which convened for the first time at a summit meeting in December 2005, and to ensure its Asian character.

A storm of anti-Japanese protests convulsed China in spring 2005. In early April, Internet-initiated campaigns against Japan's UN Security Council bid led to demonstrations in Chengdu, Shenzen and Chongquing; on 9–10 April some 10,000 demonstrators in Beijing attacked Japanese shops and offices, including the Japanese embassy and the Japanese ambassador's residence; a week later even larger protests by as many as 30,000 people took place in no fewer than ten Chinese cities, including Shanghai. In addition to opposition to Japan's UN bid, the demonstrators appeared to have been upset by controversial revisionist history textbooks approved by Japan's Education Ministry; competing Japanese and Chinese sovereignty claims over the Senkaku/Diaoyu islands; and visits to the Yasukuni shrine by Koizumi and senior LDP officials. These events were foreshadowed by a deterioration in bilateral ties dating from 2003, as well as previous Chinese popular protests against the actions of Japanese private citizens and government officials. However, the explosion of tension was on a surprising scale.

In the past, China's leaders have played the Japanese 'history card' to pressure Tokyo and to burnish their own nationalist credentials. The current shift to a more technocratic and younger Chinese leadership, represented by Hu and Wen, with no direct experience of Japanese colonial rule in the 1930s, might have been expected to lead to a more pragmatic approach to relations with Japan. However, there are clearly limits to such a change. Dispassionate analyses of the Sino-Japanese relationship by Chinese academics and think-tank specialists have often been drowned out by a chorus of emotional, and at times vitriolic, populist criticism of Japan. Leading Chinese cultural figures have been attacked verbally, and at times physically, for appearing too sympathetic to Japan. While these may be spontaneous reactions, they may also reflect the rise of competing power centres in China – for example, there were suggestions that the Shanghai protests might have been orchestrated by local municipal authorities in an effort to embarrass the national leadership.

The Beijing government stepped up diplomatic pressure on Japan in several ways. Rather than apologising to Japan for the protests or providing financial compensation, the Chinese leadership insisted the demonstrations were the result of Japan's 'incorrect understanding of history'. Vice Premier Wu Yi, on a seven-day visit to Japan in May 2005, met business and political leaders, but abruptly cut short her visit to return to Beijing, missing a scheduled meeting with Koizumi. The gesture appeared to be a calculated snub prompted by Koizumi's refusal to compromise on the Yasukuni issue. Following Koizumi's 17 October 2005 visit to the shrine, Li Zhaoxing likened the prime minister's actions to Germany's political leaders paying their respects to Adolf Hitler. Hu chose not to meet Koizumi at a November summit of Asia Pacific Economic Cooperation (APEC) in Busan, South Korea.

The Chinese leadership has not been uniformly hostile to Japan. It has attempted to limit or contain popular tensions, and launched a nationwide campaign to clamp down on any further unauthorised anti-Japanese demonstrations. Moreover, Chinese leaders have been willing to engage with some senior Japanese politicians, receiving in April 2006 a large cross-party delegation including former prime minister Ryutaro Hashimoto. Nevertheless, by spring 2006 it seemed clear that Beijing had resigned itself to a waiting-game, content to see bilateral relations remain on ice until the end of Koizumi's term in 2006 and making it clear that any future summit with Koizumi's successor would depend on the new leader making a commitment not to visit the Yasukuni shrine.

Japanese public and private responses to the rift with China have been varied. The foreign ministry has been cautious, wary of allowing alarmist Japanese public opinion to run out of control, and inclined to stress the importance of partnership with China even while allowing for the possibility of future rivalry. Similarly, the JDA, while highlighting in its 2005 White Paper the growth of and lack of transparency in China's defence spending, has been careful to stress the potential rather than the actual threat posed by China – a point echoed by the prime minister's office.

Individual politicians have been less circumspect. In December 2005, Seiji Maehara, then leader of the DPJ, characterised China unambiguously as a threat. Other politicians, including prominent members of the ruling LDP, have been even more outspoken, and in some cases inflammatory, in their comments. Health Minister Masahiro Morioka in May 2005 claimed implausibly that the 14 Class-A war criminals among those memorialised at the Yasukuni shrine were no longer viewed as war criminals in Japan. In June 2005 Japan's Education Minister Nariaki Nakayama argued against the use of the term 'comfort women' to describe Asian women forced into prostitution by Japanese troops during the Pacific War, suggesting that the term had never been used at the time and was, therefore, a historical anomaly.

Koizumi himself appears to have hoped that, by persisting in his visits to the Yasukuni shrine – the October visit was his fifth since taking office in 2001 – he would eventually persuade China to drop its criticism of Japan; he had used a similar tactic in domestic politics by adopting an uncompromising and unpopular position on postal-sector reform. In the past, analysts had argued that Koizumi's shrine visits were motivated by electoral politics and a desire to shore up his base among conservative supporters, and concern to placate key interest groups such as Izokukai (The War-Bereaved Families Association). However, this explanation was less convincing given Koizumi's impending departure from office.

The long-term importance of the shrine issue in Sino-Japanese relations will depend on who succeeds Koizumi as LDP president and prime minister. Shinzo

Abe, the chief cabinet secretary, viewed as favourite to succeed Koizumi, has firmly supported the shrine visits, although it is suggested that this stance is intended to boost his conservative credentials and that he would be more pragmatic as leader.

Another contender, Foreign Minister Taro Aso, has also taken a conservative position on the visits. However, his reputation has been damaged by some clumsy and provocative statements, including the suggestion that the emperor should visit the Yasukuni shrine and the characterisation of Taiwan as a normal 'country' that benefited from Japan's colonial rule. A third contender, Yasuo Fukuda, is more dovish on China issues and seen as less likely to visit the shrine.

Public opinion on the shrine issue is fluid and unpredictable. Ordinary voters, according to opinion polls, remain evenly divided for and against shrine visits. Across the political spectrum, there is an emerging cross-party coalition of politicians (120-strong according to one calculation) that favours building a purpose-built government war memorial – Yasukuni has no official status – as a means of depoliticising the issue. Even prominent conservative figures with strong nationalist credentials, such as former prime minister Yasuhiro Nakasone and Watanabe Tsuneo, editor of *Yomiuri Shinbun*, a leading conservative newspaper, have spoken out against Koizumi's visits.

While much attention has been focused on the shrine issue, a serious and intensifying Sino-Japanese dispute over access to the substantial and relatively underdeveloped oil and natural gas reserves in the East China Sea has perhaps been even more destabilising. The energy reserves are concentrated in the vicinity of the Senkaku/Diaoyu islands, which are claimed by Japan, China and Taiwan. At the heart of the dispute is the legal basis on which Beijing and Tokyo assert their claims to develop the resources that exist near the islands. With equal vigour, China and Japan cite the 1982 Law of the Sea Convention to support their claims. China argues, on the basis of geography and maritime law, that interstate barriers are determined by the discontinuities separating continental shelves, and points to the Okinawa Trough as a real division between the two countries. Japan, by contrast, argues that the Senkakus fall within its Exclusive Economic Zone (EEZ), which extends 200 miles beyond Japan's territory, and sees the division between Chinese and Japanese territorial waters as a 'median line' extending to the west of Okinawa – fewer than 400 nautical miles separate China and Japan.

Over the last two years both China and Japan have substantially stepped up efforts to explore and extract resources from this region. In April 2005, Japan's Ministry of Economy, Trade and Industry (METI) granted drilling rights to Japanese companies in the contested areas of the East China Sea. In August 2005, China confirmed that it would begin gas production in the Chunxiao (Shirakaba) field to the west of the median line. Subsequently, in September, China apparently began to extract natural gas from the Tianwaitian field further west of Chunxiao and in areas that China argues are not contested by Japan. The two sides have since haggled over compromise proposals, with China proposing joint development of resources on the eastern side of the median line and Japan calling for joint development on either side of the line, as well as demanding that China halt its existing development plans and provide details of explorations to date. Japan is worried that the geological features of the region are such that even Chinese extraction activity confined to the western side of the demarcation line will indirectly lead to depletion of energy stocks on the eastern side.

In spite of these tensions, economic links between Japan and China have been expanding. According to METI, China (including Hong Kong) became Japan's biggest trading partner in 2005, with trade growing 12.7%. Japan still exported more to the United States than to China, but the trend was moving towards China. Similarly Japanese direct investment in China has been rising sharply and falling in the United States. These trends were expected to continue.

Japan and the two Koreas

Japanese relations with both of the Koreas have been especially tense during 2005–06. Japan has largely followed Washington's lead with regard to North Korea, relying on the Six-Party Talks as a venue for tackling the nuclear issue. While the Japanese Foreign Ministry has maintained a characteristically pragmatic approach in dealing with North Korea – echoed by Koizumi in his public commitment to normalising bilateral relations before he leaves office – Japanese public opinion has remained inflexibly committed to understanding and resolving the fate of those Japanese citizens abducted by North Korea in the 1970s and 1980s.

Pyongyang, however, has shown little inclination to reopen the abduction issue, seeking instead to isolate Japan and detach it from its allies in the Six-Party Talks. Despite this, a modest breakthrough occurred following the fifth round of Six-Party Talks in Beijing in November 2005, when Japan and North Korea agreed to set up bilateral working groups to discuss three sets of concerns: abductions, national security and bilateral normalisation. On this basis, the two sides convened talks in February 2006, the first since October 2002, but did not make visible progress. As a result, the mood in Japan hardened appreciably by spring 2006, prompting – much to Pyongyang's annoyance – a crack-down by the Japanese government on the financial resources of Chosensoren (or Chongryun), the pro-North Korean General Association of Korean Residents in Japan; and the drafting in March 2006 of legislation threatening further economic sanctions against Pyongyang if there was no progress on the abductee issue.

The deterioration in relations has taken its toll economically, with trade between North Korea and Japan in 2005 falling to $190m, the lowest level since 1977. By mid-2006, as Pyongyang unsuccessfully attempted a test launch of its second generation *Taepo-dong* 2 medium-range ballistic missile, relations looked set to deteriorate even further.

The past year has also seen considerable disharmony between Seoul and Tokyo. As with China, the controversy surrounding Koizumi's Yasukuni shrine visits and the existence of revisionist Japanese history textbooks have caused acute discontent in South Korea. On 20 June 2005, Koizumi met Roh for a summit that produced limited and mixed results. Meeting again on the margins of the APEC summit in Busan in November, the encounter between the two leaders was even more perfunctory – a mere 20 minutes of discussion. Relations between the two men have since become even frostier, with Roh making it clear that he is not prepared to travel to Japan for a reciprocal summit unless Koizumi agrees to end the shrine visits. Though some in Japan see Roh's actions as an attempt to boost his domestic popularity, this interpretation seems seriously to underestimate the extent and intensity of South Korean irritation with Japan. In one August 2005 opinion poll, 44% of Korean students described Japan as the country to which they feel least positively inclined.

Other controversies have hampered bilateral relations. In May 2005, Japan's Vice-Foreign Minister Shotaro Yachi was reported – despite having made his remarks in an off-the-record setting – as having said that Japan was unable to share intelligence with South Korea due to US distrust of the South. The report prompted a torrent of criticism in the Korean media. In June 2005, Japan and South Korea issued an extensive report on the four-years' work of a bilateral history commission, revealing differences in interpretation and understanding of key issues in the history of relations between the two countries. However, recent relations have not been uniformly negative and there have been modest examples of cooperation and the potential for renewed dialogue. In summer 2005, Japanese and South Korean Coast Guard personnel conducted joint exercises near Tsushima, and senior officers from both countries met to discuss bilateral military exchanges. In October 2005, *Bukgwandaecheopbi*, a monument commemorating Korea's sixteenth-century defeat of Japan's invading army, was returned by Japan to South Korea, having been held by the Japanese since the Russo-Japanese War of 1904–05. In March 2006, Park Geun-hye, leader of South Korea's opposition Grand National Party, had constructive talks in Tokyo with Koizumi in which she reportedly suggested that Japan and South Korea cooperate in drafting a joint history textbook.

Economically, bilateral relations have been very positive. While progress in reaching a free-trade agreement stalled due to differences over liberalising the agricultural sectors of both countries, trade, investment and tourism have remained relatively buoyant and Korean and Japanese officials have taken the first steps towards Asian financial integration through the signing in May 2005 of a currency-swap deal, expanded in February 2006.

However, a long-standing territorial dispute over sovereignty over Takeshima (known to the Koreans as Dokto) threatens further disruption of relations. In late April 2006, the countries narrowly averted a physical confrontation following

Japan's attempt to challenge Seoul's plan to assign Korean names to some of the underwater terrain features in the vicinity of the disputed islands. With Japan threatening to send scientific exploration ships into South Korea's territorial waters, a clash was averted only by a compromise under which Seoul agreed to delay the naming initiative and Japan cancelled its survey mission. Notwithstanding this tactical concession, Seoul responded vigorously to what it saw as an ill-judged effort by Tokyo to assert its claim to the territory. In sharply worded language, Roh on 25 April accused Japan of violating 'the universal values and standards of the international community' and of being still encumbered by 'the dark chapter of its history of past imperial aggressions'. Roh said 'as long as Japan continues to glorify its past wrongs and claim rights based on such history, friendly relations between Korea and Japan cannot be established properly'.

Leadership change

An earthquake in Japan's domestic politics was triggered by the Lower House elections of September 2005. Confronting a group of conservative rebels within the LDP opposed to postal-sector reform, Koizumi unexpectedly dissolved the Lower House in August 2005, announced a snap election and embarked on a high-risk three-point strategy of expelling his critics from the LDP; recruiting a new cohort of high-profile, telegenic candidates, informally dubbed Koizumi's 'assassins' (many of whom, unusually for Japanese politics, were women); and selling himself to the electorate as a bold and decisive leader.

The strategy worked extremely well, delivering the LDP 296 of the 480 seats, a 60-seat increase on the party's pre-election total. When combined with the LDP's coalition partner Komeito, the government had 327 seats, more than the two-thirds required to effect major legislative and constitutional change. The outcome was significant because the LDP performed well in urban constituencies and amongst floating voters, allowing it to present itself as a new, reinvigorated party, less dependent on the pork-barrel politics that had characterised it for much of the post-war period. In turn, this allowed the prime minister to wrap himself more tightly in the mantle of reformist politics and to paint the opposition DPJ as out of touch and overly dependent on the support of special interests. The DPJ saw their representation in the Lower House fall dramatically from 177 to 113, prompting turmoil in the ranks of a fractious and ideologically heterogeneous party. A closely fought leadership contest saw Seiji Maehara chosen as the new DPJ leader by one vote in September 2005. However, the DPJ, after a damaging scandal involving faked e-mails and an unsuccessful effort to discredit an LDP politician, was later forced to change its leader again. Maehara was replaced by a more seasoned leader, Ichiro Ozawa, in April 2006.

The LDP's ability to capitalise on its election success should not be exaggerated. Its strong performance was concentrated in single-member districts where the first-past-the-post element of Japan's hybrid electoral system magnified a 38% share of the popular vote into 73% of seats in the Lower House. The government's fortunes could change markedly if the electorate's party loyalties were to shift suddenly. In 2006, the LDP's success became somewhat tarnished following corruption scandals and as the pace of economic reform slowed.

Ozawa is a long-time political survivor and behind-the-scenes tactician, a former LDP politician who played a key role in reshaping Japanese politics in the early 1990s. He has re-defined the strategy of the PDJ away from the pattern of accommodation with the LDP on foreign and security policies favoured by Maehara towards a more distinctly adversarial stance, challenging the government at both the national and local level. The result is that the DPJ has appeared more united as it approaches the Upper House election of 2007, in which it has a chance of overturning the government's 14-seat majority.

With Komeito also set to select a new leader in the autumn, all of Japan's leading political parties will have relatively new leaders in place by September 2006. This opens the door for new directions in foreign and domestic policy. Koizumi has embraced an anti-establishment, iconoclastic rhetoric and style, and it is difficult to judge whether any potential successor will seek to emulate this approach. Ozawa, in his early career, was keen to present himself as a radical politician, but current electoral logic may induce him to reach out to the more instinctively conservative, sectional interests that in the past underpinned the LDP. In terms of leadership style, Ozawa has tended to favour an assertive manner, at odds with the consensual norms of post-war Japanese politics. Shinzo Abe and Yasuo Fukuda, frontrunners for the LDP succession, are in some respects mainstream politicians: both are grandsons of prime ministers (Nobusuke Kishi and Takeo Fukuda respectively), and may be inclined to retreat into the comfort-zone of traditional party politics.

Whoever he is, the new prime minister is set to preside over significant changes as the new US–Japan alliance comes to fruition and as he addresses continuing issues with the country's most important friends and neighbours.

9 | **Prospectives**

The attempted merger between idealism and realpolitik at the core of American foreign policy was laid to rest during 2005, and was informally buried by mid 2006. Of course the strategic language at the highest level still paid tribute to the ideal of the universal spread of democracy and the ending of tyranny. But the diplomatic practice, now controlled largely by the US secretary of state, delivered much greater homage to the need to solve problems and deal with the world on the terms America found it, rather than on the terms the United States might wish to create.

This was all the more so because the political, military and diplomatic imbroglio established in Iraq had, by 2006, sapped the entrepreneurial flair with which the first-term Bush presidency had sought to conduct foreign policy. Creating a 'market need' for democracy and then selling it to as many who could be persuaded to 'buy' was an impractical way to maintain and build alliances for the so-called 'war on terror'. Similarly, the electoral outcome in Palestine that saw Hamas take power by popular assent, and the successes of characters such as Hugo Chávez in Venezuela, were sharp reminders that elections can be won and power secured by those with unpalatable agendas.

Different colours other than black and white – even a bit of grey – are therefore slowly being re-introduced to the American diplomatic palette. This is welcome, though it naturally means passing through a phase of apparent double standards and rhetorical contradiction. The United States favours ending tyranny and promoting democracy, but finds itself supporting strategically important autocrats who shun elections. Democracy for all is not a realisable goal, and its unqualified pursuit would lead to more instability. On the other hand, working with the status quo without regard for democratic values will only disenchant those abroad with liberal programmes and strengthen cynical usurpers of power.

The compromise between sticking to a distant goal and making a full U-turn is to adjust the aim. The United States and its democratic allies would be well advised to focus on 'good governance' as a key foreign-policy goal, one that if achieved would serve most of the security requirements putatively addressed by smooth democratisation. Championing the effects of good governance and the practices that lead to it would be a more effective way, too, of recognising the different pace of economic and political reform to which other societies can reasonably commit. Defining good governance to include many of the attributes enjoyed by modern well-established democracies, while accepting that good governance can be practised by leaders with benign intent who owe their legitimacy more to consent than to poll results, permits a freer and fuller dialogue with developing societies. It need not mean abandonment of the goal that power be checked.

A society that allows the space for private institutions to flourish, the media to speak, non-governmental organisations to operate, parties to form and foreign direct investment to flourish, reasonable individual freedom to develop within the rule of law, and the protection of private property, creates its own checks on the unbridled exercise of executive power. These are also necessary, if insufficient, steps along the road to full democratic practices. Building a democratic society is not a race and skipping steps can cause more problems than it solves.

Good governance without full electoral democracy is probably safer strategically than is democracy without transparent and effective good governance. Trying to find the right balance among the advocacy of democracy, the promotion of good governance and the conduct of practical relations with strategically important actors will create many challenges for the United States and its democratic partners in the years to come.

The end of the entrepreneurial phase of US foreign policy also means a return to a more classic strategic dictionary. If 'regime change' cannot be the answer to all strategic disquiet and, badly managed, can lead to more instability, then it follows that the principles of deterrence and containment will need to be applied with more care and determination in the face of difficult challenges.

This may become particularly the case in the Persian Gulf. There is a growing consensus that the regime in Iran is pursuing a military nuclear capacity. Any military action taken would delay, but not definitively end, the known elements of that programme, and could accelerate efforts later to develop a clandestine capability. Whether military action is taken or not, therefore, consideration would need to be given to containing and deterring now, or in the future, an Iranian nuclear capability.

In the latter part of 2006, the United States will therefore likely develop a stronger strategic dialogue with the member-states of the Gulf Co-operation

Council (GCC) to ascertain their appetite for a stronger security relationship with Washington and, if needed, a more open policy of containment of Iran should the regime not bend to diplomatic pressures. That more open strategic dialogue could weigh in the strategic calculations of Iran. For if its reluctance to suspend enrichment activities only results in its Arab neighbours importing more US interest and military presence, that result would run counter to the declared aim of Iran to rid the region of the United States and assert its rightful place in regional calculations. Just as leaving the military option on the table can in theory affect Iran's calculations so, too, and perhaps even more persuasively, brandishing the containment option could change the cost–benefit analysis in Tehran. And if diplomacy were to fail, the United States will have at least prepared the regional ground more effectively for deterring Iran or taking firmer action of another kind.

But just as the United States needs to dust off its classic strategic textbooks, so it must continue to burnish its contemporary strategic anthropology. The tribal calculations in Iraq alone would tax most experts. But these are also set against the complex regional Sunni–Shia rivalry that Iraq's instability, Iran's renaissance and Sunni-Arab malaise has fostered. At the same time, a major struggle is being fought throughout the Islamic world among conservative, liberal and extremist forces who all want to occupy the same political ground.

Divining a way to influence the outcomes of these struggles is a task that the United States can only hope to perform in collaboration with other countries and key actors in the region. Constant diplomatic activity and consultations will be required before new grand designs are drafted. Developing a new regional security arrangement will require skills that are more horticultural than architectural. Planting the seeds of a new security arrangement in the Gulf region would need to be part of a more comprehensive strategy to secure stability in the area.

While the United States adjusts its entrepreneurial goals and lowers it strategic sights, others are becoming more extrovert and trying to define more clearly their national interests.

India is stepping out of its previously hyphenated relationship with Pakistan to claim a more significant place in international affairs. Beyond seeking a UN Security Council seat and supporting an Indian candidate for the office of secretary-general, this has meant taking a number of significant steps. The most far reaching has been to develop a strategic partnership with the United States and to seek to play, diplomatically and even militarily, an extra-regional role. The spirit of the Non Aligned Movement (NAM) still lurks in the Indian political consciousness, but the motivating force behind much Indian diplomacy is to position the country as a leader on its own terms. Non alignment with the NAM will be a regular and permissible feature of this more individualistic external policy.

While India celebrates its status as the world's largest democracy and therefore implicitly admits to the role that values can play, even if quietly, as part of its external image, China is attempting to portray its foreign policy as value free. The 'peaceful rise of China' thesis has it that China needs to fuel its economy and that its economic growth will be of general benefit. Its principles of peaceful reso-lution of disputes and non-interference in the internal affairs of other countries need not be shifted as its GNP catapults forward. Suggestions from the outside that China should seek to be a 'responsible stakeholder' in the international system are met with quizzical consternation. Protests that its foreign-policy con-nections to Sudan or Venezuela speak to a more malign intent in foreign policy are rebutted by the argument that China is simply doing the business it needs to secure its economic future. China's entrepreneurial foreign policy is just that: securing the commodities for domestic growth and stability from whatever market that can provide them.

Whether China can sustain a foreign policy that is genuinely extrovert and truly value free will be an interesting question to see answered in the years ahead. Neutrality always carries its own form of intervention with it, and it is hard for the Chinese leadership to sustain the argument that its extroversion has no impact. It is certainly interested in supporting regional organisations in which the United States plays no formal part, whether that is the Shanghai Co-operation Organisation or the East Asia Summit. More important than this will be the way its business interests in strategically significant areas, like the Middle East, in time affect its foreign-policy choices. As the country becomes more entwined in the eco-nomics of the Gulf, it may find it difficult to absent itself from the politics of the region. If it does, it will demonstrate a skill no outsider has ever shown.

Meanwhile Europe, following the collapse of the constitutional referendums, is not only gazing at its own navel, but formally announcing that this period of 'reflection' will be extended. Foreign-policy initiatives will therefore have a 'directoire' quality to them, with the E3 of the UK, France and Germany, playing the lead role, newly empowered by their success in bringing the United States, if certain conditions are met, to agree to negotiate with Iran. That accomplish-ment, coupled to America's new-found diplomatic energy, has restored a certain harmony to transatlantic affairs, even if the mood is still very melodic minor: ascending, but with crucial pauses.

German Chancellor Angela Merkel helped the ascent, by establishing a strong relationship with President George W. Bush while still carrying the 'European argument' that the United States should find its way towards talking to Iran. Pause was provided by events such as Vice President's Dick Cheney's remarks about Russia, which even if seen by many in Europe as having some analytical merit, were thought shrill and misjudged, except as part of a 'good cop–bad cop' routine. It is likely that in the security realm transatlantic relations will continue to warm as the work on the difficult issues becomes ever more collaborative. Sadly, collaboration with Russia will be fleeting. Moscow will continue to view the West with suspicion, with merry talk of Ukrainian membership of NATO, and the West will find dealing with Putin's Kremlin, so opaquely absorbed by succession politics, tiresomely complex.

In these shifting circumstances, African civil wars, and populist Latin American politics, regularly grab headlines, but remain second-order strategic issues for those not immediately affected. The global strategic agenda in the immediate future will still be centred on challenges in the Persian Gulf, the development of Great-Power relations in Asia, and the management of terrorism and proliferation risks. The crises in and with Afghanistan, Iraq, North Korea and Iran, and the ever-present prospect of a terrorist surprise, can still provide shocks to the international system, and therefore command the most attention by national security advisers.

In the main, a sense of steadied pragmatism has returned to the conduct of international affairs among most states, especially given the passing of America's revolutionary moment during which it aimed actively to change the status quo in unstable places. But this should not signal the end of entrepreneurship in foreign policy. Addressing even the minimalist global strategic agenda discussed here will require innovation, rather than the repetition of old techniques. Finding the right balance between idealism and realpolitik does not mean abandoning the moral element in foreign policy. Setting the moral compass on such uncertain strategic terrain nevertheless carries risks that need to be measured and then countered. Those who rightly argue that America does not have the answers to all these questions have an ever-increasing burden to offer some of their own. For the civilised world, it will be important that America's enemies do not provide the more compelling arguments.

Index